THE CUTTING EDGE

The Cutting Edge

How Churches Speak
on Social Issues

MARK ELLINGSEN

Published for the
INSTITUTE FOR ECUMENICAL RESEARCH, STRASBOURG, FRANCE
by
WCC PUBLICATIONS, GENEVA
and
WILLIAM B. EERDMANS PUBLISHING COMPANY, GRAND RAPIDS

First published jointly 1993 by WCC Publications
World Council of Churches, 150 route de Ferney, 1211 Geneva 2, Switzerland
and
Wm. B. Eerdmans Publishing Co.
255 Jefferson Ave. S.E., Grand Rapids, Michigan 49503

Printed in the United States of America

WCC ISBN 2-8254-1097-7
Eerdmans ISBN 0-8028-0710-0

To
the youngest Ellingsens,
Elizabeth Ann and Peter,
and to Betsey
their mother and midwife
of this (and all my) books

Table of Contents

Preface

Ecumenical memory is all too often all too limited. A small number of texts are referred to repeatedly while countless others fall into obscurity, deserved or undeserved. The comprehensive picture of what has been said and argued in the past is lost.

Mark Ellingsen's study corrects the limits of memory and does more. He has collected an exhaustive documentation of statements from churches and church agencies worldwide over the last thirty years dealing with a range of socio-ethical issues. These texts are analyzed both in terms of the positions taken and in terms of the kinds of theological warrants appealed to in support of the position taken. On the basis of Dr Ellingsen's work, discussions of the social positions of the churches on various topics can now be carried out with much greater precision.

This study has been conducted in the framework of the Institute for Ecumenical Research in Strasbourg, France, where the collected church statements are now deposited and can be consulted by interested scholars. The Institute is grateful for substantial financial support in the publication of this volume from the Department of Theology and Studies of the Lutheran World Federation, Pro Fide et Christianismo (Sweden), and the North Carolina Synod of the Evangelical Lutheran Church in America.

Strasbourg, February 1993

MICHAEL ROOT
Director
Institute for Ecumenical Research
Strasbourg, France

Acknowledgments

For a book for which I am indebted to so many collaborators, these remarks are embarrassingly brief. In some sense, the Dedication and the Introduction say most of what needs to be said. The latter sketches the origins of this book and indicates my indebtedness to the Institute for Ecumenical Research in Strasbourg, France. I have not mentioned names of colleagues in this, my former institution, for fear that I would fail to give everyone their due. Consequently, let it be said that almost everyone associated with the Strasbourg Institute from 1982 to 1988 deserves credit in some way for the contents of this book, and to these deserving associates I tip my hat.

I am grateful to my editors at the World Council of Churches (WCC) and to prepublication critics such as Paul Abrecht. Their input on this project has been invaluable.

The second group to thank is those who helped me obtain the material. One of the monumental tasks of this study was to assemble an international collection of church social statements, when previously no comparable collection truly existed. In the task of obtaining these statements, an administrative undertaking to which I devoted much time during my years in Strasbourg, I depended heavily on the churches themselves to respond to my contacts. In only a few cases was I disappointed. Many church officers combed through synod and assembly meetings of the past twenty-five or thirty years to identify the statements needed for this study. In addition to such efforts, these church leaders often extended their personal encouragement to my work; I am truly grateful for their graciousness and collegiality.

Other thanks are gratefully extended to those who translated documents from languages inaccessible to me. Here I have in mind Per Lønning, Sven Oppegaard, Kees van der Zwaard, Paolo Ricca, Harding Meyer, and Betsey Ellingsen. Collaboration with these translators represented a highlight of the research and writing process.

Reference to the last translator on my list brings me to a brief commentary on the Dedication. When a family helps an author write his books as much and as skilfully as all the Ellingsens contribute to my work, I face the delightful problem of deciding to whom a new book should be dedicated. The odd fact about the choice for this book is that one important family member is missing from the Dedication. Of course a father loves all his children equally. But what is a father to do when he has recently dedicated another book to his only child, just before learning that two more would come into his life? The newcomers need their book too (one apiece someday, if possible). Thanks to Peter and Elizabeth Ann for coming into our lives. They have made a delightful contribution to this book by providing enjoyable study breaks from tedious editing.

When they learn to talk, some day they may rival their older brother in asking penetrating children's questions which would help any author write more clearly.

This book would never have reached the manuscript stage had it not been for Betsey Shaw Ellingsen. She knows why, and I was so aware of her numerous contributions that I tried to persuade her to put her name on the cover alongside mine. When her modesty prevailed, the Dedication seemed like a natural, until the two new Ellingsens made the scene and needed their book too. That's why this book is for the three of them, though I love their brother/eldest son too. How's that for social justice in a book about ethics?

Introduction

What business is it of the church to get itself tied up in political issues? What right does the church have to make statements on such issues? Such questions are quite commonly heard in the parishes of many nations, particularly but not exclusively those in the Northern hemisphere. The involvement of the churches in contemporary socio-political challenges is itself one of the more controversial issues of the day within the Christian community.

There are good indications that this issue will not go away. To a great extent the leadership of our churches is agreed that the personal and socio-political dimensions of Christian faith cannot be divided but must be related.[1] There is indeed biblical warrant for this commitment (Isa. 58:6-12; Amos 5:21-24; 1 Sam. 10:25; Matt. 25:31-46; Rom. 13:1-7; 1 Pet. 2:13-17).

The controversy about the churches' involvement in the social and ethical questions of the day is even more striking in view of its implications for the ecumenical movement. Questions have been raised by some whether the disunity between the Protestant and Roman Catholic churches does not in fact manifest itself in their division on social ethics, so as to make a common social witness impossible. No less a figure than Pope John Paul II has suggested this connection.[2] Despite the impressive convergence on doctrinal questions between Protestant and Roman Catholic churches, consensus may perhaps be incomplete until the dialogue between these traditions can demonstrate convergence on socio-ethical thinking.[3]

Another challenging development for ecumenism in the area of social ethics has been the utilization by a few church organizations of the concept *status confessionis* in order to condemn apartheid unequivocally and in one case to underline for Christians the significance of the nuclear arms race for the peace question.[4] That is to say, these issues have been deemed matters that Christian faith by its very nature must condemn; not to reject these practices must be deemed a heresy. As such, these particular socio-ethical questions in principle can divide the churches, since no church fellowship would be possible among Christians on opposite sides of a *status confessionis*. One would be deemed a heretic in the eyes of the other.

Reflections on Structure, Method, and Purpose

In view of the controversial character and ecumenical relevance of the churches' engagement with contemporary socio-ethical issues, the Institute for Ecumenical Research (associated with the Lutheran World Federation) originally commissioned this study in hopes that it might address some of the challenges which have been raised. Carried out in the context of the institute's long-term research project on the doctrine of creation, this study first and foremost aims to provide information concerning the positions taken by the churches of the world on nine families of cutting-edge contemporary socio-ethical challenges. This information is to be gained through a descriptive analysis of the churches' official social statements (i.e., those approved by the churches' highest governing authorities) issued since 1964 concerning nine issues selected by the institute's board of trustees.

The rationale for this undertaking is that such a study might serve the churches and address the challenges to socio-ethical engagement already noted in several ways. Providing information about what the churches are actually saying and how they are arriving at their conclusions on several controversial questions permits those who are uneasy about their own church's position (which is perhaps viewed as too liberal or as too conservative) to see how their church actually compares with others. They will note a rather broad consensus among the churches on many issues. On those issues where the churches do disagree with each other (often only over matters of strategy), there is no discernible pattern to the disagreement. There are certain exceptions to this rule, as a few churches do tend to exhibit certain socio-political biases, and some tend to address certain issues more than others. (The Orthodox churches, in particular, have been quite selective in which issues they address. And many churches in Asia and Africa, such as the Lutheran churches in India, have not formulated social statements.) Generally speaking, however, as the information in the Appendix shows, if a church takes a so-called liberal position on one issue, it is just as likely to be more conservative on another.

Likewise, there seems to be no recognizable correlation between church disagreements and differences in theology or in cultural context. To be sure, a church from a given cultural context is often more prone to be concerned about certain social issues than churches from other regions. Abortion, for example, is a question addressed largely by churches of the Northern hemisphere.[5] On the whole, however, on a given social issue a church is often just as likely to be in agreement with other churches from its own region as it is to be in disagreement with them. Thus, on the question of the compatibility of Christianity and Communism, one could find churches located in Communist nations on both sides of the question. And on both sides of the question the churches in these nations could find church organizations in the democratic capitalist nations which agreed with them.[6]

As the Appendix clearly indicates, theological disagreements among the churches do not correlate directly with disagreements on social ethics. Thus, though certain tendencies to the contrary can be observed, one cannot speak unequivocally of a bias towards liberal social positions by certain theological orientations and of a corresponding bias towards conservative positions by others. On any given socio-ethical issue considered, one can find churches using diverse theological arguments arriving at the same ethical conclusion, while churches relying on the same theological warrants may conclude in ethical disagreement. Thus we shall see that theological disagreements do not necessarily lead to disagreements in ethics. The determining factors in ethical disagreements are often cultural or philosophical, dependent on the implicit ontology or interpretive categories used in describing the Christian doctrines warranting the ethical conclusions.

This conclusion need not be a source of vexation for readers who come to this book troubled by their churches' involvement in socio-ethical issues. One of the features of the text is that it will not just analyze the theological and ethical positions taken by the churches. Their theological positions will also be compared with their historic confessional approaches to social ethics.

Such a comparison largely takes place in the book's Conclusion. At that point a brief sketch of the historic approach to social ethics of the various confessional families is offered. Then follows a comparison between the approach of each confessional family and the social statements by the member churches of the given confession. With some exceptions, a remarkable correspondence is reflected between the social statements and their historic confessional position.

Challenges to the validity of the modern church's socio-ethical engagements are dealt with by this descriptive study of church social statements in two ways. Not only is it usually unfair to charge a given church with being unduly liberal or unduly conservative in relation to other churches. There exists a more or less catholic consensus among the churches on the broader values for contemporary ethical decision making. It is equally inaccurate to claim that the churches are forfeiting their confessional heritage as a consequence of their contemporary engagement in the issues of the day. The general fidelity to a given church's confessional heritage which is reflected in its social statements suggests at least a compatibility between the churches' historic confessional positions and the positions taken on contemporary social issues.

This descriptive study of contemporary church social statements speaks not just to this skepticism about church engagement with the social issues of the day. It may also address the ecumenical problematic raised earlier. The observation concerning the general lack of impact which theological disagreements have on disagreements over social ethics is pertinent at this point. Insofar as disagreements about social ethics are not related to differences between the churches about the nature of the Christian faith, it seems fair to pose the question whether such ethical disagreements in fact should be deemed *status confessionis,* or church-dividing issues. If theological differences are not at stake in these issues, then the gospel is not at stake. And if the gospel is not at stake in a disagreement among churches, there seems to be no other genuinely valid grounds for regarding the issue in disagreement as worthy of sanctioning continuing division of the churches in question.

To the degree, then, that this study of church social statements shows that socio-ethical disagreements among the churches are not necessarily or even largely related to disagreements about the nature of the Christian faith, it may make a contribution to diffusing socio-ethical differences as a potential barrier to church unity. The Conclusion subsequently offers suggestions concerning how the churches' contemporary social engagements may constructively serve the cause of church unity, specifically by reviving the Life and Work approach to unity and thereby placing the importance of theological disagreements among the churches in a new light. This descriptive analysis of church social statements thus aims to serve ecumenical concerns for church unity as well as the concerns of the churches' constituencies regarding the appropriateness of their socio-ethical engagements.

Methodological Limitations

Because of the large number of social statements published by the churches, it has been necessary to set limits for this study. Virtually all of these limits have been set by the board of trustees of the Institute for Ecumenical Research and so do not reflect merely personal prejudice on the part of the author.

First, the assignment itself to study church social statements as a means of understanding contemporary social engagement by the churches came from the institute's board. Other than official reports of bilateral ecumenical dialogues, the only statements analyzed here are those that have the official authorization of an individual church body's highest level of authority. [7]

A second limit is that the focus of attention has been given only to statements issued from 1964 through 1985, and in some cases, into the 1990s. In only a few cases, involving statements of unusual importance, have earlier statements or those lacking official authorization been considered. [8] Furthermore, only those statements issued since 1965 which have drawn international attention and been widely distributed have been considered. The rationale for this second limit was that about the mid-1960s the churches showed a marked upsurge in the production of social statements. Thus the board decided that this point would be a good one for marking the beginning of social statements that one could consider "contemporary".

A third methodological decision was that church statements addressing only nine selected issues would be analyzed. These issues appear as the chapter titles of the nine numbered chapters of this book. The board of trustees judged these international socio-ethical issues to be among the day's most urgent. Such a decision overlooks a number of other important issues which I would have wished to consider, most notably women's rights and homosexuality, but I have appreciated my colleagues' sensitivity to lightening my workload.

A fourth methodological decision concerned how to obtain the statements and from which church organizations. The decision was made to request official statements on the nine selected issues from all churches belonging to the WCC, a few of the significant non-member churches (e.g., the Roman Catholic Church and larger churches associated with the evangelical movement), and significant regional and national ecumenical councils of churches. Also the larger national Roman Catholic bishops' conferences and the WCC itself were contacted.

As far as possible, the analysis in the text and the Appendix is complete with respect to statements formulated by these organizations on the nine selected issues, although not all churches and organizations responded to my request. Thus it is possible that some church social statements on these issues in the period under consideration have not been included. Yet the claim to completeness is not totally undermined, since it can be observed that I have apparently collected all "official" church statements on these topics issued during the period in question and publicly available to the church catholic. Statements not sent by their framers in response to my request are apparently not generally available and so cannot possibly be exerting much impact or influence on the whole church.

Even with this stipulation, however, a few statements worthy of consideration may have been overlooked. The very nature of the assignment — to examine statements issued primarily between the years 1964 and 1985 — means that my analysis, though supplemented by the most significant documents after 1985, is already a bit out of date or partially incomplete with respect to more recent statements at the time of publication. The Institute for Ecumenical Research wishes to be informed about statements which have inadvertently been overlooked. Outdated or partially incomplete though this analysis may be already, perhaps it lays sufficient groundwork for others interested in keeping the analysis of church social statements up to date.

A final methodological limitation to be considered relates to the decision to examine church social statements as a means of entrée to the broader issues raised by the churches' social engagements. The first question is whether the statements really provide an accurate understanding of the respective churches' actual social engagement. This question is well worth asking. Is it not more important to examine what the churches are actually doing in social ethics than what they are merely saying?

It is not clear, however, how one could measure the churches' actual socio-ethical involvements or determine their theological rationale for these involvements. In the final analysis, could the statements, albeit imperfect, be the best tool available to us?

A related problem in the analysis of social statements pertains to the validity of drawing conclusions about the actual impact theological warrants given in the statements really had on the ethical position finally taken. Those of us who have been involved in the formulation of church statements know that at least sometimes theological considerations are not the most important criteria in determining the statements' conclusions. Also the unsystematic character of these documents, their frequent lack of theological specificity, often make it difficult to determine which theological loci are being proposed as authorization for the position taken. Often the theological point at issue can be determined only indirectly, from implications of what is found explicitly in the statement.

Such difficulties notwithstanding, the attempt is still made in many of the statements to relate the socio-ethical position taken to a traditional theological rationale, often that of the confessional heritage of the church in question. In some cases, which I acknowledge, this theological grounding may not be done with sufficient clarity. Such statements, particularly those with no theological warrants, may well deserve the critique of the skeptics of church engagement in social ethics.

When theological warrants are clearly articulated in the statements, however, they provide us with indications of how the leaders of these churches regard the connection between their historic theological heritage and their present socio-ethical position. This intention in itself would seem sufficient to respond to skepticism concerning the churches' socio-ethical engagements. At least such statements show that the social positions of the churches which drew them up are not necessarily in logical conflict with historic theological positions. If such a conflict between the ethical conclusion and the theological warrant existed, even if the warrant was a mere afterthought, the statement could not have been made coherently.

Likewise, the fact that statements can articulate a relationship between their ethical conclusion and some theological warrants makes it possible to render some judgments on the ecumenical question of whether respective views on social ethics might be church dividing or church uniting. Thus, for example, if several statements show that it is possible to justify logically and appropriately two conflicting socio-ethical positions with the same theological argument, then regardless of the actual warrants utilized by these churches in arriving at their ethical conclusions, one can conclude that the ethical differences between them are not necessarily theologically related. If these disagreements on ethical questions are not theologically related, and so not related to a disagreement about the nature of the Christian faith, might one not also conclude that there is no legitimate basis for considering these disagreements about ethics to be church dividing?

In view of these considerations and in view of the vast number of documents which must be considered in this study, historical-critical judgments regarding the actual authorization for the position of a given statement will not be made. It is not my task to determine the actual intention of the framers of these statements, whether their positions were theologically inspired, or whether theological rhetoric was merely invoked to justify some prior socio-political motivation. Such a task would entail historical-critical study and redaction criticism of roughly a thousand statements. In many instances such information concerning the actual intention of the statements' framers would no longer be accessible.

This is not to imply that no attention has been given to the broader historical context in which the statements were formulated. What follows, however, is primarily a conceptual study. It is an endeavor to determine what the statements are saying about contemporary socio-ethical challenges and what role theological concepts play in the statements' ethical conclusions. It is in this sense that we shall speak of ethical warrants for the positions taken in the statements. A given doctrine warrants a statement's ethical conclusion in the sense that, for the reader, it authorizes or justifies the conclusion.

We have already noted that the role of theological doctrines in the statements' ethical conclusions will allow us to make judgments about at least the compatibility between the churches' contemporary socio-ethical positions and their historic confessional orientation to social ethics. In like manner we have noted how obtaining such information about the literary function of these theological doctrines in the statements is sufficient for determining whether a disagreement on ethics between churches is necessarily related to theological differences and so is church dividing.

It is readily apparent that as a result of these methodological limitations, this study of social statements must be quite modest with respect to the claims it makes on behalf of its conclusions. Nevertheless, for many statements the identification of theological loci functioning as theological authorization in the statements themselves may also indicate how the ethical conclusions of the statements were actually determined in the course of their formulation.

Even in those statements where the theological rationale for the position taken seems to be merely an afterthought, on grounds of much modern theology it does not seem to be a theological distortion to speak of the stated theological rationale as a warrant for the ethical position in question. Since Schleiermacher, much modern theology has employed traditional theological concepts as a kind of afterthought, as tools to provide a Christian explanation for a more fundamental core human experience.[9] Thus on such grounds one speaks of the resurrection of Jesus as the warrant for the Christian's authentic experience of salvation. What really authorizes the experience of salvation, however, is not the bodily resurrection but the experience of renewed faith.[10] Given these widely accepted suppositions, it would not seem unreasonable to take at face value a statement's claim that its ethical position was warranted by Christology, even if in fact its ethical conclusion was originally formulated in response to a general sense of love for one's fellows. In such an instance, Christology can be taken to function as warrant for the statement's position in the sense that Christology can be considered a theological interpretation or depiction of the core human experience which actually warranted the position.

In such cases, where the statements' conclusions are formulated largely in response to non-theological warrants, a conceptual study of the theological rationale given by the statement for the ethical position it assumes at least provides an accurate depiction of the theological thought process which went into the actual formulation of the statement. In that sense it does not seem inappropriate to designate a statement's theological reflections as the theological warrant given for its ethical conclusions.

At least in this qualified sense of a theological authorization for a statement, we shall speak of warrants for ethical positions taken by the churches. Far from providing a mere literary fiction, conclusions drawn from a conceptual study of the statements provide genuine and valid historical information about the theological thought processes which went into the formulation of the statements' ethical conclusions.

Guides for Using This Book

This book has been written with three somewhat distinct though related audiences in mind. These diverse audiences have in turn influenced the book's structure to some extent.

One audience for this book is parish pastors and lay leaders who want to obtain a handy summary of their church's social teachings, particularly in comparison to that of other churches, and to learn a bit more about some of the burning contemporary social issues themselves. Each of the nine chapters addresses this concern.

Because of the large number of statements devoted to each issue, and in view of the concern to address a more general audience in these chapters, the results of the actual analysis of each pertinent statement are recorded in the corresponding section of the Appendix. In each section there, the ethical position and theological warrant of every statement addressing a particular issue is noted. The statements are grouped in clusters according to the position they have taken on the social issue in question and then subdivided again into sub-groups, depending on the theological warrant employed in the statements.

As a result of this manner of dealing with all of the statements listed in the Appendix, it will not be necessary to analyze each pertinent statement in the chapters themselves. Rather, it will be sufficient simply to introduce the most important questions associated with the contemporary social issue under investigation and then proceed to describe, compare, and criticize the various types or clusters of positions on the issue taken by the statements. I do refer explicitly to some of the statements in order to exemplify the various clusters. But if these chapters are to function as planned, as handy introductions to the social issues and explanations of the various church responses to these issues, such that the book might be used by a general audience, an exhaustive analysis of each and every statement is neither desirable nor necessary.

Such a summarizing approach has its problems. One may argue with some justification that to group all statements on a given ethical question which are authorized by a particular locus such as Christology or creation is unduly insensitive to the diverse ways in which a given doctrine may be employed in an ethical argument. For example, to lump together arguments which appeal to Christology as an example with arguments in which Christology functions instrumentally (supplying the criteria for decision making) or only emotively (as mere motivation for the position taken) may be regarded as a kind of undue oversimplification of important distinctions in modes of ethical argumentation.

I am sensitive to such critical questions and do admit my discomfort with the mode of presentation in the book. The large amount of material considered, however, seems to warrant a presentation in the broad strokes I have provided. Besides, as interesting as such distinctions in the mode of ethical argumentation are, it is not clear that they are crucial for the general reader or even for the ecumenist in assessing disagreements and agreements among the churches. Finally, the discerning reader will note that these technical distinctions do appear in the text and in the Appendix at crucial points, particularly where they have implications for discerning the relationship between particular church statements. Thus I have distinguished the use of a doctrine instrumentally (as mere motive) from the same doctrine's use as warrant (as criterion) and in turn have distinguished what specific content of the doctrine has been considered (e.g., whether the person of Christ or his work of redemption is the authorization for an argument).

My method of summarizing most of the statements in broad strokes succeeds in taking into account other valid agenda items. The abridged analysis does not deprive readers of information concerning the social teachings of particular churches, especially as these teachings compare broadly with those of others. Such information can be obtained first by consulting the appropriate section in the Appendix. Then, after digesting the information there concerning the rudiments of the particular church's position and the cluster of churches with which it is identified, readers can turn to the corresponding chapter, paying special attention to its analysis of the particular socio-ethical and theological position that the church in which they are interested maintains. What is said about this particular position — its strengths and weaknesses, and its relationship to the other socio-ethical and theological positions — will pertain to the church in question and its relationship to the statements of those church organizations maintaining these other positions.

In addition to this more general audience, which is concerned to learn more about the nine social issues in general or the teachings of particular churches, the book addresses two other types of readers — those with ecclesiastical responsibility for social statements in their own churches, and scholars of ecumenism concerned about the question of whether differences in social ethics might serve further to divide or to unite the churches. With the exception of their identification of certain catholic trends in the churches' collective treatment of the nine social issues, the nine chapters will perhaps not provide new information for these expert readers.

The information in the Appendix, however, is designed to be of genuine service to administrators responsible for social statements. It provides a ready means of evaluating the position of their churches in comparison to that of other churches. Such information could be particularly valuable for church bodies still in the process of formulating a statement on one of the issues dealt with in the book.

The concerns of scholars of ecumenism have also been kept in mind in developing the Appendix and particularly in writing the Conclusion. In the latter, the ecumenical problematic of whether the churches' differences on social ethics serve further to unite or to divide them is taken up. The data in the whole book serve to help readers evaluate the warrants for my own response to this important ecumenical question.

NOTES

[1] Two of the numerous examples of this commitment on the part of church leadership are evident in the WCC Nairobi Assembly, *Confessing Christ Today* (1975), 18, and in the comments of André Appel, president of the Eglise de la Confession d'Augsbourg d'Alsace et de Lorraine, in a television interview, Station FR3, Alsace Regional Channel, Strasbourg, France, 29 March 1986.

[2] John Paul II, "Address to Ecumenical Leaders", Washington, D.C., 7 October 1979, in *Origins* 9:295; Thomas Sieger Derr, *Barriers to Ecumenism* (Maryknoll, N.Y.: Orbis Books, 1983), 7-8, 9ff., esp. p. 79. A more hopeful prospect for Protestant-Roman Catholic rapprochement on ethics has been sketched by James M. Gustafson, *Protestant and Roman Catholic Ethics* (London: SCM Press, 1979).

[3] A recommendation to examine social ethics as an issue for ecumenical dialogues came in the final report of the Roman Catholic-Lutheran-Reformed Study Commission, *Theology of Marriage and the Problem of Mixed Marriage* (1976), 108.

[4] See three statements by the World Alliance of Reformed Churches: *Racism and South Africa* (1982), I; *Southern Africa* (1989); and *Towards a Common Testimony of Faith* (1989), 2 (though it is rather guarded in its appeal to the concept). See also Lutheran World Federation, *Statements of the Assembly* (1977), 54-56; Nederduitse Gereformeerde Sendingkerk, *Confession of Faith* (1982); Moderamens of the Reformed Alliance [FRG], *Das Bekenntnis zu Jesus Christus und die Friedensverantwortung der Kirche* (1981), vol. 1; *Entschliessung der Generalsynode der Vereinigten Evangelisch-Lutherischen Kirche Deutschlands zur "Zusammenarbeit und Gemeinschaft mit den lutherischen Kirchen im Südlichen Afrika"* (1981). Six groups have designated apartheid as a heresy: Lutheran World Federation, *Statement on Human Rights* (1984), I.3; South African Council of Churches, *A Theological Rationale and a Call to Prayer for the End to Unjust Rule* (1985); Presbyterian Church of Southern Africa, *A Declaration of Faith for the Church in South Africa* (1981); Church of the Province of Southern Africa [Anglican], *Apartheid a Heresy — Support for the Dutch Reformed Mission Church* (1982); Evangelical Lutheran Church in Southern Africa, *Apartheid as Heresy* (1982); and United Church of Canada, *Apartheid as Heresy* (1984). Also see Eglise Evangélique Luthérienne de France, *Voeux et décisions du synode général* (1986), 10. A precedent for the use of the concept of *status confessionis* in this way may be evident in the WCC Uppsala Assembly section report *Towards Justice and Peace in International Affairs* (1968), 28, where it is stated that "racial discrimination is a blatant denial of the Christian faith." Cf. South African Catholic Bishops' Conference, *An Urgent Message to the State President* (1986), 1, which cites an earlier 1957 *Statement on Apartheid* by the conference in making this point; Reformed Church in America, *Report of the Advisory Committee on Christian Unity* (1982), R-9. Also see the identification of nuclear weapons as an issue of faithfulness to the gospel by the WCC Vancouver Assembly, *Statement on Peace and Justice* (1983), 25; cf. Netherlands Reformed Church, *Pastoral Letter of the General Synod on the Question of Nuclear Armaments* (1980); World Alliance of Reformed Churches, *The Theatre of Glory and a Threatened Creation's Hope* (1982).

[5] See chapter 6, as well as the section on abortion in the Appendix.

[6] See chapter 9 and the final section of the Appendix.

[7] A number of German church bodies have issued statements approved by their highest executive boards, which in turn claim to have the same "highest" authority as those issued by these churches. However, because of the volume of these additional statements and the disparity involved in comparing them with statements of other churches which are issued only by their highest legislative bodies, these German church executive committee statements have been considered only when such statements have had a special impact on their church bodies' legislative organizations or on the wider ecumenical community.

[8] In certain cases, unofficial and official documents of the earlier period have been considered: (1) if the statements in question are recognized as influential by knowledgeable people in the field; (2) if they are cited in other documents to be considered; (3) if they are necessary for a proper understanding of other relevant documents; and (4) if the official texts seem to converge with positions taken by the earlier or unofficial statements of the church organization in question.

[9] See Friedrich Schleiermacher, *The Christian Faith,* vol. 1, ed. H.R. Mackintosh and J.S. Stewart (New York: Harper & Row, 1963), 76, 125-26.

[10] A good example of this approach is evidenced in the theology of Rudolf Bultmann; see his "New Testament and Mythology", in *Kerygma and Myth,* vol. 1, ed. H.W. Bartsch (New York: Harper & Row, 1961), 39ff.

1. Apartheid and Racism

In some respects the practice of apartheid, or separate development, has been indigenous to the Republic of South Africa. In other respects it is a manifestation of a seemingly innate human tendency for like to seek out like. When this tendency to congregate, socialize, and cooperate only with persons of a similar racial and ethnic background leads to persecution or prejudice against other groups outside the privileged class, the outcome is racism. Given this definition, the practice of apartheid appears to embody racism. Nevertheless, in deference to a distinction between the two made by a number of church statements to be considered, not least of all by the Dutch Reformed Church (South Africa), as much as possible church statements on the two topics will be dealt with separately. We begin with a consideration of the specific issue of apartheid and an analysis of church statements which address the topic.

Interestingly enough, the Dutch Reformed Church (South Africa) has taken credit for the development of apartheid in South Africa. Its mission strategy was to ensure "that each man could hear and preach, in his own language, the great deeds of God". As a result separate churches were developed along racial lines in South Africa. The church claims that the results of such a mission strategy were so blessed that it had an impact on later political thinking.[1] Apartheid thus has its roots in interpersonal dynamics and structures of segregation that were in place long before the present governing party, the Nationalist Party, came to power in South Africa in 1948. At that time the term "apartheid" (literally "apartness") was coined.

The aim of apartheid considered from a political and economic viewpoint is quite obvious: to perpetuate the political and economic control of the white minority in South Africa. In order to ensure this end and to keep the indigenous black majority "in its place", the government established strict standards of racial segregation in 1950 in its Group Areas Act. Under this law about 13 percent of the country was set aside as reservations for indigenous Africans (the Homelands). Those blacks and persons of racially mixed origin who were allowed to remain in the white-dominated areas to perform menial work had few legal rights. Until recently, they were restricted to residing only in certain designated areas, they have had to carry permits, their movements and occupations have been controlled, and they have been subject to expulsion.

Much has been written about the human degradation, suffering, and international controversy which has ensued as a result of South African apartheid structures. Thus it is not necessary to elaborate further on this point or on recent, apparently liberalizing moves by the South African government. At any rate, the overwhelming reaction of the churches has consistently been one of condemnation — hardly surprising, given certain biblical mandates concerning the oneness of all Christians, the unity of humankind, and the Golden Rule (Gal. 3:28; Acts 17:26; Luke 6:31; Matt. 7:12). The majority of statements issued in condemnation of the practice was formulated by church bodies from the West or by international church agencies such as the WCC, the Lutheran World Federation, the World Alliance of Reformed Churches, and the World Methodist Council. The section in the Appendix which categorizes the churches' statements on apartheid shows the significant ecumenical consensus which is building on the issue. Protestant churches of virtually every confessional heritage in Africa have addressed the matter in virtue of condemnations of apartheid issued by the All Africa Conference of Churches and the South African Council of Churches.

It should be noted that among the confessional traditions the largest number of statements against apartheid has been issued by Presbyterian-Reformed and Lutheran churches. Outside of the African context the problem has really not been addressed by the Roman Catholic Church. Also worthy of note is the relatively recent date when the churches outside Africa first began to address the evils of apartheid. Virtually no statements were issued before the mid-1970s, with the exception of a few cutting-edge, prophetic statements by the WCC, the British Council of Churches, the World Alliance of Reformed Churches, the United Free Church of Scotland, the World Methodist Council Conference, the Anglican Church of Canada, the Associated Churches of Christ in New Zealand, the USA's United Church of Christ, the United Church of Canada, and the USA's Christian Church (Disciples of Christ).

Differences can indeed be observed among the statements which condemn apartheid. As we shall note subsequently in detail, they differ concerning their theological rationale. They also seem to differ concerning their assessment of the gravity of the problem. At least five church bodies have deemed the issue so important as to assert that it constitutes or calls for a *status confessionis,* and so consider the nature of the gospel to be at stake in the dispute.[2] But all the other statements on the subject do not seem to assign such a degree of gravity to the issue.

Differences also can be observed in the statements with regard to strategies proposed for implementing opposition to apartheid. Some opt for economic sanctions against the Republic of South Africa; others do not. A second controversial question pertains to the degree to which supporters of the anti-apartheid groups in South Africa fear Communist influence on the groups. Explicit warnings about this problem have been issued by the South African Catholic Bishops' Conference in its 1986 pastoral letter to the president of South Africa. In addition, the WCC Program to Combat Racism has stimulated some controversy with regard to questions concerning the degree to which the churches can support specific political movements or advocate the use of violence as a means of overcoming apartheid. The Vereinigte Evangelisch-Lutherische Kirche Deutschlands has been notably vocal in its criticisms on these points. On the basis of a different theological argument, a similar critique has been offered by a South African church, the Church of the Province of Southern Africa [Anglican]. A bit more sympathetic openness to the WCC efforts has been shown by the Bund der Evangelischen Kirchen in der DDR, by a 1971 resolution of the Evangelische Kirche in Deutschland, and by the Netherlands Reformed Church.[3]

Despite these matters of dispute, the overwhelming impression one gains from a consideration of the church statements on apartheid is that they represent an amazing consensus. Yet an examination of this consensus is nevertheless warranted for several reasons, particularly in relation to the one church statement, issued by the Dutch

Reformed Church (South Africa), which has sought to justify the practice. The importance of the issue is reason enough to consider the church's reactions. At least for those church bodies which have designated it a *status confessionis,* the issue of apartheid has significance for church unity. For them, a position which differs from the consensus opposition to apartheid constitutes heresy.

Also it is interesting to consider the churches' reactions to apartheid, because in the midst of Christian consensus in condemning apartheid, we still can discern a variety of theological authorizations offered by the churches. Church statements on apartheid thus raise yet a second issue pertaining to church unity. Specifically, they provide our first data for considering the possibility that at least certain theological differences might not be church dividing insofar as they do not mandate differences in praxis.

The comparison between the numerous statements condemning apartheid and the one statement which sought to authorize it also provides an opportunity to assess one of the commonly accepted truisms in modern theological circles — namely, what we might call the wisdom of the Barmen Declaration.

This declaration was a statement drawn up in 1934 by a group of German Protestants who formed the Confessional Synod in opposition to the policies of the German Evangelical Church during the Hitler regime and also with reference to the apparently unequivocal support of National Socialism by the church. In the declaration these false practices were condemned by an appeal to Christology, with its affirmation that Christ is Lord of all realms, including the sphere of politics. In contrast, the supposed Christians who were in control of the German churches largely authorized their support of the National Socialist status quo by appeal to the nature of the creation (specifically, the necessity to respect the so-called orders of creation). This dynamic thus seems to suggest that an ethic authorized by the doctrine of creation leads to conservative — even reactionary — social positions. Those who would assume a position in social ethics which is revolutionary or progressive can do so only by appealing to Christology or the gospel for authorization. Such sentiments are very much a part of the theological and ecclesiastical air we breathe these days.[4]

We already have observed a kind of confirmation of these sentiments by the reticence of the Vereinigte Evangelisch-Lutherische Kirche Deutschlands to endorse concrete political actions for overcoming apartheid. Such a position clearly implies a relatively conservative socio-political stance, since no concrete measures for overcoming the status quo are proposed. And it is significant that the VELKD articulates its position with obvious reference to a distinction between the political realm and the saving will of God, precisely the distinction which characterizes the Lutheran two-kingdom ethic and its appeal to the doctrine of creation as authorization for social ethics.

At any rate, a comparative study of church statements on apartheid seems in part to confirm the wisdom associated with the Barmen Declaration. But such an analysis, coupled with attention to church statements on racism, help show where the common wisdom must be revised and what adjustments must be made in a social ethic authorized by the doctrine of creation in order that such an ethic can be open to arriving at revolutionary or progressive conclusions. A first step in achieving these ends is to consider the former, 1974 statement of the Dutch Reformed Church (South Africa) on apartheid.

In Defence of Apartheid

Until October 1986 the official statement of the Dutch Reformed Church (South Africa) concerning apartheid and separate development was a 1974 report largely approved by the church's synod, with final formulation of certain portions handled by the church's Executive Council in the course of the next year. Although a new report was approved in 1986 (confirmed in 1990, using language a bit more critical of apartheid) which explicitly insists that apartheid cannot be justified on a biblical basis, there is good reason to consider the older statement in detail. A study of the new statements in comparison with the 1974 statement suggests that the actual substance of the 1986 statement and even to some extent the 1990 statement could be interpreted as little more than a reiteration of the substance of the older statement but now packaged in a manner more amenable to good public relations. At best, even the 1990 statement is very much a moderate, compromise statement reflecting many of the commitments of the older statement.

The 1986 statement does not condemn in principle the apartheid structures in South Africa. Objection is raised to apartheid only insofar as it benefits one group of people at the expense of another. Despite its claim that in practice apartheid has functioned sinfully, the 1990 statement largely concurs with its predecessor. No less noteworthy is the fact that the earlier 1986 statement expresses the church's ongoing support of segregated education. Granted, both documents expressed an openness to allowing blacks to join the Dutch Reformed Church, but only with the stipulation that local congregations set their own membership policies. On a national level the church does not explicitly advocate merger with black Reformed churches. Perhaps the new statements refuse to provide biblical warrants to authorize apartheid and concede that earlier attempts to provide such warrants were a mistake. As we shall see, however, the older statement bypassed biblical warrants, preferring instead to authorize apartheid on the basis of natural warrants, or those based on creation. Like the older 1974 statement, they appear to restrict severely the church's role in reforming the structures of the South African government.[5] Generally speaking, the Dutch Reformed Church seems to be lagging behind the South African government's recent efforts to open things up for minorities.

In view of these factors, and inasmuch as the older statement provides interesting insights about the nature of Reformed theology as well as the conventional wisdom associated with the Barmen Declaration, not to mention the insight it can give concerning what may go wrong with an ethic authorized by the orders of creation, detailed consideration of the older 1974 statement of the Dutch Reformed Church (South Africa) seems warranted. This is all the more the case if one compares the theological arguments of this statement with those in the church's more recent, open statement.

With regard to insights the older statement gives concerning the nature of Reformed social ethics, it should be observed that the Dutch Reformed Church and the South African people have had a symbiotic relationship which in some respects may be one of the closest parallels to a theocracy that exists in the twentieth-century Western world. We have noted already how the church has itself taken credit for inspiring the development of apartheid. In fact, it regards its very existence as inseparable from South Africa's history.

In view of these suppositions, it is hardly surprising that at some points in the 1974 statement on apartheid a characteristic Reformed, if not theocratic, social ethic is made quite explicit. The church, it is observed, should ensure that certain scriptural norms are applied in all spheres of life in respect to the state and society. The "principles of the Kingdom of God" apply "in the sphere of politics".[6] Such commitments certainly echo classic Reformed confessional statements on the subject of the relationship between church and civil government, at least insofar as they recognized that it was the function of government to preserve and promote religion and to carry out its duties in accord with the Word of God.[7]

When its concerns focus on the more specific question of apartheid, however, the Dutch Reformed Church's statement appears to shift its theological orientation somewhat. At one point it is asserted that "a political system based on the autogenous or separate development of various population groups can be justified from the Bible."[8] With the exception of identifying some allegedly biblical precedent for maintaining separate churches in South Africa along racial and ethnic lines, however, no specific biblical backing for this claim is offered.[9]

The statement enters into dialogue with a view which prevailed previously in the church, namely, the attempt of the church's 1966 statement to authorize apartheid by appeal to salvation history and the separatist, segregationist propensities of ancient Israel. The official resolution of the synod asserts that the practice of ancient Israel "cannot be applied directly, but certainly by way of analogy, to the situation of the present day". But this stronger wording concerning the appropriateness of salvation history as authorization for apartheid is immediately watered down when it is stated that "it would therefore be inadvisable for the church to draw unwarranted conclusions from it to be applied to relations between the peoples of our times."[10]

In fact, elsewhere the inapplicability of Scripture to the apartheid situation is stated more sharply. It is noted that the Bible does not use the term "race" or any other word to express this concept. Biblical concepts thus cannot simply be transferred to the present situation concerning racial problems in South Africa. Therefore any possible role for Scripture as a regulator of conduct with regard to the racial issue is denied.[11] This exclusion opens the door for other criteria to function as authorization for the justification of apartheid. There are indications that this is also the logic of the 1986 statement. In any case, in the 1974 statement the doctrine of creation and themes associated either with it or with the natural order are called on to function as criteria for judgments about the validity of apartheid.

One of the arguments made by the Dutch Reformed statement in order to make possible this appeal to the creation doctrine for authorizing its position is that, despite earlier affirmations of the legitimate influence and role of Christian faith on civil government, church and state are radically distinguished, virtually separated in their functions. Such a distinction is somewhat reminiscent of the Lutheran version of the two-kingdom ethic. By distinguishing the political sphere from the sphere of the gospel, this historic position also made it possible for Lutherans to use the doctrine of creation rather than the gospel or Christology as the criterion for social ethics.[12]

In the case of the Dutch Reformed Church and the apartheid question, however, the distinction between the realms of church and state becomes a separation in a way not envisaged by the two-kingdom ethic. The South African church states that "it is not part of the church's calling to dictate to the authorities, for instance, exactly how they should regulate the intercourse and relationships between the various groups in a multinational or multiracial situation."[13] The church seems to have nothing to say to the apartheid question!

Nevertheless the Dutch Reformed Church in fact does proceed to provide theological authorization for the practice of apartheid. It does so using the only ground left to it — the doctrine of creation.

Concerned as it is with the question of race relations, the church's statement takes up the issue of racial diversity. Such diversity is said to be "in accordance with the will of God for this dispensation".[14] Some initial indecision is shown regarding whether racial diversity is to be rooted in the doctrine of creation or in the doctrine of sin (as a consequence of the confusion of tongues beginning at the Tower of Babel). The choice between these explanations is said to "make no essential difference".[15]

Almost in the same section of the report, however, the Dutch Reformed Church proceeds to assert that "we must therefore assume that differentiation of 'peoples' is implicit in the command of the creation and that the events of Babel merely give it a new momentum and character."[16] The conclusion seems evident. Racial diversity and so apartheid apparently have been authorized by the very nature of God's creation.

Subsequently in the statement this viewpoint is made more explicit. It is asserted that "in considering its position [on social justice] in respect of the various disparate peoples inhabiting the same country, the church should take cognizance of both the unity and diversity of the human race."[17] Here the criterion for making judgments about the justice of the apartheid system is the empirical, presumably created reality of the diversity of races. But then one additional criterion for making such judgments is added: "In its teaching of social justice and Christian relationships in Southern Africa, the church must at all times take into account the actual, practical situation."[18]

Insofar as the present political situation must be taken into account and the political reality granted its own autonomy, a kind of two-kingdom ethic again seems to be in operation. Given the nature of the first criterion, however, the "natural diversity of the races" apparently rooted in God's will for creation, there appears to be no basis for challenging "the actual, practical situation". In fact, given this criterion, if the actual present situation of apartheid and separate development must be taken into account in the church's ethical judgments, the only valid conclusion seems to be that insofar as these practices quite obviously succeed all too well in maintaining the diversity of the human race, the created order must be taken as authorizing separate development and apartheid.

Elsewhere in the statement this sort of appeal to the creation doctrine as a sanction for apartheid is almost explicitly made. Apparently in an effort to justify its practice of segregated churches, appeal is made to "the natural diversity of people".[19] What else can the concept of natural diversity connote but an appeal to the nature of creation, to the so-called orders of creation, as warrant for this practice?

In this context the statement proceeds to identify what it regards as the real nature of racial distinctiveness. Separate movements are said to respect "ontological and cosmological elements".[20] In effect, the statement has posited an ontological character to racial distinctions and commends separatism and apartheid for taking account of this ontology. Thus these practices actually are warranted by appeal to the doctrine of creation, specifically by a certain kind of ontology used by the Dutch Reformed Church in developing its doctrine of creation, its way of conceiving the created orders.

Some might be tempted to discount the seriousness of these theological arguments on behalf of apartheid by maintaining that, by appealing to the creation doctrine and a kind of two-kingdom ethic as authorization for its position, the Dutch Reformed Church has forfeited its Reformed heritage. Thus the theological arguments in the statement represent little more than an attempt to "baptize" a politically and economically inspired policy of oppression.

It is quite possible that the latter observation is accurate. But since our interest at this time is restricted to the question of how the concepts of creation, Christology, and the like function in theological arguments to authorize ethical positions, we need not focus on the problem of the actual intention of the framers of the Dutch Reformed Church statement. Nevertheless it can be observed that this church's mode of theological argumentation is not necessarily a departure from the Reformed theological heritage.

For example, a careful reading of Calvin's *Institutes* suggests that at some points he maintained a kind of two-kingdom ethic. In his anthropology he insisted that the believer was under both spiritual and political governments and that the demands of the two must be distinguished. This commitment was further undergirded by his affirmation of a concept of natural law, the idea that the law is accessible to all human beings, regardless of their faith commitments. Despite his theocratic tendencies, Calvin never held a pure theocracy, as he did not grant the church authority to compel obedience by force.[21] Thus the Dutch Reformed Church's reliance on a kind of two-kingdom ethic does not necessarily entail a departure from the Reformed heritage.

It could be argued that the South African church's use of the two-kingdom formulation breaks with Calvin insofar as it appears to posit a kind of separation, not just a distinction, between the realm of the church and the realm of the state. To the extent, however, that this separation of the realms is characteristic of a dispensationalism surfacing at some points in the South African church's report, even this step cannot be deemed totally inimical to all segments of the Reformed tradition.[22] One finds a dispensationalist orientation in the seventeenth-century Westminster Confession, with its notion of two distinct, almost conflicting covenants, and different dispensations in each covenant.[23]

Nor is the Dutch Reformed Church's appeal to the doctrine of creation as authorization for its ethical conclusions totally atypical of the historic Reformed tradition. In fact, prominent nineteenth-century Reformed theologians in the Netherlands advocated freeing different life spheres from ecclesiastical control so that they might function in accord with the "common grace" accessible to all in creation. It is precisely this heritage which the South African church claims to appropriate.[24]

It is quite apparent, then, that the theological arguments of the Dutch Reformed Church represent a legitimate genre of Reformed and Christian theological thinking. What has gone wrong with these arguments, such that they can be used to justify the heinous ethical conclusions we have observed? Have we in this case identified a contemporary confirmation of the conventional theological wisdom associated with the Barmen Declaration? In the case of apartheid a social ethic authorized by the doctrine of creation, trading on a distinction (if not separation) of the two kingdoms, has resulted in a reactionary socio-political conclusion. A conceptual study of several other church social statements devoted to the issue of apartheid (and a few other issues related to questions of human liberation and peace) seems to confirm further the popular wisdom associated with Barmen. For one finds that a great number of these statements which condemn apartheid or take a revolutionary or progressive stance on other issues authorize their position by theological warrants drawn from Christology or related areas of doctrine.

Opposition to Apartheid: The Wisdom of Barmen

As a matter of fact, the majority of officially authorized church statements which condemn apartheid authorize their position by appeal to some doctrinal loci associated with the second article of the Nicene Creed. Numerous examples include statements from general councils of the World Alliance of Reformed Churches, a 1976 statement of the World Methodist Council Assembly, several statements approved by the WCC Vancouver Assembly, a policy statement by the USA's National Council of Churches, a 1986 resolution of the Lutheran Church-Missouri Synod, two statements of the Evangelical Lutheran Church in Southern Africa, and at least two statements of the South African Council of Churches.[25]

In order to illustrate the arguments used by these statements, a 1982 resolution of the General Council of the World Alliance of Reformed Churches (reaffirmed by the alliance in 1989) will receive some specific attention. Besides its typical theological arguments, this statement is particularly worthy of note because of its pertinence to the arguments of the Dutch Reformed Church (South Africa) on behalf of apartheid. In this statement, the World Alliance of Reformed Churches not only declared that apartheid calls for a *status confessionis* (i.e., apartheid is regarded as an issue "on which it is not possible to differ without seriously jeopardizing the integrity of [a] common confession", an issue over which disagreement would divide churches) but also suspended the Dutch Reformed Church and a sister church in South Africa from membership in the alliance.[26]

The theological viewpoint of this statement by the World Alliance of Reformed Churches is transparent. Apartheid, it is argued, is "sinful and incompatible with the Gospel". The practice is alleged to be "based on a fundamental irreconcilability of human beings, thus rendering ineffective the reconciling and uniting power of our Lord Jesus Christ".[27] The function of Christology or the gospel as authorizing the condemnation of apartheid is readily apparent. Elsewhere in the statement similar appeals are made to Christology and in a few cases to the doctrine of the church and eschatology. Earlier statements by the alliance using the same kind of theological arguments against apartheid are also cited.[28] But the gospel or Christology provides the ultimate warrant for the Reformed Alliance's action. The two South African member churches which are suspended are said to have "misused the Gospel". Thus on grounds of the gospel they are suspended, and apartheid is deemed a *status confessionis*.[29] There are important reasons for the alliance to emphasize that the gospel is at stake in its objections to the South African church, because on Reformed grounds (at least Calvin's), scandalous behavior among Christians is in itself no grounds for schism.[30]

In any case, the same line of argumentation concerning the evils of apartheid is reflected in the additional church statements I have identified in this section, as well as in other such statements. It applies even in the case of several statements, such as a 1983 declaration of the South African Council of Churches or two 1982 declarations of the Evangelical Lutheran Church in Southern Africa, which condemn apartheid by arguments which link appeals both to Christology and some doctrinal locus associated with the third article of the creed. The conventional wisdom drawn from the Barmen Declaration seems at this point to be reflected in the apartheid controversy. An ethic grounded in Christology or the gospel authorizes an open, progressive ethic that denounces apartheid, and an ethic rooted primarily in the doctrine of creation has authorized a reactionary defence of apartheid.[31]

A number of church statements which condemn apartheid do so by appeal to the doctrine of the church or to some other third-article locus for authorization, and some do not provide a clear theological rationale for their collective position. Yet this fact does nothing to negate the conventional wisdom associated with the Barmen Declaration. Statements without a theological authorization include two additional resolutions of the World Methodist Council, a 1974 statement issued by the All Africa Conference of Churches, and the much-discussed 1977 statement of the Lutheran World Federation which stated that apartheid constitutes a *status confessionis*. I would submit that this statement and a similar one issued in 1980 by the American Lutheran Church and in 1981 by the Vereinigte Evangelisch-Lutherische Kirche Deutschlands belong in this group of statements insofar as they fail to provide reasons concerning precisely why apartheid represents a *status confessionis*. But the idea that apartheid would conflict with the implications of confessional subscription suggests that the gospel and other second- and third-article loci are seen as being compromised by apartheid. Thus these doctrinal loci are functioning de facto as the theological authorization for condemning apartheid. At least in the case of the Lutheran World Federation statement, there are suggestions that confessional subscription has implications for living the gospel and for worship which are incompatible with apartheid. In any event, one might cite these statements as a further indication that it seems to be necessary for the churches to avoid reference to the doctrine of creation in order to overcome the reactionary thinking which might otherwise impede a condemnation of apartheid.

Even in the case of statements appealing to the doctrines of the church, eschatology, or the Holy Spirit as authorization for the condemnation of apartheid, these observations seem confirmed. Insofar as the church functions as a "sign" for the "renewed society" free of apartheid, as it does in a 1978 statement of the Vereinigte Evangelisch-Lutherische Kirche Deutschlands, elements of the gospel of redemption are functioning without explicit reference to the doctrine of creation in the condemnation of apartheid. The same kind of argument functions with regard to the appeal to the Holy Spirit as warrant by a 1975 statement of the USA's United Church of Christ.

Similar Arguments, Similar Conclusions

A survey of recent church statements addressing issues at least tangentially related to apartheid appears to confirm further the theological tendencies we have observed. When we take up the issue of racism, we shall note that numerous statements which condemn racism in general — in fact the majority of church statements that take this position — rely on warrants drawn from Christology or from some theological locus related to the second article of the creed.[32] A survey of church statements dealing with questions about women's rights or homosexuality also makes evident that a similar Christocentric ethic authorizes "progressive", liberal positions on these issues. This connection is illustrated nicely in a 1974 resolution of the Moravian Church in America, Northern Province, a 1976 resolution of the World Methodist Council, and an issue group report from the WCC Vancouver Assembly. All three take pro-feminist positions authorized by appeal to the teaching or the ministry of Christ.[33] Likewise pertinent is the fact that the United Church of Christ [USA] authorizes its advocacy of increased involvement of homosexuals in the leadership of the church by appeal to the work of Christ and the inclusive nature of divine grace.[34]

In a subsequent chapter we shall note that the association of theological arguments authorized by appeals to Christology with liberal or progressive ethical conclusions is also evident on the peace question. The greatest number of officially approved church statements advocating peace authorize their position by appeal to Christology or to the nature of the gospel. In fact some appeal to Christology appears in most of the statements advocating peace and opposing nuclear deterrence. In all but a handful of cases, even when church statements supporting these positions do appeal to the doctrine of creation for authorization, the creation doctrine is always in correlation with the gospel or Christology.[35]

Besides the tendency so far noted of theological appeals to Christology serving as ethical warrants authorizing liberal, even radical, ethical perspectives, a consideration of the predominance of such a Christocentric ethic in liberation theology seems further to strengthen the case. Thus Rubem Alves offers a "christological interpretation of the cosmos". For Alves, the cosmos is to be regarded from the perspective of liberation, so that Christology is the power and warrant for liberation. Likewise Gustavo Gutierrez follows suit in subordinating creation to redemption and in maintaining that the liberating gift of Christ is the precondition for a just society and liberation.[36]

As one may identify many instances when an ethic authorized by Christology leads to liberal or radical ethical positions, so some contemporary church statements offer confirmation of the fact that an ethic authorized by appeal to the doctrine of creation will inevitably be conservative, even reactionary. At any rate we can say that virtually every church social statement which assumes a politically and ethically reactionary or extremely conservative position appears to do so by way of an appeal to the doctrine of creation. Thus in addition to the Dutch Reformed Church's defense of apartheid, one also finds the National Association of Evangelicals [USA] taking an anti-feminist position, the Roman Catholic Church rejecting abortion as well as repudiating Communism, and the Assemblies of God rejecting homosexuality as a sin on the basis of warrants and criteria drawn from the doctrine of creation.[37] Even on the issue of nuclear deterrence, the more conservative positions of the National Conference of Catholic Bishops [USA] and the Lutheran Church in America, which advocate or tolerate continued use of deterrence as a strategy for peace, also appear to authorize their position by appeal to theological loci associated with the doctrine of creation.[38]

Creation Says No to Apartheid

Given the evidence which seems to support the critique by both Barth and the Barmen Declaration of an ethic authorized by the creation doctrine, and noting this ethic's propensity to authorize reactionary social positions or at least those out of step with the times, one is tempted to conclude that the most appropriate Christian social ethic may well be one which employs Christology or related doctrinal loci as its warrant and criterion. Certainly there seems to be a kind of ecumenical consensus on this point.[39] Nevertheless, there are exceptions. A few statements which condemn apartheid and racism make at least some reliance on the doctrine of creation or the concept of the orders of creation as a warrant for the position. Although the majority of these statements have been issued by Lutheran churches, at least one representative of many of the confessional traditions has issued such a statement. The geographical spectrum of such statements is also broad. Collectively they provide insights concerning theological arguments which can offer the safeguards necessary to ensure that a creation-based ethic is able to avoid its tendency to authorize ruthlessly reactionary or at least outmoded social ethical positions. Also their consideration makes possible an appreciation of the fact that apartheid has been condemned by different modes of theological argumentation, an insight which relates to the question whether differences on social ethics must be church-dividing issues.

With regard to the issue of apartheid and its condemnation authorized by the doctrine of creation, one pertinent statement is a 1981 resolution of the Church Council of the American Lutheran Church. Granted that with the creation of the new Evangelical Lutheran Church in America, the resolution is no longer binding on any of the American Lutheran churches; yet the resolution still warrants careful consideration both because at the time of writing and for the period we are considering it had official status, but also and most especially because of its clarity and pertinence for illustrating the argument against apartheid and racism with authorization by the doctrine of creation.

The 1981 resolution follows up on a 1980 General Convention resolution which condemned apartheid and declared it a *status confessionis*. It states: "The entire weight of biblical witness regarding the unity of human creation, of equal opportunity for development of gifts divinely given, of justice for all peoples, is cited in support of opposition to apartheid." Subsequently the resolution cites relevant biblical texts, first citing Acts 17:26a: "And he made from one every nation of men."[40] Clearly the doctrine of creation understood as a reality which unites humankind is being called upon to authorize the condemnation of apartheid. An ethic authorized by the creation doctrine thus need not necessarily fail to authorize a progressive ethic which can challenge the status quo. A closer examination of the resolution indicates that some adjustments have been made in this appeal to the creation doctrine in comparison with the version of the two-kingdom ethic we observed in the statement of the Dutch Reformed Church (South Africa).

The first point that strikes the reader is that the gospel and the created order (and by implication the two realms of the two-kingdom ethic) are not separated by the American Lutheran Church, as we found to be the case in at least those portions of the Dutch Reformed Church statement pertaining directly to apartheid. Rather, creation is correlated with the gospel, Christology, and theological loci associated with the third article of the creed. This correlation is evident insofar as the resolution also cites biblical passages pertaining to Christology (Eph. 2:14-15) or the new life in Christ (Gal. 3:28) in support of its condemnation of apartheid.[41] Elsewhere it is noted that apartheid is to be rejected because of the nature of the church, which will permit no requirements for unity among Christians in addition to agreement on the proclamation of the Word and the administration of the sacraments.[42]

One could read these statements as indicating that the American Lutheran Church has moved away from the classic Lutheran orientation of grounding its social ethic in the doctrine of creation. The passages cited seem to suggest that Christology, the gospel, and the doctrine of the church have also been called on to function as warrants for authorizing the denunciation of apartheid. Or perhaps, unlike in the earlier appeal to creation, these doctrines function less as criteria which structure the reaction or argument against apartheid and more as what we might call ethical motives, awakening believers to the evil of apartheid and creating an unspecified divine mandate for struggling against it, but not themselves structuring the argument against apartheid or proposing remedial social structures.

Nevertheless, the introduction of possible additional warrants does not necessarily entail a fundamental change in the Lutheran two-kingdom model for ethics. The appeal to the doctrine of creation, to the orders or the structures of creation, as primary warrant and criterion for ethics is not rejected. Nor are this appeal and the doctrine of creation subordinated to redemption, Christology, and similar doctrinal loci. In the resolution considered, the appeal to creation as warrant for condemning apartheid still stands on its own. The logic and authority for its argument is not contingent on these additional supporting warrants drawn from other doctrinal loci. It is simply the case, as the resolution puts it, that "the entire biblical witness . . . support[s] opposition to apartheid."[43]

Each of the major doctrinal themes of the biblical witness could presumably be called on independently to authorize a condemnation of apartheid. Thus it seems to follow that the content of these various doctrinal themes must correlate with each other, insofar as appeals to these distinct theological themes as authorization still provide the same ethical conclusions (i.e., that apartheid is evil). In short, the resolution reflects the Nicene faith, its core insight that God's work as Father (in creation) is compatible with his work in Jesus Christ (redemption) and his work as Spirit (sanctification). Creation is correlated with redemption and sanctification by both the creed and the American Lutheran Church statement.[44]

That a two-kingdom ethic seems compatible with this Nicene theological context is more or less indicated by the American Lutheran Church statement in other ways. First, insofar as creation and redemption are correlated, even if Christians were to appeal to Christology or the doctrine of the church as warrants for condemning apartheid, the ethical content of their appeal to these loci would provide them with no deeper insights into the issue than non-Christians could gain. For non-Christians would gain ethical insights into the matter by virtue of their living in creation. And insofar as creation and redemption are correlated in their content, the ethical wisdom drawn from each is similar. Thus the ethical insights gained by Christians from Christology would correlate with the ethical insights drawn by non-Christians from creation. It is certainly a core commitment of the two-kingdom ethic to affirm that Christians possess no superior ethical insight in relation to non-Christians. By contrast, a typically Reformed Christocentric position — as embodied in most of that tradition's historic confessional statements — has a more difficult time acknowledging that Christians possess no superior ethical insights on issues because of their faith.[45]

Also the American Lutheran Church's statement seems to differ from this Reformed Christocentrism in that unlike the latter, it does not advocate legislating norms drawn from Christology, ecclesiology, or the gospel as a means of overthrowing apartheid. For this and the other reasons cited, the two-kingdom ethic does not seem undercut by the American Lutheran Church's appeal to the creation doctrine as an ethical warrant correlated with appeals to other theological loci related to the theme of redemption.

This correlation of creation and redemption does indeed distinguish the American Lutheran Church's use of a creation-warranted ethic from the version that appeals to the orders of creation and that holds a two-kingdom ethic, such as we found in the Dutch Reformed Church and most other statements with a similar theological mode of argumentation and a similar reactionary social ethic. Positing such a creation-redemption correlation, however, appears to have other consequences.

We noted earlier that a crucial point for the Dutch Reformed Church's argument was its ontology, which emphasized that diversity, including even the racially segregated character of humanity, is given in creation. By contrast, although it does not explicitly refer to an ontology, the American Lutheran Church resolution posits a different kind of ontology to develop its doctrine of creation. It emphasizes that instead of distinguishing or dividing human beings, creation unifies them.[46]

Granted, a similar affirmation was also made by the Dutch Reformed Church (South Africa) in 1974, which even referred to the "unity and solidarity of the human race".[47] This affirmation, however, plays no role in the church's subsequent reflections concerning the most appropriate political structures for regulating race relations in South Africa. Rather, at that point the appeal is made to an ontology which emphasizes not unity but diversity.

The American Lutheran Church's decision to apply ontology emphasizing human unity to the apartheid question may be regarded as a consequence of correlating creation and redemption/the gospel in their resolution. This correlation entails that the orders of creation, an ontology used in developing the doctrine of creation, must not contradict the central commitments of the gospel. The gospel clearly removes all barriers between human beings (Gal. 3:28), a truth that Paul's controversy with the Jewish Christians illustrates. If a doctrine of creation is to be correlated with this particular interpretation of redemption, it thus would also reflect the unity of human beings as the American Lutheran Church statement has.

These observations help further explain the Dutch Reformed Church (South Africa) statement. As we noted, it did not correlate, but tended rather to separate, the realms of creation and the gospel. Thus the content of the gospel was not related to the ontology used in depicting the doctrine of creation. This separation was readily apparent insofar as the statement's ontology of creation emphasized the diversity of people in contrast to the unifying thrust of the gospel.

This difference in the respective ontologies employed by the two statements we have been examining ultimately accounts for their differences over apartheid. The prevailing ontology used by the Dutch Reformed Church, one which depicts reality in terms of diversity of the races, endorses separate development as being in harmony with the orders of creation. The American Lutheran Church, in contrast, has an ontology which depicts reality in terms of the unity of human beings and thus finds apartheid to be in conflict with the orders of creation.

If the disagreement over apartheid among at least a few of the churches ultimately relates to differences in the ontology they employ in developing the doctrine of creation and perhaps in the intentions of the different proponents of these diverse ontologies, one may raise the question whether a real doctrinal disagreement about the nature of the Christian faith is at stake in the debate over apartheid. In that case can one legitimately speak of apartheid as constituting a *status confessionis,* an issue which can divide churches? We may grant that non-theological factors, including degrees of sincerity in holding the faith, may presently contribute to differences among the churches. But can churches be divided legitimately over issues not occasioned by disagreements about the logic or character of the Christian faith? Indeed not, insist the Reformers.[48] It perhaps could be argued that a theological difference is at stake here, that by refusing to correlate and instead by separating creation and redemption, the Dutch Reformed Church compromised the Nicene faith in its 1974 statement. This point can be extended when one recognizes that in its more recent 1986 statement the Dutch Reformed Church's more critical perspective on apartheid emerges when it more closely correlates creation and redemption than it did in its 1974 statement.[49] An examination of the ecumenical significance of the positing of a relation of creation and redemption, along with its consequences for church unity, is beyond the scope of this book.

In addition to the two modifications of an ethical argument warranted by the creation doctrine which we have observed in the Lutheran statement, a third modification is implied. Specifically, a certain kind of anthropology seems logically entailed by the creation ontology, which was itself entailed by the correlation of creation and redemption/the gospel. If creation is depicted by means of an ontology which speaks of the unity of human persons, then human persons must be conceived of in relational terms. That is, a human being must be understood in such a way that it is necessarily related to and influenced by other human persons and its environment. This anthropology and its related ontology as well as the positing of a correlation between creation and redemption appear to be adequate safeguards to ensure that an ethic warranted by the doctrine of creation need not necessarily result in reactionary or even conservative ethical positions.

The three adjustments which we have observed in the statement of the American Lutheran Church are not peculiar to it. A consideration of other official church statements on apartheid which rely on theological warrants drawn from the doctrine of creation but do not lapse into reactionary or conservative socio-political ethical positions indicates that they have also made similar adjustments. For example, an ontology which emphasizes the unity of human persons underlies the condemnation of apartheid by appeal to the doctrine of human persons in a 1972 decision of the Associated Churches of Christ in New Zealand and in a 1986 resolution of the Anglican Church of Canada. Likewise in a 1984 statement the Evangelisch-Lutherische Kirche in Bayern condemns apartheid, or more specifically the South African policy of resettlement, by arguing that it contradicts the orders of creation. But it also states that apartheid is confounded by testimony to the unity of Christ's body and the Eucharist.[50] Insofar as Christ's body, the sacrament, and the orders of creation contradict apartheid, they must have some affinities with one another. Thus like the American Lutheran Church, the Bavarian church has formulated its conception of the doctrine of creation in such a way that its content is correlated with loci associated with the doctrine of redemption.

Similar examples are provided by at least six African and several German church bodies, not to mention a 1966 declaration of the World Methodist Council, a 1984 statement of the Reformed Church in Japan, a 1987 policy statement on Africa by the American Baptist Churches, probably a 1979 resolution on South Africa by the British Council of Churches, and to some extent a 1971 resolution of the Anglican Church of Canada. (This last item may actually subordinate creation to redemption.) Thus in South Africa, apartheid has been condemned by the Broederkring of the Dutch Reformed Church [South Africa], the Presbyterian Church of South Africa, the Federation of Lutheran Churches in South Africa, the Evangelical Lutheran Church in Southern Africa, and perhaps on one occasion the Church of the Province of Southern Africa [Anglican] as well as the All Africa Conference of Churches by appeal to the doctrine of creation, albeit correlated with appeals to loci related both to the second and third articles of the creed as warrants for their position. Creation and redemption are surely correlated in these statements. Appeal to the one locus as warrant presumably results in the same conclusion (i.e., the condemnation of apartheid) as results from an appeal to the other locus. But the statements also assert that an appeal to the creation doctrine as warrant, even when creation is considered in isolation from other doctrinal themes, is sufficient to authorize rejection of apartheid.[51] This commitment indicates the compatibility of these statements with something like an ethic based on orders of creation and the two-kingdom idea, despite their appeal to other theological loci as supplementary warrants. (Again it is interesting to note that not just Lutheran and Anglican but also Reformed churches find it possible to authorize their social ethic to some extent by way of appeal to the doctrine of creation.)

These African church statements, however, are self-consciously aware that an appeal to the doctrine of creation must be supplemented by its correlation with some other theological locus, lest the doctrine and ethical conclusions based on it be distorted, as happens in the case of the Dutch Reformed Church. This concern is made quite explicit in the statement by the Federation of Lutheran Churches in South Africa, where a challenge is issued to those who (like the Dutch Reformed Church) say that the structures of society are shaped only by natural laws without exposure to the criterion of God's love. Of similar interest is the fact that an anthropology and ontology which explicitly embrace the relational character of existence is expressly advocated by the Presbyterian Church of Southern Africa.[52] It is apparent that all of the adjustments to a creation-warranted ethic which we identified in the statement of the American Lutheran Church have been reflected in the statements of these African churches in authorizing their liberal, progressive ethic.

Theological and Ecumenical Implications

The data which we have assembled in our consideration of statements on apartheid both do and do not seem to confirm the conventional wisdom associated with the Barmen Declaration. We have noted a tendency in certain appeals to the doctrine of creation to authorize a conservative, even reactionary ethic. There likewise seems to be a tendency for an ethic authorized by appeals to Christology or related doctrinal loci to lead to liberal or even radical socio-ethical positions.

There are exceptions to these tendencies, which challenge the conventional wisdom. Thus the pre-1974 position of the Dutch Reformed Church (South Africa) seemed to authorize apartheid by something like an appeal to salvation history and the gospel. And as we have noted, a number of statements warrant denunciations of apartheid or take other liberal stances by way of appeal to the doctrine of creation.

The fact that one can identify a condemnation of apartheid in statements which are authorized by Christology and similar condemnations in other statements authorized by appeal to the doctrine of creation has several interesting implications for questions concerning church unity. It is evident that theological disagreements need not be at stake in the debate over apartheid, for we have identified churches on both sides of the issue which authorize their distinct positions by a similar mode of theological argument in appealing to the doctrine of creation. On the one hand we have already noted that use of such a common ground entails that apartheid may not truly be a *status confessionis*. The only grounds for arguing that the dispute over apartheid is related to the nature of the Christian faith and so is church dividing seem to relate to the question whether the Dutch Reformed Church (South Africa) has so distinguished creation from redemption as to distort the Nicene faith. This question perhaps could be posed to certain Lutheran theologians.

On the other hand an appreciation of the fact that differences over the mode of theological argument do not necessarily mandate differences on the question of apartheid has implications for church unity in another way. In this light a stronger case could be made for arguing that the differences between the churches in their respective characteristic theological orientations for dealing with social ethics need not divide the churches. For these differences, whether an ethic should be authorized by appeals to the doctrine of creation or to Christology seems to have no practical consequences, at least not on the question of apartheid. It might properly be asked whether doctrinal differences with no practical consequences are important enough to divide the churches.

The data likewise seem to call into question another piece of conventional wisdom. It is frequently maintained in ecumenical circles that all theology is context-bound, that different cultural contexts mandate different viewpoints in both theology and ethics.[53] In the positions taken by the six South African church bodies in condemning apartheid at least with some reference to the doctrine of creation, we have some examples of churches from the Southern hemisphere taking precisely the same position on ethics (and for the same theological reasons) as a church from the Western world (the American Lutheran Church). Likewise apartheid was condemned by appeal to Christology as authorization both by an African church, the Evangelical Lutheran Church in Tanzania, and a group of American Christians, the National Council of Churches [USA]. In fact, differences in cultural context do not appear to mandate different positions in theology and ethics.

Racism

The theological and ecumenical implications of the churches' statements on apartheid also pertain largely to their statements on racism. As we observed in certain statements against apartheid, so here some of the arguments use a creation-warranted ethic as a means of authorizing statements which condemn racism.

An examination of the relevant section in the Appendix and its documentation for the following observations indicates that the kind of unanimity which we observed in church statements on apartheid is perhaps even more pronounced in the statements on racism. One can identify condemnations of racism in statements from virtually all the major confessional traditions, including the Roman Catholic Church, Eastern Orthodoxy, and the Christian Restorationist movement. For example, condemnations of the practice are registered in the Second Vatican Council as well as by the Romanian Orthodox Church and in several statements of the Christian Church (Disciples of Christ). Even the evangelical movement is represented in these condemnations, as the Mennonite Brethren Church, the Brethren in Christ Church, the National Association of Evangelicals [USA], and the Reformed Ecumenical Synod, which condemned racism respectively in 1963 (subsequently also in 1966), 1963 (again in 1964 and 1972), 1963 (subsequently also in 1964, 1965, 1968, and several other times in the 1980s), and 1968 (more recently also in 1980 and 1984) statements, normally are associated with the evangelical movement.

The catholicity of this crusade against racism is also evident geographically insofar as one can identify pertinent statements issued by church organizations on virtually every continent. In Latin America, for example, the practice has been condemned by the Presbyterian-Reformed Church in Cuba, and in Asia by the Christian Conference of Asia. Also statements against racism appear in the earliest stages of the period under review, although, with the notable exception of the United Free Church of Scotland, it has not so much been a topic of concern to national churches outside North America until the 1970s.

Despite this widespread consensus, differences emerge. There are varying opinions concerning the role of the state in combating racism. Notable in this regard is a 1982 statement of the [Catholic] Bishops of the Netherlands which criticized government intervention in this sphere.[54] Another area of divergence among the statements pertains to the different means that they employ for authorizing their common condemnation of racism. A significant number of these statements base their open, progressive ethical position of condemning racism on some doctrine associated with the second article of the creed. For example, church bodies as diverse as the Southern African Catholic Bishops' Conference, the Romanian Orthodox Church, the 1968 Lambeth Conference, the Lutheran Church-Missouri Synod, the Baptist World Alliance, the USA's National Association of Evangelicals and various WCC assemblies have condemned racism by appeal to related themes such as the redemptive work of Christ, Christ's command, the gospel, and the criterion of what is Christ-like.[55] Especially noteworthy in this connection is a statement of the WCC Uppsala Assembly which claimed that the Christian faith is denied by racial discrimination.[56]

A large number of statements on the subject authorize their position by means of this sort of appeal to Christology or the gospel, in combination with references to some theological theme associated with the doctrine of creation and, at least in eight cases, with the doctrines of the church, baptism, or eschatology. Such an orientation appears in a significant number of WCC statements from the New Delhi and Uppsala assemblies. It also is reflected in statements of the British Council of Churches, the Baptist World Alliance, the World Alliance of Reformed Churches; in some statements by representatives of the Lutheran tradition, such as a 1979 statement of the Church of Norway and a 1963 assembly resolution of the Lutheran World Federation; as well as in some Roman Catholic statements such as the Second Vatican Council's *Gaudium et Spes* and in statements in 1966, 1968, and 1976 of the USA's National Conference of Catholic Bishops. Methodist churches like the Methodist Church in Malaysia, Moravian churches like the USA's Moravian Church, Northern Province, Brethren churches like the Brethren in Christ, and United churches like the USA's United Church of Christ also have issued condemnations of racism with this sort of argument.[57]

This sort of correlation of various theological arguments for authorizing the condemnation of racism is pushed to its logical extreme in the following statements, which invoke theological loci from all three articles of the creed: at least a few statements of the WCC Evanston and New Delhi assemblies, a 1980 policy statement on the Middle East of the USA's National Council of Churches, a 1966 declaration of the World Methodist Council Conference, a 1979 resolution on the Ku Klux Klan of the USA's Episcopal Church, 1963 and 1981 resolutions of the Christian Church (Disciples of Christ), a resolution of the 1984 Lutheran World Federation Assembly, a 1976 statement of the American Lutheran Church, a 1964 statement of the World Alliance of Reformed Churches, a 1968 declaration of the Christian Reformed Church in North America, a 1976 policy statement of the American Baptist Churches, a 1985 resolution on congregational openness and affirmation by the United Church of Christ [USA], perhaps a 1979 pastoral letter of the USA's National Conference of Catholic Bishops, a 1987 Roman Catholic papal encyclical of John Paul II, and a 1971 resolution on racism by the Evangelische Kirche im Rheinland. The reliance in these statements on appeals drawn from the third article of the creed characterizes several other statements, among them resolutions in 1969, 1977, and 1979 of the USA's United Church of Christ as well as selected WCC statements from its New Delhi and

Uppsala assemblies, which authorize the condemnation of racism solely by appeal to the doctrines of the church or eschatology.

The 1966 World Methodist Council Conference statement is particularly interesting in its argument, especially as it sheds light on the Methodist heritage. Authorization for dealing with the issues of the day is drawn from Methodist ecclesiology, specifically the emphasis on itinerancy in the Wesleyan heritage. In a related manner, a particularly revealing argument against racism and sexism appears in a 1985 resolution concerning Desmond Tutu by the Episcopal Church [USA]. It authorizes its position by appeal to the example of this modern Christian saint. Could this mode of argument be indicative of the theological ethos of the Anglican tradition (at least its Catholic inheritance)?[58]

In addition to these statements and a number of others which fail to provide any theological rationale for their position, one can even identify a few statements which exhibit other genres of theological argumentation for condemning racism. For example, some statements make their point by way of appeals only to the doctrine of creation or the doctrine of human persons. Among these statements are a number issued by the British Council of Churches, the Evangelische Kirche in Deutschland, the Konferenz der Evangelischen Kirchenleitungen in der DDR, the Church of Norway, the Lutheran Church-Missouri Synod, the Lutheran Church in America, the Reformed Ecumenical Synod, the Reformed Church in America, the Anglican Church of Canada, the Evangelische Kirche im Rheinland, the American Baptist Churches, the Associated Churches of Christ in New Zealand, as well as perhaps a 1967 pastoral letter on the hundredth year of the Canadian Confederation issued by the Canadian Catholic Conference, and the papal encyclicals *Pacem in Terris* (1963) and *Populorum Progressio* (1967). In most of these statements creation and redemption (or Christology) are in some sense correlated. For example, the latter papal encyclical rules out discrimination on the basis of the nature of human beings as God created them, asserting also a distinction between the two kingdoms. It is also added that the fight against present injustices is "authorized" by the gospel.[59]

It is even possible to read both encyclicals at this point as expressing a view more akin to the tendency of the Second Vatican Council, notably in *Gaudium et Spes,* to subordinate the ontological structures of nature to grace.[60] If this indeed is the position of both encyclicals, then the condemnation of racism would ultimately be on the basis of the gospel, on the basis of creation in light of the gospel. These encyclicals, however, nowhere make this point explicitly.

In both encyclicals the pope does urge Christians to "infuse a Christian spirit" or "Christian principles" into the laws of the community.[61] Yet no Christian theological position would aim to deny that a value like opposing racism conflicts with something like the "Christian spirit". The two encyclicals, after insisting to some extent on the autonomy of the civil realm, proceed to condemn racism at some points by appealing to the doctrine of creation independent of reference to, and apparent influence by, redemption. At the very least, then, the encyclicals' conceptual vagueness on the precise nature of the relationship between creation and redemption allows it to be cited as evidence that as long as creation is not entirely separated from redemption, the creation doctrine can stand alone to authorize more progressive, liberal ethical conclusions. The same observations may be confirmed at least by some of the statements we have noted which appeal both to creation and redemption (in separate arguments) as authorization for the critique of racism.

A 1967 statement of the Lutheran Church-Missouri Synod provides a more explicit example of the nature of the correlation between creation and redemption apparently posited by the other statements. The synod observes that "creation, too, must be understood in the light of the work and words of Jesus Christ."[62] One may speak here of an epistemological priority of redemption over creation, but the ontological structures of creation appear to have their own integrity apart from any consideration of the gospel's transforming power.

The implicit ontology or anthropology of these statements is also interesting to identify. A statement of church leaders of the GDR claims that racism must be opposed because "through it humans are denied as partners given by God".[63] Creation is conceptualized here in a way which expresses the unity of human persons, namely, that they have a common task, vocation, and nature as partners to each other. We seem to find this emphasis on the unity of human persons expressed in the implicit ontology underlying all the statements which depict the creation doctrine in such a way that it does not conflict with God's redemptive work. The same ontology is openly stated in a number of other documents which condemn racism by appeal to some locus drawn from the first article of the creed. Examples include a 1972 decision of the Associated Churches of Christ in New Zealand, a 1984 resolution on race relations by the British Council of Churches, and a 1966 declaration of the World Methodist Conference.

The ontological suppositions of the Lutheran Church-Missouri Synod statement (though now largely disregarded by the church) are no less intriguing. It asserted that "the biblical teaching concerning creation does not rule out ongoing changes within the world of creatures."[64] The statement thus indicates an openness to process or change in the orders of creation, a kind of ontology which can further ensure that appeals to the doctrine of creation as a warrant for an ethical position do not necessarily reinforce the status quo.

It is apparent from these statements that once again the conventional wisdom associated with the Barmen Declaration has been called into question. An ethic authorized by the doctrine of creation can in fact lead to progressive, liberal conclusions. Similarly, in churches' positions on women's rights, we can also identify liberal positions on this issue authorized at least in part by the doctrine of creation. See, for example, statements issued by the Latin American Protestant Conference, the Southern Baptist Convention [USA], the Lutheran World Federation, and the American Lutheran Church.[65]

We also observe in these statements that in order to ensure that appeals to the doctrine of creation do not necessarily lapse into a reactionary ethic, at least some of the three adaptations of this approach identified here have been appropriated: (1) correlating creation and redemption (i.e., the two realms of the two-kingdom ethic), such that redemption is conceived as re-creating or restoring the original structures of creation; (2) construing the orders of creation so that they correlate with and do not conflict with the gospel (in this connection an ontology which conveys the idea that the orders of creation are in process or still developing and changing could also serve); and (3) speaking of human persons in such a way that by nature they are related to each other and their environment. A further elaboration on the ecumenical and theological significance of these points can be provided in subsequent chapters and in the Conclusion.

In any case, the statements on racism are also significant for calling into question the conventional wisdom which asserts that context plays a determinative role on theology and ethics. Thus we have identified both churches from the West (e. g., the Church of Norway) and from Eastern Europe (e. g., the Konferenz der Evangelischen Kirchenleitungen in der DDR) which share in the condemnation of racism and rely on the same kind of theological authorization. At least in these cases a common theological heritage seems more influential than each church's cultural context. Likewise one finds racism condemned with authorization from Christology by churches from radically distinct cultural contexts. For example, both the South African Catholic Bishops' Conference and the Christian Church (Disciples of Christ) share a similar mode of theological argument and a common ethic, despite their radically distinct cultural contexts in Africa and North America.

In the final analysis, however, perhaps the most significant observation to be made in our study of the statements considered in this chapter is that a consensus seems to exist concerning racism and to some extent concerning apartheid. The overwhelming consensus is that they are evils which the church must condemn. To be sure, some disagreements may exist among the churches regarding the strategy for putting an end to these evils. We have already noted, for example, the debate over the viability of economic sanctions against the South African Republic as a means of combating apartheid. Nevertheless the agreement on principles is so entirely unanimous on racism and virtually unanimous on apartheid that one is tempted to speak of a kind of catholic consensus on these issues.

In that light, the fact that the churches rely on different theological authorizations to arrive at these positions is all the more significant. It suggests that theological disagreements on questions about ethics may not call into question the church's catholic consensus, and so these differences need not be church dividing.

NOTES

[1] Nederduitse Gereformeerde Kerk, *Human Relations and the South African Scene in the Light of Scripture* (Cape Town and Pretoria: Dutch Reformed Church Publishers, 1976), 5.
[2] Lutheran World Federation, *Statements of the Assembly* (1977), 54-56; World Alliance of Reformed Churches, *Racism and South Africa* (1982), I (this position was reaffirmed in its *Southern Africa* [1989] and *Towards a Common Testimony of Faith* [1989], 2); Nederduitse Gereformeerde Sendingkerk, *Confession of Faith* (1982); American Lutheran Church, *Opposition to Apartheid* (1980); *Entschliessung der Generalsynode der Vereinigten Evangelisch-Lutherischen Kirche Deutschlands zur "Zusammenarbeit und Gemeinschaft mit den lutherischen Kirchen im Südlichen Afrika"* (1981). Also note the churches cited in note 4 of the Introduction which, although they do not label apartheid a *status confessionis*, still deem it a heresy. For the documentation which confirms the preceding and following summary of trends in statements on apartheid, see the section on apartheid in the Appendix.
[3] *Beschluss der Generalsynode der Vereinigten Evangelisch-Lutherischen Kirche Deutschlands zur Rolle der Kirche in bezug auf das Südliche Afrika* (1978), 2; Vereinigte Evangelisch-Lutherische Kirche Deutschlands, *Sonderfonds des Antirassismusprograms des ÖRK* (1980); Church of the Province of Southern Africa [Anglican], *World Council of Churches* (1979), 2; Evangelische Landeskirche in Württemberg, *Mitteilung an die Gemeinden zum Programm des Ökumenischen Rates der Kirchen zur Bekämpfung des Rassismus* (1970), II, I; Eglise de la Confession d'Augsbourg d'Alsace et de Lorraine, *Résolution* [concernant le Programme de Lutte contre le Racisme] (1978), Int.; Bund der Evangelischen Kirchen in der DDR, *Erklärung der Synode des Bundes zur Situation in Südafrika* (1985); *Votum der Konferenz der Evangelischen Kirchenleitungen in der DDR vom 6/7. Juli 1979 zur Frage der Gewaltanwendung im Kampf gegen den Rassismus im südlichen Afrika*, 2.5; 3.2; *Entschliessung der Synode der Evangelischen Kirche in Deutschland betreffend das ökumenische Programm zur Bekämpfung des Rassismus* (1971); Netherlands Reformed Church, *Resolutions* (1982); Evangelische Kirche in Hessen und Nassau, *Synodalbeschlüsse: 4. Kirchensynode, 8. Tagung* (1970), 15.

For a middle-ground position on the WCC's Program to Combat Racism, see Evangelisch-Lutherische Landeskirche Hannovers, *Kirche und Rassismus* (1975), II, affirming the program but critical of its special fund; Evangelisch-Lutherische Landeskirche Hannovers, *Die Stellungnahme der Landessynode vom 21. Juni 1974*, which is critical of the program's special fund and the impression that it promotes violence; Evangelische Kirche im Rheinland, *Sonderfonds zur Bekämpfung des Rassismus* (1979), esp. 57.3-5, which endorses the special fund and the program in general for their humanitarian concerns but criticizes the fund's support of certain liberation movements; Evangelische Kirche in Deutschland, *Entschliessung zur Rassendiskriminierung* (1974), affirming the program but critical of its special fund.

[4] A typical though strongly stated argument for this position has been advanced by Ernst Bloch, *Atheismus im Christentum. Zur Religion des Exodus und des Reichs* (Frankfurt: Suhrkamp, 1968), 59-64. See *The Theological Declaration of Barmen* (1934), II, for its Christocentric social ethic. For a related critique of a social ethic appealing primarily to the doctrine of creation for authorization, specifically of the Lutheran two-kingdom ethic for fostering the reactionary politics of National Socialism, see Karl Barth, "Ein Brief nach Frankreich" (letter to Pastor Westphal, December 1939), in *Eine schweizer Stimme, 1938-1945* (Zollikon and Zurich: Evangelischer Verlag, 1945), esp. 113.

[5] Nederduitse Gereformeerde Kerk, *Kerk en samelewing* (1986), 306, 375-76, 270, 276, 256-58, 305; Nederduitse Gereformeerde Kerk, *Kerk en samelewing* (1990), 260, 279-81, 330, 334. For a similar critical assessment, at least of the 1986 statement, see World Alliance of Reformed Churches, *Southern Africa* (1989).

[6] Nederduitse Gereformeerde Kerk, *Ras, volk en nasie en volkereverhoudinge in die lig van die Skrif* (1974), 5; 46.2; 49.2, 7.

[7] For a few examples of these commitments, see Second Helvetic Confession (1566), chap. 30; Westminster Confession (1646), chap. 23; Scots Confession (1560), chap. 24; John Calvin, *Institutes of the Christian Religion* (1559), 4.20.9, 2, 3. It should also be noted that Calvin did maintain a kind of two-kingdom ethic in ibid. 2.8.1; 3.19.15; 4.11.3-5; 4.20.1, insofar as he neither supported an encroachment of the authority of the magistrate in the affairs of the church nor granted the church the authority to force or compel obedience. Rather, he insisted that believers were subject to both the spiritual and the political governments.

[8] Nederduitse Gereformeerde Kerk, *Ras, volk en nasie*, 49.6; 13.6.

[9] Ibid., 14-14.6.

[10] Ibid., 10. For the earlier statement, see Nederduitse Gereformeerde Kerk, *Human Relations in South Africa* (1966).

[11] Nederduitse Gereformeerde Kerk, *Ras, volk en nasie*, 7; 49.1.

[12] Ibid., 49. For pertinent statements of the historic Lutheran position, esp. see Martin Luther, *Temporal Authority: To What Extent It Should Be Obeyed* (1523), WA 11:251-52, 22ff./LW 45:91-92; Luther, *Predigten über das 2. Buch Mose* (1524-27), WA 16:353, 26; Luther, *Commentary on Psalm 101* (1534), WA 51, 242, 1-8, 15-19/LW 13:198; *Apology of the Augsburg Confession* (1531) 16.2-8; 28.10-18.

[13] Nederduitse Gereformeerde Kerk, *Ras, volk en nasie*, 49.1. Perhaps it could be argued that many times since the sixteenth century, notably during World War II among German Lutherans, practitioners of the two-kingdom ethic did not merely distinguish but actually separated the two kingdoms, so that the church abdicated its socio-political responsibilities. It is not our task to evaluate the validity of this argument. It should be noted, however, that at least in the Lutheran confessions (e.g., Augsburg Confession [1530], 16.7), the distinction of the realms is not deemed to authorize an apolitical stance on the part of Christians.

[14] Nederduitse Gereformeerde Kerk, *Ras, volk en nasie*, 9.

[15] Ibid.

[16] Ibid., 9.3.

[17] Ibid., 47.2.

[18] Ibid.

[19] Ibid., 14.5; cf. ibid., 29-30, 60.

[20] Ibid., 60.

[21] See note 7 for pertinent references. The case for this point has been made by Brian Gerrish, "Strasbourg Revisited: A Reformed Perspective", in *The Augsburg Confession in Ecumenical Perspective*, ed. Harding Meyer, *LWF Report* 6-7 (December 1979): 146-47.

[22] Dispensationalist themes are expressed in Nederduitse Gereformeerde Kerk, *Ras, volk en nasie*, 29-30.

[23] Westminster Confession, chap. 7. This connection between the arguments of the Dutch Reformed Church (South Africa) and the Westminster Confession has been observed by Alasdair Heron, "Creation in Light of Covenant" (paper presented at the Institute for Ecumenical Research Consultation "The Theology of

Creation — Contributions and Deficiencies of Our Confessional Traditions", Strasbourg, France, 13 October 1983), 11.

[24] Abraham Kuyper, *Lectures on Calvinism* (Grand Rapids, Mich., 1961), 46-54, 59-73, 100.

[25] Three items by the World Alliance of Reformed Churches: *Southern Africa* (1989); *Racism and South Africa* (1982), I-II; and *Reconciliation and Society: The Freedom of a Just Order* (1970), 8, Int.; World Methodist Council Assembly Resolution, *Youth Resolution on South Africa* (1976); WCC Vancouver Assembly, *Statement on Southern Africa* (1983), 1ff.; WCC Vancouver Assembly Issue Group Report, *Struggling for Justice and Human Dignity* (1983), 7.1; 9; 11; 13; 23; National Council of Churches [USA], *Southern Africa* (1977), 6-7, 1; Lutheran Church-Missouri Synod, *To Urge Support for Oppressed* (1986); Evangelical Lutheran Church in Southern Africa, *Apartheid as Heresy* (1982) and *Social Services in Independent States and Homelands* (1982), citing a 1982 resolution of the South African Council of Churches; South African Council of Churches, *The Republic of South Africa Constitution Bill* (1983) and *Apartheid as a Heresy* (1983). The last two items also include appeals to the doctrine of the church as warrant.

This list of statements and other lists which are provided in the notes to support generalizations are not complete catalogues of all pertinent church statements. For references to other statements dealing with apartheid and racism, see the relevant sections in the Appendix.

[26] World Alliance of Reformed Churches, *Racism and South Africa*, I-III. See below for a discussion of an earlier denunciation of apartheid as a *status confessionis* by the Lutheran World Federation, *Statements of the Assembly* (1977), 54-56.

[27] World Alliance of Reformed Churches, *Racism and South Africa*, II.

[28] Ibid., I-II.

[29] Ibid., I.

[30] Calvin, *Institutes* 4.1.13, 15.

[31] This observation seems not undermined, but even strengthened in the case of a number of statements which condemn apartheid by linking arguments rooted in Christology or redemption with theological arguments against apartheid which are related to doctrinal themes associated with the doctrine of creation. A number of these statements, notably South African Council of Churches, *A Message to the People of South Africa* (1968), and the 1982 statement of the Nederduitse Gereformeerde Sendingkerk, are able to use the doctrine of creation as a basis for condemning apartheid insofar as Christology or the gospel does most of the work in refuting this practice. As such, these statements differ markedly from a few documents, discussed and cited below in notes 50-51, where arguments against apartheid founded in the doctrine of creation are linked with arguments against apartheid drawn from other doctrinal themes. In the case of the latter group of statements, the doctrine of creation is able to stand alone in authorizing the condemnation of apartheid. In the present cases, however, the doctrine of creation requires or depends on supplementation of the gospel in order to authorize the statements' progressive conclusions. In that sense these statements confirm the conclusion that only an ethic rooted in Christology can arrive at satisfactory ethical conclusions.

[32] For references to these statements and others subsequently cited which condemn racism, see the section on racism in the Appendix.

[33] Moravian Church in America, Northern Province, *Resolutions* (1974); World Methodist Council Assembly, *Participation of Women* (1976); WCC Vancouver Assembly Issue Group Report, *Healing and Sharing Life in Community* (1983), 15-18; cf. Baptist World Alliance Congress, *Resolution on Sponsoring Youth Work* (1970); Christian Conference of Asia, *Justice and Service* (1977), A, D.; United Church of Christ [USA], *The Status of Women in Church and Society* (1971).

[34] United Church of Christ [USA], *Resolution on Recommending Inclusiveness on Association Church and Ministry Committees within the United Church of Christ* (1983). Cf. Episcopal Church [USA], *General Convention Resolution* [on homosexuality and the ordination of homosexuals] (1979), which is authorized by an appeal to the Holy Spirit.

[35] For a few examples of this Christocentric approach to the peace question and disarmament, see Lambeth Conference (1968) Section Report, *The Renewal of the Church in Faith;* Southern Baptist Convention [USA], *The Baptist Faith and Message* (1963), XVI; Roman Catholic Church, Vatican II, *Gaudium et Spes* (1965), 77-78; Moderamens of the Reformed Alliance [FRG], *Das Bekenntnis zu Jesus Christus und die Friedensverantwortung der Kirche* (1981), I; Erl. II, which exemplifies the combination of warrants drawn from Christology or the gospel with those drawn from the doctrine of creation. Nor should one overlook the fact that at least one of the historic peace churches, the Mennonite Brethren Churches (see its *Confession of Faith* [1975], art. 15), authorizes its position on pacifism by appeal to the example of Christ. One of the few statements calling for peace solely on the basis of a warrant drawn from the

doctrine of creation is an assembly report of the Lutheran World Federation, *Responsible Participation in Today's Society* (1970), 59ff., 26. For a more complete list of pertinent references, see the section on nuclear armaments in the Appendix.

[36] Rubem A. Alves, *A Theology of Human Hope* (St. Meinard, Ind.: Abbey Press, 1974), 149-50; Gustavo Gutierrez, *A Theology of Liberation*, trans. and ed. Sister Caridad Inda and John Eagleson (Maryknoll, N.Y.: Orbis Books, 1973), 154, 175-78.

[37] National Association of Evangelicals [USA], *Man and Woman* (1979); Roman Catholic Church, *Humanae Vitae* (1968), 14, 11, and *Divini Redemptoris* (1937), 4, 10-12, 27-28, 31; Assemblies of God [USA], *Homosexuality* (1979).

[38] National Conference of Catholic Bishops [USA], *The Challenge of Peace: God's Promise and Our Response* (1983), 167-99 (esp. 196), 203-14, 245, 258, 274, 295, 331, 333, 335, 339, 2, 13-15; Lutheran Church in America, *Peace and Politics* (1984), 4-5, 7-8. This observation should perhaps be qualified somewhat with regard to the bishops' letter. The doctrine of creation is not the only theological warrant employed by the statement. Particularly significant is the way in which it correlates creation and redemption (ibid., I). It could be possible to interpret the letter's claim that each person "is the expression of God's creative work and the meaning of Christ's redemptive ministry" in light of the tendency of the Second Vatican Council to subordinate nature to grace (*Gaudium et Spes*, 22, 77). The latter document is repeatedly cited by the bishops but never with explicit reference to the theological authorization the council gives for its positions on peace and disarmament.

[39] One can perhaps identify a kind of ecumenical consensus concerning an almost monolithic reliance on a social ethic grounded in Christology by examining statements approved by the various WCC assemblies. In all of these assemblies, each issuing numerous statements and each statement marshalling several different theological arguments to address several distinct issues, one can at most identify no more than nine statements, and perhaps only six, where arguments for a given point are solely or at least predominantly grounded in the doctrine of creation. At least one statement in each assembly — but never more than two — displays this sort of theological authorization.

[40] American Lutheran Church, *Apartheid* (1981), II/1, and *Opposition to Apartheid*.

[41] American Lutheran Church, *Apartheid*, II/1.

[42] Ibid., II/2.

[43] Ibid., II/1.

[44] For this notion that the correlation of creation and redemption was one of the crucial issues at stake in the Nicene Council's response to Arianism, I am indebted to Jaroslav Pelikan, *The Emergence of the Catholic Tradition (100-600)*, vol. 1 of *The Christian Tradition*, 5 vols. (Chicago: University of Chicago Press, 1971), 203. A condemnation of apartheid by the Lutheran World Federation, *Racism in Church and Society* (1984), 10.6; ii; i, could be understood to employ a model of argumentation like that of the American Lutheran Church. The statement has not been analyzed, however, because the statement's theological authorization did not have approval of the assembly. Christology may be functioning as the statement's primary warrant.

[45] The Second Helvetic Confession, chap. 30, maintains that Christians have deeper insights into social ethics in view of their faith, insofar as the document regards Christians as the best rulers. But such a notion was rejected by Martin Luther, *Commentary on Psalm 101* (1535), WA 51:242, 4-8/LW 13:198. Although it must be granted that in his *Lectures on Psalm 127* (1532-33), WA 40 III, 222f., 24ff., he seemed to indicate that he favored Christian rulers.

[46] American Lutheran Church, *Apartheid*, II/1.

[47] Nederduitse Gereformeerde Kerk, *Ras, volk en nasie*, 13.2.

[48] Calvin, *Institutes* 4.1.13, 15.

[49] Nederduitse Gereformeerde Kerk, *Kerk en samelewing*, 306, 160-67.

[50] Associated Churches of Christ in New Zealand, *Decisions Relating to Public Issues* (1972); Anglican Church of Canada, *South Africa* (1986), 1, 2, 5; Evangelisch-Lutherische Kirche in Bayern, *Brief an den Gemeinden zum südlichen Afrika* (1984). Also see Bund der Evangelischen Kirchen in der DDR, *Erklärung der Synode des Bundes zur Situation in Südafrika* (1985). Its appeal for fellowship of black and white in South Africa, that they live with one another reconciled, suggests this sort of ontology. The statement is worth noting as an example of a condemnation of apartheid from the former Eastern block. Also see a similar vision of the solidarity of all peoples expressed in *Pastoral Letter of the Roman Catholic Bishops in Mozambique* (1976), as another appeal is apparently made to the doctrine of creation in condemning apartheid.

[51] Broederkring of the Dutch Reformed Church [South Africa], *Theological Declaration* (1979); Presbyterian Church of Southern Africa, *A Declaration of Faith for the Church in South Africa* (1981); Federation

of Lutheran Churches in South Africa, *The Swakopmund Declaration* (1975), 4-6, 9ff., 23; Evangelical Lutheran Church in Southern Africa, *New Political Dispensation* (1984); Church of the Province of Southern Africa [Anglican], *Policy of Apartheid* (1982); All Africa Conference of Churches, *The Gospel — Good News to the Poor and Oppressed* (1981); Evangelische Kirche in Deutschland, *Erklärung des Rates der EKD zur gegenwärtigen Lage im südlichen Afrika* (1985), III, IV; Evangelische Kirche im Rheinland, *Geschäftsbeziehungendeutscher Banken zu Südafrika* (1986); World Methodist Council Conference, *Council Message to the Methodists of the World* (1966); Reformed Church in Japan, *Comments on "Human Relations and the South African Scene in the Light of Scripture"* (1984); American Baptist Churches, *Policy Statement on Africa* (1987), 1, 3; British Council of Churches, *Political Change in South Africa: Britain's Responsibility* (1979); Anglican Church of Canada, *Resolutions on South Africa* (1971).

[52] Presbyterian Church of Southern Africa, *A Declaration of Faith for the Church in South Africa.*

[53] Something like these commitments have been articulated by the WCC Conference on Faith, Science and the Future, *Towards a New Christian Social Ethic and New Social Policies for the Churches* (Cambridge, Mass., 12-24 July 1979), 2; WCC Uppsala Assembly, *Towards New Styles of Living* (1968), 27; *Message of the Holy Synod of the Russian Orthodox Church on War in a Nuclear Age* (1986), 1.4.

[54] The [Catholic] Bishops of the Netherlands, *Gelijke behandeling* (1982), 3, 4-5.

[55] See *Pastoral Letter of the Southern African Bishops Conference on the Proposed New Constitution for South Africa* (1983), 6, 9; Evangelical Lutheran Church in Tanzania, *Discrimination* (1968); *Irenic Letter of the Patriarch Justinian of the Romanian Orthodox Church* (1982); Lambeth Conference (1968), *The Renewal of the Church in Faith;* Lutheran Church-Missouri Synod, *To Urge Support for Oppressed* (1986); Baptist World Alliance, *Resolution on Brotherhood and Equality* (1965); Christian Church (Disciples of Christ), *A Message from the General Board* (1969); National Association of Evangelicals [USA], *On Civil Rights* (1965); WCC Uppsala Assembly, *Towards New Styles of Living* (1968), 13-14. For a more complete list of statements on racism pertinent to this and the two succeeding notes as well as to the preceding discussion, see the section on racism in the Appendix.

[56] WCC Uppsala Assembly, *Towards Justice and Peace in International Affairs* (1968), 28. Also see Reformed Church in America, *Report of the Advisory Committee on Christian Unity* (1982), R-9.

[57] WCC New Delhi Assembly, *Report of the Committee on the Commission of International Affairs* (1961), 42-47, 59; WCC Uppsala Assembly, *The Holy Spirit and the Catholicity of the Church* (1968), 22, 21; Lutheran-Episcopal Dialogue, series III [USA], *Implications of the Gospel* (1988), 122, 60; British Council of Churches, *Community and Race Relations Unit* (1982); Baptist World Alliance, *Resolution on Reconciliation and Racial Discrimination* (1970); three items of the World Alliance of Reformed Churches: *Reconciliation and Man: The Freedom of the New Man* (1970); *The People of the Covenant and the Mission of the Kingdom* (1982), 7, 5, 4, 3, 1; and *Racism and South Africa* (1982), I; Church of Norway, *Kirken og innvandrerne* (1979), 8-9; Lutheran World Federation, *Resolutions of the LWF Assembly,* Eleventh Plenary Session, 10 August 1963, 11; *Gaudium et Spes* (1965), 29, 22, 76-77; four items of the National Conference of Catholic Bishops [USA]: *Race Relations and Poverty* (1966), 1-3, 7, 8, 12, 22; *The National Race Crisis* (1968), 1, 8, 17-18; *Society and the Aged: Toward Reconciliation* (1976), 7-9, 34; and *To Live in Jesus Christ: A Pastoral Reflection on the Moral Life* (1976), 2, 30, 31, 70-74, 115-16); Methodist Church in Malaysia, *Social Principles* (n.d.), III/D/1; II; I; Moravian Church in America, Northern Province, *U.S. Senate Ratification of the Convention on the Prevention and Punishment of the Crime of Genocide* (1982); Brethren in Christ Church [USA], *The Christian and Society* (1972), and *Elimination of Racist Statements and Attitudes* (1970); three items of the United Church of Christ [USA]: *Jesus Christ Frees and Unites* (1975), *Economic Justice* (1973), and *Affirmative Action* (1979).

[58] Statements appealing to all three articles of the creed include WCC Evanston Assembly, *International Affairs — Christians in the Struggle for World Community* (1954), VI, and *Inter-Group Relations — The Church amid Racial and Ethnic Tensions* (1954), Res.; II; III; WCC New Delhi Assembly, *Resolution on Racial and Ethnic Tensions* (1961), 4.1; National Council of Churches [USA], *Middle East* (1980); World Methodist Council Conference, *Council Message to the Methodists of the World* (1966); Episcopal Church [USA], *General Convention Resolution* [on condemning resurgence of activity of Ku Klux Klan] (1979); Christian Church (Disciples of Christ), *Concerning Racial Integration* (1963); Lutheran World Federation, *Statement on Human Rights* (1984), II; American Lutheran Church, *Issues and Opportunities That Bind and Free* (1976); American Baptist Churches, *Policy Statement on Human Rights* (1976); United Church of Christ [USA], *Calling on United Church of Christ Congregations to Declare Themselves Open and Affirming* (1985); National Conference of Catholic Bishops [USA], *Brothers and Sisters to Us: A Pastoral Letter on Racism* (1979); Roman Catholic Church, *Sollicitudo Rei Socialis*

(1987), 15, 1, 3, 7-8, 40, 47-49; Evangelische Kirche im Rheinland, *Zum überwindung des Rassismus* (1971). Another 1984 statement of the Lutheran World Federation could be understood to assume a similar position; see note 44 for details. Some statements, like that of the Nederduitse Gereformeerde Sendingkerk, *A Confession of Faith* (1982), rely on third-article warrants more as supplements to the main warrant. Especially see South African Council of Churches, *A Message to the People of South Africa* (1968).

Ecclesiology or eschatology functions as the main authorization for United Church of Christ [USA] items *Racial Justice* (1979) and *Economic Life* (1969); WCC Uppsala Assembly statements *Message* (1968) and *The Holy Spirit and the Catholicity of the Church* (1968), 22, 21; WCC New Delhi Assembly, *Message to Christians in South Africa* (1961); Evangelische Landeskirche in Baden, *Einheit der Kirche in der Zerrissenheit zwischen Ost und West und Nord und Süd* (1981), II/1.2; Evangelisch-Lutherische Kirche in Bayern, *Menschenrechtsverletzungen* (1985); United Free Church of Scotland, *Deliverance of the General Assembly* [on nuclear questions] (1980), 1, 3; Caribbean Conference of Churches, *Thine Is the Kingdom, the Power and the Glory* (1981); Eglise Protestante Unie de Belgique, *Motion du District Antwerpen-Brabant-Limburg concernant l'attitude de l'église envers les migrants* (1984).

Also see the condemnation of racism by appeal to sacramentology as argued by the WCC Faith and Order Commission, *Baptism, Eucharist and Ministry* (1981), 20, and the appeal to both sacramentology and ecclesiology by the United Church of Christ [USA], *Racism and Sexism* (1977).

For reference to the appeal to the example of a modern saint by the Episcopal Church [USA], see its *Affirm Witness of Bishop Desmond Tutu and Church in Africa* (1985).

[59] Roman Catholic Church, *Populorum Progressio* (1967), 34, 62-63, 32, 81, 13, and *Pacem in Terris* (1963), 86, 85, 80, 10, 23, 31, 147, 157; British Council of Churches, *Community and Race Relations Unit* (1984); *Entschliessung der Synode der Evangelischen Kirche in Deutschland betreffend das ökumenische Programm zur Bekämpfung des Rassismus* (1971); *Votum der Konferenz der Evangelischen Kirchenleitungen in der DDR*, 1.3; 2.1; Lutheran Church-Missouri Synod, *Creation in Biblical Perspective* (1967), VI.5, 1; V.2; Int.; Church of Norway, *Kirken og innvandrerne* (1979), 8-9; Lutheran Church in America, *Race Relations* (1964); Reformed Ecumenical Synod, *Race Relations* (1984), art. 103, rec. 2; Reformed Church in America, *Report of the Christian Action Commission* (1966), R6, R2-R3; Anglican Church of Canada, *South Africa* (1986); Evangelische Kirche im Rheinland, *Sonderfonds zur Bekämpfung des Rassismus* (1979), 1; American Baptist Churches, *Policy Statement on Housing* (1983); Associated Churches of Christ in New Zealand, *Decisions Relating to Public Issues* (1972).

[60] *Gaudium et Spes*, 22.

[61] *Populorum Progressio*, 81; *Pacem in Terris*, 147.

[62] Lutheran Church-Missouri Synod, *Creation in Biblical Perspective*, VI.1.

[63] *Votum der Konferenz der Evangelischen Kirchenleitungen in der DDR*, 1.3.

[64] Lutheran Church-Missouri Synod, *Creation in Biblical Perspective*, VI.14.

[65] Latin American Protestant Conference, *United to Meet the Demands of the Present Time* (1978); Southern Baptist Convention [USA], *A Statement of Social Principles* (1979), 1, 3; Lutheran World Federation Assembly Resolution, *Women in Church and Society* (1977); American Lutheran Church, *Women and Men in Church and Society* (1972), 2, 8-10, and *Manifesto for Our Nation's Third Century* (1976), IV.

2. Economic Development and Unemployment

Since its inception the church has been concerned to help the poor, to assist those in a less favorable economic situation (Gal. 2:10; 2 Cor. 8:1-5; James 2:15-16; Matt. 25:35-40; Isa. 58:6-10). There is general agreement in the historic Christian community that this is a mandate for Christian ethics. An examination of the section in the Appendix pertaining to economic development makes this common position readily apparent, inasmuch as all the church statements it lists exhibit at least some concern with the problem of economic equality, if not economic assistance for the poor.

The Appendix also indicates that the concern to address the problem of helping the economically disadvantaged through strategies of transnational economic development is a problem which Christians more typically address in the context of international Christian fellowships. Relatively few national churches have addressed the issue, and those that have are almost exclusively European or North American. (The issue has received particularly frequent attention from the Church of Norway.)

An interesting pattern may be observed with respect to the dates of these statements and the location of the churches issuing them. The few church organizations from the Southern hemisphere which have addressed the matter largely did so before the mid-1970s. Since that time the churches of Asia and Africa (with the notable exception of the All Africa Conference of Churches in 1981) have rarely spoken to the issue. In contrast, only since the mid-1970s have church organizations in Europe and North America taken up the matter. With the exception of four or so American denominations — the United Church of Christ, the American Lutheran Church, the Lutheran Church in America, and the Mennonite Church, as well as perhaps the Mennonite Church, General Conference, and the Christian Church (Disciples of Christ) — and national ecumenical organizations such as the USA's National Council of Churches and the British Council of Churches, only international bodies like the WCC, the Reformed Ecumenical Synod, and the Roman Catholic Church addressed the question in the early 1970s and in the 1960s. These patterns in the churches' statements pertaining to economic development are indicators of disagreements within the Christian community regarding strategies for helping the economically disadvantaged, particularly when the church is challenged to aid not just isolated individuals but entire peoples, nations, or regions.

At least since the end of the colonial period, if not since its inception, the common-sense response to the challenge posed by the encounter with the economically disadvantaged, particularly those in the Southern hemisphere, has been to advocate full-fledged programs of economic development for underdeveloped regions. In recent years disagreements have emerged among development experts concerning the proper strategies or models for carrying out economic development of these underdeveloped regions. It thus is not surprising that these disagreements have also emerged among Christians. Such differences concerning the most appropriate models for economic development reflect in turn in the churches' statements on the issue.

The original models for economic development tend to reflect fundamental operating modes of capitalist economic systems. They may best be described by the phrase "transfer of technology". For ease of reference, and inasmuch as these models represent the first approaches to development, we shall refer to such approaches as the older models for development.

The supposition behind this older model is that underdeveloped nations and peoples need advanced technology in order to elevate their standard of living. Inevitably it is the industrialized nations and their multinational corporations, usually those of the West, which have access to such advanced technology and can supply it readily to the underdeveloped nations.

The technology of these industrialized nations is specially geared and suited for their own needs and situations. It is not economically feasible, however, nor until recently did it perhaps even occur to the transnational corporations or capitalists who owned the technology, to adapt this technology to local needs of the underdeveloped nations. One could thus speak quite literally of this development model as a transfer of technology. Western technology is directly transferred to the underdeveloped nations.

No doubt the motivations and warrants for leaders of corporations and governments who offered their technology to underdeveloped nations were in some cases humanitarian or rooted in their religious convictions. Certainly this is true of those church statements, many issued prior to this decade, which called for a direct transfer of technology. Those advocating something like such a model for development include a 1963 assembly resolution of the Lutheran World Federation, two early WCC assemblies, the Presbyterian-Reformed Church in Cuba, and perhaps a 1969 statement by the All Africa Conference of Churches. A variety of theological warrants are employed by these statements in authorizing this relatively common position. The call for such transfer of technology has been on the grounds variously of the "new life in Christ", the love of God, the gospel, the understanding of human persons as stewards of creation, or a view of natural law as requiring it. [1]

I have noted that a propelling dynamic for these older models of development tends to be the fundamental operating modes of the capitalist systems where those with the available technology are based. To be sure, this economically inspired warrant for encouraging the owner of existing technology to share it is in no way explicitly embraced by any of the church statements advocating the older models of development. Nevertheless, the investment gains for owners of existing technology which can be realized by sharing such technology with underdeveloped nations are readily apparent.

If corporations move into or sell their technology in underdeveloped nations, they immediately open potential doors in that nation for it to become a secondary market for the products of the technology. Also the proximity to sources of raw materials, cheap labor, and less stringent controls in the underdeveloped nation make it an attractive site for the holder of the technology in which to relocate. Thus the profit motive may not be the least of the warrants inspiring this older model of development. It is a warrant which may account for the interest in transferring technology to underdeveloped nations not just by Western capitalist economies but also by socialist nations.

But there may be a related, more insidious warrant undergirding this model. Its critics claim that the transfer of technology helps perpetuate a kind of neo-colonialism. Certainly this model helps to perpetuate a dependency relationship between recipient and donor. Insofar as no effort is made to develop indigenous technology in the underdeveloped nations, they remain dependent upon the industrialized nation or multinational corporation in order to keep their newly developed industries functioning efficiently.

The critics note other abuses which are said to follow from this older model for development. The neo-colonial dynamic created by the importing of technology leads to the same outcomes as did the older version of colonialism. Thus in addition to importing Western technology, underdeveloped nations will also import the social values of the West or of the socialist bloc which are associated with this technology. The result is that underdeveloped nations may compromise their unique social fabric and receive in its stead the maladies of pollution, consumerism, alcohol abuse, and the like.

Because the technology which is transferred is largely geared for Western cultures and seldom adapted to meet indigenous needs, so the arguments run, it is not likely to appreciate the real needs of the population. Indeed the capitalist mind-set of those consultants running the technology in the underdeveloped setting dictates that the new technology will cater to and thereby probably be of profit to only the technical, managerial, and scientific elite in the underdeveloped nations. There is some evidence to suggest that this has been the outcome of development aid to several of these nations. Ultimately it has only helped the rich get richer and the poor get poorer.[2]

New Indigenous Models

Given the force of these criticisms, it is not surprising that they have been taken up by the churches, particularly in some recent statements issued at WCC meetings and as early as 1973 by the Christian Conference of Asia.[3] These critiques largely reflect a similarity to those made by liberation theology and so in turn seem to reflect the influence of liberation theology on the ecumenical movement.[4] In response to these critiques one finds new models for development being articulated in the more recent statements, models which implicitly if not explicitly break with the older ideas of development as a transfer of technology to underdeveloped nations.

It is not easy to describe fully the components of these newer models. I have used the term "indigenous" in the subtitle to describe them. I do so because one of the key commitments of these new models is that development and its associated technology should itself be indigenous and thereby appropriate.

In this newer model of development the first question to be raised for under-developed regions is not how to get existing technology but what are the needs, culture, and environment of the society. This information is then used to develop technology suitable to that region. Presumably if an industrial nation is facilitating this development process, it cannot so easily dominate the underdeveloped region as can happen with mere transfer of technology. In this new model the industrial nation or corporation does not enter the underdeveloped nation with a ready-made product which will inevitably begin to exert Western/Eastern influence on the indigenous culture. Unlike the transfer-of-technology model, there is no "supplier" as such who can exert undue control over the developing nation by ever threatening to withdraw the needed technology.

Rather, in this alternative newer model the industrial nation or corporation no longer plays the paternalistic role of the emergency care-giver providing the proverbial economic band-aid. Instead, the initiator of development is to transfer capabilities by which technologies appropriate to local conditions could be developed in the receiving nations. In this sense the industrial nations and corporations facilitating development become dispensable to the developing nation, just as teachers are ultimately dispensable to students, once teachers have taught their lessons. In a very real sense, those providing the technology now are not the initiators of development, for a fundamental tenet of the new models is that developers must cultivate self-reliance and self-initiative on the part of the underdeveloped nation.

Possibilities for control by the initiator of development are further undercut with this model. Its reliance on indigenous technology entails that resources used in development are already on the scene in the underdeveloped nations. Thus these underdeveloped nations need not be dependent upon industrial nations or their multinational corporations for necessary fuel or other technological components.

These new models for development distinguish themselves from the older model in other ways. One of the consequences of their concern always to ask as a prior question about the needs, culture, and environment of a society is that development is not to be measured solely in terms of economic growth. Rather, development must also be assessed in relation to the quality of life that is engendered.

Proponents of the older model indeed exhibit some sensitivity to development in areas of human life other than that of economics. This is evident in a 1969 statement of the All Africa Conference of Churches which relates education to development. Yet while this statement and other proponents of the older model tended to focus on economic development and to regard the development of culture as a by-product, the newer models do not tend to share these priorities.[5]

The newer model's concern for quality of life as an outcome of development is reflected in a number of church statements maintaining this kind of approach to development. Most notable is the presence of this theme in Vatican II's pastoral constitution *Gaudium et Spes*. The appearance of this model in a statement of the council indicates that as early as the 1960s the seeds were already being sown for the construction of an alternative to the older model of development as mere transfer of technology. In fact the origin of the newer model can also be identified in the 1960s in WCC statements that mention "the criteria of the human" during the period of the WCC Uppsala Assembly. Thus it seems that the new model of development has its origins in the period when the WCC was being dominated by a school of thought often called secular ecumenism.

As a result of this model's correlation of development and human development, it is not surprising to see that proponents of newer models include many of the best human values under the rubric of development. For example, the WCC Nairobi Assembly claimed that development must include seeking justice. More recently the WCC Sub-Unit on Church and Society has related development to ecology.

At least in the organized ecumenical movement the predominance of this approach to development has been quite apparent in the last two decades. As was the case with church statements advocating the older model of development, a variety of theological warrants are employed by these statements to authorize advocacy of the new model. Some, like the Vatican II statement *Gaudium et Spes,* a 1975 pronouncement of the United Church of Christ [USA], and a 1974 statement of the All Africa Conference of

Churches, appeal to the nature of human persons. (In the Roman Catholic documents, human persons are understood in the light of grace, for nature is subordinated to grace.) An apparently direct appeal to the doctrine of creation, drawing upon a kind of Lutheran two-kingdom ethic stipulating a "natural ethic" accessible to all reasonable people, provides theological authorization for a more or less official 1978 statement of the Church of Norway. By contrast, Christology functions as warrant and criterion for others advocating this model. (Something like the Eastern Orthodox concept of *theosis* may function as background warrant in a 1982 report of the WCC Sub-Unit on Church and Society advocating a new model of development. At least reference seems to be made to Christ's presence in creation in the context of an earlier statement that development should be based on corporate growth "towards the measure of the . . . fullness of Christ".)

In some statements advocating this approach to development, one can even identify simultaneous appeals to several different doctrines. A 1980 statement of the theologically conservative Reformed Ecumenical Synod, authorizing its position by appeals both to Christology and eschatology, nicely illustrates this orientation. Apparently something like an appeal to several theological loci, albeit with creation or anthropology subordinated to Christology, is also evident in the Vatican II statement already cited as well as several papal encyclicals. In fact, some reference to loci from all three articles of the creed, albeit with all these themes also subordinated to Christology, appears in a 1987 papal encyclical and in a 1976 statement of the USA's National Conference of Catholic Bishops.[6]

A number of the statements advocating this model of development, however, do not appear to articulate any theological warrant for their position. A resolution of the 1978 Lambeth Conference, several resolutions of the 1960s by the USA's United Church of Christ, and some recent statements of the WCC illustrate this tendency. Could it be that the absence of a theological warrant for authorizing the new development model in such statements is related to the origins of this model in the period when "secular ecumenism" dominated ecumenical social thought? At any rate it is once again apparent, as we have previously observed, that differences in theology do not seem to mandate differences in social ethics.

Evaluation of the Models

When one considers all the attractive values linked to development by the newer models and contrasts this with the critiques raised against the older model, it appears at first glance that the only possible Christian ethic of development would be one which endorses the new indigenous model. In fact, though, there are advantages and disadvantages on each side of the debate. The new model may have as its disadvantage what is one of its strengths. Given all the positive values it associates with development, one may rightly ask how development can actually be accomplished. At least the statements which advocate this model are sufficiently vague about details of implementation that one might perhaps acknowledge the validity of criticisms concerning the model's practicality.

Details concerning implementation of development in accord with the new model have not been sufficiently provided perhaps because this new model is a relatively recent creation or because its sensitivity to responding to the local situation makes it difficult to articulate more than the broadest general principles. Insofar as the theory of this model is over twenty years old, however, one wonders whether the failure to elaborate concrete plans for its implementation could be symptomatic of a certain impracticality associated with its impressive theoretical formulations.

The older model, advocating transfer of technology, at least seems to have a concrete practical agenda for implementation of development. The underdeveloped nation asks for specific technology or aid, or the multinational corporation creates and fills the need for such technology. For all its potential abuses, the idea of transfer of technology may provide more attractive motivation for the donor to participate in the development process. The profit motive is quite clear for the corporate donor. And for nations or charitable organizations donating aid on grounds of charity, the results of such aid may be more immediately tangible than with the new model. Lack of immediately tangible results from development investments, given the new model's operating procedures, could to some extent frustrate charitable contributions to development projects.

As we have noted, the most tangible results of development aid with the older model may be that it enhances the position of the rich and already powerful in the underdeveloped nations without noticeable improvement in the living standards of the poor. Such abuses, however, could no doubt also occur when the new model is implemented. Since, on its suppositions, decisions about development projects, including the expenditure of development funding, are to be made on the local level in underdeveloped nations, it is quite easy to imagine scenarios in which the elite and the local power brokers in these nations could manipulate such projects to their advantage. Perhaps they could do it even more easily than when the older models direct development efforts. For with the new development models the donors of the development projects no longer exercise any control over the disposition of the donated resources.

To continue our comparison, there is a genuine attractiveness to the new development models insofar as they have been advocated quite strongly in ecumenical circles by third-world leaders. This commendation would seem to suggest that this model is superior, because it is apparently sensitive to the concerns of those who are the principal subjects and objects of development.

The point is not so easily made, however, when one considers church social statements devoted to the issue of development. For one can also identify several advocates from the third world of the older, transfer-of-technology model. At least it seems to have been the position of African churches before the 1970s, and it still today is the orientation of two churches in nations that until recently practised socialism. When one is in dire need of development technology or its products, the relative efficiency of the older model in delivering the goods needed immediately may outweigh the model's potential for abuse.

This last series of observations encapsulates the best conclusion that can be made of our evaluation of the two development models. Each has its strengths and weaknesses. The superiority of one over the other is not easily determined.

In our discussion I have sharply distinguished between two models of development in order to clarify the issues in the debate over development. In view of the relative toss-up between these models in terms of their strengths and weaknesses, however, and in view of the fact that all typologies such as the one we have sketched are imperfect, it is hardly surprising to find that a number of church statements take a position which appears to be somewhere in between the two models.[7]

For example, the Evangelical Church of Lutheran Confession in Brazil calls for development which will provide jobs and improve the standard of living. But it does not clarify who will own the technology bringing about such development or how decisions concerning appropriate technology should be made. In presenting its case for this approach to development, the statement appears to draw on theological warrants usually associated with liberation theology. Appeals are made to the person of Christ as liberator and example. The doctrine of creation also appears to function as a warrant.

Several statements seem to advocate aspects of both of the development models we have sketched. Good examples are provided by a 1969 resolution on world economic development by the Christian Church (Disciples of Christ), Pope Paul VI's *Populorum Progressio,* one by the [Catholic] Bishops of the Netherlands, and a joint statement by the Presbyterian Church in the U.S. and the United Presbyterian Church just before their merger, all of which advocate both the transfer of technology or capital to underdeveloped nations and also a number of the values associated with the new development models.

No theological warrant is evident in the Disciples' statement. The Presbyterian statement probably appeals to Christology as its warrant and ethical criterion, but this analysis is by no means clear. And Paul's encyclical is predominantly though not exclusively warranted by the creation doctrine. In fact, if the encyclical is intended to be read in light of the Vatican II documents it cites, the references to Christology should perhaps be deemed the principal authorization for its position on development, because creation seems to be understood in light of redemption by some of the conciliar documents. That is, these documents subordinate nature to grace.

The papal encyclical explicitly advocates so many of the values associated with the new model of development that one can only conclude that it is basically advocating the new model as has been sketched, with some modifications. With the other statements in question, however, we cannot tell which model they more closely approximate.

Perhaps the inability of the interpreter to categorize these statements is a consequence of their having been carefully crafted in order to avoid the pitfalls associated with both the newer and older models of development. The interpretive dilemma they pose is perhaps simply a consequence of their vagueness. Others must judge.

At any rate, the statements in this middle category, not quite embodying either of the development models we have sketched, authorize their middle-ground position with the same kind of variety of theological arguments which we have observed in church statements holding other positions. With this observation, it is appropriate to begin evaluating the ecumenical implications of the theological diversity which is evident among those church statements holding to similar positions on development.

Theological Evaluation

There does not appear to be any readily discernible theological pattern to the agreements and disagreements among the churches on the issue of development. Perhaps one observes relatively few appeals in the statements to the creation doctrine in isolation as warrant for the position taken on development. But this relative neglect of a creation-based ethic in favor of appeals to other doctrinal loci, notably Christology, is typical of the statements concerning many of the issues we shall consider. As we have observed, some correlation of the creation doctrine with Christology and redemption may be especially appropriate.

The one pattern which may exist in the statements collectively considered pertains to a possible relationship between the date when they were released and the particular position they take with regard to development. As one would expect, statements advocating the older model tend to predominate in the 1950s and 1960s. The majority of statements issued on development in the 1970s and 1980s tend to opt for the newer indigenous models. This trend is hardly surprising, since it was only in the 1960s that criticism of transfer of technology first emerged among development experts. As is typical, the churches, particularly the ecumenical establishment, soon seized on this important new trend.

However, we have already observed significant exceptions to this pattern. Something like the new development models were already emerging in church statements in the mid-1960s, particularly in some WCC and Roman Catholic statements, and on the American scene in a 1967 pronouncement of the United Church of Christ, in a 1966 statement of the former American Lutheran Church, as well as perhaps in a policy statement of the same year on the consequences of a rapidly changing technology by the USA's National Council of Churches. Also the old model has still been advocated in the last ten years, notably by churches in the Soviet sphere of influence or in the third world. It might be possible to understand in this way a 1985 resolution of the British Council of Churches concerning aid for Africa, one of the resolutions of the 1984 Lutheran World Federation Assembly, and a 1983 resolution of the Moravian Church in America, Southern Province, as the statements respectively merely urge industrialized nations to "assist" developing nations or urge programs of aid for "economic development." Another resolution of the assembly, on economic and social justice, seems to have opted for the newer model.

With regard to theological arguments in the statements, the lack of influence theological positions have on disagreements over development is readily apparent. A church advocating the new development model is as likely to authorize its position by appeal to some theological locus like the doctrine of human persons, for example, as is a church opting for the transfer of technology. In a number of cases we have observed that churches with different theological orientations hold the same position on development (as was evident from the variety of theological warrants used by the churches in authorizing any one of the development models). Unlike the pattern we noted in the case of apartheid, a given theological orientation does not seem to entail a tendency to assume one position rather than another with regard to the debate over development.

Nor can it be argued too facilely that the reason why theological positions appear not ultimately to determine the position churches take on development is because the statements are devoid of theological reflection. This is perhaps true in a few cases where no theological warrants are given in the statements. It is significant to note, however, that on the whole the churches' statements reflect the traditional theological orientation associated with the confessional family to which they belong. Thus most of the Lutheran statements embody a kind of two-kingdom ethic insofar as they largely appeal to the doctrine of creation to authorize their position on development. (The statement of the Eglise de la Confession d'Augsbourg d'Alsace et de Lorraine is a notable exception.) And Reformed-Presbyterian statements such as that of the Presbyterian-Reformed Church in Cuba and the joint statement of the Presbyterian Church in the U.S. and the United Presbyterian Church follow the most prominent Calvinist heritage in authorizing their positions by appealing to doctrinal themes derived from the gospel and redemption.[8]

Yet despite the reflection of sound theology in some of the statements, the failure ultimately of the theological positions to determine an approach to development is also reflected in the fact that in some cases members of the same confessional family employing the same theological arguments wind up on different sides of the question concerning models of development. Most notable here is the Presbyterian-Reformed tradition and the Roman Catholic Church, which generated statements supporting both the new and the old models of development. Theological agreement does not ensure agreement on ethics, for disagreements over ethics and social strategy are not necessarily theologically related. In fact, theological disagreement need not entail ethical disagreement.

In addition to these potentially ecumenically significant observations, consideration of church statements on development speaks to a truism which, as we noted earlier, is largely accepted in ecumenical circles. I refer to the conventional wisdom that all theology is context bound, that different cultural contexts will produce differences in both theology and ethics.[9]

In fact, our analysis of church statements on development indicates that differences in cultural context do not seem to mandate differences in ethics or theology. As we have seen, churches from similar cultural contexts are likely to take opposite positions concerning the most appropriate model of development. For example, some church organizations from the third world, notably the All Africa Conference of Churches (at least in 1969) and the Presbyterian-Reformed Church in Cuba, opt for old models of development; new models are advocated by others from the third world, notably the Christian Conference of Asia. Both groups of these third-world bodies find Western church groups agreeing with them in their respective positions concerning development.

Our example clearly illustrates an occasion in which churches from distinctly different cultural contexts come to agreement on ethics, even employing similar theological arguments, while churches from the same cultural context may entirely disagree on these same ethical issues. Such data compel us to ask whether the present ecumenical consensus regarding the determinative role of one's context in shaping theology does not deserve critical reconsideration. Likewise, the questions we posed in connection with our consideration of the treatment of apartheid by the various churches should be raised anew in concluding our theological evaluation of the statements devoted to development. What are the implications of the fact that many ethical disagreements among the churches are not related to doctrinal differences for the concern that disagreements on social ethics might divide the churches? Might there be implications for church unity in the fact that theological differences do not necessarily entail disagreements in praxis?

Related Issues

We have noted that, particularly on grounds of the new models of development, a number of important contemporary social issues should be related to the topic of development. Two such issues are those of energy consumption and of unemployment. The decisions made about energy consumption may dictate the agenda for development, and overcoming unemployment should be one of the goals of development.

Energy Consumption

Inasmuch as we will be considering further in chapter 3 the churches' treatment of the question of energy consumption, I comment here only briefly on this matter. Suffice it to say that the corresponding section in the Appendix which analyzes statements on this issue shows that the vast majority of church statements addressing it opts for some kind of reduction in the consumption of energy, particularly by industrialized nations. With the exception of the WCC, which has addressed this matter, all the statements concerned with energy consumption have been issued by churches in Europe or North America. And it is only since the late 1970s that such statements have begun to appear. This fact is hardly surprising, since only recently has the controversy about energy consumption been a Western issue of concern.

To a great extent, agreement on the desirability of reduced energy consumption is ecumenical in character, at least in the sense that various bodies among both Protestants and Roman Catholics have taken this position. Yet the unanimity is by no means complete. Disagreements are identifiable over the question of whether the reduction in energy consumption should be qualified so as not to alter drastically the standard of living in these nations or to undercut efforts in developing underdeveloped peoples. But even those who argue for an unqualified reduction of energy consumption seem (at least implicitly) to have the question of development in view. A number of these churches, such as the Church of Norway as well as the now-merged Presbyterian Church in the U.S. and the United Presbyterian Church, maintain explicitly what the others may imply, namely, that by reducing energy consumption, excess resources would be made more readily available for underdeveloped nations. [10]

Of statements available to me, I have found only one which seems to break radically with both of these proposals by advocating that industrialized nations in fact should aim to produce more goods in order to aid the poor. Unlike the other statements, this particular document, the 1967 papal encyclical *Populorum Progressio,* 48, 34, seems to imply the advocacy of more energy consumption on the part of these nations in order to facilitate the development of underdeveloped peoples.

Since further analysis of the churches' treatments of this issue of energy consumption will be offered in the next chapter, we may note here only that the theological patterns already observed in other church social statements pertain also to this issue. (The tendency for cultural context not to play a determinative role in the ethical position taken by the statements does not really apply to this case, since all the church bodies addressing this statement are located or theologically rooted in the West.) Again it is evident that theological disagreements do not mandate differences in ethics.

In some instances the papal encyclical *Populorum Progressio,* whose position on this matter seems authorized by the doctrine of creation (the duty of human solidarity accessible to all persons of good will), stands in contrast to churches advocating reduced energy consumption on grounds of the gospel or Christology. (Statements by the Southern Baptist Convention [USA] and the [Lutheran] Church of the Augsburg Confession of Alsace and Lorraine serve to illustrate this position.) In these cases theological differences do reflect in disagreements on ethical questions.

By the same token, one finds advocates of some level of reduced energy consumption (e. g., in statements of the Evangelisch-Lutherische Kirche im Rheinland-Westfalen and the Church of Norway) which seem to authorize their position by appeals to the doctrine of creation correlated with some other theological locus. Insofar as one can identify at this point theological arguments which seem somewhat analogous to the 1967 papal encyclical, they in fact lead to different conclusions concerning energy consumption. It is once again apparent that disagreement on social strategy and ethics is often not related to theological disagreements.

The point can be underlined even further if one recalls that this encyclical could be read in light of Vatican II documents, so that its references to the creation doctrine might be regarded as subordinate to redemption. But even if *Populorum Progressio* is ultimately warranted by redemption or Christology, if its actual ethical criterion is best described as humanity under grace, it still follows that we have identified some church statements which opt for basically the same theological orientation but nevertheless differ in their conclusions concerning social strategy on the use of energy. The relative inconsequentiality of theological differences as factors in determining disagreements on questions of social strategy and ethics is evident once more.

In like manner, among those statements advocating reduction of energy consumption one finds appeals to a variety of distinct doctrinal loci to warrant the positions of both those advocating unqualified reduction and those advocating reduction with some qualification. In these cases theological disagreements thus do not mandate differences on social strategy. Likewise it follows that churches on one side of the issue can find a church on the other side of the issue which employs the same theological argument but arrives at different conclusions about the proper strategy for reduction. For example, both the Evangelische Landeskirche in Baden and the Eglise de la Confession d'Augsbourg d'Alsace et de Lorraine authorize their positions on reduced energy consumption by appeal to Christology as warrant. But only the former qualifies the degree of reduction (specifying that it must not endanger development).

Unemployment

The same patterns concerning the relationship (or lack thereof) between theological and ethical disagreements is evident in the churches' treatment of the problem of unemployment. There is profound unanimity on this issue.

It is true that a 1977 statement of the German [Catholic] Bishops' Conference, backed by no clear theological warrant, would subordinate the concern for full employment in society to the concern to reduce energy consumption. The conference seems to advocate sacrificing jobs for the sake of lower levels of consumption.[11] And there is a 1979 statement of the Church of Norway which, while expressing concern for Norway's unemployed, does not advocate Norwegian efforts to find resources for helping the unemployed by means of diminishing aid for underdeveloped nations. Likewise a 1983 deliverance of the United Free Church of Scotland, while concerned about unemployment and proposing plans to deal with it, insists that "no action that we take should result in the impoverishment of people in another part of the world."

A 1966 statement of the Lutheran Church in America even conceded that there may be some nations where a full employment economy is not possible. But it simultaneously insisted that in all cases adequate income for all should be provided, and at least in developed nations full employment should be an economic goal. Another anomaly is a 1983 statement of the Church of Ireland, which rejects quotas as a means of equalizing employment in Northern Ireland. The church does proceed to urge steps to ensure employment and perhaps a basic minimum income for all citizens.

On the whole, though, the positions of these statements are quite atypical. By contrast, every other statement addressing the subject of unemployment calls for government, entrepreneurial, and in some cases ecclesiastical efforts to ensure employment, or at least it deems employment a human right. These statements emerge predominantly, though not exclusively, from churches in Western nations, particularly from churches in the USA and the Federal Republic of Germany — by churches as diverse as the Southern Baptist Convention [USA] and the Evangelisch-Lutherische Kirche in Bayern. One also finds the issue addressed in two 1970 statements by one of the Christian world communions, in the WCC Evanston and Uppsala assemblies, and even in a 1984 pastoral letter of the Liberian Catholic Bishops' Conference as well as in a couple of statements from Latin America. But the fact that a majority of the statements is issued by Western churches suggests that a Christian concern with unemployment is, not surprisingly, largely a Western problem. Nevertheless, it seems to be an ecumenical concern. Although most of the statements are issued by Protestant church bodies which represent most of the confessional traditions, the Roman Catholic Church has issued a good portion of statements on the problem as well.

Because of a general lack of clarity or elaboration by most of the statements, it is not possible to determine definitively whether the statements might differ, particularly with regard to their proposed strategies for overcoming unemployment. A typical proposal is the call for public works projects, as characterizes, to name just a few examples, a 1973 statement of the USA's United Church of Christ, a 1984 statement of the United Church of Canada, and a 1986 pastoral letter of the USA's National Conference of Catholic Bishops. Other statements, like the 1981 papal encyclical *Laborem Exercens,* call for unemployment benefits. In this connection a 1977 statement of the Evangelische Kirche in Deutschland is particularly noteworthy. Not only does it sketch a strategy for stimulating employment through new entrepreneurial investments, government public works projects, and more management-labor cooperation. It is also noteworthy in observing the psychological and communal problems associated with unemployment. Some of its more fully explicated strategies for overcoming unemployment have indeed been appropriated by several German Landeskirchen. For example, the proposal to reinvest profits in order to create new jobs is also endorsed by the Evangelisch-Lutherische Landeskirche Hannovers in its resolution on the subject.

Another statement which warrants mention is a 1977 statement of the Evangelisch-Lutherische Kirche in Bayern. It demonstrates a sensitivity to women's rights in a very concrete way by deploring the discrimination women often encounter in the world of industry. It offers in addition the interesting proposal that in obedience to the gospel command, Christians should share the available work with the unemployed. (Though it did not provide theological authorization for its position, a 1983 vote of the Fédération Protestante de France also suggested job sharing in order to create more employment opportunities. Apparently by way of appeal to the Bible and to eschatology, job sharing was also advocated by the 1983 deliverance of the United Free Church of Scotland.) With a similar tendency to look to the gospel for some kind of authorization, a related proposal was also offered in 1983 and 1984 by the Church of Ireland and by the Evangelische Landeskirche in Württemberg in a 1985 resolution entitled *Entschliessung zur Kirche und Arbeitswelt.*

Despite its qualifications, the resolution of the German church did not perhaps reflect the Bavarian church's sensitivity to women's equality, insofar as it is suggested that the unemployment crisis might be alleviated by raising questions about the appropriateness of both partners of a marriage working outside the home. A similar conservatism with regard to women in the working place is reflected in a 1979 joint pastoral letter of the Roman Catholic Bishops of Kenya. After urging the necessity of suitable employment, the bishops criticize working mothers. [12]

At any rate, in view of the general unanimity of the statements, it is not possible at this time to offer much analysis concerning disagreements among the churches on the issue of unemployment. It is perhaps worthy of note that the gospel plays an apparent role as the main authorization for the more "socialist" proposals to overcome unemployment by sharing work. This appeal, however, is not made without reference to the doctrine of creation or the natural law in all cases. In fact, the call for unemployment benefits and an openness to the socialization of certain goods by the 1981 papal encyclical *Laborem Exercens* is authorized by a kind of appeal to creation or the moral order, which shows again that a liberal ethic can be maintained on the basis of arguments rooted in the doctrine of creation. [13]

Even with respect to the disagreements we can identify, between the bulk of the statements on one side and those of the German Catholic Bishops, the Church of Norway, and the United Free Church of Scotland on the other, precise theological analysis of the disagreements ultimately is not possible. The German bishops did not provide clear theological warrants for their position so as to make theological analysis possible. The Norwegian Church refers to the fact that because all are created in God's image, all have equal rights. This appeal to the doctrine of creation, however, is accompanied by reference to Jesus' showing the danger of wealth and a comment that increased material growth in Norway is a threat to the new life in Christ. Neither remark is clearly related to the proposal concerning unemployment. Similarly, while the Free Church of Scotland does refer to the Bible and eschatology to authorize its claim about the importance of work, neither of these themes is expressly invoked to authorize its positions on how to deal with unemployment. The theological ambiguity of these statements, then, must qualify any comparison made with other statements.

Concerning the Church of Norway's statement, even if one or both of the two theological references made in it might be said to serve as a warrant for its atypical position on unemployment, it would not follow that the disagreements between this church and those advocating full employment in an unqualified way were occasioned by theological differences. With respect to those churches united in their agreement to overcome unemployment, one discerns a variety of theological warrants taken for their common position. (As was the case with statements on development and energy consumption, many, if not most, of the statements authorize their position by means of theological arguments consistent with their own confessional heritage. It is also interesting to note that in the case of statements on unemployment, various churches and ecumenical organizations at least appeal to the creation doctrine in some manner.) There thus could be cases when the Church of Norway and its partner in a disagreement over the question of unemployment might hold different theological rationales for their respective positions. However, the wide variety of views represented by those church organizations committed to overcoming unemployment affords a logical guarantee that at least some of these organizations, while disagreeing with the Church of Norway on how best to dispose of unemployment, would share the Norwegian church's theological rationale. Insofar as in these cases disagreements over unemployment between the Church of Norway and some other churches would not be theologically related, it cannot be said that theological disagreements are the determining factor in disagreements among the churches about how to deal with this social and ethical challenge.

Conclusions about the nature of disagreements between the United Free Church of Scotland and other churches concerning strategies for dealing with unemployment are much the same. Theological disagreements cannot be the determining factor in any disagreements about strategy. Even if we presume, as we did in the case of the Church of Norway statement, that any theological references in the deliverance of the United Free Church of Scotland actually authorize its atypical position on how to handle unemployment, it is soon evident that theological disagreements do not mandate the disagreements on strategies for dealing with unemployment that the Scottish church might have with other churches.

To be sure, many churches which disagree with the Scottish church's strategy authorize their position by appeal to Christology, the doctrine of creation, and some combination of these themes, and so hold theological positions in conflict with the Scottish Presbyterians. However, a number of church statements advocating the more predominant strategy for dealing with unemployment authorize their position by appeal to themes derived from all three articles of the creed. At least two statements — a 1979 letter on racism by the USA's National Council of Churches and a 1984 *Statement on Human Rights* of the Lutheran World Federation — even seem to appeal to the same eschatological themes which undergird the deliverance of the Scottish church. In these cases, disagreements about the proper strategy for dealing with unemployment are obviously not theologically related, inasmuch as the partners to the disagreement share common theological commitments. Once again it is evident that even though in some cases disagreements about unemployment may be between parties with distinct theological orientations, theological disagreements are not the ultimate occasion for the disagreements about unemployment. The rich theological diversity among church statements addressing the unemployment dilemma and their disagreements about the best strategy ought not to divide the churches. Theology, or the nature of the Christian faith, is not ultimately at stake in disagreements among the churches over unemployment. [14]

The fact that a wide variety of churches assume a similar position on how to deal with the challenge of unemployment warrants notice for another reason. It illustrates once again that distinct cultural contexts do not necessarily mandate different positions on ethics. Thus a church in the Southern hemisphere, the Evangelical Church of Lutheran Confession in Brazil, joins hands with various churches in the North in vowing to work to counteract unemployment. It is also especially interesting to note the heavy reliance of the Brazilian church's statement on the themes of liberation theology; these theological commitments, however, do not lead it to any ethical conclusions which are radically distinct from those of Northern hemisphere churches.

It is evident that with respect to the broader issues associated with economic development, including theological rationale for the positions taken, there is much agreement among the churches and their cooperative organizations. One cannot fairly speak of some churches being more "liberal" than others. One may well speak of a catholic consensus on the morality of Christian involvement in the area of economic development.

NOTES

[1] For references to these statements and others cited subsequently in the chapter explicitly dealing with this topic, see the section on economic development in the Appendix.

[2] For these criticisms I am indebted to a section report from the WCC Conference on Faith, Science and the Future, *Science/Technology, Political Power and a More Just World Order* (Cambridge, Mass., 12-24 July 1979), 1-2. For a similar critique of this development model, see WCC Sub-Unit on Church and Society, *Report of the Advisory Group of the Energy for My Neighbour Programme* (1982), VI. Similar criticisms, especially with reference to the way the poor are exploited by this model of development, were originally articulated by churches in the third world. See especially Christian Conference of Asia, *Justice and Service* (1973), Pre.; cf. [Catholic] Episcopal Conference of the Pacific, *The Pacific and Peace* (1986), IV.

[3] Christian Conference of Asia, *Justice and Service*.

[4] See Rubem A. Alves, *A Theology of Human Hope* (St. Meinard, Ind.: Abbey Press, 1974), 7, 113; Thomas Odhiambo, "An African Perspective", in "Perspectives in Developing Countries", in *Faith and Science in an Unjust World,* vol. 1, ed. Roger Shinn (Philadelphia: Fortress Press, 1980), 159, 163; Carlos Chagos, "A Latin American Perspective", in ibid., 169.

[5] All Africa Conference of Churches, *Working with Christ in the Contemporary Social, Economic and Political Situation* (1969). For references to subsequent statements cited, see the subsection entitled "Development by Initiating Indigenous Technology..." in the section on economic development in the Appendix. For the preceding description of the characteristics of this new development model, I am especially indebted to the WCC statements cited above in note 2.

[6] The encyclicals to which reference is first made are *Populorum Progressio* (1967), 5, 12-15, 20-21, 32, 34, 39, 42, 44, 48, 54, 70-73, 77, 81, 83-87; *Redemptor Hominis* (1979), 13-17; and *Sollicitudo Rei Socialis* (1987), 1, 3, 7-10, 28-49. Also see Third General Conference of Latin American [Catholic] Bishops, *The Puebla Message* (1979). For references to the documents appealing to themes from all articles of the creed, see *Solicitudo Rei Socialis* (1987), 1-3, 7-10, 28-49; National Conference of Catholic Bishops [USA], *To Live in Jesus Christ: A Pastoral Reflection on the Moral Life* (1976), 20, 30, 31, 88, 91-94, 115-16.

[7] For references to these statements and others which take a similar position, see the comments following the Appendix section on economic development.

[8] More detailed analysis of the historic confessional positions of these churches is provided in the Conclusion. For pertinent references, see chapter 1, notes 6, 11.

[9] See chapter 1, note 53, for pertinent references.

[10] For references to these statements and others cited subsequently in this section, see the section on energy consumption in the Appendix.

[11] For references to this statement and others cited in this section, see the section on unemployment in the Appendix. The Appendix also provides information concerning the degree to which my analysis is complete.

[12] A similar conservatism is also evident in a 1975 declaration of the Conférence Episcopale Française, *A propos de la conjoncture économique et sociale,* 2, which claims that most mothers of families would prefer to stay home if they received monthly allocations and suggests that such a policy could be instituted in order to assure employment for other women who are seeking it.

[13] Roman Catholic Church, *Laborem Exercens* (1981), 14, 18.

[14] This observation even pertains in the case of a comparison between the Church of Norway statement and the 1987 Roman Catholic papal encyclical *Sollicitudo Rei Socialis,* 49, which authorized its call for an end to unemployment by appeal to Mariology. This theological argument appears to be in marked contrast to the Church of Norway's theological authorization for its contrasting conclusion. A careful examination of the papal encyclical, however, suggests a convergence with the theological orientation of the Norwegian statement (see pp. 29, 27), insofar as, like the Norwegian statement, the papal encyclical also refers to the doctrine of human persons and Christology as supporting warrants for its position (see 1-3, 7-8, 47-49). Thus a compatibility in the theological arguments of these otherwise conflicting statements exists. Their disagreement is not simply reducible to disagreements about the nature of the Christian faith.

3. Ecology

The mandate placed upon humans to assume responsibility for helping to preserve God's creation is a fundamental Judeo-Christian theme, though one largely overlooked until the last decades. The divine command in creation that humanity rule over the earth (Gen. 1:26; Ps. 8:6) testifies to this mandate for the human stewardship of creation. The biblical witness gives further testimony to a belief that relationships among living things in creation are intended to be harmonious — ecologically balanced, as it were. One can only conclude that this sort of balance has been intended by God since the time of creation, not just on the basis of the Genesis creation accounts, but also insofar as this image of perfect ecological harmony evidences itself in several biblical passages which depict the eschatological vision, the fulfilment of what God has always intended for his creation (Isa. 11:6-9; cf. Rom. 8:19-22). By contrast, the mandate to dominate the world, to make it serve humanity's ends, is not part of this Judeo-Christian vision of God's purpose in creation. Rather, this image of humanity's function as the creature who dominates the earth, the creature to whose purposes the earth must conform in fear, appears in the biblical witness in the context of the doctrine of sin — as a vision of humanity's relation to the earth after the Fall and then the Flood (Gen. 9:2ff.).

Despite the biblical witness to an ecological concern and its picture of humanity in harmony with nature, it has been the second set of images — the idea that human beings should subdue the earth — which largely has characterized the Christian community's thinking, at least since the onset of the Industrial Revolution in the West. That such an intimate relationship exists between this neglect of an ecological concern and a Western confidence in technology is suggested quite clearly by patterns observable in modern church statements on ecology. By and large, the churches did not begin to address the problem of ecology until after the so-called limits-to-growth debate made itself fully felt in the ecumenical movement during the WCC Nairobi Assembly in 1975, and perhaps earlier in the council's 1974 conference on Science and Technology for Human Development, held in Bucharest. Exceptions include 1970 and 1972 statements of the former Lutheran Church in America, a 1970 statement of the American Lutheran Church, a 1969 resolution of the Lutheran Church-Missouri Synod, deliverances in 1970, 1972, and 1973 of the United Free Church of Scotland, a 1968 declaration of Anglicanism's Lambeth Conference, a 1971 declaration of the Church of Norway, a 1970 declaration of the Baptist World Alliance, a 1970 statement of the Baptist Union of New Zealand, a 1970 declaration of the World Alliance of Reformed Churches, a 1971 papal encyclical *Octogesima Adveniens,* resolutions in 1971, 1972, and 1973 by the USA's National Conference of Catholic Bishops, a 1973 resolution of the Christian Conference of Asia, a 1966 policy statement of the USA's National Council of Churches, and, significantly enough, resolutions in 1970 and 1971 of the USA's National Association of Evangelicals.[1]

The limits-to-growth debate, whose impact is still very much felt today in ecumenical ethics, grows out of the idea that there has been an undue naïvety in the ecumenical movement's earlier confidence that progress in science and technology would be beneficial in all situations. Societies heavily dependent on science and technology were seen to be in serious predicaments. Thus more critical evaluation of the aims and methods of technology are now thought to be necessary. An important consequence of this line of thinking is that for the first time it opened the ecumenical movement and the churches to reflect systematically on the depletion of physical resources and environmental pollution by an unrestrained, voracious technology. The result was that the way was opened to a preoccupation with ecology, a fact given testimony by the large amount of church statements issued on ecology since the WCC Nairobi Assembly and the council's Bucharest Conference.[2] The data certainly seem to verify the contention that the modern church's failure until recent years to take the ecological mandate seriously was related to its uncritical confidence in modern technology. Only after the churches had begun to take a critical perspective towards technology did they seem able to reappropriate the previously overlooked ecological emphases of the biblical tradition.

In directing attention to these ecological concerns, the limits-to-growth debate has been related to another development in ecumenical ethics which challenged earlier prevailing trends. In a previous chapter we noted the general acceptance in ecumenical circles of what might be termed the wisdom of Barmen. That is, theological arguments made on the basis of appeals to the doctrine of creation or a related theme are thought to issue in conservative, even reactionary positions on social ethics. Only by using arguments rooted in Christology or some locus related to the third article of the creed, it is maintained, can liberal, open ethical conclusions be attained.

Previous chapters have cited evidence which disconfirms this conventional wisdom. However, we have also observed trends which seem to confirm this wisdom — and will continue to observe them, particularly in the chapter on peace and nuclear weapons, as well as in the final chapter on Christianity and socio-political ideologies. The prejudice against theological arguments rooted in the doctrine of creation is still very much alive in ecumenical ethics. Yet when the churches address the challenge of ecology, there seems to be emerging a genuine acknowledgment that the conventional wisdom does not apply. Appeals to the doctrine of creation for authorizing the ecological concern are made in larger number by the churches than those church bodies which seek to authorize ecology by way of arguments that completely ignore the doctrine in favor of appeals to Christology or doctrines associated with the final segment of the Nicene Creed. This pattern thoroughly refutes the so-called wisdom of Barmen. The numerous church arguments on behalf of an ecological concern which have been authorized by appeals to the doctrine of creation clearly demonstrate that such appeals need not result in conservative or reactionary ethical proposals.

We have observed other contemporary ethical and social issues for which the facts refuted the conventional wisdom of Barmen. What makes the churches' treatment of the ecological agenda different is that so many church organizations, insofar as they have appealed to the doctrine of creation to authorize their concern with ecology, have indicated that at least with respect to ecological concerns, they do not accept the conventional wisdom. It is clear, then, that the limits-to-growth debate, insofar as it has directed ecumenical attention to environmental concerns, has contributed to a rekindling of confidence and interest in the doctrine of creation. It has not, however, totally eradicated the discomfort felt in ecumenical circles with appeals to the doctrine of creation to authorize positions on certain other social and ethical issues, for fear that such appeals can lead only to conservatism. Already we have examined some of the valid reasons for this concern and will continue to do so in subsequent chapters. For the present, it is sufficient to note that the ecological agenda of the churches has created a climate in which critiques of the conventional wisdom associated with the Barmen Declaration are less likely to be ignored.

To this juncture, common themes in the churches' statements pertaining to ecology have been highlighted. Interesting and significant diversity exists within this group of statements, however, with regard to the context in which each one was formulated, the theological authorization each provides, and the specific concerns each associates with ecology. Of specific concerns often associated with ecology by the church statements, two are particularly worthy of attention: energy consumption and the use of nuclear energy. Consequently, we shall devote explicit attention later in this chapter to church statements which explicitly address these issues. First, however, we consider in more detail the diversity among the church statements devoted to ecology, and the broader implications of this diversity.

The Diverse Approaches to Ecology

Along with the diversity in the churches' approaches to ecology, we should note that the overwhelming majority of church statements which have dealt with ecology are by churches located in Western nations or by international church organizations (which commonly endorse Western social agendas). Exceptions to this pattern include the following: a 1977 document of the Presbyterian-Reformed Church in Cuba, declarations of the Christian Conference of Asia in 1977 and in 1973, a 1986 statement of the [Catholic] Episcopal Conference of the Pacific, a 1988 pastoral letter of the Catholic bishops of the Philippines, an unspecified statement of the Methodist Church in Malaysia, a 1975 statement of the Presbyterian Church in Taiwan, a 1984 declaration of the Presbyterian Church of Korea, a 1978 letter from the Latin American Protestant Conference, a 1982 statement of the Evangelical Church of Lutheran Confession in Brazil, a 1981 statement of the Czechoslovak Hussite Church, statements in 1986 and 1983 of the Russian Orthodox Church, a variety of church statements issued by church bodies in East Germany — among them resolutions in 1980, 1982, 1984, and 1987 of the Bund der Evangelischen Kirchen in der Deutschen Demokratischen Republik, a 1977 resolution of the Vereinigte Evangelisch-Lutherische Kirche in der DDR, a 1985 resolution of the Evangelisch-Lutherische Landeskirche Sachsens, as well as two different 1984 and three different 1985 documents of the neighboring Evangelische Kirche der Kirchenprovinz Sachsen. (Interestingly, no statements on ecology have been received from African church bodies.)

Despite the articulation of an ecological concern by a few church bodies in the third world, the geographical location of the overwhelming majority of statements on ecology seems to confirm a common criticism of the limits-to-growth orientation and its ecological concern. This orientation appears to be a response to an exclusively Western social and economic agenda.[3] In one sense there is broad ecumenical consensus among the churches on ecology. In addition to the numerous statements issued by ecumenical organizations on the subject, every major denominational family has at least one member which has issued a statement expressing ecological concern. Even a number of church groups associated with the evangelical movement have called for more ecological sensitivity. Such a call appears in the 1973 *Chicago Declaration of Evangelicals to Social Concern,* in a 1974 document of the Billy Graham-inspired International Congress on World Evangelization, as well as in 1970, 1971, 1979, 1982, and 1990 resolutions of the National Association of Evangelicals [USA]. Ecology thus does not divide evangelicals and the mainline church estab-lishment. Despite the impressive convergence of concerns, however, the geographi-cally parochial character of Christian ecological concern raises serious questions about the degree to which one may legitimately speak of a truly ecumenical consensus regarding ecology.

Given the origins of the Christian concern about ecology in the myriad issues associated with the limits-to-growth movement, and in view of the controversy it has sparked among those who regard this agenda as a Western retreat from the West's responsibilities for social justice and developmental concerns in the Southern hemis-phere, it is hardly surprising that ecology has come to include a great variety of concerns for the churches. To be sure, some concerns linked to ecology appear repeatedly in a number of the statements, such as the concern to reduce energy consumption, specifically the use of non-renewable resources.[4] And in many cases the churches link the ecological concern with the nuclear problem in some form. The development of nuclear energy and nuclear arms (as a threat to peace) are cited as factors of grave ecological concern.[5]

Criticisms levelled against the new ecological agenda as a retreat from global responsibility by Western nations have inspired certain specific responses from the churches. For example, ecology is linked to social justice or justice in a 1972 statement of the former Lutheran Church in America, in various 1980s statements of the United Church of Canada, and a statement from a 1979 conference of the WCC. It is interesting to note that the Lutheran statement's position is authorized by an appeal to themes associated with the doctrine of creation, specifically to a kind of relational view of human persons, as described in previous chapters.

A few church statements insist that the ecological concern must not lead to a neglect of facilitating development of poorer nations. Such a commitment is articu-lated by statements like a 1980 declaration of the Arbeitsgemeinschaft Christlicher Kirchen in der Bundesrepublik Deutschland und Berlin (West), a 1978 pastoral letter of the Swiss Catholic bishops, statements in 1980 and 1977 of the German [Catholic] Bishops' Conference, as well as in the more radical wing of the American Evangelical Movement's *Chicago Declaration of Evangelicals to Social Concern* (1973). Most of these statements arrive at their position by way of arguments that draw upon a combination of doctrinal themes.

In other statements one finds a concern to relate the new consciousness of environmental protection to the needs of the poor. For example, in a 1977 statement authorized by Christology, the Evangelische Landeskirche in Baden insisted that the ecological concern and a commitment to reduced energy consumption must not override the commitment to equality in economic development. Likewise, a 1979 statement of the USA's National Council of Churches, a 1982 statement of the Church of Ireland, a 1984 statement of the United Church of Canada, and a 1985 statement of the Evangelisch-Lutherische Kirche in Bayern suggest that in some way the introduction of new environmental policies in their nations could create new jobs for the unemployed. Other statements, such as one of the resolutions of the WCC Vancouver Assembly, *Statement on the International Food Disorder,* would relate ecology to increased food production for the sake of the hungry. Correspondingly, in a 1977 statement entitled *Resolution on the Report on Racial and Economic Justice,* the United Church of Christ [USA] to some extent related the ecological concern to racial and economic justice.[6]

These diverse though somewhat related proposals for dealing with the ecological crisis are attempts to take into account the valid criticisms levelled against the new ecological agenda. In a sense, all of the statements noted in the preceding paragraphs are in sympathy with a rather pointed claim of a 1973 statement of the Christian Conference of Asia that, though environmental pollution and a reduction in demand for material goods are important, economic justice is "a more basic need".

Church bodies other than those in the Southern hemisphere have explicitly reminded the oikoumene that ecology should be a second-level concern. A 1983 statement of the Church of Ireland, for example, claims that nuclear weaponry is an issue which overshadows all of the day's cutting-edge issues, including ecology. It is quite evident how criticisms of the new ecological concern have opened the churches to considering a broad range of issues involving or related to ecology.

Several statements link certain surprising, even idiosyncratic agenda items with ecology. For example, a 1970 resolution of the Baptist World Alliance relates ecology to the problem of adequate health care. A 1971 declaration of the Church of Norway relates ecology to the pro-life position on abortion, as it regarded both as related to a similar mind-set. A 1973 resolution of the Reformed Church in America relates ecology to the need for birth control and the overall population problem. A 1986 statement of the USA's National Council of Churches, a 1987 proclamation of the Evangelische Kirche in Deutschland, and a 1989 report of the World Alliance of Reformed Churches express concerns about the environmental impact of genetic engineering. In a 1985 resolution on violence awareness, the USA's Episcopal Church related ecology not only to the overcoming of violence but also to the overcoming of racism, ageism, and drug dependency. No less idiosyncratic is a 1984 statement of the Evangelisch-Lutherische Kirche in Bayern which posits a relationship between environmental protection and setting automobile speed limits in Germany. Perhaps the most striking claim emerges in the *Confession of Faith* of the Presbyterian-Reformed Church in Cuba, which asserts that Marxism affords the best system for technological and ecological development!

This diversity among church statements with regard to differences in ecological concerns manifests no overall geographical or theological pattern. Granted, in the case of the last two statements cited, particularly the one of the Cuban church, the context has influenced the concerns associated with ecology. But we have also observed instances where church bodies from completely different contexts, such as from Asia, North America, and Western Europe, concur about the necessity of relating ecology to a given concern like justice. This commonality is evident in a 1973 statement of the Christian Conference of Asia, a 1979 statement of the USA's National Council of Churches, a 1977 statement of the Evangelische Landeskirche in Baden, and a 1980 document of the Arbeitsgemeinschaft Christlicher Kirchen in der Bundesrepublik Deutschland und Berlin (West), all of which insist that ecology must necessarily be related to a concern for justice. The American and German statements share with the other Northern hemisphere statements noted earlier the Asian Conference's inclination to subordinate the ecological concern to other social and ethical agendas. Again it is evident that differences in context do not mandate differences in ethics.

By the same token, diversity among the church statements with regard to issues associated with ecology is not theologically related. For example, in the statements described in the preceding paragraph, while the American Council authorizes its position by appeal to the doctrine of creation and a relational view of human persons, the German Council of Churches argues to a similar conclusion by appealing primarily to the lordship of Christ and the doctrine of redemption (with the doctrine of creation functioning only as a subordinate warrant), and the Baden church makes its point by exclusive appeal to the redeeming work of Christ.

Theological agreement, however, does not entail that the churches will speak in the same way about ecology and what it entails. Thus, for example, two 1984 assembly statements of the Lutheran World Federation share a similar theological orientation with the 1979 statement of the National Council of Churches, which we have been considering. Unlike the statement of the American Council, however, the Lutheran Federation statements do not speak of any relationship between ecology and justice. Similar examples could be cited. The differences among church statements concerning what ecology entails are not related to theological differences or disagreements about any matter essential to the Christian faith.

The preceding discussion concerning the lack of impact theological disagreements have on church statements pertaining to ecology brings us to the final area of diversity among the statements. In addressing the ecological challenge, the statements of the churches exhibit a significant number of distinct theological arguments.

Previously it was noted that perhaps the most characteristic theological posture of the statements devoted to ecology was the argument for ecology based on some theme related to the doctrine of creation. It must also be noted, however, that a number of statements have made their case for ecological concern with authorization drawn from Christology or the gospel, particularly from the Presbyterian/Reformed and the United church families, at least two by ecumenical organizations in Western Europe, perhaps a 1977 statement of the Christian Conference of Asia, one statement each by an Anglican, Baptist, and Mennonite church body, two statements by national Roman Catholic bishops' conferences, perhaps two by the Eastern Orthodox family of churches, at least two by Lutheran churches, and one by the WCC. Also see two 1973 resolutions of the Christian Church (Disciples of Christ) and the 1984 statement of the United Church of Canada, which authorizes its position by appeal to the commandment to love.

In addition to these appeals, a number of statements employ arguments drawing upon various combinations of doctrinal themes. Notable among such statements are nine which seem to combine themes from all three articles of the creed: a 1982 statement of the World Alliance of Reformed Churches entitled *The Theatre of Glory and a Threatened Creation's Hope*, a 1976 *Policy Statement on Human Rights* of the American Baptist Churches, probably a WCC statement entitled *Human Development: Ambiguities of Power, Technology and Quality of Life*, from the council's Nairobi Assembly, a 1987 proclamation of the Evangelische Kirche in Deutschland, a 1987 Roman Catholic papal encyclical entitled *Sollicitudo Rei Socialis*, perhaps a 1976 statement of the USA's National Conference of Catholic Bishops, a 1989 statement on the environment by the Mennonite Church [USA], a 1977 statement of the Church of the Brethren [USA], as well as a 1976 resolution of the former American Lutheran Church entitled *Issues and Opportunities That Bind and Free*.

In addition to these sorts of arguments, a fairly large number of church statements on ecology offer no clear authorization for their conclusions. Examples of this kind include several statements of the WCC Vancouver Assembly, a 1982 European Commission Anglican-Lutheran Dialogue report, a number of statements of the Uniting Church in Australia, the United Church of Canada, and the United Free Church of Scotland, as well as, uncharacteristically, a number of statements of the Roman Catholic Church (both Vatican documents and statements of national bishops' conferences). As we have seen, theological disagreements are not decisive for the churches' consideration of ecology. All of the statements enumerated in the preceding several paragraphs disagree theologically, yet all agree that ecology must be pursued.

The church statements that address the ecological challenge, particularly those which authorize their position by means of an appeal to the doctrine of creation, shed further light on what sorts of theological adjustments must be made to the doctrine of creation in order for it to function successfully in authorizing open, progressive ethical conclusions (such as fostering an ecological sensibility). All the necessary adjustments to the doctrine, which have been observed in previous chapters, are reflected in pertinent statements pertaining to ecology.

The previously noted adjustments made to the doctrine of creation in statements where the doctrine authorizes open, progressive ethical conclusions pertain to anthropology (human persons are depicted relationally, as inherently related to each other and their environment), ontology (in some respects creation is construed as ongoing, still in process), and theology (creation and redemption are correlated, so that the orders of creation do not conflict with the gospel). In two of the statements where ecology is authorized by the doctrine of creation, both by the former Lutheran Church in America (in 1972 and 1978 statements), all three of these adjustments are evident. Several other statements in this category endorse the relational anthropology and a continuity of creation and redemption, notably one in 1970 on world community by the Lutheran Church in America, a 1979 statement on energy use by the USA's National Council of Churches, a 1979 statement of human rights by the United Church of Christ, as well as a 1985 resolution of the Evangelische Kirche der Kirchenprovinz Sachsen. (The anthropology is alone explicitly affirmed in a 1977 statement of the Moravian Church in America, Southern Province.) In the majority of the rest of the statements authorizing their position on ecology by appeal to creation alone for authorization, at least some sort of continuity between creation and redemption is posited. In no case, at least, is such a continuity denied.[7] The case can be strengthened further for arguing that creation must be construed in such a way that it correlates with the basic themes of the gospel if the doctrine of creation is to function successfully in authorizing liberal, open ethical conclusions. It can be strengthened by noting again the number of statements on ecology whose arguments are dependent on some combination or correlation of creation with another doctrinal theme from the creed's second or third article.

The numerous church statements on ecology which authorize their position in some way by appeal to the doctrine of creation seem to signal in ecumenical circles a kind of renewed sensitivity to or recovery of the doctrine of creation. It is also evident, however, that this "new" theological emphasis, especially if it incorporates at least some of the theological adjustments previously identified, is to some extent irrelevant for ecology and formal church fellowship. Such a theological approach does not necessarily lead to any different conclusions for ethics, at least not on ecological questions. In that sense the churches are not divided by their theological disagreements. These same patterns reappear in church statements devoted to two other issues closely related to ecology — energy consumption and the use of nuclear energy.

Energy Consumption

In describing church statements which address the ecological challenge, it was noted that a significant number of these statements related ecology to reduced energy consumption. [8] In fact, the churches' treatment of this issue of energy consumption was raised for the first time in the context of the chapter on development. At that point most attention was devoted to the disagreement between the many churches advocating some degree of reduction in the use of energy and a 1967 papal encyclical *Populorum Progressio,* which seems to advocate increased energy consumption on the part of industrialized nations in order to facilitate the development of underdeveloped peoples. Since the previous discussion of this disagreement demonstrated that it was not of a church-dividing character, it is possible to concentrate at this point on the disagreement among those church bodies advocating less energy consumption. [9]

The previous discussion of these church statements noted that, like the statements on ecology, the concern with energy consumption is basically a Western agenda which, with the exception of just a handful of old East German church statements, is dealt with only by church bodies located in Western nations or by international church bodies following a Western agenda. (This limitation is hardly surprising, since most of the church statements which have dealt with energy consumption also have advocated ecology.) As with church statements on ecology, this Western agenda is tempered somewhat by a sensitivity on the part of at least some of the statements to the needs of the poor and of developing nations in the Southern hemisphere. Indeed, the disagreement among the churches on energy consumption is occasioned by precisely this sensitivity to the poor, or lack of it.

The disagreement turns on the question of whether a reduction in the use of energy may have adverse effects on the poor, in both hemispheres. The concern is to convert the surplus of energy use in Western nations to the development of the underprivileged. If drastic cuts are made in these nations in energy use, however, the place to cut will be in development programs for the poor. Consequently, a handful of church bodies have argued that, though the West must reduce energy consumption, it must not be to the point of destabilizing Western economies and their potential for aiding the poor. The other group of church statements, in contrast, advocates the reduction of energy consumption in an unqualified manner, without regard for the consequences such reductions might have on the economy and the poor.

The first group of statements — what we may call the qualified reductionists — is a rather exclusive group. It comprises statements by the German [Catholic] Bishops' Conference, a statement by a United church in the Federal Republic of Germany (the Evangelische Landeskirche in Baden), and statements of several Western European ecumenical councils of churches as well as a 1982 report of the WCC. On the whole, the dominant theological perspective of this group of statements in arguing for their open, progressive conclusion, with a concern for the poor and welfare of people, is Christological.

The theological profiles reveal some diversity, as illustrated by two statements of the German [Catholic] Bishops' Conference. Both statements argue their case in some sense from the perspective of the doctrine of creation or the doctrine of human beings. Although there is some ambiguity in both statements, the texts suggest that references to creation have been subordinated to Christology and the gospel (a position which, as we shall subsequently see, has a legitimate place in the conciliar heritage of the Roman Catholic tradition).[10] Thus in the bishops' 1980 statement it is asserted that Christ is "the Source and Center of Creation".[11]

Even if we take into account the possibility that references to the doctrine of creation in the bishops' statements are ultimately reducible to appeals to the gospel, one must acknowledge that these statements do differ from the others advocating a qualified reduction of energy consumption. For it still must be acknowledged in these cases that themes related to the doctrine of creation have some role in the arguments, in a way that these themes do not, at least in the 1977 statement of the Evangelische Landeskirche in Baden concerning nuclear energy. (Most of the statements which argue from a Christological basis do include at least a passing reference to the doctrine of creation, such as, for example, a 1978 statement on atomic energy of the Synod of the Protestant Church in Austria or a 1982 WCC report on energy.) In this sense we may observe another example of how theological differences do not affect ethics.

The diversity among statements in our second group — those opting for a reduction of energy consumption without qualification — is both more and less pronounced than we observed among the statements opting for a qualified reduction of consumption. A richer diversity of denominational traditions is represented in this second group, as we have statements from Lutherans (e.g., 1978 statements of the Church of Norway and by the Eglise de la Confession d'Augsbourg d'Alsace et de Lorraine), Presbyterian and Reformed churches (a 1977 resolution of the Congregational Union of Scotland, a 1978 decision of the Reformed Church of Alsace-Lorraine, as well as a 1981 joint statement of the Presbyterian Church in the U.S. and the United Presbyterian Church), Baptists (the USA's Southern Baptist Convention), Roman Catholics (a 1978 *Pastoral Letter of the Catholic Swiss Bishops*), and others. In terms of theological diversity, the predominant model of argument appears to be the total neglect of reference to the doctrine of creation. Only a few statements seem to draw primarily on some theme related to the doctrine of creation in authorizing their unqualified calls for a reduction of energy consumption, including the one by the Church of Norway, a 1986 declaration of the Evangelische Kirche in Hessen und Nassau, to some extent perhaps a 1980 statement of the Landessynode der Evangelischen Kirche im Rheinland-Westfalen, a 1977 resolution of the USA's Mennonite Church, General Conference, a 1979 statement on energy of the United Church of Christ [USA], and a 1977 statement of the American Baptist Churches. The rest of the statements taking this position tend to rely more heavily upon themes related to the gospel or Christology.

In fact, this theological diversity is not very significant. Almost all of these statements calling for unqualified reduction of energy consumption to some extent allude to themes related to the doctrinal loci from segments of the creed other than the particular doctrinal theme they emphasize. For example, the Church of Norway statement includes in its appeal to the doctrine of creation some reference to Christian responsibility (a so-called third use of the law). The argument for reduced energy consumption on grounds of creation by the United Church in Rheinland-Westphalia is correlated with an argument based on Christian hope. On the other side of the theological spectrum, both the 1981 joint statement by two predecessor bodies of the Presbyterian Church (USA) and the 1978 *Pastoral Letter of the Catholic Swiss Bishops* incorporate references to the doctrine of creation and some other theme (either eschatology or ecclesiology) in their call for reduced energy consumption on grounds of the gospel or Christology. This overlap of the statements, insofar as most seem to embrace each other's characteristic theological themes, justifies the conclusion that theological differences between the churches calling for unqualified reduction of energy consumption are not very significant.

This observation makes possible a comparison between the two groups — those calling for a qualified reduction of consumption, and those who do not make such qualifications. The tendency of the statements opting for unqualified reduction to affirm several distinct theological themes allows us to reiterate a point made in the preceding chapter. This characteristic of these statements entails that one can always find certain theological compatibilities between these statements and those which opted for a qualified reduction of consumption patterns. As we have seen, some statements opting for such qualified reduction still incorporated a second subordinate doctrinal theme to supplement their primary theological authorization.

For example, at first glance it appears that the disagreement on energy consumption between a 1977 statement of the German [Catholic] Bishops' Conference and the 1978 *Pastoral Letter of the Catholic Swiss Bishops* seems to be theologically related — the German bishops arguing for qualifications in reduced energy consumption on grounds of anthropology (the nature of human beings as creatures), and the Swiss bishops arguing with no thought of such qualifications primarily from the overall perspective of the gospel and the doctrine of redemption (with reference to ecclesiology as a subordinate authorization). However, the theological arguments overlap. The Swiss bishops also refer to the doctrine of creation; they speak of energy as God's gift. With this affirmation they tend to take a theological stance akin to the German bishops. In their own way, however, the German bishops are just as oriented towards the creed's second article as are their Swiss counterparts. Though the statement is not completely clear, the Germans' reference to the doctrine of human beings may ultimately be subordinated to an overriding commitment to charity (the gospel) as the ultimate norm for ethics. In this case the differences between the two bishops' conferences on energy consumption do not appear to be the result of totally irreconcilable theological commitments.

The case for arguing that theological disagreements do not have the final word in determining disagreements among the churches on strategies for energy reduction can be strengthened further when it is noted that proponents of the same theological orientation sometimes disagree on the question of whether reduced energy consumption should be qualified or not. For example, a 1977 statement of the Evangelische Landeskirche in Baden clearly relies on an appeal to the doctrine of Christ's redemption to authorize a qualified reduction of consumption. The German church's disagreement with the unofficial 1978 statement of the Church of Norway concerning whether reduction of consumption should be a qualified reduction would appear to be theologically related. Unlike the Baden church, the Norwegians appeal to the doctrine of creation, a kind of natural law for authorization of their position.

The Norwegian lack of concern about qualifying the reduction of energy use is shared by a more or less official statement in 1979 by the USA's Southern Baptist

Convention. In contrast to the Norwegians but more like the Evangelische Landes-kirche in Baden, the Baptists authorize their position by appeal to distinctively Christian themes and insights (the gospel). In this case, then, a disagreement between the Baptists and the Baden church on the reduction of energy consumption is not theologically related. This conclusion suggests in turn that the theological disa-greement between the Baden church and the Church of Norway may not be so crucial after all in determining their disagreement about strategies for the reduction of energy consumption.

If such a theological disagreement were determinative of a disagreement in ethics, why could the Norwegian church and the Southern Baptist Convention maintain a common disregard for qualifying reductions in energy consumption while disagreeing theologically? Theological disagreements do not seem necessarily determinative for disagreements among the churches concerning their approach to the use of energy. Disagreements on the reduction of energy consumption seem to be matters of strategy, not matters of theology which affect church fellowship.

Nuclear Energy

Since Hiroshima, world opinion has anxiously contemplated the prospects of nuclear catastrophe. In the last decade or more, however, the terrible tragedies and chaos of nuclear accidents in Three-Mile Island and Chernobyl have placed the international community on guard even with regard to nuclear energy. What was once hailed as the answer to the depletion of non-renewable fuels has become a source of deep concern.

These concerns appeared in the church statements on ecology,[12] which is quite natural because some regard the use of nuclear energy as a threat to the environment. Given the widespread concern about the use of nuclear energy, it seems appropriate to examine church statements solely with reference to what they say about this topic. This is all the more relevant, because the widespread debate in international society concerning whether nuclear power should continue to be developed and used or whether instead a moratorium should be declared has come to be reflected inside the Christian community. The church statements concerning nuclear energy tend to take sides in this debate.[13]

Before analyzing the different positions taken by the churches in this debate, it is helpful to describe briefly the overall character of church statements on nuclear energy. We have noted that a number of church statements on ecology also dealt with nuclear energy. Consequently, a number of the same statements considered in the first two sections of this chapter are dealt with again in connection with nuclear energy. As a result, we see again many of the same patterns already identified.

Like ecology and the use of energy, nuclear energy is basically an item on the Western agenda. At least this contextual bias is reflected in the church statements on nuclear energy. Although nuclear energy is also an issue on the social agenda of much of Eastern Europe, at the time of publication only one church statement from that region had been identified as addressing the issue: a 1986 resolution of the Evangelische Kirche der Union — Bereich Deutsche Demokratische Republik. Every statement, except for two 1977 statements of the Christian Conference of Asia and a 1986 declaration of the [Catholic] Episcopal Conference of the Pacific, are by church bodies located in the West. The relative newness of the concern about nuclear energy is reflected in the fact that, except for a 1970 statement of the USA's Church of the

Brethren in support of nuclear energy, none of the statements was drafted before the mid-1970s. There is at least a rich diversity in the confessional/denominational traditions taking up the question. Virtually every denominational family is represented by at least one member church body, except the Orthodox, Baptist, and Christian Restorationist traditions. Thirteen statements have been formulated by ecumenical councils.

For purposes of analysis, we may divide church statements on nuclear energy into two categories — those in favor and those against (the latter favoring some moratorium or less dependence on nuclear energy). A third group are those that do not fall neatly into one of the first two.

The analyst is immediately struck by the relative dearth of statements in support of nuclear energy. The largest number clearly opt for some moratorium (usually on the construction of new nuclear power plants) or for less dependence generally on nuclear energy. The remainder fall in the third category, which includes statements that seem vaguely to criticize nuclear energy or to call for a reduction in its use but still are apparently open to continuing dependence.

This third group of statements warrants attention because several of them offer some interesting observations. Most of them offer no clear theological warrant for their conclusions, however, which makes the debate between the first two groups of statements more pertinent to the ecumenical problematic and thus deserving prior consideration.

Two points strike the observer with reference to debate among the churches on nuclear energy. One is the lack of unqualified support for its continued use, which we have noted and which is all the more striking when one considers that there is a kind of equivocation in the support that a number of statements, which are otherwise favorable, give to nuclear energy. Only a minority opinion recorded at a 1979 conference of the WCC (in which the official report called for a moratorium on nuclear energy) and the previously noted 1970 statement of the Church of the Brethren expressly endorse the use of nuclear energy. More qualified support is provided by 1977 and 1980 statements of the German [Catholic] Bishops' Conference. The bishops express a willingness to proceed with the use of nuclear energy only if no better way to ensure adequate energy supplies can be found.

The approval of nuclear energy by three French church bodies (a 1978 statement of the Fédération Protestante de France and two Alsatian churches which subscribed to it) is even more qualified. The claim is made that a middle path will be sought between the perils of a nuclear program and the perils of an energy shortage caused by not carrying it out. In view of these qualifications and the larger number of statements calling for a moratorium, one cannot but reflect seriously on the question of whether, at this point, the churches may not have unwittingly accepted the latest Western social fad.

The second point is the diversity of theological warrants proposed by churches on both sides of the debate. Many indeed provide no warrant, especially among those calling for a moratorium. This is true of both Christian Conference of Asia statements on the subject as well as various statements by bodies as diverse as the Council of Churches in the Netherlands, the British Council of Churches, and the United Church of Canada. Among those statements that do provide a theological warrant, relatively few appeal exclusively to themes related to the doctrine of creation.

The theological diversity among the statements on both sides of the debate has its usual implications for considering questions of church unity, specifically, whether nuclear energy might be an issue about which disagreement warrants church division. Given this diversity, one can find church statements which disagree on the question of nuclear energy but share a common theological authorization. For example, in its 1977 statement on nuclear energy the Evangelische Landeskirche in Baden expresses a desire to reduce dependence on nuclear energy; as previously noted, the statement relies on an appeal to Christ's redemptive work. (A similar position was taken by the 1978 joint statement of predecessor bodies of the Presbyterian Church (USA).) But to the degree that the French church statements previously noted (those of the Fédération Protestante de France, the Reformed Church of Alsace-Lorraine, and the Eglise de la Confession d'Augsbourg d'Alsace et de Lorraine) can be understood as supporting continuing reliance on nuclear energy, it follows that any disagreement they have about nuclear energy with the Baden church cannot be theologically related. A similar point can be made with regard to the apparent disagreement about nuclear energy between the Church of Norway and the German Catholic bishops, in which both make some appeal to the doctrine of creation in authorizing their conclusions.

The data indicate that disagreements among the churches on nuclear energy are not necessarily theologically related. Once again in this disagreement, we can conclude that nuclear energy is not an issue about which disagreements can or should divide the churches, inasmuch as issues of theology — that is, of the nature of the Christian faith — are not at stake.

The disagreement among the churches on nuclear energy does have a contextual dimension. All of the statements of church bodies located in the Southern hemisphere concerning nuclear energy are critical of it. Does this uniformity suggest that the disagreements on nuclear energy are contextually related, a confirmation of the ecumenical truism that in different cultural contexts Christians will disagree about ethics and theology? In this case, there may be some validity to such an insight. It must be qualified, however, by the recognition that contextual differences between these statements and Western churches which share their critical perspective on nuclear energy have not precluded their agreement on these matters. (No judgments can be made about the impact of different contexts on the theology of these statements, because none of the three statements by church bodies in the Southern hemisphere offers theological authorization for its critque of nuclear energy.)

In view of the impasse in the dialogue between those church bodies which would continue to rely on nuclear energy and those which would declare a moratorium, the observation of one statement may be helpful in evaluating the controversy. A 1982 document by the WCC Sub-Unit on Church and Society claims at one point that debate on the issue of a moratorium on nuclear energy has been dampened. Since 1979, the argument goes, the nuclear energy industry has been in a struggle to survive, so that a de facto moratorium on its growth has been in effect. Perhaps a combination of public pressure, a reduction of energy consumption, and the development of new, safer energy technologies will solve the problem of nuclear energy. These are matters of resolve and technology, but not a question of the faith.

The churches' responses to the challenges posed by nuclear energy do have a bearing on at least one theological issue which pertains to the whole chapter. The statements on this topic as well as those pertaining to energy consumption continue to be characterized by a certain wariness about theological appeals to the doctrine of creation for warranting ethical positions. This wariness is especially evident in statements of ecumenical organizations such as the WCC, the Fédération Protestante de France, the Arbeitsgemeinschaft Christlicher Kirchen in der Bundesrepublik Deutschland und Berlin (West), the Swedish Ecumenical Council, and the Council of Churches in the Netherlands.[14] Since an ethic rooted in the doctrine of creation represents the historic approach to ethics of at least some of these organizations' constituencies, the failure of these statements to utilize such a model of ethical argumentation raises questions about why they have declined to do so. Why is an ethic which appeals to the gospel or Christology for authorization still more inclined to characterize the statements of ecumenical organizations, even when they address questions related to ecology and the limits-to-growth debate? Perhaps the new interest in the doctrine of creation brought about by this debate has not fully succeeded in challenging the old stereotypes after all. An examination of statements concerning nuclear armaments and peace raises this question anew.

NOTES

[1] WCC Nairobi Assembly Section Report, *Human Development: Ambiguities of Power, Technology and Quality of Life* (1975), 13. Also see the account of Paulos Gregorios's intervention at the Nairobi Assembly, as reported in David M. Paton, ed., *Breaking Barriers: Nairobi 1975* (London: SPCK; Grand Rapids, Mich.: Wm. B. Eerdmans, 1976), 24. For a sketch of the emergence of concerns about the limits of growth and the influence of the Bucharest Conference on ecumenical social thought, see Paul Abrecht, "Introduction", in *Faith and Science in an Unjust World,* vol. 2, ed. Paul Abrecht (Philadelphia: Fortress Press, 1980), 1-2.

[2] For references to these statements and others dealing with ecology which will subsequently be mentioned, see the section on ecology in the Appendix.

[3] For such a typical criticism, see C.T. Kurien, "A Third World Perspective", in *Faith and Science in an Unjust World,* vol. 1, ed. Roger Shinn (Philadelphia: Fortress Press, 1980), 221-24. Also see WCC Conference on Faith, Science and the Future, *Economics of a Just, Participatory and Sustainable Society* (Cambridge, Mass., 12-24 July 1979).

[4] For a few examples, see Church of Norway, *Statement on Nuclear Energy* (1978); National Council of Churches [USA], *Policy Statement: The Ethical Implications of Energy Production and Use* (1979); Eglise de la Confession d'Augsbourg d'Alsace et de Lorraine, *Le problème nucléaire* (1978); Nordelbische Evangelisch-Lutherische Kirche, *Unsere Verantwortung vor Gott für seine Schöpfung* (1988); Presbyterian Church in the U.S./United Presbyterian Church, *The Power to Speak Truth to Power* (1981), pts. 1, 1/III, 2, 3; *Social Principles of the United Methodist Church (USA)* (1984), I; Landessynode der Evangelischen Kirche im Rheinland-Westfalen, *Wort zur Energiediskussion* (1980), 2 (a, b, c, e); United Church of Canada, *The Church and the Economic Crisis* (1984); British Council of Churches, *Resolution Relating to Nuclear Policy* (1977); *Pastoral Letter of the Catholic Swiss Bishops* (1978). The same point seems to be made by several statements drafted in third-world contexts which blame present ecological problems on too hasty economic growth and industrialization. See *Guiding Principles of the Social Mission Policy of the Presbyterian Church of Korea* (1984), 4; Presbyterian Church in Taiwan, *Our Appeal* (1975), I.5; Christian Conference of Asia, *Justice and Service* (1977), D.

[5] For some examples of this sort of analysis, see Evangelische Landeskirche in Baden, *Wort zur Kernenergie* (1977); Evangelische Kirche im Rheinland, *Ausstieg aus der Atomenergie* (1987), I; Nordelbische Evangelisch-Lutherische Kirche, *Unsere Verantwortung vor Gott für seine Schöpfung,* (1988); *Statements of the Joint Session of the Waldensian Synod and the Methodist Conference (Italy)* (1978); United Church of Canada, *Energy and the Church* (1982), 2 (c-e); National Conference of Catholic Bishops [USA], *The Challenge of Peace: God's Promise and Our Response* (1983), 270-72; [Catholic] Episcopal Conference of the Pacific, *The Pacific and Peace* (1986), IV, VIII, IX; Roman Catholic Church, *Redemptor Hominis* (1979), 13-17, 8; Anglicanism, *The Resolutions of the Lambeth Conference (1978),* 1; Uniting Church in Australia, *Re Pacific Churches* (1985), 85.104; United Church of Canada, *Nuclear Power* (1980); United Church of Christ [USA], *Disarmament* (1977); Evangelical

Church of Lutheran Confession in Brazil, *God's Earth . . . Land for Everyone* (1982), I, II; Evangelisch-Lutherische Kirche in Bayern, *Wort zum Umweltschutz* (1984); Lutheran World Federation, *Caring for God's Endangered Creation* (1984), 9.1.2; 9.1.6.2; World Alliance of Reformed Churches, *The Theatre of Glory and a Threatened Creation's Hope* (1982); Christian Conference of Asia, *Justice and Service* (1973), III; Thrust Paper, IV.

[6] Also see the American Lutheran Church, *Issues and Opportunities That Bind and Free* (1976), Canadian Conference of Catholic Bishops, *Ethical Choices and Political Challenges* (1983), 19, and the statement in note 5 above of the World Alliance of Reformed Churches, which also relates the ecological crisis to economic injustice.

[7] For references, see the list of statements in the section on ecology in the Appendix, listed under the heading "Appeal to Creation/View of Human Persons". Other statements on this list which exhibit a continuity of creation and redemption include Anglicanism, *The Resolutions of the Lambeth Conference (1968)*, 6; German [Catholic] Bishops' Conference, *Statement of the Commissariat* (1977); Social *Principles of the United Methodist Church (USA)* (1980), I, VII; United Church of Christ [USA], *Energy* (1979), III/B/1; III/A/2; WCC Conference on Faith, Science and the Future, *Technology, Resources, Environment and Population* (Cambridge, Mass., 12-24 July 1979), esp. 4, 3, Int.; Evangelisch-Lutherische Kirche in Bayern, *Wort zum Umweltschutz;* Evangelische Kirche der Kirchenprovinz Sachsen, *Brief der Synode an die Gemeinden zur Friedensverantwortung* (1984).

[8] For references, see note 4 above.

[9] For the earlier discussion and pertinent references, see the subsection "Energy Consumption" in chapter 2 above. For references to the documents cited and discussed in this section, see the section on energy consumption in the Appendix.

[10] For the subsequent discussion of this tendency in the Roman Catholic tradition, see the section "Diversity in the Roman Catholic Tradition", in chapter 6 below. See Roman Catholic Church, Vatican II, *Gaudium et Spes* (1965), 22.

[11] German Catholic Bishops' Conference, *Zukunft der Schöpfung — Zukunft der Menschheit* (1980), II.7. Also see German Catholic Bishops' Conference, *Statement of the Commissariat* (1977).

[12] For a few references, see note 5 above.

[13] For references to the documents cited and discussed in this section, see the section on nuclear energy in the Appendix.

[14] WCC Sub-Unit on Church and Society, *Report of the Advisory Group of the Energy for My Neighbour Programme* (1982), VI, I; Fédération Protestante de France, *The Question of Nuclear Energy* (1978), V, II, Int.; Arbeitsgemeinschaft Christlicher Kirchen in der Bundesrepublik Deutschland und Berlin (West), *Neuer Lebenstil aus Christlicher Verantwortung* (1980), 1-3, 5; Swedish Ecumenical Council/Church of Sweden, *Nuclear Power, Energy and Questions Pertaining to the Style and Quality of Life* (1978), III.6-8, 4,1; Council of Churches in the Netherlands, *Letter to the Minister-President* (1978).

4. Nuclear Armaments (Peace and War)

Peace is an indisputably central theme in the Christian tradition (Isa. 2:4; Micah 4:1-3; Matt. 5:9, 44; John 14:27; Rom. 5:1; Gal. 6:16). Nevertheless, there has been much debate among Christians about the implications of the peace that God gives. Most notably, Christians since the earliest centuries have been engaged in debate over the question of what the appropriate attitude of the Christian should be towards war.

In view of the historic unanimity among Christians concerning the mandate for peace, and insofar as this unanimity has been reflected, since its inception, in a programmatic commitment of the modern ecumenical movement to strive for peace, it is hardly surprising to observe pronounced unanimity among recent church social statements concerning peace.[1] This unanimity cuts across denominational and geographical boundaries. Official calls for peace have been offered by the Roman Catholic Church — at the level of conciliar statements such as *Gaudium et Spes,* papal encyclicals such as *Laborem Exercens,* not to mention statements of national bishops' conferences from contexts as diverse as the USA (especially see its 1983 statement), Latin America (the Medellín Conference of 1968), the German Democratic Republic, Spain, Italy, Mozambique, South Africa, and the Philippines — as well as by the Orthodox Church (statements have been issued by both the Russian Orthodox and the Romanian Orthodox churches). Similar calls have arisen from groups at the other end of the spectrum, including a variety of Baptist and United church traditions such as the Associated Churches of Christ in New Zealand, the United Church of Christ in Japan, the Baptist World Alliance, the Christian Evangelical Baptist Union in Italy, the Bund der Evangelischen Kirchen in der DDR, the All-Union Council of Evangelical Christians-Baptists (in the USSR), the USA's United Church of Christ, the Evangelische Kirche von Kurhessen-Waldeck, and the Evangelische Kirche in Deutschland.[2]

The spectrum of churches calling for peace extends to denominational families in between these two poles — for example, to Anglican church organizations (such as the Lusitanian Catholic Apostolic Evangelical Church [Portugal], the Anglican Church of Canada, the Church of the Province of Southern Africa [Anglican], and the Lambeth Conference), Methodist churches (e. g., the Methodist Church [England], in a 1988 and in two 1978 statements; the Methodist Church of Malaysia; the Synod of the Waldensian and Methodist Churches in Italy; and the United Methodist Church [USA]), Brethren churches (such as the Church of the Brethren [USA] and the Brethren in Christ Church [USA]), Restorationist churches (such as the Christian Church [Disciples of Christ]), Reformed/Presbyterian church bodies (e. g., the Netherlands Reformed Church, the Eglise Réformée de France, the Evangelical

Presbyterian Church of Chile, the Nederduitse Gereformeerde Sendingkerk [South Africa], and the World Alliance of Reformed Churches), and even Lutheran church bodies (such as the Church of Norway, the Vereinigte Evangelisch-Lutherische Kirche Deutschlands, the Evangelisch-Lutherische Kirche in Bayern, the American Lutheran Church, the former Lutheran Church in America, and the Lutheran World Federation). Virtually every denominational family seems to have at least one member body which has drafted a statement advocating peace.

The ecumenical character of this consensus concerning peace is undergirded further by an awareness of the large number of ecumenical organizations which have advocated peace. In harmony with its earliest ethical suppositions, the WCC has approved at least one statement on the subject in every one of its assemblies. In addition, national and regional councils of churches in contexts as diverse as Romania (the Assembly of Religions in Romania), Italy (the Federation of Evangelical Churches in Italy), Ireland (the Irish Council of Churches), South Africa (the South African Council of Churches), the African continent (the All Africa Conference of Churches), and Asia (the Christian Conference of Asia) have drafted statements on peace. The consensus even cuts across the divide between mainline and conservative evangelical groups, as several church bodies associated with the evangelical movement, such as the Brethren in Christ Church [USA], the Reformed Ecumenical Synod, and the West Germany Konferenz Bekennender Gemeinschaften, also have issued statements calling for peace.

The preceding discussion clearly documents the broad ecumenical consensus on peace and demonstrates how this consensus cuts across geographical lines. The consensus also seems to permeate the entire time span of the period considered in our study of social statements. In almost every year from 1964 to 1986 a comparable number of statements were issued.

Within this broad consensus, significant differences can be noted with regard to the shape of peace and how it can best be achieved, and with regard to differences in the mode of theological arguments on behalf of peace. In the church statements explicitly devoted to peace, differences about the character of the peace desired are partially related to geographical or other contextual differences. Statements by churches located in the first world and the second world as well as those by international church organizations tend to be preoccupied with world peace and super-power relationships. Statements from church bodies in Asia, Africa, and Latin America, however, tend to be more specific in their concern about peace, usually calling for peace particularly in their own region of the world.[3]

There are exceptions to this tendency. Some church bodies with roots in European and other Western nations are on record as issuing statements calling for peace in particular geographical regions. Thus we have calls for peace in *South Africa* issued by West Germany's Vereinigte Evangelisch-Lutherische Kirche Deutschlands, the British Council of Churches, the Reformed Church in America, the Mennonite Church [USA], the National Association of Evangelicals [USA], the 1988 Lambeth Conference, the Anglican Church of Canada, the Evangelische Kirche im Rheinland (concerning Namibia), and the Christian Church (Disciples of Christ); calls for peace in *Rhodesia and Nigeria* by the United Free Church of Scotland; calls for peace in *the Middle East* by the Russian Orthodox Church, the 1988 Lambeth Conference, the USA's National Conference of Catholic Bishops, the USA's National Council of Churches, the British Council of Churches, the United Church of Canada, the United

Free Church of Scotland, the Evangelisch-Lutherische Landeskirche Sachsens, the Evangelische Kirche im Rheinland, the Episcopal Church [USA], the United Church of Christ [USA], the Christian Church (Disciples of Christ), the Church of the Brethren [USA], and the National Association of Evangelicals [USA]; calls for peace in *Northern Ireland* by the Church of Ireland, the Presbyterian Church in Ireland, the United Free Church of Scotland, the 1988 Lambeth Conference, and the British Council of Churches; calls for peace in *Vietnam* by the USA's National Conference of Catholic Bishops, the USA's National Council of Churches, the Fédération Protestante de France, the British Council of Churches, the United Free Church of Scotland, the Evangelische Kirche in Hessen und Nassau, the Evangelische Kirche im Rheinland, the Christian Church (Disciples of Christ), the USA's United Church of Christ, the Episcopal Church [USA], the Reformed Church in America, the Mennonite World Conference, as well as the World Methodist Council Conference; calls for peace in *Northeast Asia* (Korea) by the Christian Church (Disciples of Christ), the United Church of Christ [USA], and the World Alliance of Reformed Churches; and calls for peace in *Afghanistan* by the USA's United Church of Christ.

In Italy a call for peace was even issued by that nation's Christian Evangelical Baptist Union, pertaining to the Argentine-British conflict in the early 1980s, just as a call for peace in El Salvador was put forth by the Christian Church (Disciples of Christ), a concern for peace in Latin America and the Sudan was expressed by the 1988 Lambeth Conference, a concern for peace in Central America was expressed by the Presbyterian Church (USA), and a concern for peace in Germany was expressed by the Evangelische Kirche der Union — Bereich Bundesrepublik Deutschland und Berlin-West.[4] In like manner, a more global viewpoint on peace is articulated by a few church bodies located in the third world, for example, the Methodist Church in Malaysia, the Evangelical Church of Lutheran Confession in Brazil, and the Latin American [Catholic] Bishops' Conference.[5]

It may be, then, that churches located in Asian, African, and Latin American contexts are a bit more inclined to address peace in terms of the threats to their local situation. But insofar as we have identified church bodies in Europe and North America similarly preoccupied with peace in local situations and have observed a more global perspective on peace in church bodies located in the third world, it seems that contextual differences do not necessarily entail differences among the churches in their approach to the peace question. We thus have one more rebuttal of the old ecumenical truism that differences in cultural contexts mandate differences in theology and ethics. The propensity of the church statements from the third world to focus a bit more on local questions pertaining to peace may be nothing more than a consequence of the fact that churches in the first and second worlds are not so directly facing violence in their own backyards as the first group and so are less inclined to think about peace in some specific region but rather more globally.

If differences in cultural context are not significant factors in the churches' treatments of the peace question, it seems just as possible to argue that differences in their mode of theological argument on behalf of peace are not significant. An initial glance at the section on peace in the Appendix seems to confirm the conventional wisdom (and its prejudices) concerning the propensity of arguments which rely on Christology and third-article doctrinal loci to authorize more open, liberal positions, in contrast to the more ethically conservative conclusions of arguments relying on the doctrine of creation. Significantly more church statements call for peace by appealing to doctrinal themes not associated with the doctrine of creation than those that do appeal to that doctrine.

This correlation of the more liberal concern for peace with theological arguments drawn from Christology, ecclesiology, eschatology, and pneumatology is characteristic of the statements of churches from all traditions. Consequently, as was noted here and there in previous chapters, we can observe a tendency to ignore the doctrine of creation when formulating arguments on behalf of more liberal ethical positions, even among certain church bodies associated with traditions such as Lutheranism, Roman Catholicism, and to some extent Anglicanism, which have historically employed ethical arguments that rely upon this doctrine. This propensity, which even seems to override historic denominational and theological commitments, surfaces in statements on peace such as two 1970 and 1984 assembly resolutions of the Lutheran World Federation, a 1981 general synod resolution of the Vereinigte Evangelisch-Lutherische Kirche Deutschlands, a 1985 declaration on human rights of the Evangelisch-Lutherische Kirche in Bayern, perhaps in two statements of the past decade issued by the Evangelische Landeskirche in Württemberg, as well as in other statements by at least two other German Lutheran church bodies, a 1965 declaration of the Anglican Church of Canada, two 1985 statements of the Church of the Province of Southern Africa [Anglican], and numerous statements of various regional and national Roman Catholic bishops' conferences, especially though not exclusively those located in Latin America.[6]

Such tendencies for statements on peace to bypass the doctrine of creation in fact have their exceptions. Several church statements call for peace on this basis, including the following: several Lutheran statements such as the 1970 assembly resolution of the Lutheran World Federation entitled *Responsible Participation in Today's Society,* a 1984 statement of the former Lutheran Church in America, two statements issued during the past decade by the Church of Norway, statements in 1974 and 1982 by German Lutheran church bodies, a 1968 decision of the Associated Churches of Christ in New Zealand, a 1978 policy statement of the American Baptist Churches, a 1978 statement of the Methodist Church [England], a 1968 policy statement on civil disobedience of the USA's National Council of Churches, a resolution from a 1983 conference of the WCC, and perhaps Roman Catholic statements such as a 1980 pastoral letter on Communism by the USA's National Conference of Catholic Bishops, a 1967 pastoral letter on the centennial of the Canadian Confederation issued by the Canadian Conference of Catholic Bishops, a 1982 letter of the Japanese [Catholic] Bishops, and the 1967 papal encyclical *Populorum Progressio,* as well as 1977 and 1975 declarations of the Russian Orthodox Church.

Such statements indicate once again that appeals to the doctrine of creation need not necessarily result in a conservative ethic. In like manner, this data provide one more indication that theological disagreements need not be church dividing, at least not on the peace question. Different theological approaches here have no practical consequence and can authorize the same ethical conclusion, namely, a call for peace. The problems concerning the role that theological disagreements may play in causing disagreements on ethics, as well as the tendency of appeals to the doctrine of creation to render open, liberal ethical conclusions impossible, are more pressing with regard to statements on pacifism, just war, and nuclear armaments, which we consider subsequently in this chapter. I return to these questions again in those contexts.

It would be incorrect to leave the impression that the only arguments used by the churches on behalf of peace are either those which appeal only to the doctrine of creation or those which totally avoid reference to the doctrine. In fact, there are a number of mixed arguments where an appeal is made both to creation and to Christology or the gospel. Some of the numerous examples of this type include a 1982 declaration of the Bund der Evangelischen Kirchen in der DDR, a 1982 resolution by the Eglise de la Confession d'Augsbourg d'Alsace et de Lorraine, several statements of the [Catholic] Bishops' Conference of Mozambique, a statement of the Medellín Conference of the Latin American [Catholic] Bishops, several statements by national conferences of Catholic bishops of the USA and Canada, the USA's United Church of Christ, a 1974 Christmas message of the [Orthodox] Ecumenical Patriarchate of Constantinople, several statements of the Russian Orthodox Church, a number of statements of several assemblies of the WCC, a 1977 policy statement on the United Nations, as well as a 1968 policy statement on disarmament by the USA's National Council of Churches, and perhaps even the 1977 report of the Reformed-Roman Catholic International dialogue. In addition, one observes some statements, like the 1964 papal encyclical *Ecclesiam Suam* and the Second Vatican Council's *Gaudium et Spes,* as well as the 1983 joint statement of the United Presbyterian Church and the Presbyterian Church in the U.S. (predecessor bodies of the Presbyterian Church (USA)), where the doctrine of creation is subordinated to Christology.

Something like the Orthodox Church's concept of *theosis* may operate in the 1964 papal encyclical. In that connection one could perhaps read the 1981 and 1984 calls for peace by the Romanian Orthodox Church in this light. Its appeal to a general human desire for peace, a kind of argument from the doctrine of creation, may be trading on the concept of *theosis*. The general human desire for peace could be deemed the result of the universal transformation (deification) of creation by Christ.

In addition to these types of arguments, some statements link the doctrine of creation with other doctrinal themes, such as ecclesiology or eschatology. Examples include a 1985 declaration of the [Catholic] Bishops of the Netherlands and a 1986 statement of Portugal's Lusitanian Catholic Apostolic Evangelical Church. In other cases, appeals to the doctrine of creation are part of a Trinitarian argument for peace. This mode of argumentation is evident in the 1971 papal encyclical *Octogesima Adveniens,* probably in a 1987 encyclical *Sollicitudo Rei Socialis* and an earlier 1963 encyclical *Pacem in Terris,* in 1983 as well as to some extent in 1976 and 1967 in statements of the USA's National Conference of Catholic Bishops, a declaration of the Haitian [Catholic] Episcopal Conference of the same year, a 1977 statement of the Canadian Conference of Catholic Bishops, a 1986 message on war and peace of the Russian Orthodox Church (3.5), a 1982 declaration of the Evangelical Church of Lutheran Confession in Brazil, perhaps a 1984 statement of the Lutheran World Federation, as well as a 1989 report on mission and unity by the World Alliance of Reformed Churches, a 1979 resolution on the Ku Klux Klan and a 1986 policy statement on Korea by the Episcopal Church [USA], 1977, 1980, and 1985 statements by the Church of the Brethren [USA], a 1983 joint statement of the Mennonite Church [USA] and the Mennonite Church, General Conference [USA], a 1982 statement on the search for peace of the United Church of Canada, a 1985 pronouncement on just peace by the USA's United Church of Christ, a 1988 declaration of the National Council of Churches in Korea, 1980 and 1986 policy statements of the USA's National Council of Churches, a 1981 resolution of the Christian Church (Disciples of Christ) (in virtue of affirming the USA council's 1980 statement), as well as a resolution of the WCC Evanston Assembly, just to name a few examples.

We cannot cease giving an account of the diverse number of theological arguments on behalf of peace, which are identifiable in the statements, without noting that a large number of the statements provide no obvious theological rationale for their position. There are examples of such statements in most of the denominational families, as well as ecumenical organizations, located in most of the major regions of the world.

The statements I have observed which authorize peace by correlating appeals to the doctrine of creation with other doctrinal themes suggest further insights regarding the kinds of theological adjustments that enable appeals to the doctrine of creation to authorize more liberal, open ethical conclusions. In previous chapters we acknowledged that there was some truth to the conventional wisdom concerning the propensity of arguments rooted in the doctrine of creation or related themes to authorize more conservative ethical conclusions — unless certain adjustments are made to the creation doctrine. These necessary adjustments seem to include correlating creation and redemption and perhaps speaking of human persons in a relational way (i.e., as by nature related to each other and to their environment).

These adjustments, particularly the correlation of creation and redemption, characterize more than the church statements just noted in which peace was authorized by dual appeals to the doctrine of creation and some other doctrinal theme drawn from the second or third article of the creed. Virtually all of the statements which authorize peace solely by appeal to some doctrinal theme associated with the doctrine of creation still posit a correlation of creation and themes associated with redemption. (A particularly explicit expression of this commitment is evident in a 1987 policy statement of the American Baptist Churches.) As a matter of fact, in at least two of these statements, notably a 1984 statement of the former Lutheran Church in America and to some extent a 1986 resolution of the Anglican Church of Canada, a kind of relational view of human persons is employed in the argument for peace.[7] The churches' statements on peace seem to confirm previous findings concerning the theological adaptations which are made on the doctrine of creation when it functions successfully as a warrant for more open, liberal ethical conclusions.

One other theologically related difference among the church statements on peace must be noted in closing this section. This point relates to the question of differences that exist among the churches concerning their views on how peace can best be achieved. As such, this consideration provides an entrée for a subsequent consideration of the churches' positions on pacifism and war.

Although a 1965 proposal to the Evangelische Kirche in Hessen und Nassau that peace might well be nurtured by refusing to give children toy soldiers as Christmas gifts and a similar proposal in a 1988 policy statement of the Presbyterian Church (USA) represent a most unique suggestion, the crucial text to consider at this point is a 1981 declaration of West Germany's Moderamens of the Reformed Alliance. In this statement, to which we previously alluded, it was claimed that the peace question is a matter of confession.[8] In short, peace constitutes a *status confessionis*.

With the possible exception of a 1982 document of the World Alliance of Reformed Churches (to be considered more fully in the final section), this controversial German Reformed statement stands alone in its approach to peace, specifically with regard to its contribution to the question of how to achieve peace.[9] Of all the church statements devoted to peace, it alone takes a militant position on peace, asserting that the nature of the Christian faith demands peace.

This sort of argument may be the type made by the pacifist churches like the USA's Mennonite Church, Mennonite Brethren Church, and the Brethren in Christ Church. [10] There seem to be some analogues at this point between these churches and the position of the German Reformed Alliance, at least with reference to their position in relation to those with whom they disagree. This point seems further strengthened in that the statement of the alliance itself addresses the issue of the degree to which the absolute pacifist position should be endorsed by today's Christians.

The position of these German heirs of Calvin raises anew questions concerning whether disagreements on issues in the realm of ethics may divide the churches, in the sense of precluding formal church fellowship. Specifically, in this case one must ask whether the disagreement between the Reformed Alliance and church bodies which are at least open to violations of peace through participation in a "just war" might constitute a church-dividing disagreement. The same question could be raised regarding the disagreement between the alliance and church bodies which explicitly reject the use of the concept *status confessionis* as applied to questions of peace, as seems to be the case in a 1983 resolution of the Bund der Evangelischen Kirchen in der Deutschen Demokratischen Republik and, with regard to applying the concept to nuclear weapons and militarization, in a 1988 policy statement of the Presbyterian Church (USA).

Among numerous statements expressing an openness to such participation in a just war are statements by Lutheran bodies such as the Church of Norway, the Lutheran Church-Missouri Synod, and the Evangelical Lutheran Church in Tanzania. Similar statements are a 1983 statement of the Netherlands [Catholic] Bishops' Conference, a 1983 statement by the USA's National Conference of Catholic Bishops, perhaps the Second Vatican Council's *Gaudium et Spes,* several decisions by a Reformed body, the Christian Reformed Church in North America, Anglican church statements like a 1985 resolution of the Church of the Province of Southern Africa [Anglican] entitled *Conscientious Objection,* and certain statements by ecumenical organizations in Africa like the All Africa Conference of Churches in a 1981 document and the South African Council of Churches in 1974. (Virtually all church statements which explicitly reject nuclear war as a legitimate option and support conscientious objection — particularly, selective conscientious objection — seem to reflect an openness to participation in a just war.) On grounds of the German Reformed Alliance, insofar as these statements endorse an openness to relinquishing peace in interests of defending one's nation, they would appear to be violating the nature of the Christian faith.

Yet as we have raised critical questions with regard to other claims that disagreements on ethical matters (such as apartheid) constitute a *status confessionis,* so it must be asked in this case whether the nature of the Christian faith is necessarily at stake in the disagreements that the Reformed Alliance has with the statements already noted. The Reformed Alliance authorizes its position on peace by appeal to Christology. Creation functions in the statement only to help authorize its position against the development and use of nuclear weapons. [11] Thus any of the church statements countenancing a just war which were authorized by theological warrants other than the Christological orientation of the German alliance would be engaged in a disagreement with the alliance about peace which would be related to the nature of the Christian faith.

Such disagreements related to the nature of the Christian faith may be at stake in some cases. In a number of the documents we have noted that the authorization for the position taken on a just war is unclear. This is true in the case of statements of the Evangelical Lutheran Church in Tanzania, the Church of Norway, the Lutheran Church-Missouri Synod, and a 1982 document of the former American Lutheran Church, not to mention the previously noted statement of the Church of the Province of Southern Africa [Anglican]. In some cases, however, it is possible that disagreements with the Reformed Alliance concerning the validity of violating peace for the sake of a just war could be theologically related. Certainly such a disagreement seems involved in a comparison of the alliance's statement and a 1982 declaration of the Church of Norway, and perhaps in a 1966 statement of the former American Lutheran Church, whose affirmations of the validity of the concept of a just war emerge from a perspective that maintains a two-kingdom ethic and natural law.

In like manner, two Roman Catholic statements noted above — the 1983 statement on peace by the USA's National Conference of Catholic Bishops and the Vatican Council's *Gaudium et Spes* — could differ with the German Alliance on theological grounds. The Roman Catholic statements seem to share with the Reformed document a commitment to subordinating all theological claims to a Christocentric gospel, such that Christology is the main warrant. In the case of providing justification for a just war, however, the Roman Catholic statements, particularly the statement of the council, focus attention on the natural law as authorization for justifying participation in a just war. Granted, these warrants probably ultimately are subordinated to Christology or the gospel.[12] On the surface, however, the apparent disagreement between these statements and Germany's Reformed Alliance on the use of war rather than peace is theologically related — the Catholics rely on the doctrine of creation, and the Reformed appeal to Christology. In that sense their disagreement on the appropriateness of violating peace seems indeed to constitute a *status confessionis,* a situation in which the nature of the Christian faith is at stake.

This is not the whole story regarding the relationship between the Reformed Alliance's militant position on peace and those church bodies open to participation in a just war. One statement which supports the concept of a just war, a 1969 policy statement of the former United Presbyterian Church [USA], made its case by appeal to both natural law (creation) and the gospel. The latter theme converges with the Christological argument employed by the German Reformed Alliance in rejecting this concept. In this case, then, theology does not occasion disagreements about the validity of a just war.

It is also worth noting, by the same token, that at least two church statements by ecumenical organizations in Africa — a 1981 statement of the All Africa Conference of Churches and a 1974 declaration of the South African Council of Churches — as well as 1969 and 1973 decisions of the Christian Reformed Church in North America authorize a just war (or at least participation in military action for a just cause) by appealing to second-article themes (combined with reference to eschatology in the case of the All Africa Conference, or by appealing to "Christian duty" in the case of the American Reformed decisions). The German Reformed statement did likewise when it designated peace a *status confessionis.* In like manner, even the 1983 resolution of the Bund der Evangelischen Kirchen in der Deutschen Demokratischen Republik, which may have expressed unwillingness to employ the concept *status confessionis* in a manner like the Bund's Reformed brethren, still shared the Reformed Alliance's appeal to second-article themes to authorize the call for peace. At least in these particular cases, then, similar theological arguments have been used to authorize apparently conflicting ethical positions on peace. To the degree that a position in defense of a just war conflicts with the militant call for peace of the Reformed Alliance, it cannot be that such a disagreement is necessarily theologically related. Consequently it does not seem so easy to conclude that a departure from the militant stance towards peace as taken by the German Reformed Alliance represents a *status confessionis*. The nature of faith is not necessarily at stake, inasmuch as conclusions conflicting with the alliance's proposal for how best to achieve peace can be reached by means of theological commitments similar to those of the alliance. Thus we can conclude, at least in this case, that disagreements among the churches concerning how best to achieve peace need not necessarily be church dividing, for disagreements about the Christian faith (theological disagreements) are not necessarily at stake.

The Reformed Alliance's claim that peace constitutes a *status confessionis* by no means represents the only disagreement among the churches concerning how best to achieve or maintain peace. There is disagreement between proponents of pacifism or absolute non-resistance, and proponents of a just war. There is a related disagreement among certain proponents of conscientious objection and the pacifists. And there is disagreement on what may have been, at least until the deterioration of the Soviet empire, the most explosive issue of the day concerning peace — the question of the validity of nuclear deterrence.

The controversial character of deterrence explains why it is featured in this chapter. We shall consider it in full in the final section of the chapter. First, though, we take up the discussion among the churches on pacifism and its alternatives.

Just War and Pacifism

The biblical witness offers a mixed message on the Christian attitude towards war and absolute non-resistance or pacifism. Certainly some texts seem to authorize absolute non-resistance (Matt. 26:52; John 18:36; 2 Cor. 10:3-6; Eph. 6:12). In contrast, at numerous points in the Old Testament Yahweh appears to identify with the faithful in the wars and to approve their involvement in fighting certain wars (Num. 31:7; Deut. 25:19; 1 Sam. 15:1-3; 17:46ff.; 2 Sam. 5:19; 1 Chron. 14:10; Ps. 144:1).

In view of this apparent conflict, it is hardly surprising that, at least since the time of Constantine, Christians have taken different positions concerning the validity of participating in wars that are fought for just purposes (in self-defense of a nation). This debate continues in the modern church statements.

Previously we noted a number of statements of the Mennonite and Brethren church traditions which continue to advocate absolute non-resistance. At least five of these statements — 1969 and 1987 documents of the USA's Mennonite Church, a 1971 statement on peace of the USA's Mennonite Church, General Conference, as well as 1970 and 1980 declarations of the Church of the Brethren — take militant pacifist positions in the extreme insofar as they are open to total non-compliance with the American Selective Service System (i.e., the military draft). (Four statements of the USA's Mennonite Church, General Conference, and at least four statements of the USA's Mennonite Church, as well as a 1988 policy statement of the Presbyterian Church (USA), went even further when they raised the question, either by appeal to Christology or with no authorization, of whether to abstain from paying taxes earmarked for military purposes.) As such, these statements advocating non-resistance seem to confirm the conventional wisdom concerning the tendency of Christology and the gospel to be the most appropriate theological warrants for more liberal, idealistic, and radical ethical positions. In the case of all but three of the statements advocating pacifism to which we have access, whenever theological authorization is provided, appeals are made either to Christology, to the gospel or, in one case, to ecclesiology. (One of these cases, a 1966 statement of the USA's Mennonite Brethren Churches, employs a Trinitarian argument.)

On the whole, the doctrine of creation appears to be deficient for authorizing the kind of radical ethical challenge to the establishment which is characteristic of absolute non-resistance. This point concerning the deficiencies of an ethic rooted in the doctrine of creation and the corresponding bias of theological arguments based on Christology or the gospel to authorize the more liberal positions seems further supported by a consideration of the church statements supporting conscientious objection. Only a handful of them appeal exclusively to some theme related to the doctrine of creation. The vast majority appeal at least in some way to Christology as a way of making their points for the more liberal position which advocacy of conscientious objection represents.

These theological considerations, insofar as they seem to confirm the conventional wisdom associated with the Barmen Declaration, raise the question of whether the position of the churches advocating pacifism might entail that their position be considered church dividing in relation to churches who do not share a commitment to absolute non-resistance. After all, in the previous section we noted at least two Lutheran and two Roman Catholic documents — specifically the Second Vatican Council's *Gaudium et Spes* and a 1983 statement on peace by the USA's National Conference of Catholic Bishops — which advocated the authenticity of a just war by appeal to the natural law. In addition, one also should consider that a few church statements which express opposition to a nuclear war, but do not agree with the pacifist position of denying the validity of a just war, do so by appeal to the doctrine of creation.

Such an argument appears in a 1984 statement of the former Lutheran Church in America, if not in its 1970 statement on community, as well as in two 1984 statements of the United Church of Canada (one is against false apocalypticism, the other concerns a nuclear freeze), a 1982 word to the congregations by the Evangelische Landeskirche in Baden, a 1968 statement on disarmament of the USA's National Council of Churches, a 1982 statement of the Canadian Conference of Catholic Bishops, and even probably including a 1963 Roman Catholic papal encyclical *Pacem in Terris,* and a 1988 policy statement of the Presbyterian Church (USA). They as well as 1983 and 1987 statements of the Russian Orthodox Church, a 1985 resolution of the Episcopal Church [USA], and the Roman Catholic documents noted above also authorize their position on nuclear war by appeal to themes associated with the doctrine of creation, though in these latter statements these themes are in turn subordinated to Christology. Also to be considered are the numerous statements, framed by a variety of denominational traditions and ecumenical organizations, which combine creation-centered arguments against nuclear war with appeals to Christology or the gospel as well as with themes derived from the third article of the creed.

The data indicate that disagreements on these points between churches advocating absolute non-resistance and church bodies not advocating pacifism seem related to theological differences. To the degree that such theological disagreements are at stake,

the nature of the Christian faith would seem to be at stake. To that extent, disagreements about absolute non-resistance might seem to be church dividing. But this is
not the whole story.

Considerations raised in the preceding section of this chapter are relevant here.
Recall that we identified two statements by African ecumenical organizations, two
decisions of the Christian Reformed Church in North America, and a 1969 policy
statement of the former United Presbyterian Church [USA] as seeming to affirm the
validity of participation in a just war by appealing to second-article themes. The 1981
statement of the All Africa Conference of Churches added also a reference to
eschatology; the Reformed decisions appealed to "Christian duty"; and the Presbyterian statement apparently referred to natural law. [13] Thus these statements employ
precisely the same kind of theological profile as do most of the Mennonite and
Brethren churches which opt for absolute non-resistance. At this point, then, the
disagreement between the just-war and the pacifist positions is not theologically
related.

A similar point can be made with regard to a significant number of church
statements which, while denying that a nuclear war is a just war, do not endorse the
pacifist position of absolute non-resistance. See the following, for example, some of
which draw their authorization from Christology: a 1983 statement of the Anglican
Church of Canada, a 1982 statement of the World Alliance of Reformed Churches,
perhaps a 1980 policy statement of the former United Presbyterian Church [USA], a
1984 notice of the Baptist Union of New Zealand, a 1984 statement of the United
Church of Canada entitled *Confessing Our Faith in a Nuclear Age,* and one resolution
in both the 1982 and 1983 synods of the Bund der Evangelischen Kirchen in der
Deutschen Demokratischen Republik.

A similar kind of argument against nuclear war, by appeal to the Word of God,
was marshalled in a 1982 statement of the Christian Reformed Church in North
America. Also worth considering are the numerous statements which reject nuclear
war, though not a just war, by appeal to the doctrine of creation combined with appeals
to Christology and the gospel along with themes derived from the creed's third article.
In appending these doctrinal themes to the doctrine of creation, these church bodies
share the largely Christocentric theological orientation of the pacifist churches.
Consequently, any disagreement they might have with the historic pacifist churches
also is not theologically related.

In like manner, these observations would seem to pertain to statements, noted
above, which explicitly remain open to the legitimacy of a just war (even if they have
rejected nuclear war as a viable option) but authorize their position by appeal to themes
related to the doctrine of creation. For at least one of the Mennonite statements which
advocate pacifism, a 1971 statement entitled *Killing,* by the USA's Mennonite
Church, General Conference, also advocated its pacifist position with warrants drawn
from the doctrine of creation (anthropology). In this instance theological disagreements are irrelevant for determining disagreements concerning the validity of a
just war (or the rejection of a nuclear war).

It follows that disagreements between these churches which remain open to the
concept of a just war on grounds of the nature of creation and the Mennonite and
Brethren churches which espouse pacifism by appealing to Christology or the gospel
cannot be essentially related to the theological differences between them. After all,
these churches' disagreement on pacifism with at least one other Mennonite body is

not theologically related. Therefore, it seems legitimate to conclude that a church's position on pacifism need not divide it from the churches opting for some openness to participating in a just war, since theological differences (i.e., disagreements about the nature of the Christian faith) are not ultimately determinative of whether two churches will disagree about pacifism.

The preceding observations seem pertinent to understanding the relationship between the advocates of pacifism and church bodies advocating conscientious objection in some form. At this point an important consideration pertains first to the development of a modified version of conscientious objection — selective conscientious objection.

Selective conscientious objection is the idea that one may be a conscientious objector to a given war without objecting to war in principle. With the exception of a 1970 statement of the Lutheran Church of Australia, a 1983 statement of the Irish [Catholic] Episcopal Conference, a 1973 resolution of the British Council of Churches, and a WCC Uppsala Assembly statement entitled *Towards Justice and Peace in International Affairs,* this conception is present only in church statements drafted by American church bodies such as the Christian Church (Disciples of Christ) (in a 1968 statement), the Episcopal Church [USA] (in a 1985 resolution), the National Council of Churches (in a 1967 policy statement), the United Church of Christ (in a 1967 pronouncement on the subject), the National Conference of Catholic Bishops (in 1968 and 1976 statements), the former American Lutheran Church (in 1982 and 1970 statements), the Lutheran Church-Missouri Synod (in a 1969 statement), the former Lutheran Church in America (in a 1984 statement), the Presbyterian Church (USA) (in a 1988 policy statement and in a 1969 policy statement of one of its predecessor bodies), the Reformed Church in America (in a 1968 deliverance), and the Christian Reformed Church in North America (in 1939, 1969, 1973, and 1977 resolutions).[14] To a great extent, with the exception of the last of these churches, the development of this concept was related to the Vietnam War and the dilemma faced by many churches of having so many young anti-war, draftable members.

Such selective conscientious objection represents a commitment in disagreement with the historic pacifist position of the various Mennonite and Brethren churches. Unlike their pacifism, selective conscientious objection allows for the possibility that the objector in principle might be willing to fight in some war. In that sense church bodies maintaining this position endorse the concept of a just war. Likewise there is a sense in which church bodies like the United Methodist Church [USA], the Methodist Church in Malaysia, international Anglicanism (in its 1968 Lambeth Conference), the Eglise de la Confession d'Augsbourg d'Alsace et de Lorraine, the Lutheran World Federation (in its 1984 assembly), the Presbyterian Church of Southern Africa, the South African Council of Churches, the WCC (in its Vancouver Assembly), and the Roman Catholic Church (both in the Second Vatican Council and in the church's 1987 instruction on genetic engineering), all of which have opted for conscientious objection in its classical form (i.e., as conscientious objection by an individual to any war), remain open to the concept of a just war. For these church bodies do not insist that everyone in their membership be a conscientious objector. In that sense also, these statements likewise seem to be in disagreement with the historic pacifist positions of the Mennonite and Brethren churches which we have noted.

The fact that the two Methodist churches on the immediately preceding list as well as international Anglicanism, the WCC, the South African Council of Churches, and

others have authorized their affirmation of conscientious objection in its classical form
by way of an appeal to Christology or the gospel is significant for the status of their
debate with the peace question. These church bodies share a common theological
orientation with most of the historic pacifist churches, which, as we have seen,
likewise argue their case from the perspective of Christology (in one case, ecclesiology). Here again it is evident that any disagreement between these churches and
particular church bodies subscribing to conscientious objection on grounds of Christology is not theologically related. The nature of the Christian faith is not at stake on this
point.

The same conclusion would seem to pertain to those few church bodies which to
some extent authorize classical conscientious objection with authorization drawn from
themes related to the doctrine of creation. Here we may include perhaps a 1966
resolution of the USA's National Council of Churches, a 1982 resolution of the
Church of Norway, a 1982 resolution of the Evangelische Kirche im Rheinland, and
the Second Vatican Council's *Gaudium et Spes*. These church bodies seem to be in
theological disagreement with most of the statements of the historic pacifist churches.
Thus their disagreement about an openness to participation in a just war could be
theologically related. At this point, however, we must recognize that the WCC and
Roman Catholic statements are in theological disagreement with other church bodies
advocating conscientious objection by appeal to Christology. Yet their theological
disagreement does not lead to a disagreement in ethical conclusion regarding their
position on conscientious objection and an openness to the possibility of a just war.
Therefore one could not logically conclude that the same theological disagreement the
WCC and the Roman Catholic statements may have with the historic pacifist churches
is necessarily the cause of their distinct positions concerning just war and pacifism.
Why should a theological disagreement be regarded as the cause of one ethical
disagreement, when in another case the same theological disagreement has not
manifested itself in ethical disagreement? Consequently the disagreement between the
historic pacifist churches and all church bodies opting for conscientious objection in its
classical form is not necessarily theologically related. To the degree that the nature of
the Christian faith is not at stake at this point, such a disagreement does not seem to
warrant a division of the churches.

This point can be made even more sharply when we recall that at least two of the
pacifist statements authorize their position by way of some kind of appeal to themes
drawn from the doctrine of creation. Most notable here is a 1971 statement of the
USA's Mennonite Church, General Conference, entitled *Killing*. This statement
shares a similar theological position with the Second Vatican Council's *Gaudium et
Spes* and the 1968 WCC Assembly statement opting for conscientious objection.
Consequently, whatever disagreements the Mennonite pacifist position has with these
statements are not theologically related. Again it is evident that disagreements between
pacifism and the classical conscientious objector position (insofar as it retains an
openness to participation in a just war) are not essentially related to disagreements
about the nature of the Christian faith. Thus such a disagreement is not church
dividing.

The case for this point may also be made with regard to the church bodies opting
for selective conscientious objection. As was previously noted, a number of the church
bodies which hold this position are Lutheran. In faithfulness to their denominational
and confessional heritage, these church bodies largely argued their case for selective

conscientious objection on the grounds of themes related to the doctrine of creation.[15] (Such fidelity to the characteristic Lutheran position is not always in evidence. For example, in its 1982 statement on the subject, the Eglise de la Confession d'Augsbourg d'Alsace et de Lorraine argued for the classical form of conscientious objection on grounds of Christ's teaching.) Consequently, in these cases, the difference concerning an openness to participation in a just war between these church bodies and the more Christocentric ethical orientation of almost all of the Mennonite and Brethren churches seems to be theologically related.

Once again the appeal of at least two of the pacifist statements to the doctrine of creation must be considered. Insofar as the 1971 statement of the USA's Mennonite Church, General Conference, shares the same theological perspective as do the Lutheran statements opting for selective conscientious objection, it is evident that differences between these positions over an openness to participation in a just war are not always or necessarily theologically related. And if such disagreements between statements advocating selective conscientious objection and the historic peace churches are not always related to their disagreement about the nature of the Christian faith, such disagreements also do not seem to warrant a division of the churches. Besides, at least one of the historic peace churches, the USA's Mennonite Church, General Conference, in its 1971 statement *The Way of Peace,* has claimed that no fundamental disagreement between its pacifist position and selective conscientious objection exists. The American Mennonites go so far as to assert their "recognition" and "respect" for selective objectors.

Careful attention has been given to the relationship between non-resistance and every possible alternative to it which the churches espouse. The reasons are obvious. In order to continue to ensure the full participation of the historic pacifist churches in the ecumenical movement, it is necessary to assure them systematically that those with whom they disagree concerning systematic non-resistance are not advocating a different Christianity. The fact that the disagreements among modern church statements concerning this issue are not necessarily theologically related seems to demonstrate that the nature of the Christian faith (i.e., the issue of orthodoxy vs. heresy) is not at stake in the church's disagreement about pacifism.

The preceding discussion revealed one other disagreement among the churches, whose potentially problematic character for church unity warrants attention. This is the debate among proponents of conscientious objection, between those advocating the more classical form of conscientious objection and those advocating selective conscientious objection. The debate has been sharpened in particular by a 1967 statement of the National Association of Evangelicals [USA]. In this statement, the evangelicals criticize the concept of selective conscientious objection and opt for the more classical form with an argument rooted in Christology (faith in the Lord Jesus Christ). In view of the number of Lutheran, Roman Catholic, Anglican, and ecumenical statements previously noted which opt for selective conscientious objection with arguments authorized by themes related to the doctrine of creation, do we not have here a disagreement about conscientious objection which is theologically related and so (potentially) church dividing?

Possible ecclesiastical tensions at this point can be alleviated quite promptly. It is true that a significant number of church statements which support conscientious objection in its more classical form do so with authorization drawn from Christology or the gospel.[16] But at least one statement, a 1982 statement of the Church of Norway, seems to opt for conscientious objection in its classical form with a perspective informed by the two-kingdom ethic (the idea that ethical norms are drawn from the doctrine of creation). Consequently it follows that the Church of Norway shares the same theological position as the Lutheran churches from Australia and America (as well as, among others, the WCC Uppsala Assembly statement *Towards Justice and Peace in International Affairs* and the 1985 resolution on peace by the Episcopal Church (USA)), which opt for selective conscientious objection. Obviously, then, a difference in the form of conscientious objection for which one opts is not necessarily theologically related. [17] As such, we can conclude that differences between the churches on the debate over selective conscientious objection are not intrinsically related to disagreements about the nature of the Christian faith, and so are not church dividing. Besides, as we have already noted, a proponent of the most radical form of conscientious objection, absolute pacifism, has gone on record as recognizing the validity of selective conscientious objection in a 1971 statement of the USA's Mennonite Church, General Conference.

One final point in this analysis of statements related to the problematic of just war versus pacifism must be noted. We have observed that a number of churches state their support for the concept of a just war in the context of rejecting the validity of nuclear war. Representative statements issued by virtually every major denominational family (except the historic pacifist churches and the Christian Restorationist and Eastern Orthodox traditions) and statements by various ecumenical organizations have taken such a position. A few church bodies simply endorse the concept of a just war without the qualifications concerning nuclear war (for example, the Evangelical Lutheran Church in Tanzania, the Church of Norway [in 1971 and 1982], the All Africa Conference of Churches [in 1981], the South African Council of Churches [in 1974], the Lutheran Church-Missouri Synod, the former American Lutheran Church, and the third round of the USA's Lutheran-Episcopal Dialogue). In this comparison an assertion by the WCC Vancouver Assembly statement entitled *Statement on Peace and Justice* is potentially problematic. Paragraph 25 states: "We believe that the time has come when the churches must unequivocally declare that the production and deployment as well as the use of nuclear weapons are a crime against humanity and that such activities must be condemned on ethical and theological grounds. The nuclear weapons issue is, in its import and threat to humanity, a question of Christian discipline and faithfulness to the Gospel."

Nuclear weapons, both their use in a nuclear war and their deployment (presumably for deterrence), are said to be matters of faith. It is as if the assembly had invoked the concept of a *status confessionis*. The immediate problem is whether this assertion relates to the church bodies who have defended the concept of a just war without corresponding rejection of nuclear war. Is the latter group of churches divided by a matter of faith from the WCC Vancouver Assembly and other church bodies which have condemned nuclear war?

An immediate response might be to note that the churches which have spoken affirmatively about the concept of a just war without strictures on nuclear war were not disagreeing with the Vancouver Assembly and like-minded statements. Rather, the question of nuclear war was simply not an agenda item for them. The fact that three of these statements were issued by African church bodies and that only nine (three by the same theologically conservative denomination) were issued by churches in a nation with nuclear armaments (the USA) would seem to support this conclusion. [18]

A stronger case might be made for arguing that the churches failing to condemn nuclear war are not engaged in a church-dividing disagreement with those which have by noting that in several cases church bodies on both sides share a common vision of the Christian faith, a common theological profile. For example, in its 1974 statement on conscientious objection the South African Council of Churches endorses the concept of a just war (without attention to nuclear war) in the context of a second-article emphasis on redemption. Likewise in a 1981 statement entitled *The Gospel of Reconciliation,* the All Africa Conference of Churches took a similar position (insofar as it expressed an openness to the use of violence to overcome oppression), authorizing it by appeal to the gospel of forgiveness and eschatology.

The theological orientation of these African statements, largely around the second article of the creed, is precisely that of the WCC Vancouver Assembly statement against nuclear war and similar statements. See, for example, a statement entitled *International Affairs — Christians in the Struggle for World Community* of the WCC Evanston Assembly, a 1983 policy proposal of the British Council of Churches, a 1964 declaration of the Baptist Union of Great Britain and Ireland, a 1981 statement of the World Methodist Council, and a 1982 declaration of the World Alliance of Reformed Churches. In view of such data, it is difficult to see how the WCC Vancouver Assembly statement that the issue of nuclear weapons is one of "faithfulness to the Gospel" could apply to the statements on just war which do not explicitly condemn the use of nuclear weapons. The gospel is not at stake in these instances, since there is theological agreement among the statements. Consequently any other disagreements with regard to nuclear war which might emerge between church bodies open to a just war would not necessarily be related to theological disagreements. In that sense the WCC Vancouver Assembly statement is challenged: Nuclear weapons is *not* necessarily a matter of faith.

Nuclear Armaments

The preceding discussion of nuclear war and the WCC statement that not just the use but also the production and deployment of nuclear weapons is a matter of faith leads quite logically to a consideration of the churches' statements on nuclear armaments. In post-Hiroshima, international society the fear of nuclear holocaust has been pervasive. Quite obviously the church has felt this pressure. The response has taken the form of lobbying efforts and numerous social statements devoted to disarmament. A brief survey of the section on nuclear armaments in the Appendix quickly indicates to the reader the large number of statements issued by the churches on the subject, especially prior to the demise of the Soviet empire.

The fact that church statements on disarmament have been listed under the category of nuclear armaments is no mere accident of categorization. After Hiroshima, disarmament means *nuclear* disarmament.

In view of the unanimity in international society and so the church about disarmament and the need for it, there would seem to be little startling or controversial about what the churches might say concerning the matter. In a qualified sense, there is some validity to this point. The churches are unanimous in seeing the need for (nuclear) disarmament. Churches from every denominational family and several major ecumenical bodies and from every continent except Africa have formulated statements on the subject. [19]

Given the unanimity on these matters, no separate analysis of the church statements on disarmament as such has been undertaken. With regard to disarmament, little
needs to be said, and there is little that is striking in the statements. Perhaps it is of
interest to note how many of the statements (from virtually every continent and from
most denominational families) relate disarmament to economic development, being
concerned that the arms race stifles development. [20]

A second general observation concerns the way in which the concern for disarmament cuts across not just geographical and denominational contexts but also theological lines. In several cases one can find church bodies in completely different cultural
contexts and from different confessional traditions employing different modes of
theological argumentation but still agreeing on the need for disarmament. [21]

The real point of discussion on disarmament concerns not the commitment to
disarmament but strategies to be used. Should it proceed by means of unilateral
initiatives or only through bilateral agreements? Is the maintaining of a nuclear force
for the sake of deterrence an appropriate strategy for ensuring peace?

At the time decisions were being made about topics to consider for this analysis,
the question of the validity of nuclear deterrence was the primary international
problematic (at least in the Northern hemisphere), most certainly at least for the
churches. With the Bush-Gorbachev and Bush-Yeltsin arms negotiations, some of the
urgency of this question has diminished. The case for the utility of the deterrence
theory has been strengthened.

At least among the churches and in ecumenical social ethics, during the period of
the cold war the question of nuclear deterrence was a sensitive issue. Previously we
noted the WCC Vancouver Assembly statement which asserted that not just the use but
even the production and deployment of nuclear arms (i.e., the maintaining of a nuclear
deterrent) is an issue of faithfulness to the gospel. Similar arguments in opposition to
the maintaining of a nuclear deterrent have been offered by a 1982 document of the
World Alliance of Reformed Churches (perhaps only with regard to peace) and a 1980
statement of the Netherlands Reformed Church. By implication, a case seems to be
made by these statements not unlike points made by various church bodies regarding
apartheid as constituting a *status confessionis* (or the claim of the Moderamens of the
Reformed Alliance that the peace question is a matter of confession). They appear to
be implying that failure to renounce nuclear deterrence is a church-dividing issue. As
such, deterrence is still a most pressing ecumenical question.

Of the churches which have explicitly addressed the deterrence question, the
majority have opted for opposition to it. In view of the statements already cited as well
as the patterns we have observed in analyzing church statements concerning peace, it
is hardly surprising that the prevailing mode of theological argumentation for these
statements is to rely on authorization drawn from Christology or the gospel. (The one
or perhaps two statements which make this point by way of appeal to some theme
derived from the third article of the creed are also making their case against deterrence
by way of appeal to the gospel.) In a few statements, such appeals to second-article
themes are linked to doctrinal themes associated with other articles of the creed.
Examples here include the Trinitarian argument of a 1983 statement of the Moravian
Church in America, Southern Province, a 1987 resolution of the Bund der Evangelischen Kirchen in der Deutschen Demokratischen Republik, as well as perhaps a WCC
Evanston Assembly statement and a 1985 pronouncement on just peace issued by the
USA's United Church of Christ.

In addition, several of these statements appeal to the doctrine of creation in some way, though supplemented strongly by appeal to other doctrinal themes. The Moderamens of the Reformed Alliance [FRG] in its 1981 statement claiming peace is a *status confessionis* as well as a 1986 declaration of the United Church of Christ in Japan and a 1982 Church of Norway statement on peace provide examples of this sort of theological argument in opposition to the idea of deterrence. Only seven or perhaps eight others seem to opt for an end to deterrence strategy (at least in a qualified way) entirely by means of authorization drawn from the doctrine of creation: a 1984 statement of the Baptist Union of Great Britain and Ireland, two statements of the United Church of Canada (a 1982 statement proposing a nuclear weapons freeze and a 1984 statement pleading for a nuclear freeze), a 1987 pastoral letter of the Russian Orthodox Church as well as its earlier 1986 message on war and peace, and, at least by implication, a 1980 pastoral letter on Communism by the USA's National Conference of Catholic Bishops, a 1971 letter of the Japanese [Catholic] Bishops, as well as perhaps the 1963 papal encyclical *Pacem in Terris*. A number of other church statements opting for this negative evaluation of nuclear deterrence do so without any clear theological rationale.

By contrast, those church statements which continue to opt for the toleration of nuclear deterrence, at least temporarily, are in the minority of the statements which address the issue. Most of those open to it are inclined to argue their position by appeal to the doctrine of creation. The most prominent examples of this approach include a 1984 statement of the former Lutheran Church in America, a 1983 pastoral letter of the National Conference of Catholic Bishops [USA], a 1983 statement of the Catholic Bishops of the GDR, as well as perhaps a 1983 policy proposal of the British Council of Churches and the Second Vatican Council's *Gaudium et Spes*. (The latter two heavily correlate their references to creation with doctrinal themes related to the second article of the creed.) In addition to this theological approach, several statements which remain open to deterrence do not offer clear theological authorization.

In terms of their ecumenical implications, perhaps the most significant observation relates to the identification of arguments authorized by appeals to Christology on behalf of a kind of nuclear deterrence in three statements by Western European church bodies — a 1983 statement of the Netherlands [Catholic] Bishops' Conference, a 1964 resolution of the Baptist Union of Great Britain and Ireland, and a 1985 resolution of the Federation of Evangelical Churches in Italy. One statement, a 1985 resolution on peace by the Episcopal Church [USA], seems to have authorized its position by appeal to both faith and the doctrine of creation; another, the Second Vatican Council's *Gaudium et Spes,* grounded its appeal to the doctrine of creation in Christology.

Parenthetically it should be noted that a third grouping of statements related to deterrence could be identified. [22] This group is characterized by its vagueness concerning the validity of deterrence. All of these statements do urge disarmament. Most tend either to be vague in the theological authorization they offer for their position, or else they rely on authorization drawn from themes related to the second article of the creed, such as Christology, redemption, the gospel, and the like.

Some of these particular statements perhaps merely repeat slogans, as when the Moravian Church in America, Northern Province, and the Russian Orthodox Church called for a "freeze" on nuclear weapons in 1982 and 1983 respectively, or when in 1985 the Evangelisch-Lutherische Kirche in Bayern called for an end to the arms race. Several statements, including a 1977 statement of the USA's United Church of Christ, a 1982 resolution of the Uniting Church in Australia, a 1979 declaration of the Russian Orthodox Church, and two statements of the 1979 WCC Conference on Faith, Science and the Future, support the Salt II treaty of the late 1970s between the USSR and the USA. One suspects that such a position may involve concession to the idea of nuclear deterrence as a kind of necessary evil, but this is not clear.

Several statements in this third group suggest a promising middle ground between the "for" and "against" positions regarding nuclear deterrence. One which may be noted immediately emerges in several statements of the Council of Churches in the Netherlands. For example, a 1984 statement speaks of disarmament "in the parameters of the system of deterrence". Other mediating positions will be noted in closing.

At this point the relationship between the two more extreme positions requires assessment. Given the fact that most of the anti-deterrence statements tend to be authorized by appeals to Christology or the gospel, while most of those still open to deterrence as a viable approach to peace employ authorization drawn from the doctrine of creation, the case made by the WCC Vancouver Assembly statement and other church statements that the question of nuclear deterrence is a matter of faith seems vindicated. In fact, though, the diversity of theological modes of argument in the statements supporting each position calls this thesis into question. A few examples suffice.

We have noted that the WCC Vancouver Assembly and other church statements (such as the 1980 declaration of the Netherlands Reformed Church) which vehemently oppose deterrence as a matter of faith do so by appeal to themes related to the gospel and redemption. However, these same themes authorize the apparent openness of several church bodies to deterrence, as, for example, the affirmation of the temporary acceptability of deterrence by a 1983 statement of the Netherlands [Catholic] Bishops' Conference and the openness to international control of nuclear deterrence by the Baptist Union of Great Britain and Ireland in 1964. The endorsement of nuclear deterrence by the Second Vatican Council may ultimately also rely on an appeal to second-article themes, insofar as the statement in question, *Gaudium et Spes,* in fact subordinates creation to Christology.[23] It is also important to note that the British Baptists seem to have changed their position in 1984 to an opposition to deterrence. In these cases the disagreement about the validity of nuclear deterrence is not theologically related.

Likewise, although appeals to the doctrine of creation more characteristically typify the statements that defend the concept of nuclear deterrence, the theological profile of such statements as the 1983 pastoral letter of the National Conference of Catholic Bishops [USA] and the 1984 statement of the former Lutheran Church in America, which take this position, is precisely that of several documents which reject the concept of deterrence. Examples of the latter include a 1984 statement of the Baptist Union of Great Britain and Ireland, 1982 and 1984 statements of the United Church of Canada, to some extent a 1981 statement of the Moderamens of the Reformed Alliance [FRG], a 1980 pastoral letter on Communism by the USA's National Conference of Catholic Bishops, a 1971 letter of the Japanese [Catholic] Bishops, as well as 1986 and 1987 documents of the Russian Orthodox Church. Contrary to the statement on the subject of deterrence by the WCC Vancouver Assembly and other militant opponents of nuclear deterrence, nuclear deterrence does not appear to be a matter of faith; theological differences are not at stake. The plea of two 1981 German church texts — one by the Evangelische Kirche in Deutschland and the other by the Evangelische Kirche von Kurhessen-Waldeck — seems vindicated: conflicting views on nuclear deterrence ought not to separate Christians. [24]

Vindication of the plea of the German churches can be pursued further by reflecting more on how the characteristic theological profiles of the two main responses to the deterrence question relate. Certainly the conventional wisdom associated with the Barmen Declaration seems vindicated by these characteristic theological profiles. The more conservative deterrence position has most of its supporting statements authorized by the doctrine of creation, whereas the statements opting for the more open, progressive position are largely authorized by Christology or the gospel. Insofar as Christology seems more naturally to play such a role in authorizing most of the statements opposed to deterrence and in favor of unilateral disarmament, the conventional wisdom seems to invite rephrasing. Appeals to Christology tend to authorize not just liberal ethical conclusions but those that are more idealistic and less tolerant of ambiguity.

As with other issues which have been considered, however, the pattern associated with the conventional wisdom breaks down. One notes a few cases where the so-called conservative deterrence position is authorized by doctrinal themes related to Christology. Likewise the doctrine of creation serves to authorize opposition to deterrence in perhaps two instances.

When considering church statements on several previous issues, we were able to identify certain adjustments made to the doctrine of creation when church bodies employed it to avoid necessarily authorizing more conservative, even reactionary ethical conclusions. In the case of church statements on nuclear deterrence, such adjustments are not identifiable. It is true, however, that one of the adjustments to the creation doctrine which we have previously observed in church statements that appeal to it but still arrive at more liberal ethical conclusions does appear in church statements which oppose nuclear deterrence. The 1981 statement of the Moderamens of the Reformed Alliance [FRG], the 1982 statement of the Church of Norway, the 1984 statement of the Baptist Union of Great Britain and Ireland, and apparently the 1986 message of the Russian Orthodox Church as well as the 1980 pastoral letter on Communism of the USA's National Conference of Catholic Bishops all correlate creation and redemption in the course of arguing against deterrence. The Russian Orthodox message at least seems to correlate its references to the doctrine of creation with other references to the "Christian tradition" (2.25-26), and the pastoral letter of the USA's Catholic Bishops' Conference seems to correlate its references to themes associated with the doctrine of creation with other references to eschatology (43).

The same sort of correlation of creation and redemption, however, is posited in statements by church bodies drawing upon the doctrine of creation in some way to authorize their defence of the conservative strategy of nuclear deterrence. In fact three of these statements — the Second Vatican Council's *Gaudium et Spes,* the much-discussed 1983 pastoral letter on peace of the USA's National Conference of Catholic Bishops, and the 1984 statement on peace of the former Lutheran Church of America — endorse a view of human persons which previously has been identified as one of the necessary adjustments made to the doctrine of creation by statements using the doctrine to opt for more liberal positions. Each of these three statements posits what we might call a relational view of human persons — the idea that humans are by nature related to their environment and to each other. [25]

These considerations indicate that there are absolutely no theological or philosophical differences at stake in the disagreement between the churches on nuclear deterrence. The hope expressed by the Evangelische Kirche in Deutschland seems further confirmed. Conflicting views on deterrence ought not to separate Christians. Indeed, the fact that some church statements (such as the American Lutheran and the two Roman Catholic statements noted above) can employ theological perspectives in authorizing nuclear deterrence which ordinarily issue in more liberal ethical conclusions suggests another insight concerning the debate about deterrence. It may be that such a theological perspective could authorize a positive assessment of nuclear deterrence simply because such a position is not more conservative than is opposition to deterrence more liberal. The disagreement about deterrence may have nothing more to do with being liberal versus conservative than it has to do with a disagreement about the nature of the Christian faith. In the final analysis it may be nothing more than a debate about the most effective political strategy.

In view of these considerations, the question emerges concerning how the debate might be resolved. Perhaps the middle-ground positions of the third group of church statements we identified could be explored. One intriguing option is a suggestion made by a 1963 resolution of the United Church of Christ [USA] (based on an earlier 1959 statement by the church), a 1968 resolution on world order by the Christian Church (Disciples of Christ), a 1964 statement of the Baptist Union of Great Britain and Ireland (based on a 1963 resolution of the British Council of Churches), a deliverance of the same year by the United Free Church of Scotland, as well as 1965 and 1983 statements of the Anglican Church of Canada. These churches called for the "international control of nuclear arms," or at least "shared control of the deterrent". No concrete specifics were provided, but the church statements on this topic include no more provocative suggestions.

Such a proposal may have been too idealistic, and perhaps could not have been implemented effectively, given the realities of international cooperation and international law at the time these statements were issued. In our present post-cold war context, however, their proposal can be considered as viable and visionary. Nevertheless, the recent USSR-USA arms agreements may be having the final word on deterrence. The deterrence strategy clearly played a role in facilitating these recent advances. With such speculations, however, we are back to matters of political strategy, not matters of faith and church unity. This also seems to be a lesson taught by the church statements.

NOTES

[1] For the argument that a commitment to strive for peace has been part of the modern ecumenical movement since its inception, even prior to the formation of the WCC, see Paul Abrecht, "From Oxford to Vancouver: Lessons from Fifty Years of Ecumenical Work for Economic and Social Justice", *Ecumenical Review* 40, no. 2 (April 1988): 148-50. For documentation on the commitment to peace in the earliest days of the WCC, see WCC Amsterdam Assembly, *The Church and the International Disorder* (1948), Int., II; WCC Evanston Assembly, *International Affairs — Christians in the Struggle for World Community* (1954), I, II, VI, Res. I.

[2] For references to the statements to which I have alluded and to others mentioned subsequently in this introductory section of the chapter, see the section on peace in the Appendix.

[3] For a few examples, see Catholic Bishops' Conference of the Philippines, *The Fruit of Justice is Peace* (1987); Presbyterian Church in Taiwan, *Our Appeal* (1975), Int., II.3, II.5; [Catholic] Bishops' Conference of Mozambique, *Um apelo à paz* (1983), 6-9; Evangelical Lutheran Church in Southern Africa, *Lesotho Killings* (1982); Moravian Church in Nicaragua, *"Communicado": Referencia: El diálogo, la reconciliación, la justicia y la paz* (1986).

[4] Vereinigte Evangelisch-Lutherische Kirche Deutschlands, *Erklärung der Generalsynode zum Rassismus* (1970); *Beschluss der Generalsynode der Vereinigten Evangelisch-Lutherische Kirche Deutschlands zur Rolle der Kirchen in bezug auf das Südliche Afrika* (1978), 2; British Council of Churches, *Southern Africa* (1963); Reformed Church in America, *Report of the General Synod Executive Committee* (1980), R-15; Mennonite Church [USA], *Resolution on South Africa* (1987); National Association of Evangelicals [USA], *Resolution on Apartheid* (1986); Anglican Church of Canada, *South Africa* (1986); Evangelische Kirche im Rheinland, *Gespräche mit dem namibischen Kirchenrat* (1983), 3; Christian Church (Disciples of Christ), *Concerning Southern Africa* (1977); United Free Church of Scotland, *Deliverance of the General Assembly* [on public questions] (1968), 11; Russian Orthodox Church, *Erklärung des Patriarchen zum israelischen Überfall auf den Beiruter Flughafen* (1969); National Conference of Catholic Bishops [USA], *Resolution towards Peace in the Middle East* (1973), 1, 2, 8; National Council of Churches [USA], *Middle East* (1980); British Council of Churches, three publications entitled *Middle East,* dated 1973, 1984, and 1985; United Church of Canada, *The Middle East* (1977); United Free Church of Scotland, *Deliverance of the General Assembly* [on public questions] (1971), 1; ibid. (1969), 1, 13; ibid. (1967), 12, 10; Evangelisch-Lutherische Landeskirche Sachsens, *Wort der Landessynode vom 24.10.1973;* Evangelische Kirche im Rheinland, *Erklärung zur Lage im Nahost* (1968); Episcopal Church [USA], *General Convention Resolution* [on thankfulness for Israeli-Egyptian peace treaty] (1979) and *Middle East Affairs* (1982); United Church of Christ [USA], *Resolution on the Middle East* (1967) and *The Israeli-Palestinian Conflict* (1987); Christian Church (Disciples of Christ), *Concerning the United Nations' Peace-Keeping Role in the Middle East* (1973) and *Concerning a Policy Statement on the Middle East* (1981); Church of the Brethren [USA], *The Time So Urgent: Threats to Peace* (1980), 5-8; National Association of Evangelicals [USA], *Middle East Resolution* (1978); Church of Ireland, *The Report of the Role of the Church Committee* (1984), 4; ibid. (1983), 6, 3, 2; Presbyterian Church in Ireland, *Resolution on the Northern Ireland Situation* (1979); United Free Church of Scotland, *Deliverance of the General Assembly* [on public questions] (1972), 1, 11; ibid. (1974), 1, 10, 12; ibid. (1977), 10; British Council of Churches, *A Message from the BCC Assembly to Churches and Governments in Britain and Ireland* (1985) and *BCC Fund for Ireland* (1979); four items by the National Conference of Catholic Bishops [USA]: two entitled *Resolution on Peace* (1967 and 1968), *Resolution on Southeast Asia* (1971), 2-4), and *Resolution on Imperatives of Peace* (1972), 1, 6; National Council of Churches [USA], *On Viet-nam* (1965); Fédération Protestante de France, *Pour la paix au Vietnam* (1966); British Council of Churches, *Policy Statement on Vietnam* (1967); Entschliessung der Kirchensynode der Evangelischen Kirche in Hessen und Nassau zum Vietnam-Krieg* (1968); four statements of the Evangelische Kirche im Rheinland: *Beschlussanträge des Öffentlichkeitsausschusses* (1966), Bes. 86; *Wort zum Vietnamkrieg* (1967), Bes. 62; *Erklärung der Landessynode zum Krieg in Vietnam* (1968), Bes. 66; and *Erklärung zur Lage in Vietnam* (1973); three items by the Christian Church (Disciples of Christ): *Concerning Church, Nation, and Black Disciples* (1971), 9; *Appeal to the Churches on Vietnam* (1967); and *Substitute Resolution on Vietnam* (1966); three documents of the United Church of Christ [USA]: *Report of the Council for Christian Social Action, as Finally Adopted* (1965), 13; *On Justice and Peace in Vietnam* (1967); and *Joint Statement on Vietnam* (1969); Episcopal Church [USA], *The War in Vietnam* (1967); six reports of the Christian Action Commission of the Reformed Church in America: in 1973 (R-7 Floor Motion), 1972 (R-4 Floor Motion), 1970 (R-2, R-4), 1969 (R-10), 1966 (R-4), and 1965 (Addendum to report to the 1965 General Synod); Mennonite World Conference, *The Conference Message* (1967), III; World Methodist Council, *Conference Message to the Methodists of the World* (1966); Christian Church (Disciples of Christ), *Concerning North and South Korea* (1979); United Church of Christ [USA], *Peace and the Reunification of Korea* (1987), II; World Alliance of Reformed Churches, *Korean Peace and Reunification* (1989); United Church of Christ [USA], *Peace in Afghanistan* (1987); *General Assembly of the Christian Evangelical Baptist Union in Italy* (1982); Christian Church (Disciples of Christ), *Concerning El Salvador* (1981); Anglicanism, *The Resolutions of the Lambeth Conference* (1988), 24, 37, 39, 62, 73; Presbyterian Church (USA), *Our Response to the Crisis in Central America: An Appeal to Presbyterians and Other Churches in the United States* (1988); Evangelische Kirche der Union — Bereich Bundesrepublik Deutschland und Berlin-West, *Telegramm an der SACC* (1982).

[5] The Methodist Church in Malaysia, *Social Principles* (n.d.), III/E; III/B.1; Evangelical Church of Lutheran Confession in Brazil, *God's Earth . . . Land for Everyone* (1982), II; Third General Conference of Latin American [Catholic] Bishops, *The Puebla Message* (1979).

[6] For documentation concerning Lutheranism's historic commitment to a reliance on arguments grounded in the doctrine of creation for authorizing social ethical positions, as per its two-kingdom ethic, see chapter 1, note 12. For similar commitments in the Roman Catholic heritage, see Vatican II, *Gaudium et Spes* (1965), 76; Thomas Aquinas, *De Regimine Principium* (1260-65), I.1; Thomas Aquinas, *Summa Theologica* (1267-73), IIa, IIae, q. 63, art. 2; Ia, IIae, q. 91; I, q. 96, art. 4. The historic reliance of Anglicanism on a tradition of natural-law ethics has been argued by James M. Gustafson, *Protestant and Roman Catholic Ethics: Prospects for Rapprochement* (London: SCM Press, 1979), 60, 12, 3, 2; see the Church of England's Articles of Religion (1571), art. 37; Richard Hooker, *Of the Laws of Ecclesiastical Polity*, vol. 1 (London: Dent, 1954), 147-232.

[7] Lutheran Church in America, *Peace and Politics* (1984), 1; Anglican Church of Canada, *South Africa* (1986).

[8] Moderamens of the Reformed Alliance [FRG], *Das Bekenntnis zu Jesus Christus und die Friedensverantwortung der Kirche* (1981), I.

[9] For information concerning the controversies surrounding the declaration, see Günter Baadte, Armin Boyens, and Ortwin Buchbender, eds., *Frieden stiften die Christen zur Abrüstung: Eine Dokumentation* (Munich: Verlag C.H. Beck, 1984), 79-80. Also see World Alliance of Reformed Churches, *The Theatre of Glory and a Threatened Creation's Hope* (1982). The pertinent passage reads as follows: "The WARC calls upon its member churches and the individual members thereof to regard the question of peace not merely as a political question but as one that immediately concerns our commitment to the God of peace." Also see the claim of the United Church of Christ [USA], *Report of the Council of Christian Social Action, as Finally Adopted* (1965), 14, that "war is incompatible with Christian teaching."

[10] For references to these statements and those cited in the next section, see the section on just war and pacifism in the Appendix.

[11] Moderamens of the Reformed Alliance [FRG], *Das Bekenntnis zu Jesus Christus und die Friedensverantwortung der Kirche*, I, III; Erl. II; Erl. III; Erl. V.

[12] Roman Catholic Church, Vatican II, *Gaudium et Spes* (1965), 79, 22; National Conference of Catholic Bishops [USA], *The Challenge of Peace: God's Promise and Our Response* (1983), 71-73, 79-100, 120-22, 125, 15, 2. A number of other Roman Catholic documents employing a similar model of argumentation are listed in the section on just war and pacifism in the Appendix.

[13] These statements are identified earlier in this chapter (see pp. 63-64).

[14] For references to these statements and others cited in this section, see the subsection on just war and pacifism in the Appendix.

[15] For documentation of the historic Lutheran position, see chapter 1, note 12.

[16] In addition to the relevant section in the appendix, see earlier in this section for the pertinent statements, esp. p. 67-68.

[17] For another illustration of this point, note that both the Christian Church (Disciples of Christ), *Responsibilities of Conscience Regarding Participation in War* (1968), and the Vatican II document *Gaudium et Spes*, 79, 77, 76, 22, espouse support for conscientious objection (the Disciples support a selective conscientious objection, and the Vatican Council its classical form) by way of warrants drawn from both creation and Christology. Also note the appeal of the Presbyterian Church (USA), *Christian Obedience in a Nuclear Age* (1988), 26, 28, to the Christian faith in order to authorize selective conscientious objection, a theme compatible with the appeals to Christology offered by a number of other churches in support of conscientious objection in its classical form.

[18] For the statements in question, see the section on just war and pacifism in the Appendix.

[19] For these statements and others cited in this section of the chapter, see the first section under nuclear armaments in the Appendix.

[20] For a few examples, see WCC Vancouver Assembly Issue Group Report, *Statement on Peace and Justice* (1983), 7; WCC Uppsala Assembly, *Message* (1968), 38; *Message of the Holy Synod of the Russian Orthodox Church on War and Peace in a Nuclear Age* (1986), 2.27; Second General Conference of Latin American (Catholic) Bishops Medellín Conference, *Message to the People of Latin America* (1968); [Catholic] Episcopal Conference of the Pacific, *The Pacific and Peace* (1986), VIII; Church of Norway, *Kirken og freden* (1982), VIII; Evangelische Kirche in Deutschland, *Wir müssen mehr tun* (1986), II, III; United Church of Canada, *The Search for Peace in the Eighties —Statement* (1982), Rec. C/9.

[21] For an example of such a case, compare the argument for disarmament based on ecclesiology, perhaps grounded in Christology, of the Methodist Church in Malaysia, *Social Principles*, III/E; III/B.1; I, with the argument for disarmament based on creation and Christology of the Russian Orthodox Church, *Open Letter to the President of the USA, Ronald W. Reagan* (1983), and with the argument on grounds of the doctrine of creation by the Lutheran Church-Missouri Synod, *To Encourage Peacemaking and the Study of Problems concerning the Church and Nuclear Arms* (1983).

[22] For references to this third group of statements, see the end of the first section in the Appendix on nuclear armaments.

[23] For the pertinent quotation for making this point, see the section "Diversity in the Roman Catholic Tradition" in chapter 6 below, p. 92.

[24] Evangelische Kirche in Deutschland, *Kundgebung zur Veröffentlichung der Denkschrift "Frieden wahren, fördern und erneuern"* (1981); Evangelische Kirche von Kurhessen-Waldeck, *Beschluss der Landessynode über den Antrag der Kreissynode Hanau-Stadt zur Friedensfrage* (1981).

[25] For references to this relational view of human beings, see p. 12 of *Gaudium et Spes,* p. 196 of the American Catholic bishops' pastoral letter, and p. 1 of the statement by the Lutheran Church in America. A similar ontology, emphasizing the unity of human persons (and so, their mutual interdependence), is maintained by at least one statement which takes the more liberal, anti-deterrence statement, namely, United Church of Canada, *Nuclear Weapons Free Zone* (1982).

5. Divorce, Remarriage, and Polygamy

According to the biblical witness, Jesus lauded the married state and, along with a few other biblical authors, insisted on its indissoluble character (Mark 10:8-12; Matt. 19:6-9; cf. Matt. 5:31-32; 1 Cor. 7:11; Mal. 2:10-16). In contrast, some Old Testament texts and even Paul in one circumstance seem to countenance divorce (Deut. 24:1; Ezra 10:2-3; Jer. 3:8; 1 Cor. 7:15).

A similar ambiguity can be identified with regard to polygamy. According to Paul, at least bishops are to remain monogamous (1 Tim. 3:1-2). Numerous instances in the Old Testament, however, can be cited in support of polygamy (see Gen. 29-30; 2 Sam. 12:11; 1 Kings 10:8 LXX).

Although the subsequent history of the church in Western culture tended to settle the biblical ambiguity on these issues, they are by no means resolved today for the churches. The extension of the church's mission into indigenous cultures in the Southern hemisphere, where polygamy is still practised, raised the issue anew of whether the church could endorse or at least countenance the practice. In the Northern hemisphere the inroads of Enlightenment critical thinking and the breakdown of the most venerable cultural institutions have had their impact on the stability of the institution of marriage. Divorce rates are climbing in most nations north of the equator. As a result, the churches in these nations are faced with a situation in which divorce has touched large segments of their memberships as well as potential converts. Consequently a reassessment of divorce and the validity of the church's role in blessing the remarriage of the divorced has been imposed on the churches of the Northern hemisphere in consequence of the cultural agenda of these nations.

These reflections on the impact new cultural contexts have had for reopening questions about polygamy and about divorce and remarriage call our attention to the fact that the tensions in the biblical witness on these matters seem themselves to be related to the different contexts addressed by the biblical authors. This observation in turn leads one to suspect that present disagreements among the churches may be more a function of contextual, non-theological factors than they are direct consequences of theological disagreements. Certainly, contextual factors influence modern church statements on these subjects. I have found only four church statements that address the issue of polygamy, two of which were drafted in Africa, where polygamy is a local concern. No statement by a church body responsible only for members in the Northern hemisphere has come to the Strasbourg Institute's attention.[1]

By the same token, one can detect cultural biases in the statements dealing with remarriage after a divorce. All the statements received (except for two in which regret about divorce is expressed in passing) have been issued by churches located in the

Northern hemisphere (specifically in the West) and by a few international bilateral dialogues, whose agenda, most agree, is usually set by Western socio-theological concerns.[2] These observations do not in themselves verify the claim that dis-agreements among the churches on polygamy or concerning remarriage after divorce are not theologically related (and so not church dividing) because the disagreements are more related to contextual, denominational, non-theological factors. In order to develop the arguments for the non-theological character of the churches' dis-agreements on the issues considered in this chapter, it is necessary to provide a survey of the theological arguments used by the statements. We postpone consideration of the more complex question of remarriage after divorce and focus initially on those handful of official church statements which have dealt with polygamy.

Polygamy

When the Board of Trustees of the Institute for Ecumenical Research determined that official church statements on polygamy should be examined, their supposition was that in view of the controversial character of this issue on the mission fields of Africa and Asia, there would be many official church statements addressed to this topic. In fact, this seems to be an issue primarily only for Westerners working on the mission fields. As previously noted, only four official church statements have come to our attention. Yet even these statements reflect the well-known Roman Catholic conserva-tism on marital issues. As such, the topic of polygamy, even with the limited number of statements available for consideration, is pertinent to consider as another test case for assessing whether disagreements on ethical questions are necessarily church dividing.

The earliest statement to be considered, the trend-setter for the Roman Catholic approach to polygamy, is the Second Vatican Council's *Gaudium et Spes*. The statement as a whole subordinates creation to grace and Christology. In the paragraph germane for our purposes, however, marriage is located in the context of natural law, thus making an appeal to creation the basis for condemning various abuses of marriage, including polygamy, divorce, and free love.

This conciliar statement is authoritative for all Roman Catholic moral theology. Thus it is significant to compare one of the two Roman Catholic statements from Africa, a 1972 document of the Catholic hierarchy of Ghana, with another African church statement, a 1974 declaration of the All Africa Conference of Churches. The Ghanian Catholics follow the conciliar statement in condemning polygamy. In contrast, a certain degree of openness to the practice is expressed by the African ecumenical conference. The theological arguments for these positions present an interesting pattern.

The other statement on the subject by African Catholic bishops, a 1981 pronounce-ment of the [Catholic] Episcopal Conference of Africa and Madagascar, also con-demned polygamy, by way of appeal to the gospel. This regional conference, however, is a bit softer than the other two earlier Roman Catholic statements, insofar as the bishops insist that their rejection of polygamy does not imply the abandonment of Christians and catechumens engaged in polygamous relationships.

The Ghanian Catholics appeal to "Christian ethics". This vague appeal to a kind of special Christian insight on ethical questions seems to conflict with the appeal to the natural law of the Vatican II pastoral constitution. Insofar as the latter document subordinates creation to distinctively Christian themes such as grace or Christology, so that even references to the natural law may be read as appeals to distinctively Christian realities, the disagreement with the Ghanian Catholic mode of argument may not be so great. But to the degree one may refer here to two different theological arguments for the condemnation of polygamy, it is again apparent that theological disagreements concerning ethical questions need not divide the churches. Distinct theological approaches can live together in one Christian family and even can give rise to the same ethical conclusion.

In this context, clarifying the 1974 statement of the All Africa Conference of Churches is crucial. The conference does not explicitly advocate polygamy but merely raises the question: What does the practice of polygamy do to the image or concept of humankind, both male and female? From this perspective (one oriented to anthropology) it is stated: "The tendency to approach the problem of polygamy with a humanistic understanding and a caution to regard only monogamy were expressed." It would seem to be a responsible reading of the text to conclude that the conference has expressed an openness to polygamy from an anthropological perspective. To the degree this is the case, one could refer to a disagreement on polygamy between the conference and the Roman Catholic Church. The disagreement here regarding polygamy would be theologically related and perhaps even church dividing, insofar as it represents a disagreement about the nature of the Christian faith. While the All Africa Conference of Churches spoke of polygamy in terms of anthropology, the Ghanian Catholics in citing "Christian ethics" had appealed to privileged (Christian) information.

Any spectre of a church-dividing character to this disagreement seems rapidly dismissed as soon as the position of *Gaudium et Spes* is assessed. It condemns polygamy by way of appeal to a theme related to the doctrine of creation as much as the All Africa Conference of Churches appeals to a theme related to that doctrine in seeming to express an openness to the practice. In short, similar or related theological perspectives appear to issue in different appraisals of polygamy. In this case, then, any disagreement on polygamy is not theologically related. Consequently it can be said, more generally, that any disagreement among the churches about polygamy (including the one between the All Africa Conference of Churches and the Ghanian Catholics) is not necessarily theologically related. To the degree such disagreement is not theologically related, it represents no disagreement about the nature of the Christian faith and so is not church dividing.

The same point pertains to a 1988 Lambeth Conference resolution which seems to express some openness to polygamy insofar as converted polygamists are recommended for baptism and are not compelled to divorce any of their wives. The resolution, however, does not offer any theological authorization for the position it takes, other than a reference to "God's plan", which is said to uphold monogamy. Consequently, a theological disagreement does not seem to be at stake in any disagreement that the Anglican bishops might have with those church bodies which seem to reject polygamy outright.

If consideration of church statements on polygamy was not of interest in itself for such an ecumenical insight concerning the relationship between ethics and church unity, our survey is useful in its challenge to another piece of conventional ecumenical wisdom. The possible disagreement between the All Africa Conference of Churches and the Catholic hierarchy of Ghana (coupled with the Ghanian agreement with the documents of Vatican II) challenges the idea that one's context necessarily makes a significant contribution to determining theological and ethical positions. In this case the two African church bodies disagree, despite their shared context. In fact, the one African body shares more in common with the international statement of the Vatican Council, which actually follows a largely Western agenda. As with other topics already considered, church statements on polygamy and, as we shall see, those on divorce and remarriage are determined more by denominational and confessional identification than by the context of a church body's theological and ethical perspective.

Divorce and Remarriage

Although input from the Orthodox Church will be of crucial import for our purposes, the debate on remarriage after divorce has largely been an affair of Protestant-Roman Catholic relationships. This is evident from the fact that documents from bilateral dialogues concerning this issue, involving the Roman Catholic Church and one or more Protestant traditions, are crucial texts for assessing the churches' recent positions on divorce and remarriage. The consideration of this issue by these dialogues bespeaks its sensitive and practically relevant character in the life of the Christian community.

In connection with the sensitive character of this issue, it is also significant to observe that although in the period of our study a number of Protestant churches have addressed the question of remarriage after divorce, no statement by an ecumenical body addressing the issue has been brought to our attention. This silence on the issue by such organizations is one more indication of how sensitive the topic of divorce and remarriage is for ecumenical relationships. Such sensitivity is reflected in the careful treatment of the issue by the dialogues which have addressed it.

The conclusions of these dialogues and the statements of the Protestant churches which have addressed the topic in one sense come as no surprise and, to some extent, simply confirm stereotypes. Roman Catholics unequivocally reject divorce and so the remarriage of those who have been divorced. On the other side, the Protestant churches deplore divorce but express concern for those who must go through the ordeal and, with the possible exception of a 1968 and an earlier 1947 decision of the Christian Reformed Church in North America, are open to solemnizing the remarriage of the divorced, given the proper circumstances.

Even the Anglican tradition, which has historically withheld blessing the remarriage of divorced persons, is on record as being open to remarriage in certain circumstances, as affirmed in its 1975 international dialogue with the Roman Catholic Church as well as in a 1973 resolution of the Episcopal Church [USA] and in a 1981 resolution of the Church of England.[3] Likewise even a segment of the Mennonite tradition, the USA's Brethren in Christ Church, a denomination related to the evangelical movement, as early as 1974 went on record as expressing an openness to remarriage after divorce.

The Protestant commitment possesses a kind of interconfessional character. It cuts across denominational boundaries as well as theological differences, insofar as the Protestant statements which express an openness to divorce and remarriage are authorized by different theological bases. Some, like a 1970 statement of the Lutheran Church of Australia, authorize their position by referring to the doctrine of creation; others, like a 1974 statement of the Moravian Church in America, Northern Province, authorize their position by appeal to Christology; others, like a 1982 statement of the former American Lutheran Church, by combining various authorizations; still others, like a 1981 report of the Church of England, offer no clear authorization. The data again indicate that theological differences do not necessarily entail disagreements on questions pertaining to ethics. The churches' statements often suggest that doctrinal disagreements are often transcended by a unity of praxis.

In contrast, theological factors begin to emerge as apparently quite significant when comparing the characteristic Protestant and the Roman Catholic views on divorce and remarriage. The bilateral dialogues devoted to the subject as well as a pregnant passage in the Second Vatican Council's *Gaudium et Spes* point to these factors and their potentially problematic character. The council's contribution provides a useful starting point, since it provides the guiding principles for positions taken by Roman Catholics in the dialogues: "Endorsed by mutual fidelity and, above all, consecrated by Christ's sacrament, this love abides faithfully in mind and body in prosperity and adversity and hence excludes adultery and divorce."[4]

The passage seems to point to the sacramental status of marriage ("above all . . . Christ's sacrament") as the primary reason why divorce is excluded. This is not to say that the sacramental character of marriage is the only authorization for the church's position on divorce. Marriage also is related to the doctrine of creation, and in turn to the gospel by the council's pastoral constitution.[5] These other warrants, however, only support the main argument against divorce on grounds of marriage's sacramental character. In fact, the supporting warrants — creation and the gospel — are at least partially shared by all of the Protestant churches who have taken a position contrary to the Roman Catholic Church on remarriage after divorce. But none holds to the sacramental character of marriage, at least not in the statements addressing this topic.[6] Consequently it seems to follow that the disagreements between these Protestant statements and the Vatican Council relate to the Roman Catholic Church's insistence on the sacramental character of marriage. In short, the disagreement appears to be theologically related.

The internal logic for such an argument is apparent. It seems logical to rule out divorce and remarriage if marriage is a valid sacrament. Given such suppositions, remarriage after divorce would desecrate the sacramental status of marriage as much as rebaptism of adults would represent a challenge to the sacramental character of infant baptism.

This sort of grounds for disagreement between Roman Catholics and Protestants on divorce and remarriage surfaces in all but one of the interconfessional dialogues which have dealt with this subject. (The 1971 *Denver Report* of the International Roman Catholic-Methodist Joint Commission did not offer any theological rationale for the disagreement between these two traditions on the issue.) Thus in the report of the International Lutheran-Reformed-Roman Catholic Study Commission, the difference between the two sides is identified in terms of the Roman Catholic Church's insistence on the sacramental character of marriage, a commitment not endorsed by the Reformation churches. (The Reformation churches also criticize the Roman Catholic tradition for not sufficiently grounding marriage in the doctrine of creation.)[7] Likewise the report of the Anglican-Roman Catholic International Commission suggests that the Roman Catholic Church's rejection of divorce and remarriage relates to its endorsement of marriage's sacramental character and that the disagreement between it and Anglicanism relates to their different concepts of the church.[8]

It is interesting to note that none of the dialogues in question finds these disagreements necessarily problematic with regard to their implications for formal church fellowship. In fact, the Lutheran-Reformed-Roman Catholic conversations conclude that divisions among these traditions are not theological in nature but pertain to pastoral work.[9] The role that the distinct Roman Catholic sacramentology and ecclesiology play in influencing its disagreement on divorce and remarriage, however, seem to challenge the dialogue's conclusions. In the divorce-remarriage debate between Roman Catholics and Protestants, the disagreement appears related to a theological disagreement.

Only by bringing the Eastern Orthodox Church into the conversation does it seem possible to avoid the conclusion that theological differences — that is, potentially church-dividing disagreements about the nature of the faith — are at stake in the churches' differences on the divorce-remarriage question. The Orthodox share with the Roman Catholic tradition a belief in the sacramental character of marriage. But the Greek Orthodox tradition, at least in North and South America, also adheres to the practice of "oikonomia" — a showing of mercy as a witness to the gospel by allowing for the remarriage (within limits) of those divorced.[10]

The Greek Orthodox viewpoint, then, puts an entirely different character on the nature of the debate between the Roman Catholic and Protestant traditions concerning divorce and remarriage. Because Orthodox practices converge with Protestantism while its theological commitments converge with Roman Catholicism, it follows that the disagreement it has with the Catholic Church in practice is not theologically related. Consequently, the final conclusion can only be that disagreements between the Roman Catholic and Protestant traditions on this matter, despite their distinct theological perspectives, are *not necessarily* theologically related. Such considerations show genuine promise for lessening tensions in this previously problematic ecumenical issue.

What, then, is the underlying cause of these traditions' disagreement about divorce and remarriage? The suggestion of the Lutheran-Reformed-Roman Catholic Study Commission, that we are concerned here with different approaches to pastoral care, may be a valuable line to pursue in future ecumenical work, along with sensitivity to the possible impact distinct ecclesiologies and distinct ways of conceptualizing the created order may have on the issue. Liberated from at least some of the anxieties about the possible church-dividing character of divorce and remarriage, could this not be a set of contemporary challenges to which ecumenical ethics might now fruitfully respond?

NOTES

[1] For references to these statements, see the section in the Appendix on divorce, remarriage, and polygamy.

[2] For references to these statements, see Appendix.

[3] *The Report of the Anglican-Roman Catholic International Commission on the Theology of Marriage and Its Application to Mixed Marriages* (1975), 44; Episcopal Church [USA], *General Convention Resolution* [on the implementation date of new marriage canons] (1973), can. 1:18, sec. 3; Church of England, *Marriage and Divorce* (1981). Also see Christian Reformed Church in North America, *Decisions of 1968*, 60, 61, and *Decisions of 1947*, 65-69.

[4] Roman Catholic Church, Vatican II, *Gaudium et Spes* (1965), 49.

[5] Ibid., 48, 46.

[6] Among Protestant churches there is some historic precedent in the Lutheran and Anglican traditions for regarding marriage in terms of a sacramental character. See *Apology of the Augsburg Confession* (1537/1531), 13.14ff.; *An Outline of the Faith,* in *The Book of Common Prayer* (New York: Seabury, 1979), 860-61.

[7] Lutheran-Reformed-Roman Catholic Study Commission, *Theology of Marriage and the Problem of Mixed Marriage* (1976), 29, 26, 18, 12.

[8] Anglican-Roman Catholic International Commission, *Report,* 15, 36.

[9] Lutheran-Reformed-Roman Catholic Study Commission, *Theology of Marriage,* 25, 43-45; cf. Anglican-Roman Catholic International Commission, *Report,* 21. The Roman Catholic-Methodist Joint Commission, *Denver Report,* 75, simply notes the disagreement and offers no comment on its implications for church unity.

[10] Greek Orthodox Archdiocese of North and South America, *Protocol Number 206A* (1973); cf. *The Rudder of the Orthodox Christians; or, All the Sacred and Divine Canons* (1800), canon 3, "Form for a Canonical Divorce". For a description of the concept of oikonomia, see Lutheran-Reformed-Roman Catholic Study Commission, *Theology of Marriage,* 32, 43.

6. Abortion

Respect for human life is a central Christian commitment. The Decalogue is virtually unambiguous on this point (Ex. 20:13; Deut. 5:17; Gen. 9:6). This commitment relates quite naturally to the deep-seated human and religious emotions associated with the birth of children. The clan or tribal mentality of early Semitic culture with its tendency to regard the birth of children as a sign of future blessing continues to appear at several crucial points in the Christian faith (Gen. 17, 21; Ps. 128:3; Matt. 2:10-11; Luke 1:67ff.; 2:10-12, 34).

Given the logical interconnections between these commitments, it is hardly surprising that historically the church has tended to regard with skepticism, if not criticism, efforts to interfere artifically with the birth process. In fact, a certain kind of biblical appeal has been made for such traditional opposition to abortion. There are several suggestions that some of the biblical authors may have considered the fetus in the womb a living human being. Luke 1:41 reports that the babe in Elizabeth's womb leaped when Mary paid a visit during her pregnancy; Psalm 139:13, 16 speaks poetically as if life began in the womb. Thus it would follow that abortion would be murder, a violation of the Fifth Commandment. Indeed, the editors of ancient Israel's covenant code could be understood as regarding artificially induced miscarriages as criminal offenses (Ex. 21:22-25).

Particularly in our century, though, a combination of historical criticism and the tragic realities of back-alley "coat-hanger" abortion have had their impact on the earlier Christian consensus. The vast majority of churches now have become willing to concede that abortion might be legitimate, at least in some circumstances. There is some ambiguity in several statements, for example, a 1970 statement of the Baptist World Alliance, two statements of the Evangelical Lutheran Free Church of Norway, as well as several other Baptist, Reformed, United, Mennonite, and Orthodox statements, concerning whether they might ever countenance an abortion.[1] Only the Roman Catholic Church has steadfastly and unambiguously refused officially to grant the validity of abortion in any circumstances. As a result, the question of abortion has come to be seen in terms of a Roman Catholic-Protestant controversy. A study of the churches' statements on the subject, though, quickly reveals that such conclusions are too simplistic.

It must be conceded at the outset that certain patterns are identifiable in the churches' statements on abortion. Unquestionably there is a geographical pattern. Of the statements we have received from the churches, only twenty-six were formulated outside of North America and Western Europe. Nineteen of these twenty-six emerge from thoroughly industrialized cultures with a Northern hemisphere ethos — from

Australia (the Lutheran Church of Australia and the Australian [Catholic] Episcopal Conference), from New Zealand (the New Zealand Catholic Bishops' Conference, two resolutions of the Baptist Union of New Zealand, and two annual conference decisions of the Associated Churches of Christ in New Zealand), from Korea (the [Catholic] Episcopal Conference), and from several Eastern European nations. There is at least one statement by the WCC which has spoken to the subject, but like many statements of international church organizations it likely reflects to some extent a Western cultural agenda. Among the sole possible exceptions to this Western influence in setting the agenda for this issue are 1981 and 1984 statements issued in Africa (specifically by the [Catholic] Episcopal Conference of Africa and Madagascar, the Presbyterian Church of Southern Africa, and the Liberian Catholic Bishops Conference), a 1979 pastoral letter issued in Pakistan (by the [Catholic] Bishops of Pakistan), a 1984 statement issued on Taiwan (by the Chinese Catholic Bishops' Conference), and a 1983 statement issued in Haiti (by the Haitian [Catholic] Episcopal Conference).[2] In any case, it is quite apparent that abortion is not an issue of pressing concern for the churches in the Southern hemisphere and perhaps not in Eastern Europe. In another context it might be interesting to speculate on why this is the case and to ask whether it suggests that the Western capitalist system is characterized by certain structures or pressures which render pregnancy problematic, something other than the natural situation it is in other cultures.

The Roman Catholic Church seems to stand alone in its unequivocal rejection of abortion, although at least ten Protestant statements on the subject seem to reject abortion without qualification and so could be in complete harmony with Rome at this point. But the position of Protestant churches is much more differentiated than that of a mere rejection of the Roman Catholic position and an affirmation of abortion's legitimacy. Rather, Protestant churches and organizations speaking on the subject tend to disagree on the question of the circumstances in which abortion might be legitimate and the related questions of what sort of procedure abortion really is (is it murder?), in view of the status of the fetus (is the fetus a human life?). In addition, these statements also differ with regard to their sensitivity to the relationship between abortion and socio-economic factors. Several statements, notably a 1980 declaration of the Evangelische Kirche in Deutschland, a 1979 statement of the Evangelische Landes-kirche in Württemberg, and several statements of the National Conference of Catholic Bishops [USA], demonstrate their sensitivity to the socio-economic pressures which force many women to contemplate abortion insofar as these statements urge the creation of socio-economic conditions and institutions which support the pregnant mother.[3]

Another pattern which one might at first glance associate with the statements on abortion relates to the fact that various Roman Catholic statements are authorized by the doctrine of creation, appealing to natural law or anthropology. This basis could suggest once again that a correlation exists between conservative positions on social ethics and arguments drawn from the doctrine of creation. In fact, a closer examination of the statements shows once again that the conventional wisdom associated with the Barmen Declaration is not substantiated.

Rome contra Abortion

Although in the modern period the Roman Catholic Church has issued numerous statements on the subject of abortion, the best-known and most controversial is a 1968 encyclical issued by Pope Paul VI entitled *Humanae Vitae*. Its evaluation of abortion can be understood properly only in the context of its concern with the broader questions of birth control and in the context of its overall theological orientation. Given its impact on the discussion of abortion, it warrants some detailed considera- tion. [4]

The encyclical opens by stating that the duty of transmitting human life entails the collaboration of married persons with God the Creator. [5] This correlation of human sexuality with the doctrine of creation subsequently is made more explicit in the context of the encyclical's reflections on the magisterium's competency to address the moral issues related to marriage and sexuality. The church's teaching is said to be "founded on the natural law, illuminated and enriched by divine revelation" (5). Elsewhere this theological commitment to reflecting on human sexuality from the perspective of theological loci associated with the doctrine of creation is reiterated when it is stated that "the problem of birth, like every other problem regarding human life, is to be considered . . . in light of an integral vision of man and of his vocation" (7).

After establishing this theological framework, the encyclical proceeds to reflect on the character of marriage as "the wise institution of the Creator" (8). By nature, marriage is said to be "ordained toward the begetting and educating of children" (9). The Second Vatican Council's pastoral constitution *Gaudium et Spes* is cited in support of the latter affirmation. [6] This inextricable connection envisaged at this point between marriage and human procreation dictates the encyclical's subsequent conclu- sions regarding abortion and appropriate birth control techniques.

Insofar as the natural order of creation orients marriage towards procreation, it follows, the encyclical asserts, that "each and every marriage act [*quilibet matrimonii usus*] must remain open to the transmission of life". Natural law is invoked as authorization for this commitment (11). From this it follows that any sexual act which jeopardizes the responsibility to transmit life is in contradiction with human nature and natural law (13). On this basis all artificial means of birth control are rejected. Only the so-called rhythm method is deemed acceptable, for only it is in accord with natural law. Artificial means of contraception, by contrast, are said to "impede the develop- ment of natural processes" (16).

Given these commitments, the encyclical's unconditional rejection of abortion and even sterilization follows logically. Even if undertaken for therapeutic or medical reasons to save the mother's life, abortion must be excluded as a licit means of birth control. To render conjugal acts infertile by such artificial means is to contradict the natural order, with its interconnectedness of sex and procreation, as well as to violate the nature of human persons as "the minister of the design established by the Creator" (14, 13). The doctrine of creation — specifically natural law and the doctrine of human persons — has functioned to authorize the most conservative of positions on the abortion question.

This is not the whole story, however, with regard to the churches' teachings on abortion. In fact, the prevailing mode of theological argumentation employed in *Humanae Vitae* is only one of several arguments employed by the Roman Catholic Church in articulating its "no" to abortion.

Diversity in the Roman Catholic Tradition

Immediately after *Humanae Vitae* was issued, a number of national Roman Catholic bishops' conferences issued statements endorsing and defending the encyclical. Of these, perhaps the most interesting one is a 1968 letter of the bishops of Belgium. It argued, without the encyclical's own qualifications, that the papal encyclical did not forbid the use of legitimate therapeutic (i.e., artificial?) means of birth control. [7] In any case, many of these bishops' conferences moved beyond a mere endorsement of the papal encyclical's position and actually argued the case against abortion.

Quite a few of these national Roman Catholic bishops' conferences have framed such statements condemning abortion in a manner which is theologically consistent with *Humanae Vitae*'s appeal to the doctrine of creation as authorization for their common position. Perhaps the most prominent of these declarations is a 1984 statement of the Chinese Catholic Bishops' Conference, a 1983 decision of the New Zealand Catholic Bishops' Conference, a 1978 note of the Portuguese Episcopal Conference, and two or perhaps four statements in the period 1969-70 (as well as a more recent 1989 statement) issued by the National Conference of Catholic Bishops [USA]. But even in the case of these statements, some emphases distinct from *Humanae Vitae* are apparent.

Perhaps the most obvious difference in these statements is that they tend to neglect referring to the concept of natural law and to abortion primarily as a violation of the sexual order as God has created it. In place of such arguments these statements have tended to deny abortion's validity on grounds of the nature of human persons. Specifically, a commitment to the dignity or sacredness of human life is their starting point. All agree, however, and most explicitly affirm that human life begins at conception. Thus to terminate a pregnancy by means of abortion amounts to murder. Several of these statements make this conclusion explicit.

This drift away from arguments rooted in the concept of natural law and the status of the sexual act in such a framework in favor of arguments which are rooted in the doctrine of human persons is not embodied in all of these statements. At least in two 1969 statements of the USA's National Conference of Catholic Bishops, a 1974 statement of the bishops of the Netherlands, a 1977 declaration of the Episcopal Conference of Belgium, a 1978 declaration of the Italian Episcopal Conference, and a 1984 statement of the Episcopal Conference of Portugal something like the idea of natural law surfaces insofar as these five bishops' conferences claim that in urging opposition to abortion, they are not urging one ethical conviction as the sole basis of public policy. All five invoke the natural-law notion that ethical truths are accessible to all rational human beings. Thus the American bishops claim that their position is also held by persons of other faiths and by specialists in the fields of medicine, law, and so forth. Both the Dutch and Belgian bishops argue that their views represent "general human values". Likewise, the call of the New Zealand Catholic Bishops' Conference for the support of "all people of goodwill, of whatever religious persuasion or none" reflects these same commitments. [8]

In several Roman Catholic statements concerning abortion issued since *Humanae Vitae* was released, though, one can identify at least suggestions of positions that are less nuanced than those in the papal encyclical's natural-law mode of argumentation. One example is a 1980 statement of the Australian [Catholic] Episcopal Conference in which both the gospel and anthropology authorize a criticism of abortion. Two more pertinent examples include a 1983 pastoral letter on peace and nuclear armaments issued by the USA's National Conference of Catholic Bishops and a 1979 declaration by the Roman Catholic Bishops of France. Although the authorization for the French bishops' statement is somewhat ambiguous, at least one unambiguous theological warrant appears in the context of a discussion of the activities of various persons who are challenging the abortion mentality in France. Reference is made to the work of Christ and the gospel. Christ is said to make us alive to establish such signs of hope in the face of the evil of abortion. The gospel is said to be at cause in these endeavors.[9]

This tendency to bypass the doctrine of creation in favor of an appeal to other theological loci for authorization of the position against abortion also is suggested in the 1983 American Roman Catholic bishops' pastoral, as it takes up the question of abortion in relationship to the peace question. The bishops perceive such a relationship insofar as they argue that peace is impossible "without a full awareness of the worth and dignity of every human person, and of the sacredness of all human life". Abortion is then condemned for "blunt[ing] a sense of the sacredness of human life."

There is a sense in which these references to the sacredness of human life could be construed as appeals to the doctrine of creation or to the doctrine of human persons as authorization for the rejection of abortion. A similar appeal is evident in the French bishops' pastoral letter. Like the French bishops' letter, however, these references to themes associated with the doctrine of creation do not have the final word for the American bishops. They have correlated their views on abortion with peace. And peace, it is argued, rests ultimately in conversion. Spiritual exercises and especially the Mass are said to be the particular means for creating the conditions essential for peace. Thus it seems to follow that just as the quest for peace is authorized by these various spiritual exercises, particularly by the Eucharist, and inasmuch as the bishops relate peace and their opposition to abortion, their position on abortion seems likewise authorized at least to some extent by these themes. Moreover when the American bishops claim to be examining the contemporary problems in light of the gospel, it appears that this locus also authorizes their position on abortion.[10]

We have noted in previous chapters that this mode of social and ethical argumentation, which bypasses the doctrine of creation in favor of other theological loci, is a legitimate part of the Roman Catholic heritage. A kind of "Christomonism", wherein all theological themes are subordinated to Christology or redemptive grace, is evident in some documents of the Second Vatican Council and may be reflected in the statement of the American bishops described above. Thus it is reflected in the council's condemnation of abortion in the pastoral constitution *Gaudium et Spes*.

The council fathers initiate their treatment of the subject in a manner consistent with Pope Paul's later treatment of the subject in *Humanae Vitae*. The concept of natural law is introduced. Marriage is conceived of as an institution of the divine law which is "by nature ordered to the procreation and education of children". Thus the regulation of birth must be in accord with these characteristics of natural law. In making such judgments, the council states: "The objective criteria must be . . . drawn from the nature of the human person and human action." On the grounds of these criteria abortion is rejected as an "abominable crime".[11] Elsewhere the constitution rejects abortion merely on the grounds that it is "an offense against life itself".[12] This mode of argumentation, however, is not the whole story.

Immediately following the condemnation of abortion on the grounds of natural law, the pastoral constitution adds that "the true evaluation and full meaning [of human life and its transmission] can only be understood in reference to man's eternal destiny".[13] At this point the perspective of the gospel or eschatology seems to function as authorization for the rejection of abortion. In itself this does not appear to be a dramatic alteration of the mode of argumentation we have observed in most of the abortion statements already considered. *Humanae Vitae* also correlates its argument against abortion authorized by natural law with a supplementary reference to "divine revelation" or "the law of the Gospel" (4). [14] What is striking in *Gaudium et Spes* is that the council fathers have subordinated creation to redemption. This is particularly apparent in paragraph 22. The pastoral constitution states: "The Christian is certainly bound both by need and by duty to struggle with evil through many afflictions and to suffer death. But, linked with the paschal mystery and patterned on the dying Christ, he will hasten forward to resurrection. . . . *All this holds true* not for Christians only but also *for all men of good will in whose hearts grace is active invisibly*" (italics mine).

The idea that all humans of good will embody redeeming grace seems to entail that nature is created in grace. Consequently, the invocation of natural law by *Gaudium et Spes* in order to authorize the condemnation of abortion seems to entail de facto an appeal to redemptive grace. Thus it follows that the rejection of abortion on grounds of redemption or some other locus related to the gospel, as we observed in the American Catholic bishops' pastoral on peace and perhaps in the 1979 declaration of the French bishops, is a legitimate Roman Catholic position with council authorization. The condemnation of abortion in a 1983 declaration of the Haitian [Catholic] Episcopal Conference as well as in other statements by several additional national bishops' conferences, including two other statements by the USA bishops, may also move in this direction.

We have previously encountered this kind of diversity in Roman Catholic moral theology. The presence of this diversity in the case of abortion has several consequences. It reminds us that there is no necessary bias with regard to socio-ethical orientation associated with certain modes of theological argumentation. Appeals to the gospel or Christology do not always result in liberal or radical social ethical positions. Thus in the case of abortion such appeals when used in *Gaudium et Spes* and elsewhere have resulted in the most conservative of positions on the subject.

In addition, the diversity we have observed in Roman Catholic treatments of abortion suggests another important, ecumenically significant insight: that theological disagreements do not entail disagreements concerning the churches' positions on abortion. An examination of Protestant statements on the subject further illustrates this point.

Before proceeding to an examination of Protestant statements, we should note one additional Roman Catholic statement which exhibits these more recent tendencies, appealing to several loci in addition to natural-law anthropology in order to authorize its rejection of abortion. This is a 1971 statement of the Nordic Catholic bishops. The major arguments of the pronouncement authorize the bishops' position against abortion by appeal to some theme associated with the doctrine of creation; sometimes reference is made to natural law, another time the nature of human life, and on one occasion to fundamental human values. [15] These appeals, however, are correlated with subordinate appeals to the "Christian viewpoint" and Christology. [16] Most striking about the statement is not these arguments but the conclusions, arrived at without clear theological authorization, that Catholic doctors should obey government laws which permit abortion, even to the point of being sure to refer patients to other doctors who do respect the law. [17] In addition, the Nordic bishops proceed even further. While affirming *Humanae Vitae*'s rejection of artificial means of contraception, they appear to endorse contraception as valid socially as a means of reducing abortion. [18]

There are only four comparable Roman Catholic statements. One is a 1976 declaration of the German Bishops' Conference which conceded an openness to the participation of medical personnel in an abortion which might help save the mother's life (at least there was an unwillingness to criticize such participation). The second is a 1968 statement of the Canadian Catholic Conference which claimed to represent the views of the Second Vatican Council in stating that, although the direct taking of fetal life is condemned, nothing precludes treatments to save a mother's life, "even if they sometimes result in the unwanted and unsought death of the foetus". The third is a 1984 pastoral letter of the Liberian Catholic Bishops' Conference. It was even willing to endorse "therapeutic abortions" in order to save the mother's life, in addition to advocating "indirect abortions", as did the Canadians. A similar openness to the use of abortion if it is necessary in order to save the mother's life is endorsed by the fourth statement, a 1973 pastoral letter of the [Catholic] Episcopal Conference of Korea. [19]

In view of the tendencies, previously observed, of ethics authorized by Christology or the gospel to arrive at more liberal conclusions, one is tempted to ask whether this pattern might pertain in the case of the more open Roman Catholic statements on abortion. In fact, it does not pertain, at least in the case of the Nordic Catholic bishops' statement, insofar as its more open positions have no readily apparent theological authorization. Besides, the Protestant statements to be examined indicated that conservative positions on abortion do not necessarily ensue from appeals to the doctrine of creation.

Evangelical Liberty on Abortion

In examining Protestant statements on the subject of abortion, one is tempted to raise the question of whether the liberty of the gospel has set these churches free to minister more flexibly to the needs of those facing the burden of an unwanted, potentially destructive pregnancy. Of the numerous statements on the subject, perhaps those of the USA's United Church of Christ, the Moravian Church in America, Northern Province, the Lutheran Church in America, a 1976 resolution of the United Methodist Church [USA], and Great Britain's Methodist Church are among the most striking alternatives to the position of the Roman Catholic Church. As such, an examination of these particular statements provides a useful entrée to a report on Protestant statements concerning the subject.

Most, if not all, of the statements of these churches affirm more than just an openness to the use of abortion. As we have noted, such an affirmation characterizes all the Protestant statements on the subject. What is distinct about the statements of these particular churches is that they suggest so comparatively few qualifications concerning when abortion might be legitimate. Also unlike most of the Protestant statements, they differ with the Roman Catholic Church insofar as they do not unambiguously recognize the fetus as a human life. Thus abortion is not murder in their view.

Another noteworthy element in these statements is the theological consciousness which they exhibit. Though there are exceptions, most of them exhibit solid theological rationale. Granted, the language of "freedom of choice" does appear at least in some statements of the United Church of Christ [USA], the Presbyterian Church (USA), its earlier predecessor body the United Presbyterian Church [USA], the

Reformed Church in America (a 1971 guideline which by 1973 was largely rejected), the Christian Church (Disciples of Christ), and the British Methodists. But the secularist's rhetoric concerning the mother's rights to control her own body is happily missing. Instead these statements reflect a concern to deal with abortion in light of Christian and humanitarian concerns.

In connection with this matter the theological diversity exhibited by these statements is no less noteworthy. For example, a 1970 statement of the Lutheran Church in America, the 1976 statement of the British Methodists, and a 1971 statement of the United Church of Christ authorize their position by appeal to the doctrine of creation or the doctrine of human persons. It is possible that this is also the position of a 1974 resolution (reaffirmed in 1982) of the Moravian Church, Northern Province (USA), insofar as it appeals to "the sacredness of life" as authorization for its position. By contrast, Christology or the life and teachings of Christ authorize two 1979 statements of the United Church of Christ.[20] Again it is apparent that theological differences do not mandate disagreements on the topic of abortion. This point is markedly illustrated by a 1983 policy statement of the former United Presbyterian Church [USA], which argued for the open position on abortion by appealing to doctrinal themes from each of the three articles of the creed. Nor can one say that the churches' disagreements about abortion are necessarily theologically related. Even the characteristic Roman Catholic mode of argument against abortion based on the doctrine of creation is reflected in some Protestant statements which are open to abortion. Insofar as theology and the gospel are not at stake in the disagreement over abortion, it thus is appropriate to reflect on whether in principle it needs to be a church-dividing issue.

The fact that Protestant and Roman Catholic churches can agree on their basic theological orientation for approaching the problem of abortion and still disagree on their conclusions raises the question of what causes their disagreement. This problem can be dispatched with more clarity after a consideration of additional diversity within the Protestant community on the abortion question.

The Diversity of Protestant Responses

The position on abortion which we have observed in the Protestant statements thus far considered is by no means typical of the Protestant community. The vast majority of Protestant statements on the subject are more qualified in their openness to abortion, allowing abortion in only limited circumstances, usually only when the mother's life is endangered. A number of them insist that abortion is not a legitimate means of birth control. Of Protestant statements which take a more open position on abortion, the British Methodists also insist that abortion is no means of contraception and even go so far as to claim that the fetus is "biologically identifiable as belonging to the human race".[21] The gravity of abortion is further emphasized in these statements by their contention that abortion is the taking of a human life. By implication these Protestant churches side with the Roman Catholic Church over against the other group of Protestant church statements by suggesting that human life begins in the mother's womb.

In many ways the position of the Protestant churches which we have been describing represents a mediating position between that of the Roman Catholic Church and the more radical Protestant viewpoint. Henceforth I shall identify it as the "mediating Protestant position". Like the position of those who are more radical, this mediating position is open to the use of abortion in circumstances where the birth of the fetus might be a greater evil than artificial termination of pregnancy. These Protestant churches still share the Roman Catholic Church's critical perspective on abortion, however, partly in consequence of their seeming to agree that the unborn fetus is a human life.

This group of church statements includes many that provide no clear theological rationale for the position they take. This is true in the case of the various Protestant churches in Ireland, a 1982 declaration of the Eglise de la Confession d'Augsbourg d'Alsace et de Lorraine, a 1972 resolution of the Evangelische Landeskirche in Württemberg, two statements of the Lutheran Church of Australia, as well as 1973 and 1982 decisions of the Associated Churches of Christ in New Zealand. This may also be the status of the resolution of the 1984 Lutheran World Federation Assembly, though, to be sure, the resolution does see abortion as a form of violence and expresses a concern for the "dignity of all human life".

It is also possible that some statements have authorized their mediating position on abortion by way of appeals simultaneously both to the doctrine of creation (or the doctrine of human persons) and some locus associated with the doctrine of redemption. Such an approach seems reflected in a 1980 declaration of the Evangelische Kirche in Deutschland as it authorizes its position on abortion not only by appeal to the law and life as God's gift (themes related to the doctrine of creation) but also to the teaching of Christ. Indeed, the gospel alone may function to authorize this sort of position on abortion in a 1980 resolution of the Anglican Church of Canada. Likewise, among others, the USA's Southern Baptist Convention has endorsed abortion only in the most special circumstances by appeal to the nature of human persons as created by God. But this argument is made in the context of a 1979 statement which seemed to subordinate creation to redemption insofar as it claimed that democracies, and so effective socio-political institutions, require Christian influence.

Nevertheless, the majority of Protestant statements which assume the mediating position on abortion do so by way of appeal to the doctrine of creation or the doctrine of human persons. Among the more prominent of such statements are several declarations of the Church of Norway, a 1971 resolution of the USA's National Association of Evangelicals, perhaps the *Social Principles of the United Methodist Church,* a 1975 statement of the USA's Mennonite Church, several resolutions since 1971 issued by the USA's Southern Baptist Convention, a 1987 statement of the Evangelische Kirche in Deutschland (endorsing a 1980 declaration of its Rat), 1979 and 1986 declarations of the Evangelische Landeskirche in Württemberg, a 1979 official discussion paper of the Eglise de la Confession d'Augsbourg d'Alsace et de Lorraine, and a 1980 statement of the American Lutheran Church.

The latter three statements and that of the American Methodists do posit explicitly a correlation of creation and redemption. In fact, in the statements of the American Lutheran Church and the Eglise de la Confession d'Augsbourg d'Alsace et de Lorraine, Christology appears to function as a warrant to authorize Christians to care for those experiencing or contemplating an abortion. In all of these instances, however, only themes related to the doctrine of creation appear to authorize the judgment made or which is to be made concerning abortion. In this regard the American Lutheran Church's 1980 statement differed from the arguments made in its 1974 statement, wherein a similar mediating position on abortion was taken by way of appeal to loci drawn from all three articles of the creed.

The fact that appeal is made to the doctrine of creation to authorize this mediating position on abortion and that the same kind of theological argument also authorizes the two extreme positions (for and against abortion) reminds us again that theological differences or disagreements about the nature of Christian faith do not appear to be at stake in the disagreements among the churches about abortion. Thus one might rightly ask again whether the abortion controversy need be church dividing.

Since churches often agree about the contribution of Christian faith to the abortion question yet still disagree about abortion itself, we again need to determine what causes their disagreement. The crucial point or basic difference appears to be the question of when human life begins.

When Human Life Begins: The Crucial Theological-Ethical Question?

To some extent the difference between Protestant statements taking the so-called mediating position on abortion and those statements which are more radical in their openness to abortion is simply one of regarding versus not regarding the embryo or fetus as a human being. Locating the basic difference between these sets of statements in the question of when human life begins, however, is more than merely a point of logic. This means of distinguishing the Protestant statements on abortion provides a clue to recognizing that these statements may differ concerning their philosophical conceptions, if not concerning their view of human persons. This point is particularly clear in two of the more radical statements on abortion.

As we have noted, a 1976 statement by the Methodist Church [England] and a 1970 statement by the Lutheran Church in America both endorse abortion as legitimate, not just in cases where the mother's life is at stake, but also if the parents are unable to deal with the new responsibilities which would accompany the birth of a child. Also both take the position that the crucial issue in abortion is the status of the unborn fetus, which they regard as not fully human.

In both cases the latter claim is justified by appeal to a similar view of human persons. Both endorse what we have identified in previous chapters as a relational view of persons. That is, human beings are understood as those who are necessarily related to and influenced by interactions with other persons and with their environment. This affirmation is made explicitly by the British Methodists, as they state that "man is made for relationships". In the Lutheran Church in America statement the point is made that "a qualitative distinction must be made between [the fetus's] claims and the rights of a responsible person made in God's image who is living in relationships."[22]

The correlation between these statements' reliance on a relational view of human persons and their position on abortion is self-evident. Because the nature of human persons is to be in relation, to affect and be affected by others, the unborn fetus cannot be considered fully and properly a human being. It may be in relation to the mother and perhaps affects other persons. In this capacity, however, the unborn fetus functions more like an object for the projections of human persons. It does not function in relationships as an independent I which relates to a Thou, not even with the sort of independence or freedom which infants and the severely disabled exhibit in their relationships with others. Thus it follows that the termination of pregnancy in abortion is not the termination of a human life in the fullest sense.

To be sure, the British Methodists speak of the fetus's "human significance", and the American Lutherans of its being "the organic beginning of human life". Consequently, both assert that abortion is a serious matter. Yet both also assert that the claims of the fetus, as something other than a full human life, should not supersede the rights of one who is in God's image as a being in relationship with others.[23] It is the relational view of human persons which ultimately authorizes these statements' assessments of the status of the human fetus and also of abortion.

A more biological, less philosophical argument is employed by at least one church statement advocating the more open position on abortion. A 1983 policy statement of the former United Presbyterian Church [USA] argues in favor of an openness to abortion, at least up to the time of the viability of the fetus.[24] By implication, then, the American Presbyterians, at least in the early 1980s, also seemed to regard the embryo as something other than a full human life.

A quite distinct view of human persons appears to underlie the more cautious Protestant statements on abortion as well as those of the Roman Catholic Church. Insofar as these statements contend that human life does indeed begin in the mother's womb, they appear to presuppose a more static, less relational view of human being. If human life begins in the womb, the nature of human being cannot be essentially relational, at least not in the sense of being constituted through I-Thou relationships. Rather, the embryo is human merely in virtue of its physical and spiritual substance created by the union of sperm and egg. The fetus is not a human being in virtue of its being constituted through its relationship to some Thou to whom it relates as an independent subject (and not simply as an object). At least one Roman Catholic statement, a 1973 declaration of the Episcopal Conference of Belgium, articulates these philosophical suppositions explicitly. A more cautious way of making this point from the Roman Catholic side was offered by the bishops of the Netherlands in a 1974 statement. They simply noted the impossibility of determining when a fetus possesses an individual human life, with the implication that the fetus must then be treated as a human life, since we cannot concretely determine its subhuman character.[25] This point may warrant further consideration in efforts to achieve rapprochement on the question of abortion.

In any case, the difference between the most radically open statements on abortion and the more conservative statements seems to relate to a difference between a relational-activist view of human persons and a view of humans as static substances, akin to the anthropology of classical philosophy. The validity of this observation is supported when we recall the great impact classical Greek philosophy has had on Roman Catholic ontology and anthropology. It seems undergirded further by consideration of a 1974 statement of the former American Lutheran Church on abortion. The statement appears to opt for the mediating Protestant position that abortion is murder, but at the point where it seeks to argue for the appropriateness of abortion in certain circumstances, it appeals to a relational view of persons. It thus seems that not just the question of when human life begins but the deeper issue of how to describe human persons ultimately accounts for differences among the churches about the appropriateness of abortion.

Such an analysis has several consequences. It might be asked whether contemporary social scientific data and the present intellectual ethos do not suggest the superiority of the relational view of human persons in comparison to the model of human persons as static substances. Also the reliance we have noted on a relational view of persons in so many of the church statements on other social issues is worthy of note. Such data would seem to have consequences for determining the most appropriate Christian position on abortion. It indeed seems that endeavoring to determine the most appropriate mode of describing the nature of human persons is a fruitful way for Christians to proceed in the debate on abortion.

Consequences for church unity follow from these reflections. If differences about the nature of human beings — specifically differences over the most appropriate philosophical conception of the human person — ultimately underlie disagreements over abortion, then it would seem to follow that these disagreements need not be church dividing. Since the nature of the Christian faith is not really at stake in the dispute over abortion, but rather an issue of philosophy, one must ask whether such a difference is sufficient to divide churches.[26]

Final Reflections

The preceding discussion has clarified the fundamental underlying issues in the disagreements between the most radical group of Protestant statements on abortion and both groups of the more conservative statements issued on the subject. Though we have identified what ultimately may be at stake in the disagreement between the liberal Protestants and the Roman Catholic Church, as well as the core issues at stake in the intra-Protestant dispute, it is still necessary to reflect on what ultimately might distinguish the mediating Protestant position on abortion from the Roman Catholic position. There are no easy answers.

We have noted previously that there are numerous instances where the Roman Catholic statements and those of the Protestant statements reflecting the mediating position advocate fundamentally the same theological mode of argumentation. The understanding of the nature of Christian faith is thus not the determinative factor in the disagreement among these churches on abortion. Perhaps their differences are more ones of philosophy or ontology.

The clue to this observation is derived from the more liberal Protestant position of the Lutheran Church in America. In its 1970 statement which dealt with abortion and other issues related to sexuality and family, it stated that "people have a right not to have children without being accused of selfishness or a betrayal of the divine plan."[27] This assertion suggests that in addition to its view of human persons, the Lutheran Church in America distinguished itself from several Roman Catholic Church statements by means of a different construal of the orders of creation (i.e., of natural law). Whereas in several Roman Catholic statements, notably *Humanae Vitae*, the natural order was said to be so structured that every marriage act must be open to procreation, sexuality is not conceived by the Lutheran Church in America to have this relationship to procreation in the created order.[28] In short, the statements differ in their view of the created order — specifically, the place of sexual activity in the created order. The disagreement between these churches about abortion and birth control is related to this difference. Because not every act of sexual intercourse must be open to the transmission of life, the Lutheran Church in America can be more open in principle to a procedure such as abortion, even though it prevents the development of human life from a legitimate sexual transaction.

Although Protestant statements which maintain the mediating position on abortion do not explicitly address the question of natural law or the orders of creation as the Lutheran Church in America has, insofar as they do not mandate an inextricable connection between procreation and every act of sexual intercourse, perhaps an underlying cause of the disagreement between Protestant statements and the Roman

Catholic Church relates to their different ways of construing the created order. If so, it is one more indication that abortion need not necessarily be a church-dividing issue.

In developing a Christian anthropology, theology typically relies heavily on philosophy in depicting the structures of creation. Thus one might conclude that the disagreement which seems to exist between the Roman Catholic Church and various Protestant statements concerning the orders of creation fundamentally is related to the different philosophical constructs or models they employ. It also entails that the abortion question is no more worthy of fracturing Roman Catholic-Protestant church unity than are any philosophical differences worthy of dividing the church. If arguments about philosophy do not preclude church fellowship, neither should disagreements over abortion.

The preceding reflections have suggested a possible cause of the disagreement between certain Roman Catholic statements and Protestant statements, like those of the Church of Norway, the Evangelische Kirche in Deutschland, the United Methodist Church [USA], and the like, which maintain the mediating position on abortion. The distinction between these positions, however, simply does not apply in the case of many Roman Catholic statements. We have noted that a majority of Roman Catholic statements do not appeal to the concept of natural law as such in order to authorize their position. Thus they do not posit a necessary interconnection between every act of sexual intercourse and human procreation. Differences that the mediating Protestant statements have with them on abortion thus cannot be traced to this issue.

Thus the question remains: On what grounds can the mediating Protestant position on abortion differentiate itself from the official Roman Catholic position? The similarities are profound, for both consider the fetus a human life. Ultimately there may be no logical way of accounting for why the statements representing these positions diverge.

The two extreme positions on abortion are eminently logical. The Roman Catholic Church regards the fetus as a human life. Therefore abortion would be termination of that life and so would amount to murder. Abortion is thus precluded in all circumstances. Radical Protestant statements, however, such as those of the Methodist Church [England] and the Lutheran Church in America, do not concede human status to the fetus. Thus abortion is legitimate in some circumstances precisely because it is not murder.

What, then, is the logic of the mediating Protestant position? If the fetus and the embryo are a human life, how can abortion be legitimated under any circumstances? The argument for this position is put forth well by the Church of Norway by contending that we must be willing to accept the lesser evil if suffering and destructive consequences would ensue from a birth.[29]

But questions must be posed about the logic of such a viewpoint. Though the statement we have cited is an exception, the vast majority of statements exhibiting this orientation on abortion have not been careful enough. Insufficient detail or rationale is provided for justifying and determining the grounds for engaging in the "murder" of the fetus/embryo. There is a frightening logic to the position that murder is sometimes justified. If we can murder an unborn infant in order to protect a woman's life, what prevents us from terminating other persons or groups which cause us or our society undue suffering?

To be sure, the intention of those who would still remain open to abortion while deeming the fetus and the embryo a human life is not at all akin to the extermination policies of National Socialism. But the question remains whether the logic of the argument is not potentially the same. (The analogy between abortion as murder and killing in self-defence is not quite adequate, for an act of self-defence is not premeditated homicide in the way abortion would be, on the grounds of the mediating Protestant position.) The matter is all the more disconcerting in view of the fact that the vast majority of churches which have spoken on the subject of abortion have taken this mediating position. Perhaps its consequences need to be rethought or at least articulated more carefully. In the final analysis the crucial question with which the church may need to wrestle in resolving the debate on abortion is the question of the status of the fetus/embryo and the related question of the character of human life. It may be necessary to concede that the position one takes on these questions must be the determining factor in what to make of abortion.

Our analysis has pointed out some of the bitter controversy among the churches concerning abortion. It has also identified some rays of hope. We have observed that insofar as disagreements about the nature of the Christian faith (i.e., theological disagreements) are not necessarily at stake in the controversy about abortion, this issue is not necessarily symptomatic of a church-dividing difference between Protestants and Roman Catholics. Indeed, if the churches could work together in ecumenical cooperation on the question of how best to construe the doctrine of human persons in our day, an exercise in philosophical theology which should in principle be possible across confessional lines, they might be able to restore some consensus concerning the status of the fetus/embryo and the question of abortion. Perhaps then the controversy could end, the social statements cease to be issued, and a ministry to the suffering genuinely begin.

NOTES

[1] Baptist World Alliance, *Resolution on Man's Stewardship and Survival on Earth* (1970); Evangelical Lutheran Free Church [Norway], *Prenatal diagnostik og "de funksjonshemmedes år"* (1981); *Resolusjon fra den Evangelisk Lutherske Frikirkes Synodemøte til det Norske Storting* (1979). For the other statements of this genre, see the commentary at the end of the section on abortion in the Appendix.

[2] Lutheran Church of Australia, *Abortion* (1970); Australian [Catholic] Episcopal Conference, *Message of Australian Bishops to Members of Federal Parliament* (1985; see also eight other statements by the bishops, listed in the section on abortion in the Appendix); New Zealand Catholic Bishops' Conference, *For Life* (1983); Baptist Union of New Zealand, *Notice of Motion* (1988), 13.1-13.2, and *Public Questions* (1970); Associated Churches of Christ in New Zealand, *Decision* (1983 and 1973); [Catholic] Episcopal Conference of Korea, *Pastoral Letter* [on the Mother-Child Health Law] (1973); WCC Conference on Faith, Science and the Future, *Technology, Resources, Environment and Population* (Cambridge, Mass., 12-24 July 1979), 5; cf. [Catholic] Episcopal Conference of Africa and Madagascar, *Recommendations and Conclusions on Christian Family and Marriage in Africa Today* (1981), 2.3.4; Presbyterian Church of Southern Africa, *Church and Nation* (1984), 338, clauses 2-3; *Pastoral Letter on Abortion by the Catholic Bishops of Liberia* (1984); [Catholic] Bishops of Pakistan, *Joint Pastoral Letter on Abortion and Contraception* (1975); [Catholic] Bishops of Vietnam, *To Build Peace* (1969); *Statements and Proposals of the Chinese Catholic Bishops' Conference on the Issue "Should abortion be legalized?"* (1984); Haitian [Catholic] Episcopal Conference, *The Foundation for the Church's Involvement in Local and Political Arenas* (1983), 17, 19, 2, 5; *Call of the Polish (Catholic) Episcopacy before the Threats against Life* (1970), II-IV; Polish [Catholic] Episcopal Conference, *The Christian Family and the Gift of Life* (1979); Hungarian [Catholic] Episcopal Conference, *Responsibility in Defense of Human Life* (1978). For references to statements issued by churches in the West, see the section on abortion in the Appendix.

[3] Evangelische Kirche in Deutschland, *Erklärung des Rates der EKD zum Schwangerschaftsabbruch* (1980); Evangelische Landeskirche in Württemberg, *Stellungnahme zum Abbruch der Schwangerschaft* (1979); National Conference of Catholic Bishops [USA], *Statement on Abortion* (1970) and *Declaration on Abortion* (1970). For references to other statements cited in the chapter, see the section on abortion in the Appendix.

[4] One of the hotly debated issues of the day inside the Roman Catholic Church, a debate with broad ecumenical implications, pertains to the status of *Humanae Vitae* — specifically, whether it should be deemed infallible. This point has been argued by Ermenegildo Lio, *Humanae Vitae e infallibilita — Il Concilio, Paulo VI e Giovanni Paolo II* (Rome: Libreria Editrice Vaticana, 1986), who appeals to the Second Vatican Council's *Lumen Gentium* (1964), 25.

[5] Roman Catholic Church, *Humanae Vitae* (1968), 1. Subsequent paragraph references in the text are to this encyclical.

[6] Roman Catholic Church, Vatican II, *Gaudium et Spes* (1965), 50. This statement also parallels the encyclical insofar as it situates its reflections on marriage in the context of the doctrine of creation (see ibid., 48). Subsequent exposition will show, however, that there are significant differences between the council's theological authorization for rejecting abortion and the theological authorization provided by *Humanae Vitae*.

[7] *Lettre des évêques belges sur l'encyclique "Humanae Vitae"* (1968), II; cf. *Humanae Vitae*, 15. Also see the statements listed in the concluding commentary at the end of the section on abortion in the Appendix.

[8] National Conference of Catholic Bishops [USA], *Statement on Abortion* (1969) and *Statement in Protest of U.S. Government Programs against the Right to Life* (1969), 6; *Statement from the Bishops of the Netherlands on Abortion* (1974); [Catholic] Episcopal Conference of Belgium, *Pour la défense des plus faibles* (1977); *Declaration of the Italian Episcopal Conference on Abortion* (1978), 3; Episcopal Conference of Portugal, *The Legalization of Abortion in Portugal* (1984), 4; New Zealand Catholic Bishops' Conference, *For Life* (1983). The other relevant statements by the various national conferences of Catholic bishops are cited in the section on abortion in the Appendix.

[9] Conseil permanent de l'épiscopat aux Catholiques de France, *L'accueil de l'enfant a naître* (1979), 8; Australian [Catholic] Episcopal Conference, *Abortion* (1980), I-II.

[10] National Conference of Catholic Bishops [USA], *The Challenge of Peace: God's Promise and Our Response* (1983), 284-95, 13; cf. Conseil permanent de l'épiscopat aux Catholiques de France, *L'accueil de l'enfant a naître*, 2.

[11] *Gaudium et Spes,* 48, 50, 51.

[12] Ibid., 27.

[13] Ibid., 51.

[14] Also see Conferencia Episcopal Española, *La despenalización del aborto* (1983), 2, 4, 6-9, 12. In like manner the New Zealand Catholic Bishops' Conference, *For Life,* correlated its appeal to the doctrine of creation in condemnation of abortion with a reference to eschatology. Also the citation of *Gaudium et Spes* by the National Conference of Catholic Bishops [USA], *Declaration on Abortion,* may indicate that it follows the council's manner of correlating creation-related arguments for social questions with redemption. For a similar, perhaps clearer articulation of this sort of theological argument, see the National Conference of Catholic Bishops [USA], *To Live in Jesus Christ: A Pastoral Reflection on the Moral Life* (1976), 2, 30, 31, 63-65, 115-16.

[15] Nordic Catholic Bishops, *Svangerskabs afbrydelse og kristent ansvar* (1971), 6, 8, 12, 21.

[16] Ibid., 9.

[17] Ibid., 12.

[18] Nordic Catholic Bishops, *Svangerskabs afbrydelse og kristent ansvar,* 17.

[19] German Catholic Bishops, *Concerning the New Legislation on Abortion* (1976); *Canadian Catholic Conference Statement on Proposed Change of Canadian Law on Abortion* (1968), I; *Pastoral Letter on Abortion by the Catholic Bishops of Liberia* (1984), 3, 11; [Catholic] Episcopal Conference of Korea, *Pastoral Letter* [on the New Mother-Child Health Law] (1973).

[20] References for these statements are provided in the section on abortion in the Appendix. It is possible that Christology may authorize the openness to abortion of the United Methodist Church [USA], *Resolution on Responsible Parenthood* (1976); the resolution explicitly appeals to "Christian judgment" (and so by implication to the knowledge given in Christ) for authorization. For information about the status of statements by the Lutheran Church in America as well as those of the American Lutheran Church, see pp. 10ff. above.

[21] Methodist Church [England], *Abortion* (1976), 14, 9, 8. For references to statements by Protestant churches which hold this majority viewpoint, see the section on abortion in the Appendix.

[22] Ibid., esp. 3; Lutheran Church in America, *Sex, Marriage, and Family* (1970), esp. 5.

[23] Methodist Church [England], *Abortion,* 14, 3; Lutheran Church in America, *Sex, Marriage, and Family,* 5.

[24] United Presbyterian Church [USA], *Covenant and Creation: Theological Reflections on Contraception and Abortion* (1983), policy statement.

[25] *Statement from the Bishops of the Netherlands on Abortion* (1974); cf. Episcopal Conference of Belgium, *Déclaration sur l'avortement* (1973), I/3.

[26] The conclusion that disagreements on abortion need not rupture Christian fellowship was offered by the Church of the Brethren, *Statement on Abortion* (1984), in a statement which, interestingly enough, rejects abortion without any clear qualifications of circumstances in which Brethren might legitimately choose to abort.

[27] Lutheran Church in America, *Sex, Marriage, and Family,* 5.

[28] See *Humanae Vitae,* 11.

[29] Church of Norway, *Abortspørsmalet* (1971), 1-2; cf. Church of Sweden, *Yttrande över genetisk integritet* (1984), 3, 4.

7. Genetic Engineering

Inasmuch as the techniques of genetic engineering and the ethical questions they raise are distinctively modern developments of the late twentieth century, the biblical witness and the history of the Christian tradition have no direct word to speak to these matters. Of course the Christian community does not feel itself bereft of guidance from its tradition. The insistence of the biblical witness on respect for human life, the affirmation that human life is God's creation and his creation alone (Ps. 100:3), as well as considerations already noted in the discussion of abortion provide a certain guidance to the church in grappling with these exciting new medical possibilities and techniques. Nevertheless, given the relative dearth of concrete guidance on the subject which the Christian tradition can provide, it is hardly surprising that disagreement exists among contemporary church statements on this range of questions. In fact, so imposing are some of these disagreements, particularly between certain Protestant bodies and the Roman Catholic Church, that questions have been raised about whether such disagreements could preclude formal church fellowship between these bodies, or at least be symptomatic of basic differences which preclude church fellowship. Consequently, this particular issue demands our careful scrutiny.

Before taking up the main problematic of the implications of genetic engineering for church unity or church division, we first must clarify the phrase "genetic engineering". By this phrase I refer to recent breakthroughs in medical science which enable doctors and other practitioners to manipulate or operate on certain hereditary characteristics of human life or life in general, before birth. Specifically I have in mind three techniques which the church statements considered collectively examine: (1) prenatal diagnosis of the fetus and genetic counselling prior to conception; (2) research and experimentation on the human fetus, including pharmacology and gene therapy; and (3) techniques of artificial fertilization, including both in vitro fertilization (fertilization procedures transpiring outside the mother's womb through artificial techniques) and artificial insemination (transfer into a woman's genital tract of previously collected sperm). Only positions taken by modern church statements on these techniques will be examined in this chapter.

The minimal amount of specific guidance provided by the tradition for dealing with these challenges does not just manifest itself in disagreements among a number of churches. The silence of the tradition on these matters not surprisingly has given rise to a minimum of specificity in a large number of the church statements which have addressed these topics. Thus many documents, such as statements of the WCC Vancouver Assembly, an earlier statement of the council's Nairobi Assembly, a 1985 declaration of the Church of Norway, a 1983 resolution of the Church of Ireland, a

1982 resolution of the British Council of Churches, as well as earlier resolutions of the Moravian Church in America, Northern Province, and the Associated Churches of Christ in New Zealand, merely note the challenges posed by genetic engineering and then recommend further study, express reservations, or praise the potential of these techniques. A 1981 resolution of the National Association of Evangelicals [USA] was especially critical, in a very general sense, of "nonbiblical views about . . . genetic engineering".[1] It is perhaps worth noting that in cases where any theological authorization is given for these conclusions, reference is usually made to some doctrinal theme associated with the doctrine of creation. In fact, this observation concerning the theological warrants pertains to almost all church statements on genetic engineering, regardless of their conclusions.

In view of the lack of specificity of a number of church statements, a useful entrée for the analysis may be to concentrate attention on a document which is quite specific in its proposals and theological arguments. This might be the basis for comparing other statements which have addressed the topic of genetic engineering but without comparable specificity. Given the present concerns about the potentially problematic character of genetic engineering for Roman Catholic-Protestant relationships, and inasmuch as the most recent (in fact, the only) statement of the Roman Catholic hierarchy on the subject is commendable in its specificity and careful argumentation, the focal point for an analytic comparison of the church statements will be a 1987 instruction of the Vatican's Congregation for the Doctrine of the Faith (the so-called Ratzinger Commission) entitled *Instruction on Respect for Human Life in Its Origin and on the Dignity of Procreation*. This document does not possess the same authority as the other statements of the Roman Catholic hierarchy that we have considered, but it is appropriate to consider it as a valid exception to our methodological suppositions, both because of its quality and inasmuch as it has received so much attention in the present debate about ecumenical social ethics.

The Vatican's Critical Perspective: A Dialogue

The Vatican's statement on genetic engineering does not stand alone. The issue has been addressed in statements by several Protestant church bodies representing a variety of denominational traditions (particularly in the United States, Continental Europe, and the British Isles), national Catholic bishops' conferences in Portugal, the United States, and New Zealand, and by two ecumenical organizations (the USA's National Council of Churches as well as conference and assembly statements of the WCC). The geographical distribution of these statements is revealing. With the exception of a 1969 decision of the Associated Churches of New Zealand concerning organ transplants and a 1984 statement of the New Zealand Catholic Bishops on in vitro fertilization, all of the statements (except WCC statements) were drawn up by church bodies in capitalist nations of the Northern hemisphere. Genetic technology and its ethical implications are, at least for the present, a Western agenda item. Even the churches seem to recognize this limitation, in the sense that it has been categorized by at least one church, the Church of Ireland in a 1983 statement, as a concern subordinate to the issue of super-power nuclear weaponry.

Although these Protestant statements often lack specificity, certain other patterns in these statements considered collectively can be observed. Generally speaking, those church bodies which speak to the issue oppose the use of genetic techniques to allow for abortion of a deformed or handicapped fetus. Given their position on abortion, the

Church of Norway and the Evangelische Kirche in Deutschland are especially critical of this practice; they are joined in this critique by the Evangelical Lutheran Free Church [Norway] and a 1979 conference of the WCC. There is a general rejection of experimentation on human embryos or experimentation on all human life which is not undertaken voluntarily. It is said to be preferable that genetic modification be attempted only for therapeutic purposes of endeavoring to cure illness. (At least one of these commitments is endorsed by the 1979 WCC conference, the WCC Vancouver Assembly, a 1986 statement of the USA's National Council of Churches, a 1984 statement of the Church of Sweden, and, to some extent, a 1985 document of the Church of Ireland.) And euthanasia in the sense of "negative euthanasia", the withholding of artificial means to keep the terminally ill alive, is endorsed, at least by the Southern Baptist Convention [USA] and the 1979 WCC conference.

With regard to the even more controversial issue of artificial fertilization, the Protestant consensus is more tenuous. On the question of artificial insemination, there is a general rejection of the technique when the contributors to fertilization are not married to each other. Consequently, surrogate motherhood is ruled out. The latter is explicitly rejected, albeit with no theological rationale offered, in a 1985 statement of the Church of Ireland. The 1979 conference of the WCC, a 1987 proclamation of the Evangelische Kirche in Deutschland, a 1980 statement of the former American Lutheran Church, and to some extent a statement of the Congregational Union of Scotland took similar positions. Only the 1979 WCC conference, a 1983 statement of the former United Presbyterian Church [USA], and a 1987 statement of the Lutheran Church of Australia explicitly endorsed artificial insemination, and only if a woman is impregnated with her husband's sperm. One church statement, the proclamation of the Evangelische Kirche in Deutschland noted above, actually seems to advise against all forms of artificial fertilization, though it was especially critical of procedures involving a donor from outside the marriage relationship.

Protestant church bodies have been even more hesitant in articulating a position on in vitro fertilization. Concerns for regulation of the procedure were sketched by a 1985 declaration of the Church of Ireland and a 1986 resolution of the Congregational Union of Scotland. The 1986 policy statement of the USA's National Council of Churches merely stated the contrasting viewpoints currently taken by Christians on the question. Of the statements accessible at the time of writing, only a 1982 General Convention resolution on the subject by the Episcopal Church [USA] and a 1983 policy statement of the former United Presbyterian Church (USA) supported the procedure. (The Episcopalians, at least, supported the procedure only when it involves the sperm and egg of marriage partners.)

A final pattern in the Protestant statements, considered collectively, should be noted. This point relates to the theological authorization given for the positions taken, or the the lack of clear theological authorization. In a few of these cases — for example, a 1979 resolution of the Evangelical Lutheran Free Church [Norway] and a 1989 report of the World Alliance of Reformed Churches — it may be that a kind of second-article emphasis prevails (i.e., one of Christology or the gospel). And the doctrine of the Trinity functions as an overall background warrant for the positions on genetic engineering taken by a 1987 proclamation of the Evangelische Kirche in Deutschland. As we have observed on certain select issues, however, particularly in the case of ecological questions, the doctrine of creation or a related theme functions as the primary warrant in most of these Protestant statements on genetic engineering. It is also the primary authorization employed in most of the positions taken by the recent Roman Catholic statement, soon to be considered.

The predominance in these statements of arguments drawn from the doctrine of creation is perhaps a function of the fact that the largest number of statements on genetic engineering from the Protestant side are by Lutheran churches. Thus at this point these churches simply seem to be reflecting their historic confessional position. It is significant, however, that this sort of theological orientation is endorsed by statements of churches from other traditions, including a 1982 statement of the Moravian Church in America, Northern Province, a 1969 decision of the Associated Churches of Christ in New Zealand, and perhaps a 1986 statement of the Congregational Union of Scotland. Perhaps even more striking is the reliance on such a perspective in ecumenical documents of the USA's National Council of Churches and of the WCC. Appeals to the doctrine of human persons tend to predominate as authorization for several of the points made by the previously mentioned 1987 proclamation of the Evangelische Kirche in Deutschland. Could it be that the lessons learned by the ecumenical movement with regard to its new appreciation of the doctrine of creation for dealing with new questions raised by the limits-to-growth debate have been applied to this recently emerging issue of genetic engineering? Or is it rather more the case that certain cutting-edge issues lend themselves better to treatment by theological perspectives drawn from the doctrine of creation, while for other issues, such as peace, Christology provides a more helpful theological approach?

It is with these Protestant statements in the background, with their generally cautious openness to the uses and potential of the new genetic technologies, that the 1987 instruction of the Vatican's Congregation for the Doctrine of the Faith takes on special importance. Both in its specificity and in its more critical appraisal of the new genetic technology, it stands in contrast to the Protestant tendencies just summarized.

The Vatican statement (which a 1983 statement of the Episcopal Conference of Portugal generally endorses) shares a number of commonalities with the Protestant statements. Its approach to the problem in terms of the doctrine of creation and natural law accords with the theological perspective of most of the Protestant statements which have articulated some sort of theological rationale for their positions. (Granted, in accord with the working suppositions of certain documents of the Second Vatican Council, the recent Vatican statement does correlate creation and redemption, and at one point there is even a suggestion [though never carried out] of a subordination of creation to Christology.)[2] In addition, the Vatican document also shares with most of the Protestant statements an openness to the use of therapeutic processes on human embryos, but only if such genetic modification aims towards healing the embryo.

Similar general Protestant-Roman Catholic convergences on genetic engineering can be identified at other points. Both sides also endorse prenatal diagnosis as a valid procedure, as long as this procedure is not carried on with an eye towards aborting a deformed or handicapped fetus. Such a position is perfectly consistent with Roman Catholic views on abortion. (It is also consistent with the prevailing mediating position among Protestants. This observation suggests the convergence between the Protestant mediating position and the Roman Catholic view on abortion.)

One final convergence pertains to artificial fertilization. Along with all the Protestant statements which speak to the issue, the Roman Catholic document, along with the earlier Portuguese and New Zealand Catholic statements, rejects artificial insemination whenever those contributing to the fertilization are not married to each other. Consequently, surrogate motherhood is explicitly rejected.

As we begin to consider other matters related to artificial means of procreation, the more cautious, critical perspective of the Vatican document becomes apparent. Consistent with its other positions on sexual ethics, the Vatican statement places more strictures on the use of artificial insemination than do most of the Protestant statements which have addressed the subject. Although the Vatican expresses the Protestant majority's openness to artificial insemination involving marriage partners, it limits this affirmation very strictly. The use of such techniques, it is argued, must be a mere extension of sexual intercourse among the marriage partners. (The earlier Portuguese and New Zealand Catholic statements largely endorse these commitments, at least by implication, though an earlier 1981 statement of the U.S. bishops, citing John Paul II, seems a bit more cautious, even critical.)

At this point the Vatican document appeals to the concept of natural law, specifically in harmony with its articulation by the papal encyclical *Humanae Vitae,* which we examined in the last chapter. That 1968 encyclical posited that an inseparable connection exists between the two meanings of the conjugal act — its unitive meaning (the oneness of husband and wife) and its procreative meaning.[3] It was on this basis that artificial contraception must be rejected by Roman Catholics, for it separates the unitive meaning of the sex act from its procreative meaning. By the same token it is necessary for the Vatican document to conclude that "procreation is deprived of its proper perfection when it is not desired as the fruit of the conjugal act."[4] It is on these grounds that artificial insemination, even involving marriage partners, must never function as a substitute for the conjugal act. The usual manner of obtaining the sperm, through masturbation, is not permitted. The restrictions placed on the use of artificial insemination by the Roman Catholic Church, in comparison to the more open posture of the Protestant statements on the subject, extend even into the bedroom and to techniques in obtaining the sperm.

As depicted by the Vatican document, the nature of the natural law has implications for two additional strictures, not typical of the Protestant statements, which the document places on genetic technology. By ruling out procreation not linked to the sexual act, all forms of in vitro fertilization must be rejected. From the Roman Catholic perspective, in vitro fertilization is suspect on other grounds. Inasmuch as Roman Catholic anthropology presumes that human life begins in the womb, and given the fact that present in vitro techniques usually require numerous fertilizations and destructions of human embryos (since not all fertilized embryos are transferred into the genital tract of the woman), in vitro fertilization must be rejected as a kind of murder of human life.[5]

The Protestant statements previously examined assumed a very careful, hesitant evaluation of in vitro fertilization. With the possible exception of a 1987 proclamation of the Evangelische Kirche in Deutschland, however, they did not go to the extreme that the Roman Catholic Church has in rejecting it. Nor, for that matter, did a 1984 statement on the subject by the New Zealand Catholic Bishops' Conference, which, perhaps because it was prepared three years before the Vatican instruction, did not rule out in vitro fertilization in principle — as long as the procedure involves only marriage partners and is not divorced from the sexual union.

The second stricture placed on genetic technology by the Roman Catholic Church is related to the previous one. The rejection of in vitro fertilization coupled with the insistence that human life begins at conception entails placing strict restrictions on genetic research. Because the embryo is a human life, the Vatican document proceeds to condemn the destruction of embryos obtained in vitro solely for purposes of research. As one might expect, this point was made as early as 1984 by the New Zealand Catholic Bishops' Conference.[6] On their part, all of the Protestant statements are hesitant about the use of human embryos in experimentation, and most by implication may reject it, insofar as they insist that experimentation on the human being should be undertaken only with the person's voluntary consent. However, only the Church of Sweden in a 1984 statement, the Church in Wales in a 1989 statement (6), and the Lutheran Church of Australia in a 1987 statement (c) appear to affirm anything like the Roman Catholic outright rejection of experimentation on the human embryo. If not with regard to this question of genetic research, at least with regard to artificial fertilization, there is a critical edge to the Roman Catholic position on genetic engineering that is not shared by any Protestant statement which addresses this range of issues, except perhaps for the previously mentioned proclamation of the Evangelische Kirche in Deutschland.

Theological and Ecumenical Evaluation

What accounts for the generally more critical perspective towards genetic engineering of the Roman Catholic tradition, as represented by the Vatican commission? Is this critical perspective symptomatic of a basic, church-dividing difference between the Roman Catholic and Protestant traditions? Though a Protestant conservatism about genetic engineering is emerging in some circles, suspicions are presently in the air in ecumenical circles that the answer is yes. One hears the allegation that a Greek philosophical view of human persons employed in the Vatican document is the culprit.

At one level, theological considerations indeed do not divide the churches with regard to distinct positions taken concerning genetic engineering. We already have observed the role that the doctrine of creation or the doctrine of human persons plays in authorizing most of the Protestant statements as well as the more critical Roman Catholic instruction. Insofar as both groups share a common theological perspective, it would seem to follow that their disagreements in assessing genetic engineering or the validity of certain of its techniques are not related to different conceptions of the nature of Christian faith, and so not necessarily church dividing.

The contention that differences between the Roman Catholic instruction and the majority of Protestant church bodies are a consequence of the Roman Catholic reliance on an anthropology rooted in Greek philosophy requires assessment. In a sense it is true, as was evident in the preceding chapter, that the Roman Catholic tradition relies on such an anthropology, insofar as its position on abortion presupposes the idea of human persons as static substances. This conception is involved on several occasions in the instruction on genetic engineering.[7]

As we have noted, however, it also is the case that Protestant churches maintaining the so-called mediating position on abortion likewise tend to endorse this "static substance", Greek view of persons. Such an anthropology operates explicitly in several of the Protestant statements concerning genetic engineering which reject the use of genetic counseling to allow for the abortion of a deformed fetus. Statements of 1971 and 1982 of the Church of Norway, a 1984 statement of the Church of Sweden, a 1987 statement of the Lutheran Church of Australia (c), a 1987 proclamation of the

Evangelische Kirche in Deutschland (III/6, III/5[g], III/5[e]), and perhaps a report from a 1979 WCC conference seem to endorse explicitly this view of human persons as static substances.

It is evident that the more conservative, critical position of the Roman Catholic Church cannot be solely reduced to its reliance on Greek philosophy in articulating its view of the human person. Other Protestant statements which do not entirely concur with the Vatican's critical perspective on genetic engineering yet employ a similar view of human beings. Besides, the recent Vatican document cannot unequivocally be said to opt for a Greek philosophical anthropology. At one point the document speaks of the human person as a "unified totality", as a "substantial union" of soul and body.[8] Such language bears a much stronger family resemblance to the relational view of human persons described in earlier chapters than to an anthropology totally indebted to classical Greek philosophy.

In the final analysis, then, what seems to divide the Roman Catholic position on genetic engineering from the prevailing commitments of the Protestant consensus concerning this new technology is precisely the same set of issues noted in the previous chapter pertaining to the relationship between the Roman Catholic tradition and the mediating Protestant position on abortion. Once again, the disagreement boils down to a matter of philosophy or ontology — specifically, to a question of how the natural order is conceptualized. Thus, as in the case of its statements concerning abortion, the Roman Catholic tradition has insisted on construing the natural order in such a way that the marriage act is necessarily correlated with procreation (or an openness to procreation). Precisely this correlation of the sex act and procreation entailed the Roman Catholic critique or severe limitation of almost all artificial modes of reproduction. In contrast, the Protestant statements which did not posit such restrictions on genetic engineering also did not posit this sort of Roman Catholic conception of the natural order. The difference between the Vatican's most recent version of the Roman Catholic tradition and the consensus of many Protestant statements concerning genetic engineering (specifically, artificial fertilization) seems ultimately, then, to be nothing more than a disagreement about how to conceptualize natural law or orders of creation.

A similar combination of philosophial or psychological disagreements over how to construe the orders of creation or human nature may account for the internal debate among Protestants between the critical perspective of the Evangelische Kirche in Deutschland and those Protestant bodies which are more open to artificial fertilization. The German Protestant union seems ultimately to base its critique of artificial fertilization on its vision of family order as requiring that children be reared by those who gave birth to them, such that a deviation from this order can cause objective psychosomatic effects.[9] As in the case of statements on abortion, such disagreements pertain more to philosophy than to theology.

A disagreement about the nature of the faith cannot be the cause of the apparent disagreement between the Roman Catholic tradition and the Episcopal Church [USA] concerning the legitimacy of in vitro fertilization; the Episcopalians offer no theological rationale for their favorable assessment of the procedure. Likewise, theological disagreements cannot be at the root of the same disagreement between the Roman Catholic tradition and the former United Presbyterian Church [USA], since both appeal to the doctrine of creation in some manner in order to authorize their respective positions. As such, and in view of the fact that at least one Protestant statement, the

1987 proclamation of the Evangelische Kirche in Deutschland, takes an even more critical view of artificial fertilization than does the Vatican statement we have analyzed (and both took more conservative positions on in vitro fertilization than did a certain Roman Catholic statement, the 1984 statement of the New Zealand Catholic Bishops' Conference), is it not fair to conclude that, contrary to the concerns of some, the Roman Catholic-Protestant debate on genetic engineering is not church dividing? It is no more worthy of fracturing church unity than are any other philosophical differences worthy of dividing the church.

NOTES

[1] For references to these statements and others cited subsequently in the chapter explicitly dealing with this topic, see the section on genetic engineering in the Appendix.

[2] Roman Catholic Church, Congregation for the Doctrine of the Faith, *Instruction on Respect for Human Life in Its Origin and on the Dignity of Procreation* (1987), 2, 1. For a reference to this set of commitments in the council's most important document devoted to social ethics, see pp.89ff. above.

[3] Roman Catholic Church, *Humanae Vitae* (1968), 12.

[4] Roman Catholic Church, Congregation for the Doctrine of the Faith, *Instruction on Respect for Human Life in Its Origin and on the Dignity of Procreation*, II.B.4.

[5] Ibid., II,I.1, 5, Int. 4.

[6] Ibid., I.5,4; *A Statement from the New Zealand Catholic Bishops on the Morality of In Vitro Fertilization* (1984), 4.

[7] Roman Catholic Congregation for the Doctrine of the Faith, *Instruction on Respect for Human Life in Its Origin and on the Dignity of Procreation*, Int. 4, 5, I.1.

[8] Ibid., Int. 3.

[9] Evangelische Kirche in Deutschland, *Zur Achtung vor dem Leben* (1987), III/5(d), III/5(a). The concern that the birth processes associated with genetic technology might cause negative psychosomatic effects on the child is maintained explicitly in a statement endorsed by ibid., III/5; see Evangelische Kirche in Deutschland, *Von der Würde werdenden Lebens* (1985), 2.5.

8. Social Justice

A concern for justice — indeed, social justice — is a theme with deep roots in the biblical witness, most notably though not exclusively in the literature of the Old Testament prophets (Amos 5:21-24; Micah 6:8; Isa. 1:10-17; 28:17; Ex. 22:21-23). Given the communal, tribal mentality of the Hebrew people in the pre-Christian era, it is logical to conclude that at least Old Testament references to justice pertain to the whole community, and so refer to social justice.

In view of the unanimity of the biblical witness pertaining to the intimate relationship between social justice and faith in Yahweh, it is hardly surprising to find a similar unanimity among modern church statements on the topic of social justice. This unanimity may also be related to the fact that since its inception in the mid-1920s, ecumenical social thought has made social justice one of its main priorities. [1] In the last twenty-five years or so, every single statement issued by the churches on this subject affirms the duty Christians have to be concerned about social justice and to seek to implement it.

Differences do exist in the midst of this broad ecumenical consensus. As with all the issues considered in previous chapters, the churches disagree theologically insofar as they employ different kinds of theological arguments in arriving at the same conclusions concerning ethics. To a great extent this theological diversity is a function of the different confessional traditions represented in the statements. Though there are exceptions, especially evident in a number of statements of the Roman Catholic tradition which authorize their call for social justice by way of appeal to Christology or the gospel, there is much consistency with the churches' historical positions. For example, at least some of the Roman Catholic statements and the greatest number of the Lutheran statements endorse their traditions' historic fidelity to ethical arguments which are related to the doctrine of creation. [2]

The ecumenical significance of the preceding point has been previously observed and will be elaborated again in this chapter. Two additional areas of disagreement among the churches, however, also require consideration. One pertains to the question of what social justice is — What particular concerns fall under this general concept? A second, more controversial question relates to the implementation of social justice — Is it ever legitimate for Christians to resort to violent means in order to establish justice in a society presently marked by injustice? We begin with the first.

What Is Social Justice?

Webster's New World Dictionary defines justice as "the use of authority and power to uphold what is right, just [elsewhere defined as 'fair, equitable, important'], or lawful". The idea that justice entails more than merely what is the law of the land, but also pertains to that which is given by some higher authority (what is right, fair, equitable, etc.), seems to entail that the concept of social justice is a broad one, pertaining to a whole range of social and ethical concerns. Given such lexical considerations, it is hardly surprising to note that modern church statements include a broad range of items under the rubric of social justice.

One favorite theme, about which there is broad ecumenical consensus, is that social justice includes peace. Church bodies from as diverse contexts and denominational backgrounds as the Lutheran World Federation (in resolutions in 1970 and 1984), the Moravian Church in Nicaragua (in a 1986 statement), the Conference of Latin American [Catholic] Bishops (at their Medellín Conference), the 1967 papal encyclical *Populorum Progressio,* the 1963 encyclical *Pacem in Terris,* the Synod of the Waldensian and Methodist Churches, the Lusitanian Catholic Apostolic Evangelical Church (in a 1986 statement), the United Church of Canada (in a 1982 resolution on the search for peace), as well as the WCC in its Vancouver, Nairobi, New Delhi, and Amsterdam assemblies make this affirmation.

Another recurring theme is that social justice includes racial equality. Such an affirmation appears in statements as diverse as a 1973 statement of the Christian Conference of Asia, a 1977 statement of the South African Catholic Bishops, a 1978 statement of the Methodist Church [England], 1981 and 1973 statements of the USA's United Church of Christ, 1963, 1968, 1969, and 1981 statements of the Moravian Church in America, Southern Province, a 1980 declaration of the Vereinigte Evangelisch-Lutherische Kirche Deutschlands, a 1980 statement of the Reformed Ecumenical Synod, a 1970 statement of the World Alliance of Reformed Churches, and a statement of the WCC Uppsala Assembly entitled *Towards Justice and Peace in International Affairs.*

A third characteristic theme is the correlation of social justice with economic development or economic justice. This commitment appears in the statements of church bodies as diverse as the Lutheran World Federation (in two statements of its 1984 assembly), the United Church of Christ [USA] (in 1973, 1975, 1977, and 1979 statements), the World Alliance of Reformed Churches (in a 1982 statement authorized, interestingly enough, by appeal to the doctrine of creation), the Presbyterian Church of Korea (in a 1984 statement), the Methodist Church in Malaysia (in its *Social Principles*), the All Africa Conference of Churches (in 1974 and 1981 statements), the Conference of Latin American Bishops (in its Medellín Conference of 1968), the Roman Catholic hierarchy (in its two more recent statements on liberation theology, in its 1987 encyclical *Sollicitudo Rei Socialis,* in the 1971 encyclical *Octogesima Adveniens,* and in the Second Vatican Council's *Gaudium et Spes*), the Bund der Evangelischen Kirchen in der Deutschen Demokratischen Republik (in a 1980 resolution), and the WCC (in statements of its Amsterdam, Evanston, and New Delhi assemblies). No doubt the profound impact that liberation theology has had in recent decades on the ecumenical movement is reflected in this widespread tendency to link social justice to the alleviation of poverty.[3]

Another item which is increasingly coming to be subsumed under the rubric of social justice is quite relevant to the new focus of the WCC on the correlation of "justice, peace, and the integrity of creation". In a few church statements issued even some time before the council turned its attention to this set of themes, one can identify the correlation of social justice with concerns of ecology or sustainability. Such statements include 1972 and 1980 documents of the former Lutheran Church in America, 1979 statements of the USA's United Church of Christ, a 1982 statement of the World Alliance of Reformed Churches, a 1982 statement of the Anglican Church of Canada, a 1982 statement of the Evangelical Church of Lutheran Confession in Brazil, and a 1979 statement of the USA's National Council of Churches.

In addition to the preceding concerns, which the churches more characteristically associate with social justice, certain statements have related more peculiar or parochial concerns to social justice. Examples of such concerns include (1) medical care (mentioned in a 1978 statement of the Lutheran Church in America and a 1979 conference of the WCC); (2) overpopulation (in a 1975 document of the Presbyterian Church in Taiwan); (3) the freedom of couples, not constrained by government authority, to make their own decisions concerning the number of children they may have (in a 1983 statement of the Episcopal Conference of Portugal); (4) land ownership (in a 1983 document of the Paraguay [Catholic] Bishops' Conference, a 1986 document of the [Catholic] Episcopal Conference of the Pacific, and several resolutions of the Uniting Church in Australia); (5) the proper disposal of toxic and hazardous waste (in a 1985 pronouncement on the subject by the United Church of Christ [USA]); (6) nation building (in a 1981 statement of the All Africa Conference of Churches); (7) legislation prohibiting abortion (in a 1973 declaration of the Episcopal Conference of Belgium and a 1985 document of the Spanish Bishops' Conference); and (8) evangelism (in the WCC New Delhi Assembly statement entitled *Witness* and in a 1976 policy statement on evangelism of the USA's National Council of Churches). In the category of a parochial or peculiar concern related to social justice might even be one reference to social justice and the classless society in the 1977 *Letters of the Holy Synods to the Soviet Government* by the Russian Orthodox Church.

Such examples clearly confirm the churches' use of "social justice" in a broad, generic sense. This usage provides an interesting insight into the current practice of Christian social ethics by the churches and by the ecumenical movement. These ecclesiastical organizations tend to see links between a wide variety of contemporary social issues and problems, all of which reflects the impact that the ecumenical movement's preoccupation with "root causes" in dealing with social ills has had on all the churches.

In examining the churches' propensity to link together a number of issues under the rubric of social justice, we can gain at least one other ecumenical insight, one that represents a further challenge to the conventional wisdom concerning the necessary impact a church's context has on its theological and ethical point of view. The churches cited above (except perhaps those which have expressed the more peculiar concerns) come from widely diverse cultural contexts but yet tend to say similar things about what is entailed by social justice. As we have observed in church statements pertaining to other issues, differences in cultural contexts do not necessarily entail different ethics.

By the same token, the preceding considerations about what issues the churches relate to social justice provide further examples demonstrating that differences in theological perspective are not necessarily entailed by the doing of theology in different cultural contexts. For example, both the [Catholic] Bishops of Mozambique (in statements made in 1979 and 1983) and the United Church of Christ [USA] (in a 1977 statement on exploitative broadcasting) relate social justice and peace. And both make their appeal on these matters on the basis of themes related to the doctrine of creation.

These theological considerations point to a final insight revealed by a considera-tion of the churches' propensity to link a variety of different contemporary issues under the rubric of social justice. On every one of the issues we noted which characteristically are associated with social justice (peace, racial equality, economic development, ecology), one can identify at least two church statements which maintain different theological positions but yet agree in concluding that one of these issues is properly a dimension of social justice. In these cases it is evident once again that theological disagreements do not necessarily manifest themselves in dis-agreements about ethics. On questions of the substance of social justice, theology does not divide the churches.

The Debate about Violence

The potentially divisive aspect of social justice appears in the present debate over the legitimacy of employing violence to achieve social justice in the face of grave injustice. This consideration moves us squarely into the debate about liberation theology and its impact on Christian social ethics.

In some respects the debate about the legitimacy of the use of violence in achieving social aims is primarily a Roman Catholic debate.[4] Only thirty-two non-Roman Catholic statements have taken up the problem.[5] The problem for the Roman Catholic Church is basically that part of its community is open to the use of violence, even while the church officially condemns violence. Some national bishops' conferences in the Southern hemisphere have expressed an openness to the use of "counter-violence" on behalf of resistance and revolution. A 1986 communication of the Southern African Catholic Bishops' Conference, a 1979 pastoral letter of the Nicaraguan bishops (which contradicted the conference's earlier 1977 criticism of the use of violence), and the document entitled *Peace* of the 1968 Medellín Conference of Latin American Bishops express some openness to the use of violence or at least avoid outright condemnation of such recourse to violence. (At one point the Latin American bishops indeed reject the use of violence, but they also state that "revolutionary insurrection can be legitimate in the case of prolonged tyranny"; i.e., counter-violence by the oppressed is not totally condemned.) The Roman Catholic hierarchy, however — notably in the 1984 and 1986 instructions concerning liberation theology of its Congregation for the Doctrine of the Faith, and following the 1963 papal encyclical *Pacem in Terris* — has condemned the use of violence.

There are indications that the Vatican's concerns are having an impact. Thus the more recent 1979 conference meeting of the Latin American bishops (the Puebla Conference) did not take up the subject of violence at all. No doubt under papal influence the conference also shied away from the language of liberation theology concerning "the preferential option for the poor". Reference is made only to the responsibility of Christians to make the cause of the poor one's own.[6] Not unexpec-tedly, the Vatican's way seems to prevail in the intra-Catholic debate.

One cannot conclude, however, that the debate about a legitimate use of violence is simply one between the Northern and Southern hemispheres and thus reduce the issue to one of the impact distinct cultural contexts have on Christian thought and praxis. In one instance, there does seem to be this correlation. The Southern hemisphere bishops' conferences of Latin America and Southern Africa are pitted against the Northern hemisphere, which is dominated by the Vatican hierarchy (with the Northern agenda of non-violence prevailing).

However, there is another side to the story. One can identify at least two cases in which the debate about the legitimacy of violence is carried on by church bodies from more or less the same context within the Southern hemisphere. The previously cited 1981 statement of the All Africa Conference of Churches expresses an openness to, or at least understanding of, the use of violence against oppression. But the South African Council of Churches rejected such a use of violence in 1974. Here disagreements about the use of violence in the face of oppression do not seem necessarily to be a function of distinct cultural contexts. Likewise in the South American context, the Latin American bishops expressed some openness to the use of violence to overcome tyranny at its 1968 Medellín Conference, while in the same year the bishops of Chile condemned the use of such violence. In the case of both the African and the Latin American debates, theological disagreements are also not at stake, since all four of the church bodies in question appeal to some theme related to the second article of the creed (either to redemption or forgiveness) for authorization of their respective positions.

The debate about the legitimacy of the use of violence by Christians in order to achieve justice is still continuing as a particularly sensitive issue inside the Roman Catholic Church. But unless historical critical research on church statements could demonstrate that Southern hemisphere statements opposing violence, like that of the South African Council, have been coopted by the Northern hemisphere agenda, the debate among the churches concerning the use of violence cannot be deemed as merely the product of distinct regional, contextual agendas.

Concluding Theological and Ecumenical Reflections

The preceding exposition pointed out the diverse theological approaches employed by the different churches in reaching the same conclusion about social justice. Consequently the churches' treatment of social justice may point a way to another avenue for overcoming the present divisions of the churches. Their theological disagreements do not preclude common action or a common praxis, at least with regard to social justice.

The statements devoted to the challenge of social justice provide other insights. Virtually every logically conceivable theological mode of argumentation is employed by at least one church statement. Some base their argument for social justice on the doctrine of creation (as in a 1985 statement of the Evangelisch-Lutherische Landeskirche Hannovers). Others appeal to themes from all three articles of the creed. See, for example, two WCC assembly statements from Nairobi (1975) and Uppsala (1968), three policy statements from the years 1983, 1980, and 1975 of the USA's National Council of Churches, the papal encyclicals *Laborem Exercens* (1981) and *Octogesima Adveniens* (1971), a 1982 statement of the Nederduitse Gereformeerde Sendingkerk (South Africa), to some extent the 1987 papal encyclical *Sollicitudo Rei Socialis* and the 1963 encyclical *Pacem in Terris,* and at least by implication a 1981 resolution on the Middle East by the Christian Church (Disciples of Christ). Furthermore, a significant number of the statements urge social justice without providing any clear theological rationale.

To be sure, there are exceptions, as some argue their case on the basis of Christology or the gospel. Here we may include assorted statements of several Roman

Catholic bishops' conferences in the Southern hemisphere such as a 1984 document of the Peruvian [Catholic] Episcopal Conference, a 1983 statement of the Netherlands [Catholic] Bishops Conference, a 1971 statement of the Polish [Catholic] Bishops' Conference, a 1987 pastoral statement of the [Catholic] Episcopal Conference of Portugal, 1972 and 1971 statements of the former Canadian Catholic Conference, 1980 and 1978 statements of the USA's National Conference of Catholic Bishops, two 1984 assembly statements of the Lutheran World Federation, and assorted statements from the years 1985 and 1982 of the Uniting Church in Australia. As we previously noted, however, churches for the most part employ theological arguments which are consistent with their historic confessional positions.

It is striking, though, that a significant number of the statements addressing social justice are authorized by appeal to the doctrine of creation. This mode of argument appears more than just in the statements of the Roman Catholic, Lutheran, and Anglican churches. Such authorization for social justice appears in a number of statements of Union churches (such as those of the USA's United Church of Christ), Baptist churches (as evidenced in a 1984 policy statement of the American Baptist Churches), conservative evangelical churches of the Reformed-Presbyterian tradition (as evidenced in a 1984 resolution of the Reformed Ecumenical Synod), and ecumenical organizations (including at least four WCC statements). The dates of the statements of these church bodies indicate that they are not simply reflecting the influence of more recent limits-to-growth debate, which has fostered a return to the doctrine of creation. It is one more evidence of the fact that ethical arguments which appeal to the doctrine of creation for authorization do not necessarily lead to conservative or reactionary ethical conclusions.

It is interesting to note how the doctrine of creation is construed by the churches which appeal to the doctrine for authorization for their call to social justice. The same adaptations to the doctrine previously noted in other church statements which appealed to the doctrine of creation in order to authorize more liberal, progressive ethical conclusions are made in these statements which deal with social justice. All but three of them — a 1986 declaration of the Anglican Church of Canada, a 1973 deliverance of the United Free Church of Scotland, and the 1973 *Resolution on Farm Labor* by the USA's National Conference of Catholic Bishops (as well as perhaps a 1987 resolution of the USA's United Church of Christ and a 1972 statement on population by the USA's National Conference of Catholic Bishops) — posit a continuity between the structures of creation and redemption. And at least the Canadian church exhibits another one of the adaptations we have observed in statements concerning other issues which appealed to the doctrine of creation to authorize more liberal ethical positions. The Canadian Anglicans posit a view of human persons as relational, as by nature related to one another.

Several statements, notably those of 1980, 1978, as well as a 1972 statement on ecology of the former Lutheran Church in America which deal with social justice, include all three of the adaptations to the doctrine of creation which have been observed previously in more liberal position papers authorized by this doctrine. Not only is a continuity of creation and redemption posited along with a relational view of human persons, but also creation is construed as ongoing, as in process. We thus have further evidence challenging the conventional wisdom associated with the Barmen Declaration, namely, the idea that an ethic rooted in the doctrine of creation necessarily leads to conservative or reactionary ethical positions.

The churches' statements on social justice may serve to confirm at least one item of conventional wisdom — the wisdom inherent in the Life and Work Movement. If one considers the unanimity among the churches concerning the importance of social justice, their commitment to facilitating its achievement, then perhaps, despite disagreements on details, one may speak of a catholic consensus about social justice. In that sense church statements concerned with social justice seem to bear testimony to something like the Life and Work motto: Service/ethical commitment unites, and doctrine does not necessarily divide.

NOTES

[1] For a full discussion of the formative role a commitment to social justice has had on the WCC since the time of its inception and in the previous development of ecumenical social ethics, see Paul Abrecht, "From Oxford to Vancouver: Lessons from Fifty Years of Ecumenical Work for Economic and Social Justice", *Ecumenical Review* 40, no. 2 (April 1988): 148-52. For documentation of the commitment to social justice in the earliest documents of ecumenical social thought, see two section reports from the WCC Amsterdam Assembly, *The Church and the Disorder of Society* (1948), III, and *The Church and the International Disorder* (1948), I. See also J.H. Oldham, *The Oxford Conference: Official Report* (New York: Willett, Clark, 1937), 77.

[2] For reference to these statements and others cited subsequently in the chapter, see the section on social justice in the Appendix. Note the significant number of United or Union churches which appeal to some theme associated with the doctrine of creation as authorization for social justice. For documentation of the historic positions of the Lutheran and Roman Catholic heritages, see note 6 in chapter 4 above, as well as the discussion in the Conclusion below.

[3] The concern of liberation theology to relate justice to the alleviation of poverty is well illustrated by its preferential option for the poor. For an example of this commitment, see Gustavo Gutierrez, *The Power of the Poor in History* (Maryknoll, N.Y.: Orbis Books, 1981). For a discussion of the great recent impact of liberation theology on the ecumenical movement, see Abrecht, "From Oxford to Vancouver," 159-62.

For some of the numerous other examples of church statements which seem to reflect the commitments and influence of liberation theology, see Latin American Protestant Conference, *United to Meet the Demands of the Present Time* (1978); All Africa Conference of Churches, *Working with Christ for the Renewal of the Church* (1969), IB; Peruvian [Catholic] Episcopal Conference, *La justicia en el mundo* (1971), 3; *Christian Commitment for a New Nicaragua: Pastoral Letter of the Nicaraguan [Catholic] Bishops* (1979), I, II(a)-(e); Canadian Conference of Catholic Bishops, *Ethical Choices and Political Challenges* (1983), 15; Evangelical Church of Lutheran Confession in Brazil, *Our Social Responsibility* (1976), 2; Presbyterian Church in the Republic of Korea, *Statement of Korean Christians* (1973); Evangelical Methodist Church of Argentina, *Social Service and Action: Foundations in Biblical Theology* (n.d.), I; World Methodist Council, *Statement on Poverty and the North-South Debate* (1981); United Church of Canada, *Human Rights and International Affairs: Do Not Let the World Forget Us* (1982); United Church of Christ [USA], *Global Debt Crisis* (1987); National Conference of Catholic Bishops [USA], *Economic Justice for All* (1986), PM 16, 87-88, 258, 260, 274; Reformed-Roman Catholic Joint Commission, *The Presence of Christ in Church and World* (1977), 49, 54; WCC Vancouver Assembly, *Message from the Sixth Assembly of the WCC* (1983); WCC Vancouver Assembly Issue Group Report, *Moving towards Participation* (1983), Int.

[4] For a discussion of the debate in the Roman Catholic Church about violence, see Charles Villa-Vicencio, *Between Christ and Caesar* (Grand Rapids, Mich.: Wm. B. Eerdmans, 1986), 130-33. Also cited is a papal speech calling for non-violence. For an example of liberation theology's openness to the use of violence, see G. Gutierrez, *A Theology of Liberation* (Maryknoll, N.Y.: Orbis Books, 1988), 108-9, 126.

[5] The thirty-two are a 1983 policy statement on Latin America and a 1975 policy statement on the Middle East of the USA's National Council of Churches, a 1971 resolution on the WCC Program to Combat Racism by the Evangelische Kirche in Deutschland, a 1984 statement of Chile's Fellowship of Christian Churches, a 1981 declaration of the All Africa Conference of Churches, a 1982 message of the [Orthodox] Ecumenical Patriarchate of Constantinople, 1975 and 1970 statements of the Evangelisch-

Lutherische Landeskirche Hannovers, a 1974 word of the Evangelisch-Lutherische Kirche in Bayern, a 1970 pronouncement on the WCC Program to Combat Racism by the Evangelische Landeskirche in Württemberg, a 1971 resolution on the same subject as well as a 1974 word on violence by the Evangelisch-Lutherische Kirche in Bayern, a 1978 resolution of the Eglise de la Confession d'Augsbourg d'Alsace et de Lorraine, 1980 and 1979 statements of the Presbyterian Church of Southern Africa, 1963 and 1964 resolutions of the Reformed Church in America, a 1988 policy statement of the Presbyterian Church (USA), a resolution on war and violence (5) by the Anglican community's Lambeth Conference, a 1979 resolution on war of the Episcopal Church [USA] (which endorsed the Lambeth Conference resolution), a 1970 resolution devoted only to the WCC's Program to Combat Racism by the Evangelische Kirche in Hessen und Nassau, a 1971 declaration on the same subject by the Evangelische Kirche im Rheinland, a 1982 declaration on peace by the Evangelische Kirche von Westfalen, a 1968 resolution concerning revolution by the Christian Church (Disciples of Christ), as well as a 1974 statement of the South African Council of Churches, a 1987 resolution of the Mennonite Church [USA], a joint 1983 statement of the Mennonite Church, General Conference [USA], and the Mennonite Church [USA], a 1977 resolution of the Church of the Brethren [USA], a 1970 statement of the Baptist Union of Great Britain and Ireland, and, by the National Association of Evangelicals [USA], a 1987 anniversary resolution, a 1986 resolution on apartheid, and a 1965 resolution on civil rights.

See also Eglise de la Confession d'Augsbourg d'Alsace et de Lorraine, *Résolution* [concernant le Programme de Lutte contre le Racisme], 1978, (5); *Entschliessung der Synode der Evangelischen Kirche in Deutschland betreffend das ökumenische Programm zur Bekämpfung des Rassismus* (1971); Presbyterian Church of Southern Africa, *Church and Nation* (1980), 229, clause 10; Presbyterian Church of Southern Africa, *Church and Nation, South Africa* (1979), clauses 25, 26, 28; Evangelische Kirche im Rheinland, *Erklärung und Beschlüsse der Landessynode 1971 zum ökumenischen Programm zur Bekämpfung des Rassismus* (1971), B, D/1. All of the other pertinent statements are noted in the section on social justice in the Appendix.

[6] For a full discussion, see Villa-Vicencio, *Between Christ and Caesar,* 130-33.

9. Socio-political Ideologies

"I am the Lord your God, who brought you out of the land of Egypt, out of the house of bondage. You shall have no other gods before me" (Ex. 20:1-2); "Learn not the ways of the nations, nor be dismayed at the signs of the heavens because the nations are dismayed at them, for the customs of the people are false" (Jer. 10:2-3). Such biblical injunctions clearly suggest the critical perspective enjoined on the Judeo-Christian community with regard to its attitude towards socio-political ideologies. But with regard to Christianity's relationship to the two prevailing socio-political ideologies of the last half of our century — capitalism and communism — the situation is more complex.

Analysts of social history have long noted the complex though intimate relationship between Christianity's cultural dominance in the West and the emergence of liberal capitalism. One could cite a certain biblical precedent for this development. The impressive economic success of the Solomonic Empire and of the two kingdoms after their civil war, the result of their wise capitalist investments and ventures, is clearly presented by the biblical accounts as in no way incompatible with Israel's faith (1 Kings 10:11-12, 22-29; 2 Kings 3:4; 2 Chron. 9:21-22). And a kind of capitalism, at least private ownership in the sense of land ownership by the tribes, seems to have been sanctioned by Yahweh, through Joshua and Moses as his spokesmen (Josh. 13-21; Num. 32:1-42; 33:54). Also note the private property legitimately possessed by the patriarchs (Gen. 13:3; 17:8; cf. Lev. 25:13ff.).

The biblical witness, however, also suggests that Christianity is compatible with certain forms of socialism. The early church's praxis of sharing all goods in common represented a kind of premodern form of communist praxis (Acts 4:32-37). And certain propensities in the direction of the collective ownership of property are evident in the Old Testament as well (Deut. 24:19-22).

Given the diversity of the biblical witness and the church's history on these matters, it is hardly surprising to identify pronounced diversity among the churches with regard to their attitudes concerning Christianity's relationship to ideologies such as capitalism and communism. (Henceforth in discussing communism, we will have in mind only its realization in the modern Communist movement — and thus will speak of a capital-C Communism.) As with the other issues already considered, these differences among the churches are largely not related to theological disagreements but rather to contextual, or geographical, differences. Even such geographical considerations, however, do not fully succeed in explaining the disagreements among the churches with regard to their views on Christianity's relationship to capitalism and Communism. My suspicion is that sociological differences — namely, the social class of the majority of those responsible for drafting the statements — may be the determinative factor in differences among the churches on Christianity's relationship to these ideologies. This speculation warrants further study. In this context, however, our task is to summarize prevailing trends in the statements on these subjects. We first consider those which address the relationship of Christianity to Communism or socialism.

The Relation of Christianity to Communism/Socialism

Although there has been marked disagreement among the churches on this issue, at least before the recent socio-economic and political developments in Eastern Europe, a report on the statements addressed to the question which were issued before these Eastern bloc developments can be decidedly brief. In short, there are no patterns to be observed in the disagreements among the churches with regard to the Christian attitude towards Communism or socialism. Disagreements among church bodies on this issue are not necessarily conditioned by their different geographical contexts or by theological differences with one another.[1]

On the whole, church bodies issuing statements on this question authorize their positions with theological arguments compatible with the characteristically historic approach of their respective denominational tradition. For example, the Presbyterian-Reformed Church in Cuba, in harmony with the prevailing emphases of the Calvinist heritage, argues for its support for Communism in a 1977 statement by appeal to the gospel. Likewise one can identify a number of Roman Catholic statements on the subject which authorize their positions by appeal to something like the classic natural-law tradition.[2]

In fact a large number of the statements concerning this matter are issued by Roman Catholic bodies. This is indicative of the present controversy inside the Catholic Church brought about by the impact of liberation theology on certain segments of the church.[3] In any case, a significant number of these statements follow the theological orientation after Vatican II of arguing from a perspective informed by the doctrine of creation, but one in which creation is construed as subordinated to redemption.[4] This viewpoint is espoused by statements critical of Communism such as the 1964 papal encyclical *Ecclesiam Suam,* the 1981 encyclical *Laborem Exercens,* the 1984 instruction on liberation theology by the Vatican's Congregation for the Doctrine of the Faith, a 1984 document of the Peruvian [Catholic] Episcopal Conference, and to some extent the 1971 papal encyclical *Octogesima Adveniens.*

There are exceptions to the churches' reliance on their historic denominational perspective. For example, the [Catholic] Bishops' Conference of the Philippines criticizes Communism by way of an appeal to the gospel in their 1987 statement on justice and peace. Also see the 1968 pastoral letter of the bishops of Chile, a 1964 collective letter of the National Conference of [Catholic] Bishops of Brazil, a 1983 statement of the Irish Episcopal Conference, a 1977 statement of the Canadian Conference of Catholic Bishops, and the encyclical *Octogesima Adveniens.* A 1968 resolution of the Evangelical Lutheran Church in Tanzania authorizes its openness to socialism on grounds of ecclesiology (or the "inheritance of the church").

Statements of ecumenical organizations generally tend to rely on mixed arguments, incorporating appeals both to some theme related to the doctrine of creation and to another theme related to Christology. A 1971 statement of the Fédération Protestante de France in support of socialism as well as criticisms of such an ideology by a

1981 statement of the All Africa Conference of Churches (entitled *The Gospel — Good News for the Poor and Oppressed*) and a 1966 resolution of the USA's National Association of Evangelicals employ this sort of theological viewpoint. WCC statements on the subject, before the beginnings of the limits-to-growth debate, tend to reflect the council's tendency to distrust ethical arguments rooted in the doctrine of creation or a related theme. It is true that anthropology, perhaps related to eschatology and Christology, authorizes a statement of the Amsterdam Assembly concerning Communism and capitalism. In subsequent assemblies through 1975, however, the WCC's pronouncements on the subject shied away from arguments rooted in the doctrine of creation.

The lack of patterns, either contextual or theological, concerning the disagreements among the churches about Christianity's compatibility with Communism/socialism is readily apparent. Once again such data challenge the conventional wisdom about ecumenical social ethics.

With regard to context, one finds church bodies located in the third world on both sides of the issue. For example, the Presbyterian-Reformed Church in Cuba and the 1971 Peruvian [Catholic] Episcopal Conference expressed support for at least certain values of Communism. (The Presbyterian position was authorized by appeal to the gospel; the Peruvian Catholics argued on the basis of the character of the created order.) But church bodies from the same general regions, specifically Roman Catholic bishops' conferences in Latin America, Peru (in 1984), Chile, the Philippines, and to some extent Southern Africa, as well as a 1981 statement of the All Africa Conference of Churches *(The Gospel — Good News to the Poor and Oppressed)* and a 1986 declaration of the Dutch Reformed Church (South Africa) offer critiques of Communism or socialism. (Each of these church bodies relies on a different configuration of theological warrants.)

It is evident that sharing a similar context is not a factor that determines common ethical or theological perspectives. This point is further supported when we note the disagreement among five statements issued with a clear position on the subject by church bodies then located in Communist nations. The Presbyterian-Reformed Church in Cuba and a 1986 message of the Russian Orthodox Church (3.34) express approval of Communist themes, while a 1971 document of the Bund der Evangelischen Kirchen in der DDR, a 1980 resolution of the Vereinigte Evangelisch-Lutherische Kirche in der DDR, and a 1968 pastoral letter of the Catholic Bishops of Chile note the tensions between Marxism and the Christian faith. (The second and third statements appeal to themes related to the doctrine of creation to authorize their respective positions.)

When one considers the fact that for the position taken by every one of the statements cited in the preceding paragraphs there is at least one statement issued by a church body from the West or an international organization which takes the same position on Communism as one of the former Eastern bloc or third-world church statements we have noted, it is evident that the conventional wisdom concerning the supposedly necessary impact distinct contexts have on ethics and theology is once again called into question. In these cases, some church bodies share more in common in their assessment of Communism with church bodies located in radically different contexts than they do with church bodies in their own context. In different contexts, theology and ethics do not necessarily differ.

A second pattern missing in the statements pertains to theology. Already we have observed instances where church bodies shared similar conclusions about Communism/socialism, though they disagreed on theological authorization. For example, in rejecting Communism, a 1967 statement of the USA's National Association of Evangelicals appeals to the gospel, whereas the important 1937 papal encyclical *Divini Redemptoris* does so by appeal to natural law.

By the same token, virtually every argument employed by church statements condemning Communism has been utilized by other church bodies who see a compatibility between Christianity and Communism or socialism. For example, the argument by American evangelicals on grounds of the gospel is shared by the 1977 statement of the Presbyterian-Reformed Church in Cuba. The Cubans, however, employ the argument to highlight the compatibility of Communism with Christianity.

In like manner the argument against Communism by way of appeal to themes related to the doctrine of creation, offered by the 1937 papal encyclical and by the statement on justice of the 1968 Medellín Conference of the Latin American [Catholic] Bishops, is shared by the 1971 statement of the Peruvian [Catholic] Episcopal Conference in lauding Communist compatibility with Christianity.

It is evident from these examples that the theological disagreements are not the primary cause of disagreements among the churches concerning their attitudes towards Communism and socialism. Such theological disagreements do not necessarily mandate disagreements on the question of Communism.

The foregoing reflections lead to the question of what does account for disagreements among the churches with regard to a proper Christian attitude towards Communism. No unequivocally valid generalizations have been ascertained. With regard to disagreements between church bodies which agree on a common theological orientation, however, some suggestions can be offered. These are seen most clearly in the case of statements which share a common theological orientation in dealing with ethics from the perspective of the doctrine of creation but disagree in their assessment of Communism.

On the side of a positive evaluation of Communism from the perspective of the doctrine of creation, we find the 1971 statement of the Peruvian [Catholic] Episcopal Conference. It speaks of creation in terms of the good which God created to be placed at the service of all. By contrast, when construing creation as their authorization for rejecting Communism, both the papal encyclical *Divini Redemptoris* and the Latin American [Catholic] Bishops' Medellín Conference statement on justice emphasize individuality or freedom in creation.

What seems to divide these pairs of statements is the respective portrayals of the structures of creation. This is a matter for philosophy, since theology characteristically relies on philosophical concepts in the task of depicting an ontology of the created order. Consequently, it follows that much like the factors which distinguished the church statements on apartheid and a few other issues, the churches' disagreements on social issues (at least with respect to Communism/socialism) seem related to philosophical disagreements concerning the most appropriate philosophical conceptions to emphasize in depicting the created order. Such disagreements, then, are not disagreements about the nature of the Christian faith. Consequently it seems to follow that disagreements among the churches about the proper attitude towards Communism do not authorize schism between the churches; they are simply not church-dividing disagreements.

The reference to church bodies which rely on the doctrine of creation for authorization for their particular position on Communism raises one additional point which challenges the conventional wisdom on ecumenical social ethics. The fact that the 1971 statement of the Peruvian [Catholic] Episcopal Conference as well as to some extent a document of the WCC Amsterdam Assembly (entitled *The Church and the Disorder of Society*) and a 1986 message on war and peace of the Russian Orthodox Church (3.34) discern certain compatibilities between Christianity and Communism by way of arguments rooted in doctrinal themes related to the doctrine of creation certainly entails a challenge to the conventional wisdom associated with the Barmen Declaration. In this case, contrary to the conventional wisdom, appeals to themes related to the doctrine of creation have not issued in a conservative, reactionary ethic, but rather in the most radical of ethics imaginable to Western intellectuals in a post-1950s, pre-Soviet disintegration era — the endorsement of Communism. Likewise, recall how Christology or the gospel authorizes more conservative ethical positions, such as condemnation of Communism by the USA's National Association of Evangelicals (in 1967) and by the WCC Evanston and Nairobi assemblies.

The three creation-oriented affirmations of Communism also share a common construal of the doctrine of creation which confirms an observation gradually developed in this volume. It has been noted in numerous cases that when the doctrine of creation succeeds in authorizing a more liberal ethic, the statement invariably makes one of several adjustments to the doctrine. One of the adjustments we have observed repeatedly is that such church statements construe creation's structures as correlating, and not conflicting, with the structures of the gospel. The three statements in question at this point all posit such a correlation, at least insofar as they posit appeals to theological themes other than the doctrine of creation at other points in each statement for purposes of authorizing positions taken on other issues. (The themes of liberation theology seem especially evident in the Peruvian Catholic statement, insofar as an appeal is made to identify with the oppressed in response to the call of Christ.)

Each of the three statements we have been considering — the 1986 message on war and peace of the Russian Orthodox Church, the 1971 statement of the Peruvian [Catholic] Episcopal Conference, and the pertinent WCC Amsterdam Assembly statement *The Church and the Disorder of Society* — provides a pertinent insight regarding the present overall climate in the ecumenical grappling with issues of Christianity's relationship to Marxism. The Russian statement raised the question of how it and other church bodies in the Soviet Union would evaluate Communism in view of the new freedoms granted by the Gorbachev reforms. The Peruvian statement highlights tensions on this issue inside the Roman Catholic Church. The Amsterdam Assembly statement bespeaks the WCC's overall efforts to plead for a Christian pluralism with regard to the Christian attitude towards Communism and capitalism. Both of these matters belong together to some extent.

At the outset of this section, several documents of the Roman Catholic hierarchy which are quite critical of Communism were cited. This critical Vatican perspective dates to at least 1937 and the encyclical *Divini Redemptoris*. In more recent years, however, especially as related to the controversy inside the Roman Catholic Church over liberation theology, the hierarchy has turned up the heat on Communism to a fever pitch. (The 1984 instruction on liberation theology by the Congregation for the Doctrine of the Faith is the most well known but by no means sole instance of this pressure.)

The Vatican pressure has had its impact. It may be manifest in critical perspectives towards Communism taken in 1987 by the [Catholic] Bishops' Conference of the

Philippines and in 1986 by the Southern African Catholic Bishops' Conference. It is also likely that the political dynamics in these regions may have played more of a role in these statements' negative evaluation of Communism. (Note the critique of Communism in 1968 by the Catholic Bishops of Chile.) But the pressure seems most apparent in a 1986 document of the Peruvian [Catholic] Episcopal Conference, the same conference which endorsed a kind of Communist vision in 1971.

In the more recent Peruvian Catholic statement, one finds none of the earlier rhetoric about Christians seeing in socialist currents certain aspirations which correspond to Christian aspirations. Rather, there is only criticism of Communism. In fact, a kind of affirmation of capitalism is provided, at least insofar as the right of private property or ownership is endorsed. (It is interesting to note that although the document relies on the doctrines of human persons and creation at these points, these first-article themes are subordinated to the gospel in a manner akin to other post-Vatican II denunciations of Communism by the Roman Catholic hierarchy.) The Peruvian bishops' apparent retraction of their earlier 1971 views on Communism confirms an observation made in the chapter concerning church statements on social justice. It is evident that in controversial matters inside the Catholic Church, at least with respect to official church documents, the Vatican hierarchy is still influencing positions taken.

In such influence, however, the Vatican is not imposing a merely Western agenda on the Southern hemisphere with regard to anti-Communism, any more than such a case could be made in the controversy about the use of violence in the quest for social justice. There is at least one non-Roman Catholic statement from a church body in the Southern hemisphere which opposes Communism. The 1981 statement of the All Africa Conference of Churches *(The Gospel — Good News for the Poor and Oppressed)* took such a position. With church bodies in the Southern hemisphere still firmly on both sides of the debate about Communism, it is perhaps unfair to characterize the debate inside the Roman Catholic Church merely in terms of a struggle between different cultural agendas.

Indeed, the argument that the Vatican is exercising a Western cultural dominance on bishops' conferences in the South overlooks the reciprocal impact that the debate seems to have had on the hierarchy. One further observation concerning the more recent 1984 statement of the Peruvian [Catholic] Episcopal Conference is pertinent.

The bishops do condemn Marxism and endorse capitalism in the sense of private ownership. In their call for "universal ownership", however, one senses an openness to a kind of collectivism. Such modification of the concept of private ownership in the direction of the socialist emphasis on the social responsibility one has in handling goods has had its impact on the Roman Catholic hierarchy, as we shall see when examining Roman Catholic statements on capitalism.

This development in Roman Catholic social thought is in harmony with long-standing commitments of the ecumenical movement. The pertinent WCC Amsterdam Assembly statement, *The Church and the Disorder of Society,* provides an illustrative glimpse of this commitment. As such, it warrants consideration as a helpful entrée for a consideration of the churches' statements pertaining to capitalism as well as in shedding further light on present Roman Catholic social thought.

Previously in this section, we noted that the WCC has largely been committed to pleading for a kind of pluralism with regard to the relationship between Communism and capitalism. Except for some relatively recent statements without its assemblies' approval, the council has sought to assess critically the strengths and weaknesses of both capitalism and Communism, to sketch paths which might hold promise for a rapprochement of these ideologies without taking sides.[5]

These commitments clearly were foreshadowed in the council's Amsterdam Assembly.[6] Though only receiving the document, the assembly took official cognizance of the debate between capitalism and Communism, claiming that "the Church cannot resolve the debate." Weaknesses of both ideologies are criticized. Subsequently, following references to the doctrine of man as "created and called to be a free being", the statement recognizes how Communism makes a strong appeal to the masses and suggests that "the hand of God" should be recognized in certain Communist movements. Then follows a final laudatory comment: "Christians should realize that for many, especially for many young men and women, Communism seems to stand for a vision of human equality and universal brotherhood for which they were prepared by Christian influences."[7] The pertinent section of the document closes with another critique of both Communism and capitalism. It is asserted that these two extremes are not the only alternatives. Subsequently a plea is made to seek new solutions.

This sort of irenic approach to the relationship between Communism and capitalism, endeavoring to appreciate the ambiguities and refusing to pick sides, typifies other WCC assembly statements, such as its Evanston Assembly statement *Social Problems — The Responsible Society in a World Perspective*. Even in the more critical evaluations of Communism by the WCC Nairobi Assembly, at least one of the relevant statements, *Seeking Community: The Common Search of People of Various Faiths, Cultures, and Ideologies,* does acknowledge some practical areas in which this ideology and Christian faith might be compatible.

Despite the recent neglect inside segments of the council itself of this more irenic approach to the problem of relating Communism and capitalism (the WCC Vancouver Assembly only tangentially addressed the question of the relationship of Christianity to ideologies, though it still may have relied on this sort of irenic approach), exposition of the churches' statements on Christianity's relation to capitalism shows further how the irenic approach which dominated in the WCC's earlier days has developed and seems to be having an influence on some Roman Catholic thinking.[8] An analysis of these statements concerning the relationship of Christianity and capitalism shows that, just as is the case in regard to church statements on Communism, so these statements challenge many of the conventional stereotypes about ecumenical social ethics.

The Relation of Christianity to Capitalism

Since relatively few church statements have addressed the theoretical question of Christianity's relationship to capitalism, under this rubric I consider also the relatively more numerous statements which have taken up a practical side of this more theoretical question, namely, the issue of the proper Christian attitude towards private property. Inasmuch as so many of these statements are the same statements as those which addressed the relationship of Christianity and Communism, the results of the analysis in this section are akin to the data adduced with regard to the question of Christianity's relationship to Communism. We shall observe once again that differences in geographical context and theological disagreements are not necessarily determinative of disagreements in ethics. To some extent the statements devoted to this issue confirm aspects of the conventional wisdom associated with the Barmen Declaration. The data, however, again show some exceptions to this propensity.

With regard to the fundamental irrelevance of geographical context in determining disagreements on the subject of Christianity's relationship to capitalism, it should be noted that no church body in Eastern Europe has addressed the issue; only one church from a Communist nation, the Presbyterian-Reformed Church in Cuba, has done so.[9] Also it should be noted that more of the significant statements condemn capitalism than endorse it. In terms of the Southern and Northern hemispheres, however, it can be noted that church bodies from both hemispheres can be found on either side of the debate concerning capitalism or private property. For example, the right to private ownership is affirmed in both a 1970 statement of the Lutheran Church of Australia, a 1986 statement of the [Catholic] Episcopal Conference of the Pacific, and a 1983 statement of the Paraguay (Catholic) Bishops' Conference. (The first two authorize their position from the doctrine of creation.) In contrast, capitalism is condemned in both a 1981 statement of the All Africa Conference of Churches and a statement on justice of the 1968 Medellín Conference of the Latin American [Catholic] Bishops. (The latter document is authorized by an appeal to the doctrine of human persons.)

It is evident that differences in cultural context do not mandate disagreements among church bodies on the question of Christianity's relationship to capitalism. For every disagreement one of these Southern hemisphere church bodies might have with a church body from the West or an international organization, there is another church body from the same context with which it is in disagreement. Even the fact that they share a common geographical location and a common denominational heritage did not preclude the apparent disagreement about capitalism between the Conference of Latin American Bishops and the Paraguay Bishops' Conference.

This observation confirms a point made repeatedly throughout this book. The ecumenical establishment needs to begin seriously to reconsider one of its basic suppositions, namely, its stress on contextual theology and the role of context. Analysis of the churches' social statements suggests that different contexts do not necessarily lead to a difference in theology or ethics.

The preceding also provides further evidence for the case that the disagreements among the churches concerning their respective evaluations of capitalism and private ownership are not necessarily theologically related. In the Southern hemisphere church bodies noted, we identified at least one on each side of the issue which had appealed to a theme related to the doctrine of creation in order to make its particular point. Likewise on both sides of the debate one can find arguments which draw upon both the doctrine of creation and Christology or the gospel in some way. On the side of those who condemn capitalism with such warrants we can identify a 1981 statement of the All Africa Conference of Churches entitled *The Gospel — Good News to the Poor and Oppressed.* On the side of those which endorse capitalism in some form by means of an appeal to the doctrine of creation, likely grounded in Christology, is the Second Vatican Council's pastoral constitution *Gaudium et Spes,* a 1981 papal encyclical *Laborem Exercens,* a 1983 statement of the Italian [Catholic] Episcopal Conference, and a 1980 statement of the Arbeitsgemeinschaft Christlicher Kirchen in des Bundesrepublik Deutschland und Berlin (West).

To the extent that proponents of the same theological orientation can still disagree about capitalism, it follows that the disagreement itself is not ultimately based on theology. In cases, then, where the partners in a disagreement about capitalism also disagree theologically, it cannot be the case that theology itself is necessarily the deepest level of their disagreement. The conclusion is by now familiar. Insofar as theological disagreement is not ultimately at stake in the disagreement among the churches about capitalism, then the disagreement cannot be a matter of the faith. As such, there are no legitimate grounds for considering it to be a church-dividing issue.

The statements pertaining to capitalism also shed light on the validity of the conventional wisdom associated with the Barmen Declaration. In a sense this wisdom, with regard to the propensity of theological arguments rooted in Christology to authorize a more liberal ethic, seems confirmed to some extent. There is perhaps only one church statement, a 1978 statement on justice of the USA's National Conference of Catholic Bishops, which seems to argue for the more conservative defense of capitalism on grounds of an appeal to Christology or the gospel. Rather, the prevailing argument for endorsement of this more conservative position is an appeal to the doctrine of creation or some theme associated with it.

There is indeed something accurate about the perceptions of the conventional wisdom. One can identify a certain conservative propensity, at least a tolerance for ambiguity, which is associated with theological arguments for an ethic rooted in the doctrine of creation. Correspondingly, there is a drift in the direction of at least idealism, if not liberalism, in an ethic authorized by Christology. The data indicate, however, that these are tendencies, not logically unavoidable outcomes.

In at least the one instance previously noted, Christology does not authorize the more liberal position in the debate on capitalism but is actually employed by the USA's National Conference of Catholic Bishops to endorse capitalism (or at least private property), which represents the more conservative position. Likewise, the doctrine of creation is employed by several church bodies in order to authorize their more liberal conclusion about capitalism, namely, to criticize it. Such a theological orientation characterizes the criticism of free-market economy in a 1982 report of the WCC Sub-Unit on Church and Society, in a document of the council's Amsterdam Assembly entitled *The Church and the Disorder of Society,* in a document entitled *Justice* of the 1968 Medellín Conference of the Latin American [Catholic] Bishops, in a 1985 statement of the [Catholic] Bishops of the Netherlands, and perhaps in a 1984 statement of Chile's Fellowship of Christian Churches. The same previously observed patterns of adjustments made to the doctrine of creation when the doctrine functions to authorize more liberal ethical positions pertain in this case. All of these statements posit a continuity of creation and redemption; the structures of the created order are construed, not as in conflict with, but as complementary to, the gospel. For example, a kind of Eastern Orthodox notion of *theosis,* the idea that creation is becoming divinized and more akin to the stature of Christ, is endorsed by the WCC's 1982 report. Other statements which condemn capitalism while positing a continuity of creation and redemption, at least by implication, are the 1981 statement of the All Africa Conference of Churches and the 1971 statement of the Peruvian [Catholic] Episcopal Conference which we have been considering.

Once again it is evident how the conventional wisdom must be challenged. Given the proper theological adjustments, the doctrine of creation need not necessarily function to authorize only a conservative, reactionary ethic.

The preceding references to the statements of the WCC as well as of the two Roman Catholic bishops' conferences, which criticized capitalism from the perspective of the doctrine of creation, open the way to a final consideration in this chapter. In the previous section, a kind of irenic, mediating position was observed in the WCC, and increasingly in the Roman Catholic Church, with regard to the relationship between capitalism and Communism. Three of these statements exhibit these commitments, tempering their critique of capitalism with critiques of Communism or socialism. A final evaluation of such a perspective, as articulated in the statements, requires consideration.

The Debate on Capitalism versus Marxism

We have noted the general Roman Catholic critique of non-capitalist, socialist/ Marxist economics. Consequently, it is all the more striking to reflect again on the critiques of capitalism in the bishops' conference statements of Latin American, Peruvian, and Netherlander bishops. The point is made even more strikingly by an appreciation of the fact that in at least two documents of the Roman Catholic hierarchy, which otherwise endorse capitalism, one finds critiques of certain aspects of capitalism. The two encyclicals in question are *Populorum Progressio* (1967) and *Laborem Exercens* (1981). Some of their points also reappear in *Instruction on Christian Freedom and Liberation,* issued in 1986 by the church's Congregation for the Doctrine of the Faith, as well as in a 1986 pastoral letter on the economy by the USA's National Conference of Catholic Bishops.

Other interpreters have noted a developing maturation in Roman Catholic moral theology on the question of private property, and so of capitalism. We first noticed something of this in the 1984 statement of the Peruvian [Catholic] Episcopal Conference. The Peruvians endorsed capitalism, but in a qualified sense. It was speculated whether their position might be chastened by the bishops' earlier endorsement of Marxism.[10]

In any case, the documents of the Roman Catholic hierarchy cited above seem to follow in this line of thought. Ownership of private property is endorsed, but not as an absolute right. Also affirmed are competitive, presumably capitalistic markets. However, ownership of goods must be understood in relation to the right of all to the common use of goods. In short, private ownership must always be subordinated to the common good. To the extent that Western capitalist economies violate these principles, or place a "priority on capital over labor", these Roman Catholic documents subject capitalism to criticism.

With regard to the speculation that perhaps at this point the Roman Catholic hierarchy has felt some of the influences of the Marxism associated with proponents of liberation theology in the church, it is also worth noting the calls for participatory management by *Populorum Progressio* as well as for a kind of socialization of goods by *Laborem Exercens* and by the 1986 Vatican document on liberation theology, and to some extent by its 1987 encyclical *Sollicitudo Rei Socialis*. It is interesting to note that in all of these statements but one, the doctrine of creation plays some role in the statements, even as authorization for this openness to socializing tendencies. In all cases, however, creation is subordinated to Christology or redemption, in line with developments in the Second Vatican Council. It is also interesting to note that a view of human beings as by nature related to each other and to their environment also is employed by at least three of the statements.[11]

Though with a prejudice towards capitalism, these three statements seem to propose a kind of middle ground, a way of reconciling capitalism and Marxism/ socialism. That this may be a way of understanding this recent direction in contemporary Roman Catholic thought is further supported by noting that the critiques of capitalism already cited in the 1968 Medellín Conference statement of the Conference of Latin American Bishops and the 1985 statement of the [Catholic] Bishops of the Netherlands also include critiques of Communism or state socialism. A similar effort to find a middle ground was expressed by the USA's National Conference of Catholic Bishops in its 1974 *Statement on the World Food Crisis,* as the American bishops expressed an openness to modifying the free-market system "when it stands in the way of justice". There appears to be a genuine movement in Roman Catholic moral theology, at the highest levels, towards finding an irenic middle ground, not unlike that which has characterized many statements of the WCC, in the dispute between Marxism/Communism and capitalism.

The case for understanding the WCC's normative or historic position as an effort to find a middle way between Marxism and capitalism is somewhat strengthened in light of its statements on capitalism. It is true that five WCC assembly statements do criticize capitalism. Of these five, however, two either include a critique of Communism or try to propose a middle ground between Communism and capitalism. Of all the statements, only one (from Vancouver) is from an assembly which did not have a single statement issued which advocated such a middle ground. Perhaps the Vancouver Assembly statement is indicative of a certain recent decline in influence of this orientation in the council. But even this statement is quite irenic in its critique of capitalism.

In any case, some segments of the WCC have continued to develop this irenic posture towards the debate on the virtues of capitalism and Communism. To that extent, the more recent directions of the council and of the Roman Catholic hierarchy provide interesting mutual support.

One of the more interesting recent turns in the development of the WCC's pluralistic, irenic approach to the problem deserves attention in closing. In the WCC's 1979 Conference on Faith, Science and the Future, in the fifth section of a report entitled *Restructuring the Industrial and Urban Environment,* the conference offers a purportedly descriptive remark which is of genuine interest in resolving the debate. The report reads: "However, in this century, especially since the depression of the thirties and World War II, nations have sought ways of managing their economies that fall somewhere between the polarized extremes of Adam Smith and Karl Marx. Over this period, we have therefore witnessed the emergence in some western countries of the 'mixed' economy with the balance of investment more or less evenly divided between the demands of the public and the private sectors."[12]

To the degree that these descriptive remarks can be considered to possess a prescriptive status, the WCC was apparently opening new lanes for resolving the debate between capitalism and Communism. Already the analysis here has shown how and why the disagreements about Christianity's relationship to these ideologies need not be church dividing. However, the reflections of the main lines of the WCC in tandem with newer directions in the Roman Catholic Church suggest that perhaps ecumenical ethics (at least by articulating and calling attention to the present economic realities) might be able to contribute at least in some small way to the task of overcoming the theoretical disagreement between Communism and capitalism, a disagreement which the recent events in Eastern Europe in themselves will not likely resolve. The debate will remain relevant, deserving serious theological attention, as long as the Western democracies continue to endorse socialist-inspired government programs and even use those programs to stimulate their economies.

NOTES

¹ For references to these statements and others cited in this section, see the section in the Appendix on the relationship of Christianity to Communism/socialism.

² For a discussion and documentation of the historic positions of the Reformed, Lutheran, and Roman Catholic traditions, see chapter 1, notes 7, 12, 21-24, and chapter 4, note 6.

³ For a description of this debate, see Charles Villa-Vicencio, *Between Christ and Caesar* (Grand Rapids, Mich.: Wm. B. Eerdmans, 1986), 134-35.

⁴ The pertinent text in the Second Vatican Council which maintains the subordination of creation to redemption and the gospel is cited on p.92 above. This tendency has more venerable roots, tracing back at least to the 1302 papal bull *Unam Sanctam*.

⁵ For a description of the council's movement away from this agenda to a more parochial advocacy of socialism, see Paul Abrecht, "From Oxford to Vancouver: Lessons from Fifty Years of Ecumenical Work for Economic and Social Justice", *Ecumenical Review* 40, no. 2 (April 1988): 164. As a prime example of such a parochial document, largely marked by the influence of liberation theology, Abrecht cites a report prepared by the council's Commission for the Churches' Participation in Development, *Towards a Church in Solidarity with the Poor* (1980), which was approved by the council's Central Committee.

⁶ WCC Amsterdam Assembly Section Report, *The Church and the Disorder of Society* (1948), II-IV.

⁷ For reference to the quotation and the following exposition of the statement, see ibid., IV.

⁸ For the relevant statement in the WCC Vancouver Assembly, see *Message from the Sixth Assembly* (1983).

⁹ For references to these statements and others cited in this section, see the section in the Appendix on the relationship of Christianity to capitalism. It is true that during the transition stage to the Sandinista government, the Nicaraguan [Catholic] Bishops, in *Christian Commitment for a New Nicaragua* (1979), I, did criticize capitalism.

¹⁰ *Document of the Peruvian [Catholic] Episcopal Conference on the Theology of Liberation* (1984), 41-49, 51, 80, 28, 15-16. For reference to an interpreter who has identified this development, see Joseph Gremillion, "Overview and Prospectus", in *The Gospel of Peace and Justice: Catholic Social Teaching since Pope John* (Maryknoll, N.Y.: Orbis Books, 1976), 27.

¹¹ The relevant documents of the Roman Catholic Church are *Populorum Progressio* (1967), 28, 23, 22, 17; *Laborem Exercens* (1981), 12-16, 27, 1; Congregation for the Doctrine of the Faith, *Instruction on Christian Freedom and Liberation* (1986), 86, 89, 99, 80-82, 74, 73, 64, 60, 54, 30, 27; *Sollicitudo Rei Socialis* (1987), 42, 41, 21, 20, 47-49, 33, 1-3. Cf. the Vatican II document *Gaudium et Spes,* 22. The development of an appeal to a kind of relational view of human beings when dealing with these issues, with a greater emphasis on human interdependence, has been noted by Gremillion, "Overview and Prospectus", 24ff. He sees its origins in the 1961 papal encyclical *Mater et Magistra,* 59ff.

¹² For a similar proposal, see Reformed Ecumenical Synod, *Pastoral Statement: A Call to Commitment and Action* (1984), XII/F.

Conclusion

Must Social Ethics Divide the Churches?
Possibilities for Rapprochement

In a sense, data which enable an answer to the question posed in the title of this Conclusion have been given repeatedly in most of the preceding chapters. The data seem to authorize a resounding no — though at the same time, one that is somewhat cautious. No, social ethics need not divide the churches. No, even disagreements among the churches on contemporary social and ethical questions need not be church dividing. Indeed, none of the issues which we have considered seems to have sufficient theological consequences at stake for disagreements among the churches to be thought of as constituting a *status confessionis*. At least such a conclusion seems possible because of the relatively small number of disagreements on ethical questions among the churches which are related to, or manifestations of, theological disagreements.

The various sections in the Appendix show that only a few hundred such disagreements among churches, among the myriad disagreements that are logically possible, can be identified. Correspondingly, the analysis has indicated that for every contemporary issue in which one of these theologically related disagreements between church bodies emerges, one also can identify instances where one of the partners to the disagreement participates in another disagreement with a different church body on the ethical question involved but disagrees on considerations other than those of theology. Thus it follows, in the case of every modern cutting-edge issue dealt with in this volume, that disagreements among the church bodies are not necessarily theologically related.

If ethical disagreements are not theologically related, then such disagreements are not essentially related to the nature of the Christian faith. And if disagreements are not related to the nature of the faith, they do not seem to merit breaking formal church fellowship. Consequently, disagreements among the churches on the cutting-edge issues of the day do not seem to be church dividing. At least if these disagreements would merit being considered church dividing, the grounds for such an argument would have to be other than theological.

The logic of this last observation holds true even if, with the passing of years, numerous other church statements devoted to the issues covered in this book appear. In the strictest sense, with regard to its conclusions, this book will not be outdated in the foreseeable future. To the extent that the preceding analysis has identified church statements in disagreement on any given issue and has shown that their disagreement is not theologically related, it follows that precedent is now established for showing that disagreements on the issue in question are not theologically related (i.e., presumably not a function of different understandings of the Christian faith and thus not church dividing). Disagreements on the same issue between other churches with divergent theological perspectives may occur, but having established a precedent for non-theologically related disagreement on the issue in question, the disagreement between these two other churches cannot be shown to be occasioned essentially or necessarily by their theological differences.

The logic of this point holds true no matter how many new partners, with distinct theological perspectives, are shown to have a disagreement on the issue in question. Thus, no matter how many new statements on a given issue might be released in the future, regardless of their theological rationale for the position they take, as long as precedents for non-theologically related disagreements on the issue in question have been established (as we have done in this study), it should still follow logically that that issue is not church dividing. On that basis it seems warranted to conclude that the conclusions of this book, concerning the non-theological character of church dis-agreements on the nine families of issues considered, remain valid, regardless of future developments in the churches' social ethics.

The analysis in the preceding chapters has thus shown that if disagreements among the churches on the issues considered are church dividing, then the grounds for such division must be other than theological in nature. It perhaps will be helpful here to provide an overall summary of the consensus points one finds in the church statements considered as a whole. The data gleaned from such a summary of other findings of this study provide additional grounds for concluding that ethics may not even divide the churches on such non-theological grounds. Furthermore, the trends which have been identified point to a certain kind of catholic consensus among the churches in the way in which they do ethics. Finally, taken as a whole, the data even point to a fruitful avenue for ecumenical advance.

Trends in the Church Statements: New Ecumenical Insights

The first of our trends to be identified or reiterated relates directly to possible non-theological factors impeding church unity. Subsequent trends will pertain to the almost catholic theological consensus found in the statements considered as a whole. Then final non-theological factors will be considered in closing this summary.

The first trend to be considered might be classified under the rubric of contextual-ity. This point has been reiterated numerous times, in virtually each chapter. Contrary to the conventional wisdom, differences in the geographical context of church bodies do not necessarily mandate different approaches to ethics or different ways of doing theology. On numerous occasions, in virtually every chapter and on every cutting-edge issue, we have observed instances where church bodies from radically distinct geographical and cultural contexts have reached agreement on ethical questions, by means of the same theological mode of argumentation. At the same time, in these cases, church bodies from the same context could be observed which disagree with each other theologically and in their ethical conclusions.[1]

The context of a church body does have a tendency to influence that church to address certain concerns with more regularity than do churches located in a different context. Thus we have observed less concern about abortion and ecology, and in fact no interest in genetic engineering, by churches in the third world. In fact, the churches in these regions are generally less inclined than those in the West to issue any church statements at all. Occasionally a church's context does affect its perceptions in intriguing ways. A good example of this phenomenon is evident in the 1985 *Letter to President Reagan* of the Russian Orthodox Church. Perhaps under special influence by their context or Russian political authorities, the Orthodox sharply criticize the Reagan administration for its alleged civil rights and social justice violations. (Also see the church's 1986 *Message of the Holy Synod of the Russian Orthodox Church on War and Peace in a Nuclear Age,* I.2.) Perhaps an even more memorable example is evident in a 1974 message of the Synod of the Romanian Orthodox Church addressed to then-president Nicolae Ceausescu, which praises the years under Communist rule as decades in which the Romanian people have never known greater economic prosperity and peaceful cooperation with the state, governed as they are by the nation's best sons.

The context in which a church body is located inevitably has its impact on that church's overall ethical agenda and perhaps on certain details of its perspective on a given ethical question. The data gleaned by an analysis of the church statements, however, show that heretofore too much attention has been given recently to context. Context is apparently not determinative of theological and ethical differences. Some rethinking of these matters by the ecumenical community seems warranted. Contextual factors do not seem as viable a candidate as a non-theological factor for disrupting church unity, for such contextual factors apparently lack the requisite impact on interpretations of the Christian faith and the good to warrant church division.

The next trends to be considered are the common theological commitments which appear again and again in the church statements. These themes are so commonly met in the statements that one is tempted to speak of them in terms of their representing a catholic consensus.

First, in all but perhaps one of the documents which touch upon the issue, one can identify the positing of a continuity between creation and redemption.[2] This continuity is the idea that redemption completes God's creative purpose. The structures of creation are not opposed to God's redemptive purpose, as is suggested by certain theologians such as Werner Elert.[3] In view of the numerous appeals made in the statements to Christology as authorization for an ethic, the number of times a continuity between creation and redemption is posited is hardly surprising. The one statement which may not unambiguously avoid conflict with this commitment is the 1974 statement on race relations of the Dutch Reformed Church (South Africa), as it asserts that the natural diversity of people is an ontological matter not overturned by the unifying character of the gospel.[4]

Previously we observed that nothing less than the Nicene faith seems to be at stake in this affirmation of a continuity between creation and redemption. In the first chapter we noted the argument of at least one prominent church historian who has maintained that one of the crucial issues at the Council of Nicea was the positing of a continuity between creation and redemption. In response to the Arian heresy, which denied such a continuity, the council presupposed that only the one who had created the world could redeem it. By establishing that Jesus is God, the Nicene fathers also linked the work of Christ to the Father's work in creation. Consequently, as Jesus and the Father are one, yet distinct, so the work of the Father (creation) must be likened to and correlated with the work of the Son (redemption).[5] This line of thought brings us now to a question filled with profound ecumenical implications: To the degree the contemporary church statements on ethics posit a continuity of creation and redemption, could this be construed as an expression of a common Nicene faith incarnate in the churches?

Related to this point is the question of whether church statements which seem to contradict such a creation-redemption continuity might in turn be in conflict with the Nicene faith and so unalterably divided from fellowship with other churches. As previously noted, this question perhaps could be germane in the case of the 1974 statement of the Dutch Reformed Church (South Africa) pertaining to whether apartheid in fact constitutes a church-dividing *status confessionis*. However, although the question of the degree to which the 1974 statement has denied the creation-redemption continuity and so the Nicene faith is a subject worth more detailed study, it may no longer be so germane for questions of church unity. For the more recent 1986 and 1990 statements of the Dutch Reformed moves more clearly in the direction of positing a creation-redemption continuity.[6] Consequently, the South African church (and so perhaps its views on apartheid, which is not condemned in principle by the more recent statements) does not seem necessarily to be departing from the Nicene faith. The prospect of a catholic consensus among church statements on this issue of a continuity between creation and redemption may warrant further investigation. At least in their common service to the world (i.e., in their ethics), the churches unite even on doctrine.

A second theological trend which characterizes many of the statements (though with significant exceptions) relates to a common anthropological perspective. This viewpoint is relevant particularly in the abortion and genetic engineering statements which assume more conservative positions as they hold that human life begins with conception. In other cases, however, the prevailing view of human persons at least implied in the statements from all denominations and geographical regions is a kind of agentic-relational view.[7] By "relational", I refer to a view of human beings which regards them not as static essences but as intimately related to each other and to their environment, such that priority is given to construing a person's being as to a large extent determined by his or her interactions with others. This sort of anthropology is certainly consistent with the ecumenical movement's more recent preoccupation with the ecological emphases of the limits-to-growth movement.

This general anthropological viewpoint leads to a series of questions. The preceding chapters have raised the question of whether on at least a few issues — notably apartheid, abortion, and genetic engineering — ontology might be an ecumenically significant issue which causes division among the churches. To the degree that this relational view of human beings is being employed by so many churches, not just in the Northern but also in the Southern hemisphere, one is tempted to ask whether this view and its associated philosophical suppositions might play some role in the construction of an ontology acceptable to many churches in the interest of overcoming divisions among them. The relational view of human beings which has been identified in the church statements at least points to the kind of common understanding of human persons for which the 1983 WCC Vancouver Assembly called upon the churches to search.[8]

The appreciation that the churches of the world are functioning in their praxis with a relatively common ontology of human beings brings us to a consideration of two more trends — namely, a striking degree of agreement on social ethics and often on theology. In the area of theology, one observes much diversity in theological warrants offered by the churches for their ethical positions. However, at least until the new sensitivity to the doctrine of creation began to emerge, partly as a reaction to the limits-to-growth debate, the prevailing way of doing ethics in the statements was to authorize the position taken by appeal to Christology or some related theme. (Here we must note that the second most prominent authorization for the statements was actually "no clear authorization given". This fact unfortunately bespeaks the shallow quality of too many of the statements, a shallowness not just pertaining to theological depth but also relating to a dearth of penetrating insight on ethical questions.)

No doubt the Christocentric emphases in the statements considered as a whole are related to denominational factors. For as we shall note again, the majority of confessional traditions have tended historically to opt for authorizing their ethical positions by appeal to Christology or the gospel. In addition, the influence of Karl Barth on the modern ecumenical movement — specifically, his "Christomonism" — cannot be overlooked. (Recall that for Barth, creation is in the Man Jesus Christ, so that creation is subordinated to redemption.)

A related factor in the tendency of many church bodies since the Second World War to avoid appeal to the creation doctrine may be conditioned by the conventional wisdom associated with the Barmen Declaration — the belief that ethics authorized by the doctrine of creation must inevitably lead to reactionary or conservative conclusions, while only an ethic authorized by Christology or the gospel can avoid such unfortunate ethical conclusions. Such developments may have helped open the door for the profound impact liberation theology has had on the ecumenical movement; this South American theology characteristically opts for the same Christocentric emphasis as did Barth and the Barmen Declaration.[9]

Throughout the book we have observed instances which challenge the conventional wisdom. In these situations the doctrine of creation has functioned to authorize a more liberal, open ethical conclusion. In fact, in some instances one finds church statements using such a creation-based argument which come to more liberal, less conservative conclusions than conservative positions taken by church statements authorized by Christology or the gospel.[10]

Our analysis has confirmed that there is indeed some truth to the conventional wisdom. Arguments for ethical positions which are authorized by themes related to the doctrine of creation tend to issue in more conservative conclusions, more often than do statements issued by churches which appeal to Christology or the gospel. The Appendix likewise seems to support the conclusion that arguments authorized on grounds of Christology or the Christian faith more often than not tend to issue in ethical conclusions that are liberal, even idealistic. For example, note the predominance of these sorts of arguments in authorizing the idealism of outright opposition to nuclear deterrence, the practice of non-resistance, and even the invocation of the concept of *status confessionis*. These are only tendencies, however, not absolute outcomes of these theological positions.

In statements in which the doctrine of creation or themes related to this doctrine functioned to authorize more liberal ethical programs, we have ascertained that at least one of the following adjustments to the doctrine of creation was made: (1) creation has been correlated with redemption, such that redemption is conceived of as re-creating or restoring the original structures of creation; (2) the orders of creation, or ontology, are contrued in such a way that they correlate with and do not conflict with the gospel, perhaps using an ontology which conveys the idea that the orders of creation are in process or still developing and changing; and (3) human persons are spoken of in terms of a relational anthropology. Those committed by theological propensity and denominational tradition to doing social ethics from the perspective of the doctrine of creation may find it helpful to take these adjustments into account, to learn from the statements these lessons about how to do constructive ethics.

When one or more of these adjustments are made, church bodies arguing from the perspective of the doctrine of creation are almost always in a position to agree in their ethical conclusions with church bodies which have authorized the same position by appeal to a different theological authorization. On other occasions, church statements which appeal to Christology also come to agreement about the matter at hand with church statements arguing from the perspective of ecclesiology or pneumatology. All this is one more confirmation of the opening remarks of this Conclusion, pertaining to the irrelevance of theological disagreements in ethical disagreements.

In fact, there is even ecumenical precedence for this conclusion. Something like this point has even been made in an official ecumenical document. In the 1981 *Honolulu Report* of the International Methodist-Roman Catholic Conversations, it is stated: "Therefore moral theologies based on natural law and those that appeal more directly to an 'ethic of revelation' need not be in conflict" (par. 45). This observation and the data do indeed seem to point in the direction of a revivified, slightly modified Life and Work approach to ecumenics. With a paraphrase of the Life and Work motto, one is tempted to say, "Service unites, and doctrine doesn't necessarily divide!"

This reference to the uniting character of service leads quite naturally to the final collective trend we have identified in the church statements. This trend pertains to a non-theological matter — specifically, to the statements' ethical conclusions. The degree of unanimity among the churches on these matters is striking. To be sure, we have noted disagreements about nuclear deterrence, strategies for development, the superiority of Christianity or Communism, the possibility of remarriage after divorce, abortion, and genetic engineering. (Birth control, the ordination of women, and homosexuality also could be added to the list.) On the whole, however, these are disagreements about strategy.

Even disagreements on genetic engineering and abortion (particularly between the more open and the mediating Protestant positions) really amount to questions about strategy, about how and when to use otherwise usable techniques. Ultimately, we have suggested, the debate about the validity of remarriage after divorce may be a question of different strategies or styles of pastoral care. Certainly the debate about non-resistance and the just-war theory seems to relate to a question of strategy — specifically, about the most effective means of keeping peace. No reference is here made to the substantive disagreement on apartheid because this is an issue about which there is not widespread disagreement. These disagreements consequently do not override the impressive catholic consensus among the churches on the basic values such as social justice, peace, disarmament, an end to military conflict, support for the United Nations, the need for development of underdeveloped peoples, opposition to drug abuse, concern about unemployment, foreign domination, and feminism, as well as a generally critical perspective on divorce.

What is striking in the enumeration of these areas of consensus is that the churches' areas of ethical consensus are uncannily consistent with the values of Western democratic liberalism. The fact that churches on both sides of the old Iron Curtain and in both hemispheres have this sort of ethical consensus compels us again to ask whether the present ecumenical consensus regarding the necessary role of one's context in shaping theology and ethics does not deserve new critical consideration. This observation in turn suggests two other possibilities. Is it possible that certain values and patterns of theological thought associated with the West are of perduring and central value to the Christian faith, which accounts for the consensus of the church statements regarding these "Western" values? Or is it rather the case that the church statements reflect Western values because the social-statement format is essentially a Western innovation which inevitably forces the Western ethical agenda on those who employ it? These are questions which the churches will eventually need to consider. Particularly the latter question will demand consideration as the churches begin to tackle more seriously the issue of finding better mediums by which to do ethics.

Perhaps one final observation about the statements considered collectively should be made. Although, as we have noted, Christology tends to be the prevailing warrant in most of the statements, the diversity of warrants employed in the statements cannot be overlooked. This diversity appears even within denominational traditions, and even within particular churches. Consequently it follows, as we have observed in a number of chapters, that sometimes the churches employ arguments for their ethic which are not characteristic of their denominational heritages.[11]

This phenomenon raises questions about the conclusions reached in this study concerning the ecumenical implications of the data. The conclusion that theological differences among the churches are not ultimately significant in determining their ethical disagreements, and therefore that ethical disagreements are not ultimately church dividing, would be compromised if it could be shown that the social statements we have considered were theologically irresponsible or not representative of the theology of the churches which issued them.

In one sense I am in complete agreement with several analysts who have criticized both the ethical and the theological profile of the statements considered collectively.[12] Far too many statements fail to recognize the complexities of the social issues they consider or fail to provide any theological authorization for their ethical proposals. In other cases, theological reflection offered is too often superficial. The issue at hand, however, is whether the diverse theological approaches one finds a given church and denominational tradition employing in these statements represent a break with the historical confessional heritage of that church. Consequently, an all too brief survey of the approaches to social ethics historically advocated by the major confessional families will be provided.

Ethics in the Heritage of the Confessional Traditions

When all the church statements are grouped together by confessional family, one generally finds at least two or more distinct warrants employed by the modern social statements of each confessional family. In addition to authorizing their ethical conclusions by appeal to Christology or the gospel, the statements of all but one of the major confessional families combine such appeals with arguments drawn from the doctrine of creation or some related locus. Contrary to the general impressions readers may have of the historical positions of the confessional families, this sort of theological diversity represents a legitimate appropriation of the various confessional heritages.

Orthodoxy

When one considers Orthodoxy, the image of a kind of Christologically authorized ethic immediately comes to mind. The Orthodox concept of *theosis,* or the divinization of creation through Christ's identification with it, entails that the being of Christ is the norm for the redeemed created order. Certainly one can identify passages in the historic canons of the Orthodox Church which authorize a position on ethics by appeal to doctrinal themes associated with Christology or the gospel.[13] However, some modern Orthodox theologians have emphasized that, because Orthodoxy is the catholic tradition, embodying the Trinitarian catholic faith, its commitments may not be defined in a precisionistic Western manner. Much more, its ethic must be understood as embodying catholic richness. As such, Orthodoxy exhibits an ethic that is rich enough to employ different approaches to ethics in different contexts or when dealing with distinct issues.[14]

The concept of *theosis*, Christ's transformation of the created order into an image of the divine, would seem to authorize this kind of diversity in ethical approaches. On such grounds, though Christology would provide the primary criteria for judgments about the world, access to Christ could be provided by the transformed world. In that sense, if creation is understood as filled with Christ (or transformed by him), it could function legitimately on Orthodox grounds to provide criteria for making ethical judgments (since it is full of Christ).

One can adduce some data in the Orthodox heritage in support of this argument that appeals to the doctrine of creation for authorizing ethics are legitimate in the Orthodox tradition. A prominent Orthodox scholar has argued for the presence of a natural-law tradition in Orthodoxy. Certainly one can identify something like this appeal, an appeal to what is "natural" as authorization for an ethic, in one of the historic canons of the Orthodox Church.[15] In this case, the doctrine of creation seems to operate as an ethical warrant. Such considerations themselves seem to support the conclusion that Orthodox social statements which authorize their position by appeal to the doctrine of creation or some related theme are as faithful to the Orthodox heritage as those arguing for an ethical position on grounds of Christology, or *theosis*.

Roman Catholicism

At numerous points in this book we have noted the diverse approaches which characterize the Roman Catholic social statements. One would expect to encounter statements exhibiting what is ordinarily deemed characteristic of the Roman Catholic tradition, such as an appeal to natural law (creation) for authorization. Such a model for moral theology has its roots in Thomas Aquinas, if not in earlier theologians.[16] It also evidences itself in the Second Vatican Council, where a kind of two-kingdom ethic is endorsed. *Lumen Gentium* reads: "Because of the very economy of salvation the faithful should learn to distinguish carefully between the rights and duties which they have as belonging to the Church and those which fall to them as members of the human society."[17]

Despite this heritage, the development of a distinct strand of moral theology in recent Roman Catholic statements is quite legitimate. The appearance in the Roman Catholic Church of a strand of argumentation for ethics on grounds of Christology (a strand noted by other observers) has its roots in one of the church's councils — specifically, in Vatican II.[18] In two relevant texts (one cited earlier), creation is subordinated to redemption: "The Christian is certainly bound both by need and by duty to struggle with evil through many afflictions and to suffer death. But, linked with the paschal mystery and patterned on the dying Christ, he will hasten forward to resurrection. . . . All this holds true not for Christians only but also for all men of good will in whose hearts grace is active invisibly."[19] Furthermore, the task of the laity is "to cultivate a properly informed conscience and to impress the divine law on the affairs of the earthly city".[20]

The concept conveyed by these passages — the idea of creation (i.e., the entire natural order) being conformed to Christ — is not merely a twentieth-century development. It is rooted in the medieval period's infatuation with theocratic tendencies, well expressed in the 1302 papal bull *Unam Sanctam*. The state, it was maintained, would disintegrate without the church. Aquinas himself did refer to the subordination of the state to the church in several passages, most notably in his *Commentary on the Sentences* (1253-55), though even then he continued to argue for a distinction between the realms of church and secular authority.[21]

It is apparent that modern Roman Catholic statements which argue for ethical positions on the basis of the structures of creation, understood as rooted in Christology, have a venerable authoritative base in the Roman Catholic tradition. Insofar as such appeals to the doctrine of creation ultimately refer to a Christological base, Roman Catholic church statements appealing only to Christology as the criterion for an ethical judgment would seem consistent with this strand.

The Reformed Tradition

In chapter 1 we noted, contrary to normal stereotypes, the Reformed tradition's tolerance of appeals to the doctrine of creation as a warrant for ethics. The theocratic strand, however, whereby the gospel or Christology provides the criteria for all ethical decisions, is the predominant strand. (It is also the predominant authorization used in most of the statements by Reformed churches.) This principle is stated in several of the historic Reformed confessional statements. A fine statement of this point from the Second Helvetic Confession (1566) may be cited: "Let [the magistrate], therefore, hold the Word of God in his hands, and take care lest anything contrary to it is taught. Likewise let him govern the people entrusted to him by God with good laws made according to the Word of God, and let him keep them in discipline, duty and obedience."[22]

As we noted, however, the appeals made by a few contemporary Reformed statements to the doctrine of creation as authorization for an ethical position have a legitimate basis in the Reformed heritage. Not just in the nineteenth-century Dutch Reformed tradition of Abraham Kuyper or in the dispensationalist strands of the Westminster Confession (1646) do we find the positing of a distinction between creation and the realm of the gospel in such a way that creation is capable of standing alone, without depending on the gospel to authorize ethical decision making.[23] This sort of two-kingdom ethic was explicitly endorsed by John Calvin: "Therefore, in order that none of us may stumble on that stone, let us first consider that there is a twofold government in man: one aspect is spiritual, whereby the conscience is instructed in piety and in reverencing God; the second is political, whereby man is educated for the duties of humanity and citizenship. . . . Now these two, as we have divided them, must always be examined separately."[24] Modern church statements authorized by the doctrine of creation are by no means out of place in the Reformed tradition.

Lutheranism

If any tradition might be thought to rule out alternatives to its single-minded devotion to the idea that all ethical arguments must be related to the doctrine of creation, Lutheranism would seem to be the candidate. Certainly its affirmation of the two-kingdom ethic, previously described, entails that creation (i.e., the law) is the only legitimate warrant for social ethics inasmuch as the realm of the gospel has been distinguished from the political kingdom. Among the classic sixteenth-century Lutheran texts which make this point, the *Apology of the Augsburg Confession* may be cited: "The writings of our theologians have profitably illumined this whole question of the distinction between Christ's kingdom and a political kingdom. . . . The Gospel does not introduce any new laws about the civil estate, but commands us to obey the existing laws, whether they were formulated by heathen or by others, and in this obedience to practice love."[25]

Given this background, church statements issued by Lutheran bodies which appeal to Christology for ethical authorization would seem to be distortions of the Lutheran heritage. However, this may not be the whole story. Martin Luther's *Large Catechism* contains a passage which suggests a subordination of creation to redemption in a manner akin to the more recent Christological orientation of the Roman Catholic Church. According to Luther, God "created us for this very purpose, to redeem and sanctify us".[26]

If creation's original purpose was for the sake of redemption, then its content must be like that of redemption. Consequently, a certain Lutheran tolerance for ethical arguments authorized by Christology, the gospel, or redemption seems presupposed by this text. When Christians refer to creation as a warrant for their ethic, they also seem implicitly to appeal to redemption which is, after all, the content of creation. It is in this way that the significant minority of Lutheran statements, which argue their position on Christological grounds, must be understood.

Anglicanism

The predisposition of the Anglican tradition to authorize its ethics by appeal to the doctrine of creation or the natural law is generally recognized. Actually this conclusion about Anglicanism's traditional social ethical posture is based fundamentally only on the writings of certain particular individuals.[27] The Thirty-Nine Articles of Anglicanism do not provide much guidance concerning social ethics. Article 37 in the original 1571 edition, however, does distinguish the realms of spiritual and temporal government in a manner suggestive of the Lutheran two-kingdom ethic and its consequent need to endorse the doctrine of creation as sole authorization for ethical judgments in the social sphere.

Given this background, it seems difficult to recognize the full validity of Anglican social statements which appeal to Christology or the Christian faith as a warrant. However, some precedent in the Anglican heritage perhaps could be found for these sorts of arguments. One thinks of the role the Church of England historically has attributed to the British government, namely, that of the protector of the faith. The English monarch is the head of the Church of England, according to Parliament's 1534 Act of Supremacy. This role is sufficiently reminiscent of Reformed views on state-church relationships that perhaps it is fair to conclude that a Reformed-like use of Christology or the gospel to authorize a social ethic would be appropriately employed in the historic Anglican tradition.

Methodism

Although historic Methodism has by no means been devoid of a social consciousness (as early as 1789 it condemned slavery), little explicit reflection is given in its authoritative documents to theological suppositions for social ethics. [28] Consequently, it may be fair to conclude that "any warrant goes" for Methodism—that the appeal by Methodist statements to any valid doctrine for ethical authorization still represents keeping faith with the tradition.

A closer look at the historic, authoritative Methodist documents suggests that second-article warrants and perhaps something like creation are the historically normative Methodist warrants for social ethics. A first clue in this connection is a re-examination of the condemnation of slavery by the Methodist *General Rules*. The condemnation is said to be a consequence of the fact that the faithful evidence "their desire to salvation". [29] In this one historically authoritative instance, the Methodist Church has relied on the gospel or sanctification for authorization of its ethic. Should this be taken as the historically preferred paradigm for Methodist social ethics?

Hints that an ethic rooted in the doctrine of creation may be an appropriate Methodist position perhaps appear in the authoritative *Articles of Religion,* first composed by Wesley. In an article devoted to rulers he recognizes the sovereignty of government and the duty of Christians to be obedient to the government. [30] The commitments are sufficiently reminiscent of the confessional Lutheran approach to state-church relationships that one is tempted to speculate whether Methodism is implicitly endorsing the Lutheran creation-based approach to social ethics. At least this possibility is not unequivocally denied by historic Methodism. As such, the diversity of warrants which characterizes modern Methodist social statements does not appear to be illegitimate. Appeal to the second article, however, is probably the more characteristic Methodist approach.

The Mennonite Tradition

Diversity of theological warrants is even evident in the Mennonite church statements which have been considered. The predominant collective warrants, however, are doctrinal loci derived from portions of the creed concerning Christology and pneumatology. In fact, this focus has precedent in the historic Mennonite, Anabaptist tradition. Although the earliest Mennonites were separatists in a sense that Mennonite bodies issuing social statements are not, the earliest Mennonites tended to authorize such separatism by appeal to Christology and, to some extent, third-article warrants. [31]

There seems to be some historic precedent, however, for the present occasional Mennonite approach to social issues by way of the doctrine of creation. At least a certain reading of article 37 of the 1580 Mennonite Waterland Confession could be taken that way. The confession states: "Government or civil Magistrate is a necessary ordinance of God, instituted for the government of common human society and preservation of natural life and civil good." The idea of government as an ordinance built into the very fiber of the created order could be regarded as the touchstone for authorizing modern examination by Mennonites of present social issues. Much of the modern Mennonite tradition has gone its own way in relation to the classical Mennonite heritage. At least with regard to the theological perspective of modern Mennonite social statements, however, there seems to be some continuity with the past.

The Baptist Tradition

Given the somewhat common heritage of Mennonites and Baptists, it is hardly surprising to find common features in how their heritage relates to contemporary statements on the cutting-edge issues. The preponderance of Christologically based arguments in the modern statements of Baptists is matched by this sort of orientation in confessional statements of Baptist heritage such as the New Hampshire Confession of 1833, the Second London Confession of the seventeenth century, and to some extent the 1611 *Declaration of English People Remaining at Amsterdam in Holland*.[32] The latter two statements, however, also refer to government as an "ordinance of God", so perhaps these texts also could be used to authorize the validity of appeals to the doctrine of creation which we have observed in at least a dozen or more contemporary Baptist statements.[33]

Moravian, Restorationist, and United Church Traditions

The rationale for lumping together these three distinct traditions in our brief survey of the historic positions of the churches on social ethics is that all of them share a common ecumenical self-understanding, if not as a mark of ongoing identity, at least in their origins. All had their origins and to some extent still aim to be traditions which seek to overcome old denominational schisms. Also two of these traditions, and most United churches outside Germany, share in common a non-credal, non-confessional viewpoint.

Given the ecumenical commitments of these traditions, it is quite appropriate to expect that they would embody the whole spectrum of valid theological approaches to social ethics. In fact, this is largely true of the contemporary statements of these traditions, though like the rest of oikoumene, there is a definite bias towards authorizing positions by appeal to Christology or the gospel. In view of their Biblicist, non-confessional orientation, nothing precludes the legitimacy of their endorsement of the full range of theological alternatives we have identified. Even in the case of the German United churches, their recognition of both the historic Reformed and Lutheran heritages authorizes and invites the use of a wide diversity of theological perspectives, which is reflected in the statements of all these traditions.

Summary

The preceding brief summary of the historical approaches to social ethics of the major denominational families serves to indicate that the theological diversity we have identified in the statements of most of the churches does not indicate an unfaithfulness of these churches to their respective heritages. This is a signifiant point beause it shows that conclusions drawn about the churches' relationships to each other on the basis of their contemporary social statements are valid ecumenical generalizations, perhaps applicable not just to the churches involved but to the denominational families they represent. As such, the conclusion of our analysis of the statements — namely, that the ethical questions under review in this book are not church dividing — seems to be on firmer ground.

The preceding analysis of the historic positions of the denominational families makes a further contribution to the conclusion that social ethics does not divide the churches. In almost every case, the historic positions of denominational traditions are characterized by more than one theological profile, usually a prevailing model and a supplementary model (e.g., in Lutheranism, the two-kingdom ethic, supplemented by an openness to the subordination of creation to redemption). This fact indicates further the validity of concluding that theological differences on social ethics are not church dividing. They are not church dividing insofar as theological perspectives as diverse as the characteristically Reformed Christocentric approach and the characteristically Lutheran creation-centered two-kingdom ethic have a way of living together inside certain denominational traditions, sometimes along with models drawing on pneumatology, ecclesiology, eschatology, or the like. Yet these theologically distinct approaches manage to live together without fracturing the intraconfessional fellowship. Consequently, there is no reason to argue that the same theological differences should divide different confessional bodies when they do not divide a particular church. Disagreements on social ethics, even if the disagreements are theologically related, do not seem to mandate church division.

Final Reflections

Before we can allow the conclusion to stand that social and ethical differences do not divide the churches, it is necessary to examine a bit further one other problem area and to develop the possibilities that this conclusion brings for ecumenical rapprochement. The problem relates to the present impasse in cooperation between the WCC and the Roman Catholic Church on social ethics.

It would be too much and yet too little to say that tensions are being felt in Roman Catholic-WCC relations. Cooperation in social ethics has continued unabated since 1968, when the two bodies created the Society for Development and Peace (SODEPAX). The cooperation has evolved in the development of a Joint Consultative Group on Social Thought and Action, which has emerged from the Joint Working Group of the Roman Catholic Church and the WCC.

Relations are very good between the two bodies and their personnel. On that level it is unfair to speak of a tension between them. Yet the participants have begun to give serious consideration of late as to why, after all the years of cooperation, so little has been accomplished. Questions are being asked whether there might be theological, church-dividing reasons which have precluded and will continue to preclude cooperation and joint action between these church bodies.

To a certain extent, the results of this study seem to confirm some of these concerns. We have noted that some of the major debates in ecumenical ethics today set the Roman Catholic Church over against a Protestant coalition. However, our analysis of the disagreement between the parties to the debates on these issues — such as abortion, remarriage after divorce, and genetic engineering — places a more constructive context on the present WCC-Roman Catholic discussions. The conclusions of our study, showing that theological differences are not at stake in Roman Catholic-Protestant disagreements on ethics, provide a helpful way to evaluate the question of whether the factors others see as occasioning the present Roman Catholic-WCC impasse are truly church dividing. In that connection it is no less important to keep in mind the emerging theological and ethical compatibility and mutal influencing on social ethics that we have observed in earlier chapters between the Roman Catholic Church and the WCC. No less significant an ethicist than James Gustafson has observed an emerging consensus between revisionist elements in both Protestant and Roman Catholic elements. [34]

Although several publications have analyzed the present WCC-Roman Catholic impasse, only Thomas Sieger Derr has offered a book-length analysis and so may be considered to provide the definitive analysis. Basically Derr analyzes the differences interfering with WCC-Roman Catholic cooperation in terms of methodological, structural, and substantive issues. The tendency for the Roman Catholic tradition to be more abstract than the WCC in approaching ethical questions (a feature said to be due to the Catholic tradition's more characteristic reliance on a natural-law ethic) is identified as one of the methodological issues at stake. By contrast, as the various sections in the Appendix illustrate, the prevailing approach to ethics in WCC statements has been to draw on Christology for authorization (something like Karl Barth's model of *Herrschaft Christi,* or lordship of Christ). Another issue identified includes the somewhat more critical perspective of the Roman Catholic hierarchy towards ideologies, its more "priestly" pastoral style as distinct from the more "prophetic" pastoral styles of the WCC. [35]

The structural issues which Derr points out as dividing these bodies are obvious — namely, the difference between a church (which is also a geopolitical entity) and a council of churches. Then Derr proceeds to outline substantive issues such as the use of violence in the face of injustice, racism. development, population, and women's rights as ways of illustrating how the methodological and structural differences manifest themselves in the Roman Catholic-WCC relationship. [36]

Derr's analysis is careful and points to some difficulties in enhancing Roman Catholic-WCC relationships. The only theologically related difference he was able to identify, however, was his claim that the Roman Catholic Church operates with a tradition of natural-law ethics in comparison to the WCC's "predilection for discovering the divine revelation in the freshness and uniqueness of each event". [37] As we have seen, this is not the whole story. Since the Second Vatican Council the Roman Catholic Church has moved away a bit from a natural-law ethic, while positing creation's subordination to Christology. Likewise since the onset of the limits-to-growth debate the WCC has moved towards more appreciation of a natural-law ethic, one involving the role of the doctrine of creation in authorizing ethical proposals. In short, insofar as both the Roman Catholic Church and the WCC are learning to employ each other's characteristic theological perspective, the difference between them which Derr emphasizes consequently does not seem to be of a church-dividing character; instead, it is just a difference in emphasis. Each on occasion shares the other's characteristic and theological rationale, yet their inability to cooperate on ethics remains. Does it not follow, then, that their disagreements on ethical questions are not ultimately theologically conditioned?

Derr indeed notes still other areas of disagreement. But insofar as theological differences are not at stake in the relationship between the council and the Roman Catholic Church, these other issues do not seem to be matters related to faith. Rather, they are more like disagreements over "middle axioms", or strategies. Derr has correctly pointed out some of the factors that heretofore have precluded WCC-Roman Catholic cooperation on social issues. As middle axioms, however, these matters of structure and method do not seem to bar the way insuperably to closer cooperation. Differences about the nature of the Christian faith do not seem to stand in the way.

The Catholic consensus on ethical questions, in which, our study shows, both the Roman Catholic Church and the WCC largely participate, as well as the increasing theological compatibility which our study shows is emerging between the two, puts Derr's analysis of the present barriers to Roman Catholic-WCC cooperation in a new light. Their differences are not ultimately insuperable and thus not church dividing.

The data gleaned from our analysis of the church statements suggest a negative answer to the question posed in the title of this Conclusion. Even after taking into account the present difficulties between the WCC and the Roman Catholic Church as well as after considering the historic teachings of the churches, it appears that the churches' disagreements on ethics are not necessarily theologically related. As such, these disagreements are not about the nature of the faith and so do not seem to merit schism among the churches.

To this juncture the ecumenical implications of the data have been stated negatively — the analysis shows church unity is *not* jeopardized by ethics. But could one present the catholic consensus on ethics and the apparent irrelevance of theological disagreements in determining ethical differences more positively? An examination of the data in light of certain particular Anglo-American theological presuppositions could point a path to a further reviving of the Life and Work movement.

The theological model I have in mind is one largely influenced by English analytic philosophy and its idea that the meaning of concepts is their use.[38] Endorsing these suppositions, and then noting that in relatively few instances do disagreements about theological authorization for an ethic manifest themselves in disagreements in practice among the churches, could we conclude that such theological differences are not meaningful, since they are of no practical use (and as such not church dividing)? This raises a related question. To the degree that other doctrinal differences among the churches are related to differences in the theological models they use when authorizing their particular ethic, could one also conclude that insofar as such doctrinal differences do not typically manifest themselves in ethics (i.e., in disagreements in practice), disagreements among the churches on issues such as ecclesiology, sacramentology, perhaps even the papacy are not meaningful because they are of no practical use and so are not church dividing?

The question represents a kind of reintroduction of a modified Life and Work approach to ecumenics. Is the concept articulated in this way worth further inquiry and refinement by ecumenists? That is a story for some other day. At least we can raise in closing a question for the increasing number of voices who are calling on ecumenical dialogues to incorporate consideration of ethical questions alongside doctrinal matters. In view of the consensus, or at least the lack of church-dividing disagreements on ethics, which has been revealed in this analysis of the churches' social statements, do we really need such a dialogue? Perhaps it would be of use only in showing that doctrine and doctrinal differences are ultimately not important for church praxis.

NOTES

[1] See the Appendix for the various instances in which church bodies from distinct contexts arrive at complete unanimity on ethical conclusions and on theological perspective.

[2] The most definitive statements in our texts of a creation-redemption continuity include the following (as far as possible, citing at least one text from each major confessional tradition): WCC Vancouver Assembly Issue Group Report, *Taking Steps towards Unity* (1983), 4, and *Moving towards Participation* (1983), Int.; WCC Vancouver Assembly, *Statement on Human Rights* (1983), 4; WCC Nairobi Assembly Section Report, *Education for Liberation and Community* (1975), 2, and *Structures of Injustice and Struggles for Liberation* (1975), 11; WCC Uppsala Assembly Section Report, *The Holy Spirit and the Catholicity of the Church* (1968), 21; WCC New Delhi Assembly, *Statement on Religious Liberty* (1961), 2; WCC Evanston Assembly Section Report, *Inter-Group Relations — The Church amid Racial and Ethnic Tension* (1954), III, and *The Laity — The Christian in His Vocation* (1954), IV; WCC Amsterdam Assembly Section Report, *The Universal Church in God's Design* (1948), I; WCC Department on Studies in Evangelism, *The Church for Others* (Geneva, 1967), 69; WCC Conference on Faith, Science and the Future Section Report, "Humanity, Nature and God" (Cambridge, Mass., 12-24 July 1979), 2; National Council of Churches [USA] *Genetic Science and Human Benefit* (1986) V.A., and *Southern Africa* (1977), 1; Reformed-Roman Catholic Joint Commission, *The Presence of Christ in Church and World* (1977), 44; Roman Catholic-Methodist Joint Commission, *Denver Report* (1971), 40, and *Honolulu*

Report (1981), 45; Presbyterian Church of Southern Africa, *A Declaration of Faith for the Church in South Africa* (1981); Presbyterian Church in the Republic of Korea, *Our Confession of Faith* (1976); Evangelical Methodist Church of Argentina, *Social Service and Action: Foundations in Biblical Theology* (n.d.), 1; Roman Catholic Church, Vatican II, *Gaudium et Spes* (1965), 22, 57, 61; Roman Catholic Church, *Dignitatis Humanae* (1965), 9, 12, and *Redemptor Hominis* (1979), 16; Roman Catholic Church Congregation for the Doctrine of the Faith, *Instruction on Respect for Human Life in Its Origin and on the Dignity of Procreation* (1987), Int., 11; German Bishops' Conference [FRG], *Zukunft der Schöpfung — Zukunft der Menschheit* (1980), II.7; National Conference of Catholic Bishops [USA], *The Challenge of Peace: God's Promise and Our Response* (1983), I; [Catholic] Bishops of the Netherlands, *De mens in de arbeid* (1980), 2.2; Russian Orthodox Church, *An Open Letter to the President of the USA* (1983); Lutheran Church in America, *The Human Crisis in Ecology* (1972), C; American Lutheran Church, *Peace, Justice and Human Rights* (1972), 4, and *The Land* (1982), I; Lutheran Church-Missouri Synod, *To Enourage Peacemaking and the Study of Problems concerning the Church and Nuclear Arms* (1983); Church of Norway, *Human Dignity* (1985), 1, and *En ny internasjonal økonomisk ordning* (1979), 27; Lutheran World Federation, *Justification Today* (1963), 12; Moderamens of the Reformed Alliance [FRG], *Das Bekenntnis zu Jesus Christus und die Friedensverantwortung der Kirche* (1981), Erl. III; Nederduitse Gereformeerde Kerk, *Human Relations and the South African Scene* (1974), 15, 46.1, and *Church and Society* (1986), 160-70; United Presbyterian Church [USA], *Policy Statement and Recommendations* [on homosexuality] (1978) 3-4; World Alliance of Reformed Churches, *Reconciliation and Man: The Freedom of the New Man* (1970) and *The Theatre of Glory and a Threatened Creation's Hope* (1982); Lambeth Conference (1968) Section Report, *The Renewal of the Church in Faith;* Baptist World Alliance, *Reconciliation and Racial Discrimination* (1970); Mennonite Church, General Conference, *Concerns about Abortion* (1977); Christian Church (Disciples of Christ), *Resolution concerning Nuclear Arms* (1981); United Church of Christ [USA], *Human Rights* (1979); Moravian Church in America, Southern Province, *Nuclear Arms Race* (1983).

[3] See Werner Elert, *Der christliche Glaube* (Hamburg: Furche-Verlag, 1956), 460, 145, and *The Christian Ethos,* trans. Carl J. Schindler (Philadelphia: Muhlenberg Press, 1957), 63ff., 81. An argument for this kind of discontinuity in Elert's thought is provided by André Birmelé, "Interprétation et actualisation d'une tradition confessionnelle: Werner Elert, théologien luthérien" (doctoral thesis, University of Strasbourg, 1977), 333, 314ff.

[4] Nederduitse Gereformeerde Kerk, *Ras, volk en nasie en volkereverhoudinge in die lig van die Skrif* (1974), 14.5; 60.

[5] For the earlier discussion and the relevant reference, see pp.10ff. along with chapter 1, note 44.

[6] Nederduitse Gereformeerde Kerk, *Kerk en samelewing* (1986), 306, 160-67.

[7] The most definitive statements of an agentic-relational view of persons in our texts include the following (as far as possible citing at least one from every confessional tradition, major ecumenical organization, and geographical region): WCC Uppsala Assembly Section Report, *Renewal in Mission* (1968), 7, and *Towards New Styles of Living* (1968), 27; WCC Nairobi Assembly Section Report, *Confessing Christ Today* (1975), 59; WCC Vancouver Assembly Issue Group Report, *Confronting Threats to Peace and Survival* (1983), 20; National Council of Churches [USA] Policy Statement, *The Ethical Implications of Energy Production and Use* (1979); National Council of Churches [USA], *Genetic Science for Human Benefit* (1986), II.E; V.A.3; V.C.3; All Africa Conference of Churches, *The Gospel of Reconciliation* (1981) and *Evangelism and Selfhood of the Church in Africa* (1974), 2; *Plan for the Life and Mission of the Methodist Church in Brazil* (1982), III/1; Fédération Protestante de France, *Eglise et pouvoirs* (1971), 3-1.2; Synod of the Protestant Church in Austria, *Atomic Energy in Austria* (1978), III; Roman Catholic Church, Vatican II, *Gaudium et Spes,* 25; Peruvian Catholic Bishops' Conference, *La justicia en el mundo* (1971), 6; Roman Catholic Church, *Octogesima Adveniens* (1971), 24; Roman Catholic Church Congregation for the Doctrine of the Faith, *Instruction on Christian Freedom and Liberation* (1986), 27; [Catholic] Bishops of the Netherlands, *Mens, arbeid en samenleving* (1985), 4, 10; four items by the Lutheran Church in America: *Sex, Marriage, and Family* (1970); *The Human Crisis in Ecology* (1972), C; *Human Rights* (1978), 3; and *Economic Justice* (1980), 3; three items by the American Lutheran Church, *Human Sexuality and Sexual Behavior* (1980), A/3.2; B/5; *Manifesto for Our Nation's Third Century* (1976), VI; and *The Environmental Crisis* (1970), 2; Württembergische Evangelische Landessynode, *Entschliessung zur Kirche und Arbeitswelt* (1985), 2; Presbyterian-Reformed Church in Cuba, *Confession of Faith* (1977), II/B; *Plan for the Life and the Mission of the Methodist Church in Brazil* (1982), pts. II; III.1; Methodist Church [England], *Abortion* (1976), 3, and *Christian Social and Political Responsibility* (1967), I; American Baptist Churches, *Policy Statement on Energy* (1977), II; United Church of Christ [USA], *Report on Christian Life Style and Ecology* (1977) and *Human Rights* (1979); Evangelische Kirche im Rheinland, *Hilfe zum Leben* (1986), 1.

This sort of relational ontology seems to underlie the dogmatics of Karl Barth, *Die kirchliche Dogmatik,* III/2, 2nd ed. (Zurich: Evangelischer Verlag A. G. Zollikon, 1959), 81, 188-89, 293-97; ibid., I/1, 548.

[8] WCC Vancouver Assembly Issue Group Report, *Witnessing in a Divided World* (1983), 48(b).

[9] For references in Barth to the "lordship of Christ" theme (e.g., Christ as Lord of all realms, even the political), see his *Die kirchliche Dogmatik,* IV/2 (Zurich: Evangelischer Verlag A. G. Zollikon, 1955), 293-94; ibid. II/2, 3rd ed. (Zurich: Evangelischer Verlag A. G. Zollikon, 1959), 676ff. For references to these commitments of liberation theology and its impact, see chapter 1, note 36, and chapter 8, note 3. For an example of the predominance of Christological perspectives in the statements, in the section on peace in the Appendix note the significant number of ecumenical organizations, Lutheran churches, and Anglican churches which authorize their call for peace by appeal to Christology or the gospel.

[10] For examples, see the first section in the Appendix on nuclear armaments for the position of the British Council of Churches in comparison with statements which to some extent are authorized by appeals to the doctrine of creation but still oppose nuclear deterrence. Also see the section on the relationship of Christianity to Communism/socialism.

[11] A few examples are provided in note 9 above.

[12] See Roger L. Shinn, "Christian Faith and Economic Practice", *Christian Century,* 24-31 July 1991, 720, and his citation of James M. Gustafson, *Ethics from a Theocentric Perspective* (Chicago: University of Chicago Press, 1984).

[13] *The Rudder of the Orthodox Christians or All the Sacred and Divine Canons,* canon 3: "Form for a Canonical Divorce". For the endorsement of *theosis,* see Clement, *Exhortation to the Greeks* 1.8.4; Origen, *Against Celsus* 3.28; *The Holy Catechism of Nicolas Bulgaris* 163-64, 234.

[14] Gennadios Limouris, telephone interview, 1 June 1988.

[15] For the argument on behalf of a natural-law tradition in Orthodoxy, see Stanley Samuel Harakas, *Toward Transfigured Life: The Theoria of Eastern Orthodox Ethics* (Geneva: WCC, 1983), 118ff; *The Rudder of the Orthodox Christians,* canon 80. For other historical observations, see Jaroslav Pelikan, *The Christian Tradition,* vol. 2 of *The Spirit of Eastern Christendom (600-1700),* 5, 144.

[16] Aquinas, *De Regimine Principum,* I.1; Aquinas, *Summa Theologica,* IIa, IIae, q. 63, art. 2; Ia, IIae, q. 91; I, q. 96, art. 4.

[17] Roman Catholic Church, Vatican II, *Lumen Gentium* (1964), 36: cf. *Gaudium et Spes* (1965), 76, 48, 34, 12.

[18] This development is noted by Gustafson, esp. in *Ethics from a Theocentric Perspective,* 146.

[19] *Gaudium et Spes,* 22.

[20] Ibid., 43.

[21] Thomas Aquinas, *Commentum in IV Libros Sententiarium* (1253-55), trans. E. Lewis, in *Medieval Political Ideas* (New York, 1954), 566-67; cf. Aquinas, *De Regimine Principum,* I.14.

[22] See chapter 1, note 7, for references.

[23] See chapter 1, notes 23-24, for references.

[24] Calvin, *Institutes* 3.19.15; cf. 4.20.1; 4.11.3-5; 2.8.1.

[25] *Apology of the Augsburg Confession* 16.2-3; cf. chapter 1, note 12, for other relevant references.

[26] Luther, *Large Catechism* (1529), 2.64.

[27] See chapter 4, note 6, for references.

[28] For the early Methodist condemnation of slavery, see Methodist Church, *The General Rules* (1789), 30.

[29] Ibid.

[30] Methodist Church, *Articles of Religion* (1783-84), art. 23.

[31] The Dordrecht Confession (1632), art. 13; the Waterland Confession (1580), art. 37; the Schleitheim Confession (1527).

[32] The New Hampshire Confession (1833), art. 16; the Second London Confession (1689), art. 24; *Declaration of English People Remaining at Amsterdam in Holland* (1611), 24.

[33] Second London Confession, ibid., and *Declaration of English People,* ibid.

[34] Gustafson, *Protestant and Roman Catholic Ethics: Prospects for Rapprochement* (London: SCM Press, 1979), esp. 146, 152. Also especially see the previous chapter for discussion of this emerging rapprochement.

[35] Derr, *Barriers to Ecumenism* (Maryknoll, N.Y.: Orbis Books, 1983), esp. 11ff.

[36] Ibid., 24ff.

[37] Ibid., 9.

[38] See Charles Wood, *The Formation of Christian Understanding* (Philadelphia: Westminster Press, 1981), 19; George Lindbeck, *The Nature of Doctrine* (Philadelphia: Westminster Press, 1984), 68, 114. Cf. Ludwig Wittgenstein, *Philosophical Investigations,* trans. G.E.M. Anscombe (New York: Macmillan, 1953), 20.

Postscript

Since this book was written at the very beginning of the 1990s and dealt comprehensively only with church social statements issued through the end of the 1980s, former colleagues at the Institute for Ecumenical Research and WCC publishers advised me to bring the finished product up to date by commenting, just prior to publication, on a number of the most important statements issued in the 1990s by several international church organizations. The thinking was that such an addition would truly enhance the contemporary relevance of this volume.

In fact, a careful analysis of the most influential newer statements such as those issued by the 1991 Canberra Assembly of the World Council of Churches, by the council's World Convocation on Justice, Peace and the Integrity of Creation of the previous year in Seoul, by the European Ecumenical Assembly of the Conference of European Churches in 1989 in Basel, and by the most recent (1990) assembly of the Lutheran World Federation in Curitiba, Brazil, indicates that the manuscript as it was originally prepared is still most timely. The same trends which were identified as characterizing the statements analyzed in the bulk of this volume are clearly evident in the more recent statements.

Recent social statements do have some new features, at least superficially. The World Council of Churches' statements and those of its European ecumenical counterpart reflect especially pronounced attention to the issues of justice, peace, and ecology (the integrity of creation). Yet as we have previously observed and as the Appendix which follows indicates, these issues are hardly new concerns for the churches. Statements on peace and justice were issued by churches in the earliest years of the period which we have studied, and statements on ecology appeared as early as 1966.[1] Perhaps only recently have these ethical challenges been organized in such a systematic fashion, as dimensions of the same problematic reality. Already in the 1980s, however, at least since the WCC's Vancouver Assembly, after which the council began self-consciously to consider justice, peace, and ecology as related problems, a number of church statements, influenced by the council's preparatory work, self-consciously began to address these issues collectively.[2]

There is a perception that the "new" preoccupation with ecology has led church organizations to pay more attention to the doctrine of creation and to move away from the "Christomonism" (the tendency to authorize all ethical arguments solely by appeal to Christology or some related theme) which has dominated in most modern church social statements. A careful examination of the most recent church statements, however, indicates that in fact this perception is not the whole story.

True enough, these recent statements may exhibit a bit more explicit attention to the doctrine of creation than the statements issued from 1963 to the end of the last decade, collectively considered. As we noted, however, this renewed appreciation of the doctrine of creation dates back to the beginnings of the limits-to-growth debate in the mid-1970s.

A number of the more recent statements' appeals to the doctrine of creation for authorization for their ethical proposals, especially on justice, peace, and ecology, emerge in the context of arguments which authorize their position by appeal to creation in tandem with appeals to themes derived from the other two articles of the creed. In effect, then, these statements, most notably from the WCC's 1990 World Convocation on Justice, Peace and the Integrity of Creation as well as the 1989 European Ecumenical Assembly, embody a Trinitarian approach to social ethics. (These statements also take recourse to appeal to the theme of covenant, which is itself described in Trinitarian terms by the statements.)[3]

There is some perception in ecumenical circles at present that Eastern Orthodoxy's participation in the movement is having an impact, as Christianity as a whole is giving more and more attention to the doctrine of the Trinity. Certainly it might be possible to make this point on the basis of the two aforementioned ecumenical documents. Likewise Orthodox and perhaps Roman Catholic influence is thought to be making more of an impact on the ecumenical movement and the mainline Protestant churches in general, insofar as the sacraments are also noted as authorization for the ethical positions taken both by the 1989 European Ecumenical Assembly and by the report of the WCC Canberra Assembly.[4]

In fact, however, numerous earlier statements authorized their positions on justice, peace, ecology, and other issues by appeal to themes derived from all three articles of the creed. These include both Protestant and Roman Catholic documents, such as a statement from the WCC Nairobi Assembly on human development, another on development from the council's Uppsala Assembly, a 1977 statement of the Canadian Catholic Bishops Conference, a 1968 statement of the Latin American [Catholic] Bishops Second General Conference (Medellín Conference), the 1963 papal encyclical *Pacem in Terris*, and a 1976 statement on human rights by the American Baptist Churches.[5]

Likewise, examples in earlier statements of appeals to sacramentology in order to authorize certain positions can be cited. These include appeals to sacramentology correlated with some other doctrinal theme derived from the third article in order to authorize a call to economic justice framed as early as 1977 by the United Church of Christ [USA] and in the 1988 report of the third round of the USA's Lutheran-Episcopal Dialogue. A similar mode of argument was employed to authorize an ecological concern by the German [Catholic] Bishops Conference in a 1980 statement. Even the WCC was early influenced by such sacramental emphases, as such an appeal was made for purposes of condemning racism in its Faith and Order Commission's Lima text. It is readily apparent, then, that the allegedly "new" attention that the most recent church statements are said to be giving to the doctrine of creation, the Trinity, and even to the sacraments is not a radically new development after all.

A closer study of the most recent church statements suggests that even the perception that new attention to the doctrine of creation is putting an end to the hegemony of the Christomonism which dominated in the statements collectively considered in the bulk of this volume is not an accurate conclusion. In fact, a number of examples of appeals to Christology or the gospel for ethical authorization are evident in the most recent statements, especially when these statements address issues such as disarmament, conscientious objection, and unemployment. For example, the 1989 European Ecumenical Assembly rejected the principle of nuclear deterrence by appeal to the gospel and Christology. The WCC Canberra Assembly report decried unemployment solely by appeal to the gospel. Even the Lutheran World Federation, the institutional embodiment of world Lutheranism (creation-centered heritage though it be), seems to have resorted to an appeal to Christology in a 1990 argument on behalf of conscientious objection. The tendency of church statements to bypass the doctrine of creation when formulating an ethic, in favor of attending to Christology or the gospel as the sole authorization, is by no means repudiated by the statements of the 1990s. (The reference in the 1989 European Ecumenical Assembly *Final Document* to a "preferential option for the poor" also suggests the ongoing influence of liberation theology and its Christomonist ethic on the new statements.[6])

Many of the trends previously identified in the church statements collectively considered appear clearly in the most recent statements. Another good example is evident in the anthropology which prevails in the statements since 1963. The report of the WCC Canberra Assembly (13), which among the more recent statements contains the clearest articulation of anthropological assumptions, reaffirms the same agentic-relational view of human persons which characterized the catholic consensus observed earlier.

The earlier statements' collective tendency to posit a continuity between creation and redemption is evident in the newer statements. We have previously observed this characteristic in the number of newer statements which authorized some ethical position by appeal to loci derived from all three articles of the creed or combined an appeal to the doctrine of creation with some other doctrinal theme. In these cases both creation and some other doctrinal theme are authorizing the same ethical position. They could do so, however, only if continuity exists between the structures of creation and those of redemption as depicted by the other doctrinal theme which is noted in the statement.

In several cases, the more recent statements contain the same challenge to the conventional wisdom associated with the Barmen Declaration that has appeared in other statements after 1963. One of the clearest examples of creation-centered statements authorizing a progressive social ethic, contrary to what the conventional wisdom would predict, is a 1991 resolution on gay, lesbian, and bisexual persons of the United Church of Christ [USA], which employs such a theological orientation to call for social justice, especially for the gay, lesbian, and bisexual. Another good example is the WCC Canberra Assembly report's plea for ecology and justice primarily by way of appeal to creation.

The number of newer statements we have noted, which appeal to the doctrine of creation in correlation with themes from other articles of the creed in order to authorize peace and ecology, could also be cited as challenges to the conventional wisdom. These statements, in positing a continuity of creation and redemption, as well as the previously noted WCC Canberra Assembly report, which both posits a continuity of creation and redemption and articulates an agentic-relational view of human persons, embody the same adjustments made to the doctrine of creation that are exhibited in earlier statements which likewise appeal to the doctrine of creation to authorize more liberal, progressive positions.

Church statements issued in the 1990s resemble in other ways the earlier ones on which this book has focused. All of them share common collective weaknesses.

The more recent statements are on the whole still shallow in their concrete ethical proposals, more inclined to articulate general principles than to define concrete steps to action. (For exceptions, only the European Ecumenical Assembly's call for continued economic sanctions against South Africa and its call for strict legislation concerning genetic engineering could be cited. In that connection, the reservations that both the assembly and the WCC World Convocation on Justice, Peace and the Integrity of Creation express concerning genetic engineering are striking, witness to a growing hesitation within the ecumenical establishment concerning this new technology.) Likewise, although the ecumenical documents we have been examining are notable exceptions, the more recent statements are not devoid of weak theology. Several 1990 statements and resolutions of the Lutheran World Federation pertaining to apartheid, a just peace (in Brazil), and social justice in Central America as well as the WCC Canberra Assembly report in its treatment of peace and capitalism provide no theological authorization at all for the positions taken on these issues.

For our purposes, the most intriguing consideration about the more recent statements is that when considered collectively, they confirm our earlier conclusion that disagreements on ethics among the church bodies are not necessarily theologically related. To that extent, as we have noted throughout, disagreements among the churches on the cutting-edge issues of the day do not seem to be church dividing.

These observations might be illustrated by comparing one of the more recent statements dealing with a controversial question, such as that of the validity of maintaining nuclear deterrents, with earlier statements. A good example is provided by the European Ecumenical Assembly's rejection of deterrence, which is authorized by the gospel and perhaps ecclesiology. A number of earlier statements used similar theological authorizations in order to justify the opposite conclusion, namely, that deterrents should be maintained. By the same token, a number of statements which opposed deterrence, such as the assembly did, authorize their position by way of appeal to the doctrine of creation, arriving at the same ethical conclusion as the assembly, albeit in theological disagreement with it. Once again it is evident that differences about the nature of the faith are not at stake in disagreements about social ethical questions such as that of the best strategy for nuclear disarmament.

Another illustration of the irrelevance of faith issues for social ethical disagreements is evidenced by the diverse positions on energy consumption of two of the newer ecumenical statements. The WCC World Convocation on Justice, Peace and the Integrity of Creation called for a reduction of energy consumption, but only if done in such a way that the legitimate needs of developing countries were recognized. Yet the European Ecumenical Assembly, in calling for reduced energy consumption, offered none of these qualifications. In this apparent disagreement, the two statements offered compatible theological warrants for their distinct positions — a kind of Trinitarian argument by the WCC convocation and an appeal to themes derived from the second and third articles of the creed by the European assembly. Once again we have an example of the irrelevance of theological issues in determining social ethical disagreements among the churches.

These final observations concerning the most recently released church statements on social ethical issues provide clear confirmation of the primary conclusion of the volume as a whole — namely, that because the churches' disagreements on these matters are not about the nature of the Christian faith, they are not legitimately church dividing. Likewise the consensus among the churches concerning justice, peace, and ecology, which in recent years is being heartily confirmed, suggests anew that, insofar as theological disagreements do not seem to impede consensus on social ethics, insights from a theologically sophisticated Life and Work perspective applied to Faith and Order work may provide some promise for helping break the present ecumenical impasse.

Consideration and analysis of the most recent church statements on social issues provides more than merely an update of the study of such statements as a whole. Rather, these more recent statements confirm the study's conclusions, suggesting that its insights may have ongoing value for ecumenical ethics in the foreseeable future.

NOTES

[1] For an early statement on ecology, see National Council of Churches [USA], *Christian Concern and Responsibility for Economic Life in a Rapidly Changing Technological Society* (1966). Internationally the concern was raised as early as 1968 by the Anglican community in *The Resolutions of the Lambeth Conference (1968)*, 6.

[2] For a few of the numerous examples, see World Alliance of Reformed Churches, *A Message to the Congregations of the Member Churches of the WARC* (1989); Russian Orthodox Church, *Decrees of the Holy Synod* (1983); Evangelische Kirche der Kirchenprovinz Sachsen, *Vorlage des Berichtsausschusses* (1984), 1; 2.1; *Erklärung der 22. Evangelisch-Lutherische Landessynode Sachsens vom 22. März 1988*, 1988.

[3] Especially see WCC Convocation on Justice, Peace and the Integrity of Creation, *Final Document: Entering into Covenant Solidarity for Justice, Peace and Integrity of Creation* (1990); Council of European Churches and Council of European Bishops' Conferences, *Final Document of the European Ecumenical Assembly Peace with Justice* (1989), 1-4, 10, 13, 14, 20-22, 25-30, 32-34, 36-38, 40, 42-45, 70, 72, 74, 75, 77, 83, 84, 86, 87, 91, 99; Lutheran World Federation, *I Have Heard the Cry of My People... the Assembly Message* (1990). For a recent example of another probable appeal to the doctrine of creation in tandem with appeal to other doctrinal themes, see WCC Canberra Assembly, *The Report of the Seventh Assembly* (1991), 26.

[4] Council of European Churches and Council of European Bishops' Conferences, *Final Document, 40;* WCC Canberra Assembly, *Report*, esp. 18.

[5] For other examples, see the Appendix. Also see chapter 1, note 58.

[6] Council of European Churches and Council of European Bishops' Conferences, *Final Document*, 72. For appropriate references in liberation theology concerning these commitments, see chapter 1, note 36; chapter 8, note 3.

Appendix

This Appendix lists the statements received from the various churches and church organizations relative to the nine cutting-edge social issues discussed in the text above. Within each section, items are listed by the theological warrant appealed to in support of the respective positions taken. Warrants relating primarily to the first article of the creed appear first, followed generally by those referring to Christology or other second-article themes, then those related in some way to the creed's third article or to a variety of miscellaneous theological warrants. The final listing within each section is that of statements which have no clear theological warrant at all. In some cases, unfortunately, this last category contains more statements than any other.

Within the listing under any given warrant, items are listed alphabetically by author (i.e., church, council, conference, etc.). If several statements by the same group appear in a listing, they are further ordered from earliest to most recent. Finally, two or more items from the same body in the same year are listed alphabetically by title.

A. APARTHEID AND RACISM

1-1 APARTHEID

Except for the Dutch Reformed Church (South Africa), churches and councils have uniformly condemned apartheid. The three positions taken on this issue and the various theological topics (if any) appealed to are as follows:

A.   For apartheid
    A1.   Appeal to creation

B.   Modified criticism of apartheid when it violates human dignity
    B1.   Appeal to creation and the gospel/redemption
    B2.   Appeal to Scripture and Christian conscience

C.   Condemn apartheid
    C1.   Appeal to creation
    C2.   Appeal to creation and Christology
    C3.   Appeal to creation and Christian faith
    C4.   Appeal to creation, subordinated to Christian faith
    C5.   Appeal to creation/view of human persons, supplemented by other articles of the creed
    C6.   Appeal to Christology/the gospel
    C7.   Appeal to Christology/the gospel/Christian faith
    C8.   Appeal to Christology/the gospel/Christian love
    C9.   Appeal to the gospel/Christology and the doctrine of the church
    C10. Appeal to Christology, supplemented by other articles of the creed
    C11. Appeal to ecclesiology, with reference to a kind of two-kingdom ethic
    C12. Appeal to ecclesiology and eschatology
    C13. Appeal to the Bible
    C14. Appeal to the Bible and divine justice
    C15. Appeal to the Holy Spirit
    C16. Appeal to the Trinity
    C17. No clear theological warrant given for position

A. FOR APARTHEID

A1. Appeal to creation

Dutch Reformed Church (South Africa), *Human Relations and the South African Scene* (1974), 49.6; 9; 9.1; 60.

B. MODIFIED CRITICISM OF APARTHEID WHEN IT VIOLATES HUMAN DIGNITY

B1. Appeal to creation and the gospel/redemption

Dutch Reformed Church (South Africa), *Church and Society* (1986), 306, 101, 113, 127-42, 329, 343. With some secondary appeals to the third article.

B2. Appeal to Scripture and Christian conscience

Dutch Reformed Church (South Africa), *Church and Society* (1990), 97, 109-10, 130-47, 280-85, 303. Apartheid said to be a sin when it functions to oppress some part of a population. Creation and the gospel/redemption function as strong supporting warrants.

C. CONDEMN APARTHEID

C1. Appeal to creation

American Baptist Churches, *Policy Statement on Africa* (1987), 1, 3. Correlates all references to creation with Christology; also calls for divestment.

American Lutheran Church, *Apartheid* (1981), I; II/1, 2, 8. With some reference to Christology for backing as well as to ecclesiology and the concept of *status confessionis*.

Anglican Church of Canada, *South Africa* (1986), 1, 2, 5. Includes a plea for economic sanctions against South Africa.

Associated Churches of Christ in New Zealand, *Decisions Relating to Public Issues* (1972). Appeals to the doctrine of human persons.

Bund der Evangelischen Kirchen in der Deutschen Demokratischen Republik, *Erklärung der Synode des Bundes zur Situation in Südafrika* (1985). Expresses support of the WCC Program to Combat Racism.

Evangelisch-Lutherische Kirche in Bayern, *Brief an die Gemeinden zum südlichen Afrika* (1984). Correlates appeal to the orders of creation with the unity of the church and the Lord's Supper.

Roman Catholic Bishops in Mozambique, *Pastoral Letter* (1976). At least authorizes its position by appeal to human dignity.

C2. Appeal to creation and Christology

All Africa Conference of Churches, *The Gospel — Good News to the Poor and Oppressed* (1981).

Broederkring of the Dutch Reformed Church [South Africa], *Theological Declaration* (1979).

Church of the Province of Southern Africa [Anglican], *Policy of Apartheid* (1982). Deems apartheid a heresy.

Evangelische Kirche im Rheinland, *Geschäftsbeziehungen deutscher Banken zu Südafrika* (1986).

Evangelische Kirche in Deutschland, *Beschluss der 7. Synode der EKD auf ihrer 2. Tagung zur Situation in Südafrika* (1985). Calls for a moratorium on investments in South Africa. It does refer to "obedience to almighty God" as a possible warrant at one point; insofar as the above statement is endorsed, however, this one must share the preceding one's warrants.

Evangelische Kirche in Deutschland, *Erklärung des Rates der EKD zur gegenwärtigen Lage im südlichen Afrika* (1985), III, VI. Cites an earlier 1978 resolution which may have authorized its position only by appeal to the doctrine of human persons. Also the language of the theology of hope appears at one point. The statement, which was endorsed in a 1985 *Resolution of the Seventh Synod of the EKD on Its Second Meeting on the Situation in South Africa,* advocates divestment of South African holdings.

Federation of Lutheran Churches in South Africa, *The Swakopmund Declaration* (1975), 4-6, 9ff., 23.

Presbyterian Church of Southern Africa, *A Declaration of Faith for the Church in South Africa* (1981). With reference to the Holy Spirit as well; also claims apartheid is a heresy.

Reformed Church in Japan, *Comments on "Human Relations and the South African Scene in the Light of Scripture"* (1984).

C3. Appeal to creation and Christian faith

British Council of Churches, *Political Change in South Africa: Britain's Responsibility* (1979). Advocates economic sanctions against South Africa.

Evangelical Lutheran Church in Southern Africa, *New Political Dispensation* (1984).

Evangelische Kirche von Westfalen, *Wort der Landessynode 1985 zu Südafrika*.

C4. Appeal to creation, subordinated to Christian faith

Anglican Church of Canada, *Resolutions on South Africa* (1971). Calls on Canadian government to undertake economic sanctions against South Africa.

C5. Appeal to creation/view of human persons, supplemented by other articles of the creed

World Methodist Council Conference, *Council Message to the Methodists of the World* (1966). Christology perhaps functions only as a motive.

C6. Appeal to Christology/the gospel

Anglicanism, *The Resolutions of the Lambeth Conference (1988)*, 29.

Church of the Province of Southern Africa [Anglican], *Apartheid a Heresy — Support for the Dutch Reformed Mission Church* (1982). Deems apartheid a heresy.

Church of the Province of Southern Africa [Anglican], *Mixed Marriages Act — Racial Classification* (1982). Objects to South Africa's strictures against mixed marriages.

Church of the Province of Southern Africa [Anglican], *Service in the SADF* (1982), 3(c). Condemns apartheid insofar as the church regards the South African military as protecting an immoral and unjust social order.

Eglise de la Confession d'Augsbourg d'Alsace et de Lorraine, *Décision* (November 1976). The most obvious theological authorization is an appeal to the "will of God". It does hint that the gospel is the criterion for rejecting apartheid and referred in an earlier discussion to the doctrine of human persons.

Eglise Evangélique Luthérienne de France, *Vœux et décisions du Synode général* (1986), 10. Endorses the position of the Lutheran World Federation that opposition to apartheid is a matter of faith.

Evangelical Lutheran Church in Tanzania, *Regarding Salvation and Tyranny That Is Continuing in Africa* (1978).

Evangelische Kirche der Pfalz, *Beschluss der pfälzischen Landessynode vom 28. November 1985*. Also calls for economic sanctions against South Africa.

Evangelische Kirche im Rheinland, *Antwort der Landessynode der EKR auf die Beschlüsse der Nationalkonferenz des südafrikanischen Kirchenrates* (1986), A. Suggests economic sanctions against South Africa.

Lutheran Church-Missouri Synod, *To Urge Support for Oppressed* (1986). Refers specifically to the commandment of Christ.

Mennonite Church [USA], *Resolution on South Africa* (1987). Condemns apartheid as a sin in virtue of affirming a statement by Africa Inter-Mennonite Mission, Eastern Mennonite Board of Missions, and Mennonite Central Committee, *A Commentary on Mennonite Ministries and the Crisis in Southern Africa* (1986). This statement refuses to take any organizational policy position on economic sanctions against South Africa.

National Council of Churches [USA], *Southern Africa* (1977), 6-7, 1.

Netherlands Reformed Church, *Resolutions* (1982). Urges divestment and support of the WCC Program to Combat Racism.

Nordelbische Evangelisch-Lutherische Kirche, *Erklärung der Synode der NELK zu Südafrika* (1986). Warrant not clear but suggests that endeavors to overcome apartheid are "placed under" a Christocentric interpretation of the law. It also hints that apartheid is a *status confessionis*.

Presbyterian Church of Southern Africa, *Church and Nation* (1983), 237, clause 4. Calls for non-violent action.

Presbyterian Church of Southern Africa, *Church and Nation* (1984), 234, clause 3. At least insofar as reference is made to "Christian standards".

Reformed Church in America, *Report of the General Synod Executive Committee* (1980), R-7 to R-15. Calls for economic sanctions against South Africa.

Reformed Church in America, *Report of the Advisory Committee on Christian Unity* (1982), R-8 to R-10.

Reformed Church in America, *Report of the Christian Action Commission* (1983), R-11.

United Church of Canada, *Apartheid as Heresy* (1984). Deems apartheid a heresy. It claims to be endorsing a 1982 declaration of the World Alliance of Reformed Churches which designated apartheid a *status confessionis*.

United Church of Christ [USA], *Resolution on South Africa* (1977). Appeal to the gospel possibly supplemented by an appeal to ecclesiology.

United Church of Christ [USA], *Support for Liberation Movements in Namibia and Zimbabwe* (1977).

United Church of Christ [USA], *Sanctuary and Political Asylum for South African Refugees in the U.S.* (1985).

United Church of Christ [USA], *United Church of Christ Full Divestment of All Corporations Doing Business with South Africa* (1985). Calls for economic sanctions against South Africa.

Vereinigte Evangelisch-Lutherische Kirche Deutschlands, *Entschliessung der Generalsynode der VELKD zur gegenwärtigen Situation im südlichen Afrika* (1985). Calls for economic sanctions against South Africa and is also concerned about the situation in Namibia.

World Alliance of Reformed Churches, *Reconciliation and Society: The Freedom of a Just Order* (1970), 8, Intro.

World Alliance of Reformed Churches, *The Power of Grace and the Graceless Powers* (1982).

World Alliance of Reformed Churches, *Racism and South Africa* (1982), I-II. Combined with some warrants drawn from ecclesiology and the claim that apartheid is a *status confessionis*. The statement was reaffirmed by World Alliance of Reformed Churches, *Southern Africa* (1989) and *Towards a Common Testimony of Faith* (1989), 2, although it takes a more critical, cautious position on circumstances when social issues might be identified as *status confessionis*.

WCC Vancouver Assembly, *Statement on Southern Africa* (1983), 1ff. Suggests that apartheid is a *status confessionis*.

WCC Vancouver Assembly, *Struggling for Justice and Human Dignity* (1983), 7.1; 9; 11; 13; 23.

World Methodist Council Conference, *Youth Resolution on South Africa* (1976).

World Methodist Council Conference, *Resolution on Racism* (1981).

C7. Appeal to Christology/the gospel/Christian faith

Anglican Church of Canada, *Resolutions on South Africa* (1975). Calls for the Canadian government to undertake economic sanctions against South Africa; would have the church only investigate divestment.

C8. Appeal to Christology/the gospel/Christian love

International Council of Community Churches [USA], *Statement of Concern about South Africa* (1987). Calls for an end to investments in South Africa.

C9. Appeal to the gospel/Christology and the doctrine of the church

Conference of European Churches and Council of European Bishops' Conferences, *Final Document of the European Ecumenical Assembly Peace with Justice* (1989), 84, 79, 78, 77, 25-27. Includes a reference to covenant, which itself reflects a trinitarian framework, as well as a call for continuing economic sanctions against apartheid.
Evangelical Lutheran Church in Southern Africa, *Apartheid as Heresy* (1982).
Evangelical Lutheran Church in Southern Africa, *Social Services in Independent States and Homelands* (1982). Cites a 1982 resolution of the South African Council of Churches.
Evangelische Landeskirche in Baden, *Einheit der Kirche in der Zerrissenheit zwischen Ost und West und Nord und Süd* (1981), II/1.3.1. The statement claims apartheid is related to the church's confession.
South African Council of Churches, *Apartheid as a Heresy* (1983).

C10. Appeal to Christology, supplemented by other articles of the creed

Lutheran World Federation, *Racism in Church and Society* (1984), 10, 6; ii; i. Apartheid deemed a heresy. This statement, however, and its theological authorization appear in a section of the document with no official approval.
Nederduitse Gereformeerde Sendingkerk, *Confession of Faith* (1982). Apartheid is said to constitute a *status confessionis*. Creation and to some extent ecclesiology are only background warrants, although ecclesiology plays a role perhaps equal to that of the doctrine of reconciliation.
Nederduitse Gereformeerde Sendingkerk, *The Belhar Confession* (1986), 1-3. The Triune God and ecclesiology are only background warrants, although ecclesiology plays a role perhaps equal to that of the gospel.
South African Council of Churches, *A Message to the People of South Africa* (1968). Anthropology and ecclesiology are only background warrants; it refers to Christ's lordship.
South African Council of Churches, *A Theological Rationale and a Call to Prayer for the End to Unjust Rule* (1985). Apartheid is deemed a heresy. The will of God, the church's traditions, and the doctrine of creation — cited in an appeal to all men of good will — are only background warrants.

C11. Appeal to ecclesiology, with reference to a kind of two-kingdom ethic

Vereinigte Evangelisch-Lutherische Kirche Deutschlands, *Beschluss der Generalsynode der VELKD zur Rolle der Kirche in bezug auf das südliche Afrika* (1978), 1-2. Concern for justice and freedom in the South African context seems to connote opposition to apartheid. The statement also questions the WCC Program to Combat Racism.
WCC New Delhi Assembly, *Message to Christians in South Africa* (1961). No reference to a two-kingdom ethic.

C12. Appeal to ecclesiology and eschatology

Association of the Episcopal Conference of Anglophone West Africa, *Communique, Resolutions, and Recommendations* (1986), 17.

C13. Appeal to the Bible

Christian Church (Disciples of Christ), *Concerning Investments in South Africa* (1968). Calls for economic sanctions against South Africa.

C14. Appeal to the Bible and divine justice

National Association of Evangelicals [USA], *Resolution on Apartheid* (1986).

C15. Appeal to the Holy Spirit

Southern Africa Catholic Bishops Conference, *Social Justice and Race Relations within the Church* (1977), 1-5, 21, Int.
United Church of Christ [USA], *Statement on Southern Africa* (1975).

C16. Appeal to the Trinity

Baptist Union of New Zealand, *Public Questions* (1989), (b).

C17. No clear theological warrant given for position

All Africa Conference of Churches, *The Prophetic and Serving Church* (1974).
American Lutheran Church, *Opposition to Apartheid* (1980). Claiming a *status confessionis*.
Associated Churches of Christ in New Zealand, *Decisions Relating to Public Issues* (1969).
Associated Churches of Christ in New Zealand, *Decisions Relating to Public Issues* (1971).
Associated Churches of Christ in New Zealand, *Decisions Relating to Public Issues* (1980).
Baptist Union of New Zealand, *Notices of Motion* (1984).
Bremische Evangelische Kirche, *Südafrika* (1987). Calls for divestment in banks doing business in South Africa.
British Council of Churches, *Southern Africa* (1963) (b). Supports the proposal not to export arms to the South African government.
British Council of Churches, *South Africa* (1964), ii. Not yet ready to consider economic sanctions against South Africa.
British Council of Churches, *Arms to South Africa* (1970). Cites the council's resolution *South Africa* (1964); urges prohibiting the exporting of arms to South Africa.
British Council of Churches, *Emergency Resolution — South Africa* (1985).
British Council of Churches, *Resolution on South Africa* (1985). Reaffirms the council's 1979 policy of support for progressive divestment from the South African economy.
British Council of Churches, *Staff Farewells* (1986), 1.
Christian Church (Disciples of Christ), *Concerning Membership in the United Nations* (1964).
Christian Church (Disciples of Christ), *Concerning Investments in South Africa* (1968). Some appeal to the Bible for authorization. It opposes investments in South Africa.
Christian Church (Disciples of Christ), *Concerning Human Rights* (1977).

Christian Church (Disciples of Christ), *Concerning Southern Africa* (1977). Would evaluate multinational corporate investments.

Christian Church (Disciples of Christ), *Report concerning Human Rights* (1979), I.

Church of England, *South Africa* (1986). Calls for economic sanctions against the South African government.

Church of the Province of Southern Africa [Anglican], *Civil Conflict and the SADF* (1985), 3. Labels apartheid a heresy.

Church of the Province of Southern Africa [Anglican], *Rejection of Mixed Marriages and Immorality Acts* (1982), i. Objects to South Africa's strictures against mixed marriages.

Congregational Union of Scotland, *Apartheid and Racism* (1985). Favors economic sanctions.

Council of Churches in the Netherlands, *Letter of the CCN to Its Member-Churches* (1978). Urges divestment by Dutch business in order not to support apartheid.

Eglise de la Confession d'Augsbourg d'Alsace et de Lorraine, *Résolution* [concernant le Programme de Lutte contre le Racisme] (1978), Int., (1), (2), (5), (9). Notes the church's failure to participate in the WCC Program to Combat Racism. The gospel authorizes rejection of the use of violence.

Episcopal Church [USA], *General Convention Resolution* [on Namibia (South West Africa)] (1973). Criticizes the practice of apartheid in Namibia.

Episcopal Church [USA], *General Convention Resolution* [on South Africa apartheid] (1976). Includes a call for economic sanctions against South Africa.

Episcopal Church [USA], *Apartheid/Africa* (1985), Int., 2-5, 11-12. Calls for economic sanctions against South Africa in virtue of endorsing a 1985 resolution of the church's Executive Council.

Episcopal Church [USA], *Commend Bishop Tutu* (1985). At least urges mutual regard among people of South Africa.

Episcopal Church [USA], *General Convention Resolution* [adopting Executive Council resolution on South Africa] (1988). Calls for economic sanctions against South Africa in virtue of adopting the council's May 18 (1988) resolution.

Episcopal Church [USA], *Shell, Mobil, Chevron, Texaco, BP, and Total Oil Boycott* (1988). Calls for a boycott of the above oil companies which do business in South Africa in virtue of adopting the church's May 18 (1988) Executive Council resolution.

Evangelical Lutheran Church in Southern Africa, *Marriage as Promulgated by the State* (1982). At least insofar as South Africa's strictures against mixed marriages are rejected; reference is made only to the "biblical grounds for marriage".

Evangelische Kirche der Kirchenprovinz Sachsen, *Beschluss zur Gesamtthematik der Synodaltagung* (1985), 2. The covenant/gospel is a warrant for many points in the resolution, but not clearly so in this case.

Evangelische Kirche im Rheinland, *Gemeindenzentrum Johannesburg* (1974).

Evangelische Kirche im Rheinland, *Bank- und Geschäftsbeziehungen zu rassistischen Regimen* (1985).

Evangelische Kirche im Rheinland, *Wirtschaftssanktionen gegen Südafrika* (1986). Supports economic sanctions against South Africa.

Evangelische Kirche im Rheinland, *Geschäftsverbindungen von Banken zu Südafrika* (1987). Supports economic sanctions against South Africa.

Evangelische Kirche im Rheinland, *Boykott südafrikanischer Kohle* (1988). Urges boycott of South African coal.

Evangelische Kirche im Rheinland, *Geschäftsverbindungen von Banken zu Südafrika* (1988). Advises not supporting banks which deal with South Africa.

Evangelische Kirche in Deutschland, *Entschliessung zur Rassendiskriminierung* (1974).

Evangelische Kirche in Deutschland, *Gerechtigkeit und Versöhnung für das südliche Afrika* (1984).

International Council of Community Churches [USA], *On South African Apartheid* (1985).

International Council of Community Churches [USA], *Statement of Concern for the Situation in South Africa* (1986). Advocates economic sanctions/disinvestment to help end apartheid.

Lutheran World Federation, *Statements of the Assembly* (1977), 54-56. Claims apartheid represents/constitutes a *status confessionis*.

Lutheran World Federation, *Statement on Human Rights* (1984), I.3. Claims that apartheid is a heresy. The Trinitarian warrant for condemning racism possibly functions here.

Lutheran World Federation, *Statement on Namibia* (1984), 10. Claims that the rejection of apartheid is a confessional question.

Lutheran World Federation, *Statement on Southern Africa: Confessional Integrity* (1984), 1. Reaffirms the preceding statement.

Moravian Church in America, Northern Province, *Resolutions* (1978). Seems to condemn apartheid, insofar as the abuse of political power in South Africa is decried.

Presbyterian Church in Taiwan, *Peace to South Africa* (1985). The concern to create a multiracial society may be related to the gospel in the statement.

Presbyterian Church of Southern Africa, *Church and Nation* (1985), 230, clauses 6, 8, 10. Includes rejection of South African strictures against mixed marriages.

Reformed Church in America, *Report of the Christian Action Commission* (1967), rec. 1a. Though the report itself did authorize the point by appeal to Christology.

Reformed Church in America, *Report of the Committee on Christian Unity* (1981), R-12. Though the report itself does appeal to Christ's reconciliation as a warrant.

Reformed Church in America, *Report of the General Synod Executive Committee* (1982), R-25. With the gospel/Christology as background warrant.

Reformed Church in America, *Report of the Black Council* (1985), R-11, R-12.

Reformed Ecumenical Synod, *Race Relations* (1984), art. 100, rec. D/1, 4. Reaffirms a 1980 *Statement on the Social Calling of the Church*. Consequently this statement may be implicitly authorized by Christology and the gospel such as the earlier statement was.

South African Council of Churches, *National Conference Resolutions* (1983).

South African Council of Churches, *Resolution No. 5: Disinvestment* (1985). Calls for a disinvestment in businesses carrying on commerce in South Africa.

Southern African Catholic Bishops' Conference, *An Urgent Message to the State President* (1986), 1, 6, 7, 21a. Cites 1957 *Statement on Apartheid,* by the conference, which claimed that apartheid has an "anti-Christian character".

United Church of Canada, *Southern Africa* (1971). Calls for economic sanctions.

United Church of Canada, *South Africa* (1972). Calls for disinvestment in corporations working in South Africa.

United Church of Canada, *Apartheid* (1984). Calls on industrial nations to undertake economic sanctions against South Africa.

United Church of Canada, *Disinvestment* (1986). Calls for economic sanctions against South Africa.

United Church of Christ [USA], *Report of the Council for Christian Social Action, as Finally Adopted* (1965), 15. Calls for economic sanctions against South Africa.

United Church of Christ [USA], *Resolution on South Africa* (1967). Affirms the earlier 1965 statement, which recommended economic sanctions.

United Church of Christ [USA], *Southern Africa* (1971).

United Church of Christ [USA], *Expanded Criteria for Divestment and Advocacy Related to South Africa* (1987). Calls for full divestment from all companies with ties to South Africa.

United Free Church of Scotland, *Deliverance of the General Assembly* [on public questions] (1964), 10, 1. Supports a 1963 resolution of the British Council of Churches to discontinue exporting arms to South Africa, which might enable the enforcement of apartheid.

United Free Church of Scotland, *Deliverance of the General Assembly* [on public questions] (1965), 16.

United Free Church of Scotland, *Deliverance of the General Assembly* [on public questions] (1971), 1, 9.

United Free Church of Scotland, *Deliverance of the General Assembly* [on public questions] (1973), 1.

Vereinigte Evangelisch-Lutherische Kirche Deutschlands, *Entschliessung zum Fonds für Gerechtigkeit und Versöhnung* (1973), 1-2. Seems to indicate opposition to apartheid insofar as a commitment is made to conquering racial tensions in South Africa.

Vereinigte Evangelisch-Lutherische Kirche Deutschlands, *Entschliessung der Generalsynode der VELKD zur "Zusammenarbeit und Gemeinschaft mit den lutherischen Kirchen im südlichen Afrika"* (1981), 1. Claims apartheid is a *status confessionis*. This statement was confirmed by *Beschluss der Generalsynode der VELKD zur Zusammenarbeit und Gemeinschaft mit den lutherischen Kirchen im südlichen Afrika* (1984).

World Methodist Council Conference, *Resolution on South Africa* (1976).

World Methodist Council Conference, *Resolution on South Africa* (1981). Simply states that apartheid has no biblical or theological justification.

1-2 RACISM

Churches agree in their condemnation of racism. They differ widely, however, in the theological bases appealed to in their argumentation.

1. Appeal to creation/view of human persons
2. Appeal to creation/view of human persons/moral law
3. Appeal to creation/view of human persons, supplemented by other articles of the creed
4. Appeal to creation/moral commandment/anthropology
5. Appeal to creation and Christology
6. Appeal to creation and Christology/the Christian faith/gospel, with the former grounded in the latter
7. Appeal to creation and the Christian faith/the gospel
8. Appeal to creation, possibly grounded in Christology
9. Appeal to creation, with covenant a possible supporting warrant
10. Appeal to view of human persons and kingdom of God
11. Appeal to anthropology and eschatology, with the gospel in the background
12. Appeal to Christology/the gospel
13. Appeal to Christology/the gospel/reconciliation
14. Appeal to Christology/the gospel and the Bible
15. Appeal to Christology/the gospel and pneumatology
16. Appeal to Christology/redemption, supplemented by other articles of the creed
17. Appeal to Christology/grace/reconciliation and eschatology or ecclesiology
18. Appeal to Christology, supplemented by appeal to ecclesiology and creation
19. Appeal to second-article themes, supplemented by appeal to third-article loci
20. Appeal to pneumatology
21. Appeal to ecclesiology
22. Appeal to sacramentology
23. Appeal to sacramentology and ecclesiology
24. Appeal to sacramentology, eschatology, and Christology
25. Appeal to eschatology
26. Appeal to loci derived from all articles of the creed
27. Appeal to loci derived from all articles of the creed, especially creation and eschatology
28. Appeal to loci derived from all articles of the creed, including the Eucharist, Mariology, and the saints, though all are subordinated to Christology

29. Appeal to loci derived from all articles of the creed, though likely all are rooted in redemption/evangelism
30. Appeal to loci derived from all articles of the creed and the Bible
31. Appeal to the will of God and the traditions of the church
32. Reference to the contents of Scripture
33. Reference to the contents of Scripture and Christian conscience or Christian principles
34. Appeal to Christian love
35. Appeal to Christian responsibility
36. Appeal to the church's moral imperative/Christian example
37. Appeal to the example of modern saints
38. No clear theological warrant given for position

1. Appeal to creation/view of human persons

American Baptist Churches, *Policy Statement on Housing* (1983).
American Lutheran Church, *Manifesto for Our Nation's Third Century* (1976), IV. At least authorized by human interdependence.
Baptist Union of Great Britain and Ireland, *Race Relations* (1968).
British Council of Churches, *Community and Race Relations Unit* (1984).
Canadian Catholic Conference, *On the Occasion of the Hundreth Year of Confederation* (1967), 8, 12.
Evangelische Kirche im Rheinland, *Sonderfonds zur Bekämpfung des Rassismus* (1979). Concedes that the Special Fund of the WCC Program to Combat Racism serves humanitarian mandates but will not support it as long as it is used to support certain liberation movements.
International Council of Community Churches [USA], *Statement of Concern on American Indian Rights* (1988). With a possible appeal to anthropology.
Latin American Protestant Conference, *United to Meet the Demands of the Present* (1978). Concerned about discrimination against Latin American Indians. The warrant appealed to is not completely clear.
National Council of Churches [USA], *Equal Representation Is a Right of Citizenship* (1965).
Patriarchs and Catholic Bishops of Libya, *Legality Is the Unique Guarantee of the Protection of the Fatherland* (1983), I/1.
Reformed Church in America, *Report of the Christian Action Commission* (1966), R-6, R-2 to R-3. Christology functions as a warrant in the background statement.
Reformed Ecumenical Synod, *Race Relations* (1984), art. 103, rec. 2. Appeal to anthropology is correlated with reference to the unity in Christ given to the church.
United Church of Christ [USA], *Response and Action: Racial Justice* (1971). Authorization not entirely clear but does refer to the "humanization of man".
WCC Amsterdam Assembly, *The Church and the International Disorder* (1948), IV.

2. Appeal to creation/view of human persons/moral law

Anglican Church of Canada, *South Africa* (1986).
Associated Churches of Christ in New Zealand, *Decisions Relating to Public Issues* (1968).
Associated Churches of Christ in New Zealand, *Decisions Relating to Public Issues* (1972).
Church of Norway, *Human Dignity* (1985), esp. 3. With strong affirmation of creation-redemption continuity.
Lutheran Church in America, *Race Relations* (1964). With complementary appeals to all articles.

Lutheran Church in America, *Human Rights: Doing Justice in God's World* (1978), esp. 4, 5. Insofar as racism is deemed a sin.

Lutheran Church-Missouri Synod, *Creation in Biblical Perspective* (1967ff.), VI.5. Claims we must understand creation "in the light of the words and work of Christ".

Lutheran Church-Missouri Synod, *To Affirm Investment Policies* (1986).

National Association of Evangelicals [USA], *A Declaration — Forty-fifth Anniversary Year* (1987).

National Council of Churches [USA], *Genetic Science for Human Benefit* (1986), V.A.2; V.B; V.A; V.C.3. With Christology in the background, and also perhaps ecclesiology.

Roman Catholic Church, *Pacem in Terris* (1963), 86, 85, 80, 10, 23, 31, 147, 157. Appeals to the natural law and anthropology could be subordinated to redemption. At least it posits a creation-redemption continuity, as well as a relational view of human persons.

Roman Catholic Church, *Populorum Progressio* (1967), 62-63, 81, 34, 32, 13. Depends on whether references to positions of Vatican II documents and its interest in infusing the laws with a "Christian spirit" entail that, like *Gaudium et Spes,* 22, creation is grounded in Christology.

Southern Baptist Convention [USA], *A Statement of Social Principles* (1979), 2, 3. With complementary reference to Christology on the question of racism, as well as a certain theocratic orientation later in the statement.

United Church of Christ [USA], *Resurgent Racism* (1979). Seems to presuppose a kind of natural-law perspective, though the resolution may more nearly exhibit the suppositions of secular ecumenism.

3. Appeal to creation/view of human persons, supplemented by other articles of the creed

World Methodist Council Conference, *Council Message to the Methodists of the World* (1966).

4. Appeal to creation/moral commandment/anthropology

American Lutheran Church, *The Nature of the Church and Its Relationship with Government* (1980), C6, B3a, B2b, A. Opposes tax exemptions for organizations with policies of racial discrimination. It seems to rely on a two-kingdom ethic.

Evangelische Kirche in Deutschland, *Entschliessung der Synode der EKD betreffend das ökumenische Programm zur Bekämpfung des Rassismus* (1971). Endorses something like a two-kingdom ethic. It supports in a qualified way the WCC Program to Combat Racism and would study the use of violence for achieving positive social ends.

Evangelische Kirche im Rheinland, *Erklärung und Beschlüsse der Landessynode 1971 zum ökumenischen Programm zur Bekämpfung des Rassismus* (1971). Endorses something like a two-kingdom ethic, in virtue of citing the preceding resolution. It supports the WCC Program to Combat Racism and its Special Fund and is open to the possible legitimacy of the use of violence for overcoming an oppressive power.

Evangelische Kirchenleitungen in der Deutschen Demokratischen Republik, *Votum der Konferenz der Evangelischen Kirchenleitungen in der DDR vom 6./7. Juli 1979 zur Frage der Gewaltanwendung im Kampf gegen den Rassismus im südlichen Afrika,* 1.3; 2.1. With criticism, though some support of WCC Program to Combat Racism.

Lutheran World Federation, *Responsible Participation in Today's Society* (1970), 4, 16-52, esp. 51, 48-49, 30, 29, 26. Seems to appeal to creation as warrant, inasmuch as social structures rooted in creation warrant the position taken. It is unclear, however, whether reference to the "Lord of history" might also connote an appeal to Christology for authorization, and unclear whether any authorization is really given for the position on racism.

Lutheran World Federation, *Statement on Racial Issues and Minority Problems — A Challenge for the Church* (1970). Calls for cooperation of "all men of good will".

National Council of Churches [USA], *Human Rights Policy* (1963).

National Council of Churches [USA], *Indian Affairs* (1978). Concerned about racism in the law.

National Council of Churches [USA], *Immigrants, Refugees and Migrants* (1981), II/3,1.

Message of the Holy Synod of the Russian Orthodox Church on War and Peace (1986), 3.34. At least appeals to something like the concept of the natural law as grounds for praising socialism's respect for human dignity, regardless of race.

United Church of Christ [USA], *Affirming the United Church of Christ as a Just Peace Church* (1985), Pronouncement IV/D/1/i, IV/D/1. Appeals to the concept of human rights for authorization.

WCC New Delhi Assembly, *Report of the Committee on the Commission of the Churches on International Affairs* (1961), 42-47, 59. The statement concerns discrimination. Subsequently the statement condemns discrimination, with warrants from Christology and ecclesiology.

5. Appeal to creation and Christology

American Lutheran Church, *Interracial Marriage* (1968), 1, 4, 7, 8. At least insofar as interracial marriage is not condemned.

Anglicanism, *The Resolutions of the Lambeth Conference (1968),* 16.

Baptist Union of New Zealand, *Public Questions* (1970). Endorses a related resolution of the Baptist World Alliance Congress.

Baptist World Alliance, *Resolution on Reconciliation and Racial Discrimination* (1970).

Brethren in Christ Church [USA], *Statement on Race Relations* (1963).

Brethren in Christ Church [USA], *Elimination of Racist Statements and Attitudes* (1970).

Brethren in Christ Church [USA], *The Christian and Societey* (1972).

British Council of Churches, *Southern Africa* (1963), (c), (a). Cites a statement of the WCC Central Committee, *Racial and Ethnic Tensions* (1963), which condemned racism by appeal to the gospel/Christology and anthropology. It also cites a 1951 statement of the British Council.

[Catholic] Bishops' Conference of Mozambique, *A igreja num Moçambique independente* (1974), 8. Insofar as *Gaudium et Spes* is cited, may posit a subordination of creation to redemption.

Christian Church (Disciples of Christ), *Resolution concerning Stereotypes on Television* (1979). Cites *A Message from the General Board to the Christian Church (Disciples of Christ)* (1969).

Church of Norway, *Kirken og innvandrerne* (1979), 8-9. Appeal to anthropology may be grounded in the gospel, since it is presented as "basic to biblical revelation".

Evangelische Kirche von Westfalen, *Wort der Landessynode 1985 zu Südafrika.*

Evangelische Landeskirche in Württemberg, *Mitteilung an die Gemeinden zum Programm des ökumenischen Rates der Kirchen zur Bekämpfung des Rassismus* (1970), I, II/A. The majority will not support the WCC Program to Combat Racism.

Evangelisch-Lutherische Landeskirche Hannovers, *Kirche und Rassismus* (1975). Like other statements of the church on the subject, it endorses the WCC Uppsala Assembly, *Towards Justice and Peace in International Affairs* (1968), 27-28. It also claims that racism is a sin and cites the 1974 international conference of conservative evangelicals which produced *The Lausanne Covenant,* which condemned racism (p. 5) with the same authorization. It affirms the WCC Program to Combat Racism but opts not to pledge to its Special Fund.

Lutheran World Federation, *Resolutions of the LWF Assembly* (Eleventh Plenary Session, 10 Aug. 1963), 11.

Mennonite Church, General Conference [USA], *Freedom Movement* (1965). A reaffirmation of the denomination's 1959 statement (*The Christian and Race Relations*).

Plan for the Life and Mission of the Methodist Church in Brazil (1982), III/5(a), III/5(g), 6.

Moravian Church in America, Northern Province, *U.S. Senate Ratification of the Convention on the Prevention and Punishment of the Crime of Genocide* (1982). Opposes genocide on grounds of our common humanity and because it is taught in the Bible (as revelation of the gospel).

National Conference of Catholic Bishops [USA], *Race Relations and Poverty* (1966), 1-3, 7, 8, 12, 22. Possible that creation is subordinated to Christology. It calls for affirmative action.

National Conference of Catholic Bishops [USA], *The National Race Crisis* (1968), 1, 8, 17-18.

National Conference of Catholic Bishops [USA], *Society and the Aged: Toward Reconciliation* (1976), 7-9, 34.

National Council of Churches [USA], *The United Nations and World Community* (1977). Appeal to anthropology may predominate.

Reformed Ecumenical Synod, *Race Relations (South Africa)* (1972), art. 60, C, 1, 5. Endorses the earlier 1968 resolutions and remains open to the principle of different churches for different ethnic groups.

Reformed Ecumenical Synod, *Race Relations, Resolutions* (1968), 1, 2, 4, 11. Open to mixed marriages. Yet, probably in deference to member churches in South Africa, it concedes the legitimacy of forming separate congregations differentiated by "linguistic or cultural differences".

Roman Catholic Church, Vatican II, *Nostra Aetate* (1965), 5, 4, 2. May ground the references to creation in Christology, insofar as Christ is said to be "the source of all grace".

Southern Baptist Convention [USA], *On Racism* (1989).

United Church of Christ [USA], *Affirmative Action* (1979).

Social Principles of the United Methodist Church (USA) (1980), III; III/A. Though the Christological warrants are much more explicit.

United Presbyterian Church [USA], *The Confession of 1967*, II.A.4.

World Alliance of Reformed Churches, *Reconciliation and Man: The Freedom of the New Man* (1970). Though Christology, accompanied by themes of liberation theology, may be the prevelant warrant.

WCC Amsterdam Assembly, *The Church and the International Disorder* (1948), Int., IV.

WCC New Delhi Assembly, *The Message of the Assembly to the Churches* (1961), 6, 5, 8. The statement concerns discrimination. Its directive that Christians work through secular agencies suggests that awareness of the impropriety of racism is accessible to all, rooted in creation. Could other references to following Christ's command function only as motivation, not as criteria, for the statement's conclusion?

WCC New Delhi Assembly, *Service* (1961), 29-30, 37, 50.

WCC Uppsala Assembly, *Towards Justice and Peace in International Affairs* (1968), 27-28. States that racism is a blatant denial of the Christian faith.

WCC Vancouver Assembly, *Moving towards Participation* (1983), Int.

6. Appeal to creation and Christology/the Christian faith/gospel, with the former grounded in the latter

Canadian Catholic Conference, *On Immigration Policy* (1975), 9, 2, 1.

National Conference of Catholic Bishops [USA], *To Live in Jesus Christ: A Pastoral Reflection on the Moral Life* (1976), 2, 30, 31, 70-74, 115-16. Ecclesiology functions as a background warrant.

United Presbyterian Church/Presbyterian Church in the U.S., *Reformed Faith and Politics* (1983), rec. C/2, rec. C, Policy Statement.

7. Appeal to creation and the Christian faith/the gospel

American Baptist Churches, *Policy Statement on Racial Justice* (1983). Also concerned about racist practices in the sphere of employment.

British Council of Churches, *Political Change in South Africa: Britain's Responsibility* (1979). Authorized by appeal to Christian conscience and view of human persons.

National Conference of Catholic Bishops [USA], *Statement on the Missions* (1971), 10-12.

National Council of Churches [USA], *Christian Concern and Responsibility for Economic Life in a Rapidly Changing Technological Society* (1966). Affirms the ongoing character of God's creation, which is the primary warrant.

8. Appeal to creation, possibly grounded in Christology

Canadian Conference of Catholic Bishops, *Ethical Choices and Political Challenges* (1983), 39, 38, 22, 7.

Roman Catholic Church, Vatican II, *Gaudium et Spes* (1965), 29, 22, 76-77. With explicit complementary reference to Christology but also an affirmation of the two-kingdom ethic at one point.

9. Appeal to creation, with covenant a possible supporting warrant

International Council of Community Churches [USA], *Statement of Concern on Human Interdependence* (1988). Divine grace functions as the correlated warrant.

International Council of Community Churches [USA], *Statement of Concern on Racism and Sexism* (1989).

10. Appeal to view of human persons and kingdom of God

Dutch Reformed Church (South Africa), *Church and Society* (1986), 112, 218, 329, 343.

11. Appeal to anthropology and eschatology, with the gospel in the background

Roman Catholic Church, *Octogesima Adveniens* (1971), 16, 4, 48, 46.

12. Appeal to Christology/the gospel

American Lutheran Church, *Hunger in the World* (1968), 8.

Anglicanism, Lambeth Conference, *The Renewal of the Church in Faith* (1968).

Baptist Union of Great Britain and Ireland, *Race Relations and Immigration* (1965).

Baptist Union of Great Britain and Ireland, *Racial Understanding and Racist Political Parties* (1978).

Baptist World Alliance, *Resolution on Brotherhood and Equality* (1965).

Brethren in Christ Church (USA), *Commitment to Peace, Justice and Equity* (1970).

Christian Church (Disciples of Christ), *Concerning Race Relations* (1963).

Christian Church (Disciples of Christ), *Regarding Support of Immediate Brotherhood Action in Moral and Civil Rights* (1963).

Christian Church (Disciples of Christ), *Concerning World Hunger* (1966). Authorizing position by appeal to "the Christian conscience".

Christian Church (Disciples of Christ), *Concerning Ministerial Employment without Regard to Race, Color or National Origin* (1967). Authorized by appeal to "the Christian faith".

Christian Church (Disciples of Christ), *A Call to Repentance, Reconciliation and Action* (1968).

Christian Church (Disciples of Christ), *A Message from the General Board* (1969).

Christian Conference of Asia, *Justice and Service* (1973), IV/5; IV; Thrust Paper. The last reference may include appeal to anthropology.

Christian Conference of Asia, *Justice and Service* (1977), A, D.

Christian Reformed Church in North America, *Decisions of 1968,* 18-20.

Church of England, *Immigration and Migration* (1981).

Church of the Province of Southern Africa [Anglican], *World Council of Churches* (1979), 1-4. Including some critique of the WCC Program to Combat Racism.

Eglise de la Confession d'Augsbourg d'Alsace et de Lorraine, *Décision* (Nov. 1976).

Eglise de la Confession d'Augsbourg d'Alsace et de Lorraine, *Résolution* [concernant le Programme de Lutte contre le Racisme] (1978), Int., (1), (5), (9). Takes its position and authorization by citing WCC Nairobi Assembly, *Structures of Injustice and Struggles for Liberation* (1975), 57-73. It also condemns racism as a sin and opposes the use of violence to overcome it.

Eglise de la Confession d'Augsbourg d'Alsace et de Lorraine, *Résolution* [concernant les principes fondamentaux devant guider la réfléxion et l'engagement des chrétiens en tant que citoyens] (1985).

Eglise Réformée de France, *Racisme* (1980), 1. Concerned about renewed outbreak of racism in France. In another 1980 statement, *Programme de lutte contre le racisme,* the church supports the WCC Program to Combat Racism.

Episcopal Church [USA], *General Convention Resolution* [on Indo China (Vietnam)] (1973). Authorizes position by appeal to the doctrine of reconciliation.

Episcopal Church [USA], *General Convention Resolution* [on affirming United Nations Declaration of the Rights of the Child] (1979).

Evangelical Lutheran Church in Tanzania, *Discrimination* (1968).

Evangelical Methodist Church of Argentina, *Social Service and Action: Foundations in Biblical Theology* (n.d.), 4.

Evangelisch-Lutherische Landeskirche Hannovers, *Die Stellungnahme der Landessynode vom 21. Juni 1974.* Authorization provided by the "Christian mandate". It is affirmative but joins the Rat of the Evangelische Kirche in Deutschland and the Kirchenleitung of the Vereinigte Evangelisch-Lutherische Kirche Deutschlands in criticizing the Special Fund of the WCC Program to Combat Racism.

German [Catholic] Bishops' Conference, *Gegen Gewalttat und Terror in der Welt* (1973), 3, 6, 8. Especially concerned about racism in Africa.

Greek Orthodox Archdiocese of North and South America, *Against Racism* (1963). Also refers to the commandment of Christ.

Lutheran Church-Missouri Synod, *To Support Open Housing* (1967). Citing a 1956 resolution, Christians are said to be "constrained" to take this position. Thus the nature of the Christian faith seems to provide authorization.

Lutheran Church-Missouri Synod, *To Make Every Effort to Eliminate Racism* (1979). Racism is condemned as a sin.

Lutheran Church-Missouri Synod, *To Urge Support for Oppressed* (1986). Refers specifically to the commandments of Christ.

Lutheran World Federation, *Statement on Peace and Justice* (1984).

Mennonite Church [USA], *Resolution on South Africa* (1987).

Mennonite Church [USA]/Mennonite Church, General Conference [USA], *Justice and the Christian Witness* (1983), I/B; II/E. Creation seems to function as a background warrant.

Methodist Church [England], *Statement and Programme on Race Relations* (1978), 1, 5.

Methodist Church [England], *A Statement Reaffirming That the Methodist Church Is against Racism in All Its Forms and Is Committed to Racial Justice within a Plural Society* (1988). Reaffirming a 1978 statement whose condemnation of racism also was authorized by appeal to the gospel.

Moravian Church in America, Northern Province, *Resolutions* (1974).

Moravian Church in America, Southern Province, *Relations between Races* (1968). Reaffirmed by the denomination, by appeal to a similar warrant, in its *Implementing Resolution on Race* (1969).

Moravian Church in America, Southern Province, *Action on Racial Justice* (1969).

Moravian Church in America, Southern Province, *Relations between Races* (1969).

National Association of Evangelicals [USA], *Racial Minorities* (1963).

National Association of Evangelicals [USA], *Civil Rights* (1964). To some extent also appeals to the Bible.

National Association of Evangelicals [USA], *On Civil Rights* (1965). Cites a 1956 resolution of the association. It also authorizes the position taken by appeal to the "Bible's teaching".

National Association of Evangelicals [USA], *The Crisis in the Nation* (1968). With authorization drawn from "Christian witness", it implicitly condemns racism insofar as the resolution calls for "equal opportunity".

National Association of Evangelicals [USA], *Revive Your Church, O Lord!* (1989). To some extent also appeals to repentance and holiness.

National Conference of Catholic Bishops [USA], *To Teach as Jesus Did* (1972), 29, 10. The natural law serves as background warrant.

National Conference of Catholic Bishops [USA], *The Bicentennial Consultation: A Response to the Call to Action* (1977), 13-16. The gospel is at least a background warrant.

National Conference of Catholic Bishops [USA], *Economic Justice for All* (1986). PM1, PM2, PM13, 25, 28, 73, 127, 182, 199, 229, 364. Cites the conference's *Brothers and Sisters to Us* (1974).

Netherlands [Catholic] Bishops' Conference, *Vrede en gerechtigheid* (1983), I/2, 1. Reference to Christology in this instance is ambiguous.

Erklärung der Synode der Nordelbischen Evangelisch-Lutherisches Kirche zu Südafrika (1986). Warrant not clear, but suggests that endeavors to overcome racism and apartheid are "placed under" a Christocentric interpretation of the law.

[Orthodox] Ecumenical Patriarchate of Constantinople, *Le message pascal de Sa Sainteté le Patriarche Oecuménique* (1970). At least rejects discrimination.

[Orthodox] Ecumenical Patriarchate of Constantinople, *Message de Noël* (1982).

[Orthodox] Ecumenical Patriarchate of Constantinople, *Message patriarcal des Pâques* (1986).

Presbyterian Church of Southern Africa, *Church and Nation* (1984), 234, clause 3. At least insofar as reference is made to "Christian standards".

Presbyterian-Reformed Church in Cuba, *Confession of Faith* (1977), III/C.

Reformed Church in America, *Report of the Advisory Committee on Christian Unity* (1982), R-9. Racism is said to be "a contradiction of the Christian faith".

Reformed Ecumenical Synod, *Statements on the Social Calling of the Church* (1980), 17, 2, 18. Perhaps supplemented also by appeal to eschatology as warrant.

Reformed Ecumenical Synod, *Pastoral Statement: A Call to Commitment and Action* (1984), XI, XII/C, XII/D/10. Employs liberation theology's call for a preferential option for the poor.

Reformed Ecumenical Synod, *Race Relations* (1984), art. 100, rec. D/6.

Romanian Orthodox Church, *Lettre irénique de Sa Béatitude le Patriarche Iustin, adressée aux chefs des églises Chrétiennes à l'occasion de la fête de la Nativité 1982.*

Southern African Catholic Bishops' Conference, *Pastoral Letter of the Southern African Bishops' Conference on the Proposed New Constitution for South Africa* (1983), 6, 9.

United Church of Christ [USA], *Resolution on the Report on Racial and Economic Justice* (1977).

United Church of Christ [USA], *Racism in the United Church of Christ* (1979).

United Church of Christ [USA], *Affirmative Action in Church and Society* (1981).

United Church of Christ [USA], *Faith and Racism* (1981).

United Church of Christ [USA], *Increased Racial Violence against Blacks in America* (1981). Christology may only function as a motive rather than as a warrant.

United Church of Christ [USA], *Justice in Immigration* (1981).

United Church of Christ [USA], *Economic Justice: The Crisis and a Response of the Church* (1983).

United Church of Christ [USA], *The National Toxic Injustice Crisis* (1985), Pronouncements 2, 1.

United Church of Christ [USA], *United Church of Christ Full Divestment of All Financial Resources from All Corporations Doing Business with South Africa* (1985), Pronouncement 3. Concerned about racial justice.

United Church of Christ [USA], *A United Church of Christ Ministry with Indians* (1987), Pronouncement 3.

United Free Church of Scotland, *Deliverance of the General Assembly* [on public questions] (1981), 1. Cites resolutions of the British Council of Churches on the subject.

Wesleyan Church [USA], *Special Directions* (1984), (1), Int. Authorizes position by appeal to Christian faith/faith in Christ.

World Alliance of Reformed Churches, *Reconciliation and Society: The Freedom of a Just Order* (1970), 8; Int.; Appendix. With passing reference to creation and the church as warrants of statement.

World Alliance of Reformed Churches, *The Power of Grace and the Graceless Powers* (1982).

WCC Amsterdam Assembly, *The Church and the Disorder of Society* (1948), V.

WCC Amsterdam Assembly, *Message of the Assembly* (1948).

WCC Evanston Assembly, *International Affairs — Christians in the Struggle for World Community* (1954), VI. Also refers to the "moral law" and eschatology.

WCC Nairobi Assembly, *Structures of Injustice and Struggles for Liberation* (1975), 57-73. Offers some corresponding reference to God's justice as a warrant. Racism is identified as a sin.

WCC New Delhi Assembly, *Witness* (1961), 15, 14.

WCC Uppsala Assembly, *Towards New Styles of Living* (1968), 13-14 (warrant is our Christian calling).

WCC Vancouver Assembly, *Message from the Sixth Assembly* (1983). The Eucharist may function as a background warrant. Creation also is vaguely in the background.

WCC Vancouver Assembly, *Statement on Southern Africa* (1983), 1-12, 13.

WCC Vancouver Assembly, *Struggling for Justice and Human Dignity* (1983), 9; 13; 7.1; 8; 10-11; 23.

World Methodist Council Conference, *Resolution on Racism* (1981).

13. Appeal to Christology/the gospel/reconciliation

American Baptist Churches, *Policy Statement on Health Care* (1975). Opposes discrimination in availability of health care.

Christian Church (Disciples of Christ), *Concerning Wider World Perspectives* (1973).

Christian Church (Disciples of Christ), *Resolution concerning Affirmative Action and Ministerial Leadership* (1981). Authorized by appeal to Christology and the Prophets.

Christian Church (Disciples of Christ), *Resolution concerning Guidelines and Plans for the Implementation of Affirmative Action by the Christian Church (Disciples of Christ)* (1981).

Mennonite Brethren Church, *Regarding Political Involvement* (1966), II.

Mennonite Church [USA], *Urban-Racial Concerns* (1969), 4. Appeals to "Christian compassion" for authorization.

Mennonite Church [USA], *A Church of Many Peoples Confronts Racism* (1989). Reaffirms the church's earlier statements on the subject: *The Way of Christian Love in Race Relations* (1955); *Reconciliation* (1963); *Urban Riots* (1967); *Urban-Racial Concerns* (1969). It also reaffirms Mennonite Church, General Conference [USA], *The Christian and Race Relations* (1959) and *Freedom Movement* (1965). Insofar as the last statement is endorsed, the most recent statement may share its appeal to creation and redemption to authorize condemnation of racism, as well as the earlier statement's call for peace and social justice.

United Church of Christ [USA], *A Call for Action to Fulfill Racial Justice Now* (1965). Calls for economic sanctions against corporations which practice racial discrimination.

Uniting Church in Australia, *Bicentennial Celebrations* (1982), 82.48, (2).

Uniting Church in Australia, *Commonwealth Games* (1982), 82.49, (4), (1).

World Alliance of Reformed Churches, *The Pacific, Australia, and Aotearoa/New Zealand* (1989).

World Mennonite Conference, *Conference Message* (1972), Int. III.

14. Appeal to Christology/the gospel and the Bible

Christian Church (Disciples of Christ), *Concerning the Universal Declaration of Human Rights* (1973). This position is taken insofar as the Universal Declaration of Human Rights, which rejects all forms of discrimination, is endorsed.

Christian Church (Disciples of Christ), *Concerning Priorities for the Christian Church (Disciples of Christ), 1982-1985* (1981).

Lutheran Church-Missouri Synod, *To Encourage Christian Action to Combat Racism* (1971).

15. Appeal to Christology/the gospel and pneumatology

Lutheran Church-Missouri Synod, *To Adopt Proposals on Fair Housing and Employment Practices* (1965).

16. Appeal to Christology/redemption, supplemented by other articles of the creed

American Lutheran Church, *Racism in the Church* (1974), 1, 3, 6, 9.

Lutheran World Federation, *Racism in Church and Society* (1984), 10.7, 8, 10; i. See p. 158 for details about the statement.

Nederduitse Gereformeerde Sendingkerk, *Confession of Faith* (1982). Creation and ecclesiology seem to be only background warrants, though ecclesiology plays a role akin to the one played by the doctrine of reconciliation.

Presbyterian Church (USA), *Christian Obedience in a Nuclear Age* (1988), 1-2, 9. Warrant not entirely clear, but may be authorized by Christology, the law, and the Bible, insofar as racism is said to be a matter of justice, which is itself authorized by these themes.

Presbyterian Church (USA), *Life Abundant: Values, Choices and Health Care* (1988), 15, 17.

South African Council of Churches, *A Message to the People of South Africa* (1968). Anthropology and ecclesiology are only background warrants; the statement refers to "Christ's lordship".

United Church of Christ [USA], *"The Faith Crisis": Goals and Objectives* (1971). In addition to Christology, also appeals to the prophetic tradition of the Old Testament.

United Church of Christ [USA], *Health and Wholeness in the Midst of a Pandemic* (1987), Pronouncement I-III. Creation functions as a background warrant.

World Alliance of Reformed Churches, *Racism and South Africa* (1982), I. The statement was reaffirmed by World Alliance of Reformed Churches, *Southern Africa* (1989). Eschatology plays at least some role as a warrant.

17. Appeal to Christology/grace/reconciliation and eschatology or ecclesiology

National Association of Evangelicals [USA], *Go . . . Liberate* (1986).
United Church of Canada, *Poverty Report and Recommendations* (1977), rec. 2B, Int.
United Presbyterian Church/Presbyterian Church in the U.S., *Strangers Become Neighbors: Presbyterian Response to Mexican Migration* (1981), I, II/C/6.
WCC Canberra Assembly, *The Report of the Seventh Assembly* (1991), 40, 44, 48. Pneumatology is endorsed either as a motive or as a possible warrant.

18. Appeal to Christology, supplemented by appeal to ecclesiology and creation

Methodist Church in Malaysia, *Social Principles* (n.d.), III/E; III/D.1; III/B.1; II; I.

19. Appeal to second-article themes, supplemented by appeal to third-article loci

British Council of Churches, *Community and Race Relations Unit* (1982). Takes position and theological argument in virtue of adopting the paper *Towards a Multi-Racial Britain — Why and How Grants Are Made*.
Evangelical Lutheran Church in Southern Africa, *Apartheid as Heresy* (1982).
Mennonite Brethren Church, *Race Relations* (1963). Primarily concerned about overcoming racism in the church and its practice but shows some concern to overcome racism in the broader society.
United Church of Christ [USA], *Economic Justice* (1973). With a possible appeal to creation in the background.
United Church of Christ [USA], *Jesus Christ Frees and Unites* (1975).
World Alliance of Reformed Churches, *The People of the Covenant and the Mission of the Kingdom* (1982), 7, 5, 4, 3, 1. Authorization seems to be offered by the doctrines of redemption, covenant, baptism, and perhaps eschatology.

20. Appeal to pneumatology

Federation of Protestant Churches in Switzerland, *Par une action concertée énergique en faveur du Tiers monde* (1986), II.5(e), II.14. With an appeal to a Christology possibly in the background.
Mennonite World Conference, *The Conference Message* (1967), III, I.
Southern African Catholic Bishops' Conference, *Social Justice and Race Relations Within the Church* (1977), 1-5, 21, Int.

21. Appeal to ecclesiology

Eglise Protestante Unie de Belgique, *Motion du District Antwerpen-Brabant-Limburg concernant l'attitude de l'église envers les migrants* (1984). With Christology functioning as a motive.
Evangelische Landeskirche in Baden, *Einheit der Kirche in der Zerrissenheit zwischen Ost und West und Nord und Süd* (1981), II/1.2. Though elsewhere in the statement "Christian faith" functions as authorization.
Evangelisch-Lutherische Kirche in Bayern, *Menschenrechtsverletzungen* (1985). Though appeal is also likely made to Christology.

United Church of Christ [USA], *Economic Life* (1969). (Reference is also made to our "God-given duty". Concern is expressed about equal job opportunities regardless of race.)
United Church of Christ [USA], *Racial Justice* (1979).
United Free Church of Scotland, *Deliverance of the General Assembly* [on public questions] (1980), 1, 3. With love and "Christian moral values" as background warrants.
WCC New Delhi Assembly, *Message to Christians in South Africa* (1961).
WCC Uppsala Assembly, *The Holy Spirit and the Catholicity of the Church* (1968), 22, 21. Racism is said to challenge the church's catholicity, but human unity is also rooted in both creation and Christology.
WCC Uppsala Assembly, *Message* (1968).

22. Appeal to sacramentology

World Alliance of Reformed Churches, *Come Creator Spirit, for the Calling of the Churches Together* (1964). Authorization provided by baptism. Only the resolutions of the report were approved, and they do not deal with racism.
WCC Faith and Order Commission, *Baptism, Eucharist and Ministry* (1981), 20.

23. Appeal to sacramentology and ecclesiology

United Church of Christ [USA], *Racism and Sexism* (1977).

24. Appeal to sacramentology, eschatology, and Christology

Lutheran-Episcopal Dialogue, series 3 [USA], *Implications of the Gospel* (1988), 122, 60.

25. Appeal to eschatology

Caribbean Conference of Churches, *Thine Is the Kingdom, the Power and the Glory* (1981).

26. Appeal to loci derived from all articles of the creed

American Baptist Churches, *Policy Statement on Human Rights* (1976).
American Lutheran Church, *Issues and Opportunities That Bind and Free* (1976).
Baptist Union of New Zealand, *Public Questions* (1989), (b).
Christian Church (Disciples of Christ), *Concerning Racial Integration* (1963).
Christian Reformed Church in North America, *Decision of 1969*, 50-52, 210. Takes the position and its mode of argument in virtue of ratifying a report of the Reformed Ecumenical Synod, *Resolutions on Race Relations* (1968), 2-4, 7-11.
Conference of European Churches and Council of European Bishops' Conferences, *Final Document of the European Ecumenical Assembly Peace with Justice* (1989), 84, 73, 72, 44, 43, 40, 37, 33, 25-27. Includes reference to covenant, which itself reflects a trinitarian framework.
Episcopal Church [USA], *General Convention Resolution* [on condemning the resurgence of activity of the Ku Klux Klan] (1979).
Lutheran World Federation, *Statement on Human Rights* (1984), II.
National Council of Churches [USA], *Middle East* (1980). Affirmed by Christian Church (Disciples of Christ), *Concerning a Policy Statement on the Middle East* (1981).

United Church of Christ [USA], *Calling on United Church of Christ Congregations to Declare Themselves Open and Affirming* (1985).

World Alliance of Reformed Churches, *Come Creator Spirit, for the Redemption of the World* (1964), II.

WCC Evanston Assembly, *Inter-Group Relations — The Church amid Racial and Ethnic Tensions* (1954), Res.; II; III.

WCC Evanston Assembly, *International Affairs — Christians in the Struggle for World Community* (1954), VI.

WCC New Delhi Assembly, *Resolution on Racial and Ethnic Tensions* (1961), 4, 1.

WCC World Convocation on Justice, Peace and the Integrity of Creation, *Final Document: Entering into Covenant Solidarity for Justice, Peace and the Integrity of Creation* (1990), 2.3.2.1-2.3.2.4; 2.2; 2.1. Appeals to covenant, which is defined in trinitarian terms. Christology may be the prevailing warrant.

27. Appeal to loci derived from all articles of the creed, especially creation and eschatology

Beschluss der Generalsynode der Vereinigte Evangelisch-Lutherische Kirche Deutschlands zu der "Erklärung des Friedens" des Exekutivkomitees des Lutherischen Weltbundes vom 24. Oktober 1981. Cites the LWF statement, 3, 5, mentioned in the resolution's title, which seems to posit this sort of authorization in its critique of racism.

28. Appeal to loci derived from all articles of the creed, including the Eucharist, Mariology, and the saints, though all are subordinated to Christology

Roman Catholic Church, *Sollicitudo Rei Socialis* (1987), 15, 1, 3, 7, 8, 40, 47-49. Warrant is not explicitly stated but seems implied insofar as overcoming racism is related to development, which is itself authorized by these loci.

29. Appeal to loci derived from all three articles of the creed, though likely all are rooted in redemption/evangelism

National Conference of Catholic Bishops [USA], *Brothers and Sisters to Us: A Pastoral Letter on Racism* (1979).

30. Appeal to loci derived from all articles of the creed and the Bible

Evangelische Kirche im Rheinland, *Zur Überwindung des Rassismus* (1971).

31. Appeal to the will of God and the traditions of the church

South African Council of Churches, *A Theological Rationale and a Call to Prayer for the End to Unjust Rule* (1985).

32. Reference to the contents of Scripture

Christian Church (Disciples of Christ), *Concerning Investments in South Africa* (1968).

Episcopal Church [USA], *General Convention Resolution* [on directing the Executive Council to design means to assist dioceses and congregations] (1979).

Reformed Ecumenical Synod, *Race Relations* (1984), art. 103, rec. E/2.
United Church of Christ [USA], *Justice and Peace Priority* (1985).
World Alliance of Reformed Churches, *Justice, Peace and Integrity of Creation* (1989).

33. Reference to the contents of Scripture and Christian conscience or Christian principles

Dutch Reformed Church (South Africa), *A Declaration of Christian Principles* (1990), 2.2.5; 2.2.4; 1.

34. Appeal to Christian love

Mennonite Church, General Conference [USA], *The Way of Peace* (1971).
United Church of Christ [USA], *The Hispanic Ministry of the United Church of Christ* (1987), Pronouncement II.

35. Appeal to Christian responsibility

Evangelische Kirche im Rheinland, *Antrag der Kreissynode Köln-Nord zum Rassenkonflikt im südlichen Afrika* (1974).

36. Appeal to the church's moral imperative/Christian example

Episcopal Church [USA], *General Convention Resolution* [on directing the Executive Council to develop affirmative action programs] (1979).

37. Appeal to the example of modern saints

Episcopal Church [USA], *Affirm Witness of Bishop Desmond Tutu and Church in Africa* (1985).

38. No clear theological warrant given for position

All Africa Conference of Churches, *Working with Christ in the Contemporary Social, Economic and Political Situation* (1969). Though earlier in the statement reference is made to creation, Christ, and ecclesiology as warrants for action.
American Baptist Churches, *Policy Statement on Metropolitan Ministries* (1979).
American Baptist Churches, *Policy Statement on Employment* (1981).
American Lutheran Church, *A Call to Affirmation of Human Values* (1972). Perhaps a two-kingdom ethic is in the background.
Anglican Church of Canada, *Resolutions on Anti-Semitism* (1983), Act 36. Denounces racism directed against Jews.
Anglicanism, *The Resolutions of the Lambeth Conference* (1988), 31, 58.
Fédération Protestante de France, *Vœux adoptés à l'Assemblée du Protestantisme Français à la Rochelle* (1983), 5.
Baptist Union of Great Britain and Ireland, *Politics and Peaceful Protest* (1970).
Baptist Union of Great Britain and Ireland, *Racial Harmony* (1971). Though an appeal to the doctrine of creation may be in the background.
Bremische Evangelische Kirche, *Südafrika* (1987).

Brethren in Christ Church (USA), *Racial Question* (1964).

British Council of Churches, *The Programme to Combat Racism of the World Council of Churches* (1970). Supports the program and its Special Fund to support victims of racial injustice.

British Council of Churches, *Racial Justice in Southern Africa* (1970). Concerned about racial justice.

British Council of Churches, *The Christian Response to Racial Injustice in Southern Africa and Elsewhere* (1971).

British Council of Churches, *Community and Race Relations Unit* (1978).

British Council of Churches, *Nationality and Citizenship* (1979).

British Council of Churches, *Proposed Legislation on Nationality* (1981).

British Council of Churches, *Equal Opportunities* (1983), 8. Rejects racism implicitly in the decision to have the council be an equal-opportunities employer.

British Council of Churches, *Swann Report on Multi-Cultural Education Issues* (1985).

British Council of Churches, *Equal Opportunities* (1986). Rejects racism implicitly in the decision to have the council be an equal-opportunities employer.

Canadian Catholic Bishops, *On Development and Peace* (1968), 18. Cites Roman Catholic Church, *The Development of Peoples* (1967).

[Catholic] Bishops of Netherlands, *Gelijke behandeling* (1982), 3, 4-5. Though critical of government legislation designed to combat discrimination.

Christian Church (Disciples of Christ), *Concerning Non-Discrimination on Housing* (1963).

Christian Church (Disciples of Christ), *Coordinating Committee on Moral and Civil Rights* (1964).

Christian Church (Disciples of Christ), *Concerning Investments in South Africa* (1966).

Christian Church (Disciples of Christ), *Concerning World Order, Justice and Peace* (1968). Concerned about justice for blacks.

Christian Church (Disciples of Christ), *Concerning Human Rights* (1977).

Christian Church (Disciples of Christ), *Resolution concerning Racism* (1981).

Christian Conference of Asia, *Life and Action* (1977), VIII (2), I. Though the gospel could be in the background as a warrant.

Christian Reformed Church in North America, *Decision of 1971*, 113, 114.

Church of the Brethren [USA], *Statement on Aging* (1985).

Church of the Province of Southern Africa [Anglican], *Permits and Free Assembly* (1979), 1.

Episcopal Church [USA], *Conscientious Objectors* (1967).

Episcopal Church [USA], *Desegregation of Church-related Schools* (1967).

Episcopal Church [USA], *Equal Opportunity in Clergy Placement* (1967).

Episcopal Church [USA], *General Convention Response to the Presiding Bishop's Address* (1967).

Episcopal Church [USA], *Non-discriminatory Employment Practices* (1967).

Episcopal Church [USA], *Racial Discrimination in Labor Unions* (1967).

Episcopal Church [USA], *General Convention Resolution* [on affirmation of Executive Council response to "Black Manifesto"] (1969). Calls for racial justice.

Episcopal Church [USA], *General Convention Resolution* [on help to overcome discrimination and stereotypes] (1970). Condemns racism towards American Indians and Eskimos. The Christian standpoint (the gospel) may be a background warrant.

Episcopal Church [USA], *General Convention Resolution* [on racial inequities in clergy placement] (1976).

Episcopal Church [USA], *General Convention Resolution* [on South Africa apartheid] (1976).

Episcopal Church [USA], *General Convention Resolution* [on support for ministry with Asian/Pacific Islanders in [USA] (1976). Opposes racism in the sense of endorsing a ministry to racial and ethnic minorities. The mission of the church could be a background warrant.

Episcopal Church [USA], *General Convention Resolution* [on urban ministries] (1976). Concerned about racial justice.

Episcopal Church [USA], *General Convention Resolution* [on recommending that Episcopalians resign or change policies of private clubs which discriminate against Jewish, black, or other ethnic minorities] (1979).

Episcopal Church [USA], *General Convention Resolution* [on support of affirmative action] (1979).

Episcopal Church [USA], *Affirmative Action* (1982).

Episcopal Church [USA], *Affirmative Action in Church Organizations* (1982).

Episcopal Church [USA], *Relief for Refugees* (1982).

Episcopal Church [USA], *Programs for Violence Awareness* (1985).

Episcopal Church [USA], *Establish and Fund a Commission on Racism* (1988).

Episcopal Church [USA], *Reaffirm Commitment to Affirmative Action* (1988).

Episcopal Church [USA], *Use of Inclusive Language* (1988).

Episcopal Church [USA], *Women and People of Color as Interim Pastors* (1988).

Episcopal Conference of Portugal, *The Regulation of Birth* (1983), 9, 7, 6. May appeal to anthropology or the natural law, but this is not clear. Efforts to improve the human species through birth-control techniques easily transform themselves into racism.

Evangelical Lutheran Church in Southern Africa, *New Political Dispensation* (1984). May make background appeal to anthropology and "Christian principles".

Evangelische Kirche der Kirchenprovinz Sachsen, *Beschluss zur Gesamtthematik der Synodaltagung* (1985), 2. The covenant/gospel is a warrant for many points in the resolution, but not clearly so in this case.

Evangelische Kirche der Union — Bereich Bundesrepublik Deutschland und Berlin-West, *Wort an die Gliedkirchen zur 40. Wiederkehr des Tages der Synagogenbrände im Jahre 1978*. Condemns anti-Semitism.

Evangelische Kirche der Union — Bereich Bundesrepublik Deutschland und Berlin-West, *Stellungnahme der Synode der EKU (Regionalbereich West) zu UNCTAD III* (1974).

Evangelische Kirche im Rheinland, *Stellungnahme zum Problem der weissen Einwanderung ins südliche Afrika* (1976). Concerned to avoid racial discrimination in South Africa. It endorses a 1972 resolution of the WCC Central Committee and notes a 1975 report of the Evangelische Kirche in Deutschland on South Africa and a 1973 report of the British Council of Churches.

Evangelische Kirche in Deutschland, *Entschliessung zur Rassendiskriminierung* (1974). Affirms the WCC Program to Combat Racism but criticizes and refuses to support its Special Fund.

Evangelische Kirche in Hessen und Nassau, *Synodalbeschlüsse: 4. Kirchensynode, 8. Tagung* (1970), 15. Condemns racism insofar as the resolution supports the WCC Program to Combat Racism, though it is critical of the use of violence.

Evangelische Kirche in Österreich, *Beschluss* [zum Antirassismusprogramm des Ökumenischen Rates der Kirchen] (1972). Rejects involvement in the WCC Program to Combat Racism.

Evangelisch-Lutherische Kirche in Bayern, *Beschluss der Landessynode zum ökumenischen Programm zur Bekämpfung des Rassismus* (1971). Cites an earlier 1970 declaration of the church.

Wort der Landessynode und des Landeskirchenrates der Evangelisch-Lutherische Kirche in Bayern zu Fragen des sexuellen Verhaltens und des Sexualstrafrechts (1971), II.

Erklärung der Landessynode der Evangelisch-Lutherischen Landeskirche Hannovers zu dem Anti-Rassismus Programm des Ökumenischen Rates der Kirchen (1970). Warrant not clear, though creation and Christian faith lead to the rejection of the use of violence on behalf of justice for the neighbor.

Fédération Protestante de France, *Vœux à l'Assemblée Générale* (1987), 2, 4.

Latin American [Catholic] Bishops, Second General Conference (Medellín Conference), *Peace* (1968), 2, 14, 20, 26.

Lutheran Church-Missouri Synod, *To Advocate Adequate Housing* (1977). Condemns racism in housing.

Lutheran Church-Missouri Synod, *To Involve Board of Social Ministry and World Relief with Commission on Black Ministry* (1977).
Lutheran World Federation, *Resolution on Communion of All Races* (1970). Though claims racial practices should conform with Christian principles.
Lutheran World Federation, *Statement on Southern Africa: Confessional Integrity* (1984), 7.
Mennonite Church [USA], *Telegram to President Kennedy* (1965).
Mennonite Church [USA], *Urban Riots* (1967).
Moravian Church in America, Northern Province, *Resolution on Race Relations* (1963). Though reference is made to what it means to be a Christian.
Moravian Church in America, Southern Province, *Action on Racial Justice* (1968). Reaffirmed by the denomination by means of apparent authorization drawn from Christology, in its *Implementing Resolution on Race* (1969).
Moravian Church in America, Southern Province, *Equal Rights* (1974).
Moravian Church in America, Southern Province, *Parish Placement of Ordained Women* (1980).
National Association of Evangelicals [USA], *Resolution on Apartheid* (1986). Affirms the NAE statement *Race and Racial Minorities* (1956). The Bible and divine justice may be background warrants.
National Conference of Catholic Bishops [USA], *Resolution on Crusade against Poverty* (1969), 1.
National Conference of Catholic Bishops [USA], *Statement on the Twenty-fifth Anniversary of the United Nations* (1970), 5, 17. Though creation may be a background warrant.
National Conference of Catholic Bishops [USA], *To Do the Work of Justice* (1978), 34.
National Conference of Catholic Bishops [USA]/United States Catholic Bishops, *Statement on Capital Punishment* (1980), 19.
National Council of Churches [USA], *The Concern of the Church for Seasonal Farm Workers* (1966).
National Council of Churches [USA], *The Church and Television, Radio and Cable Communication* (1972), III. Concerned about racial justice.
National Council of Churches [USA], *Policy Statement on Child Day Care* (1984), II/A/3.
A Statement from the New Zealand Catholic Bishops on the Morality of In Vitro Fertilisation (1984), 1.
Presbyterian Church (USA), *God Alone Is Lord of the Conscience* (1988), C/1, A.
Reformed Church in America, *Additional Recommendations to the Report of the Christian Action Commission to General Synod* (1963), recs. 1, 2, 4.
Reformed Church in America, *Addendum to Report of the Christian Action Commission to the 1964 General Synod*. Christology is a background warrant for the report as a whole.
Reformed Church in America, *Report of the Christian Action Commission* (1964), rec. 5.
Reformed Church in America, *Report of the Christian Action Commission* (1965), rec. 1c.
Reformed Church in America, *Report of the Christian Action Commission* (1967), rec. 4. Advocates the dismantling of racist housing practices.
Reformed Church in America, *Report of the Christian Action Commission* (1968), R-36.
Reformed Church in America, *Report of the Christian Action Commission* (1969), R-1, R-5.
Reformed Church in America, *Report of the Christian Action Commission* (1971), recs. 5, 17.
Reformed Church in America, *Report of the Christian Action Commission* (1977), R-6.
Reformed Church in America, *Report of the Christian Action Commission* (1983), R-1.
Pastoral Letter of the Roman Catholic Bishops in Mozambique (1976). An appeal to the doctrine of creation could be in the background.
Roman Catholic Church, Congregation for the Doctrine of the Faith, *Instruction on Christian Freedom and Liberation* (1986), 95. Though reference to *Gaudium et Spes* could imply the correlation of creation and redemption as warrants.
Russian Orthodox Church, *Decrees of the Holy Synod* (1986).

Southern Baptist Convention (USA), *Involvement of Blacks and Other Minorities in Southern Baptist Life* (1986).

Statement of the Sudanese Catholic Bishops' Conference to the Transitional Government of the Sudan (1985), A/2.

United Church of Canada, *South Africa* (1972), 4.

United Church of Canada, *Statement on Human Rights* (1980), 2. Cites a 1979 statement of the Church in South Africa which took a similar position.

United Church of Canada, *Apartheid* (1984).

United Church of Canada, *Compensation and Redress to Japanese Canadians Interned during WWII* (1984).

United Church of Canada, *Native Church Structures* (1984).

United Church of Canada, *Racism* (1988).

United Church of Christ [USA], *Executive Council Statement on Racial Crisis* (1963).

United Church of Christ [USA], *Fair Employment Practices and Civil Rights Legislation* (1963). Urges preference be given to firms observing fair employment practices.

United Church of Christ [USA], *Integrated Quality Education* (1965). Cites the denomination's *Executive Council Statement on Racial Crisis* (1963), as well as earlier 1961 and 1959 resolutions.

United Church of Christ [USA], *Report of the Council for Christian Action, as Finally Adopted* (1965), 2-4, 6.

United Church of Christ [USA], *Resolution on Poverty* (1965).

United Church of Christ [USA], *Poverty and Economic Justice* (1967). Especially concerned about integrated housing.

United Church of Christ [USA], *Racial Justice* (1967).

United Church of Christ [USA], *Report on the Committee for Racial Justice Now, as Finally Adopted* (1967), 1, 3.

United Church of Christ [USA], *School Integration and Housing* (1967). Particularly concerned to overcome segregation and unfair housing practices.

United Church of Christ [USA], *Action on the Report on the Committee for Racial Justice* (1969).

United Church of Christ [USA], *Hunger, Population and World Development* (1969).

United Church of Christ [USA], *Resolution to Abolish Capital Punishment* (1969). Seems to condemn racism insofar as it rejects capital punishment because it discriminates against blacks.

United Church of Christ [USA], *Peace and United States Power* (1971). Concerned about racial justice.

United Church of Christ [USA], *A Sense of Moral Breakdown Issue* (1973). Though does refer to the conscience.

United Church of Christ [USA], *Statement on Women in Church and Society* (1973).

United Church of Christ [USA], *Federal Budget* (1981). Passing reference is made to the "biblical mandate", but authorization is not clear.

United Church of Christ [USA], *Pronouncement on Public Education* (1985), IV, III. Appeals to creation and the prophetic tradition may be in the background.

United Free Church of Scotland, *Deliverance of the General Assembly* [on public questions] (1965), 15.

United Free Church of Scotland, *Deliverance of the General Assembly* [on public questions] (1968), 4, 1.

United Free Church of Scotland, *Deliverance of the General Assembly* [on public questions] (1969), 1, 10.

United Free Church of Scotland, *Deliverance of the General Assembly* [on public questions] (1970), 5.

United Free Church of Scotland, *Deliverance of the General Assembly* [on public questions] (1978), 5.

Uniting Church in Australia, *Statement to Nation* (1977). The gospel may function as a warrant.

Uniting Church in Australia, *Investment Policy* (1982), 82.55.

Uniting Church in Australia, *Response to WCC Visit* (1982), 82.51 (1), (3a).

Vereinigte Evangelisch-Lutherische Kirche Deutschlands, *Erklärung der Generalsynode zum Rassismus* (1970). Also argues that while an individual Christian may engage in violence to help a neighbor, the church itself should not promote use of violence, even for a good purpose.

Vereinigte Evangelisch-Lutherische Kirche Deutschlands, *Entschliessung zum Fonds für Gerechtigkeit und Versöhnung* (1973), 1. Cites the previous 1970 declaration.

Vereinigte Evangelisch-Lutherische Kirche Deutschlands, *Sonderfonds des Antirassismus-programms des ÖRK* (1980). Including a strong criticism of the WCC Program to Combat Racism.

World Alliance of Reformed Churches, *Come, Creator Spirit, for the Renewal of Worship and Witness* (1964), 4C, 2. Pneumatology may be a background warrant. The report was only "received".

WCC Uppsala Assembly, *World Economic and Social Development* (1968), 22-23. Though earlier in the statement some warrants are drawn from both Christology and creation doctrine.

Racism is implicitly criticized by the Reformed Church in America, *Report of the Christian Action Commission* (1976), R-7, when, authorized by Christology and pneumatology, it affirms the practice of busing students to achieve quality education.

Opposition to the proposals for a new constitution in the Republic of South Africa has been expressed by several church bodies, namely, South African Council of Churches, *The Republic of South Africa Constitution Bill* (1983); Southern African Catholic Bishops Conference, *Pastoral Letter of the Southern African Bishops Conference on the Proposed New Constitution for South Africa* (1983), 9.3; Conference of the Methodist Church of Southern Africa, *On the Proposed New Constitution* (1983). Though the last statement may not have an official status, all of these statements represent a condemnation of apartheid warranted by appeals to Christology (though the first also makes some passing reference to the creation doctrine/anthropology). Also to be considered is the advocacy of refusing to participate in athletic events involving South African athletes by the British Council of Churches, *Sport Contact with South Africa* (1984). This position, as well as the British Council's expressed support, in its *Delegation to South Africa* (1983), of the South African Council of Churches, amounts to a critique of apartheid.

Likewise the opposition expressed to the South African resettlement policy by the Church of the Province of Southern Africa (Anglican), *Orderly Movement and Settlement of Black Persons Bill* (1982), on grounds of God's creation and because he loves all people, could be taken as a condemnation of apartheid. The same position is taken, on grounds of an appeal to "Christian principles", by the Presbyterian Church of Southern Africa, *Church and Nation, South Africa* (1979), 74, clause 9. In a similar manner, apartheid is implicitly critiqued by the South African Catholic Bishops Conference, *Charter of Rights for Migrant Workers in South Africa* (1981), when, with authorization drawn from all three articles of the creed, the bishops criticize the South African government's prevention of certain people from taking up permanent residence at their place of work.

Another pertinent statement is a 1976 resolution of the Vereinigte Evangelisch-Lutherische Kirche Deutschlands, *Schreiben an die FELCSA-Konferenz in Johannesburg,* which urged South African Lutheran churches to seek unity; in so doing, it seems to oppose segregation in the churches. Cf. Vereinigte Evangelisch-Lutherische Kirche Deutschlands, *Beschluss: Schreiben an die Federation of Evangelical Lutheran Churches in Southern Africa* (1977). Opposition to the South African government's actions is expressed by the Vereinigte Evangelisch-Lutherische Kirche Deutschlands in the church's latter statement as well as in its *An die Kirchenleitungen der Vereinigten Evangelisch-Lutherischen Kirche in Südwestafrika und der Deutschen Evangelisch-*

Lutherischen Kirche in Südwestafrika (1975) and its *Brief an Premierminister P.W. Botha* (1980).

Apartheid is implicitly critiqued by the call of the United Church of Christ [USA], in its *Statement on Africa* (1973), as well as in its *Action on the Report of the Committee for Racial Justice* (1969), which calls for economic sanctions against South African governments which maintain the practice. Also see the call for disinvestment in companies engaged in the South African economy by the Church in Wales, *Resolutions of April 1983 re: South Africa* (1983, reaffirmed in 1986); Reformed Church in America, *Report of the Christian Action Commission* (1971), rec. 5; Lutheran Church-Missouri Synod, *To Affirm Investment Policies* (1986), authorized by appeal to the doctrine of creation; Church of England, *South Africa* (1982); Church of England, *South Africa* (1979). See the decision (without theological authorization) to explore instruments for economic sanctions against the South African government by the British Council of Churches, *Investment in South Africa* (1973), and the limited support of the WCC Program to Combat Racism, insofar as an openness to limited disinvestment from firms doing business in South Africa, albeit with some openness to an earlier Evangelische Kirche in Deutschland strategy of exerting pressure on South African structures through German firms investing in South Africa, as advocated (without theological authorization) by the Evangelische Kirche im Rheinland, *Antrag der Kreissynode Köln-Nord zum Rassenkonflikt im südlichen Afrika* (1974).

Opposition to apartheid is also implicit in the debate concerning support of the WCC Program to Combat Racism which has gone on inside the Evangelische Kirche im Rheinland. See its *Beschluss 57,3 der Landessynode 1979* and its *Beschluss 72 der Landessynode 1984*. For a similar debate, see Evangelische Kirche in Österreich, *Beschluss* [zum Antirassismusprogramm des Ökumenischen Rates der Kirchen] (1972); Baptist Union of Great Britain and Ireland, *WCC Programme to Combat Racism* (1979). Also see the endorsement of the program by the Associated Churches of Christ in New Zealand, *Decisions Relating to Public Issues* (1974), and the Eglise Réformée de France, *Programme de lutte contre le racisme* (1980). Cf. Evangelisch-Lutherische Landeskirche Hannovers, *Verhandlung über Anträge und Eingaben zum Anti-Rassismus-Programm des Ökumenischen Rates der Kirchen* (1971).

It is also reported that three Lutheran churches in South Africa composed largely of white membership — the German Evangelical Lutheran Church in South-West Africa, the Evangelical Lutheran Church in Southern Africa (Cape Church), and the Evangelical Lutheran Church in Southern Africa (Natal-Transvaal) — have issued declarations against apartheid. But these declarations do not appear to be statements with authorization by these churches' highest governing authorities.

Racism or apartheid is also dealt with in several statements issued by the Protestant Federation of Italy, as well as in at least three statements of the Church of Sweden: *Lag mot etnisk diskriminering i arbetslivet* (1983), *Diskrimineringsutredningens slutbetänkande* (1984), and *Betänkande am Sydafrikafrågen* (1985). But these statements also do not appear to have had authorization by these organizations' highest governing authorities. An apparently pertinent statement by the Evangelical Church of the Lutheran Confession in Brazil was never obtained. A statement on the subject of apartheid was issued in 1984 by the EKD-Synode, *Gerechtigkeit und Versöhnung für das südliche Afrika*.

Apartheid is also implicitly critiqued in criticisms of white minority rule in Rhodesia (now the nation of Zimbabwe) in two statements of the Episcopal Church [USA]: *General Convention Resolution* [on Zimbabwe (Rhodesia)] (1976) and *General Convention Resolution* [on Zimbabwe (Rhodesia)] (1973), as well as by the condemnation of racism in South Africa expressed by the Mennonite World Conference, *The Conference Message* (1967), III, I; by the call to ensure human rights for all groups in South Africa by the Reformed Ecumenical Synod, *Pastoral Statement: A Call to Commitment and Action* (1984), XII/G/2; by the support for the South African Council of Churches expressed by the Reformed Church in America, *Report of the Committee on Christian Unity* (1983), R-6a to R-6d; and by the commendation of the French government's decision not to deliver arms to South Africa by the Fédération Protestante de France, *Sur la livraison d'armes à l'Afrique du sud* (1966).

B. ECONOMIC DEVELOPMENT
AND UNEMPLOYMENT

In this section we list statements by the churches on economic development per se, and then statements specifically on unemployment.

2-1 ECONOMIC DEVELOPMENT

Views of the churches on economic development divide broadly between those supporting the exporting of Western technology and those favoring an emphasis on developing indigenous technology.

A. Development by exporting Western technology and aid to less-developed nations or advocating its techniques of controlling nature
   A1. Appeal to creation/view of human persons
   A2. Appeal to Christology/the gospel
   A3. Appeal to ecclesiology
   A4. No clear theological warrant given for position

B. Development by initiating indigenous technology, with primary aim to cultivate human values
   B1. Appeal to creation/view of human persons
   B2. Appeal to creation/view of human persons, perhaps grounded in Christology
   B3. Appeal to creation and eschatology
   B4. Appeal to creation, with other warrants drawn from loci rooted in the second and third articles of the creed
   B5. Appeal to Christology/faith/the gospel
   B6. Appeal to Christology and eschatology
   B7. Appeal to the gospel and ecclesiology
   B8. Appeal to the gospel and the doctrine of creation
   B9. Some reference to loci from all three articles of the creed
   B10. Some reference to loci from all three articles of the creed for warrants, with other warrants rooted in Christology
   B11. Appeal to the biblical vision
   B12. No clear theological warrant given for position

A. DEVELOPMENT BY EXPORTING WESTERN TECHNOLOGY AND AID TO LESS-DEVELOPED NATIONS OR ADVOCATING ITS TECHNIQUES OF CONTROLLING NATURE

A1. Appeal to creation/view of human persons

All Africa Conference of Churches, *Working with Christ in the Contemporary Social, Economic and Political Situation* (1969). There is some ambiguity in the statement regarding whether development is defined solely in terms of improved economic standards. Also ambiguous is whether appeals to the "unity of human personality" and the call to the church to cooperate with government is a first-article warrant.

German Catholic Bishops' Conference [FRG], *Statement of the Commissariat* (1977). It is unclear whether a second-article appeal or even a theocratic orientation is evident, or whether a theological warrant is actually given.

Lutheran World Federation, *Resolutions of the LWF Assembly* (Eleventh Plenary Session, 10 Aug. 1963), 10.

National Conference of Catholic Bishops (USA), *Pastoral Letter on Marxist Communism* (1980), 30, 59. Cites the papal encyclicals *Mater et Magistra* (1961) and *Populorum Progressio* (1967), 44.

WCC New Delhi Assembly, *Report of the Committee on the Commission of the Churches on International Affairs* (1961), 50ff., 45, 42.

A2. Appeal to Christology/the gospel

British Council of Churches, *Christmas Appeal* (1982), 4. Merely calls for "Christian aid"; this is also said to be "a response worthy of the good news" and so may be authorized by the gospel.

British Council of Churches, *Christmas Appeal* (1984), 3. Merely calls for "Christian aid"; this is said to be "a response to the good news" and so may be authorized by the gospel.

Canadian Conference of Catholic Bishops, *On Development and Peace* (1968), 2, 3, 11, 12, 18. Cites Roman Catholic Church, *Populorum Progressio* (1967), 1.

Dutch Reformed Church (South Africa), *Human Relations and the South African Scene* (1974), 48. With some reference to humanity's created potential as a measure of development.

Lutheran World Federation, *I Have Heard the Cry of My People... The Assembly Message* (1990). Reference is also made to scripture. Creation may be a background warrant.

Methodist Church in Malaysia, *Social Principles* (n.d.), III/A/3; II; I. The kind of model advocated is not entirely clear but refers only to "economic development", with passing reference to the spiritual development of the impoverished.

Presbyterian-Reformed Church in Cuba, *Confession of Faith* (1977), III/D. Concerned with technological development, though with some attention to its relationship to the process of humanization.

Russian Orthodox Church, *Christmas Tidings of Patriarch Pimen* (1981). Concerned only with development of the motherland.

WCC Amsterdam Assembly, *The Church and the Disorder of Society* (1948), I, III. Such a development model is said to be a matter of justice. It also includes warrants drawn from eschatology, with creation in the background.

WCC Evanston Assembly, *International Affairs — Christians in the Struggle for World Community* (1954), VI. Also includes third-article warrants (the kingdom of God and the church) as well as a reference to the "moral law".

WCC New Delhi Assembly, *An Appeal to All Governments and Peoples* (1961), 8-10. At least the statement seems to refer only to medical and economic development.

A3. Appeal to ecclesiology

United Free Church of Scotland, *Deliverance of the General Assembly* [on public questions] (1980), 1, 2. Calls for increased "overseas aid". Authorization is also provided by appeals to love and "Christian moral values".

A4. No clear theological warrant given for position

Baptist Union of New Zealand, *Aid to Underdeveloped Countries* (1969). Calls for overseas aid.

Baptist Union of New Zealand, *Overseas Aid* (1976), (a), (c). Calling only for overseas aid.

British Council of Churches, *Second United Nations Development Decade* (1970). Merely calls for overseas aid.

British Council of Churches, *Christian Aid* (1979), 4.

British Council of Churches, *Christian Aid Week* (1979), 4(b).

British Council of Churches, *Christian Aid* (1981). Merely calls for Christian aid.

British Council of Churches, *Aid* (1984), 4.

British Council of Churches, *Aid for Africa* (1985). Merely calls for overseas aid.

British Council of Churches, *Christian Aid* (1986). Merely calls for Christian aid.

Bund der Evangelischen Kirchen in der Deutschen Demokratische Republik, *Beschluss der Synode des BEK-DDR zu Fragen des Friedens* (1981). Insofar as the resolution cites a call for "development aid" by the WCC Central Committee, *Increasing Threat to Peace and the Mandate of the Churches* (1981), II/E.

Christian Church (Disciples of Christ), *Regarding Non-Violent Social Deterrence* (1963). Encourages reform in nations seeking so-called aid.

Christian Church (Disciples of Christ), *Concerning Revolutionary Movements and Threats to the Peace of the World* (1966). At least calls for the affluent nations "to provide massive economic and technical aid when needed".

Christian Church (Disciples of Christ), *Concerning Indochina* (1971). At least calls for economic assistance for Vietnam.

Christian Church (Disciples of Christ), *Concerning the Crisis in Pakistan* (1971). Insofar as it advocates aid to Pakistani refugees.

Christian Church (Disciples of Christ), *A Resolution concerning World Hunger and Development* (1975), IV, V.

Church of England, *South Africa* (1982). Calls for development aid.

Church of England, *Development Education (Let Justice Flow)* (1986). Calls for development aid.

Episcopal Church [USA], *Aid for Famine Victims* (1985).

Episcopal Church [USA], *Apartheid/Africa* (1985), 7. Endorses a 1985 resolution of the church's Executive Council which called for "aid programs for black South Africans".

Lutheran Church in America, *Poverty* (1966). The model for development is not entirely clear, speaking only of rich nations assisting to raise the "standard of living" of developing nations. The love of God in Christ is referred to as a motive for such activity.

Lutheran World Federation, *Statement on Hunger* (1984), I.

Mennonite Church [USA], *A Message concerning War in Vietnam* (1965).

Moravian Church in America, Southern Province, *Statement to U.S. Government* (1983). The model is not entirely clear, but reference is made only to giving aid for economic development.

National Council of Churches [USA], *Imperatives of Peace and Responsibilities of Power* (1968).

National Council of Churches [USA], *On the Crisis in the Middle East* (1969), III/4.

Russian Orthodox Church, *Christmas Tidings of Patriarch Pimen* (1982). Concerned only with development of the motherland.

United Church of Canada, *Military Expenditures* (1986). Calls for aid to third-world countries, yet does express a concern for "quality of life".

United Church of Canada, *Nuclear-Powered Submarines* (1988). Calls for aid to developing nations.

United Church of Christ [USA], *On Justice and Peace in Vietnam* (1967). Calls for economic assistance for Vietnam.

United Church of Christ [USA], *Statement on Southern Africa* (1975).

B. DEVELOPMENT BY INITIATING INDIGENOUS TECHNOLOGY, WITH PRIMARY AIM TO CULTIVATE HUMAN VALUES

B1. Appeal to creation/view of human persons

All Africa Conference of Churches, *The Prophetic and Serving Church* (1974). Christology seems to be a background warrant.

American Lutheran Church, *Peace, Justice, and Human Rights* (1972), 1, 6, 7, 11. But does call for providing technical assistance to younger nations. Creation with Christology as motive is implied insofar as it authorizes peace and justice, which are linked to development.

Canadian Conference of Catholic Bishops, *A Society to Be Transformed* (1977), 20, 5, 7. With the gospel as a background warrant.

Church of Norway, *Statement on Nuclear Energy and Safety* (1978). Though there is some question about the official status of the statement and also concerning whether appeal to the commandment to love one's neighbor entails a corresponding warrant drawn from the second article.

Church of Norway, *En ny internasjonal økonomisk ordning* (1979), 27-28. With correlation of creation and redemption.

National Conference of Catholic Bishops [USA], *Statement on the Government and Birth Control* (1966), 15-16.

National Conference of Catholic Bishops [USA], *Statement on the Twenty-fifth Anniversary of the United Nations* (1970), 7, 17. At least urges sharing responsibility among the nations for development. Creation is at least a background warrant.

National Conference of Catholic Bishops [USA], *Statement on Population* (1973), 6, 10.

United Church of Christ [USA], *Pronouncement on the Role of Transnational Business in Mass Economic Development* (1975). Also appeals to faith as a kind of warrant. The new model is suggested by the statement's concern about "full human development", the welfare and dignity of people.

WCC Uppsala Assembly, *Towards Justice and Peace in International Affairs* (1968), 31-33. Seems to opt for new models in virtue of insistence that paternalism must be avoided in development programs.

B2. Appeal to creation/view of human persons, perhaps grounded in Christology

Roman Catholic Church, Vatican II, *Gaudium et Spes* (1965), 64-66, 84-88, 77, 22, 24, 39, 26. Mostly concerned that development takes into account total human development, but does call for new international structures to facilitate development. The last reference does seem explicitly to include appeal to the gospel and doctrine of the Holy Spirit in addition to creation as warrant.

B3. Appeal to creation and eschatology

[Catholic] Episcopal Conference of the Pacific, *The Pacific and Peace* (1986), IV, IX, II. With possible subordination to Christology.

B4. Appeal to creation, with other warrants drawn from loci rooted in the second and third articles of the creed

Canadian Catholic Conference, *On Pastoral Implications of Political Choices* (1972).
Roman Catholic Church, *Pacem in Terris* (1963), 121-25.

Roman Catholic Church, *Populorum Progressio* (1967), 5, 12-15, 20-21, 32, 34, 39, 42, 44, 48, 54, 70-73, 77, 81, 83-87. At one point seems to advocate a transfer of technology/goods, but even then is concerned to share skills and allow indigenous development. References to the gospel and the Holy Spirit probably do not function as criteria, except for at least one suggestion that theocracy might be advocated. These affirmations perhaps play a more crucial role if the statement's references to the positions of the Vatican II documents and its interest in infusing a "Christian spirit" into the laws entail that — like *Gaudium et Spes* 22 — creation is grounded in Christology.

Roman Catholic Church, *Redemptor Hominis* (1979), 13-17, esp. 17. Though anthropology and eschatology seem to be the dominant warrants.

B5. Appeal to Christology/the gospel

American Lutheran Church, *Hunger in the World* (1968), 5, 6, 9, 2. Authorization by appeal to Christian love and God's grace. Creation may be a background warrant.

British Council of Churches, *Central America* (1983). Takes this position and its mode of argument in virtue of approving the council's policy statement *Conflict and Promise — Central America in the 1980s*, 5, 2.

Canadian Catholic Conference, *Justice in the World: Proposals to the Third International Synod of Bishops* (1971), 4.

Christian Conference of Asia, *Justice and Service* (1973), Pref.; I/1,8; II/2; Thrust Paper.

Christian Conference of Asia, *Justice and Service* (1977), B/1; D.

Evangelische Kirche in Deutschland, *Wir müssen mehr tun* (1986), I, III.

Federation of Protestant Churches of Switzerland, *Par une action concertée énergique en faveur du tiers monde* (1986), I.A, III.1, III.2, III.3, III.5(a), III.5(b), III.7, III.8, III.14. Though does refer to the need to give aid to developing nations.

Latin American [Catholic] Bishops, Third General Conference, *The Puebla Statement* (1979). Creation/anthropology seems to function only as a secondary warrant.

Lutheran World Federation, *Toward Economic and Social Justice* (1984), 8.1.1.5; 8.3.7; I; II. Authorization is given only in the portion of the statement not adopted by the assembly.

United Church of Christ [USA], *Justice in Immigration* (1981). In the sense of being concerned about social as well as economic development.

United Church of Christ [USA], *Global Debt Crisis* (1987). Employs theological insights of liberation theology.

World Alliance of Reformed Churches, *Reconciliation and Creation: The Freedom of God's World* (1970), 2. But redemption is related to creation at the outset of the statement.

WCC Sub-Unit on Church and Society, *Report of the Advisory Group of the Energy for My Neighbor Programme* (1982), VI, II. Though elsewhere the statement also calls for more attention to the creation doctrine; the Christological warrant could be articulated in terms of *theosis*.

B6. Appeal to Christology and eschatology

Reformed Ecumenical Synod, *Statements on the Social Calling of the Church* (1980), 16, 18, 2. There may be some ambiguity concerning whether the statement's critique of a social order's preoccupation with material abundance pertains to the statement's position on development.

B7. Appeal to the gospel and ecclesiology

Conference of European Churches and Council of European Catholic Bishops' Conferences, *Final Document of the European Ecumenical Assembly Peace with Justice* (1989), 84, 79, 78, 77, 25-27. Includes as a possible warrant a reference to covenant, which itself reflects trinitarian content.

B8. Appeal to the gospel and the doctrine of creation

American Baptist Churches, *Policy Statement on Hunger* (1975), VII(A), I, Int. Authorized by Christian love and the oneness of humanity.

National Conference of Catholic Bishops [USA], *Economic Justice for All* (1986), PM1, PM2, PM13, PM17, PM19, 25, 28, 127, 251, 262, 264, 271, 279, 294, 322, 364. Also calls for a cut in defence spending in order to free up funds for development programs.

National Council of Churches [USA], *Christian Concern and Responsibility for Economic Life in a Rapidly Changing Technological Society* (1966).

United Church of Christ [USA], *A Pronouncement on Justice and International Development: A Manifesto for American Action in the Struggle against World Poverty* (1967).

B9. Some reference to loci from all three articles of the creed

WCC Nairobi Assembly, *Human Development: Ambiguities of Power, Technology and Quality of Life* (1975), 11-13, 17, 37-41, 61, 3-7.

B10. Some reference to loci from all three articles of the creed for warrants, with other warrants rooted in Christology

National Conference of Catholic Bishops [USA], *To Live in Jesus Christ: A Pastoral Reflection on the Moral Life* (1976), 20, 30, 31, 88, 91-94, 115-16. Christology seems to be the prevailing warrant.

Roman Catholic Church, *Sollicitudo Rei Socialis* (1987), 1, 3, 7-10, 28-49. Also appeals to eschatology, the Eucharist, Mariology, and the saints. It posits a relational view of human persons and self-consciously endorses the points of an earlier papal encyclical, *Populorum Progressio* (1967), esp. 48. Also, it employs the language of liberation theology and solidarity with the poor.

B11. Appeal to the biblical vision

WCC Canberra Assembly, *The Report of the Seventh Assembly* (1991), 31, 25. Pneumatology may be a background warrant.

B12. No clear theological warrant given for position

American Lutheran Church, *War, Peace, and Freedom* (1966), 31-32. Statement may not be official.

Anglicanism, *The Resolutions of the Lambeth Conference (1978)*, 1.

Christian Church (Disciples of Christ), *Concerning Relationships to Third World Peoples* (1975).

Christian Church (Disciples of Christ), *Concerning the United Nations* (1977), II.

Christian Church (Disciples of Christ), *Report concerning World Hunger and Response to 1975 Resolutions 46, 47 and 61* (1977), II, I.

Evangelische Kirche der Kirchenprovinz Sachsen, *Beschluss zur Gesamtthematik der Synodaltagung* (1985), 2. Without reference to socialism, claims that the concrete shape of a just world economic order can be learned only in dialogue with advocates of the poor in poor lands. The covenant/gospel is a warrant for many points in the resolution, but not clearly in this case.

Moravian Church in America, Northern Province, *Energy in the Third World* (1982).

National Council of Churches [USA], *World Poverty and the Demands of Justice* (1968).

National Council of Churches [USA], *Human Hunger and the World Food Crisis* (1975), VII/A/1.

Presbyterian Church (USA), *Our Response to the Crisis in Central America: An Appeal to Presbyterians and Other Churches in the United States* (1988).

Roman Catholic Church, *Octogesima Adveniens* (1971), 43, 41, 46, 48. Though the gospel could be in the background as a warrant.

United Church of Christ [USA], *Report of the Council for Christian Social Action, as Finally Adopted* (1965), 20.

United Church of Christ [USA], *Hunger, Population and World Development* (1969).

United Church of Christ [USA], *Affirming the United Church of Christ as a Just Peace Church* (1985), Pronouncement IV/D/3-4. Appeal to the Trinity is in the background.

United Free Church of Scotland, *Deliverance of the General Assembly* [on public questions] (1968), 1, 12.

United Free Church of Scotland, *Deliverance of the General Assembly* [on public questions] (1970), 9, 1.

United Free Church of Scotland, *Deliverance of the General Assembly* [on public questions] (1977), 1.

United Free Church of Scotland, *Deliverance of the General Assembly* [on public questions] (1982), 1. But also refers to giving aid to the poor and oppressed.

United Free Church of Scotland, *Deliverance of the General Assembly* [on public questions] (1984), 4.

United Free Church of Scotland, *Deliverance of the General Assembly* [on public questions] (1988), 7.

United Methodist Church [USA], *Social Principles of the UMC(USA)* (1980), III/L; VI/B. Concerned that development both enhance humanization and maximize political and economic self-determination. Is humanization indicative of a reliance on creation doctrine as warrant?

WCC Conference on Faith, Science and the Future, *Science/Technology, Political Power, and a More Just World Order* (Cambridge, Mass., 12-24 July 1979), 1-2, 4.

WCC Uppsala Assembly, *World Economic and Social Development* (1968), 20ff. Not clear if concern with criteria of the human for development represents an appeal to creation doctrine.

WCC Vancouver Assembly, *Confronting Threats to Peace and Survival* (1983), 24.

WCC World Convocation on Justice, Peace and the Integrity of Creation, *Final Document: Entering into Covenant Solidarity for Justice, Peace and the Integrity of Creation* (1990), 2.3.2.1; 2.2; 2.1. The concept of covenant which reflects a trinitarian orientation may function as the document's overriding warrant.

There seems to be some theory of development in the background of all churches which have taken a position in favor of the unequivocal reduction of energy use by industrial nations. Such church statements include the following twelve: (1) Southern Baptist Convention [USA], *A Statement of Social Principles* (1979), 3; (2) Presbyterian Church in the U.S./United Presbyterian Church, *The Power to Speak Truth to Power* (1981), pts. 2, 3, 1/III, 1; (3) Landessynode der evangelischen Kirche in Rheinland-Westfalen, *Wort zur Energiediskussion* (1980), 2 (a, b, c, e); (4) Church of Norway, *Statement on Nuclear Energy and Safety* (1978); (5) Eglise de la Confession d'Augsbourg d'Alsace et de Lorraine (1978); (6) *Pastoral Letter of the Catholic Swiss Bishops* (1976); (7) Fédération Protestante de France, *The Question of Nuclear Energy* (1978), V, II, Int. (there is some ambiguity regarding whether the statement's expressed concern for satisfactory energy production might qualify the call for reduced energy consumption; the statement does appear to criticize the existing models of development); (8) Congregational Union of Scotland, *Nuclear Energy and Energy Production* (1977); (9) Evangelische Kirche in

Hessen und Nassau, *Erklärung zum Synoden-Thema "In der Schöpfung leben"* (1986), 10, 7, 2, 1; (10) Evangelische Kirche von Westfalen, *Zukunft der Arbeit — Leben und Arbeiten in Wandel* (1983), 5-6; (11) Reformed Church of Alsace-Lorraine, *Décision* (1978) (given this church's endorsement of the Fédération Protestante de France's statement on this subject, there is also some ambiguity concerning its own position on this issue); and (12) Mennonite Church, General Conference [USA], *Christian Stewardship of Energy Resources* (1977).

All the statements except those of the Church of Norway, the two German union churches, and, to some extent, the American Mennonite church appear to warrant their proposals by appeal to second-article loci (in one case to third-article loci). See the following section on energy consumption for specific identification of each statement's warrants. It is unclear, however, whether they would employ the unused energy for development of the third world or, like the Church of Norway, would see the lower level of energy consumption as making possible new models of development. Likewise there seems to be an implicit theory of development in the call for reduced energy consumption, though with qualifications, by the Arbeitsgemeinschaft Christlicher Kirchen in der Bundesrepublik Deutschland und Berlin (West), *Neuer Lebensstil aus christlicher Verantwortung* (1980), 1-3, 5.

Development is explicitly addressed as an issue of Christian concern by the Methodist Church [England], *World Development Action Campaign Programme* (1978). But it hints at elements of both development models, so that a precise determination of the strategy it supports is not possible. See the reference to "human development" in a statement of the same year, entitled *Statement and Programme on Race Relations*. Unclear in its exact orientation is a statement of the Council of Churches in the Netherlands, *Over de armoede in het Nederlands ontwikkelingsbeleid* (1985), 6.8. Its concern for social justice and partnership may reflect the new model, but its interest in "translating" development programs seems restricted to linguistic translation for purposes of informing those helped. Something like the new model may be implicit in the call for multilateral foreign aid, authorized by appeal to the common good, in a statement by the National Conference of Catholic Bishops [USA], *Life in Our Day* (1968), 129. Similarly, a statement by the [Catholic] Bishops of the Netherlands, *De mens in de arbeid* (1980), 3.3, makes a passing reference to development and suggests the new model when, without theological authorization, it raises the question about giving priority to material progress only when considering the international situation. A similar point was made by the National Conference of Catholic Bishops [USA], *Statement on the World Food Crisis: A Pastoral Plan of Action* (1974), 4, which, without clear authorization, insists that "it is not enough, however, that such development merely foster economic growth."

Development is discussed, without theological authorization, by All Africa Conference of Churches, *The Gospel and Education for Liberation* (1981); Canadian Conference of Catholic Bishops, *A Brief to the Standing Committee on External Affairs and National Defence: On Preparation for the Second Special Session of the United Nations on Disarmament* (1982), 2; [Catholic] Episcopacy of France, *Déclaration sur les événements internationaux* (1968), [Catholic] Bishops of Vietnam, *To Build Peace* (1969); Baptist Union of Great Britain and Ireland, *Her Majesty's Government and the Third World* (1980); Mennonite Church, General Conference [USA], *Resolution on Vietnam* (1965); Episcopal Church [USA], *Relief for Refugees* (1982); World Alliance of Reformed Churches, *The Pacific, Australia, and Aotearoa/ New Zealand* (1989); Reformed Ecumenical Synod, *Race Relations, Resolutions* (1968), 8; and several deliverances on public questions of the United Free Church of Scotland: *Deliverance of the General Assembly [on Public Questions]* (1986), 3, expressing concern about the deprived peoples of the world; ibid. (1981), 6, 1, with Christology perhaps in the background, merely expressing support for Christian aid; ibid. (1978), 3, merely expressing support for Christian aid; ibid. (1974), 13, expressing the same support for Christian aid; ibid. (1972), 12, expressing similar programmatic support; (1971), ibid. 1, 13, supporting world development; ibid. (1969), 11, merely supporting Christian aid; ibid. (1967), 13, expressing the same programmatic support, a program which, as per ibid. (1965), 1, may only concern itself with special emergencies. See also three items by the United Church of Christ [USA]: *Peace and United*

States Power (1971), *International Relations and International Development* (1967), and *Resolution on Poverty* (1965); three items by the Christian Church (Disciples of Christ): *Concerning Relationships to Third World Peoples* (1975), *Concerning International Women's Year, 1975* (1975), and *Concerning the Need for a Stronger World Community as a Bulwark against Nuclear War* (1963); Evangelische Kirche der Union — Bereich Bundesrepublik Deutschland und Berlin-West, *Stellungnahme der Synode der EKU (Regionalbereich West) zu UNCTAD III* (1974). Also see the call for development in Southeast Asia, authorized by appeal to the gospel and moral obligation, by the National Conference of Catholic Bishops [USA], *Resolution on Southeast Asia* (1971), 5, 6, 11.

A passing reference to development, authorized by appeal to the nature of the Christian faith, is made by the National Council of Churches [USA], *Defense and Disarmament* (1968). A similar appeal for economic development, authorized by appeal to loci derived from all three articles of the creed, is offered by the National Council of Churches [USA], *Latin America and the Caribbean* (1983), I/B, I/A, Int. Also see the call for development, probably authorized by appeal to Christology and either eschatology and ecclesiology, by the United Presbyterian Church/Presbyterian Church in the U.S., *Strangers Become Neighbors: Presbyterian Response to Mexican Migration* (1981), II/B/3, I. Development also is discussed by the All Africa Conference of Churches, this time with authorization drawn from the gospel and the doctrine of human persons, in its *Gospel in Practice* (1981). In the first and last of these cases cited in this and in the preceding paragraph as well as in a number of the others cited, reference is made to economic justice, but no particular model of development is advocated. Likewise no particular model is articulated by the All Africa Conference of Churches, *The Gospel — Good News to the Poor and Oppressed* (1981), as, authorized largely by Christological themes drawn from liberation theology, it speaks of national development. The Christian Church (Disciples of Christ), *Concerning Christian Response to Revolution* (1968), authorizes its claim by appeal to natural law.

A similar failure to provide details concerns the model for development being advocated in the references to development by the Roman Catholic Church, Congregation for the Doctrine of the Faith, *Instruction on Christian Freedom and Liberation* (1986), 89-91, 80-82, 64, 60, 54, 45, 30, 98-99; National Conference of Catholic Bishops [USA], *Peace and Vietnam* (1966), 16; Australian [Catholic] Episcopal Conference, *Morals and Human Values* (1972). Anthropology and natural law function as warrants at these points, though in the first two statements they may be subordinated to Christology (the gospel). References in the American statement to Vatican II's *Gaudium et Spes,* 22, which subordinates creation to Christology, suggest that this combination of loci may warrant the American bishops' position.

Also see American Baptist Churches, *Policy Statement on Africa* (1987), 4, 1, which probably authorizes its general concern about development in Africa by appeal to creation correlated with Christology; United Free Church of Scotland, *Deliverance of the General Assembly* [on public questions] (1973), 14, 16, authorizing its general concern about world development by appeal to natural law; and the passing reference to development, authorized by pneumatology (with creation a subordinate warrant) by the Southern African Catholic Bishops' Conference, *Social Justice and Race Relations within the Church* (1977), 17-19, Int.

Reference is made to the desirability of development by both the *Anglican-Lutheran [European Regional] Dialogue* (1982), 58, 59, 29, and the Latin American [Catholic] Bishops, Second General Conference (Medellín Conference), *Message to the People of Latin America* (1968). No authorization for this concern is explicit, but Christology, the gospel, and even creation could function as background warrants. Also see *Joint Pastoral Letter of the Bishops of Kenya on the Family and Responsible Parenthood* (1979), which is apparently authorized by Christology/the gospel and ecclesiology. More explicit reference to development, with elaboration of a development model whose values largely converge with that of the new model, has been offered by the Medellín Conference, *Introduction to the Final Documents: Presence of the Church in the Present-Day Transformation of Latin America* (1968), 6, 8, 5, 4. The statement is authorized by redemption and Christology at this point along with pneumatology, anthropology, and perhaps eschatology as background warrants. It has not been listed above only because it did not address the question of the role of developed nations in facilitating the development process. For two other statements of the same conference, which take similar positions, see *Justice*, 23, 16, 13, 11, 4, authorized by creation and the gospel; and *Peace*, 1, 14, 20, 26, whose authorization is not clear. Similarly noteworthy, though somewhat unclear statements of the same Medellín Conference, include *Pastoral Concern for the Elites*, 7, in which a view akin to the older model of development was articulated but not advocated, and *Family and Demography*, 8, in which it was simply observed that increased population is a prerequisite of development.

The Lutheran Church in America, *World Community: Ethical Imperatives in an Age of Interdependence* (1970), 5-6, also undertakes a discussion of development. However, it is likewise uncertain which development model is employed. Older, more traditional Western models of short-term development aid are criticized, yet the mobilization of support for economic and social development of the third world is urged. Likewise the Evangelical Church of Lutheran Confession in Brazil, *Our Social Responsibility* (1976), 3, calls for development which will provide jobs and improve the standard of living, but no clues are given with regard to the ownership or what kind of technology would bring about such development. Also significant in this connection is a resolution of the United Church of Christ [USA], *Action for Peace in Central America* (1985). Its use of the language of aid to describe development suggests the older models of development. But its insistence that all aid should be conditioned by the recipient's "demonstrated protection of human rights" suggests the newer models of development. Also see Christian Church (Disciples of Christ), *Concerning the Universal Declaration of Human Rights* (1973). In like manner, the Christian Church (Disciples of Christ), *Report on the Response to 1975 General Assembly World Hunger Resolutions* (1979), II, III/C, IV, employed the language of aid; apparently authorized by the doctrine of creation, however, it calls for models of self-reliance in a manner suggestive of the new models of development.

The Swedish Ecumenical Council/Church of Sweden, *Nuclear Power, Energy and Questions Pertaining to the Style and Quality of Life* (1978/1975), II; III.1, 7-8, and the Southern Baptist Convention [USA], *A Statement of Social Principles* (1979), 3, also make proposals calling for developmental models that break to some extent with the more traditional Western models. These statements have not been listed above, however, because they do not address the crucial issue of development strategies for the development of underdeveloped societies. Similar sensitivity to the issues raised by the new models of development is shown by the Mennonite Church, General Conference [USA], *Resolution on Nationalism* (1968), II/4, I, perhaps authorized by Christology and the gospel of love, when it urges that foreign aid not be given unilaterally, lest the giver interfere in the affairs of the developing nation to which the aid is given. However, this statement has not been listed above both because of its use of the language of aid (which suggests the older models of development) and because of its failure to address the issue of development strategies to be employed in developing nations.

Likewise, the Canadian Conference of Catholic Bishops, *Ethical Choices and Political Challenges* (1983), 7, 11-13, 18, 19, 53, authorized by Scripture and creation, subordinated to and including an appeal to Christology, makes several affirmations about development being more than economic growth. Rather, development is said to include social, cultural, and spiritual needs. In addition, the document insists that self-reliance is central in development. Such affirmations suggest a commitment to the new models. Once again, however, the pastoral letter does not deal much with strategies for the development of underdeveloped nations. Similarly unclear is the United Free Church of Scotland, *Deliverance of the General Assembly* [on public questions] (1976), 5, which, without theological authorization, urges development of local third-world resources. Is this the sort of call for self-initiated development which characterizes the new models?

The joint statement of the Presbyterian Church in the U.S./United Presbyterian Church, *The Power to Speak Truth to Power* (1981), pts. II, II/1/E, 1/III, 1, speaks of development, though the model it advocates (calling both for the development of models sensitive to the criterion of appropriate technology and also for the transfer of capital and depletable energy resources to poorer nations) is not readily identified. A similar proposal, drawing its authorization from Christian faith or eschatology, has been offered by the National Conference of Catholic Bishops [USA], *Brothers and Sisters to Us: A Pastoral Letter on Racism* (1979). Passing reference to the need for development, at least for the meeting of unmet social needs, is made by the United Church of Christ [USA], *Disarmament* (1977), as, without a clear theological authorization, the suggestion is made that such needs might better be met by directing resources for armaments to more peaceful purposes.

The WCC Amsterdam Assembly, *The Church and the Disorder of Society* (1948), 1, claims that justice demands that inhabitants of Asia and Africa should have the benefits of technology. Is this an advocacy of the older development model of technological transfer? One supposes this is the case, but the position of the statement in calling for such a sharing of technology is only implied, not clearly stated. The WCC Vancouver Assembly, *Learning in Community* (1983), 23ff., speaks of development in relation to justice and peace, in terms of identifying with the poor. This may suggest adherence to new development models, yet sufficient evidence to make that judgment is not provided. Likewise it could be that a new model of development was evident in the WCC Uppsala Assembly, *Towards Justice and Peace in International Affairs* (1968), 32-33, when it is urged that paternalism by developed nations be avoided. Also requiring clarification is the resolution of the Christian Church (Disciples of Christ), *Concerning World Economic Development* (1969). The resolution does quote the statement of the WCC Uppsala Assembly on development, a statement which opted for new models of development that included a concern for establishing justice in the societies of developing nations. This statement is only made in passing, however, and the bulk of attention is devoted to the transfer of capital to developing nations, to their "economic development".

The 1983 WCC Vancouver Assembly statements *Struggling for Justice and Human Dignity*, 29, and *Healing and Sharing Life in Community*, 24, 1, 2, also did not clarify what model they advocated when calling for increased church funding of development programs for the poor. Similar ambiguity is evident in the WCC Conference on Faith, Science and the Future, *Economics of a Just, Participatory and Sustainable Society* (Cambridge, Mass., 12-24 July 1979), 8, with its proposal that industrial nations make part of their GNP available for developing nations. Would this represent "transfer of technology"? A similar proposal was made by the Roman Catholic Church, *Populorum Progressio* (1967), 48. But its explicit insistence that not just technology but also skills be transferred, as well as other indications, clearly shows that the statement advocates new models of development.

What is one to make of the National Council of Churches [USA], *Policy Statement: The Ethical Implications of Energy Production and Use* (1979), which calls on the USA to share technology (suggesting the older development models), but also insists that capitalism not be imposed on developing nations? Similarly in *Viet-nam* (1965), authorized by Christian love, the council called for aid (suggesting the older development models) for Southeast Asia. But in urging that this be given through an international organization in which the beneficiary governments fully participate, the new model is suggested. For similar proposals for stimulating development through such international organizations, see Reformed Church in America, *Report of the Christian Action Commission* (1966), R4, which takes its position, authorized by appeal to Christian love, by adopting the bulk of the previously cited statement of the National Council of Churches [USA]; Church of the Brethren [USA], *Justice and Nonviolence* (1977), 9, authorizing its position by appeal to Christian faith and natural law, although the statement also refers to economic aid; and three items by the Christian Church (Disciples of Christ): *Appeal to the Church on Vietnam* (1967), which takes its position, apparently authorized by the reconciling work of Christ, by citing a resolution of the General Assembly of the National Council of Churches [USA], *An Appeal to the Churches concerning Vietnam* (1966), sec. 4; *Concerning World Hunger* (1966), apparently authorizing its position by appeal to "the Christian conscience"; and *Concerning World Order, Justice and Peace* (1968), calling (without theological authorization) for multilateral arrangements in development aid.

The Lutheran World Federation, *Sent with the Gospel* (1970), 15, 13, urges that Christians participate in development processes but gives no clues concerning what sort of model is advocated. Cf. *Resolutions of the Lutheran World Fellowship Assembly* (Eleventh Plenary Session, 10 Aug. 1963), 10. Likewise the issue of how economic progress might help to solve the problem of the apportionment of goods internationally was raised by the Evangelische Landeskirche in Württemberg, *Entschliessung zur Kirche und Arbeitswelt* (1985), 3, 2, 1, 6. But no reflections are offered on the manner in which this problem might be solved best.

Reference to development is made by the Council of Churches in the Netherlands, *Letter to the Council of Ministers and the Houses of Parliament* (1984), 3, in the sense that the arms race is said to divert expenditures of money, energy, and human resources. It is not clear, but could such language imply endorsement of the older model of development? Cf. *Message of the Holy Synod of the Russian Orthodox Church on War and Peace in a Nuclear Age* (1986), 2.33-35, 2.27; Anglican Church of Canada, *Disarmament* (1983). A concern about economic development and the responsibilities it entails is addressed by the Methodist Church in Malaysia, *Social Principles* (n.d.), III/B.3; III; I, likely with a kind of theocratic authorization drawn from Christology. But the kind of model for development advocated by the church is not clear.

Another pertinent Methodist document is the 1966 *Council Message to the Methodists of the World*, by the World Methodist Council Conference. A concern is expressed that trade and commerce as well as present military expenditures be used to enhance the "general welfare". This position, authorized by an appeal to the doctrine of human persons, enhanced by reference to Methodist ecclesiology and Christology, could perhaps be akin to the new model. Reference is made to just development by the Roman Catholic Church, *Laborem Exercens* (1981), 2, but neither the model of development nor the theological rationale is clear. The same might be said about a statement of the Christian Conference of Asia, *Life and Action* (1977), VIII(5). Some concern for economic development is implied by the United Presbyterian Church [USA], *The Confession of 1967*, A/4, when, authorized by Christology, it expresses concern for the poor.

Also of pertinence to the subject is the statement of the Evangelische Landeskirche in Baden, *Wort zur Kernenergie* (1977), which insists that the concern with ecology must not be permitted to conflict with economic development. Is the older model for development advocated in this case? A similar perspective seems to operate in a 1980 statement of the Arbeitsgemeinschaft Christlicher Kirchen in der Bundesrepublik Deutschland und Berlin (West), *Neuer Lebensstil aus christlicher Verantwortung* (1980), 1-3, 6. In all the preceding statements, warrants from the second and third articles predominate. Creation functions as the sole warrant only in the statements by the WCC Vancouver and Uppsala assemblies, the Roman Catholic Church, the Lutheran Church in America, and perhaps the Swedish Ecumenical Council.

Several statements issued by the Evangelische Kirche in Deutschland seem to address issues related to economics, if not economic development: *Die Beschäftigung ausländischer Arbeit-nehmer und die wirtschaftliche Entwicklung ihrer Herkunftsländer* (1975); *Mitbestimmung in der Wirtschaft* (1968); *Eigentumsbildung in sozialer Verantwortung* (1962); *Rüstung und Entwicklung* (1981); *Weltbevölkerungswachstum als Herausforderung an die Kirchen* (1984), esp. 9, 4; *Auf dem Weg zu einer neuen Entwicklungspolitik der Europäischen Gemeinschaft* (1984); *Transnationale Unternehmen* (1985); and *Landwirtschaft im Spannungsfeld* (1984). However, they have not been included in the analysis because, with the possible exception of the last statement, the highest governing authorities of the organization (the *Synode* or the *Rat*) do not identify themselves with the positions of these statements. Rather, the governing authorities merely recognize, receive, greet, or authorize the editing and distributing of statements, which are credited to various boards *(Kammern)* of the EKD.

The Anglican Church of Canada, *Resolutions on Guaranteed Annual Income* (1977), Act 62, without theological authorization, called for a study of world development as well as of land use and natural resources. Also, without theological authorization, a 1968 *Declaration of the Conferencia Episcopal Española on "Humanae vitae"*, 11, noted the interconnections between economic development and a family politic which is capable of assuring birth-control policies in line with the papal positions. Similarly, without clear theological authorization (though the gospel might be a background warrant), economic development is discussed in passing by the Conférence Episcopale Française, *Tout être humain a le droit de vivre* (1974). Also see Patriarchs and Catholic Bishops of Libya, *Legality Is the Unique Guarantee of the Protection of the Fatherland* (1983), I/3(e), which may have anthropology functioning as a background warrant.

2-2 UNEMPLOYMENT

Virtually all church statements addressing the issue of unemployment call for government aid and private efforts to ensure full employment, or at least they deem employment a human right. Three exceptions are the German Catholic Bishops' Conference, *Statement of the Commissariat* (1977), which with no obvious theological warrant would subordinate the concern for full employment to the concern to reduce energy consumption, so that jobs could apparently be sacrificed for the sake of lower levels of consumption; the Church of Norway, *En ny internasjonal økonomisk ordning* (1979), 29, 27, which would not sacrifice reducing assistance to developing nations for the sake of Norway's unemployed; and the United Free Church of Scotland, *Deliverance of the General Assembly* [on public questions] (1983), 1-3, which, while concerned about unemployment, would take no action that might result in the impoverishment of people in another part of the world. Church statements endorsing the majority viewpoint diverge on the theological warrants given to authorize their position.

 1. Appeal to first article
 2. Appeal to first article, with some backing from Christology/the gospel
 3. Appeal to first article, possibly grounded in Christology/the gospel
 4. Appeal to creation and redemption/Christology
 5. Appeal to creation and eschatology
 6. Appeal to creation/nature and the gospel
 7. Appeal to anthropology and the gospel, with the former subordinate to the latter
 8. Appeal to Christology/nature of Christian faith/the gospel
 9. Appeal to Christology/covenant and third-article loci
10. Appeal to Christology, supplemented by third-article loci
11. Appeal to pneumatology
12. Appeal to ecclesiology
13. Warrants likely drawn from all articles of creed/Trinitarian warrant
14. Warrants likely drawn from all articles of creed/Trinitarian warrant, with creation subordinated to Christology
15. Appeal to biblical mandate
16. Appeal to Mariology, with appeal to other loci in support
17. No clear theological warrant given for position

1. Appeal to first article

American Lutheran Church, *Toward Fairness in Public Taxing and Spending* (1982), 1-2, 4.
     This statement may not have had official status.
Associated Churches of Christ in New Zealand, *Decisions Relating to Public Issues* (1968). At
     least insofar as appeal is made to human rights.
Canadian Catholic Hierarchy, *Automation* (1964), 3, 4, 11, 13, 16, 17.
Church of Norway, *Human Dignity* (1985), esp. 3. Speaks of the right of every person to work.

Evangelisch-Lutherischen Landeskirche Hannovers, *Wort der Landessynode der ELLH vom 20. Juni 1985 zu Fragen der Arbeitslosigkeit,* II, IV.

International Council of Community Churches [USA], *Statement of Concern on American Indian Rights* (1988). With a possible appeal to anthropology.

Lutheran Church in America, *Economic Justice: Stewardship of Creation in Human Community* (1980), esp. 7, 3.

Lutheran World Federation, *Responsible Participation in Today's Society* (1970), 55, 26-32.

Lutheran World Federation, *Statement on Racial Issues and Minority Problems — A Challenge for the Church* (1970). Seems to ground position in creation, insofar as cooperation with all humans to ensure justice presupposes such an insight grounded in human nature.

National Conference of Catholic Bishops [USA], *Race Relations and Poverty* (1966), 17-18, 14, 12, 7. Though it had made earlier reference to "Christian teaching", explicit authorization for concern with employment and a liberal ethic of active government intervention is derived from natural law. It calls for affirmative action.

National Conference of Catholic Bishops [USA], *Statement on Population* (1973), 4.

National Council of Churches [USA], *Immigrants, Refugees and Migrants* (1981), II/12, 1. Cites an earlier policy statement on full employment (not shared with us by the council) which urged full employment in the USA.

Roman Catholic Church, *Pacem in Terris* (1963), 11, 20, 64, 102, 10, 23, 31, 147, 157. Appeals to natural law could be subordinated to redemption. At least it posits a creation-redemption continuity as well as a relational view of human persons.

Roman Catholic Church, *Populorum Progressio* (1967), 27, 18, 12-13, 6. Prevailing warrants in the doctrine of creation could be subordinated to other references to Christology if the statement would self-consciously have this diversity of warrants interpreted in light of Vatican II documents.

United Church of Christ [USA], *Pronouncement on the Role of Transnational Business in Mass Economic Development* (1975).

United Church of Christ [USA], *The Right to Earn a Living* (1977).

United Church of Christ [USA], *Affirming the United Church of Christ as a Just Peace Church* (1985), Pronouncement IV/D/1/d. Refers to meaningful employment as a human right.

United Methodist Church [USA], *Social Principles of the UMC[USA]* (1980), IV; III/L.

WCC Evanston Assembly, *The Laity — The Christian in His Vocation* (1954), III.

2. Appeal to first article, with some backing from Christology/the gospel

Evangelical Church of Lutheran Confession in Brazil, *Our Social Responsibility* (1976), 1-4. The appeal to a Christology warrant trades heavily on liberation theology emphases throughout the statement. Perhaps these are the main warrants.

Fellowship of Christian Churches [Chile], *Let the Floodgates of Democratic Participation Be Opened* (1984), II.1.

National Association of Evangelicals [USA], *The Crisis in the Nation* (1968).

Peruvian (Catholic) Episcopal Conference, *Document of the Peruvian Episcopal Conference on the Theology of Liberation* (1984), 11, 13, 15-16, 28, 51, 80. A kind of two-kingdom ethic, perhaps subordinated to the gospel, stands in the background of the statement.

Roman Catholic Church, *Octogesima Adveniens* (1971), 18, 14, 9, 48. Takes a very conservative position on labor trends.

Roman Catholic Church, Congregation for the Doctrine of Faith, *Instruction on Christian Freedom and Liberation* (1986), 80-88, 99, 96, 74, 64, 60, 54, 30. Christology/the gospel may function as main warrant, especially if the statement intends the correlation it posits between creation and redemption to be read in light of Vatican II's subordination of creation to redemption.

3. Appeal to first article, possibly grounded in Christology/the gospel

Haitian [Catholic] Episcopal Conference, *The Foundation for the Church's Involvement in Local and Political Arenas* (1983), 15, 19, 2, 5. Ecclesiology — the church as sacrament — may also be invoked as a background warrant along with eschatology. The statement speaks of a right to work.

Roman Catholic Church, Vatican II, *Gaudium et Spes* (1965), 70, 67, 22, 76-77. Urges that capital investment be directed to providing jobs and also affirms the autonomy of the political realm.

Roman Catholic Church, *Laborem Exercens* (1981), 1, 6, 8, 18, 27. Eschatology also may function as an overriding warrant. It does refer to the "gospel of work", but an appeal to natural law does function even to authorize a call for unemployment benefits.

4. Appeal to creation and redemption/Christology

British Council of Churches, *Moral Criteria* (1982).

Roman Catholic Church, *Redemptor Hominis* (1979), 13-17, esp. 16. Eschatology may also function as a warrant, and creation may be subordinated to redemption.

United Church of Christ [USA], *Fulfilling God's Covenant with All Children* (1987).

5. Appeal to creation and eschatology

Dutch Reformed Church (South Africa), *Church and Society* (1986), 347-49, 343, 329. With reference to the Bible as authorization as well.

National Council of Churches [USA], *Policy Statement: The Ethical Implications of Energy Production and Use* (1979).

6. Appeal to creation/nature and the gospel

British Council of Churches, *The Role of Transnationals* (1983), 4.

Canadian Conference of Catholic Bishops, *A Society to Be Transformed* (1977), 3, 5, 7.

[Catholic] Bishops of the Netherlands, *De mens in de arbeid* (1980), 1.5; Int.; 2.1; 2.2; 2.3; 2.5; Concl.

Church of Ireland, *The Report of the Role of the Church Committee* (1984), 6. Also advocates work sharing.

Evangelische Kirche von Westfalen, *Zukunft der Arbeit — Leben und Arbeiten im Wandel* (1983), 2-4, 5-6, 8, 9-10.

Evangelische Landeskirche in Württemberg, *Erklärung zur Jugendarbeitslosigkeit* (1985). These themes authorize reflections on the Christian ethos of work, but it is less clear whether they authorize proposals for job sharing and for government intervention in the employment crisis.

Evangelisch-Lutherische Kirche in Bayern, *Wort der Landessynode zum Thema "Kirche und Arbeitswelt"* (1977). Designates work as a human right, evaluates appropriate working conditions by a criterion of anthropology, and warrants proposal for overcoming unemployment by appeal to the biblical commandment, the "law of Christ".

German Catholic Bishops Conference, *Pastorale Anregungen zum Problem der Arbeitslosigkeit* (1982), Int., 2, 5. At least shows a concern for the unemployed, though not necessarily in contradiction with the 1977 statement.

National Conference of Catholic Bishops [USA], *The National Race Crisis* (1968), 23, 19. Opts for government support in this area as well as for other social programs.

National Conference of Catholic Bishops [USA], *The Economy: Human Dimensions* (1975), 1, 4, 5, 7-13, 19, 24, 25.
National Conference of Catholic Bishops [USA], *To Do the Work of Justice* (1978), 30, 28, 6, 3, 2, 1.
National Conference of Catholic Bishops [USA], *Health and Health Care* (1981), 27, 12.
National Conference of Catholic Bishops [USA], *Economic Justice for All* (1986), PM1, PM2, PM10, PM13, PM17, PM19, 3, 15, 25, 28, 41, 73, 103, 127, 136, 162-63, 167, 196, 247, 364. Employment is said to be a human right.
United Church of Christ [USA], *Energy* (1979), III/C/3; III/A/2; II. Energy policy should be sensitive to employment needs. The gospel possibly is the primary warrant.

7. Appeal to anthropology and the gospel, with the former subordinate to the latter

Canadian Conference of Catholic Bishops, *Ethical Choices and Political Challenges* (1983), 38, 29, 12, 11, 7. Scripture also functions as a warrant.
Christian Conference of Asia, *Life and Action* (1977), I. Insofar as employment is deemed a right.

8. Appeal to Christology/nature of Christian faith/the gospel

All Africa Conference of Churches, *The Gospel — Good News to the Poor and Oppressed* (1981). At least expresses a concern about employment.
[Catholic] Episcopal Conference of Nicaragua, *Renewing Christian Hope at the Beginning of 1977* (1977). Calls for guarantees of work.
Chilean [Catholic] Episcopal Conference, *Declaration on Reconciliation* (1974), Dec.
Christian Church (Disciples of Christ), *Concerning the Universal Declaration of Human Rights* (1973). This position is taken insofar as the Universal Declaration of Human Rights, which speaks of the right to work, is endorsed. The Bible also functions as authorization.
Church of Ireland, *The Report of the Role of the Church Committee* (1982), 124-27. Advocates not using temporary solutions for the sake of long-term ones. It suggests investigating job sharing.
Church of Ireland, *The Report of the Role of the Church Committee* (1983), 5, 4, 3. Advocates work sharing and guaranteed minimum income. It appeals at least to "Christian teaching" and a "common Christian ethos" as grounds for deploring unemployment.
Conférence Episcopale Française, *A propos de la conjoncture économique et sociale* (1975), 1-3.
Evangelical Church of Lutheran Confession in Brazil, *God's Earth . . . Land for Everyone* (1982), II. Strong liberation theology emphasis, with creation and perhaps eschatology as background warrants.
Evangelische Kirche im Rheinland, *Arbeitslosigkeit* (1987).
Evangelische Landeskirche in Württemberg, *Entschliessung zur Kirche und Arbeitswelt* (1985), 1-6. Although reference is made to the first and third articles of the creed, the proposals to address unemployment-related problems are dealt with from the perspective of the gospel.
Irish Episcopal Conference, *Christian Faith in a Time of Economic Depression* (1983). Calls for public-works projects and purchasing only from Irish firms.
Lutheran Church-Missouri Synod, *To Show Concern for the Unemployed and the Underpaid* (1977).
Methodist Church [England], *Statement and Programme on Race Relations* (1978), 6, 1.
Methodist Church of Malaysia, *Social Principles* (n.d.), III/B/1, 3-4, 10; II; I. With reference to the doctrine of creation.

[Orthodox] Ecumenical Patriarchate of Constantinople, *Message patriarcal des Pâques* (1986).
Presbyterian Church of Southern Africa, *Church and Nation, South Africa* (1979), 74, clause 9.
Southern Baptist Convention [USA], *A Statement of Social Principles* (1979), 3.
United Church of Christ [USA], *Justice in Immigration* (1981). Concerned about the implications of immigration for U.S. unemployment.
United Church of Christ [USA], *A United Church of Christ Ministry with Indians* (1987), Pronouncements II/1, III.
WCC Canberra Assembly, *The Report of the Seventh Assembly* (1991), 40.

9. Appeal to Christology/covenant and third-article loci

Conference of European Churches and Council of European Catholic Bishops' Conferences, *Final Document of the European Ecumenical Assembly Peace with Justice* (1989), 68, 45, 44.
Joint Pastoral Letter of the Bishops of Kenya on the Family and Responsible Parenthood (1979). Authorization not entirely clear. It criticizes working mothers.
United Church of Canada, *Poverty Report and Recommendations* (1977), Recs. 6, 5, Int. Appeals to Christology and the body of Christ.
United Church of Canada, *The Church and the Economic Crisis* (1984). Calls for a national program to create new jobs through ecology and housing programs. Employment is prioritized over the free movement of capital. Authorization is often not provided, but the gospel and eschatology give what authorization is offered.
United Church of Christ [USA], *Jesus Christ Frees and Unites* (1975).

10. Appeal to Christology, supplemented by third-article loci

United Church of Christ [USA], *Economic Justice* (1973). With the doctrine of creation possibly in the background, the statement advocates public works projects if necessary.

11. Appeal to pneumatology

Southern African Catholic Bishops' Conference, *Social Justice and Race Relations within the Church* (1977), 10, Int.

12. Appeal to ecclesiology

Mennonite Church, General Conference [USA], *Resolution on Poverty in North America* (1968).
United Church of Christ [USA], *Economic Life* (1969). Also refers to our "God-given duty" as a warrant for concern about economic ills.

13. Warrants likely drawn from all articles of creed/Trinitarian warrant

American Lutheran Church, *Issues and Opportunities That Bind and Free* (1976).
[Catholic] Bishops of the Netherlands, *Mens, arbeid en samenleving* (1985), 1-6, 9-12. Many appeals are made to the doctrine of creation and to natural law, but these may be subordinated to the gospel.

Lutheran World Federation, *Statement on Human Rights* (1984), I, II. The acts of the Triune God function as authorization, insofar as the statement in fact deems employment to be a human right.

National Conference of Catholic Bishops [USA], *Brothers and Sisters to Us: A Pastoral Letter on Racism* (1979). The explicit reference to creation/justice as warrant for the concern to aim for full employment seems rooted in redemption, in view of the letter's invocation of *Gaudium et Spes,* which advocates such a relationship between the two loci. Eschatology also functions at least as a motive and the church as a sign of unity among all peoples.

United Church of Christ [USA], *Human Rights* (1979). Speaks of the "right to earn a living".

United Church of Christ [USA], *Reversing the Arms Race* (1979).

WCC Evanston Assembly, *Social Problems — The Responsible Society in a World Perspective* (1954), I.A; Int.

14. Warrants likely drawn from all articles of creed/Trinitarian warrant, with creation subordinated to Christology

National Conference of Catholic Bishops [USA], *To Live in Jesus Christ: A Pastoral Reflection on the Moral Life* (1976), 2, 30, 31, 75-77, 115-16. Christology functions as the prevailing warrant.

15. Appeal to biblical mandate

United Church of Christ [USA], *The Homeless Poor Priority* (1987).

16. Appeal to Mariology, with appeal to other loci in support

Roman Catholic Church, *Sollicitudo Rei Socialis* (1987), 49, 48, 47, 33, 18, 8, 7, 3, 2, 1. Loci from all three articles of the creed appear as background warrants.

17. No clear theological warrant given for position

All Africa Conference of Churches, *The Gospel in Practice* (1981).

American Lutheran Church, *A Call to Affirmation of Human Values* (1972). May have a two-kingdom ethic in the background.

American Lutheran Church, *The Unfinished Reformation* (1980). May not have been an official statement.

Baptist Union of New Zealand, *Unemployment* (1980), (a)-(c).

British Council of Churches, *As Others See Us — In Mission* (1979), (v). Concerned about unemployment in the third world.

British Council of Churches, *Private Members Motion* (1981).

Catholic Bishops of Liberia, *Pastoral Letter on Abortion* (1984), 9-10. A reference is made to pneumatology, but its possible function as a warrant is not made clear.

[Catholic] Episcopal Conference of Portugal, *Aspects de la vie nationale portugaise* (1987), 7.

Christian Church (Disciples of Christ), *Report of the Response to 1975 General Assembly World Hunger Resolutions Progress Report No. II* (1979), II. Merely laments unemployment.

Church of Ireland, *The Report of the Role of the Church Committee* (1981).

Church of Ireland, *The Report of the Role of the Church Committee* (1985).

Council of Churches in the Netherlands, *Letter to Dr. R.F.M. Lubbers* (1983).

Episcopal Church [USA], *General Convention Response to the Presiding Bishop's Address* (1967).

Episcopal Church [USA], *Opportunities for American Indians* (1982). Calls for overcoming unemployment among Indian people.

Evangelische Kirche der Union — Bereich Bundesrepublik Deutschland und Berlin-West, *Beschluss zum Bericht des Ratsvorsitzenden über Aufgaben der Evangelischen Kirche der Union* (1976), I/5.

Evangelische Kirche im Rheinland, *Stellungnahme der Landessynode der EKR 1968 zum Strukturwandel in der Wirtschaft* (1968).

Evangelische Kirche in Deutschland, *Entschliessung zur Rassendiskriminierung* (1974).

Evangelischen Kirche in Deutschland, *Kundgebung der Synode der EKD zur Arbeitslosigkeit* (1977). But the statement does speak of a right to work which is grounded in the social order and so perhaps could imply that authorization for the right to work reflects an appeal to the orders of creation.

Evangelische Kirche von Kurhessen-Waldeck, *Beschlüsse der Landessynode zum Problem der Arbeitslosigkeit* (1976).

Evangelische Kirche von Westfalen, *Wort der Landessynode 1984 zum Thema "Zukunft der Arbeit"* (1984).

Evangelische Kirche von Westfalen, *Beschluss der Landessynode 1985 zur Frage der Arbeitslosigkeit*.

Evangelisch-Lutherische Kirche in Bayern, *Wort der Landessynode an alle Kirchengemeinden und Dekanate in Bayern* (1982).

Evangelisch-Lutherische Kirche in Bayern, *Wort der Landessynode zu Problemen der Arbeitslosigkeit* (1982).

Evangelisch-Lutherische Kirche in Bayern, *Erklärung der Landessynode zur Arbeitslosigkeit* (1985).

Evangelisch-Lutherische Landeskirche Hannovers, *Wort der 19. Landessynode der ELLH vom 15.3.1980 zur Berufsnot jünger Menschen und zur Jugendarbeitslosigkeit*.

Fédération Protestante de France, *Vœux adoptés à l'Assemblée du PF à la Rochelle* (1983), 2-3. Interested in possibilities of sharing jobs in order to create more employment opportunities.

International Council of Community Churches [USA], *Statement of Concern on the Homeless* (1989).

Irish Episcopal Conference, *The Storm That Threatens* (1983), 1.

Italian Episcopal Conference, *Message of the Bishops to the Catholic Communities of Italy* (1977).

Lutheran Church in America, *Poverty* (1966). Does refer to Christians being motivated by the love of God in Christ and claims that the proposals of the statement are in continuity with God's mercy. Thus Christology may be functioning as a warrant to authorize the concern for full employment or at least adequate income for all.

Lutheran Church-Missouri Synod, *To Be Concerned about Unemployment* (1975).

Methodist Church [England], *A Statement Reaffirming That the Methodist Church Is against Racism in All Its Forms and Committed to Racial Justice within a Plural Society* (1988).

National Conference of Catholic Bishops [USA], *Resolution on the Pastoral Concern of the Church for People on the Move* (1976), 9, 14. Though the gospel may be a background warrant.

National Council of Churches [USA], *The Concern of the Churches for Seasonal Farm Workers* (1966), 3.

National Council of Churches [USA], *Unemployment Insurance* (1966). Reaffirms a 1958 *Policy Statement on Christian Concern about Unemployment*.

National Council of Churches [USA], *Human Hunger and the World Food Crisis* (1975), VII/D/ 3. Calls for full employment.

Reformed Church in America, *Report of the Christian Action Commission* (1969), R-8. References to creation and Christology are made by background statement.

Reformed Ecumenical Synod, *Pastoral Statement: A Call to Commitment and Action* (1984), XII/D/6. Calls for a right to work.

South African Council of Churches, *Resolution No. 5: Disinvestment* (1985), 7.

United Church of Canada, *Collective Bargaining* (1971), 1. At least speaks of a right to work.

United Church of Canada, *Free Trade* (1986). Concerned to protect unemployment benefits.

United Church of Christ [USA], *Executive Council Statement on Racial Crisis* (1963).

United Church of Christ [USA], *Resolution on Poverty* (1965).

United Church of Christ [USA], *Poverty and Economic Justice* (1967).

United Church of Christ [USA], *Racial Justice* (1967). In virtue of its subscription to the church's 1963 declaration, *A Call for Racial Justice Now*.

United Church of Christ [USA], *Concerning Our Economic System* (1977).

United Church of Christ [USA], *Affirmative Action* (1979). Though the gospel and creation might function as authorization.

United Church of Christ [USA], *Federal Budget* (1981). With at least a passing reference to the "biblical mandate".

United Church of Christ [USA], *Increased Racial Violence against Blacks in America* (1981). Concerned about the rise of unemployment among American blacks.

United Church of Christ [USA], *Justice and Peace Priority* (1985).

United Free Church of Scotland, *Deliverance of the General Assembly* [on public questions] (1972), 1, 7.

United Free Church of Scotland, *Deliverance of the General Assembly* [on public questions] (1973), 1, 10.12.

United Free Church of Scotland, *Deliverance of the General Assembly* [on public questions] (1982), 11.

United Free Church of Scotland, *Deliverance of the General Assembly* [on public questions] (1986), 7.

United Free Church of Scotland, *Deliverance of the General Assembly* [on public questions] (1988), 5-6.

Uniting Church in Australia, *Statement to Nation* (1977). The gospel/"basic Christian values" may be functioning as authorization, but this is not clear.

Uniting Church in Australia, *Board of Church and Community* (1979), 79.20.4.

World Alliance of Reformed Churches, *The Pacific, Australia, and Aotearoa/New Zealand* (1989).

WCC Uppsala Assembly, *World Economic and Social Development* (1968), 26-28. Though earlier some warrants drawn from both Christology and creation.

WCC World Convocation on Justice, Peace and the Integrity of Creation, *Final Document: Entering into Covenant Solidarity for Justice, Peace and the Integrity of Creation* (1990), 2.2; 2.1. Especially concerned about the unemployment of youth. The concept of covenant, which reflects trinitarian themes, may function as the document's overriding warrant.

At least one statement which seems to address this issue, Evangelische Kirche in Deutschland, *Solidargemeinschaft von Arbeitenden und Arbeitslosen* (1982), has not been included in this analysis because it was only "worked on" by the EKD's synod and so does not necessarily express the views of this organization's highest governing authority. Has the authority of this statement been misconstrued, so that in fact it deserves the kind of attention given to other statements representing the views of the churches' highest governing authorities? At least one statement issued by the Church of Sweden, *Motions om arbetslösheten* (1983), considers unemployment. But the statement's status as a document of that church's highest governing authority has never been clarified by its officers, and so the statement is not included above.

Concerns about racism in current employment practices have been voiced by the American Baptist Churches, *Policy Statement on Racial Justice* (1983), and by the United Church of Christ [USA], *Executive Council Statement on Racial Crisis* (1963). Likewise concern about the rise of black unemployment in the USA has been expressed by the United Church of Christ [USA], *Increased Racial Violence against Blacks in America* (1981), though without theological authorization.

Somewhat related to these concerns are the warnings about the implications for unemployment of immigration to the USA, issued by appeal to Christology, by the United Church of

Christ [USA], *Justice in Immigration* (1981). Also see the claim, authorized by appeal to God's Word and the teachings of the church, by the Canadian Catholic Conference, *On Immigration Policy* (1975), 17, 2, which claims that immigration curbs in Canada will not solve the nation's unemployment problems. Similarly, concern for indigent laborers seems to be reflected to some extent in a statement of the Evangelische Landeskirche in Württemberg, *Ausländer und Asylanten* (1982), A, and perhaps more explicitly in a statement of the Evanglisch-Lutherische Kirche in Bayern, *Votum der Landessynode zur Schaffung von Vertretungen für ausländische Arbeitnehmer* (1974), as the church urges the government to establish representation or advocacy of the interests of foreign laborers residing in Bavaria.

Likewise the same church in *Beschluss der Landessynode zu Massnahmen zur Jugendarbeitslosigkeit* (1976) and *Wort der 19. Landessynode der Evangelisch-Lutherischen Landeskirche Hannovers vom 15.3.1980 zur Berufsnot jünger Menschen und zur Jugendarbeitslosigkeit,* also without providing a theological rationale, seek to deal with problems posed by massive youth unemployment by assisting youth to deal with the crises. A concern with the problem of unemployment, without theological rationale, has also been articulated by the Evangelische Kirche im Rheinland, *Jugendarbeitslosigkeit* (1981); cf. Evangelische Kirche im Rheinland, *Arbeitslosigkeit* (1983). In its *Stellungnahme des sozialethischen Ausschusses zum Problem der Arbeitslosigkeit* (1978), without theological authorization, the same church also called for a study of the problem of unemployment. One of the many policy statements on apartheid of the Dutch Reformed Church (South Africa), *Church and Society* (1986), 3.21, also addressed unemployment, insofar as it speaks of a human right to employment authorized by the divine commission.

The same idea of employment as a right is endorsed, authorized by appeal to anthropology and the Bible (subordinated to and including the gospel), by the Canadian Conference of Catholic Bishops, *Ethical Choices and Political Challenges* (1983), 38, 23, 12, 11, 7. Other church statements listed above which make this point include Reformed Ecumenical Synod, *Pastoral Statement: A Call to Commitment and Action* (1984), XII/D/6, without clear theological authorization; Christian Conference of Asia, *Life and Action* (1977), I, authorized by anthropology and the gospel, with the former subordinated to the latter; Haitian (Catholic) Episcopal Conference, *The Foundation for the Church's Involvement in Local and Political Arenas* (1983), 15, 19, 2, 5, authorized by creation, grounded in Christology; National Conference of Catholic Bishops (USA), *Economic Justice for All* (1986), PM1, PM2, PM10, PM13, PM17, PM19, 3, 15, 25, 28, 41, 73, 103, 127, 136, 162-63, 167, 196, 247, 364, authorized by creation and the nature of the gospel; United Church of Christ [USA], *Affirming the United Church of Christ as a Just Peace Church* (1985), Pronouncement IV/D/1/D, apparently authorized by natural law; United Church of Canada, *Collective Bargaining* (1971), 1, without theological authorization; Christian Church (Disciples of Christ), *Concerning the Universal Declaration of Human Rights* (1973), authorized by Christology and the Bible, and *Report concerning Human Rights* (1979), III; Int., authorized by biblical testimony and creation. Similarly, the duty of the regime to provide the assurance of productive work is endorsed (though without providing any theological authorization for the position) by the Patriarchs and Catholic Bishops of Libya, *Legality Is the Unique Guarantee of the Fatherland* (1983), III/4.

Without providing authorization, the United Church of Canada, *Military Expenditures* (1986), claims that "security" includes employment. The Episcopal Church [USA], in both its *General Convention Resolution* [on urban Indian concerns and parish involvement] (1970) and its *Opportunities for American Indians* (1982), without theological authorization, urges efforts to help displaced or urban Indians find employment. Also see United Church of Christ [USA], *A United Church of Christ Ministry with Indians* (1987), authorized by Christology; International Council of Community Churches, *Statement of Concern on American Indian Rights* (1988), probably authorized by anthropology. An issue related to unemployment was addressed indirectly at least by the Lutheran World Federation, *Toward Economic and Social Justice* (1984), 8.1.1.2; I, insofar as the statement speaks of "the right of all persons to receive a fair wage for their services". Also see Roman Catholic Church, *Pacem in Terris* (1963), 10, 11, 20, 23, 31, 64, 102, 147, 157.

C. ECOLOGY

3-1 ECOLOGY

All church statements explicitly addressing this issue call on the churches to work for better ecological balance. The only possible exception is a 1977 statement of the Evangelische Landeskirche in Baden, *Wort zur Kernenergie,* which insists that the concern with ecology must not be permitted to conflict with economic development. Differences emerge over the warrant they use to authorize their positions and how they relate ecology to the use of energy, particularly nuclear energy.

1. Appeal to creation/view of human persons
2. Appeal to creation and Christology/the gospel
3. Appeal to creation, subordinated to the gospel/Christology
4. Appeal to creation and Christology, with creation subordinated to Christology
5. Appeal to creation, supplemented by warrants drawn from the second or third article
6. Appeal to creation, supplemented by and perhaps subordinated to warrants drawn from the second or third article
7. Appeal to creation and eschatology
8. Appeal to Christology/the gospel
9. Appeal to Christology/the gospel, supplemented by first-article warrants
10. Appeal to Christology/the gospel, supplemented by first- and third-article warrants
11. Appeal to the gospel and eschatology
12. Appeal to loci drawn from all three articles of the creed
13. Appeal to all three articles of the creed, with creation subordinated to redemption/Christology
14. Appeal to all three articles of the creed, with anthropology perhaps the prevailing warrant
15. Appeal to the Bible
16. Appeal to the commandment to love
17. Appeal to Christian ethical considerations and social responsibilities
18. Appeal to the concept of stewardship
19. Appeal to the nature of the Christian lifestyle/sanctification
20. No clear theological warrant given for position

1. Appeal to creation/view of human persons

American Lutheran Church, *Manifesto for Our Nation's Third Century* (1976). Calls for cherishing nature.

Anglicanism, *The Resolutions of the Lambeth Conference (1968),* 6. Calls for preventing pollution and encourages soil conservation and wild life protection. In section report of conference, *The Renewal of the Church in Faith,* it is claimed that the theology of creation (the warrant for ecological concern of both the resolution and of the section report) must be worked out with an awareness that "Christ, the agent of creation [is] inaugurating a cosmic redemption."

Baptist Union of New Zealand, *Public Questions* (1989), (a). Ecology includes pursuing a responsible lifestyle as well as seeking to influence industry and agriculture to restore and protect the balance of nature.

Christian Church (Disciples of Christ), *Concerning Christian Stewardship of Food and Farm Land* (1975). Ecology includes care for the farm land in such a way that food production may be increased.

Church of Norway, *Abortspørmålet* (1971), 5. Ties emerging ecological concern to the concern for life of the anti-abortion position.

Church of Norway, *Statement on Nuclear Energy and Safety* (1978). Advocates reduced energy consumption without qualification and the curtailment of nuclear technology. The orientation is that of a two-kingdom ethic, mediated by an appeal to the commandment to love one's neighbor. Could the law in this case be the natural law grounded in creation?

Church of the Brethren [USA], *Resolution on Nuclear Power* (1979). Concerned about the impact of nuclear energy on the environment.

Episcopal Church [USA], *General Convention Resolution* [to urge careful examination of all proposals for the use of undeveloped lands] (1979). Urges ecological sensitivity in converting undeveloped lands for recreational, residential, and commercial use. It suggests an ongoing creation in the sense of ongoing stewardship responsibilities.

Evangelische Kirche der Kirchenprovinz Sachsen, *Brief der Synode an die Gemeinden zur Friedensverantwortung* (1981). Relates ecology to peace and justice.

Evangelische Kirche der Kirchenprovinz Sachsen, *Beschluss zur Gesamtthematik der Synodal Tagung* (1985), Int., 3. Relates ecology to peace, justice, and a future-oriented economic policy. Covenant and gospel/conversion are background warrants; persons are viewed relationally.

Evangelische Kirche im Rheinland, *Ausstieg aus der Atomenergie* (1987), I. Ecology includes renouncement of nuclear energy and an energy policy which does not lead to the unceasing destruction and exploitation of creation.

Evangelische Kirche in Hessen und Nassau, *Erklärung zum Synoden-Thema "In der Schöpfung leben"* (1986). Concerned about the dangers of nuclear energy and energy consumption.

Evangelische Kirche von Westfalen, *Wort der Landessynode 1984 zum Thema "Kirche und Umwelt"*, 1.2.-1.3. Ecology includes appropriate use of water, air, and land, as well as reduction of waste, recycling, and the responsible use of the automobile. It posits a kind of relational view of persons.

Evangelisch-Lutherische Kirche in Bayern, *Wort zum Umweltschutz* (1984). Relates ecology to concerns about the atmosphere, deforestation, automobile speed limits, peace, and nuclear/atomic questions. The gospel is mentioned, though only as it contributes to the kind of response made to ecological challenges, not as a warrant for this response.

Evangelisch-Lutherische Landeskirche Hannovers, *Wort der Landessynode der ELLH zum Problem der Kernenergie* (1976), II. Relates preserving nature to a concern for coming generations and the use of nuclear energy.

Evangelisch-Lutherische Landeskirche Hannovers, *Wort der Landessynode der ELLH vom 20. Juni 1985 zu Fragen der Arbeitslosigkeit*, III, II. Warrant not entirely clear, but insofar as anthropology authorizes commitment to overcome unemployment and concern for ecology emerges in the context of how to create new jobs through investment, creation may also authorize the ecological concern.

Evangelisch-Methodistische Kirche [FRG], *Gefährdung der Zukunft — Verantwortung für die Zukunft* (1978), 1, 5-7. Ecology is related to the question of the quality of life in such a way that the question of economic growth must be rethought. Boundaries or the law of creation does function in one case like a kind of third use of the law.

German Catholic Bishops' Conference [FRG], *Statement of the Commissariat* (1977). Probably creation warrants ecological concern, with Christology warranting position that reduction of energy consumption not be to the point that development is jeopardized. It also authorizes openness to continued use of nuclear power to that end. Christology is perhaps the primary warrant if the statement is to be read in light of Vatican II.

Lutheran Church in America, *World Community: Ethical Imperatives in an Age of Interdependence* (1970). Not clear whether earlier reference to human unity is grounded in creation or whether the discussion of civil authority, carried on in the spirit of the two-kingdom ethic, applies to the call for an international approach to conservation and protection of resources from pollution.

Lutheran Church in America, *The Human Crisis in Ecology* (1972). Ecology is tied to social justice; Christology functions only at one point to motivate Christians, not as a criterion for their ethical action.

Lutheran Church in America, *Human Rights: Doing Justice in God's World* (1978), esp. 3-8. Future generations are said to have a right to the world's resources and a healthful environment, a right that is related to justice. References to Christology in the statement function only as motives, as the creation doctrine or anthropology authorizes the rights designated by the statement.

Lutheran Church-Missouri Synod, *Creation in Biblical Perspective* (1967ff.), III.3; VI.6.

Lutheran Church-Missouri Synod, *To Continue Development of Natural and Human Resources* (1969). Concerned about pollution of air and water as well as the laying waste to plant and animal life.

Lutheran World Federation, *Caring for God's Endangered Creation* (1984), 9.1.2; 9.1.6.2. Industrial and military development endanger the environment.

Lutheran World Federation, *Statement on Caring for God's Endangered Creation* (1984).

Moravian Church in America, Southern Province, *Conservation of Resources* (1977). Ecological concern seems implied by call for conservation of resources. The position seems warranted by creation insofar as appeal is made to human stewardship over the world.

National Association of Evangelicals [USA], *Ecology* (1970).

National Association of Evangelicals [USA], *Environment and Ecology* (1971).

National Conference of Catholic Bishops [USA], *Christian Concern for the Environment* (1971).

National Council of Churches [USA], *Consumer Rights and Corporate Responsibility* (1972). Concerned about pollution control and justice (for consumers). Stewardship provides authorization.

National Council of Churches [USA], *Policy Statement: The Ethical Implications of Energy Production and Use* (1979). Deems ecology a question of justice. It supports reduced energy consumption but wants energy policy which employs renewable fuels and provides jobs for unemployed without raising prices. In addition to reliance on a relational anthropology, the statement includes reference to eschatology, which seems to function as motive/inspiration for the position.

Reformed Church in America, *Report of the Christian Action Commission* (1973), R-4, 1. Relates ecology to the overall population problem and the need for birth control. It appeals to humankind's "stewardship of the earth" for authorization.

Reformed Church in America, *Report of the Christian Action Commission* (1982), R-5 to R-11b. Concerned about agricultural methods for earth preservation, soil conservation, safe water, conserving natural resources, and eliminating chemicals from the atmosphere.

Russian Orthodox Church, *Message of the Holy Synod of the ROC on War and Peace in a Nuclear Age* (1986), 3.33, 2.36. Relates the ecological concern to stopping the arms race.

United Church of Canada, *South Moresby — Herida Indians* (1986). Concerned to preserve Canadian Indian land from commercial logging. It appeals to the "stewardship of creation" and a related text from the Book of Genesis.

United Church of Christ [USA], *Overture on the Domestic Impact of Energy Resource Development* (1977). Relates ecology to the development of new energy resources, specifically the mining of coal in the western USA and its impact on human persons.

United Church of Christ [USA], *Energy* (1979), III/B/1; III/A/2; II. Concern for ecology emerges from reflections on energy policy. Reference to Christology may function only as a motive, though elsewhere in the statement the Christian faith functions as a warrant for positions taken.

United Church of Christ [USA], *Human Rights* (1979). Ecology is related to human rights and is authorized by the nature of human persons as necessarily related to nature. Elsewhere in the statement, however, concern for human rights is warranted by Christology, the new creation, and the Holy Spirit.

United Church of Christ [USA], *Civil Defense (Executive Council, 6/29/83)* (1983). Relates ecological concern to peace and justice.

United Church of Christ [USA], *The Crisis of People and the Land* (1985), IV. Urges care of the land and soil conservation. It is authorized by a relational view of persons.

United Methodist Church [USA], *Social Principles of the UMC[USA]* (1980), I, VII. Ecology is related to the conservation of animals, plants, air, and soil. The statement, which supports energy conservation, is affirmed by the *Soziale Grundsätze der Evangelisch-Methodistischen Kirche (FRG)* (1984), I, Grund, but with the gospel as a background warrant.

World Alliance of Reformed Churches, *Towards a Common Testimony of Faith* (1989), I/B.

WCC Canberra Assembly, *Come, Holy Spirit: The Assembly Message* (1991). Relates ecology to justice. Christology and pneumatology stand in the background.

WCC Conference on Faith, Science and the Future, *Technology, Resources, Environment and Population* (Cambridge, Mass., 12-24 July, 1979), esp. 4, 3, Int. Because human sin brought evil to natural world, it also follows that salvation in Christ has consequences for humanity's treatment of the natural world. This reference to Christology seems to function only as motive for the ethic, not as its criterion. It claims an intimate connection between ecology and societal institutions, and thus pollution is unjust.

2. Appeal to creation and Christology/the gospel

American Baptist Churches, *Policy Statement on Hunger* (1975), V, Int. Relates ecology to the agricultural implications of land use. The oneness of humanity and Christian love provide authorization.

American Baptist Churches, *Policy Statement on Energy* (1977). Relates ecology to justice and the appropriate use of energy.

Baptist Union of New Zealand, *Public Questions* (1970). Concerned about the preservation of natural resources. It takes its position while endorsing a statement of the Baptist World Alliance Congress.

Bund der Evangelischen Kirchen in der Deutschen Demokratischen Republik, *Beschluss der Synode des Bundes zum Thema "Christliche Verantwortung für die Schöpfung" vom 25. September 1984*, 1-3. Calls for a simpler lifestyle. Christology may be the prevailing warrant.

National Conference of Catholic Bishops [USA], *Health and Health Care* (1981), 27, 12. Relates environmental issues to pollution, unemployment, lack of education, inadequate housing, and health.

National Council of Churches [USA], *Christian Concern and Responsibility for Economic Life in a Rapidly Changing Technological Society* (1966). Concerned about responsible conservation of natural resources. Authorization is provided primarily by the idea of stewardship. Creation is construed as ongoing, or dynamic.

Swedish Ecumenical Council/Church of Sweden, *Nuclear Power, Energy and Questions Pertaining to the Style and Quality of Life* (1978), III.1, 4, 6-8. Would protect environment from the high tempo of technological change. Nuclear power is not a good option. It opts for reduced consumption of energy but not to the exclusion of seeking other energy options.

Synod of the Protestant Church in Austria, *Atomic Energy in Austria* (1978), Int., I-III. Concern for ecology insofar as maintaining energy reserves has implications for nature and the future. Appeal to the law and so creation is perhaps more dominant in making these points. The statement employs a relational view of persons. The gospel functions as warrant for the decision to suspend the use of nuclear energy and to call for qualified reduction of energy consumption.

United Church of Christ [USA], *The National Toxic Injustice Crisis* (1985), Pronouncement, A Proposal for Action. Especially concerned to stop the production, transportation, and dumping of toxic substances, relating this concern to racial justice. The Holy Spirit also functions as a motive.

Uniting Church in Australia, *Militarism and Disarmament* (1982), 82.57, (i). Concerned about the effects of nuclear war on the environment. Its warrants are not perfectly clear.

World Alliance of Reformed Churches, *Justice, Peace and the Integrity of Creation* (1989). Authorization by creation and covenant. It relates ecology to justice and peace and is concerned about the so-called greenhouse effect, the production of harmful gases, the undue use of fossil fuels, the dumping of nuclear and toxic waste, the production of harmful sprays, and the possible effects of bio-technology. The statement urges the simple lifestyle and the preservation/replanting of forests.

WCC Nairobi Assembly, *Structures of Injustice and Struggles for Liberation* (1975), 2, 11. Ecology is identified as a basic human right.

WCC Sub-Unit on Church and Society, *Report of the Advisory Group of the Energy for My Neighbour Programme* (1982), VI, V, II. Relates ecological concern to the question of nuclear energy. Ecology is acknowledged as being somewhat irrelevant in underdeveloped nations. Ecology is designated as one of the criteria for determining appropriate energy assistance to underdeveloped nations in their development of indigenous technology and renewable energy resources. A small reduction in energy consumption is advocated in order to make energy available to underdeveloped nations. Perhaps Christology conceived of in terms of *theosis* prevails in warranting concerns about the ethical implications of energy policies.

3. Appeal to creation, subordinated to the gospel/Christology

Canadian Conference of Catholic Bishops, *Ethical Choices and Political Challenges* (1983), 7, 19, 22, 37. Relates ecology to economics.

National Association of Evangelicals [USA], *Stewardship: All for God's Glory* (1990). Ecology includes a concern about pollution as well as water and fuel supplies.

[Orthodox] Ecumenical Patriarchate of Constantinople, *Message de Sa Sainteté le patriarche œcuménique Dimitrios à l'occasion de Noël 1987* (1987). Ultimately appeals to the concept of *theosis*.

4. Appeal to creation and Christology, with creation subordinated to Christology

Catholic Bishops of the Philippines, *What Is Happening to Our Beautiful Land?* (1988). Ecology includes a concern about pollution of rivers, damage to corals, disappearance of forests (as this has affected eradication of certain birds and animals). It relates ecology to justice and peace and speaks of creation as an ongoing process.

5. Appeal to creation, supplemented by warrants drawn from the second or third article

American Lutheran Church, *The Environmental Crisis* (1970), 1, 2-6, 8, 9, 11, 12. References to Christology and the sacraments may only be motivations, not warrants.

American Lutheran Church, *The Land: God's Giving, Our Caring* (1982), Int.; II; II/A/1-5; III/A/2, 1; IV/A/2-3; II/B/7. Perhaps creation warrants predominate.

Brethren in Christ Church [USA], *Position Paper on Church, War and Respect for Human Life* (1976), II. Concerned to share the world's resources with those in need. It also ties ecological destruction to the evil of war.

Evangelisch-Methodistische Kirche [FRG], *Soziale Grundsätze* (1977), Prin.; I; I/A, D. Reference to Christology and the gospel could function either as criteria or as mere motivations for ethical engagement. The statement sanctions the use of reliable energy resources. Ecological responsibility is said to include concern for animals and outer space.

Lutheran Church in America, *Economic Justice: Stewardship of Creation in Human Community* (1980), esp. 3, 6, 7. Economics may not overlook ecology. The reference to Christology perhaps only provides a motive. The doctrine of human persons (anthropology) is clearly the prevailing warrant. But final reference to eschatology and the idea of the church as sign of the new creation seems to function as a warrant, at least for the task of preserving the earth.

National Conference of Catholic Bishops [USA], *Economic Justice for All* (1986), 12, 94, 216-17, 238, 246. Ecology is said to be more crucial than industrial expansion. It should be considered in all measures concerning agriculture.

Netherlands [Catholic] Bishops' Conference, *Vrede en gerechtigheid* (1983), III/1. Reference to kairos may indicate an appeal to eschatology as warrant. Conservation of nature is seen as a basic value which, along with meaningful work and education, may help cure society's ills.

United Church of Canada, *Energy and the Church* (1982), 2(c-e); 3 (1). Relates ecology to energy conservation and desirability of moratorium on use of nuclear energy. A cluster of issues relate to poverty. Are references to the church as mandate to social action or the stated concern to "express the gospel in the fundamental decisions which face our society" criteria or motives for the ethical positions? The clearest warrants are drawn from the idea of God's sovereignty over creation and the human vocation of stewardship.

Waldensian Synod and the Methodist Conference [Italy], *Statements of the Joint Session of the WSMC* (1978). Decisions about the use of nuclear energy must take account of concern for environmental protection. Creation warrants predominate in the statement, with complementary appeal to believers that they "follow their calling to bear a Christian witness".

WCC Canberra Assembly, *The Report of the Seventh Assembly* (1991), 13, 14, 18, 21, 24, 25, 33, 34. Pneumatology may only function as a motive. The biblical vision is also referred to as a motive. Creation is understood sacramentally, and a relational view of persons is endorsed. Ecology is related to economics and development, the alleviation of debts, justice, peace, demilitarization, and the rejection of racism.

6. Appeal to creation, supplemented by and perhaps subordinated to warrants drawn from the second or third article

Bund der Evangelischen Kirchen in der Deutschen Demokratischen Republik, *Beschluss der Synode des Bundes zum Bericht der Konferenz der Ev. Kirchenleitungen vom 24. September 1985*, 2. Would establish programs for the protection of the environment.

[Catholic] Episcopal Conference of the Pacific, *The Pacific and Peace* (1986), IV, VIII, IX. Relates ecological concern to development and the dangers of nuclear arms and perhaps nuclear energy.

German Catholic Bishops Conference, *Zukunft der Schöpfung — Zukunft der Menschheit* (1980), I.1, 4; II.1, 7; III.2, 3. Will not opt for reduced energy consumption to the point of jeopardizing those in present need and would keep all options open with regard to nuclear energy. Given the statement's positing of a creation-redemption continuity, it is not clear if Christology and the Eucharist are criteria or motives. It is possible that creation should be deemed a background warrant. The bishops' decision to conjoin creation and eschatological themes (see I.4; the statement's title) and to speak of Christ as the source and center of creation (I.7) are most suggestive of Vatican II statements like *Gaudium et Spes*, 22, 38, where creation is subordinated to Christology in a kind of eschatological vision.

Lutheran-Episcopal Dialogue, series 3 [USA], *Implications of the Gospel* (1988), 116, 79. Concerned about air and water purity as well as individual and corporate use of resources.

National Association of Evangelicals [USA], *Save the Family* (1982). Relates ecology to economic concerns.

Roman Catholic Church, *Redemptor Hominis* (1979), 13-14, 8. Ecological problems (pollution) as well as armed conflicts, nuclear threats, and lack of respect for the unborn are the result of immense progress.

United Church of Christ [USA], *Report on Christian Life Style and Ecology* (1977). Ecology is related to the energy dilemma and the need to alter lifestyle. Insofar as all human activity is said to tie in with God's kingdom, appeals to the doctrine of creation seem to be subordinated to eschatology and Christology.

Ustřední Rada Církve Ceskoslovenské Husitské, *Der sozialethische Orientierung* (1981), 10, 1.1, Begr. Concerned about the destruction of minerals, plants, and animals.

7. Appeal to creation and eschatology

Baptist World Alliance, *Man's Stewardship and Survival on This Earth* (1970). Relates ecology to problem of adequate health care.

Landessynode der Evangelischen Kirche in Rheinland-Westfalen, *Wort zur Energiediskussion* (1980), 2(a, b, c, e); 4(e); 5; 7. To protect environment need to place limits on energy consumption. It would place limits on the number of nuclear power plants.

8. Appeal to Christology/the gospel

American Baptist Churches, *Policy Statement on Evangelism* (1984). The new life in Christ is said to include the ecological concern as well as a concern for justice.

Canadian Conference of Catholic Bishops, *A Society to Be Transformed* (1977), 3, 5, 7. Relates ecology to overcoming the misuse of natural resources. Redemption also functions as a warrant.

Christian Church (Disciples of Christ), *Concerning Our National Priorities* (1973). Concerned about reclamation of polluted water and relates the ecological concern to education, health care, and adequate nutrition.

Christian Church (Disciples of Christ), *Concerning Wider World Perspectives* (1973). Relates ecology to racial justice, population planning, and peace.

Christian Conference of Asia, *Justice and Service* (1977), D. Environmental pollution is associated with rampant technology. It is not clear if Christology is a criterion for this ethic or merely motivates it.

Eglise de la Confession d'Augsbourg d'Alsace et de Lorraine, *Le problème nucléaire* (1978). Notes the position of the Fédération Protestante de France and calls for presumably unqualified reduction of energy consumption.

Episcopal Church [USA], *Education on Land Use* (1982). Concerned about land use, soil erosion, hunger, and arms control. The statement is authorized by appeal to "Christian responsibility".

Evangelicals for Social Action [USA], *Chicago Declaration of Evangelicals to Social Concern* (1973), 5-7. Relates problem of ecology to the need for a more just distribution of goods in the face of the injustice of international action and development, which is itself subsequently related to militarism.

Evangelische Kirche der Kirchenprovinz Sachsen, *Vorlage des Berichtsausschusses* (1984), 1, 2.1. Relates ecology to peace and justice and cites the WCC formula for relating the three. It appeals to Christian faith for authorization.

Evangelische Kirche in Deutschland, *The Preservation, Promotion and Renewal of Peace* (1981), Int.; IV.1(d); IV.1(f); V.3(a); V.4(a). Ecology, like human rights and elimination of oppression, is a consequence of peace. Some reference is also made to the Eucharist as warrant.

Evangelische Kirche in Deutschland, *Wir müssen mehr tun* (1986), II.5; III. Concerned about ecological consequences of industrialization in developing nations. Authorization or "encouragement" is given by "the mercy of God".

Evangelische Landeskirche in Baden, *Wort zur Kernenergie* (1977). Sees relation between ecological concern and questions about the use of nuclear energy. This ecological concern and commitment to reduced energy consumption cannot override the commitment to equality in economic development.

Evangelisch-Lutherische Landessynode Sachsens, *Erklärung der 22. ELLS vom 22. März 1988* (1988). Relates ecology to peace and justice.

Fédération Protestante de France, *The Question of Nuclear Energy* (1978), Int. V. Concerned with environmental impact of rate of growth and nuclear energy waste. Its position on the advisability of nuclear energy's continued use and on unqualified reduction of energy consumption is not clear, but the statement suggests these positions.

International Congress for World Evangelization, *An Answer to Lausanne* (1974), 7.

Mennonite World Conference, *Our Witness to Christ in Today's World* (1990).

Nordelbische Evangelisch-Lutherische Kirche, *"Unsere Verantwortung vor Gott für seine Schöpfung"* (1988). Ecology includes a concern to limit technology so as not to violate the intrinsic value of creation. It calls for reduced energy consumption and a phasing out of dependence on nuclear energy. The statement posits a relational view of persons and construes creation as a process.

[Orthodox] Ecumenical Patriarchate of Constantinople, *Message patriarcal des Pâques* (1986). Relates ecology to destruction caused by nuclear testing and by racism, famine, and war.

Presbyterian Church in the U.S./United Presbyterian Church, *The Power to Speak Truth to Power* (1981), pts. 1, 1/II-IV, 2; 2/I. Ethic of ecological justice is related to urging unqualified decrease in energy consumption and transfer of capital and energy resources to poorer nations. (Yet a new model of development may also be suggested.) It also favors phasing out dependence on nuclear energy. Likely Christological warrant is enhanced by appeal to eschatology at one point.

Presbyterian-Reformed Church in Cuba, *Confession of Faith* (1977), III/C, D; II/A, B. Marxism best provides for technological and ecological development. But it also includes an appeal to doctrines of creation and human persons to authorize the domination of nature.

Reformed Church of Alsace-Lorraine, *Decision* (1978). Approves statement of the Fédération Protestante de France.

World Alliance of Reformed Churches, *Reconciliation and Creation: The Freedom of God's World* (1970), 3, Int. (see section report with the same title, 1, 7[d, f]). No warrant is given in the approved statement, but it is given in the section report, from which the approved recommendation emerged. It could include supplementary appeal to creation as warrant in virtue of the approved statement's acknowledging God's good gift in nature.

World Alliance of Reformed Churches, *A Message to the Congregations of the Member Churches of the WARC* (1989). Relates ecology to peace and justice.

WCC Vancouver Assembly, *Statement on the International Food Disorder* (1983), 8-10. Relates ecology to food production. There is a hint that concern about hunger is warranted by Christology and the Eucharist.

9. Appeal to Christology/the gospel, supplemented by first-article warrants

Arbeitsgemeinschaft Christlicher Kirchen in der Bundesrepublik Deutschland und Berlin (West), *Neuer Lebensstil aus christlicher Verantwortung* (1980), 1-3, 6. Relates conservation to all elements of wealth as well as the need to recover a sense of community and personal goals. Such conservation must also be sensitive to the gap between rich and poor nations and the problem of achieving international justice.

Evangelical Church of Lutheran Confession in Brazil, *God's Earth . . . Land for Everyone* (1982), I, II. Relates the ecological concern to a concern about the arms race, justice, and peasants. Eschatology may also be a background warrant. Characteristic themes of liberation theology are emphasized.

Methodist Church in Malaysia, *Social Principles* (n.d.), III/B/8; II; I. Concerned with conservation of the soil and all natural resources in the context of reflections on town and country life. The doctrine of creation perhaps plays a more central role in authorizing the concern with ecology, though the authorization is not perfectly clear and such concerns are deemed a Christian responsibility.

10. Appeal to Christology/the gospel, supplemented by first- and third-article warrants

Presbyterian Church (USA), *Life Abundant: Values, Choices and Health Care* (1988), 15-16. Relates ecology to environmental justice, to overcoming pollution as well as chemical, nuclear, and industrial waste, to health, and to social justice.

11. Appeal to the gospel and eschatology

Eglise de la Confession d'Augsbourg d'Alsace et de Lorraine, *Texte concernant J.P.S.C.* (1989). Relates ecology to peace and justice.

12. Appeal to loci drawn from all three articles of the creed

American Baptist Churches, *Policy Statement on Human Rights* (1976). Humans are said to have a right to a secure environment, clean air, and pure water. This right is related to others such as religious liberty, freedom from discrimination, and right to basic necessities.

American Lutheran Church, *Issues and Opportunities That Bind and Free* (1976). Relates concern about pollution to urban neglect, unemployment, racism, inflation, injustice, and divorce. It strongly endorses a relational view of human persons.

Conference of European Churches and Council of European Bishops' Conferences, *Final Document of the European Ecumenical Assembly Peace with Justice* (1989), 3, 13, 14, 20-22, 29, 33, 34, 36, 40, 42, 43, 45, 70, 72, 74, 77, 83, 91, 99. Relates ecology to (economic) justice, peace, the need to re-evaluate expectations raised by science and technology, curtailing population growth, overcoming wasteful use of energy, and the need to control waste. In addition to appealing to loci derived from all three articles of the creed, the document also appeals to the concept of covenant, which itself reflects trinitarian content.

Evangelische Kirche in Deutschland, *Zur Achtung vor dem Leben* (1987), III/3, I. Concerned about the ecological and social compatibility of new developments in genetic technology.

Lutheran World Federation, *I Have Heard the Cry of My People... The Assembly Message* (1990). Relates ecology to peace, justice, economics, and genetic engineering. The biblical understanding is also cited as a supporting warrant.

World Alliance of Reformed Churches, *The Theatre of Glory and a Threatened Creation's Hope* (1982). Relates the ecological crisis to threats of nuclear war and economic injustice.

WCC Nairobi Assembly, *Human Development: Ambiguities of Power, Technology and Quality of Life* (1975), 18-20, 1-7, 56-61. Calls for a kind of "ecologically sensitive" model of development.

WCC Convocation on Justice, Peace and the Integrity of Creation, *Entering into Covenant Solidarity for Justice, Peace and the Integrity of Creation* (1990), 2.1; 2.2; 2.3.1-2.3.2.3. Ecology includes overcoming poverty and special solidarity with the poor. Themes of natural law and ecclesiology are especially emphasized. Authorization is also provided by the concept of covenant, which itself reflects a trinitarian authorization.

13. Appeal to all three articles of the creed, with creation subordinated to redemption/Christology

Catholic Swiss Bishops, *Pastoral Letter* (1978). Relates a concern for the environment to squandering energy and its implications for the poor nations. It seems to advocate energy reduction without qualification.

Mennonite Church [USA], *Stewardship of the Earth Resolution on Environment and Faith Issues* (1989). Ecology is defined in terms of overcoming global warming, depletion of the ozone, destruction of plants and animals, as well as sensitivity to the unknown ecological consequences of genetic engineering. It relates ecology to peace. All themes cited as a warrant seem subordinated to the Christian faith.

Roman Catholic Church, *Sollicitudo Rei Socialis* (1987), 47-49, 40, 34, 26, 3, 1. Relates realization of limits of available resources, respecting the cycles of nature, and a concern about pollution to health, development, and justice. Mariology and the saints also function as warrants. It posits a relational view of human persons.

14. Appeal to all three articles of the creed, with anthropology perhaps the prevailing warrant

National Council of Churches [USA], *Genetic Science for Human Benefit* (1986), III; V.A.3; V.C.3. Concerned about the impact of genetic technology on the environment, especially genetically engineered bacteria and genetic modifications of certain animals and plants.

15. Appeal to the Bible

Evangelische Kirche von Kurhessen-Waldeck, *Schöpfung! Ökologie in der Kirchengemeinde* (1988). Concerned to implement programs of ecological sensitivity in parishes.

United Church of Canada, *Statements on Human Rights* (1980), 2. Relates the care of creation to justice. It cites a 1979 statement of the church in South Africa, whose appeal to the Bible for authorization must be taken as the Canadian church's authorization for the point.

16. Appeal to the commandment to love

Evangelische Kirche der Kirchenprovinz Sachsen, *Beschluss zum Handeln in der Gesellschaft, vor allem im Umweltbereich* (1985). Relates ecology to the challenge to overcome threats posed by injustice and armaments. It encourages applying economic pressure to help the ecological cause. "Obedience to God" provides authorization.

United Church of Canada, *The Church and the Economic Crisis* (1984). Relates ecology to social justice and reduction in the use of energy consumption and non-renewable resources. It suggests creating more employment in Canada by funding jobs in areas related to ecology and housing.

17. Appeal to Christian ethical considerations and social responsibilities

Christian Church (Disciples of Christ), *Concerning Investment Policies of the CC(DC)* (1971). Relates ecology to justice, freedom, and peace and advocates a policy of church investments in order to influence the achievement of these concerns.

18. Appeal to the concept of stewardship

United Church of Canada, *The Nuclear Option for Canadians* (1980). Relates ecology to social justice and participation, as well as perhaps to the use of nuclear energy.

United Church of Canada, *Acid Rain* (1982). Relates ecology to the project of reducing acid rain and energy consumption.

19. Appeal to the nature of the Christian lifestyle/sanctification

Anglicanism, *The Resolutions of the Lambeth Conference (1988)*, 40, 35. Relates ecology to social justice and peace. In one resolution, expresses concerns about forests, fisheries, and mineral deposits of South Pacific Islands.

Nordelbische Evangelisch-Lutherische Kirche, *Beschluss am 5. Juni 1982*. Relates ecology to a concern to preserve the natural condition of swamps, deserts, moors, and cemeteries.

20. No clear theological warrant given for position

American Baptist Churches, *Policy Statement on Africa* (1987), 4, 1. Concerned about ecology in Africa, with attention to how indigenous peoples are being affected. It may have an appeal to creation correlated with Christology in the background.

Anglicanism, *The Resolutions of the Lambeth Conference (1978)*, 1. Recommends use of new alternative source of energy to counter disruption of ecological balance. This involves a proposal to limit the use of nuclear energy. No reference to warrant except that "God intends all of us to enjoy this planet and not ruin it."

Anglican-Lutheran [European Commission] Dialogue (1982), 58, 59, 29. Ecology is related to modern movements for human rights, peace, social justice, and developmental issues. A kind of two-kingdom ethic authorization may be employed at one point, as well as an appeal to Christology or the gospel at another point, but this is not clear.

Baptist Union of Great Britain and Ireland, *European Conservation Year* (1970).

Bishops of Portugal, *Pastoral Statement on the Encyclical "Humanae Vitae"* (1968), 7. Relates ecology to the creation of a socio-economic climate in which a family politic in harmony with the views of *Humanae Vitae* can emerge. It cites an earlier pastoral letter on migration.

British Council of Churches, *Resolutions Relating to Nuclear Policy* (1977). In addition to ecology, discusses energy conservation and nuclear energy. It refers to the "biblical imperative", but its connotation is not clear.

Bund der Evangelischen Kirchen in der Deutschen Demokratischen Republik, *Beschluss der Synode zu dem Bericht der Konferenz der Evangelischen Kirchenleitungen, zum Arbeitsbericht des Bundes und zum Bericht des Diakonischen Werkes — Innere Mission und Hilfswerk — vom 23. September 1980*, IV, II. The ecological challenge is said to mandate the reduction of the demand for wealth, which is also seen as related to social justice.

Bund der Evangelischen Kirchen in der Deutschen Demokratischen Republik, *Beschluss der Synode zu Gesprächen mit staatlichen Stellen* (1982). Wants to consider use of GDR citizens in alternative service to work on ecological projects and such service's relation to the socialist way of life.

Bund der Evangelischen Kirchen in der Deutschen Demokratischen Republik, *Beschluss der Synode des Bundes zum Bericht der Konferenz der Evangelischen Kirchenleitungen vom 25. September 1984*, 5. Wants to consider the use of GDR citizens in alternative service to work on ecological projects.

Bund der Evangelischen Kirchen in der Deutschen Demokratischen Republik, *Beschluss der Synode des BEK-DDR zum Bericht der Konferenz der Evangelischen Kirchenleitungen zur Friedensfrage* (1986), 1. Relates ecology to justice and peace, as per the WCC call to a conciliar process on these concerns.

Bund der Evangelischen Kirchen in der Deutschen Demokratischen Republik, *Beschluss der Synode des BEK-DDR zum "Bekennen in der Friedensfrage"* (1987), III. Relates ecological concern to peace and justice, which elsewhere in the resolution seem to be authorized by a Trinitarian warrant.

[Catholic] Bishops of the Netherlands, *Mens, arbeid en samenleving* (1985), 8. Pollution a consequence of the present economic system. This critique is possibly related to the doctrine of human persons.

Christian Church (Disciples of Christ), *A Resolution concerning World Hunger and Development* (1975), V. Concerned about ecology in such a way that food production is in harmony with ecosystems.

Christian Conference of Asia, *Justice and Service* (1973), III; Thrust Paper; IV. Pollution is said to be caused by population growth, irresponsible use of science, and false understanding of development. The statement does recognize justice as a more basic need but calls for cutting the demand for material things. A liberation-theology kind of appeal to Christology as warrant is evident in the statement, but it is not clear whether it applies to ecological concern.

Christian Conference of Asia, *Assembly Resolution on Uranium Policy in Australia* (1977). Environmental pollution is associated with nuclear energy.

Church of Ireland, *The Report of the Role of the Church Committee* (1982), 127. Would use the unemployed to help improve environment. This would help give the unemployed a sense of usefulness.

Church of Ireland, *The Report of the Role of the Church Committee* (1983), 6. Claims that nuclear weaponry eclipses ecology in importance.

Eglise Evangélique Luthérienne de France, *Vœux et décisions du synode général 1987*, 5. Relates ecology to justice and peace, as per the WCC agenda.

Eglise Réformée d'Alsace et de Lorraine, *Vœux adoptés par le Synode de l'ERAL* (1987), 2. Ecology includes energy consumption, recycling, and cleansing of chemical products. The statement relates ecology to peace and justice.

Eglise Réformée de France, *Implantation des centrales nucléaires* (1980). Concerned about the environmental destruction caused by the erection of new nuclear power plants.

Episcopal Church [USA], *General Convention Resolution* [on pollution and Christian stewardship] (1973). Appeal to "Christian stewardship" as a warrant could represent an appeal to the gospel.

Episcopal Church [USA], *Reaffirm Right to Use Birth Control* (1982). Concerned about pollution and exhaustion of natural resources. It relates ecological concern to nuclear war, hunger, and birth control.

Episcopal Church [USA], *Programs for Violence Awareness* (1985). Relates ecology to the conquest of violence, racism, ageism, poverty, and drug dependency.

Episcopal Church [USA], *Act in Response to Drought* (1988). Relates concern about the deteriorating environment to drought.

Episcopal Church [USA], *Policy Statement on the Environment* (1988). Concerned about ozone depletion and warming trends.

Evangelische Kirche der Kirchenprovinz Sachsen, *Beschluss zur Teilnahme am konziliaren Prozess* (1985). Relates ecology to justice and peace.

Evangelische Kirche der Union — Bereich Deutsche Demokratische Republik, *Beschluss der 3. ordentlichen Tagung der 6. Synode der EKU — Bereich DDR* (1986). Calls for limitation of technology for the sake of the earth entrusted to us.

Evangelische Kirche in Deutschland, *Erklärung des Rates der EKD zur gegenwärtigen Energiediskussion* (1977), II/1, 2, 5, 6; I; III. Use of energy brings ecological destruction. Nuclear energy is not deemed the real issue in energy discussions. Rather, the real issue is the volume and forms of energy use. It calls for cuts in the use of energy, but not so rash as to impede development. The only warrant mentioned is a reference to "trust in God".

Evangelische Kirche von Kurhessen-Waldeck, *Beschluss der Landessynode vom 23. November 1988 in Hofgeismar.* Speaks of a responsibility for God's creation. A project of one of the church's working groups, *Ökologie in der Kirchengemeinde,* is not analyzed here because the Landessynode merely recommended it.

Evangelische Landeskirche Anhalts, *Drucksache Nr. 44/18* (1986), 1.5. Relates energy to justice and peace.

Evangelische Landeskirche in Baden, *Entschliessung der Landessynode der ELB zum Konzil des Friedens und zur Weltversammlung für Gerechtigkeit, Frieden und Bewahrung der Schöpfung* (1985). Relates ecology to justice and peace, as per the WCC's call for an international congress on these themes. It also cites a 1985 resolution of the Evangelische Kirche in Deutschland.

Evangelisch-Lutherische Kirche in Bayern, *Erklärung der Landessynode zur Arbeitslosigkeit* (1985). Suggests that in order to remedy unemployment in FRG, new public welfare jobs be created, some of them in the area of environment protection.

Evangelisch-Lutherische Kirche in Bayern, *Kirche in der Diaspora Christ sein in der Welt* (1988), 3.2. Relates ecology to peace and justice.

Evangelisch-Lutherische Kirche in Oldenburg, *Beschlossene Fassung* (1981). Relates ecology to peace and the battle against hunger and injustice.

Evangelisch-Lutherische Landeskirche Sachsens, *Beschluss der Synode betr. Sachgespräche vom 26.3.85.* Advocates use of conscientious objectors in projects designed to protect the environment.

Federation of Evangelical Churches in Italy, *Assembly of the FECI* (1985), Act 49, a, b. Ecology related to justice and peace. Christology might function as a warrant.

Fédération Protestante de France, *Sur les problèmes éthiques soulevés par la pollution* (1975).

Fédération Protestante de France, *Vœux adoptés à l'Assemblée du PF à La Rochelle* (1983), 7. Relates ecology to the removal of pollution.

Fédération Protestante de France, *Délibération de la 18ème Assemblée Générale du PF sur le projet de "Convocation mondiale pour la justice, paix et la sauvegarde de la création"* (1987). Relates ecology to justice and peace.

Latin American Protestant Conference, *United to Meet the Demands of the Present Time* (1978). Concerned about exploitation of non-renewable resources and with biological balance.

Mennonite Church, General Conference [USA], *The Way of Peace* (1971). Relates ecology to peace.

Moravian Church in America, Northern Province, *Resolutions* (1974). Sees a link between ecology and economics.

National Association of Evangelicals (USA), *Jesus Christ: Now More Than Ever!* (1979). Especially concerned about pollution and population explosion.

National Conference of Catholic Bishops [USA], *Statement on Population* (1973), 7.

National Conference of Catholic Bishops [USA], *Pastoral Letter on Marxist Communism* (1980), 28. Relates ecology to a concern about the effect the products of the market economy have on workers and consumers.

National Conference of Catholic Bishops [USA], *The Challenge of Peace* (1982), 272, 258, 237, 13-15, 123, 125, 196, 274, 285, 290-95. Relates conservation to the peace question and to human rights. It is not clear if an earlier appeal to creation (and perhaps the gospel/ Christology and the Mass) as warrants for the position on nuclear arms applies here.

National Council of Churches [USA], *Human Hunger and the World Food Crisis* (1975), VII/B/ 4. Relates ecology to food production practices. Appeal to all articles of the creed may stand in the background.

New Zealand Catholic Bishops, *A Statement from the New Zealand Catholic Bishops on the Morality of In Vitro Fertilisation* (1984), 1. Relates ecology to a concern about the present unequal distribution of the world's resources and the squandering of non-renewable resources.

Presbyterian Church (USA), *Our Response to the Crisis in Central America: An Appeal to Presbyterians and Other Churches in the United States* (1988). Would encourage ecologically sound development.

Presbyterian Church in Taiwan, *Our Appeal* (1975), I.5. Pollution, a consequence of too hasty economic growth, is deemed a problem. Some Christology is in the background as warrant elsewhere in the statement.

Presbyterian Church of Korea, *Guiding Principles for the Social Mission Policy of the PCK* (1984), 4. Pollution a consequence of domination of industrialization.

Reformed Ecumenical Synod, *Pastoral Statement: A Call to Commitment and Action* (1984), XII/D/12. Relates ecology to the elimination of poverty. Creation may be a background warrant.

Roman Catholic Church, *Octogesima Adveniens* (1971), 21, 46, 48. Identifies the environment as a new social problem. Creation and a theocratic orientation appear as possible overall warrants in the apostolic letter.

Roman Catholic Church, *Laborem Exercens* (1981), 1. Relates ecology in increased cost of energy, automation, and human rights. Anthropology subordinate to redemption could be the warrant.

Roman Catholic Church, Congregation for the Doctrine of the Faith, *Instruction on Christian Freedom and Liberation* (1986), 11. Simply notes the environmental problem as a consequence of the modern liberation process, which has freed humanity from the dangers of nature by opening the way to technological control of nature. Elsewhere in the instruction, loci from all articles of the creed function as warrants, but no proposal is made at this point on this issue.

Russian Orthodox Church, *Decrees of the Holy Synod* (1983). Relates ecology to justice and peace.

Southern Baptist Convention [USA], *A Statement of Social Principles* (1979), 5, 4. Could be assuming statement's earlier reference to a kind of theocracy, but at this point warrant is not clear.

United Church of Canada, *Nuclear Power* (1980). Relates ecology to social justice, the development of new energy resources, the minimizing of consumption of energy resources, and the need to safeguard the use of nuclear energy.

United Church of Canada, *The Search for Peace in the Eighties — Statement* (1982). Relates ecology to alleviation of poverty, hunger, and the military threat.

United Church of Canada, *Free Trade* (1986). Concerned to protect the environment, as well as consumer rights and minimum wages in face of Canada's new free trade agreement with the USA.

United Church of Canada, *Military Expenditures* (1986). Relates ecology to social justice, participation, a reduction of armaments, employment, and economic development.

United Church of Canada, *Uranium Exports* (1988). Relates ecology to social justice, participation, and a monitoring of uranium mining and nuclear energy facilities.

United Church of Christ [USA], *Peace and United States Power* (1971). Relates ecology to development, economic justice, and racial justice.

United Church of Christ [USA], *Disarmament* (1977). At least expresses a concern for the depletion of natural resources caused by the military industry. Christology could be in the background, but this is not clear.

United Church of Christ [USA], *Resolution on the Report on Racial and Economic Justice* (1977). Somewhat relates ecology to racial and economic justice. Christology is a possible warrant, but this is not clear.

United Church of Christ [USA], *Pronouncement on Toxic and Hazardous Waste* (1983). Speaks only of a "stewardship of our natural resources".

United Free Church of Scotland, *Deliverance of the General Assembly* [on public questions] (1970), 1.

United Free Church of Scotland, *Deliverance of the General Assembly* [on public questions] (1972), 1. Concerned about pollution.

United Free Church of Scotland, *Deliverance of the General Assembly* [on public questions] (1973), 1. Concerned about possible environmental damage caused by the North Sea oil industry.

United Free Church of Scotland, *Deliverance of the General Assembly* [on public questions] (1974), 1. Concerned about threats to the environment posed by North Sea oil development.

United Free Church of Scotland, *Deliverance of the General Synod* [on public questions] (1978), 1. Calls for an ecological concern when developing energy sources.

United Presbyterian Church [USA], *The Covenant of Life and the Caring Community* (1983). Urges that bio-medical research in the natural world be ecologically considerate and treat animal subjects humanely. Insofar as grace and creation authorize genetic engineering, these loci may be background warrants for the ecological concern.

Uniting Church in Australia, *Statement to Nation* (1977). Relates protection of the environment to the wise use of energy and the human rights of future generations. Creation (universal human values) may be a background warrant.

Uniting Church in Australia, *Investment Policy* (1982), 82.55. Concerned that church investments take into account environmental concerns. It relates ecology to justice.

Uniting Church in Australia, *Response to WCC Visit* (1982), 82.51, (3e). Calls for support of Australian Aborigines concerned about mining activities on their land.

Uniting Church in Australia, *Re Pacific Churches* (1985), 85.104. Concerned that the Pacific nations keep their environment free of the effects of nuclear damage.

Vereinigte Evangelisch-Lutherische Kirche in der DDR, *Beschluss zum Tätigkeitsbericht der Kirchenleitung vom 24.9.1977*. Relates responsible interaction with the goods of nature to peace and the survival of humanity.

World Alliance of Reformed Churches, *The Pacific, Australia, and Aotearoa/New Zealand* (1989). Concerned about ocean ecology, which the alliance would remedy by ending drift-net fishing.

World Alliance of Reformed Churches, *Statement on Peace* (1989), 4.3. Relates ecology to justice and peace.

WCC Conference on Faith, Science and the Future, *Economics of a Just, Participatory and Sustainable Society* (Cambridge, Mass., 12-24 July 1979), 5. Sustainability deemed a condition of social justice, and ecology is regarded as principally a Western problem. Earlier in the statement, Christology and eschatology warrant the quest for social justice.

WCC Vancouver Assembly, *Confronting Threats to Peace and Survival* (1983), 23-24, 20. Calls for ethical guidelines which are ecologically responsible and economically just. Concerned about pollution problems associated with modern technology and calls for the use of indigenous resources. Perhaps the necessary relationship of God and nature, centrally expressed in Christ, functions as warrant for the statement.

WCC Vancouver Assembly, *Healing and Sharing Life in Community* (1983), 25, 1, 2, 10. Calls on churches to monitor government policies as they relate to sharing earth's resources. Earlier in the statement it did warrant a "sharing ethic" in the Triune God and the Eucharist.

WCC Vancouver Assembly, *Learning in Community* (1983), 18, 29. Urges churches to see that concerns about ecological survival are included in educational curriculum.

WCC Vancouver Assembly, *Witnessing in a Divided World* (1983), 27, 16. Relates environment pollution to deprivation of children. The only possible warrant is worship, which warrants Christians to fight for justice.

3-2 ENERGY CONSUMPTION

With the possible exception of the Roman Catholic papal encyclical *Populorum Progressio* (1967), 48, 34, there are no acknowledged proponents of increased energy consumption. Disagreement emerges over the appropriate level for industrialized nations to reduce their energy consumption. The statements surveyed include two basic positions, in support of which various theological warrants are appealed to.

A. Favor reduction without qualification
   A1. Appeal to creation/view of human persons
   A2. Appeal to creation/view of human persons, in the context of the Christian faith
   A3. Appeal to creation and eschatology
   A4. Appeal to Christology/the gospel
   A5. Appeal to Christology/Christian faith and creation
   A6. Appeal to the gospel and perhaps ecclesiology
   A7. Appeal to all three articles of the creed, with creation subordinated to redemption/ Christology
   A8. Appeal to Scripture
   A9. No clear theological warrant given for position

B. Oppose reduction to point of destabilizing the economy and jeopardizing aid to the poor
   B1. Appeal to creation/view of human persons
   B2. Appeal to creation, supplemented by and perhaps subordinated to warrants drawn from the second and third articles
   B3. Appeal to Christology/the gospel
   B4. Appeal to Christology/the gospel, with some background reference to creation loci
   B5. Appeal to themes derived from all three articles of the creed
   B6. No clear theological warrant given for position

A. FAVOR REDUCTION WITHOUT QUALIFICATION

A1. Appeal to creation/view of human persons

Church of Norway, *Statement on Nuclear Energy and Safety* (1978). The gospel/third use of the law stands in the background.

Evangelische Kirche in Hessen und Nassau, *Erklärung zum Synodenthema "In der Schöpfung leben"* (1986), 10, 7, 2, 1.

Evangelische Kirche von Westfalen, *Zukunft der Arbeit — Leben und Arbeiten im Wandel* (1983), 5-6.

United Methodist Church [USA], *Social Principles of the UMC(USA)* (1980), I/B. Also endorsed by *Soziale Grundsätze der Evangelisch-methodistischen Kirche (FRG)* (1984), I/ B.

A2. Appeal to creation/view of human persons, in the context of the Christian faith

Mennonite Church, General Conference [USA], *Christian Stewardship of Energy Resources* (1977).

A3. Appeal to creation and eschatology

Landessynode der Evangelischen Kirche in Rheinland-Westfalen, *Wort zur Energiediskussion* (1980), 2(a, b, c, e).

A4. Appeal to Christology/the gospel

Eglise de la Confession d'Augsbourg d'Alsace et de Lorraine, *Le problème nucléaire* (1978).
Fédération Protestante de France, *The Question of Nuclear Energy* (1978), V, II, Int. There is some ambiguity regarding whether the statement's expressed concern for satisfactory energy production might qualify the call for reduced energy consumption.
Presbyterian Church in the U.S./United Presbyterian Church, *The Power to Speak Truth to Power* (1981), pts. 2, 3, 1/III, 1. With eschatology in background. It at least shows some sensitivity to the fact that in reducing energy consumption, an equitable distribution of energy must be achieved for the sake of the poor.
Reformed Church of Alsace-Lorraine, *Décision* (1978). Given its approval of the statement of the Fédération Protestante de France, there is also some ambiguity about this church's own position on this issue.
Southern Baptist Convention [USA], *A Statement of Social Principles* (1979), 3.

A5. Appeal to Christology/Christian faith and creation

American Baptist Churches, *Policy Statement on Energy* (1977), III/B/1, III, II. Creation and anthropology are probably only background warrants.
United Church of Christ [USA], *Energy* (1979), III/A/1-2; III/C/2; IV. Possible that "Christian faith" is the prevailing warrant. It does show a concern for the implications of conservation on unemployment.

A6. Appeal to the gospel and perhaps ecclesiology

Conference of European Churches and Council of European Bishops' Conferences, *Final Document of the European Ecumenical Assembly Peace with Justice* (1989), 87, 77-79, 25-27. Covenant and its trinitarian content may be a background warrant.

A7. Appeal to all three articles of the creed, with creation subordinated to redemption/Christology

Swedish Catholic Bishops, *Pastoral Letter* (1978).

A8. Appeal to Scripture

Lutheran Church-Missouri Synod, *To Encourage Conservation of Energy* (1977).

A9. No clear theological warrant given for position

British Council of Churches, *Resolutions Relating to Nuclear Policy* (1977). Does refer to the "biblical imperative".
Christian Church (Disciples of Christ), *A Resolution concerning World Hunger and Development* (1975), V.
Church of Scotland, *Deliverance on the Report and Supplementary Report of the Church and Nation Committee* (1977).
Congregational Union of Scotland, *Nuclear Energy and Energy Production* (1977).
Evangelische Kirche der Union — Bereich Deutsche Demokratische Republik, *Beschluss der 3. Ordentlichen Tagung der 6. Synode der EKU — Bereich DDR* (1986).
Reformed Church in America, *Report of the Christian Action Commission* (1980), R-1c, R-1d.
United Church of Canada, *Nuclear Power* (1980).
United Church of Canada, *Acid Rain* (1982).

B. OPPOSE REDUCTION TO THE POINT OF DESTABILIZING THE ECONOMY AND JEOPARDIZING AID TO THE POOR

B1. Appeal to creation/view of human persons

German Catholic Bishops Conference, *Statement of the Commissariat* (1977). There is some uncertainty whether a second-article reference, even a theocratic orientation, is evident, or whether a theological warrant is actually given. It is also possible that creation is subordinated to grace, if the statement is to be read in light of Vatican II.

B2. Appeal to creation, supplemented by and perhaps subordinated to warrants drawn from the second and third articles

German Catholic Bishops Conference, *Zukunft der Schöpfung — Zukunft der Menschheit* (1980), III.2, 3; I.4; II.7. See p. 208 for stipulations about its warrants.
United Church of Christ [USA], *Report on Christian Life Style and Ecology* (1977). At least insofar as the statement would examine the role of energy in global development.

B3. Appeal to Christology/the gospel

Evangelische Landeskirche in Baden, *Wort zur Kernenergie* (1977).
WCC Sub-Unit on Church and Society, *Report of the Advisory Group of the Energy for My Neighbour Programme* (1982), VI, I. But sees energy reduction as in best interests of poor. The doctrine of creation may be in the background of the statement.

B4. Appeal to Christology/the gospel, with some background reference to creation loci

Arbeitsgemeinschaft christlicher Kirchen in der Bundesrepublik Deutschland und Berlin (West), *Neuer Lebensstil aus christlicher Verantwortung* (1980), 1-3, 5. Seems to take this position insofar as it is unwilling to resolve the tension between the need for new energy sources/conservation and the problem of how to achieve international justice.

Swedish Ecumenical Council/Church of Sweden, *Nuclear Power, Energy and Questions Pertaining to the Style and Quality of Life* (1978), III.7-8, 4, 1.
Synod of the Protestant Church in Austria, *Atomic Energy in Austria* (1978), I, Int., III.

B5. Appeal to themes derived from all three articles of the creed

WCC World Convocation on Justice, Peace and the Integrity of Creation, *Final Document: Entering into Covenant Solidarity for Justice, Peace and the Integrity of Creation* (1990), 2.3.2.3; 2.2; 2.1. Though authorization is unclear, its position on this issue may come from its trinitarian authorization for ecology insofar as the proposed reduction of energy is presented as an ecological measure.

B6. No clear theological warrant given for position

Council of Churches in the Netherlands, *Recommendations on Nuclear Energy* (1977), 2. The affirmation of a qualified reduction of energy consumption is somewhat ambiguous.
Evangelische Kirche in Deutschland, *Erklärung des Rates der EKD zur gegenwärtigen Energiediskussion* (1977), II/5-6; II. Does refer to "trust in God" as a possible warrant.

The status of the statement of the National Council of Churches [USA], *Policy Statement: The Ethical Implications of Energy Production and Use* (1979), is unclear. The position taken is probably warranted by some locus related to the creation doctrine. But is the statement's support of reduced energy consumption really unqualified, in view of the organization's call for an energy policy which will provide jobs for the unemployed and draws on renewable fuel? Is this finally a significant qualification of the support for a reduction in energy consumption? Similar questions must be posed to the Nordelbische Evangelisch-Lutherische Kirche, *Unsere Verantwortung vor Gott für seine Schöpfung* (1988), 23, 25, whether its concern (not given any theological authorization) to reduce the use of energy in order to make possible that a fair amount of the diminishing resources can be obtained by the third-world nations represents a qualification of its support of reduced energy consumption.

Also one wonders if the concern of the Council of Churches in the Netherlands, *Letter to Dr. R.F.M. Lubbers* (1985), to move the question of an energy strategy away from the status quo could be a call for reduced energy consumption. But this is not clear. Likewise unclear is a passing reference to the need to discuss energy, without theological authorization provided, by the [Catholic] Bishops of the Netherlands, *De mens in de arbeid* (1980), 3.3. Also see the Uniting Church in Australia, *Statement to Nation* (1977), and the call for controlling the rate of use of non-renewable resources by the United Church of Canada, *The Church and the Economic Crisis* (1980). The United Church of Christ [USA], *Overture on the Domestic Impact of Energy Resource Development* (1977), touches on energy consumption and seems to call for a reduction in use by claiming that we need "energy policies and sources" that are "consistent with good stewardship". It may be significant that it refers to the "polarities of conservation and development".

A 1982 resolution of the Moravian Church in America, Northern Province, *Energy in the Third World,* is relevant insofar as it calls for increased use of alternative energy sources in third-world nations and less dependence on oil. Likewise the United Free Church of Scotland, *Deliverance of the General Assembly* [on public questions] (1978), 1, 7, calls for the development of all feasible energy sources. Also perhaps pertinent is a 1978 resolution of the Methodist Church (England), *World Development Action Campaign Programme,* as apparently on the grounds of Christology or the gospel, it calls for a reduction in the wasteful use of resources. A statement of the Evangelical Lutheran Free Church (Norway), *En oppfordung til våre meigheter fra synodemøtet* (1979), in appealing for reduced consumption of all resources without qualification takes a similar position. Appeal is made to the doctrine of creation, with some reference to Christian responsibility. The general appeal for conservation of resources, authorized by an apparent appeal to the doctrine of creation, of the Moravian Church in America, Southern Province, *Conservation of Resources* (1977), also could be seen as a call for reduced energy consumption. Also see *Vœux adoptés par le Synode de l'Eglise Réformée d'Alsace et de Lorraine* (1987), 2, which, without theological authorization, expresses a concern about energy consumption in the context of ecology, and Episcopal Church [USA], *General Convention Resolution* [on continuance of the Task Force on Energy and Environment] (1979), which, authorized by creation and Christology/redemption, calls for education on the question of energy consumption (as it relates to the environment).

3-3 NUCLEAR ENERGY

The statements argue either for an acceptance of the use of nuclear energy or for some restriction — if not an outright moratorium — on its use.

A.   Favor use of nuclear energy
    A1. Appeal to creation/view of human persons
    A2. Appeal to creation, supplemented by and perhaps subordinated to warrants drawn from second and/or third article
    A3. Appeal to Christology
    A4. No clear theological warrant given for position

B.   Favor some moratorium or less dependence
    B1. Appeal to creation/view of human persons
    B2. Appeal to creation in the context of the Christian faith
    B3. Appeal to creation and Christology
    B4. Appeal to Christology
    B5. Appeal to eschatology, supplemented by reference to creation
    B6. No clear theological warrant given for position

A. FAVOR USE OF NUCLEAR ENERGY

A1. Appeal to creation/view of human persons

German Catholic Bishops Conference, *Statement of the Commissariat* (1977). It is unclear whether a second-article reference, even a theocratic orientation, is evident, or whether a theological warrant is actually given. It is also possible that creation is subordinated to grace, if the statement is to be read in light of Vatican II.

A2. Appeal to creation, supplemented by and perhaps subordinated to warrants drawn from second and/or third article

German Catholic Bishops Conference, *Zukunft der Schöpfung — Zukunft der Menschheit* (1980), III.2, 3; I.4. See p. 208 for stipulations about its warrants.

A3. Appeal to Christology

Eglise de la Confession d'Augsbourg et de Lorraine, *Le problème nucléaire* (1978). Especially insists on being informed about decisions to set up nuclear power plants. It shares the ambiguity of the subsequent statements.

Eglise Réformée d'Alsace et de Lorraine, *Décision* (1978). In virtue of its approval of the statement of the Fédération Protestante de France.

Fédération Protestante de France, *The Question of Nuclear Energy* (1978), V, Int. There is some ambiguity concerning whether the statement actually favors the use of nuclear energy.

A4. No clear theological warrant given for position

Church of the Brethren [USA], *A Statement of the CB(USA) on War* (1970), 10.

Episcopal Church [USA], *General Convention Resolution* [on nuclear arms] (1976).

United Free Church of Scotland, *Deliverance of the General Assembly* [on public questions] (1978), 1.

WCC Conference on Faith, Science and the Future, *Energy for the Future* (Cambridge, Mass., 12-24 July 1979), Minority Opinion.

B. FAVOR SOME MORATORIUM OR LESS DEPENDENCE

B1. Appeal to creation/view of human persons

Church of Norway, *Statement on Nuclear Energy and Safety* (1978). The gospel/third use of the law stands in the background.

Church of the Brethren [USA], *Resolution on Nuclear Power* (1979).

Evangelische Kirche im Rheinland, *Ausstieg aus der Atomenergie* (1987).

Evangelische Kirche in Hessen und Nassau, *Erklärung zum Synoden-Thema "In der Schöpfung leben"* (1986), 7-9, 2, 1. The declaration calls for "die weitere Nutzung der Kernenergie zu verzichten".

Evangelisch-Lutherische Landeskirche Hannovers, *Wort der Landessynode der ELLH zum Problem der Kernenergie* (1976), II-III. Would forgo reliance on nuclear energy, with consideration given to economic stability.

WCC Conference on Faith, Science and the Future, *Energy for the Future* (Cambridge, Mass., 12-24 July 1979), 3-4, 1. At least appreciates the role the doctrines of creation and vocation should play in these decisions. It called for a five-year moratorium on the construction of new nuclear power plants.

B2. Appeal to creation in the context of the Christian faith

Mennonite Church, General Conference [USA], *Christian Stewardship of Energy Resources* (1977).

B3. Appeal to creation and Christology

Swedish Ecumenical Council/Church of Sweden, *Nuclear Power, Energy and Questions Pertaining to the Style and Quality of Life* (1978), III.6-8, 1. But claims that we will need to continue using nuclear energy for some time.

Synod of the Protestant Church in Austria, *Atomic Energy in Austria* (1978), I, Int., III. Perhaps more emphasis on gospel warrants.

B4. Appeal to Christology

Evangelische Landeskirche in Baden, *Wort zur Kernenergie* (1977).
Presbyterian Church in the U.S./United Presbyterian Church, *The Power to Speak Truth to Power* (1978), pts. 2/I/L, 1/IV, 1. With eschatology also in the background.

B5. Appeal to eschatology, supplemented by reference to creation

Landessynode der Evangelischen Kirche in Rheinland-Westfalen, *Wort zur Energiediskussion* (1980), 2(c), 2(e), 4(e), 7.

B6. No clear theological warrant given for position

British Council of Churches, *Resolutions Relating to Nuclear Policy* (1977). Does refer to the "biblical imperative". It at least opposes authorization of a new nuclear reactor in the United Kingdom.
Christian Conference of Asia, *Justice and Service* (1977), D. A Christological warrant is possible.
Christian Conference of Asia, *Resolution on Uranium Policy in Australia* (1977).
Church of Scotland, *Deliverance on the Report and Supplementary Report of the Church and Nation Committee* (1978). At least raises questions about the construction of a new nuclear power reactor in the United Kingdom. See, however, the church's 1977 deliverance.
Church of the Brethren [USA], *Justice and Nonviolence* (1977), 10.
Congregational Union of Scotland, *Nuclear Energy and Energy Production* (1979).
Council of Churches in the Netherlands, *Letter to Dr. R.F.M. Lubbers* (1985).
Evangelische Kirche der Union — Bereich Deutsche Demokratische Republik, *Beschluss der 3. ordentlichen Sitzung der 6. Synode der EKU — Bereich DDR* (1986).
Evangelische Kirche in Deutschland, *Erklärung des Rates der EKD zur gegenwärtigen Energie-Diskussion* (1977), I, III. Not clear if advocating short-term use of nuclear energy.
Nordelbische Evangelisch-Lutherische Kirche, *Unsere Verantwortung vor Gott für seine Schöpfung* (1988), 17, 18.
United Church of Canada, *The Nuclear Option for Canadians* (1980).
United Church of Canada, *Energy and the Church* (1982), 2(e), 2(c). Reference made to loci from all three articles of the creed. Only creation, however, is unambiguously a warrant and not clear whether it warrants this position on a nuclear moratorium.
United Church of Canada, *Uranium Exports* (1988).
United Church of Christ [USA], *Energy* (1979), II; III/A; II/B/5. Perhaps authorization is given by the nature of the Christian faith and loci associated with the doctrine of creation, since these loci authorize the statement's overall views on energy policy.

Criticism of nuclear energy or calls for some reduction in its use are also suggested by several other statements. One is by the Council of Churches in the Netherlands, *Letter to the Minister-President* (1978) and is apparently authorized by Christology and anthropology. This affirmation was explicitly endorsed by two documents of the [Catholic] Bishops of the Netherlands: *Letter to the Ministry in Care of the Minister-President* (1978) and *Letter to the Members of the Parliament* (1979), in virtue of the bishops' subscription to the previous letter. Other such statements are the following: National Council of Churches [USA], *Policy Statement: The Ethical Implications of Energy Production and Use* (1979, warranted by creation and perhaps eschatology); [Orthodox] Ecumenical Patriarchate of Constantinople, *Message de Noël* (1980, without clear theological authorization); Evangelisch-methodistische Kirche (FRG),

Soziale Grundsätze (1977), I/A, B (warranted by creation, with Christology in the background); Presbyterian Church (USA), *Life Abundant: Values, Choices and Health Care* (1988), 7; Anglicanism, *The Resolutions of the Lambeth Conference (1978)*, 1 (with no clear theological warrant); United Church of Christ [USA], *Overture on the Domestic Impact of Energy Resource Development* (1977, with no clear theological authorization). In addition the statements of the *Joint Session of the Waldensian Synod and the Methodist Conference [Italy]* (1978) and the Evangelische Kirche im Rheinland, *Verwendung des anfallenden Atommülls* (1966), have called for a study of this issue, and the United Free Church of Scotland, *Deliverance of the General Assembly* [on public questions] (1980), 1, 6, probably authorized by ecclesiology (and love), has noted the debate on the issue.

The pertinent observations of the WCC Sub-Unit on Church and Society, *Report of the Advisory Group of the Energy for My Neighbour Programme* (1982), V, should also be noted. It is maintained in the report that since 1979 the nuclear energy industry has been in a struggle to survive, that a de facto moratorium on its growth has been in effect. Perhaps a statement by the [Catholic] Bishops of the Netherlands, *De mens in de arbeid* (1980), 3.3, as it speaks of the need to discuss the "nuclear danger", could be a call for the end of use of nuclear energy. But this is not clear. An implied critique of nuclear energy is offered by the [Catholic] Episcopal Conference of the Pacific, *The Pacific and Peace* (1986), VIII, IX, as it criticizes "nuclear pollution", but neither this nor its theological authorization are entirely clear. Criticism of the use of nuclear energy is noted in passing by the United Church of Christ [USA], *Report on Christian Life Style and Ecology* (1977).

The position of the Church of Scotland, *Deliverance on the Report and Supplementary Report of the Church and Nation Committee* (1977), is unclear. At one point questions are raised about the construction of new nuclear energy reactors in the United Kingdom. But, again without providing theological rationale, the deliverance refers to the United Kingdom as a society which "benefits from nuclear power". Likewise see similar criticisms of new nuclear energy power plants by the Eglise Réformée de France, *Implantation des centrales nucléaires* (1980), and a call (without offering theological authorization) to end experimentation on nuclear machines by the Fédération Protestante de France, *Sur l'arrêt de l'expérimentation d'engins nucléaires* (1969). The precise position of a 1980 statement of the United Church of Canada, *Nuclear Power,* is somewhat unclear. Without theological authorization, it urges safeguarding policies on nuclear energy in order to limit the proliferation of nuclear weapons. Also see the concern to control nuclear power, authorized by the gospel, Christology, and the Bible, which was expressed by the Christian Church (Disciples of Christ), *Concerning Priorities for the Christian Church (Disciples of Christ), 1982-1985* (1981).

A proposal of the Nordelbische Evangelisch-Lutherische Kirche, *Vorlage des synodalen Umweltausschusses für eine Erklärung zur Energieerzeugung durch Kernkraft* (1986), which deals with both the use of nuclear energy and ecology, has not been considered above. The proposal was only received by the *Erklärung der Nordelbischen Synode zur Energieerzeugung durch Kernkraft als ein Beitrag zu einem nordelbischen konziliaren Beratungsprozess* (1986).

D. NUCLEAR ARMAMENTS

4-1 NUCLEAR ARMAMENTS

In this largest section of the Appendix we first list statements of the churches relating to nuclear armaments, followed by those dealing with the related topic of peace and then the issue of just war versus pacifism. In their positions, churches divide over whether nuclear weapons have any rightful place in deterrence.

A. Will tolerate maintaining nuclear weapons, at least temporarily for deterrence
   A1. Appeal to creation/natural law
   A2. Appeal to creation/natural law/divine Providence, perhaps grounded in Christology
   A3. Appeal to creation/natural law and Christian faith, with anthropology grounded in faith/Christology
   A4. Appeal to creation, possibly related to the gospel
   A5. Appeal to Christology/the gospel
   A6. No clear theological warrant given for position

B. Oppose nuclear deterrence
   B1. Appeal primarily to creation
   B2. Appeal to creation, supplemented by secondary references to Christology and ecclesiology
   B3. Appeal to Christology/the gospel alone
   B4. Appeal to Christology, supplemented by appeal to creation
   B5. Appeal to Christology, with creation in the background
   B6. Appeal to Christology, with eschatology and/or sacramentality as background warrants
   B7. Appeal to Christology and pneumatology
   B8. Appeal to the gospel and perhaps ecclesiology
   B9. Appeal to all three articles of the creed
   B10. Appeal to the mercy of God
   B11. Appeal to the Bible
   B12. Appeal to the Word of God
   B13. No clear theological warrant given for position

A. WILL TOLERATE MAINTAINING NUCLEAR WEAPONS, AT LEAST TEMPORARILY FOR DETERRENCE

A1. Appeal to creation/natural law

Canadian Conference of Catholic Bishops, *A Brief to the Standing Committee on External Affairs and National Defence: On Preparation for the Second Special Session of the United Nations on Disarmament* (1982), 1.5. Cites Roman Catholic Church, *Gaudium et Spes* (1965), 80, 22, which subordinates creation/ anthropology to Christology.

Catholic Bishops of the GDR, *For an Effective Service of Peace* (1983). Though concern for peace is inspired by Christology.

Lutheran Church in America, *Peace and Politics* (1984), 4-5, 7-9. Seems to regard need for deterrence, but not as a permanent situation. It is authorized by creation insofar as the political work of peace is authorized in this way. The church's 1970 statement calling for unilateral disarmament is cited.

National Conference of Catholic Bishops [USA], *The Challenge of Peace: God's Promise and Our Response* (1983), 167-99 (esp. 196), 203-14, 245, 258, 274, 295, 331, 333, 335, 339, 2, 13-15. Calls for a halt to further testing and production. It claims that the Eucharist/Mass creates conditions for peace and also suggests looking at the arms race from the perspective of the gospel, taking its proposals as consequences of being Jesus' disciples. The warrant which directly authorizes the statement's position on deterrence is God's providential care and the Word of God, which causes us to recognize our common humanity. Common creation is identified as "*the* fundamental premise of world order in Catholic teaching".

A2. Appeal to creation/natural law/divine Providence, perhaps grounded in Christology

National Conference of Catholic Bishops [USA], *Peace and Vietnam* (1966), 8, 1. Apparent appeal to creation may be rooted in Christology, in view of the statement's citation of *Gaudium et Spes*.

Roman Catholic Church, Vatican II, *Gaudium et Spes* (1965), 82, 81, 76-79, 39, 22. Assumes call to bilateral disarmament concerns nuclear weapons; the statement does deplore the arms race.

A3. Appeal to creation/natural law and Christian faith, with anthropology grounded in faith/Christology

Episcopal Church [USA], *"To Make Peace" Report* (1985). Takes this position in virtue of approving the statement of the church's Joint Commission on Peace, *To Make Peace* (1982), I/C/3, II, Int., Aft. It may have argued its openness to deterrence with this sort of authorization.

A4. Appeal to creation, possibly related to the gospel

British Council of Churches, *Policy Proposals* (1983).

A5. Appeal to Christology/the gospel

Anglican Church of Canada, *Resolution on War and the Arms Race* (1965). At least insofar as the statement calls for the international control of nuclear deterrents.

Baptist Union of Great Britain and Ireland, *Test Ban Treaty* (1964). Endorsement of a 1963 resolution of the British Council of Churches which, by appeal to "Christian conscience", called for international control of the deterrents.

Federation of Evangelical Churches in Italy, *Assembly of the FECI* (1985), Act 38. At least approves of installation of the cruise missiles.

Netherlands [Catholic] Bishops Conference, *Vrede en gerechtigheid* (1983), II/3; I/1; III/1. Though claims deterrence cannot be accepted.

A6. No clear theological warrant given for position

American Lutheran Church, *War, Peace, and Freedom* (1966), 31b. At least calls for "multilateral reduction of armaments". The statement may not have official status.

American Lutheran Church, *Peace, Justice and Human Rights* (1972), 7. Endorses a 1966 convention action of the church in calling for multilateral disarmament, and to that extent seems open to deterrence.

American Lutheran Church, *Mandate for Peacemaking* (1982), A.10; B.1. At least supports SALT II. Christology and various third-article loci may be in the background.

British Council of Churches, *Non-Proliferation and Control of Nuclear Weapons* (1967), 2(iii). Sees national possession of nuclear weapons by a few nations as "a step towards international control and ultimate abolition". Christian conscience functions as a background warrant but does not clearly authorize this point. It reaffirms and cites the council's *Nuclear Deterrent and the Test Ban Treaty* (1963), (iv), (ii).

Church of England, *General Synod Resolutions on "The Church and the Bomb"* (1983), 1.

Congregational Union of Scotland, *Nuclear Armaments* (1981). Seems open to maintaining deterrence insofar as it calls for multilateral disarmament.

Evangelische Kirche in Deutschland, *The Preservation, Promotion and Renewal of Peace* (1981), I.4(b); V.1(a). Though does opt for an appeal to the gospel and the Eucharist to warrant the Christian commitment to preserving peace. The statement may not be official in the sense of being the organization's highest authorization.

Irish Episcopal Conference, *The Storm That Threatens* (1983), 5. A natural-law argument could be in the background, but this is not clear.

National Conference of Catholic Bishops [USA], *Human Life in Our Day* (1968), 107, 4-8. May have appeals to natural law and faith in the background.

Presbyterian Church in Ireland, *Resolution* [on the nuclear arms race] (1984). But would forswear first strike.

United Church of Christ [USA], *Supporting the U.S. Catholic Bishops' Pastoral Letter concerning Nuclear Armament and the Arms Race* (1983). Insofar as the bishops' openness to deterrence in *The Challenge of Peace* (1983) is endorsed.

B. OPPOSE NUCLEAR DETERRENCE

B1. Appeal primarily to creation

Baptist Union of Great Britain and Ireland, *Peace and Disarmament* (1984). Seems to take this position insofar as it calls for phasing out nuclear weapons unilaterally. It does seem open to retaliation, however, in the event of an attack.

Japanese [Catholic] Bishops, *International Appeal for Peace* (1982).

National Conference of Catholic Bishops [USA], *Pastoral Letter on Marxist Communism* (1980), 57. Calls for banning nuclear weapons by citing the papal encyclical *Pacem in Terris* (1963), 112.

Roman Catholic Church, *Pacem in Terris* (1963), 112-14, 5, 10, 23, 31, 147, 157. Appeals to natural law could be subordinated to redemption. It at least posits a creation-redemption continuity, as well as a relational view of persons. It urges banning nuclear weapons but calls only for reducing the stockpiles equally.

Russian Orthodox Church, *Letter to General Secretary M.S. Gorbachev* (1986). At least expresses the hope for a world without nuclear weapons.

Russian Orthodox Church, *Message of the Holy Synod of the ROC on War and Peace in a Nuclear Age* (1986), 2.25, 2.26, 2.28, 2.31. Also appeals to the Christian tradition. It would be open to a temporary *parity* of armaments and opposes the use of outer space for weapons (2.21-2.22, 2.29, 2.37, 3.34).

United Church of Canada, *Nuclear Weapons Free Zone* (1982). Calls for Canada to be free of nuclear weapons. It opposes the production and testing of cruise missiles.

United Church of Canada, *Nuclear Freeze* (1984).

B2. Appeal to creation, supplemented by secondary references to Christology and ecclesiology

Church of Norway, *Kirken og freden* (1982), II(3), II(II), I(1), I(2), III. Peace is tied to justice and development. It posits a strong creation-redemption continuity; secondary references are mere motives.

B3. Appeal to Christology/the gospel alone

All-Union Council of Evangelical Christians-Baptists [USSR], *Resolution* (1986). Seems to oppose deterrence in calling for full elimination of nuclear arms.

American Baptist Churches, *Policy Statement on Peace* (1985).

Anglicanism, Lambeth Conference (1968), *The Renewal of the Church in Faith*.

Baptist Union of New Zealand, *Public Questions Presentation* (1982).

Bund der Evangelischen Kirchen in der Deutschen Demokratischen Republik, *Beschluss der Synode des Bundes zum Bericht der Konferenz der Ev. Kirchenleitungen vom 24. September 1985*, 1. Confirms 1982 and 1983 renunciations of deterrence by the Bund.

Church of Ireland, *The Report of the Role of the Church Committee* (1981).

Church of Ireland, *The Report of the Role of the Church Committee* (1983), 6.

Evangelische Kirche der Kirchenprovinz Sachsen, *Beschluss zur Gesamtthematik der Synodaltagung* (1985), 1.

Evangelische Kirche in Deutschland, *Zur Erhaltung und Festigung des Friedens* (1983). Endorses *Wort des Rates der Evangelischen Kirche in Deutschland zur Friedensdiskussion im Herbst 1983,* which, without clear theological authorization, also rejected nuclear deterrence.

Evangelische Kirche von Westfalen, *Pastoralbrief der Generalsynode zur Frage der Kernwaffenrüstung vom November 1980.* Claims to correct the church's earlier pastoral writing *Die Frage der Kernwaffen* (1962), which had supported nuclear deterrence.

Evangelische Landeskirche in Baden, *Wort an die Gemeinden* (1982), 3, Int. Faith authorizes disarmament, and so also presumably its position on deterrence.

Evangelisch-Lutherische Landeskirche Sachsens, *Kanzelabkündigung der Landessynode, des Landesbischofs und Landeskirchenamtes vom 24.03.1982.*

Fédération Protestante de France, *La lutte pour la paix* (1983). At least calls for a nuclear freeze as a first step to unilateral de-escalation.

International Council of Community Churches [USA], *Statement of Concern on Nuclear Weapons* (1982). Authorized by appeals to covenant and faith.

Lutheran World Federation, *Statement on Peace and Justice* (1984).

Netherlands Reformed Church, *Pastoral Letter of the General Synod on the Question of Nuclear Armaments* (1980). Corrects an earlier 1962 statement, *The Question of Nuclear Weapons,* in which an openness to deterrence was expressed by appeal to God's Word. The more recent statement's authorization is an appeal to God's mercy (the gospel). The "obedience of faith" is said to be on trial, thus almost making the issue a *status confessionis.*

Presbyterian Church (USA), *Christian Obedience in a Nuclear Age* (1988), 27-28, 8, 6-7, 1. Calls for a phased elimination of all nuclear weapons by 2000 and criticizes a 1971 defence of deterrence as an interim solution, which was proposed by the United Presbyterian Church [USA].

United Church of Canada, *Confessing Our Faith in a Nuclear Age* (1984).

United Church of Canada, *Disarmament* (1986). Authorization seems to be drawn from the nature of the Christian faith. Elsewhere it merely calls for a "nuclear freeze".

United Church of Christ [USA], *Broken Arrow* (1981). At least calls for unilateral disarmament.

Vereinigte Evangelisch-Lutherische Kirche Deutschlands, *The Contribution of the Church and the Christian to Serving Peace* (1981). Authorized by Christology and the "Christian mandate", the statement at least urges participation in the dismantling of threats to human life which are posed by atomic weapons.

Waldensian and Methodist Churches in Italy, *Synod of the WMCI* (1982). Calls for unilateral disarmament.

World Alliance of Reformed Churches, *The Theatre of Glory and a Threatened Creation's Hope* (1982). At least insofar as unilateral disarmament is endorsed as a matter of Christian faith, and so presumably as a matter of the gospel.

WCC Vancouver Assembly, *Confronting Threats to Peace and Survival* (1983), 14-17. Yet does make some interim disarmament proposals, including demilitarization of space.

WCC Vancouver Assembly, *Statement on Peace and Justice* (1983), 20, 23, 24, 25. Also claims that there is no peace without justice and that the arms race stifles development. In the final article cited, passing reference is made that Christian discipline and the gospel itself are at stake in the production of and deployment of nuclear weapons. Endorsed by Evangelische Kirche im Rheinland, *Kriegsdienstverweigerung* (1988).

World Methodist Council Conference, *A Call to End the Arms Race* (1981). Refers only to the "Prince of Peace" in urging "outlawing production and use of all nuclear armaments".

B4. Appeal to Christology, supplemented by appeal to creation

Evangelisch-Lutherische Kirche in Bayern, *Erklärung zur Friedensfrage* (1983), II, I. Creation functions as the declaration's stated warrant, but insofar as it endorses *Wort des Rates der Evangelischen Kirche in Deutschland zur Friedensdiskussion im Herbst 1983,* 2, 1, Int., which took its position against deterrence by appeals to Christian responsibility and reconciliation in Christ, these themes seem to be the prevailing warrants for the Bavarians.

Moderamens of the Reformed Alliance [FRG], *Das Bekenntnis zu Jesus Christus und die Friedensverantwortung der Kirchen* (1981), I; III; Erl.II. Claims the peace question is a *status confessionis.*

Russian Orthodox Church, *Point of View of the Patriarchs on Nuclear Weapons* (1977). Would prohibit nuclear weapons.

United Church of Christ in Japan, *The Fundamental Policy for Social Action* (1966), II/A(2)(a); Int.; I/A/2.

B5. Appeal to Christology, with creation in the background

[Orthodox] Ecumenical Patriarchate of Constantinople, *Message pascal de Sa Sainteté le Patriarche œcuménique Dimitrios Ier* (1983). At least claims that the hope given by the resurrection cannot be replaced by a nuclear force aiming to give security.

B6. Appeal to Christology, with eschatology and/or sacramentality as background warrants

Baptist Union of New Zealand, *Notices of Motion* (1984).

Evangelische Kirche von Kurhessen-Waldeck, *Wort der Landessynode zum Thema "Ermutigung zum Frieden" vom 17. Mai 1984,* 3, 4. Cites WCC Vancouver Assembly, *Statement on Peace and Justice* (1983), 25, which forbids the development, possession, and supply of nuclear weapons. It also cites the 1934 Barmen Declaration, II, V, for authorization.

B7. Appeal to Christology and pneumatology

Evangelisch-Lutherische Landeskirche Hannovers, *Wort der Landessynode vom 23. November 1983 an die Gemeinden*. Cites a 1983 declaration of the Rat of the Evangelische Kirche in Deutschland which had called for a diminishing of nuclear deterrence.

B8. Appeal to the gospel and perhaps ecclesiology

Conference of European Churches and Council of European Bishops' Conferences, *Final Document of the European Ecumenical Assembly Peace with Justice* (1989), 87, 77-79, 75, 25-27, 11. While advocating a ban on nuclear tests, it also calls for a common security system. The covenant and its trinitarian orientation may be a background warrant.

B9. Appeal to all three articles of the creed

Bund der Evangelischen Kirchen in der Deutschen Demokratischen Republik, *Beschluss der Synode des BEK-DDR zum "Bekennen in der Friedensfrage"* (1987), I-II.

Moravian Church in America, Southern Province, *Nuclear Arms Race* (1983). Creation seems to be subordinated to the other articles. It is not clear whether deterrence is absolutely rejected, since the church seeks a bilateral East-West arms treaty.

National Council of Churches in Korea, *Declaration of the Churches of Korea on Reunification and Peace* (1988). With special emphasis on Christology/the gospel.

Roman Catholic Church, *Sollicitudo Rei Socialis* (1987), 24, 7-8, 3, 1, 40, 47-49. These themes are background warrants for the encyclical's position, insofar as they authorize development; the opposition to nuclear arms is argued on grounds of their stifling development.

United Church of Christ [USA], *Affirming the United Church of Christ as a Just Peace Church* (1985), Pronouncements III, IV/E/4/9, IV/E/6-8. The Trinitarian authorization for peace seems pertinent.

WCC Evanston Assembly, *International Affairs — Christians in the Struggle for World Community* (1954), Res. I; I; VI; II; Int. Claims atomic weapons should be eliminated. Other loci are probably subordinated to Christology.

B10. Appeal to the mercy of God

Russian Orthodox Church, *Easter Communication* (1988). At least calls for a nuclear-free world.

B11. Appeal to the Bible

Church of the Brethren [USA], *Statement on a Call to Halt the Nuclear Arms Race* (1982).

B12. Appeal to the Word of God

Evangelische Kirche im Rheinland, *Die Friedenszusage Gottes und unser Streit um den Frieden* (1982). Does recognize the validity of holding the deterrence position.

B13. No clear theological warrant given for position

Anglicanism, *The Resolutions of the Lambeth Conference (1988)*, 32.

Bund der Evangelischen Kirchen in der Deutschen Demokratischen Republik, *Beschluss der Synode des Bundes zum Bericht der Konferenz der Evangelischen Kirchenleitungen vom 25. September 1984*, 4. At least takes this position insofar as a critical view is taken towards the impact the stationing of nuclear missiles in Europe might have in ensuring peace.

Bund der Evangelischen Kirchen in der Deutschen Demokratischen Republik, *Beschluss der Synode des BEK-DDR zum Bericht der Konferenz der Evangelischen Kirchenleitungen zu Friedensfragen* (1986), 1. Though appeals to Christology and natural law may be in the background.

Christian Church (Disciples of Christ), *Regarding Non-Violent Social Deterrence* (1963).

Christian Evangelical Baptist Union in Italy, *General Assembly of the CEBUI* (1982).

Church of Norway, *Om nøytronbomben* (1978). Insofar as opposing development of nuclear weapons by Norway seems to oppose deterrence.

Evangelische Kirche der Union — Bereich Deutsche Demokratische Republik, *Beschluss der 3. ordentlichen Tagung der 6. Synode der EKU — Bereich DDR* (1986), Brief an den Erzbischof, Brief an die Presbyterianische Kirche (USA). Insofar as the resolutions call for the abolition of nuclear weapons.

Evangelische Kirche in Deutschland, *Ermutigung zur Fortsetzung des Weges zur Abrüstung* (1987). Cites a 1983 proclamation calling for the termination of trying to ensure peace through the equalization of nuclear arms.

Evangelische Kirche von Westfalen, *Friedensverantwortung der Kirche* (1982), III, IV. Endorses *Bericht der Konferenz der Evangelischen Kirchenleitungen in der DDR vom 24.9.1982*, which urged the development of a nuclear-free zone in Europe. The former statement was endorsed by Evangelische Kirche im Rheinland, *Friedensverantwortung der Kirche* (1983), 2, 4, which authorizes its position by appeal to ecology.

Evangelisch-Lutherische Landeskirche Sachsens, *Brief der Landessynode an die Gemeinden zur Friedensfrage vom 16.10.85.* At least calls for a "limited unilateral disarmament".

Lutheran World Federation, *Our Responsibility for Peace and Justice* (1984), 13.1.8, 11; 13.4.2.8. A reference to the gospel later in the statement perhaps authorizes the position against deterrence, but this is not clear.

Mennonite Church [USA], *Resolution concerning Security and the Current World Arms Race* (1981).

Romanian Orthodox Church, *Lettre irénique de Sa Béatitude le Patriarche Iustin: Pâques 1983* (1983). At least calls for total disarmament.

United Church of Canada, *Building a Non-Nuclear Security* (1984).

United Church of Canada, *Military Expenditures* (1986).

Vereinigte Evangelisch-Lutherische Kirche in der DDR, *Beschluss der Generalsynode zu den Berichten des leitenden Bischofs und der Kirchenleitung vom 28.6.1981.* At least rejects deterrence by implication insofar as the resolution is critical of considering armaments to be instrumental in preserving peace.

World Alliance of Reformed Churches, *Statement on Peace* (1989), 4.2.

A proclamation of the Nordelbische Evangelisch-Lutherische Kirche, *Unsere Kirche und der Frieden in der Welt* (1983), which addresses nuclear disarmament, peace, and justice, has not been included in the appropriate lists. The proclamation was merely received by the church's September 1983 Synode.

There is ambiguity regarding the position taken in several statements, including National Council of Churches [USA], *Defense and Disarmament* (1968); United Church of Christ [USA], *Weapons of Mass Destruction* (1983), authorized by the doctrine of creation and also criticizing the development of nuclear weapons; United Church of Canada, *Manifesto on Nuclear Disarmament* (1982); Baptist World Alliance, *Resolution on World Peace and Reconciliation*

(1970); Russian Orthodox Church, *Open Letter to the President of the USA Ronald W. Reagan* (1983) and *Decree of the Holy Synod* (1983), also calling for a nuclear weapons moratorium; Reformed Church in America, *Overtures* (1982), 1-2, calling for a bilateral nuclear freeze, and *Report of the Christian Action Commission* (1982), R-1a, R-1b, R-1e, urging a U.S.-Soviet nuclear freeze; Episcopal Church [USA], *Nuclear Weapons* (1982), calling for a "bilateral nuclear freeze"; and Moravian Church in America, Northern Province, *Nuclear Non-Proliferation and World Peace* (1982).

What is meant in these cases by a call to end or limit "deployment" or to a freeze of nuclear weapons? Can the existing ones still be used for deterrence? Nor is it clear what to make of calls for "a genuine disarmament", as evident in the statement by the Religious Denominations of the USSR, *Declaration on Peace* (1982). Cf. WCC Nairobi Assembly, *Public Affairs* (1975), no clear warrant; WCC New Delhi Assembly, *Service* (1968), 68, 66, authorized by Christology and ecclesiology; *Beschluss der Synode des Bundes der Evangelischen Kirchen in der DDR zu Fragen des Friedens* (1981), insofar as the resolution cites WCC Central Committee, *Increasing Threat to Peace and the Mandate of the Churches* (1981), III/H, III/G, II/C, I/B, including the WCC statement's call for a halt to the production of the neutron bomb and its call for the creation of nuclear-free zones — all without clear theological authorization, except some reference to the gospel's commandments; Bund der Evangelischen Kirchen in der Deutschen Demokratischen Republik, *Beschluss der Synode zum Bericht der Konferenz der Evangelischen Kirchenleitungen vom 26. September 1978*, 1.1, 1.3, without clear authorization; National Conference of Catholic Bishops [USA], *To Do the Work of Justice* (1978), 3, 2, 1, 6, authorized by Christology/the gospel/Christian faith; Russian Orthodox Church, *Decrees of the Holy Synod* (1986), without theological authorization, also calling for an end to nuclear testing and for negotiations leading towards the liberation of humanity from nuclear weapons; Evangelische Kirche in Hessen und Nassau, *Beschluss der Kirchensynode* (1983), 19, probably authorized by Christology; and Christian Church (Disciples of Christ), *Concerning the Need for a Stronger World Community as a Bulwark against Nuclear War* (1963), which cites a statement of the WCC New Delhi Assembly.

See also World Alliance of Reformed Churches, *Justice, Peace and the Integrity of Creation* (1989), authorized by the covenant; United Presbyterian Church [USA], *Call to Peacemaking* (1980), I, authorized by Christology; United Church of Christ [USA], *Peace and the Resolving of Conflict* (1981), authorized by appeal to covenant/gospel of love and concerned that nuclear deterrence is less effective as the sophistication of weapons increases; Evangelische Landeskirche in Württemberg, *Friedensauftrag der Kirche* (1979), insofar as the statement cites a declaration of the Rat der Evangelischen Kirche in Deutschland of 19.11.1979, which, without clear theological authorization, called for disarmament; United Presbyterian Church/Presbyterian Church in the U.S., *Reformed Faith and Politics* (1983), Rec. C/2, Policy Statement, authorized by creation and faith/Scripture, with the former subordinated to the latter; Evangelische Kirche der Kirchenprovinz Sachsen, *Beschluss zum Handeln in Gesellschaft, vor allem im Umweltbereich* (1985), authorized by our "obedience to God", and *Wort an die Gemeinden* (1983), probably authorized by Christology; Evangelische Kirche der Union — Bereich Bundesrepublik Deutschland und Berlin-West, *Beschlüsse auf Vorlage des Berichtausschusses* (1978), 5, no clear warrant, and *Telegramm der Synode der EKU — Bereich DDR* (1982), citing a telegram and official statement of the Evangelische Kirche der Union — Bereich Deutschen Demokratische Republik, which authorized its position by appeal to the gospel.

The desire to eliminate nuclear weapons, with a confession that no unanimity has been reached concerning how this might be achieved (presumably with reference to the appropriateness of deterrence), has been explicitly addressed by the Evangelische Kirche der Union — Bereich Bundesrepublik Deutschland und Berlin-West, *Politische Dimension kirchlichen Handelns* (1982). Also see the call for disarmament, authorized by appeal to God's word and the commandment, by the *Beschlüsse der 5. Tagung der III. Generalsynode der Vereinigten Evangelisch-Lutherischen Kirche in der DDR vom 8.-11. Juni 1983*, 1-3. Does its call for a "common security" among the super-powers represent a rejection of the concept of deterrence?

A similar set of questions emerges with regard to the call for an end to the development of nuclear armaments by the National Council of Churches [USA], *The United Nations and World Community* (1977), II/2, with no clear authorization; Mennonite Church [USA], *Militarism and Conscription Statement* (1979), Con.; Int., authorized by Christology and prophecy; United Church of Canada, *Civil Disobedience* (1984), perhaps authorized by Christian discipleship, and *Alternate Defence Policy for Canada* (1988), providing no theological authorization; Christian Church (Disciples of Christ), *Concerning Ending the Arms Race* (1979), without theological authorization, which also calls for an end to testing nuclear arms. Also see the call, authorized by love and pneumatology, for a nuclear arms reduction by the World Alliance of Reformed Churches, *Come Creator Spirit, for the Redemption of the World* (1964), C/1, as well as the call, without theological authorization, for broadening the "nuclear embargo" (presumably against South Africa) by Episcopal Church [USA], *Apartheid/Africa* (1985), 10, in virtue of endorsing a 1985 resolution of the church's Executive Council.

In like manner, questions about whether existing nuclear weapons might still be employed for purposes of deterrence must be posed to three statements of the Christian Church (Disciples of Christ): *Concerning Priorities for the Christian Church (Disciples of Christ), 1982-1985* (1981), which, authorized by the Bible, the gospel, and Christology, called for the control of nuclear arms; *Resolution concerning Nuclear Arms* (1981), with its call, authorized by the doctrine of creation with some reference to Christology, for new international disarmament treaties; and *Resolution concerning a Nuclear Arms Freeze* (1981). See also World Methodist Council, *Recommendation on Disarmament* (1981), authorized by the doctrine of creation; National Association of Evangelicals [USA], *Threat of Nuclear Holocaust* (1982), without clear authorization, urging arms control agreements; and WCC Uppsala Assembly, *Towards Justice and Peace in International Affairs* (1968), 11-12, perhaps authorized by Christology.

The attitude towards deterrence in the following statements needs to be clarified: Russian Orthodox Church, *Letter to John Paul II* (1986), which, without theological authorization, rejects the SDI program while supporting the USA-USSR Reykjavik summit and the annihilation of strategic nuclear weapons; Evangelische Kirche der Pfalz, *Brief an die Bundestagsabgeordneten in Bereich der Evangelischen Kirche der Pfalz* (1985), which, authorized by Christian responsibility, opposes German participation in the SDI missile program; Evangelische Kirche im Rheinland, *Weltraumrüstung* (1986), which, without theological authorization, also rejects German participation in the SDI program; United Free Church of Scotland, *Deliverance of the General Assembly* [on public questions] (1970), 10, which, without theological authorization, supports the nuclear non-proliferation treaty; Bund der Evangelischen Kirchen in der Deutschen Demokratischen Republik, *Erklärung der Synode des Bundes zur Stationierung von atomaren Mittelstreckenwaffen vom 20. September 1983*, which, without clear theological authorization, urges that new medium-range nuclear missiles not be stationed in Germany (also see the East German Bund's *Beschluss der Synode zur Frage der Stationierung von Mittelstreckenraketen in Europa vom 25. September 1979*), and those which explicitly support SALT II and other disarmament treaties.

We find support for such treaties, with no clear theological authorization in all but one of the following cases, by the United Church of Christ [USA], *Disarmament* (1977); Russian Orthodox Church, *Declaration of the Patriarchs and the Holy Synod to the SALT-II Agreement* (1979); Reformed Church in America, *Report of the Christian Action Commission* (1971), Rec. 22, which also seeks an end to the deployment and development of ABM missiles; Church of the Brethren [USA], *The Time So Urgent: Threats to Peace* (1980), 2, authorized by the doctrine of creation and also including a call for a nuclear moratorium; WCC Conference on Faith, Science and the Future, *A Resolution on Nuclear Disarmament* (Cambridge, Mass., 12-24 July 1979), authorized by the doctrine of creation; and ibid., *Science/Technology, Political Power and a More Just World Order*, 4.

The original SALT talks were supported, with creation as at least a background warrant, by the National Conference of Catholic Bishops [USA], *Statement on the Twenty-fifth Anniversary of the United Nations* (1970), 8, 17, and also, without theological authorization, by the United

Church of Christ [USA], *Peace and United States Power* (1971). The latter's priority statement also called for disarmament and an end to nuclear testing. SALT II is criticized by WCC Nairobi Assembly, *Public Affairs* (1975). The SALT talks were endorsed by Episcopal Church [USA], *General Convention Resolution* [on nuclear arms] (1976). But the resolution expresses the hope for a time when dependence on nuclear arms as a deterrent might end.

Similar support for the SALT II accord along with a call for a "bi-lateral nuclear freeze" is called for by Episcopal Church [USA], *Nuclear Freeze and Peacemaking* (1985), A, with no theological authorization. Also see Uniting Church in Australia, *Militarism and Disarmament* (1982), (6b), (4), (1c), authorized by Christology. Support for the SALT talks has also been expressed by the Christian Church (Disciples of Christ), *Concerning the United Nations* (1977), II, without theological authorization, and *Concerning Ratification by the United States Senate of the Strategic Arms Limitation Treaty with Russia* (1979), authorized by Christology. The same church also called for the postponement of the USA's ABM missile system in its *Concerning the Safeguard Anti-Ballistic Missile System and the Influence of the Military/Industrial Complex* (1969), without theological authorization. Similar lack of clarity about the precise position concerning deterrence is evident in the criticism (without theological authorization) of the neutron bomb by the (Orthodox) Patriarchate of Constantinople, *Message de Noël* (1981), and by the plea (without theological authorization) to phase out all private sector production of the cruise missiles by United Church of Canada, *The Search for Peace in the Eighties — Statement* (1982). Also see United Church of Canada, *Nuclear Weapons Free Zone* (1982), analyzed above.

Ambiguity concerning statements' positions on deterrence appears in a statement of the Lutheran Church in America, *World Community: Ethical Imperatives in an Age of Interdependence* (1970), 4-5, and its claim that nuclear war is suicidal. Although this statement insists on the appropriateness of massive arms as a means of maintaining national security and calls on the United States to undertake unilateral action on disarmament, an acknowledgment of the inevitability of violent conflict among the nations is conceded. A statement of the Bund der Evangelischen Kirchen in der DDR, *Refusing the Spirit and the Logic of Terror* (1982), II, I, authorized by creation and Christology, is perhaps also unclear. It advocates a reliance on multilateral disarmament actions leading to unilateral disarmament, but is it thereby conceding de facto the temporary validity of nuclear deterrence? Also see the similar expressed hope for "mutual reductions in nuclear and conventional arms", proposed without theological authorization, of the British Council of Churches, *A Statement on Geneva Summit Meeting* (1985).

On the Irish scene, there is lack of clarity about the legitimacy of nuclear deterrents in the call to limit stockpiling by the Church of Ireland, *Resolution of the General Synod* (1978); also see its *Resolution of the Standing Committee* (1982). See the criticism of the stockpiling of atomic weapons and of arms production by the Roman Catholic Church, *Sollicitudo Rei Socialis* (1987), 24, 7-8, 3, 1, 40, 47-49, its position authorized by appeal to all three articles of the creed, with all loci subordinated to Christology. The Methodist Church of Ireland, *Resolution of the 1984 Conference,* merely calls for the rejection of militarism without expressing a position on nuclear deterrence. And the Irish Council of Churches, *Resolution at the Annual Meeting* (1982), merely registers opposition to the arms race, with warrants drawn from Christology and the gospel. Cf. American Lutheran Church, *Hunger in the World* (1968), 3; United Church of Canada, *The Nuclear Option for Canadians* (1980); Eglise Protestante Unie de Belgique, *Assemblée synodale* (1982), with authorization from all three articles of the creed.

In similar manner, the call to taking steps to disarmament by the Methodist Church in Malaysia, *Social Principles* (n.d.), III/E; III/B.1; I, authorized by ecclesiology perhaps subordinated to Christology, could have relevance to nuclear disarmament and might imply a temporary openness to the use of deterrence. But this is by no means unambiguous. Also see *Vereinigte Evangelisch-Lutherische Kirche Deutschlands, Entschliessung der Generalsynode der VELKD zur Friedenssicherung und Friedensförderung vom 25. Juni 1980,* without theological authorization.

The position of the Congregational Union of Scotland, *Nuclear Armaments* (1984), is unclear. Its call for a "nuclear freeze" could connote an openness to deterrence, but that conclusion does not necessarily follow. Likewise ambiguous is the call, with Trinitarian authorization, for an end to competition in nuclear weapons in the *Guiding Principles for the Social Mission Policy of the Presbyterian Church of Korea* (1984), 5(3), 5; [Catholic] Episcopal Conference of the Pacific, *The Pacific and Peace* (1986), VIII. Similar questions can be raised to the National Association of Evangelicals [USA], *The Threat of War* (1979), which, without theological authorization, urges "reasonable restraint in the production and use of . . . military capability". Also see the call for a reduction of military expenditures, with a possible though not clear Trinitarian authorization, by the National Council of Churches [USA], *Human Hunger and the World Food Crisis* (1975), VII/A/5, IV, and a Trinitarian-authorized call by the council that the Middle East be made a nuclear-free zone and that the injustice of the arms race be recognized in its policy statement *Middle East* (1980). This last statement was affirmed by Christian Church (Disciples of Christ), *Concerning a Policy Statement on the Middle East* (1981).

A similar call for creating a nuclear-free zone in middle Europe was made (without theological authorization) by the Evangelische Landeskirche in Baden, *145. Entschliessung der Synode an den Rat der EKD* (1983), as well as by *Beschluss der Ev.-Luth. Landessynode Sachsens vom 23.03.1983,* which cites with favor *Beschluss der Konferenz der Evanglischen Kirchenleitung in der DDR vom 13. März 1983.* Is the Saxons' call for a reduction of weapons presently at hand still an indication of some openness to a "strategy of deterrence"? This is unclear. Also see the call for an end to nuclear testing by the Evangelisch-Lutherische Landeskirche Sachsens, *Schreiben der Landessynode an den Nationalen Christenrat der USA vom 19.03.1986.* Similar calls were issued for the establishment of nuclear-free zones, this time in Northeast Asia, probably authorized by loci derived from all three articles of the creed, by National Council of Churches [USA], *Peace and Reunification of Korea* (1986), 13, 2; by Episcopal Church [USA], *Endorse Reunification of Korea Policy Statement* (1988), in virtue of its endorsement of the preceding policy statement; by United Church of Christ [USA], *Peace and the Reunification of Korea* (1987), with no authorization; and by World Alliance of Reformed Churches, *Korean Peace and Reunification* (1989), in virtue of its endorsement of WCC Central Committee, *Peace and the Reunification of Korea* (1989), which made this point, probably authorized by the gospel/Christology.

Other churches whose position on deterrence requires clarification include the Southern Baptist Convention [USA], *A Statement of Social Principles* (1979), 4. The statement clearly opposes nuclear proliferation yet claims that "some military preparedness may be deemed necessary". Also see American Baptist Churches, *Policy Statement on Military and Foreign Policy* (1978), which, with no authorization, also calls for "multilateral disarmament". Similarly clarification on this issue is required in the case of the call for disarmament in an atomic age, albeit without theological authorization, by the Russian Orthodox Church, *Christmas Tidings of Patriarch Pimen* (1982), or in the call to end the arms race, on grounds of creation and redemption, issued by the WCC New Delhi Assembly, *An Appeal to All Governments and Peoples* (1961), 2-4, 9, 10. Cf. also WCC Uppsala Assembly, *Message* (1968); Roman Catholic Church, *Redemptor Hominis* (1979), 17, 8, 13-16, authorized primarily, though not exclusively, by eschatology; Evangelisch-Lutherische Kirche in Bayern, *Erklärung der Landessynode zur Genfer Gipfelkonferenz* (1985), with no theological authorization. Also the statement of the Council of the Federation of European Baptists, *Declaration on Disarmament* (1982), authorized by the gospel, requires clarification. The statement is unclear if its claim that we denounce the arms race and the corresponding claim that national security depends on increasing arms is a call for opposing the principle of deterrence.

The same question about the position on deterrence must be raised to all those statements calling for a halt to the escalation or proliferation of the nuclear arms race. See Anglicanism, *The Resolutions of the Lambeth Conference (1978),* 5; *Vereinigte Evangelisch-Lutherische Kirche Deutschlands, Beschluss der Generalsynode der VELKD zu der "Erklärung zum Frieden" des Exekutivkomitees des Lutherischen Weltbundes vom 24. Oktober 1981,* citing the

LWF statement (4) in the resolution's title; Vereinigte Evangelisch-Lutherische Kirche in der DDR, *Beschluss zum Tätigkeitsbericht der Kirchenleitung vom 24.9.1977;* Evangelische Kirche der Kirchenprovinz Sachsen, *Vorlage des Berichtsausschusses* (1984), 2.2; Bund der Evangelischen Kirchen in der Deutschen Demokratischen Republik, *Beschluss der Synode zur Frage der Stationierung von Mittelstreckenraketen in Europa vom 25. September 1979;* Assembly of Religions in Romania, *Motion on Peace* (1981); WCC Vancouver Assembly, *Witnessing in a Divided World* (1983), 38; WCC Nairobi Assembly, *Human Development: Ambiguities of Power, Technology and Quality of Life* (1975), 25, with no clear warrant; Evangelische Kirche in Deutschland, *Wir müssen mehr tun* (1986), II.7; III; National Council of Churches [USA], *China* (1966), with no clear authorization; United Church of Canada, *Nuclear Power* (1980), with no theological authorization; Uniting Church in Australia, *Re Peace and Disarmament* (1985), 85.76.7, with no clear authorization for the call for Australia to withdraw from support of the arms race. Also see Uniting Church in Australia, *Falkland Islands Conflict* (1980), 82.58, (3).

Also to be noted in connection with its position on nuclear armaments is the Christian Conference of Asia, *Justice and Service* (1977) and *Nuclear Testing in the Pacific* (1973); Evangelische Kirche in Deutschland, *Antrag zur Friedenssicherung/SDI* (1986); Eglise Réformée de France, *Les essais nucléaires français* (1973); Evangelische Kirche im Rheinland, *Antrag betr. Atomteststopp* (1987); and United Church of Canada, *Nuclear Arms* (1972), which oppose nuclear testing. A similar difficult statement to characterize is United Church of Christ [USA], *Reversing the Arms Race* (1979). Authorized by loci derived from all three articles of the creed, it calls for disarmament and supports the SALT II treaty. It advocates "independent initiatives toward disarmament". Is this a call to unilateral disarmament in contrast to the deterrence strategy? The implications of such a call are not made clear.

Perhaps the most difficult statement to characterize as far as its position on deterrence is the WCC Conference on Faith, Science and the Future, *A Resolution on Nuclear Disarmament* (Cambridge, Mass., 12-24 July 1979). Its call for the "eventual abolition" of nuclear weapons suggests that the statement should be listed above among those that oppose nuclear deterrence. But the resolution also supports SALT II, which could seem to entail an openness to deterrence at least for some time. The statement also raises atypically problematic questions for characterizing its theological warrants. The bulk of the statements considered in the preceding paragraphs either posit no warrants or rely on warrants drawn from the second article of the creed. (About six statements do combine warrants drawn from the creation doctrine with other loci, and in one WCC New Delhi statement Christology and the church function as warrants.) Yet only in the case of statements by the World Methodist Council and perhaps by the Lutheran Church in America, the Church of Ireland, the Christian Church (Disciples of Christ), and the Assembly of Religions in Romania are loci from the creation doctrine alone functioning as warrants. (Christology/the gospel seems to be a warrant more prevalent for "peace positions", but as we have noted, creation warrants do not prevail on most contemporary ethical issues.) At any rate, in the case of this WCC statement one discerns an unambiguous appeal to the doctrine of creation to warrant the position. But what is one to make of the suggestion that such ethical action is a "work of faith, hope and love"?

A similar position, calling for the abolition of nuclear weapons while seeming to express an openness to deterrence insofar as bilateral steps to disarmament are advocated, has also been taken by the WCC World Convocation on Justice, Peace and the Integrity of Creation, *Final Document: Entering into Covenant Solidarity for Justice, Peace and the Integrity of Creation* (1990), 2.3.2.2; 2.2; 2.1. Christology and the concept of covenant, which is shaped by themes derived from all three articles of the creed, provide authorization.

The [Catholic] Bishops of the Netherlands, *De mens in de arbeid* (1980), 2.2, argues on the basis of the "story of creation and redemption" that the present increase of nuclear weapons can be dealt with. But the bishops' position on disarmament is unclear.

An impression of openness to nuclear deterrence is given by the Council of Churches in the Netherlands, *Letter to the Council of Ministers and the Houses of Parliament* (1984), insofar as the appeal for disarmament (on the basis of the doctrine of creation, with some secondary reference to the gospel) is made "in the parameters of the system of deterrence". But the endorsement of nuclear deterrence as a necessary evil is never given. (An earlier 1982 statement, taking a similar position, is cited.) The statement also cited a 1978 declaration of the council, *Letter to the Minister-President,* which likewise maintains a kind of middle ground on deterrence. Its appeal to Christology and creation led it to reject the neutron bomb and the development of nuclear armaments, but it explicitly elected to leave open the question of how to put an end to the deployment of such armaments. Presumably a kind of temporary maintenance of nuclear arms for this purpose is not precluded. The position of this 1978 declaration also is explicitly endorsed on two occasions by the [Catholic] Bishops of the Netherlands, both times without providing theological rationale: first in their *Letter to the Ministry [in care of] the Minister-President* (1978), and again in their *Letter to the Members of the Parliament* (1979).

A similarly apparently open, though even more critical, Roman Catholic assessment of nuclear deterrence was articulated by the National Conference of Catholic Bishops [USA], *To Live in Jesus Christ: A Pastoral Reflection on the Moral Life* (1976), 2, 30, 31, 100, 101, 115-16. Authorized to some extent by themes derived from all three articles of the creed, albeit with Christology the prevailing warrant (such that references to the doctrine of creation may be subordinated to it), the American bishops claim that it is "wrong to threaten to attack them [with nuclear weapons] as a strategy of deterrence". Yet in the interim the bishops seem open to retaining such weapons, stating, "We urge the continued development and implementation of policies which seek to bring these weapons more securely under control, progressively reduce their presence in the world, and ultimately remove them entirely." The precise position of the United Free Church in Scotland, *Deliverance of the General Assembly* [on public questions] (1980), 1, 7, is also unclear. Authorized by the Christian conscience, it states its opposition to nuclear weapons. In so doing, it cites an earlier resolution of the British Council of Churches, *The Nuclear Deterrent and the Test Ban Treaty* (1963), (iv). The Scottish church also cites the British Council's subsequent proposal that the United Kingdom not replace its present nuclear deterrent. Whether this position still permits reliance on some deterrence is uncertain.

It is relevant to note a statement of the Federation of Protestant Churches in Switzerland, *Pour une action concertée énergique en faveur du tiers monde* (1986), II.12, II.13, which calls for disarmament. But no position is taken concerning deterrence, and though Christology may be in the background, no warrant is clearly stated. Also see the Uniting Church of Australia, *Nuclear Action Fund* (1982), 82.56, (I), which, without theological authorization, merely calls for a study of nuclear disarmament. A statement by the Lutheran Church-Missouri Synod, *To Encourage Peacemaking and the Study of Problems concerning the Church and Nuclear Arms* (1983), also called for the limitation of nuclear arms (largely by appeal to a kind of two-kingdom ethic), but as a matter of principle, no position was taken concerning deterrence. A rather stronger statement was made by the Evangelische Kirche der Pfalz, *Wort an die Gemeinden* (1981), when, authorized by appeal to natural law, it called for a reduction (unilateral, if necessary) of military arms. Also see the call, authorized by appeal to Christian faith and natural law, for dismantling the nuclear arsenal, issued by the Church of the Brethren [USA], *Justice and Nonviolence* (1977), 8-9; the call, authorized by the gospel/Christology, for a halt to nuclear proliferation issued in *Resolution concerning the Establishment of a Designated Peace Sunday in the Christian Church (Disciples of Christ)* (1981); the lament about the nuclear arms race, insofar as it leads to squandering funds for development, by the Evangelische Kirche in Deutschland, *Wir müssen mehr tun* (1986), II; III; and the same organization's call for arms' control and the end of nuclear testing in *Antrag zur Friedenssicherung/SDI* (1986).

A statement by the Eglise Réformée de France, *Décision VII* (1968), should be noted. Its position on nuclear deterrence is unclear. Taking a position authorized by the Christian faith, the statement merely calls for disarmament. Similar conclusions must be reached concerning a statement of the Evangelical Church of Lutheran Confession in Brazil, *God's Earth . . . Land for Everyone* (1982), I, II, authorized by the gospel, with creation and perhaps eschatology as background warrants.

A statement by the Anglican Church of Canada, *Disarmament* (1983), takes an ambiguous position on nuclear deterrence. On the one hand, it appeals to Christology to authorize a call for mutual disarmament. This affirmation suggests an openness to at least temporary reliance on nuclear deterrence. On the other hand, a subsequent claim that conflict should be resolved without recourse to the threat to use nuclear weapons seems to preclude deterrence. Perhaps this relates to the statement's interesting call for the international control of nuclear weapons. For such a proposal, also see United Church of Christ [USA], *Resolution on Nuclear Testing* (1963), citing a 1959 resolution of the church, *Call to Christian Action in Society,* which took this position apparently without clear authorization; Christian Church (Disciples of Christ), *Concerning World Order, Justice and Peace* (1968), with no clear authorization but also calling for a general and complete disarmament; Baptist Union of Great Britain and Ireland, *Test Ban Treaty* (1964), see above; Anglican Church of Canada, *Resolution on War and the Arms Race* (1965), Act 87; United Free Church of Scotland, *Deliverance of the General Assembly* [on public questions] (1964), 13, 1, authorized by the Spirit of Christ and citing WCC Central Committee, *The Test Ban Treaty and the Next Steps* (1964), in support of multilateral disarmament agreements; and three statements of the British Council of Churches: *The Nuclear Deterrent and the Test Ban Treaty* (1963), (iv), (ii), authorized by "Christian conscience" and citing the WCC Central Committee statement referred to above; *Non-Proliferation and Control of Nuclear Weapons* (1967), 1, 2(i), 2(iii), authorized by "Christian conscience" and citing the preceding statement of the British Council and its theological warrant; and *The Future of the British Nuclear Deterrent* (1979), which refers to the previously cited 1963 statement of the council.

Also worth noting is the Latin American [Catholic] Bishops, Second General Conference (Medellín Conference), *Message to the People of Latin America* (1968), which is perhaps authorized by baptism and creation along with an express appeal to the gospel. It issues a call to limit the arms race in the interests of development. No explicit position on nuclear deterrence is expressed. Cf. another document from this conference, *Peace* (1968), 29, 13, 14, 20, 26, with no clear authorization, and also Latin American [Catholic] Bishops, Third General Conference, *The Puebla Message* (1979). Also noteworthy is the proposal of the Reformed Church in America, *Report of the Christian Action Commission* (1985), R-2, R-3, without theological authorization, to divest stocks in companies dealing with the production of nuclear weapons. Cf. Reformed Church in America, *Report of the Christian Action Commission* (1983), R-9.

The last word by statements whose position on nuclear deterrence is not directly spelled out should be given to the Evangelische Kirche in Deutschland, *Kundgebung zur Veröffentlichung der Denkschrift "Frieden wahren, fördern und erneuern"* (1981). It insists that both opposing views concerning the validity of nuclear deterrence are equally concerned with peace, that they ought not separate Christians who, while working for peace under God's Word, may hold such conflicting views. The same plea is made, with a citation of the EKD material, by the Evangelische Kirche von Kurhessen-Waldeck, *Beschluss der Landessynode über den Antrag der Kreissynode Hanau-Stadt zur Friedensfrage* (1981). Also see United Free Church of Scotland, *Deliverance of the General Assembly* [on public questions] (1983), 5, 7, authorized by the Holy Spirit. Weaknesses in both of the opposing views are cited by the Evangelisch-Lutherische Kirche in Oldenburg, *Beschlossene Fassung* (1981).

4-2 PEACE

All church statements explicitly addressing the issue call for efforts on the part of their governments and all governments to aim for peace. The statements diverge on theological warrants given to authorize this call.

Only those statements explicitly issuing the call for peace are given here, although all of those listed above in calling for nuclear disarmament might also have been included in this list, as some of them also explicitly call their churches to work for peace.

1. Appeal to creation
2. Appeal to creation, correlated with Christology/the gospel
3. Appeal to creation, perhaps grounded in Christology
4. Appeal to creation/view of human persons, supplemented by other articles of the creed
5. Appeal to creation and Christology/the gospel
6. Appeal to creation and Christology/the gospel/redemption
7. Appeal to creation and divine Providence
8. Appeal to creation, Christology, and the Bible
9. Appeal to the first article, with some backing from Christology/the gospel and/or ecclesiology
10. Appeal to first- and second-article loci, with creation subordinated to Christology
11. Appeal to Christology/the gospel
12. Appeal to Christology/the gospel and third-article loci
13. Appeal to Christology/the gospel, supplemented by an appeal to the Eucharist
14. Appeal to Christology and eschatology
15. Appeal to Christology, the law, and the Bible
16. Appeal to Christology, with creation a background warrant
17. Appeal to Christology, with creation probably subordinated to Christology
18. Appeal to Christology/Christian faith, perhaps supplemented by appeal to creation
19. Appeal to Christology, with eschatology in the background
20. Appeal to Christology and the Old Testament prophetic tradition (or the doctrine of redemption)
21. Appeal to the gospel and eschatology, with creation possibly subordinated to these loci
22. Appeal to the Christian faith/Christology
23. Apparent appeal to pneumatology
24. Appeal to the Old Testament prophetic tradition
25. Apparent appeal to ecclesiology
26. Appeal to ecclesiology and Christology
27. Appeal to ecclesiology, perhaps subordinated to Christology
28. Appeal to ecclesiology, with some reference to a two-kingdom ethic
29. Appeal to the nature of the Eucharist
30. Appeal to eschatology
31. Appeal to eschatology and prophecy
32. Appeal to eschatology and perhaps creation
33. Appeal to eschatology and worship, with some reference to creation
34. Appeal to all articles of the creed
35. Appeal to all articles of the creed, with all loci subordinated to Christology
36. Authorized by loci from all articles of the creed, with Christology the prevailing warrant
37. Appeal to loci from all articles of the creed, especially creation and eschatology
38. Appeal to loci from all articles of the creed, with the first article perhaps subordinated
39. Appeal to the doctrine of God and ecclesiology
40. Appeal to the acts of the Triune God
41. Appeal to divine Providence
42. Appeal to divine justice and the Bible
43. Appeal to the will of God
44. Appeal to God's grace
45. Trust in the security of God's presence
46. Appeal to God's Word
47. Appeal to the Bible's word of renewal

48. Appeal to the Bible and creation
49. Appeal to Scripture and Christian conscience or Christian principles
50. Appeal to Christian duty/the gospel
51. Appeal to command to love
52. Appeal to faith in God
53. Appeal to Christian ethical considerations and social responsibility
54. Appeal to the example of the faithful
55. No clear theological warrant given for position

1. Appeal to creation

American Baptist Churches, *Policy Statement on Military and Foreign Policy* (1978).

American Lutheran Church, *Peace, Justice, and Human Rights* (1972), 1, 3, 4, 7, 8, 10, 11. Christology or redemption perhaps functions only as a motive.

American Lutheran Church, *The Nature of the Church and Its Relationship with Government* (1980), B3a.

American Lutheran Church, *Toward Fairness in Public Taxing and Spending* (1982), 2. Statement may not have had official status.

Anglican Church of Canada, *South Africa* (1986). Concerned about peace in South Africa.

Assembly of Religions in Romania, *Motion on Peace* (1981). Assuming that general human solidarity about a desire for peace represents a creation appeal.

Associated Churches of Christ in New Zealand, *Decisions Relating to Public Issues* (1968). Especially authorized by the nature of human persons.

Australian [Catholic] Episcopal Conference, *Morals and Human Values* (1972).

British Council of Churches, *Policy Statement on Vietnam* (1967). Calls for peace in Vietnam, citing in support the council's *United Nations* (1966), 5.

British Council of Churches, *Work for the Council* (1982), B/1.

[Catholic] Bishops Conference of Mozambique, *A paz e possivel* (1985), 4, 17ff. Christology seems to function only as a background warrant in the statement. It is especially concerned about peace in Mozambique.

Church of Norway, *Kirken og freden* (1982), III, II(3), II(2), I(2), I(1). Peace is tied to justice and development. Secondary references to Christology and ecclesiology function merely as motives.

Church of Norway, *Human Dignity* (1985), esp. 3. Also calls church to work for disarmament.

Evangelische Kirche der Kirchenprovinz Sachsen, *Brief der Synode an die Gemeinden zur Friedensverantwortung* (1984). Though authorization may be mixed with secularism.

Evangelisch-Lutherische Kirche in Bayern, *Wort der Synode zur Frage der Gewalt* (1974). Relates peace to freedom and social justice.

Japanese [Catholic] Bishops, *International Appeal for Peace* (1982).

Lutheran Church in America, *World Community: Ethical Imperatives in an Age of Interdependence* (1970).

Lutheran Church in America, *Peace and Politics* (1984), 1-3, 5, 8-9, 12. The political work of peace is authorized in this way, though Christology functions as authorization at one point, and all three articles of the creed function to authorize peace in general.

Lutheran World Federation, *Responsible Participation in Today's Society* (1970), 59ff., 26. The Sermon on the Mount functions as a secondary warrant.

Lutheran World Federation, Executive Committee, *Declaration for Peace* (1981), 3-4. Also motivated by eschatology and some reference to the doctrine of the church as warrant. It calls for non-proliferation of nuclear arms.

Methodist Church [England], *World Development Action Campaign Programme* (1978).

National Conference of Catholic Bishops [USA], *Population and the American Future: A Response* (1972), 2. Relates peace to justice and charity with fellow human beings.

National Conference of Catholic Bishops [USA], *Pastoral Letter on Marxist Communism* (1980), 57.

National Council of Churches [USA], *Religious Obedience and Civil Disobedience* (1968), III, I. The gospel seems to be correlated with the policy statement's appeal to natural law.

Roman Catholic Bishops in Mozambique, *Pastoral Letter* (1976). Anthropology is at least a background warrant.

Roman Catholic Church, *Populorum Progressio* (1967), 87, 83, 81, 76, 55, 21, 13. In two of the cited sections no explicit warrant is given. Warrant depends on whether references to positions of Vatican II documents and the encyclical's interest in infusing the laws with a "Christian spirit" entail that, like *Gaudium et Spes*, 22, creation is grounded in Christology.

Romanian Orthodox Church, *Telegram to the President of Romania* (1981). Though perhaps the warrants are drawn from a general human desire for peace, the result of *theosis*, the universal transformation of creation through Christ's work.

Russian Orthodox Church, *Message of the Patriarchs of the Holy Synod* (1975). Appeals to human consensus for authorization.

Russian Orthodox Church, *Point of View of the Patriarchs* (1977). Appeals to human consensus for authorization.

United Church of Canada, *Nuclear Weapons Free Zone* (1982).

United Church of Christ [USA], *Exploitative Broadcasting Practices* (1977), II. With eschatology functioning to authorize patience in working for a solution and the themes of liberation theology as background warrants.

Vereinigte Evangelisch-Lutherische Kirche in der DDR, *Beschluss der Generalsynode zu den Berichten des leitenden Bischofs und der Kirchenleitung vom 12. Juni 1982* (1982). Takes this position and its authorization in virtue of endorsing the report of the bishops.

WCC Conference on Faith, Science and the Future, *A Resolution on Nuclear Disarmament* (Cambridge, Mass., 12-24 July 1979).

2. Appeal to creation, correlated with Christology/the gospel

American Baptist Churches, *Policy Statement on Africa* (1987), 1, 3. Concerned only with a just peace in Namibia.

United Free Church of Scotland, *Deliverance of the General Assembly* [on public questions] (1964), I, II. Quotes WCC Executive Committee, *The Test Ban Treaty and the Next Steps* (1964), which authorized its call for peace by appeal to a concept of natural law. Elsewhere the deliverance calls for peace on Cyprus, without providing any authorization.

3. Appeal to creation, perhaps grounded in Christology

National Conference of Catholic Bishops [USA], *Peace and Vietnam* (1966), 1, 2. In view of citations from Vatican II's *Gaudium et Spes*, 22, which subordinates creation to Christology, perhaps the American statement's appeal to creation presupposes creation's subordination to Christology.

4. Appeal to creation/view of human persons, supplemented by other articles of the creed

World Methodist Council Conference, *Council Message to the Methodists of the World* (1966). Urges peace in Vietnam, citing WCC Central Committee, *Resolution on Vietman* (1966).

5. Appeal to creation and Christology/the gospel

American Baptist Churches, *Policy Statement on Peace* (1985).

American Lutheran Church, *Manifesto for Our Nation's Third Century* (1976), VI, IV, II. At least appeals to Christology and the prophets.

Anglican Church of Canada, *Disarmament* (1983).

British Council of Churches, *Peace Forum* (1983). Confirms the terms of reference of the council peace forum, *The BCC for the Future* (1983), A1, sec. 7.1, which argues the case for peace with these warrants.

Canadian Catholic Conference, *On Pastoral Implications of Political Choices* (1972). Relates peace to justice.

[Catholic] Bishops Conference of Mozambique, *Caminhos de paz* (1979), IV.2; IV.1; Int. Especially concerned about peace in Mozambique.

[Catholic] Bishops Conference of Mozambique, *Cessem a guerra: Construamos a paz* (1979), 5, 14, 16. Especially concerned about peace in Mozambique. It appeals to the Word of God and trust in God.

[Catholic] Bishops Conference of Mozambique, *Um apelo à paz* (1983), 6-9. Especially concerned about peace in Mozambique.

Church of Ireland, *The Report of the Role of the Church Committee* (1984), 4. Insofar as appeal is made to put an end to violence in Northern Ireland.

Eglise de la Confession d'Augsbourg d'Alsace et de Lorraine, *Le problème de la paix* (1982). Though creation is probably only a background warrant.

Evangelische Kirche der Pfalz, *Wort an die Gemeinden* (1981).

Federation of Evangelical Churches in the GDR, *Refusing the Spirit and the Logic of Terror* (1982), I, II.

Latin American (Catholic) Bishops, Second General Conference (Medellín Conference), *Message to the People of Latin America* (1968). Creation functions as a warrant insofar as an appeal is made to "all men of good will". Baptism may function as a background warrant.

Lutheran World Federation, *I Have Heard the Cry of My People... The Assembly Message* (1990). Christology is perhaps the prevailing warrant. Reference is also made to scripture. Peace is related to ecology and justice.

Methodist Church in Brazil, *Plan for the Life and Mission of the MCB* (1982), III/6; III/5(b); III/3; III/2.

National Conference of Catholic Bishops [USA], *Resolution on Southeast Asia* (1971), 3-7, 11. Especially concerned about peace in Vietnam; links this concern with justice.

National Conference of Catholic Bishops [USA], *Resolution towards Peace in the Middle East* (1973), 1, 2, 8, Concerned about peace and justice in the Middle East.

National Conference of Catholic Bishops [USA], *The Bicentennial Consultation: A Response to the Call to Action* (1977), 38, 29, 13, 9, 8, These two themes at least function as background warrants insofar as peace is closely related to social justice.

[Orthodox] Ecumenical Patriarchate of Constantinople, *Message de Noël du Patriarche œcuménique* (1974). Relates peace to philanthropy.

Russian Orthodox Church, *Decrees of the Holy Synod* (1983). Relates peace to justice and ecology.

Russian Orthodox Church, *Jubiläumsbotschaft zum Millennium der Taufe Russlands* (1987). Relates peace to justice. Authorization is provided by natural law and by Christian vocation.

Southern Baptist Convention [USA], *The Baptist Faith and Message* (1963), XVI.

United Church of Canada, *Manifesto on Nuclear Disarmament* (1982). Assumes this authorization if the statement's referrence to covenant as warrant for its position is a first-article appeal and the statement's reference to Christ is not merely an appeal to Christology for ethical motivation.

United Church of Canada, *False Apocalypticism and the Church* (1984).

United Church of Christ [USA], *A Pronouncement on Justice and International Development: A Manifesto for American Action in the Struggle against World Poverty* (1967). Peace is related to economic justice. Although faith/repentance plays some role in the statement, it may be that concern for peace is authorized merely by appeal to rational common sense.

United Church of Christ [USA], *A Resolution on Human Rights, with Special Emphasis on Rumania, Philippines and South Korea* (1977). With Christology perhaps only a background warrant.

United Methodist Church [USA], *Social Principles of the UMC(USA)* (1980), V/G-VI/A; VI/C; VI/D.

WCC Amsterdam Assembly, *The Church and the International Disorder* (1948), Int. II.

WCC New Delhi Assembly, *An Appeal to All Governments and Peoples* (1961), 9-10.

WCC Vancouver Assembly, *Message from the Sixth Assembly* (1983). Also states that Christians are "empowered" by the Eucharist. It calls for end to the arms race.

6. Appeal to creation and Christology/the gospel/redemption

Bund der Evangelischen Kirchen in der Deutschen Demokratischen Republik, *Beschluss der Synode des Bundes zum Bericht der Konferenz der Evangelischen Kirchenleitungen in der DDR vom 19. September 1983*, 4, 5. Relates peace to justice as per the WCC Vancouver Assembly, *Statement on Justice and Peace* (1983), 24a.

National Council of Churches [USA], *Defense and Disarmament* (1968).

National Council of Churches [USA], *The United Nations and World Community* (1977), Int.

Reformed Ecumenical Synod, *Pastoral Statement: A Call to Commitment and Action* (1984), XI, XII/D/1.

United Free Church of Scotland, *Deliverance of the General Assembly* [on public questions] (1963), 7. Also opposes nuclear testing.

7. Appeal to creation and divine Providence

Hungarian [Catholic] Episcopal Conference, *Responsibility in Defence of Human Life* (1978).

8. Appeal to creation, Christology, and the Bible

Presbyterian Church (USA), *Our Response to the Crisis in Central America: An Appeal to Presbyterians and Other Churches in the United States* (1988). Calls for a just peace in Central America.

9. Appeal to the first article, with some backing from Christology/the gospel and/or ecclesiology

Roman Catholic Church, Congregation for the Doctrine of the Faith, *Instruction on Christian Freedom and Liberation* (1986), 91, 89, 80-82, 64, 60, 54, 45, 30, 98-99. Christology/the gospel may function as the main warrant, especially if the statement intends the correlation it posits between creation and redemption to be read in light of Vatican II's subordination of creation to redemption.

10. Appeal to first- and second-article loci, with creation subordinated to Christology

Episcopal Church [USA], *General Convention Resolution* [on establishing a joint commission on peace] (1979). Cites a 1962 statement of the church's House of Bishops.

Episcopal Church [USA], *"To Make Peace" Report* (1985). Takes this position in virtue of approving the statement of the church's Joint Commission on Peace, *To Make Peace* (1982), which argued the case for peace with this sort of authorization.

Latin American [Catholic] Bishops, Third General Conference, *The Puebla Message* (1979).

National Conference of Catholic Bishops [USA], *Human Life in Our Day* (1968), 4-9, 95, 96, 101, 102, 114, 116, 126, 157. In view of the statement's citation of Vatican II's *Gaudium et Spes*, 22, which subordinates creation to Christology, perhaps this American statement is positing the same kind of subordination.

Roman Catholic Church, Vatican II, *Gaudium et Spes* (1965), 82-93, 76-79, 72, 39, 22.

United Presbyterian Church/Presbyterian Church in the U.S., *Reformed Faith and Politics* (1983), Rec. C/2, Rec. C, Policy Statement.

11. Appeal to Christology/the gospel

All-Union Council of Evangelical Christians-Baptists [USSR], *Resolution* (1986).

American Baptist Churches, *Policy Statement on Racial Justice* (1983).

Anglican Church of Canada, *Resolution on War and the Arms Race* (1965).

Anglicanism, *Resolutions of the Lambeth Conference (1978)*, 5.

Assembly of Argentine Bishops, *Before the Return to Democracy: Call of the Assembly of Argentine Bishops* (1983). Appeal to the doctrine of human persons stands in the background.

Baptist Union of Great Britain and Ireland, *Peace and Disarmament* (1984).

Baptist Union of New Zealand, *Public Questions Presentation* (1982).

Baptist World Alliance, *Resolution on Peace* (1965).

Baptist World Alliance, *Resolution on World Peace and Reconciliation* (1970). With some possible corresponding reference to creation warrants. It also includes limiting the deployment of weapons.

Baptist World Alliance Congress, *Resolution on Religious Liberty, Human Rights, World Peace and Public Morality* (1975). Also includes an appeal to end the arms race.

Brethren in Christ Church [USA], *Commitment to Peace, Justice and Equity* (1970).

Brethren in Christ Church [USA], *Position Paper on Church, War and Respect for Human Life* (1976), I, II. Some loci related to the doctrine of creation may be background warrants.

British Council of Churches, *Central America* (1983). Takes this position on peace in Central America and its mode of argumentation in virtue of approving the council's policy statement *Conflict and Promise — Central America in the 1980s*, 1, 5, 7.

Bund der Evangelischen Kirchen in der Deutschen Demokratischen Republik, *Beschluss der Synode zum Bericht der Konferenz der Evangelischen Kirchenleitungen vom 26. September 1978*, 1.1, 1.3.

Bund der Evangelischen Kirchen in der Deutschen Demokratischen Republik, *Beschluss der Synode des BEK-DDR zu Fragen des Friedens* (1981). Endorses WCC Central Committee, *Increasing Threat to Peace and the Mandate of the Churches* (1981), III/G; III/I; III/E; III/ C, which at one point authorizes peace by appeal to the gospel.

Bund der Evangelischen Kirchen in der Deutschen Demokratischen Republik, *Beschluss der Synode des BEK-DDR zum mündlichen Bericht der Konferenz der Evangelischen Kirchen- leitungen vom 28. September 1982*, II, III.

Bund der Evangelischen Kirchen in der Deutschen Demokratischen Republik, *Beschluss der Synode des Bundes zum Begriff "status confessionis" vom 19. September 1983*. May reject the application of the concept of *status confessionis* to the peace question. Theological authorization for its position on peace is drawn from the Barmen Declaration and WCC Vancouver Assembly, *Statement on Peace and Justice* (1983), 25.

Bund der Evangelischen Kirche in der Deutschen Demokratischen Republik, *Beschluss der Synode des Bundes zum Bericht der Konferenz der Evangelischen Kirchenleitungen vom 25. September 1984*, 5, 3.

Bund der Evangelischen Kirchen in der Deutschen Demokratischen Republik, *Beschluss der Synode des Bundes zum Bericht der Konferenz Evangelischen Kirchenleitungen vom 24. September 1985*, Int., 1.

Catholic Bishops of the GDR, *For an Effective Service of Peace* (1983).

[Catholic] Episcopal Conference of Nicaragua, *Renewing Christian Hope at the Beginning of 1977* (1977). Calls for peace in Nicaragua. It also claims that peace is rooted in conscience.

[Catholic] Episcopal Conference of the Philippines, *Call for Free and Honest Elections* (1986).

Catholic Swiss Bishops, *Pastoral Letter* (1978). Relates peace to energy consumption.

Christian Church (Disciples of Christ), *Concerning the Church's Witness for Peace* (1971). The law may function as a supporting warrant.

Christian Church (Disciples of Christ), *Concerning the United Nations' Peacekeeping Role in the Middle East* (1973). Concerned about peace in the Middle East.

Christian Church (Disciples of Christ), *Concerning Wider World Perspectives* (1973).

Christian Church (Disciples of Christ), *Concerning Ratification by the United States Senate of the Strategic Arms Limitation Treaty with Russia* (1979).

Christian Church (Disciples of Christ), *Concerning the Church's Witness for Peace* (1979). Takes position and authorization in virtue of citing the previously cited 1971 resolution of the same title.

Christian Conference of Asia, *Life and Action* (1977), I.

Christian Evangelical Baptist Union in Italy, *General Assembly of the CEBUI* (1980).

Church of God in Christ (Mennonite) [USA], *Principles of Faith* (1963), 36-37.

Church of Ireland, *The Report of the Role of the Church Committee* (1983), 6, 3, 2. Concerned, but not exclusively so, with peace in Northern Ireland. Anthropology, subordinated to the gospel, may vaguely function as a warrant.

Church of Ireland, *The Report of the Role of the Church Committee* (1985), 151, 154.

Church of the Brethren [USA], *A Statement of the Church of the Brethren on War* (1970), 1, 3, 11.

Church of the Province of Southern Africa [Anglican], *Cadets at School* (1985). Concerned to curtail civil conflict in South Africa.

Church of the Province of Southern Africa [Anglican], *Increasing Use of Violence* (1985).

Congregational Union of Scotland, *Nuclear Armaments* (1981). Insofar as appeal is made to "Christian conscience".

Council of the Federation of European Baptists, *Declaration on Disarmament* (1982).

Eglise Protestante Unie de Belgique, *Assemblée synodale* (1982).

Eglise Réformée de France, *Decision VII* (1968).

Episcopal Church [USA], *General Convention Resolution* [affirming Lambeth statement on war and violence] (1979).

Episcopal Church [USA], *General Convention Resolution* [on affirming United Nations Declaration of the Rights of the Child] (1979).

Episcopal Church [USA], *Non-violent War Resistance* (1982). Reaffirms the church's *General Convention Resolution* [affirming the Lambeth statement on war and violence] (1979), and so seems to share its appeal to Christology. The affirmed 1978 Lambeth statement was said to have been "enlightening, inspiring, and empowering" for the church in its *Recommend 1988 Lambeth Conference Address Issues of War* (1985).

Episcopal Church [USA], *Establish a Standing Commission on Peace* (1985).

Evangelical Church of the River Plate [Argentina], *Seek the Good of the City* (1978). Concerned about peace in Argentina; grace functions to authorize this concern.

Evangelical Methodist Church of Argentina, *Social Service and Action: Foundations in Biblical Theology* (n.d.), 1. With some reference to ecclesiology.

Evangelical Presbyterian Church of Chile, *I Believe in One God, the Fount and Future of Life: Creed of the EPCC* (1983). Ecclesiology may function as a background warrant insofar as it authorizes a concern for the oppressed, as in liberation theology.

Evangelische Kirche der Kirchenprovinz Sachsen, *Wort an die Gemeinden* (1983).

Evangelische Kirche der Union — Bereich Bundesrepublik Deutschland und Berlin-West, *Telegramm der Synode der EKU — Bereich DDR* (1982). Cites a telegram and official statement of the Evangelische Kirche der Union — Bereich Deutsche Demokratische Republik, which authorized its position by appeal to the gospel.

Evangelische Kirche im Rheinland, *Wort zum Vietnamkrieg* (1967). Calls for peace in Vietnam.

Evangelische Kirche im Rheinland, *Erklärung der Landessynode zum Krieg in Vietnam* (1968). Calls for peace in Vietnam and endorses WCC Central Committee, *Vietnam Declaration* (1967).

Evangelische Kirche in Deutschland, *Beschluss der Synode der EKD in Trier, November 1985.*

Evangelische Kirche in Deutschland, *Beschluss der 7. Synode der EKD zum ökumenischen Konzil des Friedens* (1985).

Evangelische Kirche in Hessen und Nassau, *Beschluss der Kirchensynode* (1983), 19.

Evangelische Kirche von Westfalen, *Wort der Landessynode 1984 zur Friedensverantwortung der Kirche* (1984).

Evangelische Landeskirche in Baden, *Wort an die Gemeinden* (1982), 3, 1, Int. Also refers to the contribution worship makes to peace.

Evangelische Landeskirche in Württemberg, *Zur Bundeswehr gehen? Wehrdienst verweigern?* (1985).

Evangelisch-Lutherische Landeskirche Sachsens, *Kanzelabkündigung der Landessynode, des Landesbischofs und Landeskirchenamtes von 24.03.1982.*

Evangelish-Lutherische Landessynode Sachsens, *Erklärung der 22. ELLS vom 22. März 1988.* Relates peace to justice and ecology.

Federation of Evangelical Churches in Italy, *Assembly of the FECI* (1982).

Federation of Evangelical Churches in Italy, *Assembly of the FECI* (1985), Act 38.

Federation of Evangelical Churches in Italy, *Assembly of the FECI* (1985), Act 49. Also calls for disarmament.

Fédération Protestante de France, *La lutte pour la paix* (1983).

German [Catholic] Bishops Conference, *Gegen Gewalttat und Terror in der Welt* (1973), 3-5, 8. Relates peace to justice and laments cruelties in Vietnam.

Irish Council of Churches, *Resolution at the Annual Meeting* (1982), I/1; III/1, 3. With creation and eschatology in the background.

Latin American [Catholic] Bishops, Second General Conference (Medellín Conference), *Justice* (1968), 3, 5, 16-23. Authorization by appeal to conversion and the gospel. Creation, Christology, eschatology, pneumatology, and baptism seem to be secondary warrants.

Latin American [Catholic] Bishops, Second General Conference (Medellín Conference), *Peace* (1968), 1, 14-16, 19, 20, 22, 24, 26. Creation may be a background warrant.

Lutheran-Episcopal Dialogue, series 3, *Implications of the Gospel* (1988), 123, 114, 85. One passage employs language which suggests a kind of two-kingdom ethic.

Lutheran World Federation, *Statement on Servanthood and Peace* (1970).

Lutheran World Federation, *Statement on Peace and Justice* (1984).

Lutheran World Federation, *Toward Economic and Social Justice* (1984), 8.3.4; II. Authorization is given in a part of the statement not approved by the assembly.

Mennonite Church [USA], *A Message concerning War in Vietnam* (1965).

Mennonite Church [USA], *Taxes Designated for War* (1967).

Mennonite Church [USA], *Conscription and Militarism* (1969). At least insofar as appeal is made to Christian love.

Mennonite Church [USA], *Militarism and Conscription Statement* (1979), A, Con. The Holy Spirit also functions as a motive.

Mennonite Church [USA], *Growing in Stewardship and Witness in a Militaristic World* (1987).

Mennonite Church, General Conference [USA], *A Christian Declaration on Capital Punishment* (1965). Peace is a concern of the state, but this is subordinated to the lordship of Christ.

Mennonite Church, General Conference [USA], *Freedom Movement* (1965). A reaffirmation of the denomination's 1959 statement, *The Christian and Race Relations*. Both statements were reaffirmed by Mennonite Church [USA], *A Church of Many People Confronts Racism* (1989).

Mennonite Church, General Conference [USA], *Resolution on Nationalism* (1968), II, I.

Mennonite Church, General Conference [USA], *Television Violence* (1977), Int.

Mennonite Church, General Conference [USA], *World Peace Tax Fund Act* (1977).

Mennonite World Conference, *Our Witness to Christ in Today's World* (1990).

Methodist Church [England], *Statement and Programme on Race Relations* (1978), 9, 1. Concerned about domestic peace.

Moderamens of the Reformed Alliance [FRG], *Das Bekenntnis zu Jesus Christus und die Friedensverantwortung der Kirche* (1981), I; V; VI; VII; Erl. I; Erl. VII. The warrants for the position on peace include the claim that peace is a *status confessionis*. At one point eschatology also functions as the warrant for the endeavor to maintain peace.

Moravian Church in America, Northern Province, *Nuclear Non-Proliferation and World Peace* (1982). Though an appeal to the doctrine of creation seems to stand in the background.

Moravian Church in Nicaragua, *"Communicado": Referencia: El diálogo, la reconciliación, la justicia y la paz* (1986).

National Conference of Catholic Bishops [USA], *Resolution on Peace* (1968).

National Conference of Catholic Bishops [USA], *Statement on the Twenty-fifth Anniversary of the United Nations* (1970), 3-4, 7-8. The doctrine of creation stands in the background.

National Conference of Catholic Bishops [USA], *Resolution on Imperatives of Peace* (1972), 1, 6, Calls for peace in Vietnam.

National Council of Churches [USA], *On Viet-nam* (1965). Calls for peace in Vietnam. Authorization is also provided by Christian love and by faith.

National Council of Churches [USA], *Imperatives of Peace and Responsibilities of Power* (1968), III, II, I, Int., Sum. Creation functions only as a motive.

National Council of Churches [USA], *On the Crisis in the Middle East* (1969), I, I/3, II. Calls for peace in the Middle East.

Netherlands [Catholic] Bishops' Conference, *Vrede en gerechtigheid* (1981).

Netherlands Reformed Church, *Pastoral Letter of the General Synod on the Question of Nuclear Armaments* (1980).

Nordelbische Evangelisch-Lutherische Kirche, *Erklärung der Synode der NELK zu Südafrika* (1986). Warrant not clear but suggests that endeavors to promote justice and peace in South Africa are placed under the law of Christ.

[Orthodox] Ecumenical Patriarchate of Constantinople, *Message de Noël 1971*.

[Orthodox] Ecumenical Patriarchate of Constantinople, *Message de Noël 1972*.

[Orthodox] Ecumenical Patriarchate of Constantinople, *Message patriarcal à l'occasion de Noël* (1985).

[Orthodox] Ecumenical Patriarchate of Constantinople, *Message de Sa Sainteté le Patriarche œcuménique Dimitrios à l'occasion de Noël 1987*. Authorized by grace.

Peruvian [Catholic] Episcopal Conference, *Document of the Peruvian Episcopal Conference on the Theology of Liberation* (1984), 25-28, 15-16, 51, 80. A kind of two-kingdom ethic stands in the background of the document.

Polish [Catholic] Episcopacy, *Communique of the 165th Plenary Assembly of the Polish Episcopacy* (1978), 4. Concerned about peace in Europe.

Presbyterian Church (USA), *Life Abundant: Values, Choices and Health Care* (1988), 1. Relates peace to justice.

Reformed Church in America, *Report of the General Synod Executive Committee* (1980), R-15, R-12. Calls for peace, justice, and the conquest of apartheid in South Africa. An appeal to Christology authorizes the witness against apartheid and so, by implication, seems to authorize this call for peace.

Romanian Orthodox Church, *Lettre irénique de Sa Béatitude le Patriarche Iustin, adressée aux chefs des églises chrétiennes à l'occasion de la fête de la Nativité 1982.*

Romanian Orthodox Church, *Lettre irénique de Sa Béatitude le Patriarche Iustin — Pâques 1984.* Appeals to *theosis* as warrant.

Romanian Orthodox Church, *Christmas Letter of Patriarch Theoctiste* (1987).

Southern Baptist Convention [USA], *The Baptist Faith and Message* (1963), XVI.

United Church of Canada, *Statement on Human Rights* (1980), 2. Endorses affirmations to work for peace by the Presbyterian Church in the Republic of Korea, *Statement of Faith,* and a 1979 statement of the Church in South Africa. The latter statement authorized peace by appeal to the gospel, so this authorization seems endorsed by the Canadian church.

United Church of Canada, *Human Rights and International Affairs: Do Not Let the World Forget Us* (1982).

United Church of Canada, *Cruise Missile Testing* (1988).

United Church of Christ [USA], *Disarmament* (1977). Would redirect military resources to meet unmet needs of American people.

United Church of Christ [USA], *Increased Violence against Blacks in America* (1981). The appeal to Christology may function only as a motive, not as the pronouncement's warrant.

United Church of Christ [USA], *Justice in Immigration* (1981).

United Church of Christ [USA], *Acts of Violence against Reproductive Health Care Facilities* (1985).

United Free Church of Scotland, *Deliverance of the General Assembly* [on public questions] (1969), 1, 13. Especially concerned about peace in the Middle East.

United Free Church of Scotland, *Deliverance of the General Assembly* [on public questions] (1981), 1.

United Presbyterian Church [USA], *The Confession of 1967,* II.A.4.

United Presbyterian Church [USA], *War, Peace, and Conscience* (1969).

Uniting Church in Australia, *Commonwealth Games* (1982), 82.49, (3).

Vereinigte Evangelisch-Lutherische Kirche Deutschlands General Synod, *The Contribution of the Church and Christians to Securing Peace* (1981).

Vereinigte Evangelisch-Lutherische Kirche in der DDR, *Beschluss der Generalsynode zum Bericht der Kirchenleitung vom 8. Juni 1980,* 9.

Waldensian and Methodist Churches in Italy, *Synod of the WMCI* (1982).

World Alliance of Reformed Churches, *The Theatre of Glory and a Threatened Creation's Hope* (1982).

World Alliance of Reformed Churches, *A Message to the Congregations of the Member Churches of the WARC* (1989).

World Alliance of Reformed Churches, *Southern Africa* (1989).

World Alliance of Reformed Churches, *Statement on Peace* (1989), 1-3.4; 4.3. Relates peace to justice and ecology.

WCC Vancouver Assembly, *Statement on Peace and Justice* (1983), 1-2, 6-10, 14, 20-27. This statement was adopted by the Evangelische Kirche im Rheinland, *Kriegsdienstverweigerung* (1988).

12. Appeal to Christology/the gospel and third-article loci

American Lutheran Church, *Mandate for Peacemaking* (1982), A.1-3.

[Catholic] Bishops' Conference of Mozambique, *A urgencia da paz* (1984), 15, 8.

Catholic Bishops' Conference of the Philippines, *The Fruit of Justice Is Peace* (1987).
Concerned about peace in the Philippines. It speaks of justice, mainly with reference to land
reform.

Mennonite World Conference, *The Conference Message* (1967), III. Concerned about peace in
Vietnam and elsewhere.

Roman Catholic Church, Congregation for the Doctrine of the Faith, *Instruction on Certain
Aspects of the "Theology of Liberation"* (1984), Conc.; XI.8; VII.8; V.1; IV.9-11; I.1-2.
Anthropology is a possible background warrant.

Vereinigte Evangelisch-Lutherische Kirche in der DDR, *Beschlüsse der 5. Tagung der III.
Generalsynode der VELK-DDR vom 8.-11. Juni 1983*, 2.

World Alliance of Reformed Churches, *Come Creator Spirit, for the Redemption of the World*
(1964), I/C, II.

13. Appeal to Christology/the gospel, supplemented by an appeal to the Eucharist

Evangelische Kirche in Deutschland, *The Preservation, Promotion and Renewal of Peace*
(1981), Int.; I.4(b); IV.1(d); IV/1(f); V.1(a); V.3(a); V.4(a).

14. Appeal to Christology and eschatology

Eglise de la Confession d'Augsbourg d'Alsace et de Lorraine, *Texte concernant J.P.S.C.*
(1980). Relates peace to justice and ecology.

Evangelische Kirche im Rheinland, *Friedensverantwortung der Kirche* (1983), 1, 2.4. Takes
this theological perspective in virtue of endorsing Evangelische Kirche von Westfalen,
Friedensverantwortung der Kirche (1982), and a draft of the National Conference of
Catholic Bishops [USA], *The Challenge of Peace: God's Promise and Our Response*
(1983), which collectively employ these warrants.

Federation of Protestant Churches in Switzerland, *Pour une action concertée énergique en
faveur du tiers monde* (1986), II.5(a).

Latin American Council of Churches, *Commitment for the Kingdom* (1982), I.

Reformed Ecumenical Synod, *Statements on the Social Calling of the Church* (1980), 16, 18, 2.

United Presbyterian Church/Presbyterian Church in the U.S., *Strangers Become Neighbors:
Presbyterian Response to Mexican Migration* (1981), I. Ecclesiology also provides authorization.

15. Appeal to Christology, the law, and the Bible

Christian Church (Disciples of Christ), *Concerning the Reinstitution of the Compulsory Draft in
Peacetime* (1979). The Bible is probably the prevailing model.

Presbyterian Church (USA), *Christian Obedience in a Nuclear Age* (1988), 1-2, 8-9, 16-18.
Relates peace to justice. It cites United Presbyterian Church [USA], *The Confession of
1967*, III.A.4.

16. Appeal to Christology, with creation a background warrant

Romanian Orthodox Church, *Lettre irénique à l'occasion de la fête de Pâques* (1987).

Russian Orthodox Church, *Ehre sei Gott in der Höhe und Frieden auf Erden* (1983).

17. Appeal to Christology, with creation probably subordinated to Christology

Roman Catholic Church, *Ecclesiam Suam* (1964), 16, 64, 94, 98, 104, 106. At one point uses
language of *theosis*.

18. Appeal to Christology/Christian faith, perhaps supplemented by appeal to creation

Anglican-Lutheran [European Commission] Dialogue (1982), 29, 58, 59. At least includes one reference to something like a two-kingdom ethic.
Reformed-Roman Catholic Joint Commission, *The Presence of Christ in Church and World* (1977), 53, 51, 48, 44, 23.
United Church of Christ in Japan, *The Fundamental Policy for Social Action* (1966), II/A(2)(a); Int.; I/A(2).

19. Appeal to Christology, with eschatology in the background

Evangelische Kirche von Kurhessen-Waldeck, *Wort der Landessynode zum Thema "Ermutigung zum Frieden" vom 17. Mai 1984,* 1-4. For authorization cites WCC Vancouver Assembly, *Statement on Peace and Justice* (1983), 8-10, as well as the Barmen Declaration (1934), II, V. It in turn includes a background reference to ecclesiology. Sacramentology is also a supporting warrant.
Mennonite Brethren Churches, *Mennonite Brethren Distinctives* (1966), 24-26.

20. Appeal to Christology and the Old Testament prophetic tradition (or the doctrine of redemption)

South African Council of Churches, *Conscientious Objection* (1974).
United Church of Christ [USA], *"The Faith Crisis": Goals and Objectives* (1971).

21. Appeal to the gospel and eschatology, with creation possibly subordinated to these loci

Igreja Lusitana Católica Apostólica Evangélica, *Declaração do Sínodo da ILCAE sobre o Ano Internacional da Paz* (1986), 1-4.

22. Appeal to the Christian faith/Christology

Christian Church (Disciples of Christ), *Appeal to the Churches on Vietnam* (1967). Calls for peace in Vietnam by citing National Council of Churches [USA] General Assembly, *An Appeal to the Churches concerning Vietnam* (1967), sec. 3, par. 3.
Christian Church (Disciples of Christ), *Concerning Universal Human Rights* (1977). Relates peace to justice and human rights.
Episcopal Church [USA], *General Convention Resolution* [on humane treatment of prisoners of war] (1970). Authorization is an appeal to "Christian duty".
Episcopal Church [USA], *General Convention Resolution* [on the Panama Canal Treaty] (1976). Authorization seems to be provided by the doctrine of reconciliation and perhaps also by ecclesiology.
Evangelische Kirche der Kirchenprovinz Sachsen, *Beschluss der Gesamtthematik der Synodaltagung* (1985), Int., 1, 3. Relates peace to justice and ecology. It appeals to the gospel and the concept of covenant.

Evangelische Kirche der Union — Bereich Bundesrepublik Deutschland und Berlin-West, *Telegramm an den SACC* (1982). Calls for a just peace in divided Germany.

Evangelische Kirche in Deutschland, *Zur Erhaltung und Festigung des Friedens* (1983). Endorses a *Wort des Rates der Evangelischen Kirche in Deutschland zur Friedensdiskussion im Herbst 1983*. Although the synod offered no explicit theological authorization for its call to peace, the Rat statement which it endorsed authorized its position by appeal to Christology and the doctrine of reconciliation.

Evangelische Kirche von Westfalen, *Wort der Landessynode 1984 zur Friedensarbeit in den Gemeinden* (1984).

Evangelische Landeskirche in Württemberg, *Brief der ELW an Wehrpflichtige* (1988). Redemption may be the prevailing warrant.

Evangelisch-Lutherische Kirche in Bayern, *Erklärung zur Friedensfrage* (1983), IV, I. The declaration appeals to "Christian responsibility" as authorization. It endorses *Wort des Rates der Evangelischen Kirche in Deutschland zur Friedensdiskussion im Herbst 1983*, 2, which employed the same warrant.

Evangelisch-Lutherische Landeskirche Hannovers, *Wort der Landeskirche vom 23. November 1983 an die Gemeinden*. Also authorized by appeal to the biblical witness.

International Council of Community Churches [USA], *Statement of Concern on Nuclear Weapons* (1982). Appeals to the concept of covenant.

Mennonite Church [USA], *Stewardship of the Earth Resolution on Environment and Faith Issues* (1989). With creation and eschatology as background warrants.

Mennonite Church, General Conference [USA], *The Way of Peace* (1971).

Mennonite World Conference, *Conference Message* (1972), I, II. Authorized by Christology and reconciliation.

National Conference of Catholic Bishops [USA], *To Do the Work of Justice* (1978), 1, 2, 6, 7, 14. Relates peace to social justice and human rights.

[Orthodox] Ecumenical Patriarchate of Constantinople, *Le message pascal de Sa Sainteté le patriarche œcuménique* (1970).

Russian Orthodox Church, *Christmas Greetings of Patriarch Pimen* (1981).

Russian Orthodox Church, *Decrees of the Holy Synod* (1986).

Russian Orthodox Church, *Easter Communication* (1987).

Russian Orthodox Church, *Segenwünsche* (1987).

Sudan Catholic Bishops' Conference, *Lord Come to Our Aid* (1984), G-G/b, G/d. Also appeals to Christian responsibility and love.

United Church of Canada, *Disarmament* (1986).

United Church of Christ [USA], *Peace and the Resolving of Conflict* (1981). Authorization provided by the covenant and the commandment to love one another.

United Church of Christ [USA], *Weapons of Mass Destruction* (1983).

United Church of Christ [USA], *Responding to Space Weaponry* (1985).

United Church of Christ [USA], *Fulfilling God's Covenant with All Children* (1987). Affirms a just peace.

United Church of Christ [USA], *The Israeli-Palestinian Conflict* (1987). Authorized by reconciliation and calls for a just peace in the Middle East.

Uniting Church in Australia, *Militarism and Disarmament* (1982), 82.57, (1a), (1c), (8f).

Uniting Church in Australia, *Re Pacific Churches* (1985), 85.105.2. Concerned about a peaceful independence in New Caledonia.

World Alliance of Reformed Churches, *Justice, Peace and the Integrity of Creation* (1989). Authorization also provided by covenant and the Bible. It relates peace to justice and ecology and is concerned about peace in Nicaragua and Korea.

WCC Amsterdam Assembly, *Message of the Assembly* (1948).

WCC Uppsala Assembly, *Towards Justice and Peace in International Affairs* (1968), 8.

23. Apparent appeal to pneumatology

Evangelisch-Lutherische Kirche in Bayern, *Erklärung der Landessynode der ELKB zum Vorschlag eines Friedenskonzils* (1985).

Latin American [Catholic] Bishops, Second General Conference (Medellín Conference), *Introduction to the Final Documents: Presence of the Church in the Present-Day Transformation of Latin America* (1968), 8, 5. Christology and eschatology may function as background warrants.

Polish Episcopal Conference, *Communique of the Plenary Session* (1981), 5, 2. With natural law and the gospel as background warrants in this call for peace in Poland.

Reformed Church in America, *Report of the Christian Action Commission* (1981), R-10 to R-12. At least claims that the Spirit leads to peace.

United Free Church of Scotland, *Deliverance of the General Assembly* [on public questions] (1983), 7.

World Alliance of Reformed Churches, *Come Creator Spirit, for the Re-making of Man* (1964), 3. The gospel also functions as a supporting warrant. This point was only received, not adopted.

24. Appeal to the Old Testament prophetic tradition

United Church of Christ [USA], *Pronouncement on Public Education* (1985), IV.

25. Apparent appeal to ecclesiology

Hong Kong Christian Council, *The Manifesto of the Protestant Church in Hong Kong on Religious Freedom* (1984). With creation as a background warrant.

26. Appeal to ecclesiology and Christology

Evangelisch-Lutherische Kirche in Bayern, *Menschenrechtsverletzungen* (1985). Cites a 1984 statement of the Lutheran World Federation.

Joint Pastoral Letter of the Bishops of Kenya on the Family and Responsible Parenthood (1979). Authorization not entirely clear; relates peace to development.

National Conference of Catholic Bishops [USA], *Economic Justice for All* (1986), 341, 332, 331, 320, 292, 68, 20. Also authorized by an appeal to biblical principles.

27. Appeal to ecclesiology, perhaps subordinated to Christology

Methodist Church in Malaysia, *Social Principles* (n.d.), III/E; III/B.1; II; I. Also concerned about disarmament. Creation may be a background warrant.

28. Appeal to ecclesiology, with some reference to a two-kingdom ethic

Vereinigte Evangelisch-Lutherische Kirche Deutschlands, *Beschluss der Generalsynode der VELKD zur Rolle der Kirchen in bezug auf das südliche Afrika* (1978), 2. Concerned only with domestic peace in South Africa.

29. Appeal to the nature of the Eucharist

[Catholic] Bishops of the Netherlands, *De mens in de arbeid* (1980), 2.8.

30. Appeal to eschatology

Association of the Episcopal Conference of Anglophone West Africa, *Communique, Resolutions, and Recommendations* (1986), 15.

Bund der Evangelischen Kirchen in der Deutschen Demokratischen Republik, *Beschluss der Synode des BEK-DDR zum Bericht der Konferenz der Ev. Kirchenleitungen zu Friedensfragen* (1986), 1, 5. Relates peace to justice and ecology as per the WCC call for a conciliar process on these concerns.

Caribbean Conference of Churches, *Thine Is the Kingdom, the Power and the Glory* (1981).

Nicaraguan [Catholic] Bishops, *Christian Commitment for a New Nicaragua* (1979), I.

Presbyterian Church in Ireland, *Resolution on the Northern Ireland Situation* (1979). Only concerned with peace in Northern Ireland. Some reference is made to the law of God as authorization.

Presbyterian Church in Taiwan, *An Urgent Call of the General Assembly of the PCT* (1988).

Presbyterian Church of Korea, *Guiding Principles for the Social Mission Policy of the PCK* (1984), 5(3), 5.

World Alliance of Reformed Churches, *The People of the Covenant and the Mission of the Kingdom* (1982), 7. Also refers to a concern about justice.

31. Appeal to eschatology and prophecy

Anglicanism, *The Resolutions of the Lambeth Conference (1988)*, 24, 27, 37, 39, 40, 62, 73. Calls for peace in Israel, Latin America, the Sudan, South Africa, and Northern Ireland.

32. Appeal to eschatology and perhaps creation

Methodist Church [England], *A Statement Reaffirming That the Methodist Church Is against Racism in All Its Forms and Committed to Racial Justice within a Plural Society* (1988).

33. Appeal to eschatology and worship, with some reference to creation

[Catholic] Bishops of the Netherlands, *Mens, arbeid en samenleving* (1985), 11.

34. Appeal to all articles of the creed

American Lutheran Church, *War, Peace, and Freedom* (1966), 24, 26, 31, 32, 34, 41. Authorization is drawn from anthropology, Christology, the Word, the Spirit, and the sacraments. The statement may not have official status.

American Lutheran Church, *Issues and Opportunities That Bind and Free* (1976).

Church of the Brethren [USA], *The Time So Urgent: Threats to Peace* (1980), 5-8. At one point calls for peace and justice in the Middle East.

Church of the Brethren [USA], *Resolution on Normalizing Relations with Cuba* (1985). Relates peace to justice.

Conference of European Churches and Council of European Bishops' Conferences, *Final Document of the European Ecumenical Assembly Peace with Justice* (1989), 1, 2, 4, 20, 21, 25-30, 32, 36-38, 40, 42, 45, 70, 72, 75, 77, 83, 86, 91. Relates peace to justice. Concerned about peace in the Middle East. Authorization is also provided by appeal to covenant, which itself reflects a trinitarian orientation.

Episcopal Church [USA], *General Convention Resolution* [on condemning resurgence of activity of the Ku Klux Klan] (1979).

Episcopal Church [USA], *Endorse Reunification of Korea Policy Statement* (1988). By endorsing the National Council of Churches (USA) (1986) policy statement cited below, this resolution shares its Trinitarian authorization for peace.

National Council of Churches in Korea, *Declaration of the Churches of Korea on National Reunification and Peace* (1988). Concerned about peace and justice in Korea as well as its reunification; endorsed by World Alliance of Reformed Churches, *Korean Peace and Reunification* (1989).

National Council of Churches [USA], *Middle East* (1980). Urges peace and justice in the Middle East. Approved by Christian Church (Disciples of Christ), *Concerning a Policy Statement on the Middle East* (1982).

National Council of Churches [USA], *Latin America and the Caribbean* (1983), III/C(3), III/A, III, Int. Concerned about peace in Latin America and the Caribbean. At one point the gospel functions as the primary authorization.

National Council of Churches [USA], *Peace and the Reunification of Korea* (1986), esp, 2, 9-13.

Roman Catholic Church, *Pacem in Terris* (1963), 1-3, 5, 10, 23, 31, 121, 147, 165-71. Relates peace to justice. Appeals to all loci may be subordinated to redemption. At least it posits a creation-redemption continuity, with natural law as prevailing warrant. It also posits a relational view of persons.

Russian Orthodox Church, *Message of the Holy Synod of the ROC on War and Peace in a Nuclear Age* (1986), 3.5; also see 1.4, 1.5, 1.7, 1.9, 2.3, 2.23, 3.1, 3.3, 3.10, 3.13-15, 3.18-20, 3.23, 3.25, 3.34, 4. Claims that peace depends on human efforts. At some points in the statement, Christology alone authorizes peace. At another point the liturgy provides authorization. Elsewhere the message opts for a natural-law ethic resembling the two-kingdom ethic.

United Church of Canada, *The Search for Peace in the Eighties — Statement* (1982).

United Church of Christ [USA], *Reversing the Arms Race* (1979).

United Church of Christ [USA], *Affirming the United Church of Christ as a Just Peace Church* (1985), Pronouncement, A Proposal for Action.

WCC World Convocation on Justice, Peace and the Integrity of Creation, *Final Document: Entering into Covenant Solidarity for Justice, Peace and the Integrity of Creation* (1990), 2.1; 2.2; 2.3.2; 2.3.2.2. Relates peace to justice and ecology. Authorization is also provided by appeal to the concept of covenant, which reflects a trinitarian orientation.

35. Appeal to all articles of the creed, with all loci subordinated to Christology

Roman Catholic Church, *Sollicitudo Rei Socialis* (1987), 39-41, 47-49, 10, 7-8, 1-3. Cites an earlier papal encyclical, *Populorum Progressio* (1967), 87, 55.

United Presbyterian Church [USA], *Call to Peacemaking* (1980), I, II. Relates peace to justice.

36. Authorized by loci from all articles of the creed, with Christology the prevailing warrant

WCC Evanston Assembly, *International Affairs — Christians in the Struggle for World Community* (1954), I; II; VI; Res. I; Int.

37. Appeal to loci from all articles of the creed, especially creation and eschatology

[Catholic] Episcopal Conference of the Pacific, *The Pacific and Peace* (1986), IX, VIII, VII, IV, II, I.

Evangelisch-Lutherische Kirche Deutschlands, *Beschluss der Generalsynode der VELKD zu der "Erklärung zum Frieden" des Exekutivkomitees des Lutherischen Weltbundes vom 24. Oktober 1981*. Cites the LWF statement, 3-5, in the resolution's title.

38. Appeal to loci from all articles of the creed, with the first article perhaps subordinated

Evangelical Church of Lutheran Confession in Brazil, *God's Earth . . . Land for Everyone* (1982), II. With liberation theology's emphasis on discovering God in the natural signs.

Haitian [Catholic] Episcopal Conference, *The Foundation for the Church's Involvement in Local and Political Arenas* (1983), 2, 5, 11, 12, 19.

National Conference of Catholic Bishops [USA], *The Challenge of Peace: God's Promise and Our Response* (1983), 2, 13-15, 20-125, 186, 196, 200-201, 258-59, 274-85, 289-96, 303-10, 325-27, 329, 331, 333, 339.

Roman Catholic Church, *Octogesima Adveniens* (1971), 17, 23, 37, 45, 46, 48.

United Presbyterian Church [USA], *Call to Peacemaking* (1980), I-II.

39. Appeal to the doctrine of God and ecclesiology

Nederduitse Gereformeerde Sendingkerk [South Africa], *Confession of Faith* (1982).

40. Appeal to the acts of the Triune God

Bund der Evangelischen Kirchen in der Deutschen Demokratischen Republik, *Beschluss der Synode des BEK-DDR zum "Bekennen in der Friedensfrage"* (1987), Int., I, III. Authorization seems implied, since peace is related to overcoming deterrence, which is itself rejected by appeals to the Triune God.

Lutheran World Federation, *Statement on Human Rights* (1984), I, II. Insofar as peace is a human right.

Southern African Catholic Bishops' Conference, *An Urgent Message to the State President* (1986), 2-5, 7, 23-27.

41. Appeal to divine Providence

World Alliance of Reformed Churches, *Towards a Common Testimony of Faith* (1989), 1/B.

42. Appeal to divine justice and the Bible

National Association of Evangelicals [USA], *Resolution on Apartheid* (1986). Concerned about peace and justice in South Africa.

43. Appeal to the will of God

Evangelisch-Lutherische Kirche in Oldenburg, *Beschlossene Fassung* (1981).
International Council of Community Churches [USA], *On Hiroshima Anniversary* (1985).
   Appeals to the guidance of God.
United Church of Christ (USA), *Renewed United States Support of the United Nations as Our
   Best Investment for a Just Peace* (1987). Calls for a just peace.

44. Appeal to God's grace

American Baptist Churches, *Policy Statement on Family Life* (1984).

45. Trust in the security of God's presence

Evangelische Kirche in Deutschland, *Kundgebung zur Friedenssicherung* (1980).
Nederduitse Gereformeerde Sendingkerk [South Africa], *The Belhar Confession 1986,* 4.

46. Appeal to God's Word

Evangelische Kirche im Rheinland, *Die Friedenszusage Gottes und unser Streit um dem Frieden*
   (1982).

47. Appeal to the Bible's word of renewal

Christian Reformed Church in North America, *Guidelines for Justifiable Warfare* (1982), 11,
   13. Authorized by the Word, with pneumatology providing motivation.
Evangelische Kirche im Rheinland, *Leitsätze zur Friedenserziehung in der Schule* (1982).
Evangelische Kirche in Deutschland, *Kundgebung zur Veröffentlichung der Denkschrift
   "Frieden wahren, fördern und erneuern"* (1981).
Mennonite Church [USA], *Resolution concerning Security and the Current Arms Race* (1981).
   Appeals to the "biblical message".
National Association of Evangelicals [USA], *Communism* (1963). Relates peace to social
   justice. It is authorized by appeal to "biblical principles".
National Council of Churches [USA], *Policy Statement on Child Day Care* (1984), I/C.
   Scripture is said to provide authorization.
United Church of Christ [USA], *Peace Church* (1981). The Bible provides authorization.
United Church of Christ [USA], *Justice and Peace Priority* (1985). Authorized by "the biblical
   vision of Shalom".
United Church of Christ [USA], *A Pronouncement Affirming the Wholeness of the Gospel:
   Integrating Evangelism and Church Growth and Justice and Peace* (1987), I-III.
   Authorized by "the biblical story".

48. Appeal to the Bible and creation

National Association of Evangelicals [USA], *Peace, Freedom and Human Rights* (1987).
   Relates peace to freedom, citing earlier 1952 and 1979 resolutions.

49. Appeal to Scripture and Christian conscience or Christian principles

Dutch Reformed Church (South Africa), *Church and Society 1990*. Relates peace to social justice and human dignity.

Dutch Reformed Church (South Africa), *A Declaration of Christian Principles* (1990), 2.2.3-2.2.5; 1. Relates peace to social justice and reasonableness, especially in its vision for a new constitution in South Africa.

50. Appeal to Christian duty/the gospel

Christian Reformed Church in North America, *Decision of 1969*. Takes this position and authorization in virtue of reasserting the church's 1939 decision *Testimony concerning the Christian's Attitude toward War and Peace*, which took this position with such an argument.

Christian Reformed Church in North America, *Acts of Synod* (1973), 79-81. Takes this position in virtue of reaffirming two decisions cited above.

51. Appeal to command to love

[Catholic] Bishops of Vietnam, *To Build Peace* (1969). Appeals to charity for authorization.

[Catholic] Episcopacy of France, *Déclaration sur les événements internationaux* (1968). Concerned with peace in Czechoslovakia, Biafra, and Israel.

International Council of Community Churches [USA], *Statement of Concern about Central America* (1987).

Patriarchs and Catholic Bishops of Libya, *Legality Is the Unique Guarantee of the Protection of the Fatherland* (1983), I/4, III/9. Love provides the authorization.

Reformed Church in America, *Report of the Christian Action Commission* (1966), R-4. Calls for peace and justice in Vietnam, taking this position in virtue of adopting National Council of Churches [USA], *On Viet-nam* (1965).

United Church of Canada, *The Church and the Economic Crisis* (1984).

52. Appeal to faith in God

United Church of Canada, *Peace in Central America* (1986). Calls for peace in Central America.

53. Appeal to Christian ethical considerations and social responsibility

Christian Church (Disciples of Christ), *Concerning Investment Policies of the CC(DC)* (1971).

54. Appeal to the example of the faithful

Russian Orthodox Church, *Easter Communication* (1988).

55. No clear theological warrant given for position

All Africa Conference of Churches, *The Gospel of Reconciliation* (1981). Especially concerned about the arms race in Africa.

Anglicanism, *The Resolutions of the Lambeth Conference (1968)*, 2. Also condemns the use of nuclear weapons.

Anglicanism, *Resolutions of the Lambeth Conference (1978)*, 2.

Associated Churches of Christ in New Zealand, *Decisions Relating to Public Issues* (1966). Particularly concerned about peace in Vietnam.

Baptist Union of Great Britain and Ireland, *Vietnam* (1967). Calls for peace in Vietnam.

Baptist Union of Great Britain and Ireland, *Politics and Peaceful Protest* (1970).

Baptist Union of Great Britain and Ireland, *Falklands Crisis* (1982). Calls for peace in the Falkland Islands.

Baptist Union of New Zealand, *Notices of Motion* (1984).

Bishops of Chile, *Collective Pastoral Letter* (1968). Relates peace to social justice; condemns use of violence.

Brethren in Christ Church [USA], *Call to Prayer in Observance of National Holidays* (1970).

Brethren in Christ Church [USA], *Affirmation of Commitment to Spiritual Power* (1971).

Brethren in Christ Church [USA], *Indo-China War* (1971). Opposing war in Vietnam.

Brethren in Christ Church [USA], *The Christian and Society* (1972).

British Council of Churches, *Southern Africa* (1963), (a). Calls for peace in South Africa; cites a 1951 statement of the council.

British Council of Churches, *Middle East* (1973). Urges peace in the Middle East.

British Council of Churches, *BCC Fund for Ireland* (1979). Urges peace in Ireland.

British Council of Churches, *Disarmament* (1981).

British Council of Churches, *Namibia* (1981). Calls for peace in Namibia.

British Council of Churches, Community and Race Relations Unit (1982). Adopts the paper *Towards a Multi-racial Britain – Why and How Grants Are Made*.

British Council of Churches, *The Falkland Islands* (1982). Calls for peace on the Falklands.

British Council of Churches, *Recommendations [of the council's delegation to the Middle East] Accepted by the BCC Assembly* (1982), 8.2.1. Calls for peace in the Middle East.

British Council of Churches, *Christmas Appeal* (1983), 6.

British Council of Churches, *Middle East* (1984). Comments (approves) the council's policy statement, *Statement on the Middle East* (1983), 4.3, 4.1, 2.1, which urged peace in the Middle East.

British Council of Churches, *East-West Relations* (1985).

British Council of Churches, *International Year of Peace* (1985).

British Council of Churches, *A Message from the BCC Assembly to Churches and Governments in Britain and Ireland* (1985). Calls for peace in Northern Ireland.

British Council of Churches, *Middle East* (1985). Calls for peace and justice in the Middle East.

British Council of Churches, *Statement on Geneva Summit Meeting* (1985).

British Council of Churches, *The Falkland Islands* (1986). Calls for peace on the Falklands.

Bund der Evangelischen Kirchen in der Deutschen Demokratischen Republik, *Beschluss der Generalsynode zu den Berichten des Leitenden Bischofs und der Kirchenleitung vom 28. Juni 1981*, 5. May have an appeal to natural law in the background.

Bund der Evangelischen Kirchen in der Deutschen Demokratischen Republik, *Beschluss der Synode zu Gesprächen mit staatlichen Stellen* (1982).

Bund der Evangelischen Kirchen in der Deutschen Demokratischen Republik, *Beschluss der Synode des Bundes zur Stationierung von atomaren Mittelstreckenwaffen vom 20. September 1983*.

Bund der Evangelischen Kirchen in der Deutschen Demokratischen Republik, *Erklärung der Synode des Bundes zur Vorbereitung eines "Konzils des Friedens"* (1985). Also calls for justice, though not explicitly for social justice.

Canadian Catholic Conference, *On Development and Peace* (1968), 2, 11. Cites Roman Catholic Church, *The Development of Peoples* (1967).

Canadian Conference of Catholic Bishops, *The Neutron Bomb — Enough Is Enough!* (1981), 4, 11. Relates peace to social love.

Canadian Conference of Catholic Bishops, *A Brief to the Standing Committee on External Affairs: On Preparation for the Second Special Session of the United Nations on Disarmament* (1982), Int.; 2.1.

[Catholic] Bishops of Panama, *Declaration of the Bishops of Panama concerning the Negotiations for a New Treaty on the Canal* (1975). May have an appeal to the doctrine of creation in the background.

Catholic Bishops of the Philippines, *What Is Happening to Our Beautiful Land?* (1988). Relates peace to ecology and justice. Appeal to creation and Christology, with the former subordinated to the latter, may be background warrants.

[Catholic] Episcopacy of France, *Jésus-Christ, sauveur, espérance des hommes aujourd'hui* (1968).

Christian Church (Disciples of Christ), *Concerning the Need for a Stronger World Community as a Bulwark against Nuclear War* (1963).

Christian Church (Disciples of Christ), *Concerning Membership in the United Nations* (1964).

Christian Church (Disciples of Christ), *Concerning Revolutionary Movements and Threats to the Peace of the World* (1966).

Christian Church (Disciples of Christ), *Substitute Resolution on Vietnam* (1966).

Christian Church (Disciples of Christ), *Concerning World Order, Justice and Peace* (1968).

Christian Church (Disciples of Christ), *Concerning World Peace* (1968).

Christian Church (Disciples of Christ), *Concerning a Department of Peace* (1969).

Christian Church (Disciples of Christ), *Concerning Military Draft* (1969).

Christian Church (Disciples of Christ), *Concerning the Support of Eighty United States Congressmen Who Have Proposed a United Nations Peacekeeping Force* (1969).

Christian Church (Disciples of Christ), *Concerning Church, Nation, and Black Disciples* (1971), 9. Calls for an end of American involvement in Vietnam.

Christian Church (Disciples of Christ), *Concerning Indochina* (1971). Urges peace in Indochina.

Christian Church (Disciples of Christ), *Concerning U.S.A.-China Relationships* (1971).

Christian Church (Disciples of Christ), *Concerning International Women's Year, 1975* (1975).

Christian Church (Disciples of Christ), *Concerning the Normalization of United States-China Diplomatic Relations* (1977). Urges a peaceful solution of the international status of Taiwan.

Christian Church (Disciples of Christ), *Concerning Southern Africa* (1977). Calls for peace in Southern Africa.

Christian Church (Disciples of Christ), *Concerning the United Nations* (1977).

Christian Church (Disciples of Christ), *Concerning Ending the Arms Race* (1979).

Christian Church (Disciples of Christ), *Concerning North and South Korea* (1979). Calls for peace and justice in Northeast Asia.

Christian Church (Disciples of Christ), *Concerning a National Peace Academy* (1981).

Christian Church (Disciples of Christ), *Concerning El Salvador* (1981). Supports justice, reconciliation, and peace in El Salvador.

Christian Church (Disciples of Christ), *Concerning Support for the Conscientious Objectors to War* (1981). Christian faith could function as a background warrant.

Christian Evangelical Baptist Union in Italy, *General Assembly of the CEBUI* (1982). Especially concerned about peace between Argentina and Great Britain; appeals to the Bible for authorization.

Church of England, *Defence and Disarmament* (1979).

Church of England, *South Africa* (1986). Concerned about peace in South Africa.

Church of Ireland, *The Report of the Role of the Church Committee* (1981).

Church of Ireland, *A Resolution of the Standing Committee* (1982).

Church of the Province of Southern Africa [Anglican], *Escalation of Terrorist Activities* (1983).

Conferencia Episcopal Española, *La despenalización del aborto* (1983), 9. Relates peace to the right to life.

Consultation of Religions in Romania, *Telegram to the President of Romania* (1981). The statement's appeal to the idea of peace as a fundamental right could be a creation appeal.

Eglise Evangélique Luthérienne de France, *Vœux et décisions du synode général 1987, 5.* Relates peace and justice to ecology, as per the WCC agenda.

Eglise Evangélique Luthérienne de France, *Vœux et décisions du synode général 1988,* 6. Calls for peace in New Caledonia.

Eglise Réformée d'Alsace et de Lorraine, *Vœux adoptés par le Synode de l'ERAL* (1987), 2.

Episcopal Church [USA], *The War in Vietnam* (1967). Calls for a just and durable peace in Vietnam.

Episcopal Church [USA], *General Convention Resolution* [on Ryuku Island (Okinawa)] (1969). Calls for peace and prosperity in Asia.

Episcopal Church [USA], *General Convention Resolution* [on Namibia (South-West Africa)] (1973).

Episcopal Church [USA], *General Convention Resolution* [on peace education] (1973).

Episcopal Church [USA], *General Convention Resolution* [on thankfulness for Israeli-Egyptian peace treaty] (1979). Concerned about peace in the Middle East.

Episcopal Church [USA], *Middle East Affairs* (1982). Concerned about peace in the Middle East.

Episcopal Church [USA], *Military Aid to El Salvador* (1982). Calls for a just peace in Central America.

Episcopal Church [USA], *Commend Bishop Tutu* (1985). Prays for peace in South Africa.

Episcopal Church [USA], *Encourage Contact with Episcopal Churches in Central America* (1985).

Episcopal Church [USA], *Encourage Seminary Courses on Peace* (1985).

Episcopal Church [USA], *Nuclear Freeze and Peacemaking* (1985), B, D.

Episcopal Church [USA], *Work for Peace in Nicaragua and All Central America* (1985). Calls for peace in Central America.

Evangelical Lutheran Church in Southern Africa, *Lesotho Killings* (1982). Concerned about peace on the African continent.

Evangelical Lutheran Church in Tanzania, *Regarding Salvation and Tyranny That Is Continuing in Africa* (1978). The position may be warranted by appeal to the concept "Word of God".

Evangelische Kirche der Kirchenprovinz Sachsen, *Vorlage des Berichtsausschusses* (1984), 1, 2.2.

Evangelische Kirche der Kirchenprovinz Sachsen, *Beschluss zur Teilnahme am konziliaren Prozess* (1985).

Evangelische Kirche der Union — Bereich Bundesrepublik Deutschland und Berlin-West, *Stellungnahme der Synode der EKU zu UNCTAD III* (1974). Calls for social peace.

Evangelische Kirche der Union — Bereich Bundesrepublik Deutschland und Berlin-West, *Beschlüsse auf Vorlage des Berichtsausschusses* (1978), 4. Concerned about peace in Europe.

Evangelische Kirche der Union — Bereich Bundesrepublik Deutschland und Berlin-West, *Politische Dimension kirchlichen Handelns* (1982).

Evangelische Kirche der Union — Bereich Deutsche Demokratische Republik, *Beschluss der 3. Ordentlichen Tagung der 6. Synode der EKU — Bereich DDR* (1986).

Evangelische Kirche im Rheinland, *Beschlussanträge des Öffentlichkeitsausschusses* (1966). Urges peace in Vietnam.

Evangelische Kirche im Rheinland, *Erklärung zur Lage in Nahost* (1968). Calls for peace in the Near East.

Evangelische Kirche im Rheinland, *Erklärung zur Lage in Vietnam* (1973). Concerned about peace in Vietnam; endorses Evangelische Kirche in Deutschland, *Entschliessung der Synode in Vietnam* (1973), and National Council of Churches [USA], *The Indochina War: Healing the Divisions of the Nation* (1972), which, warranted by ecclesiology and perhaps Christology, called for amnesty for Americans in legal difficulties due to the Vietnam War.

Evangelische Kirche im Rheinland, *Sonderfonds zur Bekämpfung des Rassismus* (1979), 6.

Evangelische Kirche im Rheinland, *Kriegsspielzeug* (1988). Opposes use of violence.

Evangelische Kirche in Deutschland, *Ermutigung zur Fortsetzung des Weges zur Abrüstung* (1987). Cites a 1983 statement calling for peace.

Evangelische Kirche in Hessen und Nassau, *Antrag Trautwein* (1965). Proposes refusing to give children toy soldiers as Christmas presents. The motion may not have been approved.

Evangelische Kirche in Hessen und Nassau, *Entschliessung der Kirchensynode der EKHN zum Vietnam-Krieg* (1968). Calls for peace in Vietnam; relates it to justice.

Evangelische Kirche in Hessen und Nassau, *Erklärung der Kirchensynode zur Lage in Biafra* (1969), 24, 23. Concerned about peace in Nigeria and Biafra.

Evangelische Kirche in Hessen und Nassau, *Erklärung der Synode der EKHN zum Aufruf zu einem "Ökumenischen Konzil des Friedens"* (1985). Relates justice to peace.

Evangelische Kirche in Österreich, *Beschluss der Generalsynode* [betr. Zivildienst] (1990).

Evangelische Kirche von Kurhessen-Waldeck, *Beschluss der Landessynode über den Antrag der Kreissynode Hanau-Stadt zur Friedensfrage* (1981). Reference to the Word of God may be a background warrant.

Evangelische Landeskirche Anhalts, *Drucksache 44/18* (1986), 1.5.

Evangelische Landeskirche Anhalts, *Entschliessung der Landessynode zum Bericht der Kirchenpräsidenten* (1985). Christology and Scripture may be background warrants.

Evangelische Landeskirche in Baden, *Entschliessung der Landessynode der ELB zum Konzil des Friedens und zur Weltversammlung für Gerechtigkeit, Frieden und Bewahrung der Schöpfung* (1985). Relates peace to justice and ecology.

Evangelische Landeskirche in Württemberg, *Friedensauftrag der Kirche* (1979). Insofar as the statement cites Evangelische Kirche in Deutschland und Bund der Evangelischen Kirchen in der Deutschen Demokratischen Republik, *Wort zum Frieden* (1979).

Evangelische Landeskirche in Württemberg, *Beschluss zur Friedensfrage ["Konzil des Friedens"] vom 28. November 1985.*

Evangelisch-Lutherische Kirche in Bayern, *Erklärung der Landessynode zur Genfer Gipfel-Konferenz* (1985).

Evangelisch-Lutherische Kirche in Bayern, *Kirche in der Diaspora. Christ sein in der Welt* (1988), 3.2.

Evangelisch-Lutherische Landeskirche Hannovers, *Erklärung der Landessynode der ELLH zu dem Anti-Rassismus-Programm des Ökumenischen Rates der Kirche* (1970), 2.

Evangelisch-Lutherische Landeskirche Sachsens, *Wort der Landessynode vom 24.10.1973.* Calls for just order and peace, especially in Chile and in the Near/Middle East.

Evangelisch-Lutherische Landeskirche Sachsens, *An die Gemeinden der Evangelisch-Lutherischen Landeskirche Sachsens* (1984).

Evangelisch-Lutherische Landeskirche Sachsens, *Brief der Landessynode an die Gemeinden zur Friedensfrage vom 16.10.85.*

Evangelisch-Lutherische Landessynode Sachsens, *Beschluss der ELLS vom 23.03.1983.*

Evangelisch-Lutherische Landessynode Sachsens, *Beschluss der Friedensverantwortung der ELLS vom 17.3.85.*

Evêques [catholiques] Suisses, *Déclaration des évêques suisses sur l'encyclique "Humanae Vitae"* (1968), 5.

Fédération Protestante de France, *Pour la paix au Vietnam* (1966). Concerned about peace in Vietnam.

Fédération Protestante de France, *Vœux adoptés à l'Assemblée du PF à La Rochelle* (1983), 1, 5.

Fédération Protestante de France, *Délibération de la 18ème Assemblée Générale du PF sur le projet "Convocation mondiale par la justice, la paix et la sauvegarde de la création"* (1987).

Fédération Protestante de France, *Vœux à l'Assemblée Générale* (1987), 5. Concerned about peace in New Caledonia.

Fellowship of Christian Churches (Chile), *Let the Floodgates of Democratic Participation Be Opened* (1984), III.

Greek Orthodox Archdiocese of North and South America, *Against Racism* (1963). Relates peace to justice and opposition to racism.

International Council of Community Churches [USA], *Statement of Concern* [on ecology] (1983). Claims only that peace begins with us.

Irish Episcopal Conference, *The Storm That Threatens* (1983), 2, 5.

Italian Episcopal Conference, *Message of the Bishops to the Catholic Communities of Italy* (1977).

Lippische Landeskirche, *Beschluss der Landessynode 1985 Stichwort: Friedenskonzil*.

Lutheran Church-Missouri Synod, *To Encourage Peacemaking and the Study of Problems concerning the Church and Nuclear Arms* (1983).

Lutheran World Federation, *Our Responsibility for Peace and Justice* (1984), 13.1.1, 11; 13.4.2.3, 8. In the last articles cited, peace is authorized by the gospel, but such authorization does not pertain to the entire statement.

Lutheran World Federation, *Statement on "The Unity We Seek"* (1984).

Mennonite Brethren Churches, *Regarding Political Involvement* (1966). Relates peace to love.

Mennonite Church [USA], *Telegram to President Kennedy* (1965).

Mennonite Church [USA], *Resolution on Central America* (1983).

Mennonite Church [USA], *Resolution on Conscientious Objection to Military Taxes* (1983).

Mennonite Church [USA], *Resolution on South Africa* (1987). Concerned about peace and social justice in South Africa.

Mennonite Church, General Conference [USA], *Resolution on Vietnam* (1965). Concerned with peace in Vietnam.

Methodist Church of Ireland, *Resolution of the 1984 Conference*.

National Association of Evangelicals [USA], *The Use of Force* (1977). Cites a 1952 resolution of the association.

National Association of Evangelicals [USA], *Middle East Resolution* (1978). Predestination may be a background warrant in this call for peace in the Middle East.

National Association of Evangelicals [USA], *Threat of Nuclear Holocaust* (1982). Cites a 1952 resolution of the association.

National Conference of Catholic Bishops [USA], *Resolution on Peace* (1967). Urges peace in Vietnam.

National Conference of Catholic Bishops [USA], *War in the Middle East* (1967). Urges peace in the Middle East.

National Conference of Catholic Bishops [USA], *Statement on Farm Labor* (1968), 9-10, 12. Calls for peace in dispute among American growers and farm workers. Anthropology could be a background warrant.

National Conference of Catholic Bishops [USA], *Resolution on Farm Labor* (1975), 3. Urges peace and justice in the agricultural industry.

National Council of Churches [USA], *China* (1966), Int.

National Council of Churches [USA], *World Population and the Demands of Justice* (1968).

National Council of Churches [USA], *The Church and Television, Radio and Cable Communication* (1972), III.

Nordelbische Evangelisch-Lutherische Kirche, *Beschluss der Synode vom 21. Januar 1983*. Only partially endorses, but basically criticizes, a 1980 declaration of the church's Kirchenleitung, *Erklärung zu Frieden und Abrüstung*.

[Orthodox] Ecumenical Patriarchate of Constantinople, *Message de Sa Sainteté le Patriarche œcuménique Dimitrios Ier à l'occasion de la fête de Noël 1984*.

Polish [Catholic] Bishops, *Polish Bishops Invite the Whole Nation to Prayer for the Fatherland* (1971), 1-4. Especially concerned about peace in Poland. Christology and ecclesiology may be background warrants.

Polish [Catholic] Episcopacy, *Letter* (1970).

Polish [Catholic] Episcopacy, *Communique of the 146th Plenary Assembly of the Polish Episcopacy* (1975), 1.

Presbyterian Church in Taiwan, *Our Appeal* (1975), Int.; II.3; II.5. Only concerned about peace in Taiwan.

Reformed Church in America, *Addendum to Report of the Christian Action Commission to the 1965 General Synod*. Urges peace in Vietnam.

Reformed Church in America, *Report of the Christian Action Commission* (1968), 3. Urges peace in Vietnam.

Reformed Church in America, *Report of the Christian Action Commission* (1969), R-10. Urges peace in Vietnam.

Reformed Church in America, *Report of the Christian Action Commission* (1970), R-2, R-4. Urges peace in Vietnam. Christology is in the background.

Reformed Church in America, *Report of the Christian Action Commission* (1971), Rec. 23. Urges peace in Indo-China.

Reformed Church in America, *Report of the Christian Action Commission* (1972), R-4 Floor Motion. Urges peace in Vietnam.

Reformed Church in America, *Report of the Christian Action Commission* (1973), R-7 Floor Motion. Urges peace in Vietnam.

Reformed Church in America, *Report of the Christian Action Commission* (1980), R-6.

Reformed Church in America, *Report of the Christian Action Commission* (1982), R-13, R-1a. Urges peace in El Salvador; calls for "Christian action" on peacemaking.

Reformed Church in America, *Report of the Christian Action Commission* (1983), R-9.

Reformed Church in America, *Report of the Christian Action Commission* (1985), R-3d, R-4.

Religious Denominations of the USSR, *Declaration on Peace* (1982). With appeal for disarmament, no further deployment.

Roman Catholic Church, *Redemptor Hominis* (1979), 17, 13-16. Though eschatology or loci from other articles of the creed could function as warrants.

Roman Catholic Church, *Laborem Exercens* (1981), 27, 18, 16, 2. Though the encyclical does refer to Christology in the first section cited as authorizing the Christian willingness to suffer for peace; elsewhere, however, eschatology or anthropology grounded in redemption are said to authorize the church's social concern.

Romanian Orthodox Church, *Lettre irénique adressée par Sa Béatitude le Patriarche Justinian aux chefs des Eglises chrétiennes à l'occasion de la Sainte Fête de la Nativité* (1974). Relates peace to social justice.

Romanian Orthodox Church, *Message of the Holy Synod of the ROC Addressed to A.M. Nicolae Ceauşescu, President of Romania* (1974). Concerned about peace in Romania; praises the prosperity and freedom under Ceauşescu's socialist leadership.

Romanian Orthodox Church, *Lettre irénique de Sa Béatitude le Patriarche Iustin — Pâques 1983*.

Russian Orthodox Church, *Patriarch Alexius an den sowjetischen Friedensrat* (1966).

Russian Orthodox Church, *Erklärung des Patriarchen zum israelischen überfall auf den Beiruter Flughafen* (1969). Calls for peace in the Near East.

Russian Orthodox Church, *Verfügungen des Heiligen Synods* (1973). Calls for a just peace.

Russian Orthodox Church, *Letters of the Holy Synod to the Soviet Government* (1977).

Russian Orthodox Church, *Decrees of the Holy Synod* (1980).

Russian Orthodox Church, *Decrees of the Holy Synods* (1981)

Russian Orthodox Church, *Botschaft des hochheiligen Patriarchen zur 300-Jahr-Feier des Bistums Woronesh* (1982).

Russian Orthodox Church, *Decrees of the Holy Synod* (1982). Also concerned about disarmament; would make the Indian Ocean a zone of peace.

Russian Orthodox Church, *Message of Patriarch Pimen and the Holy Synods on the Occasion of the Sixtieth Anniversary of the Founding of the USSR* (1982).

Russian Orthodox Church, *Decrees of the Holy Synod of the ROC* (1985). Relates peace to justice; is especially concerned about peace in Europe.

Russian Orthodox Church, *Decrees of the Holy Synod* (1986). Relates peace to justice and disarmament. The Holy Spirit provides motivation.

Russian Orthodox Church, *Letter to General Secretary M.S. Gorbachev* (1986).

South African Council of Churches, *Resolution No. 5: Disinvestment* (1985), B. Concerned about peace in South Africa.

Southern African Catholic Bishops Conference, *Call for an End to Conscription* (1985). Concerned about peace in Southern Africa.

Sudanese Catholic Bishops' Conference, *Statement of the SCBC to the Transitional Government of the Sudan* (1985), Conc. Concerned about peace, justice, and unity in Sudan.

United Church of Canada, *Report of the Committee on the Church and International Affairs* (1971).

United Church of Canada, *South Africa* (1972). Relates peace to the overcoming of apartheid.

United Church of Canada, *United Nations Charter Revision* (1972).

United Church of Canada, *The Middle East* (1977).

United Church of Canada, *Confessing Our Faith in a Nuclear Age* (1984). Also condemns the use of nuclear weapons.

United Church of Canada, *Conscientious Objection to War and Tax Reduction* (1986).

United Church of Canada, *Alternate Defence for Canada* (1988).

United Church of Canada, *Nuclear-Powered Submarines* (1988).

United Church of Christ [USA], *Report of the Council on Christian Social Action, as Finally Adopted* (1965), 13, 14, 19. Calls for peace in Vietnam; claims war is incompatible with Christian teaching.

United Church of Christ [USA], *International Relations and International Development* (1967). Makes a special reference to a concern for peace in Vietnam.

United Church of Christ [USA], *On Justice and Peace in Vietnam* (1967). Calls for peace in Vietnam; cites the denomination's *Report of the Council for Christian Social Action, as Finally Adopted* (1965), 13.

United Church of Christ [USA], *Resolution on the Middle East* (1967). Concerned about peace in the Middle East.

United Church of Christ [USA], *Hunger, Population and World Development* (1969).

United Church of Christ [USA], *Joint Statement on Vietnam* (1969). Refers to the denomination's 1967 resolution *On Justice and Peace in Vietnam*, in its concern about peace in Vietnam.

United Church of Christ [USA], *Peace Education* (1969).

United Church of Christ [USA], *Peace and United States Power* (1971). Especially, though not exclusively, is concerned about peace in the Middle East.

United Church of Christ [USA], *Peace and Reconciliation in Angola* (1981). Calls for peace in Angola.

United Church of Christ [USA], *All-Church Peace Offering* (1983).

United Church of Christ [USA], *Civil Defense (Executive Council, 6/29/83)* (1983). An appeal to creation may be in the background.

United Church of Christ [USA], *Developing the UCC(USA) as a Peacemaking Church* (1983).

United Church of Christ [USA], *Direct Investment in Weapons Producers* (1983). Also recommends limiting direct investments in weapons producers.

United Church of Christ [USA], *Impact of U.S. Foreign and Military Policy on Central America* (1983). Concerned about peace in Central America.

United Church of Christ [USA], *Action for Peace in Central America* (1985). Calls for peace in Central America.

United Church of Christ [USA], *Promoting East-West Citizen Dialogue* (1985).

United Church of Christ [USA], *Peace and the Reunification of Korea* (1987). Concerned about peace and justice in Korea.

United Church of Christ [USA], *Peace in Afghanistan* (1987). Concerned about peace, justice, and self-determination in Afghanistan.

United Church of Christ [USA], *Response to Comrades Invitation* (1987). Concerned about social justice and peace, especially for children.

United Free Church of Scotland, *Deliverance of the General Assembly* [on public questions] (1967), 10, 12. Especially concerned about peace in Vietnam and in the Middle East.

United Free Church of Scotland, *Deliverance of the General Assembly* [on public questions] (1968), 11, 1. Especially concerned about peace in Rhodesia, Nigeria, the Middle East, and Vietnam.

United Free Church of Scotland, *Deliverance of the General Assembly* [on public questions] (1971), 1. Urges peace in the Middle East.

United Free Church of Scotland, *Deliverance of the General Assembly* [on public questions] (1972), 1, 11. Concerned about justice and peace in Northern Ireland.

United Free Church of Scotland, *Deliverance of the General Assembly* [on public questions] (1974), 1, 10, 12. At one point is especially concerned about peace in Northern Ireland.

United Free Church of Scotland, *Deliverance of the General Assembly* [on public questions] (1976), 1, 8. Concerned about justice and peace in Northern Ireland.

United Free Church of Scotland, *Deliverance of the General Assembly* [on public questions] (1977), 10. Urges a just peace in Northern Ireland.

United Free Church of Scotland, *Deliverance of the General Assembly* [on public questions] (1982), 9, 1. Welcomes initiatives of the British Council of Churches.

United Free Church of Scotland, *Deliverance of the General Assembly* [on public questions] (1986), 4. Concerned about world peace and a general disarmament.

United Free Church of Scotland, *Deliverance of the General Assembly* [on public questions] (1987), 1, 5.

United Free Church of Scotland, *Deliverance of the General Assembly* [on public questions] (1988), 8.

Uniting Church in Australia, *Bicentennial Celebrations* (1985), 85.40.4-5.

Vereinigte Evangelisch-Lutherische Kirche Deutschlands, *Erklärung der Generalsynode zum Rassismus* (1970). Concerned only with domestic peace in South Africa.

Vereinigte Evangelisch-Lutherische Kirche Deutschlands, *Entschliessung zum Fonds für Gerechtigkeit und Versöhnung* (1973), 1. Concerned only with domestic peace in South Africa.

Vereinigte Evangelisch-Lutherische Kirche Deutschlands, *Entschliessung der Generalsynode der VELKD zur Friedenssicherung und Friedensförderung vom 25. Juni 1980.*

Vereinigte Evangelisch-Lutherische Kirche Deutschlands, *Beschluss der Generalsynode der VELKD zur Friedensfrage vom 30. Oktober 1982.* Rejects the position of the Moderamens of the Reformed Alliance, *Das Bekenntnis zu Jesus Christus und die Friedensverantwortung der Kirche* (1981), I.

Vereinigte Evangelisch-Lutherische Kirche in der DDR, *Beschluss zum Tätigkeitsbericht der Kirchenleitung vom 24.9.1977.*

Vereinigte Evangelisch-Lutherische Kirche in der DDR, *Beschluss der Generalsynode zu den Berichten des Leitenden Bischofs und der Kirchenleitung vom 28.6.1981.*

Vereinigte Evangelisch-Lutherische Kirche in der DDR, *Beschluss der Generalsynode zum Bericht des amtierenden Leitenden Bischofs vom 16. Juni 1984.*

Vereinigte Evangelisch-Lutherische Kirche in der DDR, *Beschluss der Generalsynode über den Bericht des amtierenden Leitenden Bischofs vom 16. Juni 1985, 6.*

Waldensian and Methodist Churches in Italy, *Synod of the WMCI* (1981).

World Alliance of Reformed Churches, *Sri Lanka* (1989). Calls for peace in Sri Lanka.

World Alliance of Reformed Churches, *Sudan* (1989). Calls for justice and peace in Sudan.

WCC Canberra Assembly, *The Report of the Seventh Assembly* (1991), 7, 21, 49, 51. Especially concerned about peace in the Persian Gulf. Pneumatology may be a background warrant.

WCC Nairobi Assembly, *Education for Liberation and Community* (1975), 40.

WCC New Delhi Assembly, *The Message of the Assembly to the Churches* (1961), 6. Some apparent reference is made to Christology/gospel warrants, but the Christian's need to work through secular agencies to serve humanity may suggest this value is accessible to all, grounded in creation.

WCC Vancouver Assembly, *Learning in Community* (1983), 18, 29.

4-3 JUST WAR AND PACIFISM

We may distinguish at least the following six positions of the churches on the issue of war — ranging from openness to the idea of any kind of (just) war, to an absolute rejection of any war. As usual, theological justifications of the various positions overlap almost completely.

A.   Concedes valid government involvement in war/just war
    A1.   Appeal to creation
    A2.   Appeal to creation, with Christology in the background
    A3.   Appeal to Christology/the gospel
    A4.   Appeal to the gospel/Christian duty
    A5.   Appeal to the gospel and natural law
    A6.   Appeal to redemption
    A7.   Appeal to loci drawn from the second and third articles
    A8.   Appeal to the Bible/Word of God
    A9.   No clear theological warrant given for position

B.   Views nuclear war as not a just war (though relatively open to the concept of a just war)
    B1.   Appeal to creation
    B2.   Appeal to creation, with Christology in the background
    B3.   Appeal to creation, perhaps grounded in Christology
    B4.   Appeal to creation/natural law and the gospel, with creation perhaps grounded in the gospel
    B5.   Appeal to Christology/the gospel/redemption
    B6.   Appeal to Christology and creation
    B7.   Appeal to loci drawn from the second and third articles
    B8.   Appeal to all articles of the creed
    B9.   Appeal to the Word of God
    B10. Position motivated by faith
    B11. Position motivated by the Christian faith
    B12. No clear theological warrant given for position

C.   Open to conscientious objection (though not to the exclusion of the concept of a just war)
   C1.   Appeal to creation/moral law/view of human persons
   C2.   Appeal to creation and Christology/the gospel
   C3.   Appeal to creation, perhaps grounded in Christology
   C4.   Appeal to creation and the gospel, with the former perhaps grounded in the latter
   C5.   Appeal to Christology/the gospel
   C6.   Appeal to Christology/reconciliation
   C7.   Appeal to Christology/the Christian faith
   C8.   Apparent appeal to pneumatology
   C9.   Appeal to themes from all articles of the creed, with all themes subordinated to Christology
   C10. Appeal to the Word of God
   C11. Appeal to Christian responsibility/the gospel and baptism
   C12. Appeal to the Christian faith
   C13. No clear theological warrant given for position

D.   Opposes military conscription (and rejects the concept of a just war)
   D1.   No clear theological warrant given for position

E.   Open to conscientious objection (but rejects the concept of a just war)
   E1.   Appeal to Christology
   E2.   No clear theological warrant given for position

F.   Supports absolute pacifism (non-resistance)
   F1.   Appeal to creation/anthropology
   F2.   Appeal to Christology
   F3.   Appeal to the gospel
   F4.   Appeal to Christology and pneumatology
   F5.   Appeal to ecclesiology
   F6.   Appeal to all three articles of the creed
   F7.   Appeal to the Bible
   F8.   Appeal to the Bible, the righteousness of God, and perhaps Christology
   F9.   No clear theological warrant given for position

A. CONCEDES VALID GOVERNMENT INVOLVEMENT IN WAR/JUST WAR

A1. Appeal to creation

American Lutheran Church, *War, Peace, and Freedom* (1966), 14-15, 35, 3. Statement may not have official status; relies on two-kingdom ethic.
Church of Norway, *Kirken og freden* (1982), I(4), III(2)(f). At least seems to argue from a two-kingdom ethic perspective.

A2. Appeal to creation, with Christology in the background

Presbyterian Church (USA), *Christian Obedience in a Nuclear Age* (1988), 5, 1. Primarily appeals to the concept of international law for authorization.

A3. Appeal to Christology/the gospel

Lutheran-Episcopal Dialogue, series 3 [USA], *Implications of the Gospel* (1988), 85, 123.

A4. Appeal to the gospel/Christian duty

Christian Reformed Church in North America, *Decision of 1969.* Takes this position and authorization in virtue of affirming the church's 1939 decision *Testimony concerning the Christian's Attitude toward War and Peace,* which took this position with such an argument.
Christian Reformed Church in North America, *Acts of Synod* (1973), 79-81. Takes this position in virtue of reaffirming the two decisions cited above.

A5. Appeal to the gospel and natural law

United Presbyterian Church [USA], *War, Peace, and Conscience* (1969).

A6. Appeal to redemption

South African Council of Churches, *Conscientious Objection* (1974).

A7. Appeal to loci drawn from the second and third articles

All Africa Conference of Churches, *The Gospel of Reconciliation* (1981). At least open to the use of violence in rebellion against oppression. Also see a 1983 statement of the Southern African Catholic Bishops Conference.
Conference of European Churches and Council of European Bishops' Conferences, *Final Document of the European Ecumenical Assembly Peace with Justice* (1989), 86, 77-79, 25-27. These themes likely function as warrants insofar as they appear to justify the recommendations. Appeals to the theme of covenant, which has a trinitarian content, may be in the background.

A8. Appeal to the Bible/Word of God

Christian Reformed Church in North America, *Guidelines for Ethical Decisions about War* (1977), Int. C.

A9. No clear theological warrant given for position

American Baptist Churches, *Policy Statement on Peace* (1985). Cites with some approval the 1983 pastoral on peace of the National Conference of Catholic Bishops (USA), which condemned nuclear war on just-war principles.
American Lutheran Church, *Mandate for Peacemaking* (1982), A.9; A.1-A.3. Appeals to Christology/the gospel and third-article loci are in the background.
Canadian Conference of Catholic Bishops, *A Brief to the Standing Committee on External Affairs and National Defence: On Preparation for the Second Special Session of the United Nations on Disarmament* (1982), 2.5.
Christian Reformed Church in North America, *Guidelines for Justifiable Warfare* (1982), 5-6.
Church of Norway, *Abortspørsmåalet* (1971), 2.
Evangelical Lutheran Church in Tanzania, *Regarding a Christian Use of Weapons* (1980). Could be open to conscientious objection. There is only a hint of a warrant that a Christian should "obey God rather than man".
Lutheran Church-Missouri Synod, *To Adopt a Statement on Conscientious Objection* (1969).

B. VIEWS NUCLEAR WAR AS NOT A JUST WAR
(THOUGH RELATIVELY OPEN TO THE CONCEPT OF A JUST WAR)

B1. Appeal to creation

Canadian Conference of Catholic Bishops, *A Brief to the Standing Committee on External and National Defence: On Preparation for the Second Special Session of the United Nations on Disarmament* (1982), 1.5; Int.

Evangelische Landeskirche in Baden, *Wort an die Gemeinden* (1982), 3.

Lutheran Church in America, *World Community: Ethical Imperatives in an Age of Interdependence* (1970), 4-5.

Lutheran Church in America, *Peace and Politics* (1984), 1, 9, 10.

National Council of Churches [USA], *Defense and Disarmament* (1968).

Roman Catholic Church, *Pacem in Terris* (1963), 127, 5, 10, 147, 157. Appeal to natural law could be subordinated to redemption. At least it posits a creation-redemption continuity.

Russian Orthodox Church, *Decrees of the Holy Synod* (1983).

Russian Orthodox Church, *Jubiläumsbotschaft zum Millennium der Taufe Russlands* (1987).

United Church of Canada, *False Apocalypticism and the Church* (1984). Insofar as the statement advocates the collaboration of all people in working towards common goals.

United Church of Canada, *Nuclear War* (1984). Insofar as the use of nuclear weapons is deemed a crime against humanity.

B2. Appeal to creation, with Christology in the background

Presbyterian Church (USA), *Christian Obedience in a Nuclear Age* (1988), 27, 8, 5, 2, 1. At least authorizes defence of a just war primarily by appeal to international law.

B3. Appeal to creation, perhaps grounded in Christology

Irish Episcopsal Conference, *The Storm That Threatens* (1983), 1, 3, 5. Appeal to natural law seems to function as warrant. However, in view of the statement's citation of Vatican II's *Gaudium et Spes,* 22, which subordinates creation to Christology, perhaps this Irish statement is positing such a subordination of this loci.

National Conference of Catholic Bishops [USA], *Peace and Vietnam* (1966), 6-8, 1. Apparent appeals to creation may be rooted in Christology, in view of the statement's citation of *Gaudium et Spes.*

Roman Catholic Church, Vatican II, *Gaudium et Spes* (1965), 79-80, 76-77, 22. Specifically condemns "total warfare".

Russian Orthodox Church, *Open Letter to the President of the USA Ronald W. Reagan* (1983).

B4. Appeal to creation/natural law and the gospel,
with creation perhaps grounded in the gospel

Episcopal Church [USA], *General Convention Resolution* [on establishing a Joint Commission on Peace] (1979). Cites a 1962 statement of the House of Bishops.

Episcopal Church [USA], *"To Make Peace" Report* (1985). Takes this position in virtue of approving the statement of the church's Joint Commission on Peace, *To Make Peace* (1982), I/C, For., Int., Aft., which argued its case with this sort of authorization.

National Conference of Catholic Bishops [USA], *Human Life in Our Day* (1968), 105, 99, 95. In view of citations from Vatican II's *Gaudium et Spes,* 22, which subordinates creation to redemption, perhaps this American statement's appeals to these loci entail a similar subordination.

National Conference of Catholic Bishops [USA], *The Challenge of Peace: God's Promise and Our Response* (1983), 71-100, 120-61, 284-301, 329, 333, 339, 58, 57, 13-15, 2. Perhaps with appeals to the Mass and kingdom as background warrants, insofar as the former is said to create conditions for peace. In view of citations from *Gaudium et Spes,* 22, which subordinate creation to redemption, perhaps references to the gospel are the prevailing warrants. It also expresses an openness to pacifism, inasmuch as this view is said to be rooted in the Christian tradition.

B5. Appeal to Christology/the gospel/redemption

Anglican Church of Canada, *Disarmament* (1983). This claim is implicit in the rejection of the use of nuclear arms.

Anglicanism, *Resolutions of the Lambeth Conference (1978),* 5.

Anglicanism, *The Resolutions of the Lambeth Conference (1988),* 27.

Baptist Union of Great Britain and Ireland, *Test Ban Treaty* (1964). Endorses a 1963 resolution of the British Council of Churches. At least opposes the first use of nuclear arms by the West.

British Council of Churches, *The Nuclear Deterrent and the Test Ban Treaty* (1963), (iii), (iv). Insofar as the use of nuclear weapons is said to be intolerable to the Christian conscience.

British Council of Churches, *Policy Proposals* (1983). Insofar as the use of nuclear weapons is said to be intolerable to the Christian conscience; cites the earlier 1963 decision of the council in support.

Bund der Evangelischen Kirchen in der Deutschen Demokratischen Republik, *Beschluss der Synode des BEK-DDR zum mündlichen Bericht der Konferenz der Evangelischen Kirchenleitungen vom 28. September 1982,* II.

Bund der Evangelischen Kirchen in der Deutschen Demokratischen Republik, *Beschluss der Synode des Bundes zum Bericht der Konferenz der Evangelischen Kirchenleitungen in der DDR vom 19. September 1983,* 4. Cites the WCC Vancouver Assembly, *Statement on Peace and Justice* (1983), 26, in the resolution's call for non-participation of Christians in any war.

Church of Ireland, *The Report of the Role of the Church Committee* (1983), 6. May even be opposed to the concept of a just war in the present, since it may likely lead to nuclear holocaust.

Congregational Union of Scotland, *Nuclear Armaments* (1981). Insofar as appeal is made to the Christian conscience.

Episcopal Church [USA], *General Convention Resolution* [affirming Lambeth statement *War and Violence*] (1979).

Episcopal Church [USA], *Non-violent War Resistance* (1982). Affirms the preceding 1979 resolution of the church as well as 1930, 1948, 1958, and 1968 statements of the Lambeth Conference.

Evangelische Kirche von Westfalen, *Pastoralbrief der Generalsynode zur Kernwaffenrüstung vom November 1980.*

Evangelisch-Lutherische Landeskirche Sachsens, *Kanzelabkündigung der Landessynode, des Landesbischofs und Landeskirchenamtes vom 24.03.1982.* In the sense that it is claimed that there can be no victor in a nuclear war.

Netherlands [Catholic] Bishops Conference, *Vrede en gerechtigheid* (1983), II/2; I/1. Though the latter appeal to Christology may not pertain here.

United Church of Canada, *Manifesto on Nuclear Disarmament* (1982). Insofar as, on the basis of the covenant, nuclear war is rejected.

United Church of Canada, *Confessing Our Faith in a Nuclear Age* (1984). At least an appeal to the gospel is in the background of this condemnation of the use of nuclear weapons.

World Alliance of Reformed Churches, *The Theatre of Glory and a Threatened Creation's Hope* (1982). Insofar as a call is made for nations not to use nuclear arms.

World Alliance of Reformed Churches, *Statement on Peace* (1989), 4.1; 3.2. Calls for critical study of just (and thus nuclear) war.

WCC Evanston Assembly, *International Affairs — Christians in the Struggle for World Community* (1954), Res. I; I; Int. Seems to take this position insofar as it is urged that nuclear weapons be eliminated.

WCC Vancouver Assembly, *Statement on Peace and Justice* (1983), 20, 23, 25. Statement hints that the attitude taken towards nuclear weapons is a *status confessionis,* "a question of Christian discipline and faithfulness to the gospel". Endorsed by Evangelische Kirche im Rheinland, *Kriegsdienstverweigerung* (1985).

World Methodist Council Conference, *A Call to End the Arms Race* (1981). Seems to take this position by appealing to the "Prince of Peace" and in urging the outlawing of the use of all nuclear arms.

B6. Appeal to Christology and creation

Canadian Conference of Catholic Bishops, *The Neutron Bomb — Enough!* (1981). Appeals to the nature of the Christian faith.

Council of Churches in the Netherlands, *Letter to the Minister-President* (1978). For references to two statements of the [Catholic] Bishops of the Netherlands which subscribe to this letter, see p. 224 above.

Council of Churches in the Netherlands, *Letter to the Council of Ministers and the Houses of Parliament* (1984), 2. Seems to oppose nuclear war insofar as the use of nuclear arms is condemned. Creation is the primary warrant.

Moderamens of the Reformed Alliance, *Das Bekenntnis zu Jesus Christus und die Friedens-verantwortung der Kirche* (1981), Erl. III; Erl. V. Though creation is only a background warrant.

National Conference of Catholic Bishops [USA], *Resolution on Southeast Asia* (1971), 5. Cites the encyclical *Pacem in Terris* (1963), 127.

National Conference of Catholic Bishops [USA], *Resolution towards Peace in the Middle East* (1973).

Russian Orthodox Church, *Message of the Holy Synod of the ROC on War and Peace in a Nuclear Age* (1986), 1.1, 1.2, 1.4, 1.6, 1.7, 2.14, 2.16, 2.18-2.19, 3.34, 4.

United Church of Canada, *Nuclear Arms* (1972). Insofar as the use of nuclear weapons is rejected.

United Church of Christ [USA], *Weapons of Mass Destruction* (1983). Insofar as the nations are called to forswear a first strike.

Uniting Church in Australia, *Militarism and Disarmament* (1982), 82.57, (6), (1b), (1a).

WCC Amsterdam Assembly, *The Church and the International Disorder* (1948), I. Seems to include appeal to the law, which entails a creation warrant.

WCC Uppsala Assembly, *Towards Justice and Peace in International Affairs* (1968), 4ff. Though much more explicit reference is made to Christology as warrant.

B7. Appeal to loci drawn from the second and third articles

Baptist Union of New Zealand, *Notices of Motion* (1984). Eschatology is only a background warrant.

United Presbyterian Church [USA], *Call to Peacemaking* (1980), I.

B8. Appeal to all articles of the creed

Moravian Church in America, Southern Province, *Nuclear Arms Race* (1983). Creation is likely subordinated to the other articles.

National Council of Churches in Korea, *Declaration of the Churches of Korea on National Reunification and Peace* (1988).

United Church of Christ [USA], *Reversing the Arms Race* (1979).

United Church of Christ [USA], *Affirming the United Church of Christ as a Just Peace Church* (1985), Pronouncement II-IV. The Trinitarian authorization for peace seems applicable.

Vereinigte Evangelisch-Lutherische Kirche Deutschlands, *Beschluss der Generalsynode der VELKD zu der "Erklärung zum Frieden" des Exekutivkomitees des Lutherischen Weltbundes vom 24. Oktober 1981*. Cites the LWF statement, 3-5, in the resolution's title.

Vereinigte Evangelisch-Lutherische Kirche in der DDR, *Beschluss der 5. Tagung der III. Generalsynode der VELK-DDR vom 8.-11. Juni 1983*, 1-3.

B9. Appeal to the Word of God

Christian Reformed Church in North America, *Guidelines for Justifiable Warfare* (1982), 9-11, 13. With pneumatology functioning as a motive.

Evangelische Kirche im Rheinland, *Die Friedenszusage Gottes und unser Streit um den Frieden* (1982).

International Council of Community Churches [USA], *Statement of Concern on Nuclear Weapons* (1982).

B10. Position motivated by faith

Catholic Bishops of the Philippines, *What Is Happening to Our Beautiful Land?* (1988). The gospel may be a background warrant.

B11. Position motivated by the Christian faith

World Alliance of Reformed Churches, *Justice, Peace and the Integrity of Creation* (1989). Also challenges the concept of a just war in the present context.

B12. No clear theological warrant given for position

All-Union Council of Evangelical Christians-Baptists [USSR], *Resolution* (1986). Takes this position insofar as it claims a nuclear war could not be permitted. Christology could be in the background, but this is not clear.

American Lutheran Church, *Mandate for Peacemaking* (1982), A.10; A.9; A.1-A.3. Though reference to the gospel/Christology and third-article loci may be operative.

Anglican Church of Canada, *Resolution on War and the Arms Race* (1983). At least insofar as the statement condemns a first use of nuclear weapons.

Anglicanism, *Resolutions of the Lambeth Conference (1968)*, 2. At least insofar as the use of nuclear weapons is condemned.

Bund der Evangelischen Kirchen in der Deutschen Demokratischen Republik, *Beschluss der Synode des BEK-DDR zu Fragen des Friedens* (1981). Insofar as the resolution endorses WCC Central Committee, *Increasing Threat to Peace and the Mandate of the Churches* (1983), III.

Bund der Evangelischen Kirchen in der Deutschen Demokratischen Republik, *Beschluss der Synode des BEK-DDR zum Bericht der Ev. Kirchenleitungen zu Friedensfragen* (1986), I. Cites Bund der Evangelischen Kirchen in der DDR und EKD, *Hoffnung auf Frieden,* which asserted that war is no means of conflict solution.

Bund der Evangelischen Kirchen in der Deutschen Demokratischen Republik, *Beschluss der Synode des BEK-DDR zum "Bekennen in der Friedensfrage"* (1987), II.

Catholic Bishops of the GDR, *For an Effective Service of Peace* (1983).

Christian Church (Disciples of Christ), *Regarding Non-Violent Social Deterrence* (1963).

Church of England, *General Synod Resolutions on "The Church and the Bomb"* (1983), 1. At least calls for a rejection of first use of nuclear arms. Reference to support such positions is made to "Christian teaching" and "moral obligation".

Church of Norway, *Om nøytronbomben* (1978). Insofar as the statement opposes use of nuclear weapons.

Church of the Province of Southern Africa [Anglican], *Conscientious Objection* (1985). At least endorses just-war concept.

Eglise Protestante Unie de Belgique, *Assemblée synodale* (1982).

Episcopal Church [USA], *General Convention Resolution* [on peace education] (1973).

Episcopal Church [USA], *Reaffirm the Right to Use Birth Control* (1982).

Episcopal Church [USA], *Use of Nuclear Weapons* (1982). At least insofar as the resolution condemns a first use of nuclear weapons.

Evangelische Kirche der Union — Bereich Deutsche Demokratische Republik, *Beschluss der 3. ordentlichen Tagung der 6. Synode der EKU — Bereich DDR* (1986).

Evangelische Kirche von Westfalen, *Friedensverantwortung der Kirche* (1982), II.

National Association of Evangelicals [USA], *Jesus Christ: Now More Than Ever!* (1979).

National Association of Evangelicals [USA], *Threat of Nuclear Holocaust* (1982).

Netherlands Reformed Church, *Pastoral Letter of the General Synod on the Question of Nuclear Armaments* (1980). Takes this position insofar as it endorses a 1962 resolution of the church which authorized its position by appeal to the Christian conscience.

Presbyterian Church (USA), *Life Abundant: Values, Choices and Health Care* (1988), 23, 7, 1. Though Christology may be a background warrant.

Reformed Church in America, *Report of the Christian Action Commission* (1982), R-1a.

Russian Orthodox Church, *Letter to John Paul II* (1986).

Russian Orthodox Church, *Easter Communication* (1988). Though love may be a background warrant.

United Church of Canada, *Civil Disobedience* (1984).

United Church of Canada, *Disarmament* (1986).

United Church of Christ [USA], *Developing the United Church of Christ as a Peacemaking Church* (1983).

United Church of Christ [USA], *Supporting the U.S. Catholic Bishops Pastoral Letter concerning Nuclear Armament and the Arms Race* (1983).

United Free Church of Scotland, *Deliverance of the General Assembly* [on public questions] (1969), 1.

United Free Church of Scotland, *Deliverance of the General Assembly* [on public questions] (1983), 1.

WCC Nairobi Assembly, *Public Affairs* (1975), 2. Insofar as the statement urges nations to pledge that they will not use weapons of mass destruction.

WCC World Convocation on Justice, Peace and the Integrity of Creation, *Final Document: Entering into Covenant Solidarity for Justice, Peace and the Integrity of Creation* (1990), 2.3.2.2; 2.1. At least insofar as the use of nuclear weapons and war in general are rejected. The concept of covenant, which reflects a trinitarian content, may function as the document's overriding warrant.

C. OPEN TO CONSCIENTIOUS OBJECTION
(THOUGH NOT TO THE EXCLUSION OF THE CONCEPT OF A JUST WAR)

C1. Appeal to creation/moral law/view of human persons

American Lutheran Church, *War, Peace, and Freedom* (1966), 14, 37, 38. Statement may not be official.

Church of Norway, *Kirken og freden* (1982), I(4), III(2)(f). At least seems to argue from a two-kingdom ethic perspective.

Episcopal Church [USA], *"To Make Peace" Report* (1985). Endorses selective conscientious objection, explicitly rejects pacifism, and endorses withholding taxes to be used for military expenditures in virtue of approving the statement of the church's Joint Commission on Peace, *To Make Peace* (1982), I/C, Int., For. The appeal to natural law could be subordinated to the Christian faith/revelation.

Evangelische Kirche im Rheinland, *Kriegsdienstverweigerung und Zivildienst* (1982) 1, 3. Argues that conscientious objection should include a responsibility to mandatory civil service.

Lutheran Church in America, *Conscientious Objection* (1968). Supports conscientious objection even to a particular war. Draws upon appeals to creation insofar as all persons, regardless of religious conviction, are deemed capable of conscientious objection.

Lutheran Church of Australia, *Conscientious Objection to Service in War* (1970), 2-4, 9. Strong statement of a two-kingdom ethic; open to conscientious objection only in certain contexts, not as an absolute commitment.

National Council of Churches [USA], *Rights and Responsibilities of Debate, Diversity and Dissent* (1966).

National Council of Churches [USA], *Conscientious Objection to Military Service* (1967). Supports selective conscientious objection.

Roman Catholic Church, Congregation for the Doctrine of the Faith, *Instruction on Respect for Human Life in Its Origin and the Dignity of the Human Person* (1987), III; Int.; I. Calls for conscientious objection in the sense of civil disobedience to laws which are not in conformity with natural law pertaining to sexuality and the unborn child's right to life. The gospel serves as a background warrant.

Southern Baptist Convention [USA], *A Statement of Social Principles* (1979), 4. Supports selective conscientious objection.

WCC Uppsala Assembly, *Towards Justice and Peace in International Affairs* (1968), 21, 17. Opts for selective conscientious objection.

C2. Appeal to creation and Christology/the gospel

Christian Church (Disciples of Christ), *Responsibilities of Conscience Regarding Participation in War* (1968). Supports selective conscientious objection to particular wars.

C3. Appeal to creation, perhaps grounded in Christology

National Conference of Catholic Bishops [USA], *Peace and Vietnam* (1966), 9, 6, 1. Apparent appeals to creation may be rooted in Christology, in view of the statement's citation of *Gaudium et Spes*.

Roman Catholic Church, Vatican II, *Gaudium et Spes* (1965), 79, 77, 76, 22.

C4. Appeal to creation and the gospel, with the former perhaps grounded in the latter

National Conference of Catholic Bishops [USA], *Human Life in Our Day* (1968), 150-153, 145. Supports selective conscientious objection. In view of references to Vatican II's *Gaudium et Spes,* 22, which subordinates creation to redemption, perhaps this American statement's appeals to these loci entail a similar subordination.

C5. Appeal to Christology/the gospel

Anglicanism, *The Resolutions of the Lambeth Conference (1988),* 27.

Bund der Evangelischen Kirchen in der Deutschen Demokratischen Republik, *Beschluss der Synode des BEK-DDR zum mündlichen Bericht der Konferenz der Evangelischen Kirchenleitungen vom 28. September 1982,* III. Authorized by faith, calls for an alternative service corps in the GDR.

Bund der Evangelischen Kirchen in der Deutschen Demokratischen Republik, *Beschluss der Synode des Bundes zum Bericht der Konferenz der Evangelischen Kirchenleitungen in der DDR vom 19. September 1983,* 4. Cites WCC Vancouver Assembly, *Statement on Peace and Justice* (1983), 25, 26.

Bund der Evangelischen Kirchen in der Deutschen Demokratischen Republik, *Beschluss der Synode des Bundes zum Bericht der Konferenz der Kirchenleitungen vom 25. September 1984,* 5. In the sense of suggesting alternative, non-military service as an option for GDR citizens.

Bund der Evangelischen Kirchen in der Deutschen Demokratischen Republik, *Beschluss der Synode des BEK-DDR zum Bericht der Konferenz der Ev. Kirchenleitungen zu Friedensfragen* (1986), 4. Authorized by the nature of faith.

Episcopal Church [USA], *Conscientious Objectors* (1967). Cites a 1934 resolution of the church in support.

Episcopal Church [USA], *Refusal to Participate in War* (1982).

Federation of Evangelical Churches in Italy, *Assembly of the FECI* (1982).

Lutheran World Federation, *I Have Heard the Cry of My People... The Assembly Message* (1990). Also makes reference to scripture. Creation may likewise be a background warrant.

Methodist Church in Malaysia, *Social Principles* (n.d.), III/E.2; III/B.1; II; I. With a passing reference to the doctrine of creation.

Moravian Church in America, Southern Province, *Conscientious Objection to Bearing Arms* (1968). Creates a formal process through which conscientious objectors must pass in order to be sanctioned.

National Association of Evangelicals [USA], *Military or Alternative Service* (1967). Christology seems to authorize both conscientious objection and military service. It opposes selective conscientious objection and conscientious objection without reference to religious conviction.

Presbyterian Church of Southern Africa, *Church and Nation, South Africa* (1979), 74.

Reformed Church in America, *Report of the Christian Action Commission* (1967), Rec. 2b. At least authorization was provided by Christology in a 1940 statement which was reaffirmed by the General Synod.

South African Council of Churches, *Conscientious Objection* (1974).

United Church of Christ [USA], *A Pronouncement on Selective Conscientious Objection* (1967). The love of God and his living Word authorize selective conscientious objection.

United Church of Christ [USA], *Support for Conscientious Objection to War* (1981).

United Church of Christ [USA], *War Tax Resistance* (1983). Supporting decisions of those who withhold taxes to be used by the military.

United Methodist Church [USA], *Social Principles of the UMC(USA)* (1980), V/G. Rejects enforced military service in peacetime. War is seen as incompatible with gospel.

United Presbyterian Church [USA], *War, Peace, and Conscience* (1969). Supports selective conscientious objection, even for those already serving in the military.

Uniting Church in Australia, *Militarism and Disarmament* (1982), 82.57, (4h), (1c), (1b). With the doctrine of creation possibly a background warrant.

Waldensian and Methodist Churches in Italy, *Synod of the WMCI* (1982).

WCC Vancouver Assembly, *Statement on Peace and Justice* (1983), 25. Endorsed by Evangelische Kirche im Rheinland, *Kriegsdienstverweigerung* (1988).

C6. Appeal to Christology/reconciliation

Evangelische Kirche der Pfalz, *Wort an die Gemeinden* (1981).

Evangelische Landeskirche in Württemberg, *Zur Bundeswehr gehen? Wehrdienst verweigern?* (1985).

Evangelische Landeskirche in Württemberg, *Brief der ELW an Wehrpflichtige* (1988).

C7. Appeal to Christology/the Christian faith

Anglicanism, *The Resolutions of the Lambeth Conference (1968)*, 8.

Bund der Evangelischen Kirchen in der Deutschen Demokratischen Republik, *Beschluss der Synode des BEK-DDR zum "Bekennen in der Friedensfrage"* (1987), II. Appeals to "the obedience of faith" for authorization.

Christian Church (Disciples of Christ), *Concerning Support for the Conscientious Objector to War* (1981).

Eglise de la Confession d'Augsbourg d'Alsace et de Lorraine, *Le problème de la paix* (1982).

Wesleyan Church [USA], *Special Directions* (1984), (3), Int.

C8. Apparent appeal to pneumatology

World Alliance of Reformed Churches, *Come Creator Spirit, for the Redemption of the World* (1964), C/1.

C9. Appeal to themes from all articles of the creed, with all themes subordinated to Christology

National Conference of Catholic Bishops [USA], *To Live in Jesus Christ: A Pastoral Reflection on the Moral Life* (1976), 2, 30, 31, 99, 115-16. Supports selective conscientious objection. Christology seems to be the prevailing warrant.

C10. Appeal to the Word of God

American Lutheran Church, *National Service and Selective Service* (1970), 5-7. Reference to God's Word and love could entail that the gospel is a warrant for conscientious objection, but this is not clear. It speaks of selective conscientious objection.

Christian Reformed Church in North America, *Decision of 1969*. Endorses selective conscientious objection. It reasserts the church's *Testimony concerning the Christian's Attitude toward War and Peace*, which also endorsed selective conscientious objection with the same mode of argument.

Christian Reformed Church in North America, *Acts of Synod* (1973), 79-81. Endorses selective conscientious objection in virtue of citing the church's 1939 decision cited above.

C11. Appeal to Christian responsibility/the gospel and baptism

United Church of Christ [USA], *Affirming the United Church of Christ as a Just Peace Church* (1985), A Proposal for Action IV/4, III, Pronouncement III. Earlier appeals to creation, pneumatology, ecclesiology, and eschatology could be relevant.

C12. Appeal to the Christian faith

Presbyterian Church (USA), *Christian Obedience in a Nuclear Age* (1988), 26, 28, 13. Endorses selective conscientious objection. Also, authorized by Christian conscience, it would support those who would refuse to pay specific taxes for military expenditures.

C13. No clear theological warrant given for position

American Baptist Churches, *Policy Statement on Church and State* (1986), 3.

American Lutheran Church, *Mandate for Peace* (1982), B.2; A.9; A.1-A.3. Supports selective conscientious objection. Christology/the gospel and two third-article loci could be in the background of the statement.

Baptist Union of New Zealand, *The Christian's Involvement in War* (1969).

British Council of Churches, *Selective Conscientious Objection* (1973). Supports selective conscientious objection.

Bund der Evangelischen Kirchen in der Deutschen Demokratischen Republik, *Beschluss der Generalsynode zu den Berichten des leitenden Bischofs und der Kirchenleitung vom 28. Juni 1981*, 5. At least supports those engaged in alternative service.

Bund der Evangelischen Kirchen in der Deutschen Demokratischen Republik, *Beschluss der Synode des BEK-DDR zu Fragen des Friedens* (1981). Insofar as the resolution endorses WCC Central Committee, *Increasing Threat to Peace and the Mandate of the Churches* (1981), III/G.

Bund der Evangelischen Kirchen in der Deutschen Demokratischen Republik, *Beschluss der Synode zu Gesprächen mit staatlichen Stellen* (1982). At least supports non-military service in the GDR in some form.

Bund der Evangelischen Kirchen in der Deutschen Demokratischen Republik, *Beschluss der Synode des Bundes zum Bericht der Konferenz der Ev. Kirchenleitungen vom 24. September 1985*, 2. Calls for an alternative service corps in the GDR.

Catholic Bishops of the GDR, *For an Effective Service of Peace* (1983). Though appeals to Christology elsewhere in statement.

Christian Church (Disciples of Christ), *Concerning the Church's Witness for Peace* (1971). Notes that earlier Disciples' resolutions had endorsed selective conscientious objection. Christology and the law are clearly in the background.

Christian Reformed Church in North America, *Guidelines for Ethical Decisions about War* (1977), Guideline 1.

Church of the Province of Southern Africa [Anglican], *Conscientious Objection* (1982), 2.

Church of the Province of Southern Africa [Anglican], *Conscientious Objection* (1985).

Church of the Province of Southern Africa [Anglican], *End Conscription* (1985).

Episcopal Church [USA], *The War in Vietnam* (1967).

Episcopal Church [USA], *General Convention Resolution* [on reconciliation, amnesty, and returned veterans] (1976).

Episcopal Church [USA], *General Convention Resolution* [on encouraging conscientious objectors to register] (1979).

Episcopal Church [USA], *Ministry to Conscientious Objectors* (1982).

Episcopal Church [USA], *Non-violent War Resistance* (1982).

Episcopal Church [USA], *Conscientious Objection as a Faithful Response to War* (1988).

Evangelische Kirche der Kirchenprovinz Sachsen, *Beschluss zur Gesamtthematik der Synodaltagung* (1985), 1. In the sense of calling for the option of alternative service in the social realm.

Evangelische Kirche in Hessen und Nassau, *Synodalbeschlüsse* (1978), 17. Calls for a change in procedures for testing decisions of conscience, presumably in order to allow civil service as a legitimate alternative to military service. Cites a 1973 resolution of the Evangelische Kirche in Deutschland in support.

Evangelische Kirche in Österreich, *Beschluss der Generalsynode* [betr. Zivildienst] (1990).

Evangelische Kirche von Westfalen, *Friedensverantwortung der Kirche* (1982), IV. The statement was endorsed by Evangelische Kirche im Rheinland, *Friedensverantwortung der Kirche* (1983), 2, 4, which authorizes its positions by appeal to eschatology.

Evangelische Landeskirche in Baden, *Wort an die Gemeinden* (1983), 2.

Evangelische Landeskirche in Württemberg, *Kriegsdienstverweigerung* (1970).

Evangelisch-Lutherische Kirche in Bayern, *Wort der Landessynode zu Fragen der Kriegsdienstverweigerung* (1978).

Evangelisch-Lutherische Landeskirche Sachsens, *Kanzelabkündigung der Landessynode, des Landesbischofs und Landeskirchenamtes vom 24.03.1982.* In endorsing *Erklärung der Konferenz der Evangelischen Kirchenleitungen in der DDR vom 14.03.1982,* opposes pacifism in the sense of being open to service in the military.

Evangelisch-Lutherische Landeskirche Sachsens, *Beschluss der Friedensverantwortung der ELLS vom 17.3.85.*

Evangelisch-Lutherische Landeskirche Sachsens, *Beschluss der Synode betr. Sachgespräche vom 26.3.85.*

Federation of Swiss Protestant Churches, *Declaration of the FSPC concerning the Question of Civil Service* (1983). Though does include a passing reference to human conscience.

Fédération Protestante de France, *Sur les insoumis et objecteurs de conscience* (1972).

Fédération Protestante de France, *La lutte pour la paix* (1983).

Irish Episcopal Conference, *The Storm That Threatens* (1983), 3. Favors selective conscientious objection.

Lutheran Church-Missouri Synod, *To Adopt a Statement on Conscientious Objection* (1969). Supports selective conscientious objection; some reference is made to the Word of God.

Lutheran World Federation, *Our Responsibility for Peace and Justice* (1984), 13.4.2.8, 6; 13.1.11, 10, 3. But the statement could be understood to reject the concept of a just war. In the first reference to conscientious objection, the gospel may be functioning as a warrant.

Moravian Church in America, Southern Province, *Conscientious Objection* (1983). Supports conscientious objection to bearing arms.

National Association of Evangelicals [USA], *Amnesty* (1973).

National Conference of Catholic Bishops [USA], *The Challenge of Peace: God's Promise and Our Response* (1983), 118-21, 125, 233, 185, 290, 329, 333, 339, 58, 57, 13-15, 2. Though elsewhere in statement quest for peace is warranted by the gospel, Christology, eschatology, the Mass, and a view of human persons as God's creative work; opts for selective conscientious objection.

Presbyterian Church (USA), *God Alone Is Lord of the Conscience* (1988), B/1, B/2, B/6, Sum. Supports selective conscientious objection.

Presbyterian Church of Southern Africa, *Church and Nation* (1983), 237.

Presbyterian Church of Southern Africa, *Church and Nation* (1985), 230, clause 6.

Reformed Church in America, *Report of the Christian Action Commission* (1968), 7, 5. Supports selective conscientious objection.

Reformed Church in America, *Report of the Christian Action Commission* (1971), Rec. 24.

Reformed Church in America, *Report of the Christian Action Commission* (1975), R-II/B.

Southern African Catholic Conference, *Call for an End to Conscription* (1985).

United Church of Canada, *Conscientious Objection to War and Tax Reduction* (1986). Calls for an option to allow taxpayers to allocate taxes for peaceful purposes only.

United Church of Christ [USA], *Peace and United States Power* (1971). Opts for selective conscientious objection.

Vereinigte Evangelisch-Lutherische Kirche Deutschlands, *Entschliessung der Generalsynode der VELKD zur Friedenssicherung und Friedensförderung vom 25. Juni 1980.*

Vereinigte Evangelisch-Lutherische Kirche in der DDR, *Beschluss der Generalsynode zu den Berichten des leitenden Bischofs und der Kirchenleitung vom 28.6.1981.*

Vereinigte Evangelisch-Lutherische Kirche in der DDR, *Beschlüsse der 5. Tagung der III. Generalsynode der VELK-DDR vom 8.-11. Juni 1983,* 3(b). Perhaps authorized by Christology, but not clearly.

WCC Vancouver Assembly, *Confronting Threats to Peace and Survival* (1983), 18. Though earlier in the statement one does find warrants drawn from the gospel/Christology for the position against nuclear deterrence.

WCC World Convocation on Justice, Peace and the Integrity of Creation, *Final Document: Entering into Covenant Solidarity for Justice, Peace and the Integrity of Creation* (1990), 2.2; 2.1. The concept of covenant, which reflects a trinitarian content, may function as the document's overriding warrant.

D. OPPOSES MILITARY CONSCRIPTION
(AND REJECTS THE CONCEPT OF A JUST WAR)

D1. No clear theological warrant given for position

Church of the Brethren [USA], *The Time So Urgent! Threats to Peace* (1980), 4, 7. Endorses conscientious objection to the point of supporting those refusing to register with the selective service system.

Mennonite Brethren Churches, *Regarding Political Involvement* (1966), I.

Mennonite Central Committee, *A Statement of Concern Regarding the Military Selective Service Act of 1967* (1967), 2.

E. OPEN TO CONSCIENTIOUS OBJECTION
(BUT REJECTS THE CONCEPT OF A JUST WAR)

E1. Appeal to Christology

Mennonite Church [USA], *Taxes Designated for War* (1967).

Mennonite Church [USA], *Resolution on Conscientious Objection to Military Taxes* (1983). Cites a 1979 resolution which had supported a refusal to pay a portion of one's taxes which supports military efforts.

Mennonite Church [USA], *Growing in Stewardship and Witness in a Militaristic World* (1987). Authorized by Christian faithfulness, objects to paying taxes designated for military purposes and endorses total non-compliance with the selective service system.

Mennonite Church, General Conference [USA], *The Way of Peace* (1971). Open to non-cooperation with the selective service; also open to selective conscientious objection.

E2. No clear theological warrant given for position

Church of the Brethren [USA], *Justice and Nonviolence* (1977), 10.

F. SUPPORTS ABSOLUTE PACIFISM (NON-RESISTANCE)

F1. Appeal to creation/anthropology

Mennonite Church, General Conference [USA], *Killing* (1971).

F2. Appeal to Christology

Brethren in Christ Church [USA], *Commitment to Peace, Justice and Equity* (1970).
Brethren in Christ Church [USA], *Position Paper on Church, War and Respect for Human Life* (1976), II, III. Refuses participation in military service.
Church of the Brethren [USA], *A Statement of the Church of the Brethren on War* (1970), 1-4, 6, 8. Open to non-cooperation with the selective service.
Church of the Brethren [USA], *The Time So Urgent: Threats to Peace* (1980), 7-8. Also explicitly rejects nuclear war.
Mennonite Brethren Churches, *Confession of Faith* (1965), 2-3.
Mennonite Brethren Churches, *Confession of Faith* (1975), Art. 15.
Mennonite Brethren Churches, *Seventh Revised Draft, Mennonite Brethren Confession of Faith* (1975).
Mennonite Church [USA], *Love and Nonresistance* (1963).
Mennonite Church [USA], *Conscription and Militarism* (1969). Also endorses early affirmations of 1951 and 1937; open to total noncompliance with the selective service system.
Mennonite Church [USA], *Militarism and Conscription Statement* (1979), C. Endorses total non-compliance with selective service system and also endorses legislation which would promote alternative uses for paid taxes otherwise to be devoted to military purposes.
Mennonite Church [USA], *Resolution concerning Security and the Current Arms Race* (1981).
Mennonite World Conference, *Our Witness to Christ in Today's World* (1990).

F3. Appeal to the gospel

Church of God in Christ (Mennonite) [USA], *Principles of Faith* (1963), 46-48.
Church of God in Christ (Mennonite) [USA], *Confession of Faith* (1965), no. 6.
Mennonite Church, General Conference [USA], *The Way of Peace* (1971). Open to non-cooperation with the selective service.

F4. Appeal to Christology and pneumatology

Mennonite Church [USA], *Resolution on Vietnam* (1965).

F5. Appeal to ecclesiology

Mennonite Brethren Churches, *Resolution on War and Violence* (1969).

F6. Appeal to all three articles of the creed

Mennonite Brethren Churches, *Mennonite Brethren Distinctive* (1966), 24-26. Also authorized by the Word of God.

F7. Appeal to the Bible

Church of the Brethren [USA], *Statement on a Call to Halt the Nuclear Arms Race* (1982). Also explicitly rejects nuclear war.

F8. Appeal to the Bible, the righteousness of God, and perhaps Christology

Mennonite Church [USA], *A Message concerning the War in Vietnam* (1965).

F9. No clear theological warrant given for position

Church of the Brethren [USA], *Justice and Nonviolence* (1977), 1, 2, 8. Scripture may be a background warrant. Christian faith and natural law also authorize an explicit rejection of nuclear war.

Church of the Brethren [USA], *Statement on Abortion* (1984). Endorses an earlier 1972 statement of the church. It may relate pacifism to a christologically based compassion, but this is not clear.

Pacifism, implicitly endorsed by the openness to refusing to pay taxes used for military purposes, is called for by three items of the Mennonite Church, General Conference [USA]: *World Peace Tax Fund Act* (1977), authorized by Christology/the gospel; *War Taxes* (1974), without theological authorization; and *The Way of Peace* (1971), likely authorized by Christology; and three items of the Mennonite Church [USA]: *Resolution on Military Tax Withholding* (1989), 4, without authorization; *Growing In Stewardship and Witness in a Militaristic World* (1987), authorized by Christian faithfulness; and *Resolution on Conscientious Objection to Military Taxes* (1983), authorized by Christology.

A kind of pacifist position with regard to the use of violence for political ends has been taken without theological authorization by the Church of Ireland, *The Report of the Role of the Church Committee* (1981). Similarly, see the criticism of the concept of a just war in our present context, authorized by appeal to the Covenant and the Christian faith, by the World Alliance of Reformed Churches, *Justice, Peace and the Integrity of Creation* (1989). Insofar as it would advocate that Sweden maintain its military force for defence purposes, the Church of Sweden, *Svensk säkerhetspolitik* (1985), 2-3, may advocate an openness to the concept of a just war. Its call for weapons reduction but continuing production may signal an openness to deterrence.

The Associated Churches of Christ in New Zealand, *Decisions Relating to Public Issues* (1970), claims that war is contrary to the teachings of Christ. Also see Episcopal Church [USA], *General Convention Resolutions* [on humane treatment of prisoners of war] (1970) and *General Convention Resolution* [on opposition to peacetime conscription] (1979). And the World Methodist Council Conference, *Council Message to the Methodists of the World* (1966), calls for "the abolition of war on our planet" by appeal to the doctrine of human persons (their interdependence), supplemented by references to Christology and Methodist ecclesiology (with its itinerancy). A similar point is taken, with authorization drawn from natural law and the concept of divine providence, by the Hungarian [Catholic] Episcopal Conference, *Responsibility in Defence of Human Life* (1978). Also see *Note pastorale de l'Episcopat français sur "Humanae vitae"* (1968), 22. Also making a similar point (while providing no theological authorization) is the United Church of Canada, *United Nations Charter Revision* (1972), as it calls for a charter revision which would cancel a nation's right to declare war beyond its borders.

A kind of rejection of nuclear war, by means of a possible appeal to the doctrine of creation, is offered by the Roman Catholic Church, *Laborem Exercens* (1981), 12, 1, 27, in which creation may be subordinated to redemption. But the papal position on the injustice of nuclear war is as unclear as the warrant.

A position relevant to conscientious objection has been taken by the National Council of Churches [USA], *The Indochina War: Healing the Divisions of the Nation* (1972), which, authorized by ecclesiology and perhaps Christology, calls for amnesty for all Americans in legal difficulties over their actions during the Vietnam War. Also see Christian Church (Disciples of Christ), *Concerning Reconciling the Nation through a Grant of Amnesty* (1973), which authorizes its position by appeal to Christology, and the National Conference of Catholic Bishops [USA], *Resolutions on Southeast Asia* (1971), 8, 10, 11, probably authorized by the nature of the Christian faith, with natural law in the background. Likewise conscientious objection seems implicitly endorsed by the Evangelische Kirche im Rheinland, *Kriegsdienstverweigerung* (1971), when, without theological authorization, it advocates providing pastoral care to conscientious objectors.

E. DIVORCE, REMARRIAGE, AND POLYGAMY

5-1 DIVORCE AND REMARRIAGE

Disagreements on the legitimacy of remarriage after divorce have surfaced in several bilateral dialogues. In each case, the Roman Catholic members have denied the legitimacy of remarriage. Consider the following three reports:

Roman Catholic-Methodist Joint Commission, *Denver Report* (1971), 75, 70-71. The respective theological warrants are not clear, though both parties affirm marriage as a divine institution and seem to ground it in the creation doctrine, as both commend the Vatican II decree *Gaudium et Spes* (1965), 47-52. This decree grounded marriage in natural law. But it also tended systematically to subordinate creation to Christology (22).

Lutheran-Reformed-Roman Catholic Study Commission, *Theology of Marriage and the Problem of Mixed Marriages* (1976), 24ff., 9, 12, 14. The disagreements seem related to the Roman Catholic insistence on marriage's sacramental character. For Protestants, marriage is more clearly unambiguously rooted in the creation doctrine, as part of the fundamental experience of humanity.

The Report of the Anglican-Roman Catholic International Commission on the Theology of Marriage and Its Application to Mixed Marriages (1975), 41ff., 15, 21, 36. Both sides seek to resolve the differences (48, 54). It is stated that only modern Anglicanism has granted the possibilities of remarriage after divorce (41, 42, 44). Creation and the sacramental character of marriage are noted by Roman Catholics as warrants for their position. Both sides identify differences over the respective concepts of the church as the underlying cause of the disagreement.

Church statements generally affirm the legitimacy of remarriage after divorce. The exceptions are the Vatican II document *Gaudium et Spes,* 49; a statement of the Australian (Catholic) Episcopal Conference, *Morals and Human Values* (1972), authorized by appeal to natural/moral law; a statement of the National Conference of Catholic Bishops [USA], *To Live in Jesus Christ: A Pastoral Reflection on the Moral Life* (1976), 2, 30, 31, 36, 39, 115-16, authorized by sacramentology/Christology, with creation and ecclesiology in the background; and a decision by the Christian Reformed Church in North America, *Decisions of 1968,* which, without providing theological warrant, by implication reaffirms its *Decision of 1947,* 65-69, to oppose remarriage after divorce while the former spouse remains alive.

Warrants appealed to in support of the statements differ widely.

1. Appeal to creation/view of human persons
2. Apparent appeal to the gospel
3. Appeal to Christian faith/Christology
4. Appeal to God's grace
5. Appeal to loci drawn from the first and second articles of the creed
6. No clear theological warrant given for position

1. Appeal to creation/view of human persons

Lutheran Church in America, *Sex, Marriage, and Family* (1970).
Lutheran Church of Australia, *The Attitude of the LCA to Marriage, Divorce and Remarriage* (1978), III A/3; I/1.
Southern Baptist Convention [USA], *A Statement of Social Principles* (1979), 1.

2. Apparent appeal to the gospel

Brethren in Christ Church [USA], *Position Paper on the Church's Ministry to the Divorced and Remarried* (1974).

Greek Orthodox Archdiocese of North and South America, *Protocol Number 206A* (1973).

Moravian Church in America, Northern Province, *Resolutions* (1974).

United Methodist Church [USA], *Social Principles of the UMC(USA)* (1980), II/D; II.

3. Appeal to Christian faith/Christology

Wesleyan Church [USA], *Special Directions* (1984), (6), Int.

4. Appeal to God's grace

American Baptist Churches, *Policy Statement on Family Life* (1984).

5. Appeal to loci drawn from the first and second articles of the creed

American Lutheran Church, *Teachings and Practice on Marriage, Divorce, and Remarriage* (1982), 16, 24.

6. No clear theological warrant given for position

Church of England, *Marriage and Divorce* (1981).

Church of the Brethren [USA], *Marriage and Divorce* (1977).

Eglise de la Confession d'Augsbourg d'Alsace et de Lorraine, *Règlement du remariage de divorcés* (1976). The church's blessing of such a remarriage must be the exception to the rule; divorce is said to be contrary to the gospel.

Episcopal Church [USA], *General Convention Resolution* [on implementation date of new marriage canons] (1973), Can. 1:18, sec. 3. This followed an earlier call for a study of the issue in the resolution *Human Sexuality* (1967).

Conference of the Methodist Church in the Caribbean and the Americas, *Relating to Divorced Persons* (1972).

Waldensian Church, *Divorzio* (1971), 60. Although, in principle, the statement rejects consent to a public certification of the remarriage of divorced persons, it is open to such remarriage provided that the partner who has been divorced submits to examination by the church consistory and proves that forgiveness with the previous partner has come to pass, so that the brotherly/sisterly fellowship between them may continue in the church. Christology may be a background warrant.

Without reference to remarriage and while providing no theological authorization, an openness to divorce when necessary is expressed by the Church of Ireland, *The Report of the Role of the Church Committee* (1981). A lament about the rising number of divorces in Latin America is cited by the Latin American [Catholic] Bishops, Second General Conference (Medellín Conference), *Family and Demography* (1968), 3(c). A similar concern about the growing number of divorces, probably authorized by a Trinitarian argument, was expressed by the American Lutheran Church, *Issues and Opportunities That Bind and Free* (1976). Also see three items of the National Association of Evangelicals [USA]: *A Declaration — Forty-fifth*

Anniversary Year (1987), *Save the Family* (1982), and *A Response to Secular Humanism* (1981). A concern to allow divorce in the church and to take a more compassionate attitude towards it has been expressed by the All Africa Conference of Churches, *The Church and Cultural Renewal in Africa* (1974), 1/5(c).

5-2 POLYGAMY

Of the five statements on the subject, one by the All Africa Conference of Churches, *The Church and Cultural Renewal in Africa* (1974), 1/2, asks that Christians consider the implications of polygamy on the *imago dei* in human beings and that they are cautious not "to regard only monogamy". Another statement which seems to express a certain qualified openness to polygamy is Anglicanism, *The Resolutions of the Lambeth Conference (1988)*, 26, insofar as it does advocate baptizing converted polygamists and would not compel such persons to divorce any of their wives. The resolution, however, does not offer any theological authorization for its position, other than a reference to "God's plan", which is said to uphold monogamy.

Polygamy is condemned explicitly, on grounds of "Christian ethics", in *Catholic Hierarchy of Ghana on Family Planning* (1972) and, by appeal to "the Gospel of Jesus Christ", by the [Catholic] Episcopal Conference of Africa and Madagascar, *Recommendations and Conclusions on Christian Family Life and Marriage in Africa Today* (1981), 3.2.3; 2.2.3; 1.5, although the condemnation is not meant to imply abandonment of Christians and catechumens currently involved in polygamy. In this regard these bishops' conferences follow the Second Vatican Council, *Gaudium et Spes* (1965), 47, 48, 22, which condemns polygamy by means of an appeal to creation (marriage as built into natural law) while conceiving of creation as subordinated to grace/Christology.

F. ABORTION

Statements of the churches on abortion fall into three large groups: those against abortion in all circumstances, those viewing abortion as a fully legitimate alternative, and those viewing abortion as legitimate only in certain restricted situations.

A. Against abortion in all circumstances
    A1. Appeal to creation/natural law/view of human persons
    A2. Appeal to anthropology/natural law
    A3. Appeal to creation, perhaps grounded in Christology
    A4. Appeal to creation/anthropology and Christology/the gospel
    A5. Appeal to natural law/anthropology, supplemented by the gospel
    A6. Appeal to natural law/anthropology, supplemented by the gospel, with the possibility that creation is grounded in the gospel
    A7. No clear theological warrant, but may appeal to loci derived from all three articles of the creed, with all loci subordinated to Christology
    A8. No clear theological warrant given for position

B. Abortion a legitimate alternative because the fetus is not human
    B1. Appeal to creation/view of human persons
    B2. Appeal to creation/view of human persons and grace
    B3. Appeal to Christology
    B4. Appeal to Christology, with appeal to creation possibly in background
    B5. Appeal to themes associated with all three articles of the creed
    B6. No clear theological warrant given for position

C. Abortion a legitimate alternative only in some circumstances (for it is the taking of a human life)
    C1. Appeal to creation/law/view of human persons
    C2. Appeal to creation, supplemented by Christology
    C3. Apparent appeal both to creation and to redemption/Christian faith
    C4. Appeal to the gospel
    C5. Appeal to ecclesiology
    C6. Appeal to all the articles of the creed
    C7. No clear theological warrant given for position

A. AGAINST ABORTION IN ALL CIRCUMSTANCES

A1. Appeal to creation/natural law/view of human persons

Australian [Catholic] Episcopal Conference, *Abortion* (1971).
Australian [Catholic] Episcopal Conference, *Abortion* (1972).
Australian [Catholic] Episcopal Conference, *Morals and Human Values* (1972).
Australian [Catholic] Episcopal Conference, *Abortion Clinics* (1977).
Australian [Catholic] Episcopal Conference, *Abortion* (1978).
Australian [Catholic] Episcopal Conference, *Adoption of Abortion as Official A.L.P. Policy* (1984).
Australian [Catholic] Episcopal Conference, *Message of Australian Bishops to Members of Federal Parliament* (1985).
[Catholic] Bishops of Kenya, *Joint Pastoral Letter of the Bishops of Kenya on the Family and Responsible Parenthood* (1979). With Christology and ecclesiology as possible background warrants.

Canadian Catholic Conference, *Statement on Abortion* (1970).

[Catholic] Bishops of the Netherlands, *Statement from the Bishops of the Netherlands on Abortion* (1974). Cites a 1971 letter which offers a similar argument.

Catholic Bishops Conference of India, *Statement on the Occasion of the Tenth Anniversary of "Humanae Vitae"* (1978).

[Catholic] Bishops of Vietnam, *To Build Peace* (1969). Ecclesiology is a background warrant.

[Catholic] Episcopal Conference of Belgium, *Pour la défense des plus faibles* (1977). With at least one reference to God's love.

(Catholic) Episcopal Conference of Korea, *Pastoral Letter* [on the new Mother-Child Health Law] (1973). But is open to abortion in an emergency, to save the life of the mother.

Chinese Catholic Bishops Conference, *Statement and Proposals of the CCBC on the Issue "Should abortion be legalized?"* (1984), I/1, 9.

Conférence Episcopale Française, *Tout être humain a le droit de vivre* (1974). With the gospel and the Bible as possible background warrants.

Conférence Episcopale Française, *L'avenir d'un peuple* (1982).

Episcopal Conference of Portugal, *Note of the Bishops of Portugal on Abortion* (1978).

Episcopal Conference of Portugal, *The Regulation of Birth* (1983), 6, 11.

Episcopal Conference of Portugal, *The Legalization of Abortion in Portugal* (1984), 1-6. Cites an earlier 1982 pastoral which condemned abortion by appeal to the nature of human life. This statement also authorizes its position by appeal to the natural law.

Hungarian [Catholic] Episcopal Conference, *Responsibility in Defense of Human Life* (1978).

Irish Episcopal Conference, *The Storm That Threatens* (1983), 4.

Italian Episcopal Conference, *Declaration of the IEC on Moral Problems* (1971). The gospel may function as a background warrant.

Italian Episcopal Conference, *Message to the President of the Senate, Prof. Amintore Fanfani, and the Senators of the Italian Republic* (1977).

Italian Episcopal Conference, *Declaration of the IEC on Abortion* (1978), 3.

National Conference of Catholic Bishops [USA], *Human Life in Our Day* (1968), 85-87.

National Conference of Catholic Bishops [USA], *Statement in Protest of U.S. Government Programs against the Right to Life* (1969), 6, 3, 1.

National Conference of Catholic Bishops [USA)] *Statement on Abortion* (1969).

National Conference of Catholic Bishops [USA], *Declaration on Abortion* (1970). Insofar as the declaration cites Vatican II, it could be following the council's tendency to subordinate nature to grace).

National Conference of Catholic Bishops [USA], *Statement on Abortion* (1970). Appeal to the "biblical" law to authorize position may indicate that Scripture, not creation, is ultimately the warrant.

National Conference of Catholic Bishops [USA], *Population and the American Future: A Response* (1972), 4, 6, 7.

National Conference of Catholic Bishops [USA], *Resolution on the Pro-Life Constitutional Amendment* (1973), 1-2, 4-5.

National Conference of Catholic Bishops [USA], *Resolution on Abortion* (1989). Insofar as the resolution cites Vatican II's *Gaudium et Spes*, 22, it could be following that statement's tendency to subordinate nature to grace.

New Zealand Catholic Bishops Conference, *For Life* (1983). Correlates creation and eschatology.

Polish [Catholic] Episcopacy, *Call of the Polish Episcopacy before the Threats against Life* (1970), II-IV. Christology may be a background warrant.

Roman Catholic Church, *Humanae Vitae* (1968), 14, 11.

Roman Catholic Church, Congregation for the Doctrine of the Faith, *Instruction on Respect for Human Life in Its Origin and on the Dignity of Procreation* (1987), I.1; I.2; Int.1; I. The gospel appears as a secondary warrant.

A2. Appeal to anthropology/natural law

Austrian [Catholic] Episcopacy, *Declaration of the Austrian Episcopacy on the Encyclical "Humanae Vitae"* (1968).
[Catholic] Bishops of Pakistan, *Joint Pastoral Letter on Abortion and Contraception* (1975).
Episcopat Français, *Note pastorale de l'épiscopat français sur "Humanae Vitae"* (1968), 19, 5.
National Conference of Catholic Bishops [USA], *Statement on Population* (1973), 8.
Polish [Catholic] Episcopal Conference, *The Christian Family and the Gift of Life* (1979).

A3. Appeal to creation, perhaps grounded in Christology

Canadian Catholic Conference, *For a Society Hospitable to Life* (1973). Insofar as the statement cites the Second Vatican Council's *Gaudium et Spes,* 22, which subordinates creation to Christology, it may be that the Canadian statement posits a similar subordination of its warrants.
Conferencia Episcopal Española, *Moral and Christian Attitudes over against the Decriminalization of Abortion* (1985), 2-5, 7, 18. The gospel may be a background warrant. Insofar as the statement cites the Second Vatican Council's *Gaudium et Spes,* 51 (22), which subordinates creation to the gospel, it may be that the Spanish statement posits a similar subordination of its warrants.
German [Catholic] Bishops' Conference, *Concerning the New Legislation on Abortion* (1976). Insofar as the statement cites the Second Vatican Council's *Gaudium et Spes,* 51 (22), which subordinates creation to Christology, it may be that the German statement posits a similar subordination of its warrants. Explicit appeal is made to the "biblical message". It claims that no one will condemn medical personnel who, in crisis situations where the mother's life is at stake, take a decision of conscience with reference to the concrete situation which leads them to participate in an abortion.
Haitian [Catholic] Episcopal Conference, *The Foundation for the Church's Involvement in Local and Political Arenas* (1983), 17, 19, 2.5. Ecclesiology — the church as sacrament — also may be invoked.
National Conference of Catholic Bishops [USA], *Pastoral Plan for Pro-life Activities* (1975), Int., 13, 20, 27, 58. Insofar as the statement cites the Second Vatican Council's *Gaudium et Spes,* 22, which subordinates creation to Christology, it may be that the American bishops posit a similar subordination of their two warrants.
National Conference of Catholic Bishops [USA], *To Live in Jesus Christ: A Pastoral Reflection on the Moral Life* (1976), 2, 30, 31, 63-65, 115-16. Christology and ecclesiology function as background warrants.
National Conference of Catholic Bishops [USA], *The Challenge of Peace: God's Promise and Our Response* (1983), 284-95, 13, 333. Insofar as the position on abortion is related to peace and the Mass creates conditions for peace, a supplementary warrant is possible. This is especially possible to the degree the statement is influenced by Vatican II's subordination of nature to grace.
Roman Catholic Church, Vatican II, *Gaudium et Spes* (1965), 51, 50, 39, 27, 22.

A4. Appeal to creation/anthropology and Christology/the gospel

Australian [Catholic] Episcopal Conference, *Abortion* (1980), I-II.
Catholic Bishops of Liberia, *Pastoral Letter on Abortion by the CBL* (1984). Also refers to pneumatology, which seems to function only as a motive, not as a warrant. It is open to "indirect abortion", and even "deliberative abortion", if necessary in order to save a woman's life.

[Catholic] Bishops of the Netherlands, *Pastoral Letter of the Bishops of the Netherlands on Direct Abortion* (1971). Suggests that in situations where conflict may exist between the welfare of the fetus and that of the mother, preference should be given to the former.

[Catholic] Episcopal Conference of Belgium, *Déclaration sur l'avortement* (1973), I/1a, b, I/2, I/3, Conc.

Conferencia Episcopal Española, *Abortion: The Gravest Crime against Human Life* (1974), 2, 10-12, 15-16. In situations where conflict may exist between the welfare of the fetus and that of the mother, many mothers, it is said, will give preference to saving the fetus.

German [Catholic] Bishops Conference, *Appeal to All: Protect Human Life* (1973).

Italian Episcopal Conference, *Message of the Bishops to the Catholic Communities in Italy* (1977).

Italian Episcopal Conference, *Formation of Consciences in Fidelity to the Gospel and with Love for Country* (1981), 5, 6.

National Conference of Catholic Bishops [USA], *The Bicentennial Consultation: A Response to the Call to Action* (1977), 28, 13.

A5. Appeal to natural law/anthropology, supplemented by the gospel

[Catholic] Episcopal Conference of Africa and Madagascar, *Recommendations and Conclusions on Family Life and Marriage in Africa Today* (1981), 2.3.4; 2.2.3; 1.5.

Conferencia Episcopal Española, *La despenalización del aborto* (1983), 2, 4, 6-9, 12.

Nordic Catholic Bishops, *Svangerskabs afbrydelse og krisitent ansvar* (1971), 6-9, 12, 17, 21. Reflects an openness to tolerating laws favorable to abortion and an openness to the use of contraception as a socially useful tool for reducing the number of abortions.

A6. Appeal to natural law/anthropology, supplemented by the gospel, with the possibility that creation is grounded in the gospel

Canadian Catholic Conference, *Statement on Proposed Change of Canadian Law on Abortion* (1968). Insofar as the statement cites the Second Vatican Council's *Gaudium et Spes,* 51 (22), which subordinates nature to grace, it may be that the Canadian statement posits a similar subordination of its warrants. Though condemning abortion, the statement is open to "treatments needed to save a mother's life even if they sometimes result in the unwanted and unsought death of the fetus".

A7. No clear theological warrant, but may appeal to loci derived from all three articles of the creed, with all loci subordinated to Christology

Roman Catholic Church, *Sollicitudo Rei Socialis* (1987), 26, 39-40, 47-49, 7, 2, 1. Insofar as opposition to abortion is related to peace by the encyclical, which is authorized by loci derived from the three articles of the creed, this mode of argument may pertain to the encyclical's position on abortion.

A8. No clear theological warrant given for position

Conseil Permanent de l'Episcopat aux Catholiques de France, *L'accueil de l'enfant à naître* (1979), 2, 3, 8. Reference to abortion could represent a correlated appeal to the doctrine of creation. Christology/the gospel may function as the warrant.

National Conference of Catholic Bishops [USA], *Health and Health Care* (1981), 40.

Nordic Catholic Bishops, *Pastoral Letter of the Nordic Catholic Bishops on the Encyclical "Humanae Vitae"* (1968), IV.

B. ABORTION A LEGITIMATE ALTERNATIVE
BECAUSE THE FETUS IS NOT HUMAN

B1. Appeal to creation/view of human persons

Lutheran Church in America, *Sex, Marriage, and Family* (1970).

Methodist Church (England), *Abortion* (1976), 6, 3, 8, 9. Though does not favor abortion on demand and at one point claims that the fetus "belongs to the human race".

Moravian Church in America, Northern Province, *Resolutions* (1974). Warrant not entirely clear but appeals to "sacredness of life" and status of the fetus.

Moravian Church in America, Northern Province, *Resolutions* (1982).

Unitarian Universalist Association, *General Assembly Resolution* (1987). At least appeals to the doctrine of human persons and the concept of conscience.

United Church of Christ [USA], *Freedom of Choice concerning Abortion* (1971). Affirms women's freedom of choice by appeal to the idea of God as source of life, calling humans to share in the work of creation. It is open to abortion as long as it is early in the pregnancy, before fetus is a human life. Perhaps this commitment is affirmed in another pronouncement of the same General Synod entitled *The Status of Women in Church and Society*. However the statement merely endorses legalized abortion, and it seems authorized by the gospel of God's love for all.

B2. Appeal to creation/view of human persons and grace

United Presbyterian Church [USA], *The Covenant of Life and the Caring Community* (1983), Policy Statement.

B3. Appeal to Christology

Reformed Church in America, *Report of the Christian Action Commission* (1971), Rec. 1-3. Does take a position on the status of the fetus but merely emphasizes freedom of choice on abortion. Authorization is provided by "Christian freedom" (i.e., the gospel) and, to some extent, Christology.

United Church of Christ [USA], *Abortion* (1979).

United Church of Christ [USA], *Resolution on Reaffirmation of Freedom of Choice* (1979), 8, 1.

United Methodist Church [USA], *Resolution on Responsible Parenthood* (1976). At least appeals to "Christian judgment" for authorization.

B4. Appeal to Christology, with appeal to creation possibly in background

Christian Church (Disciples of Christ), *General Assembly Resolution* (1975), Res. 7524.

B5. Appeal to themes associated with all three articles of the creed

United Presbyterian Church [USA], *Covenant and Creation: Theological Reflections on Contraception and Abortion* (1983). Viability of the fetus is made the criterion for determining the validity of abortion. In a 1985 statement of the Presbyterian Church (USA), abortion is rejected as a convenience to ease embarrassment or when employed as a method of birth control.

B6. No clear theological warrant given for position

Christian Church (Disciples of Christ), *Resolution concerning Webster vs. Reproductive Health Services* (1989).

Episcopal Church [USA], *Abortion Law Reform* (1967). Open to abortion only in cases where the mother's life is seriously threatened, where the child would be deformed, or where pregnancy was the result of rape or incest.

Episcopal Church [USA], *General Convention Resolution* (1976).

Episcopal Church [USA], *General Convention Resolution* [on abortion] (1979). Refers to the fetus as "the beginning of new human life". Appeals to an earlier 1976 resolution.

Episcopal Church [USA], *Abortion* (1982), 3, Int. Reaffirms the church's 1979, 1976, and 1967 positions.

Episcopal Church [USA], *Pre-Natal Sex Selection* (1982). Open to abortion when pre-natal diagnosis reveals serious abnormalities in the fetus.

Fédération Protestante de France, *Révision de la loi Veil* (1979). Unlike other statements which do not qualify the circumstances for abortion or stress freedom of choice, the statement seems to regard the fetus as a human life.

Moravian Church in America, Northern Province, *Resolutions* (1970). Claims that the Bible does not address the issue. But insofar as individual Christians are free to decide for themselves on basis of the interpretation of faith, reason and so creation could authorize judgments about abortion.

Reformed Church in America, *Report of the Christian Action Commission* (1968), R-38.

United Church of Canada, *Contraception and Abortion* (1980), 2.

United Church of Christ [USA], *Recommendations in Regard to the Human Sexuality Study* (1977), 11. Refers only to "women's freedom of choice" as a right.

United Free Church of Scotland, *Deliverance of the General Assembly* [on public questions] (1967), 7, 1. Though opposes abortion on demand.

United Free Church of Scotland, *Deliverance of the General Assembly* [on public questions] (1968), 1.

C. ABORTION A LEGITIMATE ALTERNATIVE ONLY IN SOME CIRCUMSTANCES (FOR IT IS THE TAKING OF A HUMAN LIFE)

C1. Appeal to creation/law/view of human persons

American Lutheran Church, *Abortion* (1980), i, b, a, k. Reference to Christology functions only as a motive in caring for those involved in an abortion.

Associated Churches of Christ in New Zealand, *Decisions Relating to Public Issues* (1983). Seems to appeal to creation/the Decalogue insofar as abortion is murder and aborting normal fetuses an evil.

Baptist Union of New Zealand, *Public Questions* (1970).

Baptist Union of New Zealand, *Notice of Motion* (1988), 13.1-13.2.

Christian Reformed Church in North America, *Acts of the Synod* (1972), 63-64.

Church of England, *Abortion* (1983).

Church of Norway, *Abortspørsmålet* (1971), 1-2, 4-6. This early statement is affirmed in Church of Norway, *Oppfølging av biskopenes uttalelse om abort* (1978).

Church of Norway, *Letter to the Storting* (1973). Though the only theological argument pertains to the human value of the fetus.

Church of Norway, *Vern om menneskeverdet i livets grensesituasjoner* (1982). Though references to the doctrine of creation are grounded in Scripture.

Church of Norway, *Human Dignity* (1985), esp. 2.

Church of Sweden, *Yttrande över genetisk integritet* (1984), 3. Though reference to a Christian-ethics perspective could entail that authorization is drawn from the second article.

Eglise de la Confession d'Augsbourg d'Alsace et de Lorraine, *Le texte suivant la discussion* (1979). Though expresses mixed feelings about placing further limitations on abortions, agrees the practice is legitimate in certain circumstances. Christology is related to creation. This reference and another to Scripture as the source for the church's insights about procreation could undermine the appeal to the doctrine of creation for authorization on this subject.

Evangelische Landeskirche in Württemberg, *Stellungnahme zum Abbruch der Schwangerschaft* (1979). Authorization not unambiguous but does refer to life as God's gift and his command to protect life, including "unborn life". This implies that the first article authorizes the statement's position.

Evangelisch-Lutherische Kirche in Bayern, *Wort zum Schwangerschaftsabbruch* (1971), III, II.

Evangelisch-Lutherische Landeskirche Hannovers, *Überlegungen des öffentlichkeits- und Presseausschusses für eine Erklärung an die Kirchengemeinden in Sachen Para. 218 StGB* (1973). Approved by the church's Landessynode. The appeal to anthropology as a warrant is made from a Christian point of view. The majority supported *Kommuniqué der Kirchenleitung der Vereinigten Evangelisch-Lutherischen Kirche Deutschlands vom 23. März 1973.*

Lutheran Church-Missouri Synod, *To State Position on Abortion* (1971). Also rejects "willful abortion".

Lutheran Church-Missouri Synod, *To State Position on Abortion* (1979).

Lutheran Church-Missouri Synod, *To Reaffirm and Implement the Synod's Pro-Life Position* (1983). Also refers to Scripture. It cites the church's 1971, 1977, 1979, and 1981 resolutions opposing "willful abortion". It is open to abortion only when the mother's life is in danger.

Mennonite Brethren Churches, *Abortion* (1972).

Mennonite Brethren Churches, *Resolution on Abortion* (1975).

Mennonite Church [USA], *Summary Statement on Abortion* (1975).

National Association of Evangelicals [USA], *Abortion* (1971). All life is a gift from God.

National Association of Evangelicals [USA], *Abortion* (1973). Also refers to the teachings of Scripture.

Reformed Church in America, *Abortion* (1973). Reaffirmed in 1974, 1975, 1980, and 1981.

Southern Baptist Convention [USA], *On Abortion* (1971). Very broad in the few restrictions the resolution would place on abortion.

Southern Baptist Convention [USA], *On Abortion and Sanctitity of Human Life* (1974).

Southern Baptist Convention [USA], *A Statement of Social Principles* (1979), 5, 4. Reticence is expressed about abortion because of the need to respect human life. It suggests that the fetus is deemed a human person and thus that it is appealing to creation. Earlier comments, however, suggest an appeal to theocratic principles.

Southern Baptist Convention [USA], *On Pro-Life Actions of SBC Agencies* (1988).

Southern Baptist Convention [USA], *On Encouraging Laws Regulating Abortion* (1989). Opposes legalized abortion.

United Methodist Church [USA], *Social Principles of the UMC(USA)* (1980), II/G; II. Appeals to the concept of the sacredness of life but earlier had claimed the "gospel understanding" primary. It also could be construed as open to abortion for reasons other than the preservation of the mother's life.

C2. Appeal to creation, supplemented by Christology

Evangelische Kirche in Deutschland, *Erklärung des Rates der EKD zum Schwangerschaftsabbruch* (1980). Proposes a social program with socialist, collectivist tendencies in order to support those who are expecting children. The position taken by the organization's Rat was largely endorsed (with authorization primarily drawn from anthropology, with the doctrine of the Trinity as a background warrant) by its synod in *Zur Achtung vor dem Leben* (1987), III/6, III/5(g), III/5(e). A similar endorsement of the declaration was given by the Evangelische Landeskirche in Württemberg, *Wort an die Gemeinden zum Schutz des ungeborenen Lebens vom 27. November 1986, 9.*

C3. Apparent appeal both to creation and to redemption/Christian faith

British Council of Churches, *Termination of Pregnancy Bill* (1967), 1-3. Appeals to the doctrine of human persons and to "Christian compassion"/gospel. The status of the fetus is implied, but not clearly stated.

Evangelische Kirche im Rheinland, *Hilfe zum Leben* (1986), 1, An. (b). At least suggests that the fetus is a human life. The authorization is not clear but suggests that the position on abortion is related to the inviolability of human life and also the fact that human life has been elected to fellowship with God.

National Association of Evangelicals [USA], *A Response To Secular Humanism* (1981). Authorized by creation and Christology.

Reformed Church in America, *Abortion* (1983).

Southern Baptist Convention [USA], *On Abortion* (1984).

Wesleyan Church [USA], *Special Directions* (1984), (II), Int.

C4. Appeal to the gospel

Anglican Church of Canada, *Resolution on Abortion* (1980), Act 42. Though taking no explicit position on the status of the fetus, it is likely that such a first-article appeal is in the background.

C5. Appeal to ecclesiology

United Free Church of Scotland, *Deliverance of the General Assembly* [on public questions] (1980), 1, 9. Love and Christian moral values may function as background warrants. It is open to abortion only in some circumstances but does not take a position on the status of the fetus. However, in a subsequent 1986 deliverance of the assembly (p. 2), the Free Church claims that human life begins at conception.

C6. Appeal to all the articles of the creed

American Lutheran Church, *Christian Counseling on Abortion* (1974), 1-3, 5. At least insofar as the statement refers to the fetus's "right of the developing life". A relational view of persons functions to authorize abortion in some circumstances.

C7. No clear theological warrant given for position

American Lutheran Church, *Human Sexuality and Sexual Behavior* (1980), D.5; A.2/2.

Anglican Church of Canada, *Resolution on Abortion* (1973). At least insofar as abortion on demand is rejected.

Assemblies of God, *Statement on Abortion* (1971). Contains only a general reference to what Scripture teaches.

Associated Churches of Christ in New Zealand, *Decision Relating to Public Issues* (1973). Seems to opt for abortion only in certain specified circumstances.

Associated Churches of Christ in New Zealand, *Decisions Relating to Public Issues* (1982). Seems open to abortion in certain circumstances and does not identify the fetus as a human life. It regards the abortion of a normal fetus, however, as inherently evil.

Church of God in Christ (Mennonite) [USA], *Birth Control and Abortion* (1974). Threatens church members who plan an abortion with excommunication.

Church of Ireland, *The Report of the Role of the Church Committee* (1981).

Church of Ireland, *Statement Issued by the Standing Committee of the Church of Ireland* (1982).

Church of Norway, *Vern om fosterets liv* (1977). Though does make reference to God's Word as a warrant and rejects abortion as the taking of a human life.

Eglise de la Confession d'Augsbourg d'Alsace et de Lorraine, *Déclaration* (1982).

Evangelische Landeskirche in Württemberg, *Beschluss der Württemburgischen Evangelischen Landessynode* (1972), 1-3. Suggests the fetus is human in calling it "unborn life".

Fédération Protestante de France, *Sur la contraception et l'avortement* (1972). But does not identify the fetus as a human life.

Lutheran Church of Australia, *Attitude to Birth Control* (1968), 8, 7. Refers only to the will of God.

Lutheran World Federation, *Partnership of Women and Men* (1984), 6.6.3; i. Does regard abortion as a form of violence which, insofar as it is related to sexism, is deemed a sin that impedes the advancement of the gospel. But it also expresses concern for "the dignity of all human life".

Methodist Church in Ireland, *Resolution of the Methodist Conference* (1981). Seems to take this position insofar as it opposes "indiscriminate abortion".

Presbyterian Church in Ireland, *Resolution of the General Assembly* (1982).

Southern Baptist Convention [USA], *On Abortion* (1982).

A number of national Roman Catholic bishops' conferences issued statements in defence of *Humanae Vitae,* almost immediately after the encyclical had been issued. These include *Lettre des évêques belges sur l'encyclique "Humanae Vitae"* (1968); *Declaration of the German (Catholic) Bishops* [on *Humanae Vitae*] (1968); [Catholic] Bishops' Conference of England and Wales, *Declaration on the Encyclical "Humanae Vitae"* (1968), 11, 6, 5, 2, 1, (may, by implication, also condemn abortion); Canadian Catholic Conference, *Declaration concerning the Encyclical "Humanae Vitae"* (1968), reaffirmed in the conference's *Precise Details on the Subject of "Humanae Vitae"* (1969); *Déclaration des évêques suisses sur l'encyclique "Humanae Vitae"* (1968); *Declaration of the Conferencia Episcopal Española on "Humanae Vitae"* (1968), esp. 10; and *Pastoral Statement of the Bishops of Portugal on the Encyclical "Humanae Vitae"* (1968). These statements have not been listed above because they do not explicitly condemn abortion. Authorization for the defence of the encyclical is not usually clear.

The Belgium bishops' letter II is of special interest, for that document expresses an openness to the use of legitimate therapeutic means of birth control (artificial means?). Likewise the German bishops expressed an openness to Roman Catholics' dissenting from the official papal rejection of artificial means of birth control.

A strongly critical appraisal of abortion was offered by the Evangelisch-Lutherische Landeskirche Hannovers, *Problem der Zunahme von Schwangerschaftsabbrüchen aus sozialer Notlage* (1987), which claims that all abortion is murder and is not in accord with the law of God. The church's Landessynode only "received" a report of the same title, one which somewhat tempered the impression of absolute rejection of abortion in all circumstances (3).

A similar ambiguity should be noted regarding the intention of the Baptist World Alliance, *Resolution on Man's Stewardship and Survival on This Earth* (1970), when it states: "We support all efforts which are rooted in the biblical concept of the sanctity of life and the integrity of human personality to limit the population of the earth." Is this an indication of complete hesitancy about the use of abortion? For similar conclusions grounded in similar modes of argument, also see Southern Baptist Convention [USA], *On Abortion* (1987) and *On Sex Education and Adolescent Pregnancy* (1986); Reformed Ecumenical Synod, *Pastoral Statement: A Call to Commitment and Action* (1984), XII/D/1; *Erklärung der Kirchensynode der Evangelischen Kirche in Hessen und Nassau zur Lage von Frauen in Schwangerschaftskonflikten und zur Beratungssituation* (1985); Baptist Union of New Zealand, *Forum Remits* (1989), (C); Mennonite Church, General Conference [USA], *Concerns about Abortion* (1977) and *Killing* (1971).

Like the Baptists, the Reformed Synod, and the Mennonites, the Church of the Brethren [USA] rejects abortion as a kind of murder of unborn life, without qualification, in its *Statement on Abortion* (1984). But perhaps unlike the Roman Catholic Church, the Brethren indicate an openness to maintaining fellowship with those who have decided on an abortion. Also see a similar possibly unqualified denial of abortion in two items by the [Orthodox] Ecumenical Patriarchate of Constantinople: *Message de Sa Sainteté le Patriarche œcuménique Dimitrios Ier à l'occasion de la fête de Noël 1984* (1984) and *Message de Noël* (1981). See a similar denial in *Stellungnahme der Evangelischen Kirche in Österreich zum Schwangerschaftsabbruch (Para. 144 StG)* (1972); National Association of Evangelicals [USA], *A Declaration — Forty-fifth Anniversary Year* (1987) and *Revive Your Church, O Lord!* (1989); and Southern Baptist Convention (USA), *On Support of the Danforth Amendment* (1987).

In several documents, the position taken on abortion is uncertain. See Southern Baptist Convention [USA], *On Human Organ Donations* (1988), which denies the validity of being construed as a document in support of abortion; National Association of Evangelicals [USA], *Save the Family* (1982), which criticizes abortion as a strategy for "relieving parents of their responsibility"; Lutheran Church-Missouri Synod, *To Implement Pro-Life Programs* (1981), which rejects "willful abortion" by citing 1971, 1977, and 1979 resolutions of the church, especially Lutheran Church-Missouri Synod, *To Support Efforts to Protect the Living but Unborn* (1977); World Alliance of Reformed Churches, *Justice, Peace and the Integrity of Creation* (1989), which condemns abortion as a means of birth control; and United Church of Christ [USA], *Freedom of Choice* (1981), which claims that "abortion should not be considered a primary method of birth control."

Also see the WCC Conference on Faith, Science and the Future, *Technology, Resources, Environment and Population* (Cambridge, Mass., 12-24 July 1979), 5, which rules out abortion "simply as a means of birth control". Cf. Presbyterian Church of Southern Africa, *Church and Nation* (1984), 338, clauses 2-3; Episcopal Church [USA], *"To Make Peace" Report* (1985). The last item takes this position in virtue of approving the statement of the church's Joint Commission on Peace, *To Make Peace* (1985), II/A.

In the case of the United Church of Christ, however, its endorsement of "freedom of choice", an openness (based on apparent appeal to the doctrine of human persons) to the possibility that human life may not begin at conception, could be regarded as an endorsement of the more liberal position on abortion. In like manner, one cannot determine precisely how the United Church of Christ [USA] regards the status of the fetus on the basis of its affirmation of the "sacredness of individual lives" in the statements *Abortion* (1979) and *Resolution on Reaffirmation of Freedom of Choice Regarding Abortion* (1979). Also see the denomination's *General Synod Resolution* (1987). Yet it should be noted that all three statements affirm something like freedom of choice.

The precise orientation concerning the status of the fetus and the validity of abortion in certain circumstances is not entirely clear in statements of the Evangelical Lutheran Free Church [Norway]. In its *Prenatal diagnostik og "de funksjonshemmedes år"* (1981), authorized by the doctrine of creation, it warns against the use of prenatal diagnosis to interrupt pregnancies of handicapped fetuses. It expresses its concern about legislation concerning the interruption of pregnancy in *Resolusjon fra den Evangelisk Lutherske Frikirkes Synodemøte til det Norske Storting* (1979) and in its *Statement on State-Church Relations* (n.d.), 2, 10.

Further clarification of the apparently open position on abortion of the Evangelical Methodist Church of Italy and the Waldensian Church, *Aborto* (1978), II, is necessary. On the one hand, without theological authorization, the statement seems open to abortion in the sense that it does not want Italian hospitals to deny the abortion option to patients. Yet on the other hand, the churches would work from a perspective of eliminating abortion. No position on the status of the fetus is taken.

One resolution of the Vereinigte Evangelisch-Lutherische Kirche Deutschlands, *Beschluss der Generalsynode betr. seelsorgerliche Beratung in Fragen des Schwangerschaftsabbruches* (1976), deals with abortion insofar as it calls on the churches to provide pastoral care and guidance to women contemplating abortion. But it takes no position on abortion as such. Cf. Evangelische Kirche im Rheinland, *Flankierende Massnahmen zu Para. 218* (1976); Evangelisch-Lutherische Kirche in Bayern, *Massnahmen in Zusammenhang mit Para. 218 StGB* (1973). A similarly vague, though perhaps more critical perspective on abortion (with reference to the fetus as "unborn life"), without its total rejection, was taken by the same church in *Schwangerschaftsabbruch und Bewahrung des Lebens* (1986). Likewise the abortion controversy and the related controversy over artificial means of contraception were noted by the WCC Nairobi Assembly, *Human Development: Ambiguities of Power, Technology, and Quality of Life* (1975), 32, but no position was taken except to affirm "the sanctity of human life".

The position of the Church of Ireland seems unclear in its *Report of the Role of the Church Committee* (1984), 3(a), as it defends opposition to an amendment to the Irish constitution that would forbid abortion, while at the same time noting that many in the church abhor abortion. Likewise, after appeal to freedom of conscience and the sacraments, the Episcopal Church [USA], *General Convention Resolution* (1988), states its opposition to legislation which would forbid abortion. But although the resolution also advocates limiting the use of abortion, no position is taken on the status of the fetus.

Also note the concern for lack of respect for unborn life, a concern not clearly authorized (though reference is made to all three articles of the creed in the encyclical) by the Roman Catholic Church, *Redemptor Hominis* (1979), 8, 12-14, 16, 17. Similarly, though with no theological authorization, regret about the increasing number of abortions is expressed by the Polish [Catholic] Episcopal Conference, *A Pastoral Letter for the Family* (1973); cf. Church of England, *Abortion* (1979). In this statement, as well as in resolutions of 1974 and 1975, the liberal abortion law of the United Kingdom was criticized. In resolutions of 1979, 1974, and 1966, all entitled *Abortion,* the Church of England speaks of the "unborn child" (in the womb).

Likewise, regret is expressed over the number of clandestine abortions in France by the Eglise Evangélique Luthérienne de France, *Sur le mariage* (1967). The statement contends that the number might be diminished if a 1920 French law was revised in order to legalize contraception. Similarly, the concern to protect unborn life was expressed by the Conference of European Churches and the Council of European Bishops' Conferences, *Final Document of the European Ecumenical Assembly Peace with Justice* (1989), 84, 77, 79, which was authorized by the gospel and ecclesiology. No clear position on abortion is taken by the Lutheran-Episcopal Dialogue, series 3, *Implications of the Gospel* (1988), 120, 117. With some possible authorization drawn from the gospel as well as the doctrine of creation, it does refer to the fetus's "embryonic humanity" and its claims on society.

At least one statement of the Vereinigte Evangelisch-Lutherische Kirche Deutschlands, *Das Leben bejahen* (1985-86), which deals with abortion, has not been included in this analysis. There is ambiguity about its status as an authorized document. It was done "on behalf of" the VELKD Bischofskonferenz and was considered by its Generalsynode. But these bodies do not explicitly identify themselves with its views.

Also note that the Presbyterian Church (USA), *General Assembly Resolution* (1988), while appealing to the Reformed faith for authorization, has mandated a new study of abortion. Likewise see the call for a similar study by the Episcopal Church [USA], *Abortion Study* (1985), as well as its earlier *Human Sexuality* (1967); Christian Church (Disciples of Christ), *Concerning World Population Growth* (1971); United Free Church of Scotland, *Deliverance of the General Assembly* [on public questions] (1965), 1, calling for a study of the proposed relaxation of abortion laws in the United Kingdom. The Presbyterian Church (USA), has more recently, in its *Support of Operation Respect* (1989), endorsed a more explicitly open position when, without clear theological authorization, it supported "freedom of choice" with respect to abortion. No clear position is taken concerning circumstances in which abortion might be legitimate or concerning the status of the fetus, but the statement does suggest that the fetus might be considered a "potential human life".

A most appealing final word on the subject has been offered by the United Church of Christ [USA], *Acts of Violence against Reproductive Health Care Facilities* (1985). It calls for moderation on both sides in the debate on abortion.

G. GENETIC ENGINEERING

In this section we consider forty-two statements of churches that address one or another topic in the broad field of genetic engineering. In a little over half of the cases, the theological warrant appealed to can be characterized simply. Three of the statements, examined at the end of the listing below, address a wider range of issues and have a more complex theological orientation.

1. Appeal to creation
2. Appeal to creation/view of human persons
3. Appeal to creation/natural law/view of human persons
4. Appeal to view of human persons
5. Appeal to the sanctity of human life
6. Appeal to natural law
7. Appeal to creation and Christology
8. Appeal to creation and probably to pneumatology
9. Appeal to grace and creation
10. Appeal to covenant
11. Appeal to the gospel and ecclesiology
12. No clear theological warrant given for position

1. Appeal to creation

Episcopal Church [USA], *Genetic Engineering* (1985). The statement encourages genetic engineering research as well as the production and use of cloned human genes designed in vitro in order to provide a source of pure human proteins for therapy. Life is viewed as a gift from God.

Evangelical Lutheran Free Church (Norway), *Prenatal diagnostik og "de funksjonshemmedes år"* (1981). Warns against the use of prenatal diagnoses to single out and interrupt pregnancies of deformed/handicapped fetuses. The strongest appeal is to the doctrine of creation, though some reference is also made to the Bible and Christian ethics.

Lutheran Church of Australia, *Reproductive Technology* (1987). The church is open to artificial insemination involving marriage partners (b, d, a). It opposes in vitro fertilization involving a donor who will not be one of the legal parents (b, d). It rejects procedures which involve the intentional harming of "embryonic human beings" (c, d). Appeal is made both to God as the giver of marital love and to the Word of God.

Moravian Church in America, Northern Province, *Genetic Engineering* (1982). Sees immense promise in genetic engineering as long as it does not sacrifice an individual's well-being. Humanity's dominion over the earth as well as creation functions as warrant.

2. Appeal to creation/view of human persons

National Council of Churches [USA], *Study Paper on Bioethical Concerns* (1982), III; III/C; II/ A, B, D. Genetic engineering raises complex questions. This preparatory study paper calls for government regulation and further study. The danger of these techniques is that the integrity of one human being might be sacrificed for anticipated social benefits. It calls for regulations on human rights for genetic research, particularly prohibition of human cross-breeding. Its theological warrant is at many points correlated with redemption/Christology and once even with eschatology.

United Methodist Church [USA], *Social Principles of the UMC(USA)* (1980/1988), III/L, III, Pre. The church welcomes development and application of gene technology for battling hunger through improved crops as well as for healing diseases by new medicine. It calls for legal control of both research and application. It rejects changing human chromosomes except for therapeutic reasons, and only if this does not include experiments which produces waste embryos or changes in germ cells. A commitment to witness to the gospel represents a background warrant.

3. Appeal to creation/natural law/view of human persons

New Zealand Catholic Bishops, *A Statement from the New Zealand Catholic Bishops on the Morality of In Vitro Fertilisation* (1984). The bishops are not in principle opposed to in vitro fertilization and artificial insemination, as long as they involve only marriage partners and are not divorced from the "expression of married love" (3); reject surrogate motherhood and artificial insemination with a donor sperm (2-3, 4); reject experimentation on embryos (4); and reject storage and discarding of fertilized ova (4).

Roman Catholic Church, Congregation for the Doctrine of the Faith, *Instruction on Respect for Human Life in Its Origin and on the Dignity of Procreation* (1987). This instruction takes a position in at least these six areas: (1) it is open to human procreation by means of artificial insemination involving marriage partners, as long as it is a mere extension of sexual intercourse (II.B.6-8; II; I; Int.); (2) it rejects artificial insemination involving persons not joined in marriage, including an explicit rejection of surrogate motherhood (II.A; II; I; Int.); (3) it rejects all forms of in vitro fertilization (II.B.4-6; II.B; II; I; Int.); (4) it rejects use of human embryos obtained by in vitro fertilization for purely research purposes, including fertilizing human and animal gametes (I.4-6; I; Int.); (5) it is open to therapeutic procedures on human embryos only if directed towards their healing (I.3; I; Int.); and (6) it is open to prenatal diagnosis as long as it is not done with the thought of inducing an abortion depending on the results of the diagnosis (I.2, 1; I; Int.). The gospel and (in the case of artificial fertilization) the tradition of the church serve as secondary warrants.

4. Appeal to view of human persons

Associated Churches of Christ in New Zealand, *Decisions Relating to Public Issues* (1969). Merely expresses reservations about organ transplants, particularly with regard to deceased donors. It affirms the value of every human life.

Church of Norway, *Vern om menneskeverdet i livets grensesituasjoner* (1982). Claims that the inviolability of human life must be respected in genetic research. The desire for normal children cannot set the agenda for genetic counseling.

Church of Norway, *Human Dignity* (1985), esp. 3. The church must "contribute to the strengthening of ethical responsibility, and to the development of legal regulations within medical research". The warrant stresses God as Creator.

Church of Sweden, *Yttrande över integritet* (1984), 2-5. This statement is generally critical of genetic engineering and is especially opposed to research on human embryos, fertilized eggs, and aborted fetuses. It is open to genetic engineering only where it can be of immediate therapeutic benefit. The primary warrant is the belief that human life begins with conception, with subordinate reference to the "Christian ethic".

Evangelische Kirche im Rheinland, *Initiativantrag der Synodalen Kowalewski betr. Gesetzesvorlage des Bundesjustizministeriums zur Pänalisierung der "Forschung an menschlichen Embryonen"* (1988). Rejects the intended destruction of human embryos in research; cites Evangelische Kirche in Deutschland, *Zur Achtung vor dem Leben* (1987).

Evangelische Landeskirche in Württemberg, *Wort an die Gemeinden zum Schutz des ungeborenen Lebens vom 27. November 1986,* 4. Opposes mandatory prenatal diagnosis.

National Conference of Catholic Bishops [USA], *Health and Health Care* (1981), 40. Cites an address of John Paul II to criticize the implicit dangers of genetic engineering and artificial insemination.

United Free Church of Scotland, *Deliverance of the General Assembly* [on public questions] (1986), 2. Rejects all experimentation on human embryos which is not designed for the benefit of these embryos.

5. Appeal to the sanctity of human life

WCC Nairobi Assembly, *Human Development: Ambiguities of Power, Technology, and Quality of Life* (1975), 32, 74. Regards these developments as opening fresh ethical questions in uncharted areas and recommends further study. The overriding concern "to preserve the sanctity of human life".

6. Appeal to natural law

Episcopal Conference of Portugal, *The Regulation of Birth* (1983), 13. Opposes artificial fertilization; rejects the use of sperm banks; and is open to artificial insemination involving marriage partners, provided that the means conform to the moral law.

7. Appeal to creation and Christology

National Association of Evangelicals [USA], *A Response to Secular Humanism* (1981). Critical of genetic engineering.

8. Appeal to creation and probably to pneumatology

WCC Canberra Assembly, *The Report of the Seventh Assembly* (1991), 26. Concern is expressed about biotechnologies which might threaten the sustainability of creation by usurping powers that belong to the Creator. Pneumatology may only function as a motive.

9. Appeal to grace and creation

United Presbyterian Church [USA], *The Covenant of Life and the Caring Community* (1983). This statement (1) speaks of the promise of genetic engineering and therapy; (2) is open to amniocentesis; (3) affirms the validity of artificial insemination by the husband; (4) affirms the validity of in vitro fertilization; (5) calls for a study of anonymous artificial insemination and surrogate motherhood; and (6) discourages the use of human embryos for experimentation except in cases of clearly demonstrable benefit. It views creation as an ongoing process.

10. Appeal to covenant

World Alliance of Reformed Churches, *Justice, Peace and the Integrity of Creation* (1989).
Finds biotechnology helpful in making it possible for couples to have children. It is also not
opposed to its use in the development of crops. The statement, however, expresses concern
about the full effects of such technology on the ecosystem. It is critical of the commerciali-
zation of childbirth and the use of new genetic techniques for sex selection.

11. Appeal to the gospel and ecclesiology

Conference of European Churches and Council of European Bishops' Conferences, *Final
Document of the European Ecumenical Assembly Peace with Justice* (1989), 87, 79, 78,
77, 25-27. Urges development of strict legislation and professional codes of conduct for
genetic research and genetic engineering. Covenant, which is formulated to reflect
trinitarian authorization, may be a background warrant.

12. No clear theological warrant given for position

American Lutheran Church, *Human Sexuality and Sexual Behavior* (1980), D/6. Raises
numerous critical questions about artificial insemination, particularly artificial insemination
in which the contributors to fertilization are not married. Genetic engineering in general
requires further study. No warrant is clear on these topics, although the overall statement is
rooted in the creation doctrine.
British Council of Churches, *Choices in Childlessness* (1982), 5. Calls for a study of the issues
raised by new medical techniques for the procreation of children.
Church in Wales, *Human Infertility Services and Embryology: Some Ethical Guidelines* (1989).
Opposes use of embryos created in vitro for research; rejects the use of abortion in order to
obtain tissues for transplant therapy; and calls for government regulations.
Church of Ireland, *The Report of the Role of the Church Committee* (1983), 6. Claims that
today's acute questions in medical ethics are a subordinate concern to the issue of the super-
powers' nuclear weaponry.
Church of Ireland, *The Report of the Role of the Church Committee* (1985). This report (1)
opposes surrogate motherhood; (2) opposes trans-species fertilization; (3) calls for close
monitoring of the use of human embryos in research; and (4) seems to set a limit of fourteen
days after fertilization as the maximum age to which embryos may be grown in vitro. The
last three commitments are endorsed only in virtue of "encouraging study" of the Warnock
Report, in which these points are made.
Church of Norway, *Abortspørsmålet* (1971), 4. Opposes use of genetic techniques to allow for
abortion of fetus which is deformed/handicapped. It is possibly authorized by appeal to the
Fifth Commandment, but that is not clear.
Conférence Episcopale Française, *L'avenir d'un peuple* (1982). Notes that genetic engineering
might work for good or evil; claims that its techniques must be controlled.
Congregational Union of Scotland, *Genetic Engineering* (1986). Compassion for the individual
in need must be the guiding principle. Care must be taken, especially when using human
embryos and in legislation with regard to commercial surrogate motherhood. The warrant is
not clear, though it could be anthropology.
Episcopal Church [USA], *"In Vitro" Fertilization* (1982). Supports in vitro fertilization for the
purpose of providing children in a marriage.
Episcopal Church [USA], *Pre-natal Sex Selection* (1982). Opposes abortion, based on biomedical diagnosis, in order to select a child's sex or after the diagnosis of cosmetic abnormalities. It supports abortion in cases where serious abnormalities are diagnosed.

Evangelical Lutheran Free Church (Norway), *Resolusjon fra den Evangelisk Lutherske Frikirke Synodemøte til det Norske Storting* (1979). Concerned about the use of prenatal diagnosis as a threat to unborn life. No theological warrant is evident, except perhaps in the concern that such practices are symptoms of "de-Christianization".

Mennonite Church [USA], *Stewardship of the Earth Resolution on Environment and Faith Issues* (1989). Concerned about the unknown consequencs of genetic engineering on the ecosystem. Although specific theological warrant is not clear, themes derived from all three articles of the creed, especially Christian faith, may function as background warrants.

Reformed Church in America, *Report of the Christian Action Commission* (1973), R-5. Calls for a study of the moral implications of genetic engineering.

Southern Baptist Convention [USA], *A Statement of Social Principles* (1979), 5. Regards genetic engineering as "potentially very dangerous". It would possibly be willing to endorse "negative euthanasia", understood as withholding artificial means to keep terminally ill alive. It perhaps is drawing on theocratic principles enunciated earlier.

United Church of Christ [USA], *Concern about the Moral and Ethical Implications of Genetic Engineering* (1983). After noting the potential of genetic engineering both to help and to harm creation, calls for a study of the discipline.

United Church of Christ [USA], *The Church and Genetic Engineering* (1987). Calls for study of the implications and issues involved in genetic engineering.

WCC Vancouver Assembly, *Confronting Threats to Peace and Survival* (1983), 28-30. Churches must monitor questions on genetic engineering. The council sees positive effects of technology for agriculture, though it is a problem for the world food market. It opposes using humans in research without their consent. The overall theological warrant is not clear, although there is one reference to the integrity of human nature.

WCC Vancouver Assembly, *Healing and Sharing Life in Community* (1983), 27. Churches must examine questions of biomedical ethics. Early in the statement an ethic of sharing and healing is warranted by the Triune God, the Eucharist, and Christ himself.

National Council of Churches [USA], *Genetic Science for Human Benefit* (1986), comments on several points: (1) it notes that genetic engineering is a matter of concern to Christians, about which they require knowledge (V.C.3; I.A.C); (2) it approves genetic counseling prior to conception (II.A); (3) it simply notes the different approaches taken by different churches on diagnosis after fertilization (II.B); (4) it is open to pharmacological treatments obtained through genetic technology (II.C); (5) it is skeptical about gene therapy (II.D); (6) it is concerned that genetic science not be used to authorize racism or be a tool for socio-political domination (II.E; V.B); (7) it is open to genetic modification to cure illness (V.A.1) but insists that genetic therapy and experimentation be voluntary and accessible to all (II.E; V.A.2; V.B.1); (8) it simply notes the contrasting Christian viewpoints on in vitro fertilization (II.F); (9) it simply reports distinct positions regarding possible environmental impact of genetic technology (III; V.A.3); (10) it opposes military use of this technology (IV.C); and (11) it calls for government regulation (V.C.3; IV). We list here seriatim the respective theological warrants for these eleven matters: (1) overall a Trinitarian authorization, with creation (even a two-kingdom ethic) perhaps the predominant theme (see esp. I.D; II.A; V); (2) anthropology; (3) perhaps anthropology; (4) perhaps anthropology; (5) probably anthropology; (6) not clear; (7) the doctrine of sin, with anthropology authorizing criteria for dispensing the technology; (8) not clear; (9) anthropology; (10) not clear; and (11) possibly a Trinitarian authorization.

A document of the WCC Conference on Faith, Science and the Future, *Ethical Issues in the Biological Manipulation of Life* (Cambridge, Mass., 12-24 July 1979) addresses many of these issues. The report (1) recommends study and closer scrutiny of genetic engineering (6; Int.); (2) holds that abortion should not be mandatory in case of abnormalities (1); (3) finds it unobjectionable for a woman to be impregnated by means of these techniques with her husband's sperm, but raises questions if the donors are not married to each other, and particularly if the woman is unmarried (1); (4) asserts that no genetic experimentation should jeopardize human consciousness (2); (5) urges caution in the development of means of controlling aspects of the personality and behavior manipulation (3); and (6) rejects euthanasia but is open to terminating care when it cannot achieve anything (4). No theological warrant is evident for the first point; for the second, creation/anthropology is possibly correlated with Christology; the view of human persons is appealed to in the third and fourth (and perhaps also the fifth) points; and creation stands behind the discussion of the sixth point.

In *Zur Achtung vor dem Leben* (1987), the Evangelische Kirche in Deutschland (1) advises against all treatments of artificial fertilization (III/5[b]), particularly all forms of artificial insemination involving a donor from outside the marriage relationship (III/5[c]); (2) opposes surrogate motherhood (III/5[d]); (3) insists on the right of the person to decline to be the subject of genetic research (III/5[f]); (4) insists that prenatal diagnosis should not automatically be bound to a decision for abortion (III/5[g]) and is generally critical of abortion except in certain exceptional circumstances (III/6.III/5[e]); and (5) opposes intended destruction of human embryos in research (III/6[i]) and warns against future technology concerning the transfer of genes (III/6[h]). It cites with favor a 1985 statement of the organization's Rat, *Von der Würde werdenden Lebens*. The Christian faith, specifically the doctrine of the Trinity (I), with a particular Christological emphasis (IV), provides the overall authorization. The view of human persons seems to provide the primary ethical warrant for the last three points. This appeal may also operate in the critique of all forms of artificial insemination, inasmuch as the cited statement of the organization's Rat (2.5) speculated on the negative psychosomatic effects such a procedure might have on the child. Also note that the anthropological argument in the rejection of surrogate motherhood is related to the statement's concern about the child's welfare.

H. SOCIAL JUSTICE

All church statements explicitly addressing this issue call for Christians to work for social justice. Differences emerge over the warrant to authorize this position, and whether a particular contemporary question is necessarily correlated with the concern for social justice. In a few cases also the proper means for achieving these aims is debated — specifically, whether violence is ever appropriate in pursuing social justice. By virtue of their position on issues such as human rights, apartheid, and development, various churches have taken a stand in favor of social justice. Yet only those *explicitly* calling for it are included here.

1. Appeal to creation/view of human persons
2. Appeal to creation, correlated with Christology or Christian ethics/Christian conscience
3. Appeal to creation and Christology/the gospel, with the former likely grounded in the latter
4. Appeal to creation and the gospel/Christology
5. Appeal to creation and the gospel/covenant/the Bible
6. Appeal to creation, Christian faith/Christology, prophecy, and the Bible
7. Appeal to creation, subordinated to covenant/the gospel
8. Appeal to anthropology, rooted in Christology and eschatology
9. Appeal to Christology/the gospel/redemption
10. Appeal to Christology and prophecy
11. Appeal to Christology, the Bible, and the law
12. Appeal to Christology and some other locus drawn from the third article
13. Appeal to the Christian message/the gospel
14. Appeal to the gospel, with creation as a subordinate warrant
15. Appeal to the gospel and eschatology, with creation possibly subordinated to these loci
16. Appeal to redemption, correlated with creation
17. Authorization drawn from pneumatology
18. Appeal to prophecy
19. Appeal to the prophetic tradition
20. Appeal to the prophetic heritage, with some reference to creation
21. Authorization apparently drawn from ecclesiology
22. Appeal to ecclesiology, with some reference to a two-kingdom ethic
23. Authorization drawn from sacramentology and ecclesiology
24. Probably warrants drawn from eschatology, with reference to creation
25. Appeal to the kingdom of God
26. Appeal to the kingdom of God and sacramentology
27. Appeal to all three articles of the creed
28. Appeal to loci from all articles of the creed, especially creation and ecclesiology or eschatology
29. Appeal to all three articles of the creed, though all may be grounded in Christology
30. Warrant drawn from all three articles of the creed, with creation subordinated to Christology
31. Appeal to God's grace
32. Warrant rooted in righteousness, the holiness of God
33. Appeal to the will of God
34. Appeal to the call of God
35. Appeal to the Word of God
36. Appeal to the Word of God/gospel and creation
37. Appeal to the Bible and the gospel/Christology
38. Appeal to the biblical vision and possibly to the Spirit
39. Appeal to the Bible and prophecy

40. Appeal to the Bible and Christian conscience or Christian principles
41. Appeal to covenant and Scripture
42. Appeal to divine justice and the Bible
43. Authorization likely drawn from the priesthood of all believers
44. Appeal to Christian love
45. Appeal to the witness of love/the gospel
46. Appeal to Christian ethical considerations and social responsibility
47. Appeal to evangelism and to all three articles of the creed, though all may be grounded in Christology
48. Appeal to Christian responsibility
49. Appeal to the Christian faith/gospel
50. Appeal to Christology supplemented by loci from the first and third articles of the creed
51. Appeal to prophecy with the Trinity doctrine in the background
52. No clear theological warrant given for position

1. Appeal to creation/view of human persons

All Africa Conference of Churches, *The Prophetic and Serving Church* (1974). Justice related to development. This vision of development is rooted in view of human persons.

American Baptist Churches, *Policy Statement on Housing* (1983). Calls for social justice in the sphere of housing. Authorization is provided by "the Christian concept of the dignity of the individual".

American Lutheran Church, *Peace, Justice, and Human Rights* (1972), 1, 4, 5, 7, 10, 11. At least concerned with international justice and the relation of justice to peace, human rights, and development. References to Christology and redemption seem to function only as motives.

American Lutheran Church, *The Unfinished Reformation* (1980). May not have been an official statement.

American Lutheran Church, *Toward Fairness in Public Training and Spending* (1982), 1-5. Justice includes peace and concern with those on society's margins. It calls for public income support as a right and also for full employment and rejects a distinction between welfare and social security. The gospel may be a motive. The statement may not have had official status.

Anglican Church of Canada, *South Africa* (1986). Concerned about justice and peace in South Africa, and so rejects apartheid and racism.

Associated Church of Christ in New Zealand, *Decisions Relating to Public Issues* (1968). Concerned about a just peace on earth, free from all forms of discrimination.

Australian [Catholic] Episcopal Conference, *Morals and Human Values* (1972). Concerned about injustices inherent in attempts to settle disputes by violence or war.

British Council of Churches, *Work for the Council* (1982), B/1, B/3. Speaks only of justice; relates it to peace.

[Catholic] Bishops Conference of Haiti, *Les élections n'ont été ni libres ni justes* (1977), 6, 3. Relates justice to truth, freedom, and respect of human rights, especially as it relates to recent elections in Haiti.

[Catholic] Bishops Conference of Mozambique, *Caminhos de paz* (1979), IV.1; IV.2; Int. Relates justice to peace. Christology or the gospel may be a background warrant.

[Catholic] Bishops Conference of Mozambique, *Um apelo à paz* (1983), 6-9. Relates justice to peace and the promotion of fundamental goods. Christology could be a background warrant.

[Catholic] Bishops of Panama, *Declaration of the Bishops of Panama concerning the Negotiations for a New Treaty on the Canal* (1975). Justice (particularly for Panama with regard to the Canal Zone), related to peace, is authorized by an appeal to all persons of good will. Elsewhere, without authorization, the declaration speaks of national and international justice.

[Catholic] Episcopal Conference of Belgium, *Déclaration sur l'avortement* (1975), I/5. Relates justice to the need to maintain enforcement of anti-abortion legislation.

Chilean [Catholic] Episcopal Conference, *Declaration on Reconciliation* (1974). Only refers to justice.

Conférence Episcopale Française, *Note pastorale de l'épiscopat français sur "Humanae Vitae"* (1968), 22. Condemns injustice and war; is concerned with respect for human life.

Episcopal Conference of Portugal, *The Regulation of Birth* (1983), 11. Social justice related to the freedom of couples, not constrained by government authority, to make their own decisions concerning the number of children they may have.

Evangelical Church of Lutheran Confession in Brazil, *The Curitiba Declaration* (1970), I/3. Church seeks to make public officials find just solutions. It adopts the framework of a two-kingdom ethic concerning the role of the state.

Evangelical Lutheran Free Church (Norway), *En oppfordring til vare menigheter fra synodemotet* (1979). Distribution of the world's resources, especially to parts of the world in need, is a matter of justice. Appeal to the doctrine of creation includes a reference to the readers' "Christian responsibility".

Evangelische Kirche der Kirchenprovinz Sachsen, *Brief der Synode an die Gemeinden zur Friedensverantwortung* (1984). Speaks only of justice, relating it to peace and ecology. Authorization is not completely clear, so the statement may draw upon models of secular ecumenism.

Evangelische Landeskirche in Württemberg, *Erklärung der 8. Württ. Evan. Landessynode zum politischen Auftrag der Kirche* (1973), 5ff. Speaks of government's role in promoting justice. Opts for a clear two-kingdom ethic point of view.

Evangelisch-Lutherische Landeskirche Hannovers, *Wort der Landessynode der ELLH vom 20. Juni 1985 zu Fragen der Arbeitslosigkeit*, IV, II. Relates social justice to the reduction of unemployment.

Fédération Protestante de France, *Sur l'action locale contre les esclavages sociaux* (1969). Justice entails the struggle against all forms of social slavery, such as alcoholism, prostitution, drugs, and homelessness. The creation doctrine seems to provide authorization insofar as appeal is made for Christians to cooperate with secular organizations. (Secular ecumenism could be operative instead at this point.)

Fédération Protestante de France, *Vœux à l'Assemblée Générale* (1987), 6, 5. In one resolution, no authorization is given for concern about justice and peace in New Caledonia. The other resolution, concerned about the just administration of the goods of the earth given by God, relates justice to the conquest of poverty.

International Council of Community Churches [USA], *Statement of Concern on Nuclear Weapons* (1982). Relates justice to disarmament and a concern for the poor. Authorization seems to be provided by appeal to the law of God.

Lutheran Church in America, *The Human Crisis in Ecology* (1972), A; C.9. The crisis in ecology is tied to international social justice.

Lutheran Church in America, *In Pursuit of Justice: Society, the Offender, and Systems of Correction* (1972), B. Relates justice to civil peace; is concerned with criminal justice. It manifests a strong two-kingdom ethic, though Christology may be in the background.

Lutheran Church in America, *Human Rights: Doing Justice in God's World* (1978), esp. 3, 4, 5. Justice is related to human rights, such as environment protection and right to adequate medical care. It is also related to economic justice.

Lutheran Church in America, *Economic Justice: Stewardship of Creation in Human Community* (1980), esp. 3, 6, 7. Relates social justice to economic justice, ecology, and private ownership. The statement does refer to Christ's work and eschatology, although they seem only to motivate, not authorize, the quest for justice. Also a reference is made to the church, which suggests that its function as a sign of the new creation is probably a warrant for the statement's concerns with ecology.

Lutheran Church-Missouri Synod, *Creation in Biblical Perspective* (1969ff.), VI.5. Creation in God's image is a powerful force for ethical behavior regarding social injustice.

Lutheran World Federation, *Responsible Participation in Today's Society* (1970), 59ff., 26. Justice and peace are related. Appeal to Romans 13 and earlier appeal to creation doctrine suggests that it functions here as warrant, though this is not completely clear.

Lutheran World Federation, *Declaration for Peace* (1981), 3-4. Justice and peace are related. The argument is also motivated by eschatology; warrants are correlated with ecclesiology and Christology.

National Association of Evangelicals [USA], *Violation of Human Rights in Uganda* (1977). Concerned about justice and human rights in Uganda.

National Conference of Catholic Bishops [USA], *Population and the American Future: A Response* (1972), 2, 3. Relates social justice to overcoming poverty, disease, and violence.

National Conference of Catholic Bishops [USA], *Resolution on Farm Labor* (1973), 2, 8. Calls for social justice for U.S. agricultural workers, to be obtained by boycotting table grapes grown on non-union farms.

National Conference of Catholic Bishops [USA], *Statement on Population* (1973), 3-5. Relates social justice to worldwide equality, decent standard of living, educational opportunities, full employment, and population control.

National Conference of Catholic Bishops [USA], *Statement on the World Food Crisis: A Pastoral Plan of Action* (1974), 17. Speaks only of justice. Would modify the free-market system when it stands in the way of justice.

National Conference of Catholic Bishops [USA], *Pastoral Plan for Pro-Life Activities* (1975), 26-27. Speaks only of justice — a just system of law.

National Conference of Catholic Bishops [USA], *Pastoral Letter on Marxist Communism* (1980), 65, 61, 59, 43-45, 30. Social justice includes development, control of greed and natural possessions, as well as concern for the oppressed. It authorizes its position by quoting the call for social justice on grounds of anthropology made by the papal encyclical *Populorum Progressio* (1967), 44.

National Conference of Catholic Bishops [USA], *The Challenge of Peace: God's Promise and Our Response* (1983), 327, 326, 301-6, 285, 283, 282, 275, 274, 57-60, 13-15, 2. Concerned only at one point with justice for all people; otherwise deals only with justice. Justice is related to peace. All the articles of the creed are called upon to authorize justice, but only "public opinion" (the kind of consent rooted in creation) authorizes social justice.

National Council of Churches [USA], *Religious Obedience and Civil Disobedience* (1968), VI, III, II, I. Speaks only of justice, relating it to peace, freedom, and an openness to civil disobedience. The gospel is correlated with the statement's appeal to natural law.

National Council of Churches [USA], *Consumer Rights and Corporate Responsibility* (1972). Concerned about justice for consumers. Stewardship of creation functions as the warrant.

Reformed Ecumenical Synod, *Race Relations* (1984), art. 103, rec. 2. Relates social justice to concern to overcome racism. Appeal to anthropology is correlated with reference to the unity in Christ given to the church.

Russian Orthodox Church, *Point of View of the Patriarchs* (1977). Calls for just relations among nations, which it relates to disarmament. It appeals to human consensus for authorization.

Russian Orthodox Church, *Decree of the Holy Synod* (1983). Relates justice to peace, ecology, and the rejection of nuclear war.

Russian Orthodox Church, *Jubiläumsbotschaft zum Millennium der Taufe Russlands* (1987). Relates justice to peace.

United Church of Christ [USA], *Executive Council Statement on Racial Crisis* (1963). Relates social justice to racial equality. Authorization is by appeal to the concept of "God-given rights to protest injustice".

United Church of Christ [USA], *Pronouncement on the Role of Transnational Business in Mass Economic Development* (1975). Relates social justice to economic justice and full human development.

United Church of Christ [USA], *Exploitative Broadcasting Practices* (1977), II. Relates community justice to peace and concern about undue sex and violence on television. Themes of liberation theology function as background warrants, and eschatology authorizes patience for dealing with these challenges. (This part of the statement may not have General Synod authorization.)

United Church of Christ [USA], *Energy* (1979), II, III/C. Relates social justice to issues of energy consumption and so ecology. Reference to Christology may function only as a motive, though elsewhere in the statement it is also a warrant.

United Church of Christ [USA], *General Synod Resolution* (1987). Relates abortion to social justice.

United Church of Christ [USA], *The Relationship between the United Church of Christ and the Jewish Community* (1989).

United Free Church of Scotland, *Deliverance of the General Assembly* [on public questions] (1973), 16.

Uniting Church in Australia, *Response to WCC Visit* (1982), 82.51, (3b). Concerned about injustices done to Aboriginal Australians by the dispossession of their land.

World Alliance of Reformed Churches, *The Theatre of Glory and a Threatened Creation's Hope* (1982). Speaks only of economic justice in its relation to ecology and the threat of nuclear war. Creation may be subordinated to redemption.

WCC Amsterdam Assembly, *The Church and the Disorder of Society* (1948), III, I, VI. Social justice is related to responsibility and freedom in society. Also concerned about economic justice. Creation may be subordinated to Christology and eschatology, which are at least background warrants.

WCC Nairobi Assembly, *Seeking Community: The Common Search of People of Various Faiths, Cultures, and Ideologies* (1976), 8, 10. Later in the statement, Christology also functions as warrant. All humanity have common concern with justice and peace.

WCC Uppsala Assembly, *Towards Justice and Peace in International Affairs* (1968), 17. Justice is achieved only when full equality of the races is established. It also demands "a common understanding" of the dignity of humankind. This creation warrant is surrounded elsewhere in the statement by appeals to Christology to warrant other positions.

WCC Vancouver Assembly, *Witnessing in a Divided World* (1983), 41, 40.

WCC Canberra Assembly, *Come, Holy Spirit... The Assembly Message* (1991). Concern for justice for the poor and marginalized is expressed. Justice is related to ecology. Christology and pneumatology stand in the background.

2. Appeal to creation, correlated with Christology or Christian ethics/Christian conscience

American Baptist Churches, *Policy Statement on Africa* (1987), 1, 3. Calls for a just peace in Namibia. Addresses other problems such as apartheid, human rights, health care, illiteracy, ecology, and development.

American Lutheran Church, *The Nature of the Church and Its Relationship with Government* (1980), B2a, B2b, B3a. Relates social justice to peace, civil rights, human rights, equal opportunity, and the promotion of the general welfare of all people.

Presbyterian Church (USA), *God Alone Is Lord of the Conscience* (1988), G, A. Speaks only of justice; at one point is concerned about justice in employment practices. Christology/faith functions only as a motive for this ethic.

3. Appeal to creation and Christology/the gospel, with the former likely grounded in the latter

Latin American [Catholic] Bishops, Third General Conference, *The Puebla Message* (1979). Relates justice to freedom, the civilization of love, and social peace. The concern for "social peace" suggests that references in the document to justice refer to social justice. A number of its themes are characteristic of liberation theology.

National Conference of Catholic Bishops [USA], *Brothers and Sisters to Us: A Pastoral Letter on Racism* (1979). Concerned with justice in the context of racial equality. Justice is said to demand full employment. The statement is possibly also authorized by eschatology.

Paraguay [Catholic] Bishops' Conference, *El campesino paraguayo y la tierra* (1983), Int. 2.2-2.5. Relates social justice to ownership of private property maintained with a sense of the common good.

Roman Catholic Church, Vatican II, *Gaudium et Spes* (1965), 22, 29, 69, 74, 76, 83. Excessive social and economic disparity is not justice. Justice is the condition of peace. The last reference roots injustice in doctrine of sin. Note a kind of two-kingdom ethic in the statement (76, 74).

United Presbyterian Church/Presbyterian Church in the U.S., *Reformed Faith and Politics* (1983), Recs. C/2, C, B/3, Policy Statement. Relates social justice to economic justice, peace, disarmament, and the overcoming of racism.

4. Appeal to creation and the gospel/Christology

All Africa Conference of Churches, *The Gospel — Good News to the Poor and Oppressed* (1981). Concerned only with economic justice.

American Lutheran Church, *Manifesto for Our Nation's Third Century* (1976), VI, II. Social justice is related to peace.

Anglican Church of Canada, *Disarmament* (1982). Relates social justice to the WCC vision of a "just, sustainable, participatory society", which is in turn seen as a basis for peace. Its warrant not entirely clear at this point.

Assembly of Argentine Bishops, *Before the Return to Democracy* (1983), 4, 6. Social justice includes concern for the poor and is also related to peace.

Bund der Evangelischen Kirchen in der Deutschen Demokratischen Republik, *Beschluss der Synode des Bundes zum Bericht der Konferenz der Evangelischen Kirchenleitungen in der DDR vom 19. September 1983*, 4, 5, 7. Refers only to justice; relates it to peace, mutual security, disarmament, human rights, development, and the overcoming of poverty. Cites WCC Vancouver Assembly, *Statement on Peace and Justice* (1983), 26, 25, 24a.

Canadian Catholic Conference, *On Pastoral Implications of Political Choices* (1972). Calls for economic justice linked to peace and love.

[Catholic] Bishops of the Netherlands, *De mens in de arbeid* (1980), 22; 28; Slut. Seems to relate injustice and the increase of nuclear weapons. Elsewhere the Eucharist provides authorization. Note the endorsement of a relational view of persons.

[Catholic] Episcopal Conference of the Pacific, *The Pacific and Peace* (1986), VII. Justice relates to ownership of the land, justice to migrants, and political independence. Eschatology may be a background warrant.

Church of Ireland, *The Report of the Role of the Church Committee* (1984), 4. Especially concerned about justice in Northern Ireland, particularly as it might help establish peace.

Evangelical Presbyterian Church of Chile, *I Believe in One God the Fount and Future of Life: Creed of the EPCC* (1983). Relates justice to peace. Creation may be the primary warrant. Ecclesiology may also function as a warrant insofar as it authorizes (as in liberation theology) the struggle against oppression.

Evangelische Landeskirche in Württemberg, *Mitteilung an die Gemeinden zum Programm des ökumenischen Rates der Kirchen zur Bekämpfung des Rassismus* (1970), I, II/A. Relates justice to the conquest of racism (though will not support the WCC Program to Combat Racism). Opposes the use of violence in the struggle against racism.

Evangelisch-Lutherische Kirche in Bayern, *Wort der Synode zur Frage der Gewalt* (1969). Relates social justice to freedom and peace; rejects the use of violence as a means of social reform. Authorization is by the law of creation, but the gospel also serves as warrant, in virtue of citing *Erklärung des Rates der Evangelischen Kirche in Deutschland vom 28. November 1974.*

Evangelisch-Lutherische Landeskirche Hannovers, *Kirche und Rassismus* (1975), I/B/2, 5. Relates justice to the conquest of racism and to evangelism. Cites the 1974 international conference of conservative evangelicals, *The Lausanne Covenant,* 5, which called for justice with the same authorization. Seems open to the use of violence, in extreme circumstances, to overcome racism and achieve justice.

Latin American [Catholic] Bishops, Second General Conference (Medellín Conference), *Message to the People of Latin America* (1968). Relates social justice to participation, cultural autonomy, and peace. Christology and baptism could be background warrants. The themes and agenda of liberation theology are reflected in the statement.

Methodist Church in Brazil, *Plan for the Life and Mission of the MCB* (1982), III/6; III/5(b); III/3; III/2; II/10. Relates social justice to peace, racial equality, and economic justice. At one point it employs themes of liberation theology.

National Conference of Catholic Bishops [USA], *The National Race Crisis* (1968), 9. Justice primarily related to racial equality, which includes concern with housing, employment, education, and welfare. It opts for heavy government intervention in achieving these aims.

National Conference of Catholic Bishops [USA], *Resolution on Southeast Asia* (1971), 4-7, 11. Relates social justice to peace. The natural law, as per a citation from *Gaudium et Spes* (1965), 82, provides authorization along with the gospel.

National Conference of Catholic Bishops [USA], *To Teach as Jesus Did* (1972), 8, 9-11, 60-61, 109. Speaks only of justice; relates it to peace. The gospel and eschatology function as background warrants.

National Conference of Catholic Bishops [USA], *Resolution towards Peace in the Middle East* (1973), 1, 2, 7, 8. Concerned about justice in the Middle East, which is related to peace in the region and to ensuring international access to Jerusalem.

National Conference of Catholic Bishops [USA], *Society and the Aged: Toward Reconciliation* (1976), 5, 6, 8, 9, 52. Social justice as healing the rupture between society and its elderly members.

National Conference of Catholic Bishops [USA], *The Bicentennial Consultation: A Response to the Call to Action* (1977), 8, 9, 13, 21, 34, 38. Relates social justice to peace, justice for women, women's rights, and justification (the transformation of human life).

National Conference of Catholic Bishops [USA], *Health and Health Care* (1981), 12-13, 52. Social justice is related to adequate health care and economic justice. In general, justice also demands that employees realize the special responsibilities they have as workers who care for the sick in a Christian facility.

National Council of Churches [USA], *Christian Concern and Responsibility for Economic Life in a Rapidly Changing Technological Society* (1966). Social justice includes the overcoming of poverty. It posits a view of creation as ongoing.

National Council of Churches [USA], *Defense and Disarmament* (1968). Refers only to justice; relates it to peace and perhaps to development.

National Council of Churches [USA], *The United Nations and World Community* (1977), Int. Concerned about international justice; relates it to peace.

Roman Catholic Church, *Populorum Progressio* (1967), 5, 22, 32, 44, 61, 76, 81. Relates justice to development, peace, international morality, and international trade relations. Besides appeal to creation (the idea that all persons of good will share common values), it appeals to a kind of theocratic vision of the church influencing civil laws. Such affirmations perhaps play a more crucial role if the statement's references to the positions of the Vatican II documents and its interest in infusing a "Christian spirit" into the laws entail that — like *Gaudium et Spes,* 22 — creation is grounded in Christology.

Roman Catholic Church, *Redemptor Hominis* (1979), 12-17 (esp. 16, 17). Relates social justice to human rights and the moral order. Eschatology and ecclesiology also stand in the background, and creation/anthropology may be subordinated to these other loci.

Russian Orthodox Church, *Message of the Holy Synod of the ROC on War and Peace in a Nuclear Age* (1986), 1.2, 1.7, 2.7, 2.9, 3.27, 3.28, 3.30, 3.34. Relates social justice to political and economic independence as well as to peace.

Sudan Catholic Bishops' Conference, *Lord Come to Our Aid* (1984), E, G-G/b, G/d. Relates justice to human rights, dignity, peace, unity, and stability. Christology authorizes the rejection of the use of violence.

United Church of Christ [USA], *A Resolution on Human Rights with Special Emphasis on Rumania, Philippines and South Korea* (1977). Concerned with social justice insofar as it relates to human rights. Christology may function only as a background warrant.

United Church of Christ [USA], *The Crisis of People and the Land* (1985), I, III, IV. Relates social justice to justice in agricultural life and to the just care of the land.

United Church of Christ [USA], *Fulfilling God's Covenant with All Children* (1987). Social justice is related to economic justice, peace, and support of programs for helping, empowering, and sustaining children.

United Methodist Church [USA], *Social Principles of the UMC(USA)* (1980), VI/D; VI/A; VI. Ties justice to peace and economic order. Christians are to seek the meaning of the gospel in dealing with this issue. The claim to commend efforts of all people seeking "peace through law" suggests a warrant rooted in creation doctrine.

United Presbyterian Church [USA], *War, Peace, and Conscience* (1969). Concerned only about justice.

World Alliance of Reformed Churches, *Reconciliation and Man: The Freedom of the New Man* (1970). Justice counteracts racial prejudice and economic inequality. But Christology, particularly themes consistent with liberation theology, may be the prevailing warrant.

WCC Amsterdam Assembly, *The Church and the International Disorder* (1948), I, Int. Relates justice to peace, claiming the pursuit of justice is an attack on the causes of war.

WCC Evanston Assembly, *Social Problems — The Responsible Society in a World Perspective* (1954), I/A; II. In providing justice, the state should take responsibility for regulating the economy and for relieving the impact of unemployment and old age. It almost opts for welfare state.

WCC New Delhi Assembly, *An Appeal to All Governments and Peoples* (1961), 9-10. Correlates justice and peace. Perhaps a somewhat more obvious appeal is made to Christology as warrant.

WCC New Delhi Assembly, *Service* (1961), 1-3, 29, 36, 39. Justice entails the state's responsibility to provide freedom and promote economic development.

WCC Uppsala Assembly, *Renewal in Mission* (1968), I/7. Seeking justice is part of the restoration of true humanity in Christ, but human nature (creation) itself demands interdependence with society.

WCC Vancouver Assembly, *Message from the Sixth Assembly* (1983). Justice is the root of peace. It also states that Christians are empowered by the Eucharist.

5. Appeal to creation and the gospel/covenant/the Bible

Baptist Union of New Zealand, *Public Questions* (1970). Concerned that even the poor receive a just share of medical technology.

United Presbyterian Church [USA], *Covenant and Creation: Theological Reflections on Contraception and Abortion* (1983), Policy Statement, Rec. 8. Concerned about justice, which includes maintaining order, improving the quality of life, and opposing the restriction of equal access to contraception and abortion regardless of race, age, and economic standing.

United Presbyterian Church [USA], *The Covenant of Life and the Caring Community* (1983), Policy Statement. Concerned about justice in the sense of providing health care to all, regardless of race, gender, age, or economic standing.

6. Appeal to creation, Christian faith/Christology, prophecy, and the Bible

Mennonite Church [USA]/Mennonite Church, General Conference [USA], *Justice and Christian Witness* (1983), I/A, I/B, II/A, II/C, II/E, III/A, III/C, IV/B, V, V/B, V/C, VI/A, VII/B, VIII/C, VIII/A. Relates justice to peace, love, evangelism, action on behalf of the oppressed, as well as overcoming racism and pollution. Christology may be the prevailing warrant. It authorizes the rejection of violence.

7. Appeal to creation, subordinated to covenant/the gospel

Catholic Bishops of the Philippines, *What Is Happening to Our Beautiful Land?* (1988). Refers only to justice; relates it to peace and ecology.

8. Appeal to anthropology, rooted in Christology and eschatology

National Conference of Catholic Bishops [USA], *Peace and Vietnam* (1966), 1-2, 15ff. Speaks only of justice as it is the starting point of peace. In view of citations from Vatican II's *Gaudium et Spes,* 22, which subordinates creation to Christology, possible appeals to anthropology in this statement should be subordinated to Christology.

Roman Catholic Church, *Laborem Exercens* (1981), 26, 20, 8, 27, 1. Cf. 18, 2. Relates social justice to human work, stressing the priority of the former to technological advances and the role of labor unions in enhancing this aim. It often calls for justice without any theological authorization or by way of appeal to Christology.

9. Appeal to Christology/the gospel/redemption

American Baptist Churches, *Policy Statement on Racial Justice* (1983). Concerned about racial justice; relates it to peace. The doctrine of human persons is a background warrant.

American Baptist Churches, *Policy Statement on Peace (1985)*. Speaks only of justice; relates it to peace.

Anglicanism, *The Resolutions of the Lambeth Conference (1978),* 5. Relates justice to peace; rejects the use of violence to achieve these aims.

Assembly of Argentine Bishops, *Before the Return to Democracy* (1983). Social justice requires investing all energies in the poor, to the point of accepting austerity. Such themes of liberation theology are complemented by appeal to the doctrine of human persons as a background warrant.

Baptist Union of Great Britain and Ireland, *Poverty and World Development* (1975). Speaks only of justice; relates it to food shortages. The doctrine of creation may authorize dealing with the food crisis.

Bishops of Chile, *Collective Pastoral Letter* (1968). Social justice related to peace. It criticizes use of violence to achieve justice. Authorization is by love, with Christology in background.

Brethren in Christ Church [USA], *Elimination of Racist Statements and Attitudes* (1970). Social justice involves overcoming racism.

British Council of Churches, *Central America* (1983). Calls for justice and peace in Nicaragua; takes this position and its authorization in virtue of approving the council's policy statement *Conflict and Promise — Central America in the 1980s*, 2, 5.

Canadian Catholic Conference, *Justice in the World: Proposals to the Third International Synod of Bishops* (1971), 2, 6, 8. Relates justice to the overcoming of unscrupulous advertising and the exploitation of the poor.

Canadian Catholic Conference, *Sharing National Income* (1972). Social justice includes the call for redistribution of income, so all may have a decent standard of living.

Canadian Catholic Conference, *Social Justice in the Church* (1972). Concerned about social justice for the poor.

Canadian Conference of Catholic Bishops, *Ethical Choices and Political Challenges* (1983), 7, 9, 15, 22. Concerned about economic justice, explicitly for the poor. Creation also functions as a background warrant in authorizing a priority for the poor.

[Catholic] Episcopal Conference of Nicaragua, *Renewing Christian Hope at the Beginning of 1977* (1977). Relates social justice to peace, civil rights, employment, and religious freedom. Violence in Nicaragua is condemned.

[Catholic] Episcopal Conference of Portugal, *Aspects de la vie nationale portugaise* (1987), 1, 8. Relates social justice to freedom.

[Catholic] Episcopal Conference of Spain, *L'église et les pauvres* (1970), 15, 14, 2. Urges justice, including economic justice, a better distribution of material goods, human dignity, agrarian reform, multiplying home constructions, and the adjustment of salaries.

[Catholic] Episcopal Conference of the Philippines, *Call for Free and Honest Elections* (1986). Calls for the election of candidates who personify the evangelical values of justice and peace.

Christian Church (Disciples of Christ), *Appeal to the Churches on Vietnam* (1967). Relates justice to peace. The statement takes its position by citing National Council of Churches (USA) General Assembly, *An Appeal to the Churches concerning Vietnam* (1967), sec. 3, par. 2.

Christian Church (Disciples of Christ), *Concerning Christian Response to Revolution* (1968). Speaks only of justice; relates it to freedom and a concern for the downtrodden. Authorization is also provided by "Christian ethics". It opposes the use of violence.

Christian Church (Disciples of Christ), *Concerning the United Nations' Peace-keeping Role in the Middle East* (1973). Concerned about justice and peace in the Middle East.

Christian Church (Disciples of Christ), *Concerning Wider World Perspectives* (1973). Concerned about racial justice as it relates to ecology, population planning, and peace.

Christian Church (Disciples of Christ), *A Resolution concerning World Hunger and Development* (1975), I, II/C, V. Speaks only of justice, which includes love, concern for people of poorer nations, an end to economic privilege, and a concern for the undernourished.

Christian Church (Disciples of Christ), *Concerning Universal Human Rights* (1977). Refers only to justice; relates it to peace and human rights.

Christian Church (Disciples of Christ), *Resolution concerning Affirmative Action and Ministerial Leadership* (1981). Speaks only of justice, especially of concern for the disadvantaged. Appeal is made to the prophets as a supporting warrant.

Christian Conference of Asia, *Justice and Service* (1973), III; IV; II/1, 2; Thrust Paper. Justice tied to racial equality, development, and liberation and is deemed more important than ecology. Reference to justice in the face of racism could possibly be authorized by creation/ view of human persons.

Christian Conference of Asia, *Life and Action: Thrust Paper* (1973), I. Concerned with development of just and creative communities. Christian faith may be the warrant, but this is not entirely clear.

Christian Conference of Asia, *Justice and Service* (1977), C, D. Health care is noted as an issue of social justice. Other related issues are hunger, political detainees, rights of workers, and military and economic domination by foreign nations.

Conférence Episcopale Française, *Tout être humain a le droit de vivre* (1974). Relates justice to the development of the rights of the oppressed and the prevention of abortion.

Eglise Protestante Unie de Belgique, *Assemblée synodale* (1982). Relates justice to peace and freedom.

Episcopal Church [USA], *General Convention Resolution* [on the Panama Canal treaty] (1976). Concerned about negotiating a just and equitable new Canal Zone treaty. Ecclesiology may function as the warrant.

Episcopal Church [USA], *General Convention Resolution* [affirming Lambeth statement on war and violence] (1979). Endorses the 1978 Lambeth Conference resolution.

Episcopal Church [USA], *Non-violent War Resistance* (1982). Endorses the 1979 resolution of the denomination, so the call for justice and peace seems to share the earlier resolution's theological warrants.

Episcopal Church [USA], *Establish a Standing Commission on Peace* (1985). Speaks only of justice; relates it to peace.

Evangelical Methodist Church of Argentina, *Social Service and Action: Foundations in Biblical Theology* (n.d.), 1. Seems to relate social justice to economic justice. Ecclesiology may be background warrant. Themes are drawn from liberation theology and secular ecumenism.

Evangelische Kirche der Kirchenprovinz Sachsen, *Beschluss zum "Fonds für ökumenische Solidarität"* (1985). Relates justice to the conquering of poverty.

Evangelische Kirche der Kirchenprovinz Sachsen, *Beschluss zur Gesamtthematik der Synodaltagung* (1985), 2, 1, Int. Concerned about a just world economic policy, including justice to the needs and values of the weak. It relates justice to peace and ecology. Insofar as it is related to peace, the concept of covenant as well as the gospel provide authorization.

Evangelische Kirche der Kirchenprovinz Sachsen, *Beschluss zum Handeln in der Gesellschaft, vor allem im Umweltbereich* (1985). Relates justice to disarmament and ecology. Obedience to God provides authorization.

Evangelische Kirche der Pfalz, *Beschluss der pfälzischen Landessynode vom 28. November 1985.* Concerned about justice for the black people in South Africa.

Evangelische Kirche der Union — Bereich Bundesrepublik Deutschland und Berlin-West, *Telegramm an den SACC* (1982). Concerned about a just peace in divided Germany.

Evangelische Kirche von Kurhessen-Waldeck, *Wort der Landessynode zum Thema "Ermutigung zum Frieden" vom 17. Mai 1984,* 3-4. Relates justice to peace; cites WCC Vancouver Assembly, *Statement on Peace and Justice* (1983), 8-10, as well as the 1934 Barmen Declaration, II, V. It in turn includes a background reference to eschatology. Sacramentology is also a supporting warrant for authorizing peace.

Evangelisch-Lutherische Landessynode Sachsens, *Erklärung der 23. ELLS vom 22. März 1988.* Speaks only of justice; relates it to peace and ecology.

Fédération Protestante de France, *La lutte pour la paix* (1983). Relates justice to peace, which is clearly authorized by the gospel of Christ.

Federation of Evangelical Churches in Italy, *Assembly of the FECI* (1982). Relates justice to peace.

Federation of Evangelical Churches in Italy, *Assembly of the FECI* (1985), Act 38. Speaks only of justice, in its relation to peace and disarmament.

Fellowship of Christian Churches [Chile], *Let the Floodgates of Democratic Participation Be Opened* (1984), II/1, II/3, III. Speaks only to justice but relates it to Chile's economic system as well as the breakdown of family life, drug addiction, hunger, and peace. Rejects the use of violence as a means of gaining power.

German [Catholic] Bishops' Conference, *Gegen Gewalttat und Terror in der Welt* (1973), 5-8. Relates justice to peace, freedom of conscience, and religious freedom; opposes the use of violence. It cites Roman Catholic Church, *Populorum Progressio* (1967), 76.

Irish Episcopal Conference, *Christian Faith in a Time of Economic Depression* (1983). Relates social justice to charity and the overcoming of unemployment.

Italian [Catholic] Episcopal Conference, *Concordant Testimony* [on duty of consistency in civil choices] (1976), 5. Relates justice to integrity and dedication to the poor.

Latin American [Catholic] Bishops, Second General Conference (Medellín Conference), *Peace* (1968), 14, 1, 15-16, 19, 20-22, 26, 27. Relates social justice to peace and development, as well as to the rights of the oppressed, human dignity, self-determination, and the satisfaction of legitimate aspirations. Creation may be a background warrant. Anthropology and the evangelical doctrine of love authorize the statement's criticism of attempts to affect violent changes in structures. In fact, the statement concedes that "revolutionary insurrection can be legitimate in the case of prolonged tyranny". Counter-violence by the oppressed is not totally condemned.

Latin American [Catholic] Bishops, Second General Conference (Medellín Conference), *Poverty and the Church* (1968), 1, 7, 18. Concerned with social justice as it relates to overcoming poverty in Latin America. Christology seems to authorize this concern insofar as poverty is said to cry out for justice and exertion to the fulfilment of Christ's mission.

Lutheran World Federation, *Seeking Economic and Social Justice* (1984), II; 8.3.8. Relates social justice to economic justice, poverty, and hunger. Authorization is provided by portions of the statement which were not ratified.

Lutheran World Federation, *Statement on Peace and Justice* (1984). Social and economic justice are prerequisites of peace and involve overcoming all forms of discrimination.

Mennonite Brethren Churches, *Regarding Political Involvement* (1966), I, II. Relates social justice to the struggle against racism.

Mennonite Brethren Churches, *Seventh Revised Draft, Mennonite Brethren Confession of Faith* (1975), XIV-XV. Relates justice to pacifism and to overturning discrimination.

Mennonite Church [USA], *Growing in Stewardship and Witness in a Militaristic World* (1987). Speaks only of justice; relates it to peace.

Mennonite Church, General Conference [USA], *A Christian Declaration on Capital Punishment* (1965). Relates justice to peace and its position against capital punishment. Justice is also said to be a concern of the state, but this is subordinated to the lordship of Christ.

Mennonite Church, General Conference [USA], *The Way of Peace* (1971). Relates justice to peace.

Mennonite World Conference, *Our Witness to Christ in Today's World* (1990). Justice includes compassion for the oppressed. Justice is related to peace and ecology.

Methodist Church [England], *Statement and Programme on Race Relations* (1978), 9, 1. Concerned about "racial justice", which is related to the concern about unemployment.

Methodist Church in Malaysia, *Social Principles* (n.d.), III/E; III/B.1; II;I. Social justice a presupposition of peace. Some reference is made to creation, but Christology/the gospel provides the primary authorization.

National Association of Evangelicals [USA], *On Civil Rights* (1965). Relates justice to the overcoming of racism. The Bible also functions as a warrant. It deplores the use of violence to secure social justice.

National Association of Evangelicals [USA], *Revive Your Church, O Lord!* (1989). Refers only to justice; seems to relate it to overcoming racism and rejecting abortion. Repentance and holiness seem to function as related warrants.

National Conference of [Catholic] Bishops of Brazil, *Après la révolution brésilienne du 1er avril* (1964). Relates social justice to the overturning of the materialistic terms of injustice.

National Conference of Catholic Bishops [USA], *The Economy: Human Dimensions* (1975), 4, 5, 19, 27. Concerned only about justice for immigrants.

National Conference of Catholic Bishops [USA], *The Plan of Pastoral Action for Family Ministry: A Vision and a Strategy* (1978), 31, 61, 62. Concerned about social justice in relation to family governmental policy; relates justice to the physical and spiritual needs of the needy.

National Conference of Catholic Bishops [USA], *To Do the Work of Justice* (1978), 1-3, 6-8, 14, 28, 32, 35, 46-48. Relates social justice to world peace, full employment, disarmament, housing, overcoming hunger and sexism, criminal justice, economic justice, human freedom, and human rights.

National Conference of Catholic Bishops [USA], *Statement on Capital Punishment* (1980), 3, 21. Relates social justice to the preservation of the social order, the protection of lives from capital punishment, and the overcoming of poverty.

National Council of Churches [USA], *On Viet-nam* (1965). Concerned about justice in Vietnam; relates it to peace and freedom. Christian love and faith also provide authorization.

National Council of Churches [USA], *The Concern of the Churches for Seasonal Farm Workers* (1966), 2. Concerned about justice in farm labor. Reconciliation functions as the warrant.

National Council of Churches [USA], *The Church as Purchaser of Goods and Services* (1968). Concerned about achieving social justice by exerting consumer pressure.

National Council of Churches [USA], *Imperatives of Peace and Responsibilities of Power* (1968), Sum., I-III. Concerned about justice among the nations. Justice includes freedom, order, and concern for the oppressed.

National Council of Churches [USA], *On the Crisis in the Middle East* (1969), I/2, III. Concerned about justice in the Middle East; relates it to peace, economic development, and social development.

National Council of Churches [USA], *Evangelism Today* (1976). Relates social justice to economic justice, the liberation of the oppressed, and evangelism.

Nederduitse Gereformeerde Sendingkerk, *The Belhar Confession 1986,* 4. Relates justice to peace. The nature of God also provides authorization.

Netherlands [Catholic] Bishops' Conference, *Vrede en gerechtigheid* (1983), I/1; III/2. Apparently references to justice connote social justice, but perhaps not. Peace is the fruit of justice. Creation and eschatology could be supporting warrants.

Nordelbische Evangelisch-Lutherische Kirche, *Erklärung der Synode der NELK zu Südafrika* (1986). Concern for justice related to the South African apartheid system. Justice is also related to peace. The warrant is not clear, but there is a suggestion that the "law of Christ" functions as warrant.

[Orthodox] Ecumenical Patriarchate of Constantinople, *Message pascal de S.S. le Patriarche Œcuménique Dimitrios* (1977). Relates justice to the distribution of wealth.

[Orthodox] Ecumenical Patriarchate of Constantinople, *Message patriarcal à l'occasion de Noël* (1985). Refers only to justice. Relates it to overcoming suffering and oppression.

[Orthodox] Ecumenical Patriarchate of Constantinople, *Message pascal de Sa Sainteté le Patriarche œcuménique Dimitrios Ier* (1987). Refers only to justice; relates it to overcoming suffering and oppression.

Patriarchs and Catholic Bishops of Libya, *Legality Is the Unique Guarantee of the Protection of the Fatherland* (1983), I/3(b), I/4, III/4. Relates social justice to peace, equality of opportunity, and prosperity, as well as perhaps the right to private property, religious liberty, and a critique of racism and sexism. Love (and so the gospel) provides authorization in most cases.

Peruvian [Catholic] Episcopal Conference, *Document of the Peruvian Episcopal Conference on the Theology of Liberation* (1984), 15-16, 5-8, 28, 51, 80. Relates social justice to overcoming poverty and the call for liberation. A kind of two-kingdom ethic stands in the background of the statement.

Presbyterian Church in Taiwan, *Our Appeal* (1975), II.5. Seems to relate social justice to the alleviation of hunger and overpopulation.

Reformed Church in America, *Report of the Christian Action Commission* (1963), Recs. 2d, 2. Relates social justice to economic justice as a challenge to Communism. "Christian truth" may function as authorization.

Reformed Church in America, *Report of the General Synod Executive Committee* (1980), R-15, R-12. Concerned about justice in South Africa as it relates to peace and the overcoming of apartheid. An appeal to Christology authorizes the witness against apartheid and so, by implication, seems to authorize the call for justice.

Roman Catholic Church, *Divini Redemptoris* (1937), 32, 52-54. Social justice demands a proper subsistence for workers; opts for public old-age insurance. Just economic order should be founded on a Christian base.

Roman Catholic Church, *Ecclesiam Suam* (1964), 95.

Russian Orthodox Church, *Easter Communication 1987*. Relates justice to peace, truth, and the striving for brotherhood.

South African Council of Churches, *Conscientious Objection* (1974). The statement's concern with justice presumably relates to social justice. Justice has implications for avoiding discrimination and as a criterion for determining whether to serve in the military. Violence as a means of achieving social aims is rejected.

Southern African Catholic Bishops' Conference, *Social Justice and Race Relations within the Church* (1977), Int. Relates social justice to a concern about race relations. Pneumatology may function as a background warrant.

United Church of Canada, *Human Rights and International Affairs: Do Not Let the World Forget Us* (1982). Relates social justice to world peace, human rights, and the sharing of wealth.

United Church of Canada, *Refugee Policy* (1988). Concerned about justice for refugees to Canada.

United Church of Christ [USA], *A Call for Action to Fulfill Racial Justice Now* (1965). Calls for racial justice.

United Church of Christ [USA], *The Ministry of Caring* (1967). Relates social justice to appropriate health and welfare legislation.

United Church of Christ [USA], *Support for Liberation Movements in Namibia and Zimbabwe* (1977). Relates social justice to the struggle against apartheid. It is more important than access to raw materials and financial gains.

United Church of Christ [USA], *Affirmative Action in Church and Society* (1981). Relates social justice to overcoming all forms of racial and gender discrimination.

United Church of Christ [USA], *Increased Racial Violence against Blacks in America* (1981). Concerned about racial justice; relates it to peace. Christology may function only as a motive for the position.

United Church of Christ [USA], *Justice in Immigration* (1981). Speaks only of justice, specifically of just policies for citizens both in nations that send immigrants and in those that receive them.

United Church of Christ [USA], *U.S. Military Aid to El Salvador* (1981). Concerned with justice to the poor and oppressed; themes of liberation theology are made quite evident.

United Church of Christ [USA], *Economic Justice: The Crisis and a Response of the Church* (1983). Speaks only of justice; relates it to economic justice and overcoming racism.

United Church of Christ [USA], *Full Divestment of All Financial Resources from All Corporations Doing Business with South Africa* (1985), Pronouncement I, III. Calls for racial and human justice in overturning apartheid.

United Church of Christ [USA], *The National Toxic Injustice Crisis* (1985), Pronouncement, A Proposal for Action. Relates social justice to racial justice and a concern about ecology, especially the proper disposal of toxic and hazardous waste.

United Church of Christ [USA], *A United Church of Christ Ministry with Indians* (1987), Pronouncement I, III, IV, A Proposal for Action IV, VI. Concerned about justice for American Indians.

United Presbyterian Church [USA], *The Confession of 1967,* II.A.4. Relates social justice to a concern about the poor, peace, and freedom.

Uniting Church in Australia, *Statement to Nation* (1977). Speaks only of justice; relates it to truth, religious liberty, welfare of the whole human race, as well as the eradication of poverty and racism. Authorization is drawn from "basic Christian values", though an appeal to the doctrine of creation may be in the background.

Uniting Church in Australia, *Bicentennial Celebrations* (1982), 82.48, (2), (3). Concerned about land justice for Aboriginal Australians.

Uniting Church in Australia, *Commonwealth Games* (1982), 82.49, (5), (2), (1). Concerned about social, legal, and economic justice for Aboriginal Australians. Earlier appeal to reconciliation seems to provide authorization, but not clearly.

Uniting Church in Australia, *Bicentennial Celebrations* (1985), 85.40.1-85, 40.6. Concerned about social justice for Aboriginal Australians and their land rights. It also relates justice to peace.

Uniting Church in Australia, *Re Pacific Churches* (1985), 85.105.2. Concerned about just and peaceful independence in New Caledonia.

Vereinigte Evangelisch-Lutherische Kirche Deutschlands, *Entschliessung der Generalsynode der VELKD zur gegenwärtigen Situation im südlichen Afrika* (1985). Speaks of justice for black people in South Africa; relates such justice to equal rights and the overcoming of apartheid without bloodshed.

Vereinigte Evangelisch-Lutherische Kirche in der DDR, *Beschluss der Generalsynode zum Bericht der Kirchenleitung vom 8. Juni 1980, 9.* Speaks only of justice; relates it to peace and freedom.

Waldensian and Methodist Churches in Italy, *Synod of the WMCI* (1982). Concerned about justice in relation to international disparities and armaments.

World Alliance of Reformed Churches, *Racism and South Africa* (1982), I-II. Speaks only of justice in government. This statement was reaffirmed by World Alliance of Reformed Churches, *Southern Africa* (1989), with special concern about justice in South Africa.

World Alliance of Reformed Churches, *A Message to the Congregations of the Member Churches of the WARC* (1989). Relates justice to peace and ecology.

World Alliance of Reformed Churches, *Statement on Peace* (1989), 1-3.4; 4.3. Relates justice to peace and ecology.

WCC Department on Studies in Evangelism, *The Church for Others* (Geneva, 1967), 79. On the basis of Christ's victory, the church may be a forum of other groups seeking justice.

WCC Evanston Assembly, *Message from the Second WCC Assembly* (1954).

WCC Nairobi Assembly, *Confessing Christ Today* (1975), 57, 59-60. Perhaps the gospel is not a criterion for justice, since later articles also include creation as warrant.

WCC New Delhi Assembly, *Witness* (1968), 29, 28. Concern for justice related to evangelism. Elsewhere in the statement, reference is also made to creation and the sacraments as components of evangelism, but no reference is made to them in conjunction with concern for justice.

WCC Vancouver Assembly, *Confronting Threats to Peace and Survival* (1983), 1.

WCC Vancouver Assembly, *Statement on Peace and Justice* (1983), 1-2, 8, 23-24. No peace without justice. It also includes passing reference to eschatology/hope for creation as warrant. The statement was endorsed by Evangelische Kirche im Rheinland, *Kriegsdienstverweigerung* (1988).

World Methodist Council, *Statement on Poverty and the North-South Debate* (1981). No justice in a world with poverty. In calling the church to become a church of the poor in obedience to Christ, the statement employs themes from liberation theology.

10. Appeal to Christology and prophecy

Mennonite World Conference, *Conference Message* (1972), III. Criticizes unjust imprisonment and persecution by violence.

11. Appeal to Christology, the Bible, and the law

Church of the Brethren [USA], *A Vision of Unity for the CB(USA) in the 1980s* (1982). Relates justice to love and peace.

Presbyterian Church (USA), *Christian Obedience in a Nuclear Age* (1988), 1-2, 8-9, 11, 13, 15-18, 23-26. Relates social justice to economic justice, racial justice, human rights, and peace. It is open to the use of violence to achieve justice in extreme cases and cites the United Presbyterian Church [USA], *The Confession of 1967*, III.A.4.

Presbyterian Church (USA), *Our Response to the Crisis in Central America: An Appeal to Presbyterians and Other Churches in the United States* (1988). Calls for a just peace in Central America, including a community of all people as well as economic and social development.

12. Appeal to Christology and some other locus drawn from the third article

Anglicanism, Lambeth Conference, *On Our Place in God's World* (1988), 1, 3. Relates justice to the more equitable sharing of resources. Authorization is drawn from eschatology, prophecy, the Christian vision, and perhaps creation, which is correlated with eschatology.

Christian Church (Disciples of Christ), *Concerning the Universal Declaration of Human Rights* (1973). Concerned about justice for the neighbor in order to overcome exploitation; also concerned about just conditions for work.

Church of Ireland, *The Report of the Role of the Church Committee* (1985), 152, 154. Concerned about justice in Northern Ireland and also about economic justice. Ecclesiology is probably the main warrant, with Christology in the background, insofar as it authorizes a ministry of reconciliation in Ireland.

Eglise de la Confession d'Augsbourg d'Alsace et de Lorraine, *Texte concernant J.P.S.C.* (1989). Speaks only of justice; relates it to peace and ecology.

Evangelical Lutheran Church in Southern Africa, *Social Services in Independent States and Homelands* (1982). Concerned about justice in the South African Homelands, and so to that extent with social justice. Ecclesiology and the gospel function as authorization.

Evangelisch-Lutherische Kirche in Bayern, *Menschenrechtsverletzungen* (1985). Justice related to peace. Ecclesiology may be the prevailing warrant. It endorses a 1984 statement of the Lutheran World Federation.

Federation of Protestant Churches in Switzerland, *Pour une action concertée énergique en faveur du tiers monde* (1986), II.5(a). Concerned about justice and peace in the pursuit of development.

Mennonite Central Committee (U.S. Ministries), *Native American Statement* (1978). Concerned about the rights of American Indians to justice.

Mennonite World Conference, *The Conference Message* (1967), III. Relates justice to peace, freedom, overcoming restricted liberties, poverty, and racism.

National Association of Evangelicals [USA], *A Declaration — Forty-fifth Anniversary Year* (1987). Concerned about structural justice, especially political and economic justice; rejects any liberation theology that advocates violent revolution.

National Council of Churches [USA], *Indian Affairs* (1978). Concerned about justice for American Indians. Love and eschatology function as warrants.

Nicaraguan [Catholic] Bishops, *Christian Commitment for a New Nicaragua* (1979), I, II(a), II(c). Relates social justice to peace and liberation of the poor. This pastoral letter reflects a liberation theology perspective. In another pastoral letter (of 2 June 1979), the gospel was used to authorize revolutionary insurrection (violence).

Reformed Ecumenical Synod, *Statements on the Social Calling of the Church* (1980), 16, 18, 2. Urges attacking unjust structures such as those perpetuating racism. Christology and eschatology function as warrants.

United Church of Canada, *Poverty: Report and Recommendations* (1977), Recs. 8B, 8A, Int. Concerned about social justice for Canada's poor.

United Church of Canada, *A Report on French/English Relations* (1980). Relates justice to concern for the rights of Francophone minorities and to liberation from discrimination.

United Church of Christ [USA], *Economic Justice* (1973). Relates social justice to economic justice and to racial and social equality. Christology may be more prevalent as a warrant than is the reference to the kingdom of God. Creation may function as a background warrant.

United Presbyterian Church/Presbyterian Church in the U.S., *Strangers Become Neighbors: Presbyterian Response to Mexican Migration* (1981), II/D, II, I, Int. Speaks only of justice; relates it to opposition to racism, peace, concern about the stranger, and preference for the poor. It is especially concerned about justice for Mexican migrants in the United States.

Ustřední Rada Církve Ceskoslovenské Husitské, *Der sozialethischen Orientierung* (1981), 1.4, 1.1, Begr. Relates social justice to the struggle for freedom and religious liberty.

World Alliance of Reformed Churches, *Come Creator Spirit, for the Redemption of the World* (1964), C/I. Relates social justice to peace, racial justice, and identification with those who suffer. The Word of God also functions as a warrant.

WCC Conference on Faith, Science and the Future, *Economics of a Just, Sustainable and Participatory Society* (Cambridge, Mass., 12-24 July 1979), 1, 7. Christology and the eschatological hope warrant quest for social justice in the socio-economic order. Justice is linked with participation and sustainability.

WCC Nairobi Assembly, *Structures of Injustice and Struggles for Liberation* (1975), 1-2, 7. Christology the principal warrant for struggling with injustice, but such struggling creates community, which is expressed in the Eucharist.

WCC Vancouver Assembly, *Healing and Sharing Life in Community* (1983), 11, 1-4. Justice determines adequate distribution of health care. Healing and sharing, which demand justice, are all originated from Christ himself and the sacrament. One reference to the Triune God as warrant appears at the beginning of the statement.

WCC Vancouver Assembly, *Message of the Sixth Assembly of the World Council of Churches* (1983). Speaks only of justice and relates it to peace. Some reference to creation may be in the background.

13. Appeal to the Christian message/the gospel

American Baptist Churches, *Policy Statement on Hunger* (1975), VIII. Relates justice to programs of assistance and development.

American Baptist Churches, *Policy Statement on Energy* (1977), III, II, I. Speaks only of justice; relates it to ecology and appropriate use of energy. Creation/anthropology is a possible background warrant.

Episcopal Church [USA], *Affirm Witness of Bishop Desmond Tutu and Church in Africa* (1985). Relates justice to overcoming racism and sexism; appeals to the example of modern saints such as Tutu.

National Conference of Catholic Bishops [USA], *Human Life in Our Day* (1968), 101-2, 34. Relates social justice to peace.

Reformed Ecumenical Synod, *Race Relations, Resolutions* (1968), 13. Relates justice to love. Also, in apparent empathy with the white South African member churches, allows for separate development of racial groups.

14. Appeal to the gospel, with creation as a subordinate warrant

American Lutheran Church, *The "Tax Revolt" and the Role of Government* (1978), D, C. Concerned with economic justice. The two-kingdom ethic is in the background. The statement may not be official.

Anglican-Lutheran [European Commission] Dialogue (1982), 29, 58, 59. Relates social justice to human rights, peace, ecology, and development. Authorization is not very clear; something like an argument based on a two-kingdom ethic could be the more dominant argument.

Evangelical Church of Lutheran Confession in Brazil, *God's Earth . . . Land for Everyone* (1982), I, II. Relates social justice to political and economic justice and ecology, as well as to the arms race and land distribution. Eschatology may function as a background warrant. Liberation theology has a strong impact on the statement.

Reformed-Roman Catholic Joint Commission, *The Presence of Christ in Church and World* (1977), 53, 51, 49, 48, 44, 23. Relates justice to peace and liberty. Creation is subordinated to the gospel. It employs insights of liberation theology.

15. Appeal to the gospel and eschatology, with creation possibly subordinated to these loci

Igreja Lusitana Católica Apostólica Evangélica, *Declaração do Sínodo da ILCAE sobre o Ano Internacional da Paz* (1986), 1-4. Relates social justice to peace.

16. Appeal to redemption, correlated with creation

United Church of Canada, *Statement on Human Rights* (1980), 1, 2. Social justice includes a concern for political and economic justice; reaffirms a 1977 statement of the church on the subject. It cites a 1976 statement of the National Council of Churches in the Philippines and a WCC Nairobi Assembly publication concerned with the root causes of unjust structures. It endorses the concern for justice affirmed in the following four statements: Presbyterian Church in the Republic of Korea, *Statement on Faith;* Presbyterian Church in Taiwan, *Our Appeal* (1975); a 1979 statement of the Church in South Africa, authorized by the gospel and the Bible; and Christian Council of Asia, *Human Rights in Asia* (1974), which is authorized by appeal to loci from all three articles of the creed and which also expresses concern for the liberation of the poor and the oppressed. With this endorsement, the Canadian church also seems to embrace a similar Trinitarian authorization for its own position.

United Church of Christ [USA], *Health and Wholeness in the Midst of a Pandemic* (1987), Pronouncement I, III, IV. Calls for just employment practices in dealing with victims of AIDS.

17. Authorization drawn from pneumatology

[Catholic] Bishops Conference of Mozambique, *A urgência da paz* (1984), 15, 10, 8. Relates justice to peace; concerned with the situation in Mozambique.

Latin American [Catholic] Bishops, Second General Conference (Medellín Conference), *Introduction to the Final Documents: Presence of the Church in the Present-Day Transformation of Latin America* (1968), 8, 5. There is no clear reference to social justice, but the themes of liberation theology clearly are reflected in the statement. Christology and eschatology may function as background warrants.

Polish Episcopal Conference, *Communique of the Plenary Session* (1981), 5, 2. Relates justice in Poland to love, peace, and the rights of workers. Natural law and "Catholic social teaching" may serve as background warrants.

World Alliance of Reformed Churches, *Come Creator Spirit, for the Re-Making of Man* (1964), 3. The Spirit, with the gospel in support, authorizes a concern about structures of justice. This point was only "received", not approved.

18. Appeal to prophecy

Church of the Brethren [USA], *Statement on Aging* (1985). Concerned about global justice and peace.

19. Appeal to the prophetic tradition

United Church of Christ [USA], *The Hispanic Ministry of the United Church of Christ* (1987), Pronouncement II. Speaks only of justice; relates it to the fight against bigotry and perhaps to a preferential option for the poor.

United Church of Christ [USA], *Opposition to Declaring English as the Exclusive Official Language of the United States* (1987). Speaks only of justice; relates it to equal access to services necessary to a safe and healthy life. Justice includes adequate police and fire protection.

20. Appeal to the prophetic heritage, with some reference to creation

United Church of Christ [USA], *Pronouncement on Public Education* (1985), I-IV. Social justice is related to healthy school systems, peace, and the overcoming of racism and sexism.

21. Authorization apparently drawn from ecclesiology

Eglise Protestante Unie de Belgique, *Motion du District Antwerpen-Brabant-Limburg concernant l'attitude de l'Eglise envers les migrants* (1984). Speaks only of justice; relates to an overcoming of racism. Christology probably functions as a motive.

Hong Kong Christian Council, *The Manifesto of the Protestant Church in Hong Kong on Religious Freedom* (1984). Relates justice (presumably social justice) to peace, service to the needy, religious freedom, and human rights (in view of Hong Kong's new relation to China). Its warrant is not entirely clear. Creation may function as a background warrant.

22. Appeal to ecclesiology, with some reference to a two-kingdom ethic

Vereinigte Evangelisch-Lutherische Kirche Deutschlands, *Beschluss der Generalsynode der VELKD zur Rolle der Kirchen in bezug auf das südliche Afrika* (1978), 2. Concerned with justice in South Africa, and so justice is related to racial integration and peace.

23. Authorization drawn from sacramentology and ecclesiology

United Church of Christ [USA], *Racism and Sexism* (1977). Refers to global justice and economic justice. It is concerned to overcome racial and sexual injustice.

24. Probably warrants drawn from eschatology, with reference to creation

Methodist Church [England], *A Statement Reaffirming That the Methodist Church Is against Racism in All Its Forms and Committed to Racial Justice within a Plural Society* (1988). Reaffirms an earlier 1978 statement; affirms social justice, racial justice, and peace. It is opposed to unemployment. Creation is a warrant insofar as Christians are encouraged to join secular efforts for justice and peace.

National Council of Churches [USA], *Policy Statement: The Ethical Implications of Energy Production and Use* (1979). Concerned with "ecological justice". The guidelines given, however — sustainability, fairness, and participation — are not explicitly derived from eschatology.

25. Appeal to the kingdom of God

Caribbean Conference of Churches, *Thine Is the Kingdom, the Power and the Glory* (1981). Concerned with caring for refugees and migrants.

Presbyterian Church in Taiwan, *An Urgent Call of the General Assembly of the PCT* (1988). Relates social justice to peace, freedom, and a more equitable agricultural policy in Taiwan.

Presbyterian Church of Korea, *Guiding Principles for the Social Ministry Policy of the PCK* (1984), 5(2), 5. Primary concern for social justice relates to economic justice.

26. Appeal to the kingdom of God and sacramentology

Lutheran-Episcopal Dialogue, series 3 [USA], *Implications of the Gospel* (1988), 122, 114. Concerned with sexism, racism, the exploitation of labor, just economic systems, and equal education. One reference could suggest a kind of two-kingdom ethic, and the gospel could be in the background.

27. Appeal to all three articles of the creed

All Africa Conference of Churches, *The Gospel and Reconciliation* (1981). Relates social justice to nation building; authorizes the use of violence against oppression.

American Baptist Churches, *Policy Statement on Human Rights* (1976). Relates social justice to human dignity.

American Lutheran Church, *Issues and Opportunities That Bind and Free* (1976). Refers only to justice; relates it to ecology, unemployment, racism, misuse of the media, and international tensions.

American Lutheran Church, *Christian Social Responsibility* (1978), A1, A3, B2, B7. Primary warrant may be a kind of two-kingdom ethic.

Anglicanism, *The Resolutions of the Lambeth Conference (1988)*, 24, 27, 36, 37, 39, 40, 73. Relates social justice to economic justice and ecology. It is concerned about peace and justice in South Africa, as well as about justice, freedom, and a higher standard of living in Latin America.

Bund der Evangelischen Kirchen in der Deutschen Demokratischen Republik, *Beschluss der Synode des BEK-DDR zum "Bekennen in der Friedensfrage"* (1987), Int. III. Relates justice to economic justice, ecology, peace, and the rejection of deterrence. Insofar as deterrence is rejected by appeal to the Triune God, this authorization seems to apply to the concern for justice.

Canadian Conference of Catholic Bishops, *A Society to Be Transformed* (1977), 1, 5, 6, 7, 9, 10, 12, 18-20. Concerned about social justice on behalf of the poor; relates it to peace, love, and equality. The Scriptures also function as warrant. It quotes Roman Catholic Church, *Octogesima Adveniens* (1971), 48.

Church of the Brethren [USA], *Justice and Nonviolence* (1977), 2, 3, 4, 7-8, 9, 10, 11. Concerned about economic justice and eco-justice; relates justice to peace, ecology, defending the rights and needs of the poor, compassion and equal respect for all persons, as well as liberation.

Church of the Brethren [USA], *The Time So Urgent: Threats to Peace* (1980), 6-8. Relates justice to peace and disarmament. At points, it is especially concerned about justice in the Middle East.

Church of the Brethren [USA], *Resolution on Normalizing Relations with Cuba* (1985). Relates justice to peace and the restoration of American diplomatic relations with Cuba.

Conference of European Churches and Council of European Bishops' Conferences, *Final Document of the European Ecumenical Assembly Peace with Justice* (1989), 1, 2, 4, 10, 14, 20, 21, 25-27, 29-32, 36-38, 40, 42, 44, 45, 52, 56, 61, 68, 70, 72, 77, 83, 84, 86, 87, 91. Justice is related to economic justice, justice in tourism, overcoming racism and sexism, lightening the debt burden on poor nations, concern for the poor and poorer nations, reduced energy consumption, employment, development, and the self-determination of national groups. It opposes the use of violence. Authorization is also provided by appeal to prophecy and to covenant, which itself reflects a trinitarian orientation. Endorses the preferential option for the poor.

Episcopal Church [USA], *General Convention Resolution* [on condemning resurgence of activity of the Ku Klux Klan] (1979). Relates justice to peace and the condemnation of racism.

Episcopal Church [USA], *Endorse Reunification of Korea Policy Statement* (1988). By endorsing the National Council of Churches [USA], *Peace and the Reunification of Korea* (1986), this resolution shares its Trinitarian authorization for justice in relation to peace, the reunification of Korea, and promotion of a participatory democracy.

Latin American [Catholic] Bishops, Second General Conference (Medellín Conference), *Justice* (1968), 3-5, 13, 16, 21, 23. Refers only to justice but is concerned about how it relates to the just distribution of goods, solidarity, as well as to liberation from hunger, misery, and oppression. Warrants include redemption, the gospel, Christology, pneumatology, baptism, conversion, and creation (entailed by a kind of two-kingdom ethic). Characteristic themes of liberation theology are reflected in the statement.

Latin American Council of Churches, *Commitment for the Kingdom* (1982), I, II. Relates justice to peace and life.

National Conference of Catholic Bishops [USA] *Economic Justice for All* (1986), PM1, PM8, PM12, PM13, PM15-PM17, 19, 20, 25, esp. 30, 38-40, 54, 55, 68-74, 77, 78, 86-88, 100, 103, 125, 127, 136, 247, 251, 258, 260, 274, 290, 292, 314, 315, 320, 322, 326-27, 331, 332, 341, 342, 364. Social justice is related to economic justice, peace, development, minimum wages, and unemployment compensation. Justice entails the participation of everyone as well as a "fundamental option for the poor". It also encourages government intervention to help promote justice.

National Council of Churches [USA], *Human Hunger and the World Food Crisis* (1975), I, III/B/1, IV, IV/B, VII/A/2-3. Relates social justice to economic justice and justice for all food-producing groups.

National Council of Churches [USA], *Middle East* (1980). Relates social justice to economic justice and peace in the Middle East. It also relates justice to rights of religious minorities, self-determination, and an end to the arms race. It opposes a reliance on violence. The statement is affirmed by Christian Church (Disciples of Christ), *Concerning a Policy Statement on the Middle East* (1981).

National Council of Churches [USA], *Latin America and the Caribbean* (1983), Int., I/B, II, III, III/A, III/G. Relates social justice to economic justice and peace and opposes the use of violence to attain these ends. Eschatology and Christology function as prevailing warrants at one point.

National Council of Churches [USA], *Peace and the Reunification of Korea* (1986), 2, 9-13. Concerned about justice in Korea; relates it to peace, the reunification of Korea, and the promotion of a participatory democracy.

Nederduitse Gereformeerde Sendingkerk, *Confession of Faith* (1982). Justice (presumably social justice) is related to peace and support for the oppressed. A Trinitarian warrant operates, assuming the statement's reference to God's will entails an appeal to first-article themes.

Roman Catholic Church, *Pacem in Terris* (1963), 166-68, 161-64, 157, 147, 121, 96, 91-92, 59, 56, 53, 37-38, 31, 23, 20, 10, 5. Social justice is related to international justice, just wages, concern for the poor and minorities, as well as peace. It opposes the use of violence in seeking to achieve justice. Appeals to all loci may be subordinated to redemption. It at least posits a creation-redemption continuity, with natural law as the prevailing warrant, and also posits a relational view of persons.

Roman Catholic Church, *Octogesima Adveniens* (1971), 1, 12, 17, 37, 41, 43, 48. Social justice is related to the new model of development.

South African Catholic Bishops' Conference, *Charter of Rights for Migrant Workers in South Africa* (1981). Concerned about justice in the sense of a just wage for workers and in the sense of allowing all workers in South Africa to be able to take up permanent residence at their place of work.

Southern African Catholic Bishops' Conference, *An Urgent Message to the State President* (1986), 3-5, 7, 19, 23-25. Social justice related to peace in society, love, freedom, and a society free of apartheid. It understands why violence might be employed by the oppressed in South Africa.

United Church of Christ [USA], *Human Rights* (1979). Social justice is related to economic justice. Does a Trinitarian warrant for human rights apply to a call for justice?

United Church of Christ [USA], *Reversing the Arms Race* (1979). Refers only to justice; relates it to peace. Authorization is provided by appeal to Christology, reason, and the Holy Spirit.

United Church of Christ [USA], *Affirming the United Church of Christ as a Just Peace Church* (1985), Pronouncement, A Proposal for Action. Relates social justice to economic justice, peace, the promotion of human welfare, and overcoming the oppression of the poor.

World Alliance of Reformed Churches, *Reconciliation and Society: The Freedom of a Just Order* (1970), App.; Int; 10. Appeal to Christology predominates early in statement, but at one point church and creation also function as warrants. It is principally concerned with racial justice.

World Alliance of Reformed Churches, *Mission and Unity* (1989). Justice is related to mission, which includes peace and the overcoming of prejudice.

World Alliance of Reformed Churches, *Towards a Common Testimony of Faith* (1989), 3. Overcoming sexism is said to be a matter of justice.

WCC Nairobi Assembly, *Human Development: Ambiguities of Power, Technology, and Quality of Life* (1975), 3-7, 11-12, 15, 37, 56, 61, 75, 77. Justice pertains to political, economic, and social objectives and so must be a component of development. It is compromised by military build-up. Warrants include God's demand for justice, the invitation to be stewards of creation on basis of love for all, expectation of the kingdom, and the liberating power of Christ. Insofar as Christians are to cooperate with all who fight injustice, the warrant for justice seems accessible to all, grounded in creation.

WCC Uppsala Assembly, *World Economic and Social Development* (1968), 3-4, 15. Relates justice to world development.

WCC World Convocation on Justice, Peace and the Integrity of Creation, *Final Document: Entering into Covenant Solidarity for Justice, Peace and the Integrity of Creation* (1990), 2.1; 2.2; 2.3.2; 2.3.2.1; 2.3.2.2. Justice includes economic justice, the overcoming of foreign debt, racism, and sexism. Concerned about the welfare of youth, human rights, development, liberation, women's rights, peace, and ecology. Rejects the use of violence. Authorization is also provided by appeal to the covenant, which itself reflects a trinitarian authorization.

28. Appeal to loci from all articles of the creed, especially creation and ecclesiology or eschatology

National Council of Churches [USA], *Immigrants, Refugees and Migrants* (1981), I, II/4, 13. Concerned about justice, especially human rights, the alleviation of suffering and racism, as well as just international relations (which may help facilitate immigration).

Vereinigte Evangelisch-Lutherische Kirche Deutschlands, *Beschluss der Generalsynode der VELKD zu der "Erklärung zum Frieden" des Exekutivkomitees des Lutherischen Weltbundes vom 24. Oktober 1981*. Social justice is related to peace, human rights, and the overcoming of hunger and racism. The resolution cites the LWF statement (3-5), mentioned in its title.

29. Appeal to all three articles of the creed, though all may be grounded in Christology

Haitian [Catholic] Episcopal Conference, *The Foundation for the Church's Involvement in Local and Political Arenas* (1983), 2, 5, 11, 12, 19. Justice is related to peace, love, and perhaps private property and employment. A strong affirmation of a relational view of human persons is employed. Ecclesiology — the idea of the church as sacrament — is invoked for authorization.

Methodist Church in Malaysia, *Social Principles* (n.d.), II; III/E. Social justice is related to economic justice, international justice, peace, and perhaps freedom from discrimination. Creation appears only once and at best functions as a secondary warrant. The appeal to ecclesiology is perhaps the strongest.

National Conference of Catholic Bishops [USA], *The Church in Our Day* (1967), 59-62. Relates social justice to peace, civil rights, and the overcoming of inhumanity. It cites various Roman Catholic statements noted in the more detailed description of the Pastoral on p.255.

National Conference of Catholic Bishops [USA], *To Live in Jesus Christ: A Pastoral Reflection on the Moral Life* (1976), 2, 19, 22, 23, 30, 31, 60, 70, 74, 78, 83, 91-92, 95, 104, 112, 115-16. Relates social justice to peace, truth, love, development, human rights, and the overcoming of racism; urges justice for farm workers. Christology may be the prevailing warrant. It cites the Vatican II document *Gaudium et Spes* (1965).

Roman Catholic Church, Congregation for the Doctrine of the Faith, *Instruction on Certain Aspects of the "Theology of Liberation"* (1984), Int.; I.1-2; IV.9-11; V.1; XI.5-8, 18; Conc.; VII.8. Relates justice to peace, freedom, human dignity, solidarity with the poor, and themes related to liberation theology, but it rejects the use of violence for achieving these ends. Appeals to eschatology function only as background warrants. The theocratic tone, the predominance of Christology, is suggested by a reference to the "Christian conception of society".

Roman Catholic Church, Congregation for the Doctrine of the Faith, *Instruction on Christian Freedom and Liberation* (1986), 30, 45, 54, 57, 60, 63-65, 76-78, 80-82, 89-91, 98-99. Relates justice to peace, development, and the alleviation of suffering. Human solidarity and its implications for property and labor-management relations also are considered. The use of violence for achieving justice is rejected. Both the sacraments and eschatology support referencnes to the first two articles of the creed.

United Church of Christ in Japan, *The Fundamental Policy for Social Action* (1966), Int.

30. Warrant drawn from all three articles of the creed, with creation subordinated to Christology

United Presbyterian Church [USA], *Call to Peacemaking* (1980), I. Concerned about political and economic justice, which are related to peace and human rights.

31. Appeal to God's grace

American Baptist Churches, *Policy Statement on Family Life* (1984). Relates social justice to peace.

United Church of Christ [USA], *The Israeli-Palestinian Conflict* (1987). Reconciliation authorizes the call for a just peace in the Middle East. Affirms US Interreligious Committee for Peace in the Middle East, *A Time for Peace in the Middle East* (1987).

32. Warrant rooted in righteousness, the holiness of God

Evangelical Church Mekane Yesus (Ethiopia), *On Human Rights* (1972). The statement calls for avoiding injustice.

Peruvian [Catholic] Episcopal Conference, *La justicia en el mundo* (1971), 7, 30. But justice is also related to love and the instruction of Christ.

33. Appeal to the will of God

United Church of Christ [USA], *Renewed United States Support of the United Nations as Our Best Investment for a Just Peace* (1987). Calls for a just peace. Relates justice to common security from violence.

34. Appeal to the call of God

United Church of Christ [USA], *Support of the Boycott of California Table Grapes* (1985). Relates justice to efforts by California farm laborers to organize a union.

35. Appeal to the Word of God

American Baptist Churches, *Policy Statement on Immigration and Refugee Policy* (1982). The biblical mandate authorizes a concern for justice in admitting immigrants and refugees to America.

American Lutheran Church, *War, Peace, and Freedom* (1966), 34, 31g, 24. Justice is related to peace, freedom, and truth. At some points, no theological authorization is provided. The statement may not be official.

Christian Church (Disciples of Christ), *Report concerning Human Rights* (1979), Int. Speaks only of justice; relates it to human rights, liberation, and fulfilment. It appeals to the "biblical testimony".

Christian Reformed Church in North America, *Guidelines for Justifiable Warfare* (1982), 11, 13. Relates social justice to peace and a stable political order in which human values are preserved. Pneumatology functions as a motive.

Episcopal Church [USA], *General Convention Resolution* [on directing the Executive Council to design means to assist dioceses and congregations] (1979). The Bible authorizes the resolution's concern for racial and economic justice.

Episcopal Church [USA], *Moral Criteria* (1982). Refers to "biblical teachings about justice".

National Association of Evangelicals [USA], *Communism* (1963). Relates social justice to peace; appeals to "biblical principles of duty and freedom".

National Association of Evangelicals [USA], *Change Your World* (1983). Refers to "the biblical principle of justice".

National Council of Churches [USA], *Policy Statement on Child Day Care* (1984), I/C. Refers only to justice, relating it to nurture. Scripture functions as the warrant.

Reformed Church in America, *Report of the Christian Action Commission* (1982), R-12a. Speaks of the biblical principle of justice; relates it to stewardship, self-sacrifice, and concern for the poor.

Reformed Church in America, *Report of the Christian Action Commission* (1983), R-4. Reaffirms the church's *Report of the Christian Action Commission* (1982), R-12a.

United Church of Canada, *Apartheid* (1984). Relates justice to the struggle against racism and apartheid. Authorization is provided by appeal to the Bible.

United Church of Christ [USA], *Peace Church* (1981). Relates justice to peace. Authorization is provided by appeal to the Bible.

United Church of Christ [USA], *Family Farm* (1985). Speaks only of justice; relates it to land and the present crisis of the American family farm. Authorization is provided by appeal to the Bible.

United Church of Christ [USA], *Justice and Peace Priority* (1985). Relates social justice to economic justice, peace, and critiques of racism, sexism, and homosexual discrimination. Authorization is provided by "the biblical vision of Shalom".

United Church of Christ [USA], *A Pronouncement Affirming the Wholeness of the Gospel: Integrating Evangelism and Church Growth and Justice and Peace* (1987), I-IV, Proposal for Action. Speaks only of justice; relates it to peace and evangelism. Though the primary authorization is the "biblical story", reference is also made to the gospel. The Spirit and the sacrament of Holy Communion function as motives.

United Church of Christ [USA], *Secretaries/Support Staff Just Employment Practices* (1987). Speaks only of justice; relates it to righteousness and fair salaries. It appeals to "biblical faith".

36. Appeal to the Word of God/gospel and creation

South African Council of Churches, *A Theological Rationale and a Call to Prayer for the End to Unjust Rule* (1985). Concerned about justice in the structures of South Africa. Ecclesiology and the church's tradition function as background warrants. Creation is invoked as a warrant insofar as an appeal is made to "all people of goodwill".

37. Appeal to the Bible and the gospel/Christology

Christian Church (Disciples of Christ), *Concerning Priorities for the Christian Church (Disciples of Christ), 1982-1985* (1981). Only refers to justice; relates it to peace, political justice, economic justice, concern for the poor and oppressed, concern about racism and nuclear proliferation, hunger, human rights, and control of nuclear power.

38. Appeal to the biblical vision and possibly to the Spirit

WCC Canberra Assembly, *The Report of the Seventh Assembly* (1991), 21, 27, 33, 39, 41, 43, 47, 51, 54, 84. Social justice is related to economic equality, development, ecology, peace, demilitarization, rejecting racism and sexism, as well as justice for indigenous peoples.

39. Appeal to the Bible and prophecy

United Church of Christ [USA], *U.S. Intervention in the Philippines* (1987). Only concerned about justice, especially in the Philippines.

40. Appeal to the Bible and Christian conscience or Christian principles

Dutch Reformed Church (South Africa), *Declaration of Christian Principles* (1990), 2.2.3-2.2.5; 1. Relates social justice to peace and reasonableness; rejects the use of violence.

41. Appeal to covenant and Scripture

World Alliance of Reformed Churches, *Justice, Peace and the Integrity of Creation* (1989). Especially concerned about economic justice; suggests this might be achieved by cancelling the debts of debtor nations. It also is concerned about economic justice for women and relates justice to peace and ecology.

42. Appeal to divine justice and the Bible

National Association of Evangelicals [USA], *Resolution on Apartheid* (1986). Concerned about justice and peace in South Africa. Affirms the Association's *Race and Racial Minorities* (1956), and quotes its *On Civil Rights* (1965), which rejected the use of violence to achieve civil rights.

43. Authorization likely drawn from the priesthood of all believers

Christian Conference of Asia, *Life and Action* (1973).

44. Appeal to Christian love

Reformed Church in America, *Report of the Christian Action Commission* (1966), R-4. Concerned about justice in Vietnam; relates it to peace and freedom in the region. Its position and the argument for it derive from its adoption of most of National Council of Churches [USA], *On Viet-nam* (1965).

45. Appeal to the witness of love/the gospel

American Baptist Churches, *Policy Statement on Evangelism* (1984). Justice is a characteristic of the new life in Christ. It is related to ecology. The love of God provides the primary authorization.

Episcopal Church [USA], *"To Make Peace" Report* (1985). Calls for justice among nations in virtue of approving the statement of the church's Joint Commission on Peace, *To Make Peace* (1982), I/C, IV/B, which argues its case by appeal to Christian love.

International Council of Community Churches [USA], *Statement of Concern about Central America* (1987). Concerned about justice in Central America; relates it to peace.

United Church of Christ [USA], *Peace and the Resolving of Conflict* (1981). Relates justice to peace. Authorization is provided by the command to love one another and by the covenant.

46. Appeal to Christian ethical considerations and social responsibility

Christian Church (Disciples of Christ), *Concerning Investment Policies of the CC(DC)* (1971). Wants the church's investments to make a positive contribution to justice, freedom, peace, and ecology.

Christian Reformed Church in North America, *Decision of 1969,* 50-52, 210. Relates justice to the avoidance of the isolation of racial groups. This position and its authorization are the result of ratifying a report of the Reformed Ecumenical Synod, *Resolutions on Race Relations* (1968), 13, which took this position for these same reasons.

47. Appeal to evangelism and to all three articles of the creed, though all may be grounded in Christology

Roman Catholic Church, *Sollicitudo Rei Socialis* (1987), 41, 47-49, 33, 10, 7-8, 1-3. Relates social justice to peace, international justice, development, and employment. It posits a relational view of human persons and claims to represent the position of an earlier papal encyclical, *Populorum Progressio* (1987), 5, 22, 32, 44, 61, 76, 81.

48. Appeal to Christian responsibility

Evangelische Kirche im Rheinland, *Antrag der Kreissynode Köln-Nord zum Rassenkonflikt im südlichen Afrika* (1974). Concerned about justice, which is related to the demolition of stuctures promoting racism.

49. Appeal to the Christian faith/gospel

Evangelisch-Lutherische Kirche in Bayern, *Erklärung zur Friedensfrage* (1983), IV. Relates justice to peace; is authorized by Christian responsibility and reconciliation.

Polish [Catholic] Episcopacy, *Catholic Bishops Invite the Whole Nation to Prayer for the Fatherland* (1971), 2, 4. Concerned about social justice in Poland; relates it to peace. It speaks of a "Christian spirit of social justice". Ecclesiology and Christology are background warrants.

United Church of Canada, *Southern Africa* (1971). Relates justice to the overcoming of apartheid.

United Church of Canada, *The Search for Peace in the Eighties — Statement* (1982). Relates social justice to peace and economic justice. The call for justice is authorized by eschatology.

United Church of Canada, *Civil Disobedience* (1984). Speaks only of justice; relates it to disarmament.

United Church of Canada, *Service to French and English Language Minorities* (1984). Relates social justice to liberation from discrimination against language minorities.

United Church of Canada, *Aboriginal Rights Entrenchment in the Constitution* (1986). Speaks only of justice for aboriginal peoples in Canada; appeals to faith for authorization.

United Church of Canada, *Disarmament* (1986). Relates justice to peace and nuclear disarmament.

United Church of Canada, *Free Trade* (1987). Speaks only of justice; relates it to a concern for the poor. It appeals to faith for authorization and reaffirms earlier 1986 and 1984 statements.

50. Appeal to Christology supplemented by loci from the first and third articles of the creed

Presbyterian Church (USA), *Values, Choices and Health Care* (1988), 1, 11-12, 13, 15, 17-18, 27. Relates social justice to environmental justice, health care, overcoming racism and sexism.

51. Appeal to prophecy with the Trinity doctrine in the background

National Council of Churches in Korea, *Declaration of the Churches of Korea on National Reunification and Peace* (1988). Concerned about social and economic justice, especially in Korea. It is endorsed by World Alliance of Reformed Churches, *Korean Peace and Reunification* (1989). Also endorses the WCC Central Committee, *Peace and the Reunification of Korea* (1989), which in turn endorses the Korean statement.

52. No clear theological warrant given for position

All Africa Conference of Churches, *The Gospel and Education for Liberation* (1981). Concerned only with economic justice, so it may not belong on this list.

All Africa Conference of Churches, *The Gospel in Practice* (1981). Concerned only with economic justice, so it may not belong on this list.

American Baptist Churches, *Policy Statement on Agricultural Labor* (1975). Speaks only of economic justice. It advocates only non-violent change.

American Baptist Churches, *Policy Statement on Military and Foreign Policy* (1978). Relates social justice to economic justice and the prevention of war.

American Baptist Churches, *Policy Statement on Native Americans* (1979). Speaks only of justice for Native Americans.

American Lutheran Church, *Hunger in the World* (1968), 3, 2, 8. Relates social injustice to hunger, economic inequities, and the arms race. Christian love and compassion (the gospel) could be a warrant, but this is not clear.

American Lutheran Church, *A Call to Affirmation of Human Values* (1972), 2. Speaks only of justice; relates it to unemployment and racism.

American Lutheran Church, *Mandate for Peacemaking* (1982), A.5; A.8. Speaks only of international justice in relation to peacemaking and curbing the arms race. Creation warrants a concern for economic justice.

Anglican Church of Canada, *Resolutions on Native Canadians* (1969), Res. no. 3. Concerned about justice for indigenous peoples in Canada.

Anglican Church of Canada, *Resolutions on South Africa* (1971). Concerned about social justice for black people in South Africa.

Anglican Church of Canada, *Resolutions on Native Canadians* (1975), Act 28. Concerned about justice for indigenous peoples in Canada.

Anglican Church of Canada, *Resolutions on Native Canadians* (1977), Act 60. Concerned about justice for indigenous peoples in Canada.

Anglican Church of Canada, *Resolutions on Native Canadians* (1983), Act 43. Concerned about justice for indigenous peoples in Canada.

Anglican Church of Canada, *Resolutions on Native Canadians* (1986), Act 29. Concerned about justice for indigenous peoples in Canada.

Australian [Catholic] Episcopal Conference, *Message of Australian Bishops to Members of Federal Parliament* (1985). Refers only to justice; relates it to human life and to the protection of the unborn fetus.

Baptist Union of Great Britain and Ireland, *The Rhodesian Crisis* (1966). Refers only to justice; calls for it and human rights in Rhodesia.

Baptist Union of Great Britain and Ireland, *Vietnam* (1967). Refers only to justice; calls for justice and peace in Vietnam.

Baptist Union of Great Britain and Ireland, *Politics and Peaceful Protest* (1970). Relates social justice to peace and the condemnation of racism. Christology authorizes rejection of the use of violence in political protests.

Baptist Union of Great Britain and Ireland, *Falklands Crisis* (1982). Calls only for justice and peace in the Falkland Islands.

Baptist Union of New Zealand, *Notice of Motion* (1984). Calls for social justice, equity, and an end to apartheid in South Africa. Earlier in the motion, justice, as the rejection of nuclear war and the use of resources for weaponry, was authorized by Christology, with eschatology in the background.

Baptist Union of New Zealand, *Public Questions* (1984). Calls for justice for the disenfranchised in South Africa.

British Council of Churches, *Policy Statement on Vietnam* (1967). Concerned about a just peace in Vietnam. Creation functions to authorize peace, but the authorization for justice is not clear.

British Council of Churches, *The Programme to Combat Racism of the World Council of Churches* (1970). Concerned about fighting for racial justice.

British Council of Churches, *Racial Justice in Southern Africa* (1970). Concerned about racial injustice in South Africa and elsewhere.

British Council of Churches, *East Pakistan — West Bengal* (1971). Concerned about a just political settlement in Pakistan.

British Council of Churches, *Christian Aid* (1981). Calls for justice and aid work.

British Council of Churches, *Ireland* (1981). Calls for justice without discrimination in Northern Ireland.

British Council of Churches, *Community and Race Relations Unit* (1982). Calls for justice and peace in a multiracial society in virtue of adopting the paper *Towards a Multi-Racial Britain — Why and How Grants Are Made,* which took these positions.

British Council of Churches, *Private Member's Motion* (1982), 6. Urges development education in search of world justice.

British Council of Churches, *Recommendations [of the council's delegation to the Middle East] Accepted by the BCC Assembly* (1982), 8.2.1. Calls for peace and justice in Palestine.

British Council of Churches, *Christmas Appeal* (1983), 6. Speaks only of justice; relates it to peace.

British Council of Churches, *Middle East* (1984). Urges justice and peace in the Middle East in virtue of commending (i.e., approving) the council policy statement *Statement on the Middle East* (1983), 4.1.

British Council of Churches, *Emergency Resolution — South Africa* (1985). Relates its call for social justice in South Africa to an end to apartheid.

British Council of Churches, *A Message from the BCC Assembly to Churches and Governments in Britain and Ireland* (1985). Urges a just and lasting peace in Northern Ireland.

British Council of Churches, *Middle East* (1985). Calls for justice and peace in the Middle East.

British Council of Churches, *Resolution on South Africa* (1985), 2, iii. Urges a more just political order in South Africa.

British Council of Churches, *Statement on Geneva Summit Meeting* (1985). Speaks only of justice; relates it to peace.

British Council of Churches, *Staff Farewells* (1986), 1. Speaks of the injustice of apartheid.

Bund der Evangelischen Kirchen in der Deutschen Demokratischen Republik, *Beschluss der Synode zu dem Bericht der Konferenz der Evangelischen Kirchenleitungen, zum Arbeitsbericht des Bundes und zum Bericht des Diakonischen Werkes — Innere Mission und Hilfswerk — vom 23. September 1980*, IV. Social justice is related to the overcoming of present misery in the third world and to present European patterns of consumption.

Bund der Evangelischen Kirchen in der Deutschen Demokratischen Republik, *Beschluss der Synode des BEK-DDR zu Fragen des Friedens* (1981). Social justice is related to economic justice, human rights, and peace, as per the resolution's citation of WCC Central Committee, *Increasing Threat to Peace and the Mandate of the Churches* (1981), II/F, III/D/3, III/D/5.

Bund der Evangelischen Kirchen in der Deutschen Demokratischen Republik, *Beschluss der Synode des Bundes zum Bericht der Konferenz der Ev. Kirchenleitungen vom 24. September 1985*, I, Int. Relates justice to peace. Since peace is authorized by Christology, the latter might also function here as a warrant.

Bund der Evangelischen Kirchen in der Deutschen Demokratischen Republik, *Erklärung der Synode des Bundes zur Situation in Südafrika* (1985). Concerned about social justice in South Africa.

Bund der Evangelischen Kirchen in der Deutschen Demokratischen Republik, *Beschluss der Synode des BEK-DDR zum Bericht der Konferenz der Ev. Kirchenleitungen zu Friedensfragen* (1986), 1, 5. Relates ecology to justice and peace, as per the WCC call for a conciliar process devoted to these issues.

Canadian Catholic Conference, *Indispensable Collaboration between Public Authorities and Intermediate Organizations* (1963), I, II. Calls for justice as the norm for disposing of goods and services. It relates this to salvation.

Canadian Catholic Conference, *On the Occasion of the Hundredth Year of Confederation* (1967), 8, 11, 34, 35. Justice is regarded as equal opportunity for all as the goal of a healthy social life. It is related to peace. The statement rejects the use of violence.

Canadian Catholic Hierarchy, *Automation* (1964), 12. Concerned that the negative results of automation be borne equally; cites a statement of the Holy See to the Halifax Social Life Conference.

Canadian Conference of Catholic Bishops, *A Brief to the Standing Committee on External Affairs and National Defence: On Preparation for the Second Special Session of the United Nations on Development* (1982), Int.; 2; 2.1. Relates social justice to development, peace, and the use of present military expenditures for development.

[Catholic] Bishops of the Netherlands, *Letter to the Members of the Parliament* (1979). Expresses this concern in the context of endorsing the bishops' 1976 statement *Leben in Veränderung*.

[Catholic] Bishops of Vietnam, *To Build Peace* (1969). Relates social justice to peace.

[Catholic] Episcopacy of France, *Jésus-Christ, sauveur, espérance des hommes aujourd'hui* (1968). Speaks only of justice; relates justice to peace.

Christian Church (Disciples of Christ), *Regarding Support of Immediate Brotherhood Action in Moral and Civil Rights* (1963). Concerned about racial justice.

Christian Church (Disciples of Christ), *Substitute Resolution on Vietnam* (1966). Calls for justice with peace.

Christian Church (Disciples of Christ), *Concerning World Order, Justice and Peace* (1968). Social justice includes economic order, arms control, political justice, and justice for blacks.

Christian Church (Disciples of Christ), *Concerning Reconciliation beyond 1972* (1971). Refers only to justice, which is said to include freedom for all and solidarity with the disadvantaged.

Christian Church (Disciples of Christ), *Concerning the United Nations* (1977), II. Only calls for justice; relates it to peace and world order.

Christian Church (Disciples of Christ), *Concerning North and South Korea* (1979). Calls for justice and peace in Northeast Asia.

Christian Church (Disciples of Christ), *Resolution concerning Guidelines and Plans for the Implementation of Affirmative Action by the Christian Church (Disciples of Christ)* (1981). Refers only to justice; relates it to affirmative action.

Church of England, *South Africa* (1979). Calls for social justice in South Africa.

Church of England, *South Africa* (1986). Calls for justice, which includes democracy, participation, and an end to racism in South Africa.

Church of Ireland, *The Report of the Role of the Church Committee* (1981). Relates justice to peace, education, and economic justice.

Church of Ireland, *The Report of the Role of the Church Committee* (1983), 2, 3. Especially concerned about justice in Northern Ireland. A theocratic perspective subordinating reference to anthropology perhaps is a warrant for this concern.

Church of the Province of Southern Africa [Anglican], *Escalation of Terrorist Activities* (1985). Concern about justice in South Africa. It relates justice to peace in the face of terrorist activities.

Conferencia Episcopal Española, *Moral and Christian Attitudes over against the Decriminalization of Abortion* (1985), 15, 5. Relates social justice to economic and legal care for the family, including the prevention of abortion.

Eglise Evangélique Luthérienne de France, *Vœux et décisions du Synode général 1987*, 5. Concerned about justice as it relates to peace and ecology, as per the WCC agenda.

Eglise Réformée d'Alsace et de Lorraine, *Vœux adoptés par le Synode de l'ERAL* (1987), 2, 8. Concerned about justice in New Caledonia. At another point it relates justice to peace and ecology.

Episcopal Church [USA], *The War in Vietnam* (1967). Calls for a just and durable peace in Vietnam.

Episcopal Church [USA], *General Convention Resolution* [on affirmation of Executive Council response to "Black Manifesto"] (1969). Concerned about racial and economic justice.

Episcopal Church [USA], *General Convention Resolution* [on Canada-MacKenzie native land claims] (1976). Calls for justice in the settlement of the Déné people's land claims.

Episcopal Church [USA], *General Convention Resolution* [on repression and racism] (1976). Concerned about justice and religious liberty.

Episcopal Church [USA], *General Convention Resolution* [on urban ministries] (1976). Concerned about racial and economic justice.

Episcopal Church [USA], *General Convention Resolution* [on support for the establishment of an Hawaiian Native Claims Settlement Commission] (1979). Concerned about justice for Hawaiian natives.

Episcopal Church [USA], *Middle East Affairs* (1982). Calls for a just peace in the Middle East.

Episcopal Church [USA], *Military Aid to El Salvador* (1982). Urges a just peace in El Salvador and elsewhere in Central America.

Episcopal Church [USA], *Advocacy for Justice* (1985).

Episcopal Church [USA], *Commend Bishop Tutu* (1985). Speaks only of justice in South Africa; relates it to peace and mutual regard among people in that nation.

Episcopal Church [USA], *Encourage Contact with Episcopal Churches in Central America* (1985). Speaks only of justice; relates it to peace.

Episcopal Church [USA], *Nuclear Freeze and Peacemaking* (1985), B, D. Speaks only of justice; relates it to peace.

Episcopal Church [USA], *Appoint Committee on Status of Women* (1988). Concerned about justice issues that affect women.

Episcopal Church [USA], *Establish and Fund Commission on Racism* (1988). Concerned about justice inside the church and its relation to racism.

Episcopal Church [USA], *Reaffirm Commitment to Affirmative Action* (1988). Relates social justice to overcoming racism through affirmative action.

Evangelische Kirche der Kirchenprovinz Sachsen, *Vorlage des Berichtsausschusses* (1984), 1, 2.3. Relates social justice to peace, ecology, and the conquest of hunger; cites the WCC formula of relating the first three.

Evangelische Kirche der Kirchenprovinz Sachsen, *Beschluss zur Teilnahme am konziliaren Prozess* (1985). Relates justice to peace and ecology.

Evangelische Kirche der Union — Bereich Bundesrepublik Deutschland und Berlin-West, *Beschluss zum Bericht des Ratsvorsitzenden über Aufgaben der EKU* (1976), I/3. Concerned about justice, land, and freedom for all in South Africa.

Evangelische Kirche der Union — Bereich Bundesrepublik Deutschland und Berlin-West, *Beschlüsse auf Vorlage des Berichtsausschusses* (1978), 4. Concerned about a just sharing of the earth's goods.

Evangelische Kirche der Union — Bereich Deutsche Demokratische Republik, *Beschluss der 3. ordentlichen Tagung der 6. Synode der EKU — Bereich DDR* (1986), Brief an die Vereinigte Kirche Christi (USA); Brief an die Presbyterianische Kirche (USA). Refers only to justice; relates it to peace.

Evangelische Kirche im Rheinland, *Sonderfonds zur Bekämpfung des Rassismus* (1979), 3. Relates social justice to political and economic justice, as well as to the overcoming of racism.

Evangelische Kirche im Rheinland, *Einsetzung einer Kommission* (1987). Speaks only of justice, urging just distribution of work and income in the church.

Evangelische Kirche im Rheinland, *Geschäftsverbindungen von Banken zu Südafrika* (1987). Speaks only of justice, especially urging justice in South Africa.

Evangelische Kirche in Deutschland, *Entschliessung zur Rassendiskriminierung* (1974). Concerned about social justice in South Africa; relates it to political justice and freedom from apartheid.

Evangelische Kirche in Hessen und Nassau, *Entschliessung der Kirchensynode der EKHN zum Vietnam-Krieg* (1968). Speaks only of justice; relates it to peace and to social and economic relationships in Vietnam.

Evangelische Kirche in Hessen und Nassau, *Erklärung der Synode der EKHN zum Aufruf zu einem "Ökumenischen Konzil des Friedens"* (1985). Speaks only of justice; relates it to peace.

Evangelische Kirche von Westfalen, *Friedensverantwortung der Kirche* (1982), I; II; IV. Relates social justice to peace, freedom, human rights, and overcoming the gap between rich and poor. It rejects the use of violence in settling disagreements. Its position was endorsed by Evangelische Kirche im Rheinland, *Friedensverantwortung der Kirche* (1983), 2, 4, which authorizes its positions by appeal to eschatology.

Evangelische Kirche von Westfalen, *Zukunft der Arbeit-Leben und Arbeiten im Wandel* (1983), 5-8, 9-10. Social justice includes defence of the social assets of the lower wage groups, just pay, just service, just taxes, just distribution of gainful employment, and socially graduated distribution of income.

Evangelische Kirchenleitungen in der Deutschen Demokratischen Republik, *Votum der Konferenz der EK-DDR vom 6/7. Juli 1979 zur Frage der Gewaltanwendung im Kampf gegen den Rassismus im südlichen Afrika*, 3.1; 2.1; 1.3. Concerned with justice in Southern Africa, and so justice is related to overcoming racism. No authorization is explicitly given for seeking justice, though condemnation of racism is authorized in part by the doctrine of human persons.

Evangelische Landeskirche Anhalts, *Drucksache Nr. 44/18* (1986), 1.5. Relates justice to ecology and peace.

Evangelische Landeskirche in Baden, *Wort an die Gemeinden* (1982), 3. Speaks only of justice; relates it to peace and freedom as well as to the absence of social and economic tensions. It cites a 1981 position of the church's Landessynode.

Evangelische Landeskirche in Baden, *Entschliessung der Landessynode der ELB zum Konzil des Friedens und zur Weltversammlung für Gerechtigkeit, Frieden und Bewahrung der Schöpfung* (1985). Relates justice to peace and ecology, as per the WCC's call for an international congress on these themes. It also cites a 1985 resolution of the Evangelische Kirche in Deutschland.

Evangelisch-Lutherische Kirche in Bayern, *Kirche in der Diaspora, Christ sein in der Welt* (1988), 3.2. Speaks only of justice; relates it to peace, ecology, human dignity, human rights, and a concern for those without a voice in society.

Evangelisch-Lutherische Kirche in Oldenburg, *Beschlossene Fassung* (1981). Speaks only of justice; relates it to ecology, peace, and disarmament.

Evangelisch-Lutherische Landeskirche Hannovers, *Erklärung der Landessynode der ELLH zu dem Anti-Rassismus-Programm des Ökumenischen Rates der Kirche* (1970), 6.

Evangelisch-Lutherische Landeskirche Hannovers, *Wort der Landessynode vom 23. November 1983 an die Gemeinden*. Speaks only of justice, which it relates to peace.

Evangelisch-Lutherische Landeskirche Sachsens, *Wort der Landessynode vom 24.10.1973*. Calls for just order and peace, especially in Chile and in the Near/Middle East.

Evangelisch-Lutherische Landeskirche Sachsens, *Brief der Landessynode an die Gemeinden zur Friedensfrage vom 16.10.85*. Speaks only of justice. It is especially concerned about a more just distribution of the earth's goods, an issue it relates to peace.

Evêques Suisses, *Déclaration des évêques suisses sur l'encyclique "Humanae Vitae"* (1968), 26, 12-14. Relates social justice to the papal position on birth control and the family.

Federation of Evangelical Churches in Italy, *Assembly of the FECI* (1985), Act 49. Speaks only of justice, in relation to peace and disarmament. Christology could be a warrant.

Fédération Protestante de France, *La situation en Irlande* (1969). Concerned about social and economic justice in Northern Ireland as well as a peaceful order which assures minorities of their rights.

Fédération Protestante de France, *Vœux adoptés à l'Assemblée du PF à la Rochelle* (1983), 4-5. Concerned about justice in South Africa and other trouble spots; relates it to freedom, peace, and the overcoming of racism.

Fédération Protestante de France, *Déliberation de la 18ème Assemblée Générale du PF sur le projet de "Convocation mondiale pour la justice, paix et la sauvegarde de la création"* (1987). Relates justice to ecology and peace.

Greek Orthodox Archdiocese of North and South America, *Against Racism* (1963). Relates justice to peace and equality.

Irish Episcopal Conference, *The Storm That Threatens* (1983), 6. Relates social justice to peace.

Lutheran Church in America, *Poverty* (1966). Establishing social justice is deemed primarily the responsibility of the government. It relates social justice to economic justice, employment, and development. With regard to the statement's authorization, it does refer to the motivation provided by the love of God in Christ and claims that its ethical proposals are in continuity with God's mercy. Thus Christology might be functioning as a warrant.

Lutheran Church in America, *Peace and Politics* (1984), 9, 1. Insofar as social justice is related to the building of peace, authorization could be provided by creation.

Luthern World Federation, *I Have Heard the Cry of My People... The Assembly Message* (1990). Concerned with economic justice and dealing with the debt crisis. Justice is related to peace, ecology, and education. Opposition to violence is asserted. Christology may function as the prevailing warrant, though this point is not clearly made.

Mennonite Church [USA], *Telegram to President Kennedy* (1965). Speaks only of justice; relates it to peace.

Mennonite Church [USA], *Urban Riots* (1967). Relates justice to race relations. Christology could be a background warrant.

Mennonite Church [USA], *Militarism and Conscription Statement* (1979), Int. Only refers to justice; relates it to freedom and well-being.

Mennonite Church [USA], *Resolution on Central America* (1983). Calls for social and economic justice in Central America, as well as for peace.

Mennonite Church [USA], *Resolution on South Africa* (1987). Calls for social justice and peace in South Africa; rejects the use of violence.

Mennonite Church, General Conference [USA], *Freedom Movement* (1965). Concern about justice in the community relates to concern about good race relations and the witness of peace. The gospel may function as warrant, but this is not clear. Re-affirmed by the Mennonite Church [USA], *A Church of Many Peoples Confronts Racism* (1989).

Moravian Church in America, Southern Province, *Action on Racial Justice* (1968). Concerned about equal opportunity for American blacks. This position is reaffirmed by the denomination, with authorization drawn from Christology, in *Implementing Resolution on Race* (1969).

Moravian Church in America, Southern Province, *Action on Racial Justice* (1969). Concerned about equal opportunity for American blacks. Christology could be providing authorization for this position, especially in light of the church's affirmation of the statement, with authorization drawn from Christology, in its *Implementing Resolution on Race* (1969).

Moravian Church in Nicaragua, *"Communicado": Referencia: El diálogo, la reconciliación, la justicia y la paz* (1986). Concerned about social justice with peace in Nicaragua. The gospel could be in the background as a warrant, but this is not clear.

National Association of Evangelicals [USA], *Control of Obscenity* (1965). Calls for justice in efforts to control obscenity.

National Association of Evangelicals [USA], *A Vital Church: Concerned, Committed, Conquering* (1969). Social justice is related to equality for all as well as concern for the poor and the oppressed.

National Association of Evangelicals [USA], *Jesus Christ: Now More Than Ever* (1979). Concerned only about justice as it relates to moral standards and ecology.

National Association of Evangelicals [USA], *Sentencing Reform* (1983). Calls only for justice, of which the punishment of criminal offenders is an expression.

National Association of Evangelicals [USA], *Tuition Tax Credits* (1983). Calls for economic justice, to be achieved by granting tax credits for those who send their children to religious schools.

National Conference of Catholic Bishops [USA], *Resolution on Peace* (1967), 3. Speaks only of a just and lasting peace in Vietnam.

National Conference of Catholic Bishops [USA], *Resolution on Peace* (1968). Speaks only of justice and calls for a just, peaceful solution in Vietnam.

National Conference of Catholic Bishops [USA], *Statement on Farm Labor* (1968), 11-12. Speaks only of justice; relates it to peace and the right of labor to organize for purposes of collective bargaining. The doctrine of human persons may be in the background as a warrant.

National Conference of Catholic Bishops [USA], *Resolution on Imperatives of Peace* (1972), 6. Refers only to justice; relates it to peace.

National Conference of Catholic Bishops [USA], *Resolution on Farm Labor* (1975), 3. Refers only to justice and peace in the agricultural industry.

National Council of Churches [USA], *Equal Representation Is a Right of Citizenship* (1965). Relates social justice to a concern for an open society, human rights, and the right to vote.

National Council of Churches [USA], *On Guaranteed Income* (1968). Concerns about achieving a justice in which we all have access to at least a minimum standard of living. It cites several statements of the council, especially *Christian Concern and Responsibility for Economic Life in a Rapidly Changing Technological Society* (1966).

National Council of Churches [USA], *World Poverty and the Demands of Justice* (1968). Speaks only of justice, which it correlates it with freedom, development, and peace.

National Council of Churches [USA] *The Church and Television, Radio and Cable Communication* (1972), III. Concerned about racial and economic justice; relates them to peace.

[Orthodox] Ecumenical Patriarchate of Constantinople, *Message de Noël* (1982). Relates justice to peace, love, truth, and freedom and opposes the use of violence.

Polish [Catholic] Episcopacy, *Call of the Polish Episcopacy before the Threats against Life* (1970), IV. Speaks only of justice; relates it to society's responsibility for the protection of children (including protection from abortion).

Polish [Catholic] Episcopacy, *Letter of the Polish Episcopacy* (1970), 4. Relates social justice to peace, religious liberty, freedom of expression, and freedom from want.

Polish [Catholic] Episcopacy, *Communique of the 146th Plenary Assembly of the Polish Episcopacy* (1975), 1. Speaks only of justice; relates it to peace and human rights.

Presbyterian Church in Taiwan, *Peace to South Africa* (1985). Social justice is related to a concern for a multiracial society in South Africa. Some reference is made to the correlation of these concerns with the gospel.

Presbyterian Church of Southern Africa, *Church and Nation* (1984), 234, clause 5. Concerned about social justice in South Africa, especially as it might be advanced by civil disobedience.

Protestant Federation of Haiti, *Declaration* (1987). Calls for justice and fidelity to Haiti's new constitution.

Reformed Church in America, *Additional Recommendations to the Report of the Christian Action Commission to General Synod* (1963), Rec. 1-4. Calls for racial justice and commends non-violent means to achieve the ends.

Reformed Church in America, *Report of the Christian Action Commission* (1964), Rec. 5D. Reaffirms the church's 1963 resolution commending non-violent means for achieving justice.

Reformed Church in America, *Report of the Christian Action Commission* (1971), 15. Concerned about justice in the USA.

Reformed Church in America, *Report of the Christian Action Commission* (1985), R-III/A. Urges justice for farm workers.

Reformed Ecumenical Synod, *Pastoral Statement: A Call to Commitment and Action* (1984), XII/D, XII/D/11, also see XI, XII/B, XII/D/1, XII/F, XII/K. Relates social justice to human rights and the assurance of an end to artificial detention. It calls for justice, which is related to peace, human rights, the critique of abortion, and a pluralistic view of societal relationships. It is authorized by Christology/redemption and creation.

Roman Catholic Bishops in Mozambique, *Pastoral Letter* (1976). Concerned about justice in South Africa, including the critique of apartheid as well as the overcoming of oppression.

Romanian Orthodox Church, *Lettre irénique adressée par Sa Béatitude le Patriarche Justinian aux chefs des églises chrétiennes à l'occasion de la Sainte Fête de la Nativité* (1974). Relates social justice to peace.

Russian Orthodox Church, *Verfügungen der Heiligen Synode* (1973). Relates justice and peace.

Russian Orthodox Church, *Message of the Patriarchs of the Holy Synod* (1975). Refers only to justice, which it relates to peace. An appeal to natural law may be in the background, but not clearly.

Russian Orthodox Church, *Letters of the Holy Synod to the Soviet Government* (1977). Relates social justice to the ideals of the classless society.

Russian Orthodox Church, *Decrees of the Holy Synod* (1985). Relates justice to peace and truth.

Russian Orthodox Church, *Letter to President Reagan* (1985). Contains stringent criticisms of alleged social justice/civil rights violations by the USA's Reagan administration.

Russian Orthodox Church, *Letter to John Paul II* (1986). Relates justice to peace.

South African Council of Churches, *Resolution No. 5: Disinvestment* (1985), B. Concerned about achieving justice and peace in South Africa; seeks to minimize reliance on violence.

Sudanese Catholic Bishops Conference, *Statement of the Sudanese Catholic Bishops' Conference to the Transitional Government of the Sudan* (1985), A/1, A/2, B/1/b, B/2, Conc. Calls for justice in the Sudan; relates it to peace, freedom, unity, overcoming discrimination, and giving priority to the poor.

United Church of Canada, *Collective Bargaining* (1971), 1-2. Concerned about economic justice as it includes collective bargaining and a commitment to fighting poverty.

United Church of Canada, *Report of the Committee on Church and International Affairs* (1971). Relates justice to peace and freedom, especially as they are threatened in situations of tyranny.

United Church of Canada, *Anicinabe Park Occupation* (1974). Concerned about a just response to native people's violent demonstration.

United Church of Canada, *French/English Relations* (1977). Affirms a statement of the church issued the same year, *A Statement on the Implications of Developments in Quebec for Canada and the Church,* which called for justice.

United Church of Canada, *The Middle East* (1977). Concerned only about justice and peace in the Middle East.

United Church of Canada, *Native Ministries* (1980). Concerned about justice and self-determination for Indian peoples.

United Church of Canada, *The Nuclear Option for Canadians* (1980). Relates social justice to participation and ecology.

United Church of Canada, *Nuclear Power* (1980). Relates social justice to ecology, participation, and the development of new energy resources.

United Church of Canada, *The Church and the Economic Crisis* (1984). Relates social justice to economic justice and ecology. But justice (related to unemployment and the overcoming of poverty) is authorized by appeal to Christology/the gospel and eschatology. The statement relies on liberation theology's commitment to the priority of the poor.

United Church of Canada, *Compensation and Redress to Japanese Canadians Interned during WWII* (1984). Concerned about justice for Japanese Canadians interned during World War II; relates this concern to a critique of racism.

United Church of Canada, *Confessing Our Faith in a Nuclear Age* (1984). Speaks only of justice; relates it to peace.

United Church of Canada, *Gift, Dilemma and Promise* (1984). Calls for social justice insofar as it supports the wholeness of the person and the values in marriage. Loci from all three articles of the creed are in the background.

United Church of Canada, *Militarization of Native Land in Labrador and Quebec* (1986). Concerned about justice for Canadians.

United Church of Canada, *Military Expenditures* (1986). Relates social justice to ecology and a reduction of armaments.

United Church of Canada, *Free Trade* (1988). Relates social justice to economic justice; cites a 1980 church document, *The Quest for the Shalom Kingdom.*

United Church of Canada, *Uranium Exports* (1988). Relates social justice to ecology, a moratorium on the expansion of nuclear energy facilities, and a critique of nuclear arms.

United Church of Christ [USA], *Integrated Quality Education* (1965). Concerned about racial justice.

United Church of Christ [USA], *Resolution on Poverty* (1965). Concerned about racial justice and problems of urbanization, deprivation, and unemployment.

United Church of Christ [USA], *On Justice and Peace in Vietnam* (1967). Concerned about justice and peace in Vietnam.

United Church of Christ [USA], *Poverty and Economic Justice* (1967). Relates social justice to the war on poverty, maximum employment, adequate income, and integrated housing. Social justice should be a consideration in church decisions about investments.

United Church of Christ [USA], *Report on the Committee for Racial Justice Now, as Finally Adopted* (1967), 3. Concerned about racial justice in employment.

United Church of Christ [USA], *Resolution on the Middle East* (1967). Concerned about justice for Arab refugees in the Middle East.

United Church of Christ [USA], *Peace and United States Power* (1971). Refers to racial and economic justice and relates it to peace, ecology, and development.

United Church of Christ [USA], *Resurgent Racism* (1979). Concerned about racial justice. Natural law could be a warrant in the background.

United Church of Christ [USA], *Federal Budget* (1981). Relates social justice to racial justice and a concern for the poor as it is reflected in the federal government's budget. It refers to the "biblical mandate" as authorization, without being very specific.

United Church of Christ [USA], *Civil Defense (Executive Council, 6/29/83)* (1983). Speaks only of justice; relates it to peace. Creation may be a background warrant.

United Church of Christ [USA], *Developing the United Church of Christ as a Peacemaking Church* (1983). Speaks only of justice; relates it to economic justice, peace, health care, food, shelter, and employment.

United Church of Christ [USA], *Impact of U.S. Foreign and Military Policy on Central America* (1983). Calls for justice in Central America; also calls for peace.

United Church of Christ [USA], *Action for Peace in Central America* (1985). Concerned about economic justice and agrarian reform as well as peace in Central America.

United Church of Christ [USA], *Family Life Priority, 1986-7* (1985). Calls for justice and love for all families.

United Church of Christ [USA], *Spiritual Renewal Priority* (1985). Merely calls for justice integrated with our spiritual lives.

United Church of Christ [USA], *Peace and the Reunification of Korea* (1987). Concerned about justice and peace in Korea.

United Church of Christ [USA], *Peace in Afghanistan* (1987). Concerned about justice, peace, and self-determination in Afghanistan.

United Church of Christ [USA], *Response to Comrades Invitation* (1987). Relates social justice (especially for children) to peace.

United Free Church of Scotland, *Deliverance of the General Assembly* [on public questions] (1964), 11. Merely urges a just peace in Cyprus.

United Free Church of Scotland, *Deliverance of the General Assembly* [on public questions] (1967), 11. Concerned about justice in Rhodesia.

United Free Church of Scotland, *Deliverance of the General Assembly* [on public questions] (1968), 11. Concerned about justice in Rhodesia.

United Free Church of Scotland, *Deliverance of the General Assembly* [on public questions] (1972), 1, 11. Urges justice and peace in Northern Ireland.

United Free Church of Scotland, *Deliverance of the General Assembly* [on public questions] (1974), 12. Refers only to justice; relates it to peace.

United Free Church of Scotland, *Deliverance of the General Assembly* [on public questions] (1976), 8. Calls for a just peace in Northern Ireland.

United Free Church of Scotland, *Deliverance of the General Assembly* [on public questions] (1977), 10. Urges a just peace in Northern Ireland.

United Free Church of Scotland, *Deliverance of the General Assembly* [on public questions] (1980), 4. Calls for justice in new legislation for civil liberties and in immigration rules.

Uniting Church in Australia, *Investment Policy* (1982), 82.55. Concerned that the church's investments give consideration to issues about the environment and justice.

Uniting Church in Australia, *Economic Justice* (1985), 85.77.5. Concerned only with economic justice and setting aside funds for eliminating poverty.

Vereinigte Evangelisch-Lutherische Kirche Deutschlands, *Erklärung der Generalsynode zum Rassismus* (1970). Concerned with justice in South Africa, and so justice is related to racial integration and peace.

Vereinigte Evangelisch-Lutherische Kirche Deutschlands, *Erschliessung zum Fonds für Gerechtigkeit und Versöhnung* (1973), 1. Concerned with justice in South Africa, and so justice is related to racial integration and peace.

Vereinigte Evangelisch-Lutherische Kirche Deutschlands, *Brief an die FELCSA* (1980). Concerned with justice in Southern Africa, and so justice is related to racial integration.

Vereinigte Evangelisch-Lutherische Kirche in der DDR, *Beschluss zum Tätigkeitsbericht der Kirchenleitung vom 24.9.1977*. Concerned with justice in South Africa, and so justice is related to racial integration and peace.

World Alliance of Reformed Churches, *Sudan* (1989). Calls for justice and peace in the Sudan.

WCC Conference on Faith, Science and the Future, *Ethical Issues in the Biological Manipulation of Life* (Cambridge, Mass., 12-24 July 1979), 4, 3. Justice determines distribution of medical resources. Not clear whether an earlier reference to human nature as ultimately understood in reference to God's creation applies to warrant this point.

WCC New Delhi Assembly, *The Message of the Assembly to the Churches* (1961), 6. Relates peace and justice. Some apparent warrants are drawn from Christology/the gospel. It is not clear, however, whether these function as criteria for ethical judgments, in view of fact that reference to the Christian's need to work through secular agencies to achieve justice could suggest that this is a value accessible to all through creation.

I. SOCIO-POLITICAL IDEOLOGIES

In this section we consider separately the views of the churches first about the relationship of Christianity to Communism/socialism and then about its relationship to capitalism.

9-1 RELATIONSHIP OF CHRISTIANITY TO COMMUNISM/SOCIALISM

The churches are divided in their conclusions about Communism/socialism. As we have seen throughout this book, so here theological justifications for the different conclusions overlap.

A. Compatible
   A1. Appeal to creation/view of human persons
   A2. Appeal both to creation and the gospel/Christology/view of human persons
   A3. Appeal to the gospel
   A4. Apeal to ecclesiology
   A5. Appeal to all articles of the faith

B. Incompatible
   B1. Appeal to creation/natural law/principles of human thought
   B2. Appeal to creation/natural law, perhaps grounded in Christology
   B3. Appeal to Christian faith/Christology
   B4. Appeal to the gospel
   B5. Appeal to first- and second-article loci
   B6. Appeal to first- and third-article loci
   B7. Appeal to the third article, supplemented by reference to the first article
   B8. Appeal to the Word of God
   B9. Appeal to the love of God
   B10. No clear theological warrant given for position

A. COMPATIBLE

A1. Appeal to creation/view of human persons

Peruvian [Catholic] Episcopal Conference, *La justicia en el mundo* (1971), 14, 16. At least affirms socialism. It closely relates appeal to creation to redemption by claiming that Christians see Christian aspirations in certain socialist currents.

Russian Orthodox Church, *Message of the Holy Synod of the ROC on War and Peace* (1986), 3.34. At least appeals to something like the concept of natural law as grounds for praising socialism.

WCC Amsterdam Assembly, *The Church and the Disorder of Society* (1948), II-IV. If not a full endorsement of Communism, the Council does note its most compatible points with Christian faith and proposes a synthesis with capitalism, a way in which these ideologies would be put in their proper place by Christian faith.

A2. Appeal both to creation and the gospel/Christology/view of human persons

Evangelical Church of Lutheran Confession in Brazil, *Our Social Responsibility* (1976), 3, 2, 1. At least advocates the redistribution of wealth.

Fédération Protestante de France, *Eglise et pouvoirs* (1971), 6-32; 6-332; 3-2; 7-12; 7-6. Opts for implementing socialism, also with some reference in the statement to warrants drawn from eschatology.

A3. Appeal to the gospel

Presbyterian-Reformed Church in Cuba, *Confession of Faith* (1977), III/C, D; II/B.

A4. Appeal to ecclesiology

Evangelical Lutheran Church in Tanzania, *Resolution* (1968), I. Compatibility with some form of socialism seems affirmed on the basis of the inheritance of the church.

A5. Appeal to all articles of the faith

Nicaraguan [Catholic] Bishops, *Christian Commitment for a New Nicaragua* (1979), I. At least opts for socialism in Nicaragua.

B. INCOMPATIBLE

B1. Appeal to creation/natural law/principles of human thought

Deutsche Demokratische Republik Evangelische Synode, *Das Verhältnis zu Staat und Gesellschaft* (1971). In its apparent reliance on a two-kingdom ethic, the statement indicates that the church can be of service to socialist society.

Latin American [Catholic] Bishops, Second General Conference (Medellín Conference), *Justice* (1968), 10-11, 22. Also criticizes capitalism; retains an openness to socialization/collective management of business enterprises.

Roman Catholic Church, *Divini Redemptoris* (1937), 4, 10-12, 27-28, 31. Cf. 41, 54, 73. Combines this warrant with a kind of theocratic vision.

Sudan Catholic Bishops' Conference, *Lord Come to Our Aid* (1984), C/1.

B2. Appeal to creation/natural law, perhaps grounded in Christology

Australian [Catholic] Episcopal Conference, *De-Christianising Influences in Australian Society* (1976), 2.

Peruvian [Catholic] Episcopal Conference, *Document of the Peruvian Episcopal Conference on the Theology of Liberation* (1984), 41-49, 51, 80, 28, 15-16. At least insofar as reference is made to building a "civilization of love" as a possible authorization for positions taken in the document.

Roman Catholic Church, *Ecclesiam Suam* (1964), 100-101, 98. Uses language of *theosis* in the last reference, though something like natural law authorizes rejection of Communism.

Roman Catholic Church, *Laborem Exercens* (1981), 14, 13, 1, 27. Retains an openness to the socialization of some goods. Eschatology also may function as a warrant, to which creation is subordinated.

Roman Catholic Church, Congregation for the Doctrine of the Faith, *Instruction on Certain Aspects of the "Theology of Liberation"* (1984), VII (esp. VII.8), Conc.

B3. Appeal to Christian faith/Christology

National Association of Evangelicals [USA], *Communism* (1963).

Reformed Church in America, *Report of the Christian Action Commission* (1963), Rec. 2.

Vereinigte Evangelisch-Lutherische Kirche in der DDR, *Beschluss der Generalsynode zum Bericht der Kirchenleitung vom 8. Juni 1980, 9.*

B4. Appeal to the gospel

Canadian Conference of Catholic Bishops, *A Society to Be Transformed* (1977), 15, 17. Also criticizes capitalism.

Catholic Bishops Conference of the Philippines, *The Fruit of Justice Is Peace* (1987). Also criticizes capitalism.

[Catholic] Bishops of Chile, *Collective Pastoral Letter* (1968).

Irish Episcopal Conference, *Christian Faith in a Time of Economic Depression* (1983). Is critical of Marxism's ability to contribute to a just society.

National Association of Evangelicals [USA], *Reconciliation of China and Cuba* (1964). The Bible is a background warrant.

National Association of Evangelicals [USA], *The Communist Threat* (1967).

National Conference of [Catholic] Bishops of Brazil, *Après la révolution brésilienne du 1er avril* (1964). Also criticizes the abuses of liberal capitalism.

Roman Catholic Church, *Octogesima Adveniens* (1971), 26-27, 30-36, 48. Also criticizes liberalism. Creation functions as warrant at several points, even in the expression of an openness to certain "historical movements" sprung from ideologies (such as Marxism). These appeals complement this appeal to the "Christian faith".

WCC Evanston Assembly, *Socialist Problems — The Responsible Society in a World Perspective* (1954), II. Does opt for allowing the Communist and capitalist systems to live side by side; earlier in the statement adovates a kind of welfare state.

WCC Nairobi Assembly, *Confessing Christ Today* (1975), 27. Claims socialist economies can obscure confession of Christ.

B5. Appeal to first- and second-article loci

All Africa Conference of Churches, *The Gospel — Good News to the Poor and Oppressed* (1981).

National Association of Evangelicals [USA], *Communist Aggression* (1966).

National Conference of Catholic Bishops [USA], *Economic Justice for All* (1986), PM1, PM2, PM13, 25, 28, 88, 115, 127, 364.

B6. Appeal to first- and third-article loci

National Conference of Catholic Bishops [USA], *Pastoral Letter on Marxist Communism* (1980), 14, 40-49.

B7. Appeal to the third article, supplemented by reference to the first article

Dutch Reformed Church (South Africa), *Church and Society* (1986), 216-18, 184-99.

B8. Appeal to the Word of God

Reformed Ecumenical Synod, *Pastoral Statement: A Call to Commitment and Action* (1984), XI.

B9. Appeal to the love of God

Mennonite Church [USA], *A Message concerning the War in Vietnam* (1965).

B10. No clear theological warrant given for position

National Association of Evangelicals [USA], *Vietnam* (1966).
National Conference of Catholic Bishops [USA], *The Challenge of Peace: God's Promise and Our Response* (1983), 246, 274, 13-15, 2. Yet relies on warrant from all three articles of the creed to authorize other positions.

While acknowledging Christianity's incompatibility with Communism due to its atheism, their compatibility is acknowledged in other areas by WCC Nairobi Assembly, *Seeking Community: The Common Search of People of Various Faiths, Cultures, and Ideologies* (1975), 38-39. No doctrinal warrant is provided for this judgment, though its subsequent call for the church to confront all ideologies (including capitalism) seems warranted by Christology and earlier the statement appealed to creation warrants for purposes of seeking community (ibid., 43-45, 8, 10, 29).

A criticism of Communism seems implied by the Southern African Catholic Bishops' Conference, *An Urgent Message to the State President* (1986), 22, as the bishops claim that more repression of the liberation, anti-apartheid groups in South Africa will only serve to facilitate these groups' dependence on Moscow and other Communist centres of power.

Also relevant is *Beschluss der Synode des Bundes der Evangelischen Kirchen in der DDR zum mündlichen Bericht der Konferenz der Evangelischen Kirchenleitungen vom 28. September 1982*, 3, as it notes a 1982 document of the Konferenz der Kirchenleitungen which claimed that the church in a socialist state participates in the society and helps it (in the freedom of faith) to seek the best for the whole. Similarly the Bund der Evangelischen Kirchen in der Deutschen Demokratischen Republik, *Beschluss der Synode des Bundes zum Bericht des Vorsitzenden der Konferenz der Evangelischen Kirchenleitungen vom 22. September 1981*, dealt with the relationship between Christianity and Communism insofar as, without theological authorization, it expresses a concern about the right to the practice of religion as well as the relationship between Communist training and the freedom of religion. Also worthy of note is the call for a dialogue with Communism, issued by the National Council of Churches in Korea, *Declaration of the Churches of Korea on National Reunification and Peace* (1988), with authorization drawn from the Trinity.

9-2 RELATIONSHIP OF CHRISTIANITY TO CAPITALISM

The churches have come to different conclusions in their evaluation of capitalism. Some explicitly endorse it (or at least the concept of private ownership); others condemn it. They have in common, however, the kinds of theological warrants appealed to.

A.   Endorse (at least de facto, by endorsing private ownership)
   A1. Appeal to creation/view of human persons
   A2. Appeal to creation, likely grounded in Christology
   A3. Appeal to Christology
   A4. Appeal to first- and second-article loci
   A5. Appeal to first- and second-article loci, with creation likely grounded in the gospel
   A6. Appeal to Scripture and Christian principles
   A7. No clear theological warrant given for position

B.   Condemn
   B1. Appeal to creation
   B2. Appeal to creation and to suppositions resembling Christocentric liberation theology
   B3. Appeal to Christology/the gospel
   B4. Appeal to eschatology and Christology
   B5. Apparent appeal to all three articles of the creed for warrants
   B6. Appeal to the Word of God
   B7. No clear theological warrant given for position

A. ENDORSE (AT LEAST DE FACTO,
BY ENDORSING PRIVATE OWNERSHIP)

A1. Appeal to creation/view of human persons

American Lutheran Church, *The Land: God's Gift, Our Caring* (1982), II; II/A/1-2; II/B/1, 3, 7.
[Catholic] Bishops of Vietnam, *To Build Peace* (1969). Also calls on government to create means to help those without property to obtain it.
[Catholic] Episcopal Conference of the Pacific, *The Pacific and Peace* (1986), VII/A. Seems to take the position insofar as the private ownership of land is endorsed.
International Council of Community Churches [USA], *Statement of Concern on American Indian Rights* (1988). At least calls for land ownership by way of a possible appeal to anthropology.
Lutheran Church in America, *Human Rights: Doing Justice in God's World* (1978), esp. 3, 5, 8. Seems to take this position insofar as private ownership is deemed not an absolute right, though it is apparently permitted.
Lutheran Church in America, *Economic Justice: Stewardship of Creation in Human Community* (1980), esp. 6-7. Endorses legitimacy of ideologies in serving political cohesion; opts for a kind of big government which would aim to ensure economic justice. The statement makes some references to Christology, but they do not seem relevant to the position on private property.
Lutheran Church of Australia, *Conscientious Objection to Service in War* (1970), 2. Insofar as the right to private property is endorsed.
Patriarchs and Catholic Bishops of Libya, *Legality Is the Unique Guarantee of the Protection of the Fatherland* (1983), I/3(d), III/8. At least endorses the right to private property.
Roman Catholic Church, *Divini Redemptoris* (1937), 27. Cf. 41, 54, 73. But a number of the statement's constructive proposals emerge from theocratic suppositions.

Roman Catholic Church, *Pacem in Terris* (1963), 21-23, 5, 10, 31, 59, 147, 157. Appeals to anthropology and natural law could be subordinated to redemption. It does posit a continuity between creation and redemption, as well as a relational view of persons.

Roman Catholic Church, Congregation for the Doctrine of the Faith, *Instruction on Christian Freedom and Liberation* (1986), 87, 85, 80-82, 99, 98, 74, 73, 64, 60, 54, 30. At least insofar as the right to private property, with a consciousness that goods are meant for all, is endorsed and collectivism is rejected. Christology/the gospel may function as the main warrant, especially if the statement intends the correlation it posits between creation and redemption to be read in light of Vatican II's subordination of creation to redemption.

United Church of Christ [USA], *Human Rights* (1979). Appeals to creation are closely related to the work of the other persons of the Trinity.

A2. Appeal to creation, likely grounded in Christology

Arbeitsgemeinschaft Christlicher Kirchen in der Bundesrepublik Deutschland und Berlin (West), *Neuer Lebensstil aus christlicher Verantwortung* (1980), 1-3, 5-6. Seems to take this position insofar as private ownership is deemed not an unconditional right, though it is apparently permitted.

Haitian [Catholic] Episcopal Conference, *The Foundation for the Church's Involvement in Local and Political Arenas* (1983), 15, 19, 2, 5. At least endorses right to property. Ecclesiology — the church as sacrament — may also be invoked as a background warrant, as well as eschatology.

Methodist Church in Malaysia, *Social Principles* (n.d.), III/B.1; II-I. Insofar as private ownership is affirmed.

Peruvian [Catholic] Episcopal Conference, *Document of the Peruvian Episcopal Conference on the Theology of Liberation* (1984), 41-42, 51, 80, 28, 15-16. At least insofar as private property is endorsed in a qualified sense and reference is made to building a "civilization of love" as a possible warrant.

Roman Catholic Church, Vatican II, *Gaudium et Spes* (1965), 22, 39, 68-71, 74, 76.

Roman Catholic Church, *Laborem Exercens* (1981), 12, 14-16, 27, 1. Eschatology may also be an overriding warrant. The encyclical endorses private ownership, but only with qualifications, and criticizes capitalism, which is said not to be sufficiently concerned about the common use of property.

A3. Appeal to Christology

National Conference of Catholic Bishops [USA], *To Do the Work of Justice* (1978), 32, 29, 1.

A4. Appeal to first- and second-article loci

National Conference of Catholic Bishops [USA], *Economic Justice for All* (1986), 364, 128-30, 114-15, 28, 25, PM19, PM13, PM2, PM1. But does insist that the church is not bound to any particular economic system; it even advocates (in 314-18) some government intervention in the economy.

A5. Appeal to first- and second-article loci, with creation likely grounded in the gospel

Paraguay [Catholic] Bishops Conference, *El campesino paraguayo y la tierra* (1983), Int., 2.1-2.5. At least endorses the right to private property, despite dependence on themes of liberation theology.

A6. Appeal to Scripture and Christian principles

Dutch Reformed Church (South Africa), *A Declaration of Christian Principles* (1990), 2.24; 1.

A7. No clear theological warrant given for position

National Council of Churches [USA], *Genetic Science for Human Benefit* (1986), IV. At least concedes the legitimacy of capitalism.

United Church of Christ [USA], *Concerning Our Economic System* (1977). Offers a qualified endorsement.

United Church of Christ [USA], *Justice and Peace Priority* (1985). At least endorses land ownership.

United Methodist Church [USA], *Social Principles of the UMC(USA)* (1980), IV/A. Makes no reference to a warrant except "trusteeship under God".

B. CONDEMN

B1. Appeal to creation

[Catholic] Bishops of the Netherlands, *Mens, arbeid en samenleving* (1985), 8. Also includes a critique of the present praxis of state socialism.

Fellowship of Christian Churches [Chile], *Let the Floodgates of Democratic Participation Be Opened* (1984), II, II/1, II/2. At least rejects the free-market system. Faith functions as a motive.

Latin American [Catholic] Bishops, Second General Conference (Medellín Conference), *Justice* (1968), 10-11, 22. Also condemns Communism.

WCC Amsterdam Assembly, *The Church and the Disorder of Society* (1948), IV, III, II, I. Though not fully clear whether earlier creation warrant applies and whether references to Christology and eschatology could be warrants.

WCC Sub-Unit on Church and Society, *Report of the Advisory Group of the Energy for My Neighbor Programme* (1982), II. May combine creation warrant with the concept of *theosis*.

B2. Appeal to creation and to suppositions resembling Christocentric liberation theology

All Africa Conference of Churches, *The Gospel — Good News to the Poor and Oppressed* (1981). Though the Christology emphasis is stronger at this point than explicitly liberation theology themes.

Peruvian Catholic Episcopal Conference, *La justicia en el mundo* (1971), 14, 3.

B3. Appeal to Christology/the gospel

Canadian Conference of Catholic Bishops, *A Society to be Transformed* (1977), 13, 17. Also criticizes Communism.

Catholic Bishops Conference of the Philippines, *The Fruit of Justice Is Peace* (1987). Also criticizes Communism.

Fédération Protestante de France, *Eglise et pouvoirs* (1971), 4; 6; 7.12.

Irish Episcopal Conference, *Christian Faith in a Time of Economic Depression* (1983). At least
  is critical of neo-capitalism's ability to contribute to a just society.
Presbyterian-Reformed Church in Cuba, *Confession of Faith* (1977), 3/A, C.
WCC Amsterdam Assembly, *Message of the Assembly* (1948). Only insofar as the statement
  rejects every program which would treat humans as though they were "means of profit".
WCC Nairobi Assembly, *Confessing Christ Today* (1975), 27. Claims that capitalism and
  socialism obscure the confession of Christ.
WCC Vancouver Assembly, *Message from the Sixth Assembly* (1983). Elsewhere in the
  statement appeals are made to creation and possibly the Eucharist; here there are only calls
  for a "new international economic order".

B4. Appeal to eschatology and Christology

Reformed Ecumenical Synod, *Statements on the Social Calling of the Church* (1980), 16, 18, 2.
  Critiques capitalism's preoccupation with material abundance.

B5. Apparent appeal to all three articles of the creed for warrants

WCC Nairobi Assembly, *Human Development: Ambiguities of Power, Technology, and Quality
  of Life* (1975), 13, 12, 37-38, 41, 3-7, 61. At least critiques the present system of
  multinational corporations.

B6. Appeal to the Word of God

Reformed Ecumenical Synod, *Pastoral Statement: A Call to Commitment and Action* (1984),
  XI.

B7. No clear theological warrant given for position

Nicaraguan [Catholic] Bishops, *Christian Commitment for a New Nicaragua* (1979), I. At least
  opposes capitalism in Nicaragua.
WCC Canberra Assembly, *The Report of the Seventh Assembly* (1991), 77. At least offers
  criticism of the free-market system.

Criticism of Communism's exploitation of the hopes and dreams of the poor is offered,
without any clear theological authorization, by the Christian Church (Disciples of Christ),
Regarding Non-Violent Social Deterrence (1963).
    An observation has been offered by the WCC Conference on Faith, Science and the Future,
Restructuring the Industrial and Urban Environment (Cambridge, Mass., 12-24 July 1979), 5,
that the capitalist and Marxist systems have been correlated to some extent in the "mixed
economies" of some nations. But the result does not receive full commendation. A similar call
for a "pluralistic view of societal relationships", one not characterized by a polarization between
capitalism and collectivism, has been offered by appeal to Scripture by the Reformed Ecumenical Synod, *Pastoral Statement: A Call to Commitment and Action* (1984), XII/F. A balanced
assessment of the relationship between Christian values and capitalism is offered by the Roman
Catholic Church, *Populorum Progressio* (1967), 22, 23, 26, 58, 59, 61. Private property is
affirmed as a right, presumably on the basis of the gospel. So also affirmed are competitive
(presumably capitalist) economic markets. But an appeal to the gospel warrants the critique of a

type of capitalism which carries no sense of social obligation. And without specific warrants (though the statement's positions on development seem rooted in the creation doctrine), it does insist on regulating prices on the international economic trade market. Also see Roman Catholic Church, *Laborem Exercens* (1981), 12, 14-16, 27, 1, cited above. Another statement in the same spirit was issued by the National Conference of Catholic Bishops [USA], *Statement on the World Food Crisis: A Pastoral Plan of Action* (1974), 14, 17, in which creation/natural law authorizes the conclusion that the operation of the free-market system should be modified "when it stands in the way of justice".

Though it takes no clear position on the Communism-capitalism debate, the Lutheran-Episcopal Dialogue, series 3 [USA], *Implications of the Gospel* (1988), 122, with authorization drawn from the gospel, supported by eschatology and sacramentology, does affirm that all economic systems are not morally neutral. Likewise, in the "Social Creed of the Methodist Church", in *Plan for the Life and Mission of the Methodist Church in Brazil* (1982), III/5(h), the church states that in individualism and in collectivism "we encounter the risks of partial humanisms." Also see the Christian Church (Disciples of Christ), *Concerning Revolutionary Movements and Threats to the Peace of the World* (1966), which, without clear theological authorization, calls for "alternatives to Communism without necessarily accepting western liberal capitalistic forms".

In a similar manner, the Canadian Conference of Catholic Bishops, *Ethical Choices and Political Challenges* (1983), 51, 43, 22, 7, without theological authorization (though Christology seems to function as the governing warrant throughout the statement), laments that "the restricted ideological choice between two systems, either capitalism or communism, tends to stifle social imagination." Yet the Canadian bishops do tend to move away from the neutral perspective at one point in advocating social ownership and control of capital and technology by communities and workers. A similar criticism of both capitalism and Communism is offered by the Roman Catholic Church, *Sollicitudo Rei Socialis* (1987), 41, 21, 20, 40, 47-49, 33, 2, 1. Insofar as this debate is related to development by the encyclical, loci from all three articles of the creed (with all loci subordinated to Christology) seem to function as warrants. However, in ibid., 42, this neutral perspective is somewhat modified, insofar as private property, though under a "social mortgage", is endorsed with authorization drawn from the nature of the Christian faith.

Index

relation of Christianity to communism/social-
ism, 344
social justice, 312, 340
Sudanese Catholic Bishops' Conference to the
Transitional Government of the Sudan
racism, 179
Swedish Catholic Bishops
energy consumption, 219
Swedish Ecumenical Council
economic development, 193
nuclear energy, 54
Swedish Ecumenical Council/Church of Sweden.
See also Church of Sweden
ecology, 206
economic development, 191
energy consumption, 221
nuclear energy, 55 n. 14, 223
Swiss Catholic Bishops. *See also* Catholic Swiss
Bishops
ecology, 44, 54 n. 4
energy consumption, 49, 50
Synod of the Protestant Church in Austria
ecology, 206
energy consumption, 221
nuclear energy, 49, 223
theological warrant discussed, 146 n. 7

Unitarian Universalist Association
abortion, 291
United Church in Rheinland-Westphalia
energy consumption, 49
United Church of Canada
abortion, 292
apartheid, 2, 157, 161
ecology, 44, 46, 47, 54 nn. 4-5, 205, 208, 212,
213, 216
economic development, 184
energy consumption, 220, 221
just war and pacifism, 65, 270, 272, 274, 280,
282
nuclear armaments, 73, 74, 78 n. 20, 79 n. 25,
228, 229, 232, 234, 235, 237
nuclear energy, 52, 224, 225
peace, 57, 60, 77 n. 4, 242, 243, 249, 252,
255, 258, 265
racism, 172, 179
social justice, 112, 117 n. 3, 318, 321, 322,
329, 331, 332, 340
unemployment, 37, 198, 201, 202
United Church of Christ in Japan
nuclear armaments, 230
peace, 56, 73, 251
social justice, 328
United Church of Christ [USA], 2, 149, 150
abortion, 93, 94, 291, 292, 296, 298
apartheid, 2, 9, 22 nn. 33-34, 157, 159, 161

ecology, 45, 47, 54 n. 5, 55 n. 7, 205, 206,
209, 216, 217
economic development, 26, 29, 30, 33, 184,
185, 186, 187, 188, 189, 191, 192
energy consumption, 49, 219, 220, 221
genetic engineering, 303
just war and pacifism, 67, 72, 273, 274, 276,
278, 280
nuclear armaments, 73, 76, 228, 229, 231, 232,
233, 234, 235, 236, 237, 239
nuclear energy, 224, 225
peace, 242, 244, 249, 251, 252, 253, 255, 257,
265, 266
peace, 56, 58, 60, 77 n. 4, 78 n. 9
racism, 17, 24 nn. 57-58, 25 n. 58, 163, 164,
165, 166, 169, 170, 171, 172, 173, 174,
175, 179, 181
relation of Christianity to capitalism, 348, 349
social justice, 112, 113, 116, 117 n. 3, 309,
312, 318, 319, 321, 322, 323, 324, 326,
328, 329, 330, 331, 341
theological warrant discussed, 146 nn. 2 and 7
unemployment, 37, 195, 196, 197, 198, 199,
201, 202
United Free Church of Scotland
abortion, 292, 294, 297
apartheid, 2, 161, 162,
ecology, 41, 47, 217
economic development, 183, 188, 189, 190,
191
energy consumption, 221
genetic engineering, 301
just war and pacifism, 274
nuclear armaments, 75, 234, 239
nuclear energy, 223, 225
peace, 57-58, 77 n. 4, 242, 244, 249, 253, 266
racism, 16, 25 n. 58, 170, 173, 179
social justice, 116, 309, 341
unemployment, 36, 37, 38, 39, 194, 201
United Methodist Church [USA]
abortion, 93, 95, 99, 101 n. 20, 291, 293
divorce and remarriage, 285
ecology, 54 n. 4, 55 n. 7, 206
economic development, 188
energy consumption, 218
genetic engineering, 300
just war and pacifism, 67, 277
peace, 56, 244
racism, 166
relation of Christianity to capitalism, 349
social justice, 312
unemployment, 195
United Presbyterian Church/Presbyterian Church in
the U.S. *See also* United Presbyterian Church
[USA]; Presbyterian Church (USA)
ecology, 54 n. 4, 210
economic development, 188, 190, 191
energy consumption, 35, 49, 219